Binding breaking
11/30/18

VICARS
Of
CHRIST

by the same author

Christ in Our World
God Our Saviour
Come, Holy Spirit
Christ and Original Sin
Jesus Who Became Christ

PETER DE ROSA

VICARS
of
CHRIST

*The Dark Side
of the Papacy*

CROWN PUBLISHERS, INC.   NEW YORK

Published in the United States of America by Crown Publishers, Inc., 225 Park Avenue South, New York, New York 10003.

Originally published in Great Britain by Bantam Press, a division of Transworld Publishers Ltd

CROWN is a trademark of Crown Publishers, Inc.

Manufactured in the United States of America

Library of Congress Cataloging-in-Publication Data
De Rosa, Peter
Vicars of Christ: the dark side of the papacy/ p. cm.
Bibliography: p.
1. Papacy—Controversial literature. I. Title.
BX1765.2.B69 1988
262'.13—dc19
88-7126
CIP

ISBN 0-517-57027-0

10 9 8 7 6 5 4 3 2 1

First American Edition

Humbly and with Penitence

to

All the Victims of the Holocaust

NOTE TO THE READER

This book is not a work of theology, still less a textbook on the papacy. It is an investigation of the role of the popes in the light of history, culture, ethics and the personalities of the pontiffs themselves. Though, like Dante, I stress here the dark side of the papacy, it is the work of a friend not an enemy.

CONTENTS

VICARS
of
CHRIST

On hearing that Ludwig Pastor had begun his great work, *The History of the Popes*, the Dominican Cardinal de Lai remarked: 'Prima la carità e poi la verità anche nella storia', 'Charity precedes truth even in the writing of history'. On hearing this, Pastor replied: 'If that were so, all history would be impossible. Fortunately, Christ said, "I am the Truth".'

PROLOGUE

The Great Cover-Up

IT IS EASILY THE BIGGEST COVER-UP IN HISTORY. It has gone on for centuries, claiming first thousands, then millions of lives. Though it is highly visible, no one seems to have noticed it. Unknowingly, many artists, great and not so great, have contributed to it. And the camouflage is nothing more alarming than a little piece of cloth – the cloth that covers the loins of Jesus on the cross.

In the beginning, the cross was never represented in art or sculpture. While Jesus was adored for his self-emptying and the cross was the centre of the faith, no one dared depict him in his utter humiliation.

It is said that Constantine's armies bore the cross on their insignia. This was not so. On shield and banner they had the first two letters of Christ's Greek name Χριστος fused like this: ☧. Only when the memory of the thousands who had died on crosses all over the Roman world dimmed did Christians feel free to depict the cross as the symbol of Christ's suffering love. It was an empty cross. Who would dare to recrucify Christ?

Later, this bare symbol of his conquest of the dark forces seemed too austere. Fifth century artists began to paint a cross with a lamb next to it, for Jesus was 'the Lamb of God' slain for the sin of the world. Then, with mounting courage, a lamb-white Jesus was himself depicted next to the cross. With only two known exceptions, not till the end of the sixth century was he shown *on* his cross. Still the artist dared not paint in the pain and humiliation. Jesus was in a long tunic, with only hands and feet bare to show in stylized fashion the nails that pinned him to the wood. This was an image of triumph; he was not suffering and dying but reigning, open-eyed and sometimes crowned, on the throne of the cross. The first tenth-century Greek representation of Jesus *suffering* on the cross was condemned by Rome as blasphemy. Soon the Church of Rome itself yielded to its fascination.

With Jesus ever more remote and with medieval theology becoming drier and more scholastic, piety demanded a more human Christ: a man they could see and almost feel, a man with the trials and tribulations they themselves met with every day of their short and suffering lives. Artists now freely depicted Christ in agony on his cross; deep wounds and blood, agony in every limb, dereliction in his eyes. His garments shrank to impress on the faithful the extent of the Lord's abasement.

There it stopped: at a loin-cloth. Had the artist gone further, who would have been brave enough to look on Christ the way he was: naked like a slave?

What stayed the artist's hand was not propriety but theology. The artists were not to be blamed. After all, how could they see that the pain of the recrucified Christ, without the ultimate truth that only complete nakedness brings, would lead to a catastrophe? In giving Jesus the final shreds of decency, that loin-cloth took from him his Jewishness. It literally covered his pride and turned him into an honorary Gentile. For what it hid was not just his sex but that knife-mark in his flesh, the circumcision, that showed he was a Jew. *That* is what Christians feared to see.

In crucifixions by Raphael and Rubens, even by Bosch and Grüne-wald, the loin-cloth becomes ornamental; its folds hang decorously. In Grünewald's Colmar crucifixion, says Husmans, Jesus is bent like a bow; the tormented body glistens palely, dotted with blood, bristling with thorns like the burr of a horse-chestnut. *This*, the artist seems to say, is what sin has done to . . . whom?

To God, is the answer of theology. This is the death of God. The more intense the agony, the less His glory shines through, the more terrifying it is. 'God died on Calvary.' It sounds good theology. It might have been but for that piece of cloth. For, the artist seems to be saying, someone is responsible for doing *that* to God. But who?

A superficial reading of Matthew's Gospel provides the answer: the Jews. They called out to Pilate: 'Crucify him. His blood be upon us and upon our children.' The word of God seems to blame Jews, Jesus' contemporaries and their descendants, for the Death of God. Jews are, therefore, deicides. One drop of that Blood would save a thousand worlds; the Jews shed it all. For them, the Blood is not salvation but an undying curse. By their unbelief, Jews continue killing God. Having murdered Christ, being guilty of the greatest imaginable crime, they were surely capable of anything. That is the calumny. That is the great heresy. Because of it, tales of Jews ritually slaughtering and drinking the blood of little Christian children fitted the pattern set by the Crime of killing God. Those fabrications still circulate.

Without the cover-up, without that piece of cloth, it would have stared everyone in the face that what took place on Calvary was also Jewicide. God was a Jew. It was not so much Jews killing God as a Jew, who was God's Son, shedding his blood for the sin of the world. Would Christians over centuries have instituted pogroms against Jews in the name of the Cross if on it Jesus had borne the mark of circumcision? Would a Jew have authorized the massacre of Jews? Would it not have been plain that Jesus was present in every pogrom saying:

4

'Why are you persecuting me; for what you do unto these the least of my brethren, you do unto *me*'?

That cover-up, now nearly twenty centuries old, was not perpetrated by a deviant sect but by main-line Christianity, by the Holy Roman Catholic and Apostolic Church. No doctrine was taught more universally, with less qualification – in Catholic terms, more infallibly – than that 'Jews are cursed for killing God', a charge still not officially withdrawn. By a bizarre twist, Jews, from whom the Saviour came, were the only ones blamed for killing him. It was not Jesus who was recrucified but the race from which he sprang.

In the Third and Fourth Councils of the Lateran (1179 and 1215), the church codified all previous enactments against Jews. They had to wear a badge of shame. In England it was saffron, in the presumed shape of the tablets of Moses. In France and Germany it was yellow and round. In Italy, the badge was a red hat, until a short-sighted Roman prelate mistook a Jew for a cardinal and the colour was changed to yellow. Jews were forbidden all contact with Christians, barred from administration, deprived of lands, forbidden to own shops, herded into ghettos which were bolted at night. No system of *apartheid* was more rigorously enforced. For refusing to deny their ancestral faith and convert to Christianity, Jews were hounded from one land to another. One pope gave them a month to quit their homes in Italy, leaving them only two places of refuge. During the Crusades, they were slaughtered in their thousands, out of devotion to Christ. A Jew who showed his nose on Good Friday was virtually committing suicide, even though the Man on the Cross had a Jewish nose. Thus down the ages, millions suffered and died. Bad art and disastrous theology had prepared the way for Hitler and his 'final solution'.

In Nazi Germany, to begin with, stars were daubed on Jewish homes and shops; it was the signal that they could be smashed and looted. Towns boasted, as they had done in medieval times, of being *Judenrein*, free from Jewish contamination. Typically, on the outskirts of the village of Obersdorf, there was a wayside shrine with a crucifix. Over Jesus' head was the inscription, INRI ('Jesus of Nazareth, King of the Jews'). In the foreground was a notice: *'Juden sind hier nicht erwünscht'* – 'Jews are not welcome here.'

In 1936, Bishop Berning of Osnabrüch had talked with the Führer for over an hour. Hitler assured his lordship there was no fundamental difference between National Socialism and the Catholic Church. Had not the church, he argued, looked on Jews as parasites and shut them in ghettos? 'I am only doing,' he boasted, 'what the church has done for fifteen hundred years, only more effectively'. Being a Catholic himself, he told Berning, he 'admired and wanted to promote Christianity'.

It never occurred to Hitler, it seems, that Jesus, whom he referred to in *Mein Kampf* as 'the Great Founder of this new creed' and the scourge of Jews, was himself a Jew; and if not, why not? From

5

September 1941, every Jew in the Reich over six years old had to wear in public, as a badge of shame, the Star of David. Why did Hitler not insist that on the loin-cloth of every crucified Christ on display in the Reich that same Star of David should be pinned? Would he have been so keen to promote his brand of Christianity if only once he had seen Jesus crucified as he really was? Suppose Jesus had appeared naked on every cross in Germany? Would the German bishops and Pius XII have kept silent for so long had *they* seen their crucified Lord without his loin-cloth?

In spite of Christian cruelty, which to some degree prepared for the Holocaust, some Catholics still say their church has never erred.

Fifteen years after the gates of Auschwitz, Bergen-Belsen, Dachau, Ravensbruch and Treblinka were mercifully opened and, as if to confound the critics who say the papacy can never change, a pope, John XXIII, composed this remarkable prayer: 'The mark of Cain is stamped upon our foreheads. Across the centuries, our brother Abel has lain in blood which we drew, and shed tears we caused by forgetting Thy love. Forgive us, Lord, for the curse we falsely attributed to their name as Jews. Forgive us for crucifying Thee a second time in their flesh. For we knew not what we did.'

It was some atonement for over a hundred anti-Semitic documents that were published by the church between the sixth and the twentieth centuries. Not one conciliar decree, not one papal encyclical, Bull or pastoral directive suggests that Jesus' command, 'Love your neighbour as yourself', applied to Jews. Against this entire tradition, John the Good pointed to the mark of Cain on his own forehead. He accepted the church's guilt in shedding Jewish blood across the centuries, in accusing them of being accursed by God. Most movingly of all, he claimed that Catholic persecution of Jews amounted to crucifying Jesus a second time in the flesh of his own people. The pope, chief representative of a holy and infallible church, begged forgiveness for these appalling sins and errors. Our only excuse, he said, was ignorance.

Before becoming Supreme Pontiff, John had been apostolic delegate to Turkey and Greece when Hitler rose to power. He issued false baptismal certificates to four thousand Jews so that they could pose as Christians and escape the Holocaust. When the war was over and he was appointed nuncio to Paris, he went to a cinema to see the first pictures of the survivors of the Belsen death camp. He emerged in tears, saying, '*This* is the Mystical Body of Christ.' Maybe that searing experience made him the first pope who saw Jesus on the cross without his loin-cloth.

Pope John found no difficulty in acknowledging that the church was wrong. Disastrously wrong – and wrong over many centuries. He was one of the few pontiffs to see that the church's only way forward was to face fearlessly its own past, however un-Christlike it may have been. Nearly a quarter of a century after his death, there are still some believers who insist that what the church now is, it must always have been – in spite of irrefutable evidence to the contrary. They, who number millions, do not find it easy to accept that the Christian church, the Roman church, inspired by popes, many of them canonized, has been so cruel. Nor that pontiff upon pontiff almost reversed the Gospel text, 'It is better for one man to die for the sake of the people' to make it read, 'It is better for a people to suffer for the sake of one man.' There is, tragically, an undeniable link between the fires, the crosses, the papal legislation, the pogroms – and the gas-chambers and crematoria of the Nazi death camps.

There are other vital matters in the areas of power, truth and love on which the church has been disastrously wrong for century after century. The Second Vatican Council called by Pope John in 1962 began to accept this. In a revolutionary way, John, supreme pontiff, became the Devil's Advocate of the church itself.

In the canonization process, the Devil's Advocate has a central role, for the holiness of a prospective saint must be subjected to the most intense scrutiny. It is as if the church leaves Satan free to throw at the saint's memory all the dirt he can find – to see if any of it sticks. Only then will that man, woman or child be worthy of public veneration. Of course, the Devil's Advocate is really the church's champion.

When Pope John said the church needs constant reformation, he seemed to suggest that it needs a permanent Devil's Advocate. As a historian, he knew the church had done much harm. As a loving and forgiving human being, he knew that had any other institution lasted as long and possessed so much power, it would probably have done far more harm and far less good. Finally, he left behind him the clear impression that the harm done by his church must not be hidden, nor history falsified.

PART ONE

Power

'All power tends to corrupt; absolute power corrupts absolutely.' LORD ACTON, in a letter to Bishop Mandell Creighton, 1887

ONE

From Calvary to
the Vatican

ON THIS GREAT FESTIVAL OF PETER AND PAUL, the twenty-ninth day of June, they have come, young and old, sinners and saints, from every corner of the world to be with the Bishop of Rome, Vicar of Christ, Successor of the Apostles, Pontifex Maximus of the Universal Church, Patriarch of the West, Primate of Italy, Archbishop and Metropolitan of the Province of Rome, State Sovereign of Vatican City, and Servant of the servants of God, Pope John Paul II. Some pilgrims are clothed sombrely, some are in the brightly coloured folk-dress of their native lands. There are tourists among them but most are pilgrims. A visit to Rome and attendance at a papal mass are the fulfilment of a life-time's ambition.

Before dawn, they began making their way out of the honeycomb that is Rome. They emerged from expensive hotels on the Veneto, from quiet convents and cheap boarding-houses.

Their brief journey has taken them past crumbling villas, past Renaissance palaces whose huge studded doors give the impression that the owners are preparing for a fresh invasion of Goths and Vandals. They walk through piazzas with bubbling fountains, hardly recognizing some of Rome's four hundred churches, many of which are open on only one day a year, their festival day. They cross the Tiber, which for centuries served the city as both sewer and unofficial cemetery. Probably Tiber has claimed more lives than any river outside China; thousands have drowned there in a day. This morning, it is sluggish and brown as the habit of a Franciscan.

Finally, the pilgrims find themselves on the Via della Conciliazione at the end of which is one of the most impressive sights in the world. In the shimmering heat of summer, the cupola of St Peter's seems to float in space. Michelangelo, who designed it, has, more than any pope, expressed the massive and enduring strength of the greatest institution the world has ever seen. It preserved the ancient heritage. It gave barbarian hordes a new religion and a rule of law. It created Europe, giving diverse peoples a loyalty and a destiny beyond all boundaries. As Lord Macaulay said more than a century ago when he pondered on the Church of Rome:

> She was great and respected before the Saxons set
> foot in Britain, before the French had passed the

Rhine, when Grecian eloquence still flourished in Antioch, when idols were still worshipped in the temple of Mecca. And she may still exist in undiminished vigour when some traveller from New Zealand shall, in the midst of a vast solitude, take his stand on a broken arch of London Bridge to sketch the ruins of St Paul's.

As the faithful enter the piazza of St Peter's, circled by Bernini's awesome colonnade, they study the window on the third floor of the apostolic palace from which the pope blesses the crowd at noon on Sundays. Few of them know just how vast the palace is. When an ageing Leo XIII wanted to enjoy a trip round the Vatican gardens, he sat down in a small chair in his study. Then bearers carried him down spiral staircases, along labyrinthine corridors, through rooms and galleries filled with some of the great art treasures of the world, for over a mile within the palace to take him to his horse-drawn carriage.

Forty years after Leo died occurred a violation of the Vatican. The only bombs ever to be dropped on it, narrowly missing St Peter's, happened to be made in Britain. One moonless night in the Second World War, a German plane dropped four bombs captured in Tobruk, to make it appear that the Allies had attacked the holiest Catholic shrine.

Though the Vatican is only the size of a golf-course, the pilgrims are overwhelmed by the scale of their surroundings. In the centre of the piazza is the 322-ton 132-foot high obelisk of Caligula. It stood originally on the spine of Nero's Circus, close to where St Peter was crucified. This monument reminds them they are on hallowed ground.

Climbing the stone steps, they reach the portico. It, too, is immense and full of history. To the right is the Holy Door, now sealed up since it is not a Jubilee Year. Over the central arch is a representation of *Navicella*, St Peter's frail bark that has withstood the storms of the ages. This fragment of mosaic which survived the demolition of the first St Peter's, was the work of Giotto, the thirteenth-century artist who impressed the reigning pope by being able to draw, free hand, a perfect circle. In front of the central door, a porphyry disc is set in the paving. It marks the spot where, on Christmas Day 800, Charlemagne, having climbed the steps on his knees, kissing each step in turn, knelt and received from Leo III the crown of the Holy Roman Empire.

Pushing aside the heavy leather curtains, the faithful step into the basilica. Even on a dull day, a golden light streams down from the high plain windows. The floor covers six acres of multicoloured marble. The nave is 600 feet long and 80 feet wide, and at the end of it, rising higher than any palace in Rome, are the spiral columns of Bernini's colonnade.

The Corinthian columns, draped on this feast of the Apostles in the red of martyrdom, support a yellow vault 133 feet high. The holy water bowls are as big as baths, the cherubs over them are six feet tall. To right and left are gigantic statues, and chapels the size of churches. Michelangelo's best-loved work, the *Pietà*, which he carved when he was twenty-five and which alone bears his name, stands behind its protective screen. There are papal tombs to which sculptors gave years of their lives. Chateaubriand, the French diarist who lived through the Revolution, remarked in his *Memoirs* that in Rome there are more tombs than corpses; and he imagines skeletons flitting from one marble resting place to another to keep cool, as a sick man might move from his bed to one more comfortable.

At the top of the left aisle there is an altar beneath which rests the body of Pope Leo the Great. One of the noblest of popes, he was the first to be buried in St Peter's in the year 688. From that time on began the custom of having more than one altar in a place of worship. Now St Peter's, more than any church in the Christian world, is filled with altars.

High in the apse there is the gigantic Chair of St Peter, in gilded bronze, supported by effigies of four Doctors of the Church. The ornamentation covers an ordinary sedan chair that dates back at least to the second century. This is arguably the most ancient of thrones. The 'Chair within the Chair' was last seen on the Feast of the Apostles in 1867. What was revealed was a piece of chipped, worn oak, patched up with acacia wood and embellished by ivory figures, some of them upside-down.

Moving clockwise round the apse to the nave, the pilgrims come to the famous bronze statue of St Peter. It is robed, on this, the saint's feast, in a cope of gold brocade and crowned with a jewelled tiara. The extended right foot has been worn smooth by the kisses of their predecessors. It is a reminder of quite recent times when a pope, in audience, was obliged to leave his foot on a convenient cushion for visitors to kiss.

On 26 September 1967, Paul VI, with death already on his face, came here, like a doomed sparrow, before opening the first Synod of Bishops. He placed a lighted candle on the ground, then in a cloud of incense bent to kiss the foot of the statue. So many pontiffs must surely have done the same, coming down on the Vigil of Peter and Paul to worship at the shrine of the Prince of the Apostles.

In the Blessed Sacrament chapel, the papal procession is readying itself. John Paul's journey has been the shortest of all; he merely left his office on the third floor of the Palace. Yet, in many ways, he has travelled further in the last few minutes than anyone. He has left behind the cares of State, the problems of Vatican City, and assumed the role he loves best: head of the church. For a while, he can put the troubles of the church into his prayers. None knows better than he that among the assembled crowd, whose murmurs he can hear, are many bewildered members of his flock. Priests are in conflict with their bishops, nuns with their superiors; laity are aroused as never before against the moral teachings of the Church. No pope has received more adulation and less obedience. In this most sacred of times, he concentrates on his role as Shepherd of the Universal Church.

Members of his rainbow-coloured retinue – prelates, chamberlains, princes, Swiss Guards – are busy forming, shuffling themselves into the order that protocol demands, making final adjustments to their uniforms. Paul VI stopped all the feather-waving, the military regalia, the naked weapons. But weapons are there all the same. Unlike any other pontiff, around Pope John Paul are the blue-suited members of the *Ufficio centrale di vigilanza*. They form the effective security arm of the tiny city-state. Not only are they armed, they have orders to shoot to kill, should the pope's life be in danger. Under their jackets their walkie-talkies are linked to Rome's city police headquarters and the offices of the *Digos*, the Italian anti-terrorist squad. The pope is, irreverently, referred to, in the security-speak, as '*Il Bersaglio*' – 'The Target.'

Finally, to the sound of trumpets, the pontiff strides down the nave, blessing the giraffing crowd. The faithful are blind to the white-vested bishops, the twinned cardinals, the purple-clad monsignori. They see only the pope who wears the white skull-cap, the man who heads a church numbering nearly a billion, with 4,000 bishops, 400,000 priests and a million nuns. Jubilant though they are in the basilica, though they kneel and clap and swoon and even elderly nuns, for the first time in years, forget their inhibitions, they all sense he is fixed on the Other, on the God whom he represents on earth and to whom alone he is accountable. The pope is no pop-idol but the vicar of Christ, and, under Christ, essential to salvation. Through waves and waves of adulation, and camera flashes and only half-heard singing by the Sistine choir of *Tu es Petrus*, 'Thou art Peter', he reaches the high altar.

His retinue fans out, taking their places on lesser chairs. The security men disappear into the side-chapels. In every sense, the pope now stands alone. It was always so with the Roman pontiff but none was ever lonelier or more vulnerable than John Paul II.

In the Vatican's lists he is called the 263rd pontiff, but the number is not certain. There have been times when no one knew who was the rightful pope of several claimants. Moreover, it was only in the year 1073 that Pope Gregory VI forbade Catholics to call anyone pope except the Bishop of Rome. Before then, many bishops were fondly addressed as 'pope' or 'papa'. Even the title 'Bishop of Rome' is now weighted with dignities it did not always have. A leader or overseer of a small early Christian community was scarcely a modern bishop with power and jurisdiction. Many other matters, too, are far from clear.

For example, how long did Peter live in Rome? There was a late fourth-century report that he was there for twenty-five years, but there is no historical basis for this. What is known is that, about the year 58, Paul the Apostle wrote another of his letters, this time to the Romans. In it, he greeted entire households and mentioned twenty-nine individuals by name. But he did not salute Peter. That is surely an astonishing omission if Peter was residing there and was Bishop of Rome. Further, Eusebius of Caesaria, acknowledged to be the Father of Church History, writing about the year 300, said: 'Peter is reported to have preached to the Jews throughout Pontius, Galatia, Bithynia, Cappadocia and, about the end of his days, tarrying at Rome, was crucified.' Today, historians suggest that Peter lived in Rome for three or four years *at most*. There is no record that he took charge of the community there. It cannot have been automatic. He had not even been bishop in Jerusalem after Jesus' death. James, the Lord's brother, was. Then there is this startling fact: in the earliest lists of bishops of Rome, Peter's name never appeared. For example, Irenaeus, Bishop of Lyons from 178–200, was the disciple of Polycarp, Bishop of Smyrna, who was himself a disciple of John the Apostle. He enumerated all the Roman bishops up to the twelfth, Eleutherius. According to Irenaeus, the first bishop of Rome was not Peter or Paul but Linus. The Apostolic Constitution in the year 270 also named Linus as first bishop of Rome, appointed by St Paul. After Linus came Clement, chosen by Peter. The mystery deepens. In all his writings, Eusebius never once spoke of Peter as Bishop of Rome.

How is this to be explained? It seems that in the minds of the early Christian commentators the apostles were in a class apart. They did not belong to any particular church, not even when they 'planted' it, that is, founded it, as Paul did throughout Asia Minor. The apostles belonged to *the whole church*. Being an apostle precluded a man from being bishop of one place. Peter, too, whatever momentous decisions he made in Jerusalem, Antioch and elsewhere, remained an apostle of the entire community.

The Catholic church has made it a point of faith that popes are successors of St Peter *as Bishop of Rome*. But Peter never had that title; he was only invested with it centuries after he died. Naturally, he would have had immense moral authority in the Jewish–Christian community in Rome but, unlike Paul who was a Roman citizen, he would have been a foreigner there. Almost two thousand years later, another foreigner, a man from a far country, sits in what is known as Peter's Chair, as the strains of a Palestrina motet soar up into the dome.

It is nearly ten years since Karol Wojtyla of Cracow became pontiff when the first John Paul died, much mourned after a thirty-three day reign. Albino Luciani emerged after his election on to the loggia of St Peter's and smiled more in a few seconds than *his* predecessor Paul VI had smiled in fifteen years, then prophetically, without addressing one word to the crowd, stepped back into the shadows of the Vatican.

In Rome, the joke is that the oldest, most secret and most powerful of all institutions is the Sacred Congregation for the Dissemination of Rumours. In the Eternal City is anything believed unless it is whispered? Word whipped round that John Paul I had been poisoned. For centuries such things had always been said when a pontiff suddenly sickened and died. Many of these rumours were untrue. Not all, though.

On 27 July 1304, nine months into his reign, Benedict XI was in Perugia when a young man veiled as a serving sister of the Order of St Petronilla presented his Holiness with a silver salver piled with figs. 'The gift of Mother Abbess,' the demure 'sister' murmured. Benedict, everyone knew, had a passion for figs. A few days later, he was buried.

Whether this or that rumour were true or not, popes were always well advised to employ a wine-taster and to inspect the figs. But in the case of John Paul II's predecessor where is the proof? A post-mortem would have settled the matter. Maybe in spite of denials a post-mortem has. The Vatican is tight-lipped about such things.

In the conclave following Luciani's unexpected death in 1978, Karol Wojtyla was elected. He looked younger at his enthronement than his fifty-eight years. Now he looks older than sixty-seven. His shoulders are more rounded. He is thinner, the cords of his neck stand out. His eyes have narrowed betraying his Slavonic origin. As his hair has receded under the skullcap, his ears have become as prominent as when he was a boy.

Many things have helped to age him. His arduous travels. The attempt on his life on 13 May 1981 which came close to success and he needed six pints of blood in a five-and-a-half-hour operation. The paperwork that piles up on his desk each day – 'To keep the pope out of mischief', as one aide put it. And the Curia. A pope and his civil servants survive at best in an uneasy accommodation. In John Paul, the Curia have a pontiff who initially knew nothing of their wiles.

Whispers – that most powerful Congregation again – reach him in the papal apartment. The few liberal prelates who have survived in Rome dislike him for what they call his intransigence.

Some conservatives in his entourage on this great festival of the Apostles are critical, too. In their eyes, John Paul has done something little short of heresy: he has demythologized the papacy. Media pictures reveal a showbiz pope in a sombrero, pope holding hands with youths as he sways to rock music, pope being cuddled Down Under by a somewhat mystified Koala. Why, these conservatives ask, does he not stay in the Vatican, a figure of mystery and awe, like old Leo XIII who was wise enough to look at the world through a window – a closed one, too, unlike, they add, that crypto-communist John XXIII who opened a window and let in a hurricane?

The pope is above such talk. His eyes are tightly closed as he prays for all his flock, not only those assembled in St Peter's but throughout the world. He is convinced that only his voice, the voice of Peter, the voice of Christ, is strong enough to halt the Gadarene rush of the modern world into the lake of death. He is appalled at the callous indifference to the unborn. He is dismayed that virginity is almost a dirty word and homosexuality has become not merely legal but romantic. He fears that even priests and nuns are losing their dedication to their vows. As the Gospel is read by a deacon, he knows that he is the Rock, he at least must stand firm. Errors can be corrected, trends reversed if only his faith does not fail.

His eyes are webbed now, pain edges his mouth. These days, his face is sad even when, more and more rarely, he smiles, as though the sadness of his native Poland has permeated his soul. At the *mémento* of every mass, he never fails to mention the living and dead of his homeland.

Being a Pole, he never expected to be pope. Not even when he was made cardinal in 1964, nor when Paul VI chose him in 1976 to give the Lenten retreat to his household did he entertain the thought. That was against the drift of history. After four and a half centuries, the papacy was all but hereditary to the Italian nation. During that Lenten retreat, Karol Wojtyla heard Pope Paul's confession and no doubt did his best to strengthen his resolve, but how could he imagine that one day he would celebrate high mass in St Peter's as supreme pontiff? His background was: industrial labourer, rock-climber, amateur actor, spiritual resistance fighter against Nazism and, later, communism, dreamer, part-time poet. One of his poems, 'The Armaments Factory-Worker', begins: 'I cannot influence the fate of the world.'

The faithful gathered in front of him at mass think, on the contrary, that his is the greatest influence for good in the world. His integrity shines forth. Here is a man who cannot be bought and sold, a prelate in the mould of Thomas à Becket who died rather than water down the church's claims. His presence, as he proceeds to the altar to begin the canon of the mass, radiates a sense of majesty.

John Paul is the last of the absolute monarchs. The Catholics in St Peter's, on whom a hush has now settled, would not have it otherwise. He is the supreme oracle, Lord of the Church, Vicar of Christ. For them, he is endowed with an infallibility that is little short of divine. It comforts them to know that of all the religious people on earth – Jews, Hindus, Protestants, Buddhists – God speaks in a special way to them through his Holiness. Their spiritual life flows from him; he, being the church's head, is the bond that unites them to God and to each other. Many, however mistakenly, think their faith derives from him and bishops get their power from him. There are not a few non-Catholics in St Peter's for this festival mass who also feel that Pope John Paul II is the world's best bulwark against atheistic communism in the East and the widespread, more subtle atheism of a secularized West.

The pope speaks softly but clearly the words of the mass. Every gesture is according to the rubrics, for he knows that if he departs from them, priests everywhere will take it into their heads to make modifications of their own. And as he proceeds, the faithful in the basilica wonder how John Paul sees himself. In a sense, it is not so difficult to know. In spite of his travels, his endless allocutions, even after Vatican II – maybe *because* of Vatican II – he realizes that this pageant in St Peter's is not the whole truth about the church he heads. As he pauses to remember the living, his widespread flock, his prayer is influenced by all those depressing statistics piled upon his desk.

Priests are the pontiff's first concern. In 1971, a study commissioned by the Sacred Congregation of the Faith was leaked to the press. It revealed that from 1963 to 1969 over 8,000 priests had asked to be dispensed from their vows and nearly 3,000 others had left without waiting for permission. The study estimated that over the next five years 20,000 would leave. The estimate proved to be far too conservative.

Matters were worst in countries that pontiffs had relied on for providing missionaries. Holland, for example, used to produce over 300 priests a year. Now, ordinations are almost as rare as mountains. In Ireland, at the end of 1987, there were 6,000 priests and over 1,000 ex-priests. In the United States of America there are reckoned to be 17,000 ex-priests. The average age of those who remain is a startlingly high 54. The future, too, looks bleak. Over the last twenty years, the number of seminarians in the States has fallen from 50,000 to 12,000.

The pontiff prays for the laity with their manifold concerns. He prays for those present and those, all over the world, who have begun to parade their disobedience. In advance of his trip to America in September 1987, he must have read a *Time* magazine poll. It revealed that 93 per cent of Catholics hold 'it is possible to disagree with the pope and still be a good Catholic'. Even in Ireland, a poll at about the same time showed that only one young person in three agrees with him on contraception. All the indicators suggest a worldwide community in Napoleonic retreat. The church is still teaching but fewer and fewer are listening.

The mass was supposed to give the pontiff a respite from the cares and burdens of office. In a sense, it deepens his worries. He has to let Jesus, whose sacrifice he is preparing to commemorate, take his burdens from him.

As the consecration draws near, perhaps John Paul's mind goes back to his childhood in Wadowice when he served at the altar and learned the Latin responses of the mass. In those days, the pope's word *was* Catholicism. It disheartens him to find that, now he is pontiff, on many issues he calls critical he is *in a minority*.

That is why, at this papal mass, he does not see the cardinals glorious as flamingos around him. Prelates like snowy-haired Ratzinger from Munich, since 1982 head of the Sacred Congregation of the Faith, once called the Holy Inquisition. The pope is equally unaware of the splashes of red and purple from prelatial robes of all degrees. He does not bother to look at the crammed tribunes in which ambassadors, obscure royal personages and obscurer princes and princesses sit in gold and diamonded splendour.

He sees no one; no one else sees anyone but him.

'This is my body.' The pope utters these words with overpowering devotion, as full of awe today as when he said them at his first mass forty years ago. 'This is my blood.' Now it is not the Vicar of Christ but Christ himself who is the focus of the silent congregation.

It is so at every mass whether it be said in the humblest village church or in a basilica like St Peter's. Jesus Christ is Lord; and the pope represents him and his teaching authority in the world today. Is not the congregation right to see the pope as the freest, most sovereign person in the world?

The truth is, the pontiff is a prisoner.

The first consequence of absolutism is that those closest to the source of power inhale the same air as the monarch. In the pope's case, faceless men, paper-shufflers, pen-pushers in dark offices in and around the Vatican, make sure the pope's vision matches theirs. They feed him selective information; they hide from him whatever would contradict a cause they wish to promote. These are the first of the pope's gaolers.

The Second Vatican Council, 1962–5, was aimed at liberalizing the Roman Church. No sooner was it over than the old bureaucrats took charge; they have been in charge ever since, interpreting liberal decrees in an illiberal way.

Even the First Vatican Council, summoned by Pius IX in 1869 to declare him infallible, refused to discuss the draft decrees drawn up by the Curia. They did not represent, the bishops said, the faith of the church, only one biased school of theology. But, in the end, the bureaucrats always win. They remain in place when the more liberally minded men have dispersed. Curial officials, many of whom are present at this mass, have always hated councils for daring to threaten their infallibility. As one embittered diocesan bishop said recently: 'The Curia is a Church Council in permanent session.'

For all his apparent muscle, John Paul continues to sign documents prepared by prelates in the Holy Office or the Secretariat of State. Someone suggests to him that a particular bishop in North America is not quite orthodox, as the Curia interprets the word. Would it not be wise to keep him under surveillance?

Then there are those voluminous files in the Holy Office on theologians like Küng of Tübingen or Curran of Washington. On other promising clerics, too. Where does this priest or that monsignor stand on Christ, on Mary, on frequent confession? Has he ever been soft on contraception? Has he ever taken part in anti-nuclear demonstrations? Does he sympathize with Karl Marx? Many an up-and-coming cleric can be kept permanently down by means of a single innuendo. Most curial poisons are administered aurally.

In this, it might be said, the pontiff is served no differently from any other leader caught in the web of his civil service. Except that the pope himself has a host of unseen 'watchers' who keep an eye on *him*.

A pontiff, more than any other monarch, is a prisoner of the past. The congregation can see signs of it in the pope's dress. In the mitre, the pallium, the Fisherman's Ring. Not just the basilica itself, the famous relics it contains; even items of dress show that the pontiff is himself a prisoner of history. But most shackles are in the mind.

The pontiff can never speak without taking account of what his predecessors have said on the same or a related topic. In any papal encyclical, for every biblical quotation there are likely to be up to a dozen references to earlier popes. All pontiffs drive by the rear-view mirror. A past long dead, often called tradition, dictates the road into the future. One dead pope is more powerful than a thousand living bishops.

'*Pax vobiscum*,' the pope says. 'Peace be with you.' The congregation embrace each other as they pass on this sign of peace. But whoever bears the burden of infallible office cannot always be a man of peace; he also brings a sword. For he cannot, out of supposed compassion, afford even once to make or risk making the slightest mistake in doctrine or morals. He has to be careful not to contradict a pontiff of seven or ten centuries ago. No wonder his Curia cannot always distinguish novelty from originality.

Pope John Paul, with eyes reverently closed, receives the body and blood of Christ. Everywhere in the basilica priests appear in cotta and stole to distribute communion, the body of Christ, to the faithful. The church herself is called the body of Christ. In receiving communion, the faithful are in touch with their crucified and risen Lord and with all their fellow Christians, living and dead. That small wafer links them sacramentally with the entire history of the church.

That history has been good and bad, full of heroic deeds and ignoble crimes. The pontiff is a prisoner even of those crimes. He knows the church was responsible for persecuting Jews, for the Inquisition, for slaughtering heretics by the thousand, for reintroducing torture into Europe as part of the judicial process. But he has to be careful. The doctrines responsible for those terrible things still underpin his position. Methods may differ, the aim remains the same. The whole world must be brought to acknowledge Christ and his church. Ruled and guided by the pope, the Catholic church has the fullness of truth to which other religions can at best approximate.

John Paul, praying as communion is distributed, would not want people to think that compassion is incompatible with inflexibility towards truth. Freedom to teach error, he believes, is mistaken. How can anyone have the *right* to teach as true what the church says is untrue or immoral? He, like every pontiff, takes it for granted that where the church is strong, her power must be used to outlaw what she condemns. Pius IX, proclaimed infallible in this very basilica in 1870, was quite open about this. In the archives of the Foreign Office in London, there is a letter dated 15 February 1865 and marked 'Confidential'. It was from Odo Russell, representative of the British government in the Vatican. He reported what the pope said to him in an audience: 'That liberty of conscience and toleration I condemn here [in Rome], I claim in England and other foreign countries for the Catholic Church.' Pius IX was only concerned with a political judgement: Would the church stand to lose or gain by refusing to others the freedom she demands for herself?

Pius IX, like the present pontiff, was convinced that the church has managed to go doctrinally unchanged throughout the ages. The faithful in St Peter's share that conviction, believing that the papacy is chiefly responsible for this almost miraculous continuity.

The fact is, the church has changed radically in even vital areas such as sex, money and salvation.

To take two of the more interesting examples.

Every pontiff up to and including the nineteenth century condemned the taking of interest on loans (usury) under *any* circumstances. It did not matter whether the interest charged was high or low, whether the loan was made to a poor peasant or an emperor. Centuries after peasant communities ceased to be the norm, the church went on condemning interest-taking and, surprisingly, has never officially withdrawn its ban. Yet today the Vatican has its own bank, established in 1942 by Pius XII, which has recently been the focus of terrible financial scandals.

A second proof of radical change concerns the Catholic teaching, 'There is no salvation outside the church'. It was first formulated to exclude all the unbaptized, such as Jews and unbelievers. Even babies born of Christians who died before baptism were said to be excluded from heaven. Today, John Paul still teaches there is no salvation outside the church but 'church' and 'salvation' are so widely interpreted that all people of goodwill, even atheists, can be saved. This linguistic trick stops Catholics seeing that traditional teaching has been *reversed*. To admit change would expose too much of the past as

21

a bad dream. That is why, like all authoritarian bodies, the Catholic church refuses to admit she has changed in essentials, even when she has improved.

Apart from these pointers, it is enough to suggest that almost every document of Vatican II would have been condemned as heretical by Vatican I. The orthodoxy of one age is not the orthodoxy of another.

The chief disadvantage of an infallible institution is that no claim can be withdrawn, no doctrine denied, no moral decision reversed, even when new arguments suggest a radical overhaul.

None of this concerns the faithful in St Peter's. They believe John Paul is infallible and, though they are not thinking expressly of that now, it influences their love and loyalty. As he makes his devotions after communion, they see him at the altar with the eyes of faith.

In front of that altar at which he alone says mass, there is an oval space. This is the Confession or Martyr's Tomb. It is lit today as on every day by ninety-three lamps in triple clusters; its walls and floors are covered with jasper, agate and porphyry. Saints like Dominic and Ignatius Loyola, emperors like Charlemagne and Frederick Barbarossa have knelt here to honour Peter. For beneath the feet of John Paul II is buried St Peter whose bones have consecrated not only this mighty basilica but also his successors in the See of Rome.

Not a single person present doubts that St Peter is buried in this church that bears his name. But is he?

The Catholic church is sometimes dogmatic when doubts, or at least reservations are in order. In fact, there is no simple answer to the question of where Peter is buried.

In the early period after Peter's death, his bones were moved a couple of times to safer sites. When troubles died down, the body was returned to where Peter gave the witness of his life. A small oratory was erected over his tomb, followed in the fourth century by Constantine's basilica which stood for eleven hundred years.

Few of the faithful in St Peter's on this festival of the apostles realize that over a thousand years ago a decision was made to separate the heads of Peter and Paul from their trunks. Those heads have been kept ever since in St John Lateran which is the pope's cathedral and the mother-church of Christendom. St John Lateran was also built by Constantine next to the Lateran palace which he bestowed on the Bishop of Rome.

By the ancient laws of Rome and the canons of Catholic theology, it follows that Peter is not really buried in St Peter's but with Paul in St John Lateran. Where the head is, so runs the ancient maxim, there is the place of burial. Even today, pastoral practice considers the head the most important part of the remains. In a case of decapitation or a mangled death, it is the head that is anointed with sacred chrism.

There was one occasion when Peter's head rejoined his trunk. In

1241, Emperor Frederick II marched on Rome. Many citizens, disgusted with the behaviour of the papacy, were preparing to throw open the city's gates to let the invaders in. Pope Gregory IX, near to death, hit on the idea of processing with the heads of the two great apostles from the Lateran to St Peter's. It worked. The citizens of Rome, realizing they stood to lose not only their heritage but their chief source of income, closed ranks and danger was averted.

In 1370, Pope Urban V enclosed the heads in silver busts encrusted with precious gems. In this way, he prepared for a further drama.

In 1438 a wealthy Venetian was on the point of death. Despairing of doctors, he prayed to Peter and Paul, promising that he would adorn their reliquaries with a pearl of great price if he recovered. He did and kept his word. Soon afterwards, a dozen pearls were found to be missing from the reliquaries, as well as two rubies of forty-seven and forty-eight carats, a sapphire and three large diamonds. The Venetian's pearl, too, had been snatched, probably on the very feast of St Peter and St Paul when the relics were on display.

The culprits were soon traced. Two cousins confessed to hiding their booty in the home of their uncle.

They became Roman sport. As a climax to a carnival in the piazza of St John Lateran, the two young men had their right hands chopped off before they were burned. Their uncle, a mere receiver, was treated more leniently. After being prodded with red-hot tongs, he was hanged.

In 1799, Napoleon's soldiers stole the reliquaries. They pocketed the gems, including the pearl, but left the relics behind. These were found, so it was said, with the original seal intact. Nothing was left but vertebrae, a jaw-bone with a few loose teeth and a portion of skull. New gold reliquaries were made, and the heads now rest in the shrine above the papal altar of the Lateran. It is there, strictly speaking, that both apostles are buried together. Since St John Lateran is also 'the Mother and Head of all the churches in the city and in the world' it is surely there that the Holy Father should have celebrated mass on the festival of St Peter and St Paul.

There is an over-riding reason why he did not do so.

The pope says mass with Peter's trunk beneath his feet. Two hundred feet above his head there is something far more important than Peter's remains: words of the Lord. In letters five feet high, running round the dome, is the most famous of all puns: '*Tu es Petrus, et super hanc petram aedificabo ecclesiam meam, et portae inferi non praevalebunt adversus eam*' – 'Thou art Peter and upon this Rock I will build my church and the gates of hell will not prevail against it.' Scholars assume that in the original Aramaic, the pun was perfect: Peter and Rock are both *Cepha*. This is the text that forms the background of all Pope John Paul's thinking. Who would doubt that he frequently takes this text, in all humility, for his meditation? This text is the reason why pontiffs now prefer to celebrate the feast of St Peter and St Paul *in St Peter's*, rather than in the more obvious place, St John Lateran. For Roman pontiffs claim to be successors not of Peter *and* Paul but of Peter *alone*. The New Testament speaks of Peter as the apostle to the Jews and Paul as apostle to the Gentiles. But in the pope's mind, Peter was Paul's superior; Peter had jurisdiction over Paul and the other disciples. This authority was given Peter by the Lord himself in those words circling the great dome. It is this supreme authority that he, John Paul II, has inherited. Why is it, his Holiness must wonder, that Protestants cannot be logical? Jesus, the Son of God, gave Peter supremacy over the church; this supremacy must remain in the church as a permanent office; he, John Paul, is the present holder of this office.

There is, however, another interpretation of this text with a better pedigree than most Catholics realize. It may jolt them to hear that the great Fathers of the church saw no connection between it and the pope. Not one of them applies 'Thou art Peter' to anyone but Peter. One after another they analyse it: Cyprian, Origen, Cyril, Hilary, Jerome, Ambrose, Augustine. They are not exactly Protestants. Not one of them calls the Bishop of Rome a Rock or applies to him *specifically* the promise of the Keys. This is as staggering to Catholics as if they were to find no mention in the Fathers of the Holy Spirit or the resurrection of the dead. The great pun, the play on words, was applied exclusively to Peter.

The surprises do not stop there. For the Fathers, it is Peter's faith – or the Lord in whom Peter has faith – which is called the Rock, not Peter. All the Councils of the church from Nicaea in the fourth century to Constance in the fifteenth agree that Christ himself is the only foundation of the church, that is, the Rock on which the church rests.

Perhaps this is why not one of the Fathers speaks of a transference of power from Peter to those who succeed him; not one speaks, as church documents do today, of an 'inheritance'. There is no hint of an abiding Petrine *office*. In so far as the Fathers speak of an office, the reference is to the episcopate in general. All bishops are successors to all the apostles.

Analysis of another important Gospel text yields the same result. Jesus said to Peter: 'I have prayed for thee that thy faith should not fail; and when thou art converted, confirm thy brethren.' This statement only applied to Peter personally. It never occurred to the eighteen or so Fathers who commented on this text that there is a promise in it to 'Peter's successors'. Peter, as an individual, had no successors.

What, then, becomes of the promises said to be made via Peter to his 'successors', the popes? Do not popes inherit infallibility and world-wide jurisdiction from Peter?

The first problem about infallibility is that the New Testament makes it plain that Peter himself made tremendous errors both before

and after Jesus died. When, for instance, Jesus insisted that he had to go up to Jerusalem where he would be crucified, Peter protested so much that Jesus called him a 'satan' in his path. Some Catholic theologians have suggested that these words, 'Get thee behind me Satan', should be added to the Petrine text already inscribed round Michelangelo's dome. After Jesus' resurrection, Peter made an equally bad blunder. 'Heresy' is not too bad a word for it. The church's greatest ever canon lawyer, Gratian, said in 1150: '*Petrus cogebat Gentes Judaizare et a veritate evangelii recedere*', 'Peter compelled the Gentiles to live as Jews and to depart from Gospel truth'.

As to worldwide jurisdiction, did it ever cross Peter's mind when he preached to his little flock at Antioch or Rome that he had command over the whole church? Such an idea had to wait until Christianity was integrated into the Roman Empire. Even then it took time for the papacy to grow to the stature that made such a pretention plausible.

The difficulties do not stop there. Popes are only said to be infallible when they address the whole church. When did they first do so? Certainly not in the first millennium. During that time, as everybody agrees, only General Councils expressed the mind of the church. Was the pope's supreme power suspended all that while? If the church managed to function without it for a thousand years, why should she need it at all? By a piece of bad luck, one of the first if not *the* first, papal document addressed to the universal church was *Unam Sanctam*, a Bull of Boniface VIII in 1302. It was so far-fetched a document, it raised ticklish questions about infallibility at the First Vatican Council in 1870.

So the early church did not look on Peter as Bishop of Rome, nor, therefore, did it think that each Bishop of Rome *succeeded* to Peter. Nevertheless, Rome was held in highest esteem for rather different reasons. In the first place, it was where Peter *and* Paul had witnessed with their lives. Secondly, Rome was a sacred spot because there the faithful, clergy and laity, kept their bodies and reverenced them. Those bodies were a kind of pledge of orthodoxy throughout the ages.

Decades passed. The Bishop of Rome became increasingly important, especially when the Imperial Court was transferred to Constantinople in the fourth century. That left an enormous political, administrative and emotional gap. The Bishops of Rome were on hand, so to speak, to fill it. From this time on, the Bishops of Rome started to separate Peter from Paul, and applied to themselves the promises made in the gospel to Peter. Such was now the prestige of the Bishop of Rome that scholars searched the scriptures for texts that would underpin his role as civil leader and patriarch of the West. What could be neater than to apply texts which in the gospels refer only to Peter to the bishop who rules in the city where Peter died? The gospels did not create the papacy; the papacy, once in being, leaned for support on the gospels. This support did not come easily; it required skill to take

statements made by a poor Carpenter to an equally poor Fisherman and apply them to a regal pontiff who was soon to be called Lord of the World.

In St Peter's on this festival, John Paul is not thinking of himself as Lord of the World but as Chief Shepherd of the flock. He gives his final blessing and the crowd breaks into applause. For the first time since entering the basilica, the pontiff allows himself to smile. The sacred liturgy is over and he returns down the nave to the Blessed Sacrament chapel, bestowing benedictions along his path. For many people as they stream out of the basilica, this has been the most memorable day of their lives.

As the basilica returns to normal, it is tempting to ask: If Peter were to arise from his tomb under the dome and be told that all this was erected in his honour, how would he react?

Of course, anyone coming back from the dead after only fifty years would be shaken to the core, and Peter died for Christ over nineteen centuries ago. Who can tell how he would respond to the marvels of modern technology: aeroplanes, cars, television, telephones? There are eighty telephone receivers in St Peter's alone – dial 3712 and the phone will ring in the shadow of the high altar. The spread of the church and its organization would also astonish him. A loose affiliation of a few Jewish fishermen and their mostly peasant converts is bound to differ from a worldwide closely knit church approaching a billion.

The only fair question is: If Peter came back as a pilgrim, how would he judge what goes on in the Vatican by the standards of the Gospel?

Jesus was born in a stable. In his ministry, he had nowhere to lay his head.

Today, his Vicar inhabits a palace with eleven thousand rooms. And then there is Castelgandolfo, overlooking the Alban Lake where pontiffs go to escape the summer heat. Beautiful Castelgandolfo, slightly larger than the Vatican, is where John Paul, at some cost, had a swimming pool built for his personal use.

Jesus renounced possessions. He constantly taught: 'Go, sell all thou hast and give to the poor, then come and follow me.' He preached doom to the rich and powerful. Lay up for yourselves treasures in heaven, he said, where neither rust nor moth can spoil it.

Christ's Vicar lives surrounded by treasures, some of pagan origin. Any suggestion that the pope should sell all he has and give to the poor is greeted with derision as impractical. The rich young man in the gospel reacted in the same way.

Throughout his life, Jesus lived simply; he died naked, offering the sacrifice of his life on the cross.

When the pope renews that sacrifice at pontifical high mass, no greater contrast could be imagined. Without any sense of irony, Christ's Vicar is clad in gold and the costliest silks. This has often been a source of scandal. For example, in the fourteenth century, the great Petrarch described a papal mass in Avignon which was far less splendid than the recent ceremony in St Peter's. 'I am astounded,' Petrarch wrote, 'as I recall the pope's predecessors, to see these men loaded with gold and clad in purple. We seem to be among the kings of the Persians or the Parthians, before whom we must fall down and worship. O apostles and early popes, ye unkempt and emaciated old men, is it for this ye laboured?'

Jesus' only title was given him by Pilate in mockery: 'King of the Jews'.

In the Pontifical Yearbook, Peter sees the pope has a dozen glorious titles, including State Sovereign. He would find Pontifex Maximus the most surprising, for in his time that was the title of the pagan high priest of Rome. Besides, Jesus was only a layman.

The pope's aides also have titles somewhat unexpected in the light of the Sermon on the Mount: Excellency, Eminence, Your Grace, My Lord, Illustrious One, Most Reverend, and so on. However, the cardinals' hats that once brought in millions to the papal coffers are now handed over free of charge. But still their Eminences dress like royalty, even if their trains have been cut back recently by several yards. Impressions *do* matter. Those who dress in purple silk, live in palaces, sit on thrones – it is not easy for them to act as servants of the servants of God or to represent the Poor Man of Nazareth to the poor and starving of the world. Only twice has John Paul called his cardinals together. Each time it was to discuss the parlous state of Vatican finances.

Peter, always penniless, would be intrigued to know that according to canon 1518 of the 1917 code his successor is 'the supreme administrator and manager of all church properties'. Also that the Vatican has its own bank to which clients are only admitted if, in addition to sound references, they can provide something Peter himself never had: a baptismal certificate.

The celibacy of the clergy, popes included, might also surprise Peter, seeing that Jesus chose him, knowing he was married.

Peter would finally be staggered at the sheer number of images in St Peter's. He and his Master, as Jews, were opposed to religious images. God, whose very name could not be uttered, could not be represented, either. Reverence for One who dwells in inaccessible light demands the utmost reticence. Even the Holy of Holies in the Jerusalem temple was but a bare dark room.

In St Peter's, Jesus is crucified at every altar. The basilica is decorated with statues of kneeling and reclining popes. Some figures are less than edifying. Pope Paul III, for instance, lies buried in the apse. His monument is adorned with reclining beauties, one of whom is Justice. Originally naked, she was fitted with a metal chemise, painted to look like the original marble, at the command of Pius IX. His Holiness had discovered that the model for Justice was Paul III's sister Giulia, the mistress of Pope Alexander VI.

Peter attended the simple ceremony of the Supper on the night before Jesus died. He knew that on the rocky knoll outside Jerusalem, Jesus, previously reviled, scourged, spat upon, his head crowned with thorns, was stripped naked and crucified between two thieves.

What connection, if any, Peter would wonder, is there between those events and a papal mass? Has all this pageantry distorted and trivialized the message of Jesus? How and by what tortuous paths has a small persecuted community traversed the seemingly infinite distance between Calvary and the Vatican?

TWO

The Quest for
Absolute Power

THE MILLIONS WHO VISIT the Vatican each year sense the power of the church. The walls, the statues, the giant pillars, that omnipresent dome, they all exude it. If they are fortunate to have an audience with the Holy Father or merely receive his blessing from his study window, most pilgrims feel a force pass from him to them. He possesses, such is their faith, the gift of God's Spirit to an eminent degree. Even a rosary blessed by the pontiff has a special significance; it is like an invisible autograph. He has great power from God and he is pledged to use it for the good of mankind.

Papal prestige today is very high. In this century, pontiffs have achieved world renown. Historic events and instant communication have contributed to make them 'Spokesmen of Religion'. Their own personalities have also had something to do with this. John Paul's recent predecessors have also been men of eminence: Pius XI, Pius XII, John XXIII, Paul VI, John Paul I. They have had their critics inside and outside the church. Few would deny that their chief aim was to follow Jesus Christ. The result is: John Paul II, by common consent, is the only leader whose standing in religion matches the political clout of the American President and the Soviet General Secretary.

Not realizing that the past is unpredictable, many Catholics take it for granted that most popes have been on this pattern. Unlearned in history, they allow themselves, in Acton's phrase 'to be governed by the Unknown Past'. They may have heard of Pope Alexander VI, the infamous Borgia. He was, no doubt, the exception that proves the rule. Besides, however bad a pope, they take it for granted, with Joseph de Maistre, the nineteenth-century historian, that 'the Bulls of these monsters were irreproachable'. Whatever their private morals, they never compromised the faith of the church. In this context, even Judas Iscariot brings comfort. If one of Jesus' closest disciples betrayed the Lord, should we be surprised if one pope or a few abused the power God gave them? Judas' betrayal led to the world's salvation. Could it be that God uses the occasional evil pope to prove that, in God's providence, even Alexander VI still mediates God's truth and love?

In 1895, Cardinal Vaughan of Westminster said in a sermon: 'The life of the papacy is like that of Christ himself, chequered by sufferings and peaceful times; today hosannas, tomorrow the passion and crucifixion;

29

but then followed by the resurrection. The Vicar of Christ and His Church are necessarily in conflict with the false maxims of the world; and sufferings and persecutions are the inevitable consequence.'

Who could forgive his hearers for concluding that most popes were Christ-figures? But this everlastingly sunny side of the papacy needs complementing by the darker side. Most Catholics go through life and never hear in school or church a word of reproach for any pope. Yet a devout Catholic like Dante had no scruple about dumping pontiff after pontiff in the deepest pit of hell. If Jews in their psalms condemn – even curse – God, cannot Catholics condemn popes when they deserve it? The history of the popes is, to borrow a phrase from Mr Gorbachev, full of blank pages. Not all popes have been saints; many were hardly Christians. Until Pius IX lost the Papal States in 1870, popes were seldom even liked. They were often hated and feared.

Distortion begins in the lists of the popes where all but one of the first thirty popes are described as martyrs. They probably were martyrs in the sense of 'witnesses of the faith'. There is no evidence that all died for Christ. Further, among the popes were a large number of married men, some of whom gave up their wives and children in exchange for the papal office. Many were sons of priests, bishops and popes; some were bastards; one was a widower, another an ex-slave; several were murderers, some unbelievers; some were hermits, some heretics, sadists and sodomites; many became popes by buying the papacy (simony), and continued their days selling holy things to rake in the money; one at least was a Satan-worshipper; some fathered illegitimate children, some were fornicators and adulterers on a grand scale; some were astonishingly old, some even more astonishingly young; some were poisoned, others strangled; worst of all were those who worshipped a granite God. As well as these, many were good, holy and selfless popes, and a few martyrs.

It is time to cease treating the papacy in terms of hagiography. The studied silence about the sins of the papacy is a scandal and a form of bad faith. Worse, it makes the present crisis in the church impossible to resolve.

The greatest of the papacy's sins, the source of most others, was the abuse of its immense power. It is strange to think that the person from whom it was allegedly derived lived and died without any power at all.

'The First Pope'

He had been so long in the dungeon he had lost track of time. The walls and floor were scabbed with blood. The heat and stench were intolerable. Flea-bitten, rat-bitten, he lay, old and thin, in a bed of damp straw. He was the happiest man in Rome, maybe in the whole world.

His gaolers called this 'solitary confinement'; the prisoner knew he was never less alone. In his heart was the Master whom he served all those years ago in their homeland by the blue waters of an inland sea. In darkness, he lived in the dazzling light of Christ. In chains, he was a free man.

The memories washed over him. He remembered the call, 'Come, follow me'. He dropped everything: nets, livelihood, independence. He gave his word and never took it back, in spite of the occasional lapse.

There *were* things to be ashamed of. When, for instance, the Master hinted that they must go to Jerusalem where death was waiting for him, Peter objected. Jesus rounded on him: 'Get thee behind me, Satan.' It still rang in his ears. Peter did not understand then. How could he?

Worse was to come. In the Garden of Gethsemane, late at night after a Passover meal, Jesus, so lonely, so afraid, had asked him to watch and pray. The prisoner was young then, he needed more sleep than now, but the memory shamed him. He could still feel the hand on his shoulder, nudging him awake, and that gentle voice, hurt but not resentful: 'Could you not watch one hour with me?' The High Priest's servants came with staves and swords to arrest Jesus. The prisoner had grabbed a sword and hacked at the ear of a servant called Malchus. Jesus hated swords. He told Peter the place for swords was the scabbard and did his best for Malchus, apologizing all the while.

That was when Peter and the rest ran away. What point in staying close to a man who refused to defend himself, who treated his enemies as he would his friends?

Peter had followed to the courtyard of the High Priest. He tried to warm himself by the fire, but the cold that gripped him was not in his limbs. Now, in the stifling heat of his cell, he shivered at the bitter memory of denying his Master before a serving girl. He would never forget the look Jesus gave him when he was led out like a lamb for slaughter. No words, just a glance. He was supposed to be tough, but he split down the middle; he left crying like a child.

Next day, he no doubt watched the crucifixion from a great distance. Was this the end? Or would God intervene and rescue Jesus, pull out the nails, restore him to his followers, unharmed and triumphant? If so, it would prove he was the Messiah, God's Anointed, who would lead them on to glory. The extraordinary thing was *nothing happened*. No angel came to comfort him. He just died.

Peter saw soldiers take down his body and those of the two crucified with him. He was devastated. The cross seemed to show Jesus was, for all his lovableness, a false messiah, deluded like so many others. With his Galilean friends, Peter went home. It was in Galilee, where Jesus had once called him beside the lake, that he had a resurrection experience. Paul was to say that Peter first *saw* the Lord. By an inspiration, a vision not attributable to flesh and blood, he grasped that the cross was not the end but the beginning; it was both scandal *and* salvation. He convinced the other disciples; they had the same experience. They, too, saw the Lord.

Later, intricate stories, spread about Jesus being buried in an unused rock-tomb, and how, on what was to be called Easter Day, the rock was rolled away to reveal an empty grave. The stories contradicted one another at many points. But they expressed in a Jewish way the disciples' experience: Jesus was not cursed on the cross; he became by means of it Lord and Christ. He *was* the Messiah, after all. He was risen.

The disciples had returned to Jerusalem, preaching their faith. Their stories told of eating and drinking with Jesus after his resurrection to help others believe. Special prestige attached to Peter. He was the Rock on which the new grouping – later called 'the church' – was built. His faith had confirmed his brethren. He was the shepherd who brought into one fold the flock of lost sheep. He was chief fisher of men. He was the first Christian.

Together, the disciples read again Moses and the prophets. These, too, made it plain that the cross was part of God's plan. Men must live their lives in the shadow of the cross which would save them as it had once lifted Jesus from agony to glory.

The prisoner spent all his days smiling in the darkness of the Mamertine. Nothing mattered to him or the disciples once they knew that the Lord was risen from the dead. He was the Suffering Servant of God. What else had he preached about and shown them except that he had come not to be served but to serve, to give his life for others? This explained why he turned his back on force, why he laughed at the idea of a sword helping to promote his message. He had come not to wound and kill but to be wounded and, if need be, to die, so that God's love and compassion would shine through the gaping wounds of his body.

For some while, one thing bothered Peter: Who were eligible to be Jesus' disciples? Only Jews? If Gentiles too, would they have to become Jews first? He found the answer in a strange dream that convinced him that nothing was required of Gentile converts but faith in Christ.

Later, he back-tracked. He urged Gentiles to abide by Jewish dietary laws. That was when a forceful new convert showed his mettle. 'When Cephas [Peter] came to Antioch,' Paul said, 'I opposed him to his face because he was so obviously wrong. . . . I said to Cephas in front of everyone, "You are a Jew yet you live like a Gentile. How can you force Gentiles to live like Jews?"'

Peter accepted correction. He had made an awful mistake. Had Paul not put him right, the message that man is only justified by faith would have been ruined from the start. After this, Peter and Paul divided up the mission: Peter preached to Jews and Paul, a Roman citizen, to Gentiles.

After organizing the church in many places, Peter, much later, felt drawn to the capital of the Empire. When Jesus was born, he was enrolled in a census ordered by Augustus. He was executed by Romans. Since they were masters of the world, it was in Rome, where, according to Tacitus, all the shame and vice of the world congregate, that Peter had to make converts.

Jews were long established in Rome. They were looked on with suspicion because of their refusal to worship, as polite immigrants usually did, the gods of the Pantheon. This amounted to treason, but Romans were generally tolerant in matters of religion. The Jews survived, were given exemption from worshipping the *manes*. In time, they were even given legal status.

Peter had a hard job preaching Jesus to his fellow Jews. To them, Peter was a heretic. He accepted the Jewish Bible but not circumcision. He honoured Abraham, Moses and David, but did not keep their festivals. He even worshipped God on a Sabbath of his own. Above all, Jews did not take to the idea of a crucified Messiah. Jesus convinced no one while he lived, he died like the brigand he was, and his so-called resurrection was based on the testimony of a few crazy women.

In the Rome of Peter's day, the Forum and the Palatine were impressive even at a distance. The palace of Augustus glistened white in the sun. Peter was glad Christians owned nothing but a few underground burial-places.

He could not help contrasting the Caesars and his Master. Jesus had no armies, no weapons apart from one rusty sword a follower had picked up by the way. His only authority was love; it was the only authority he bequeathed his disciples. All forms of compulsion and worldly titles were alien to him. He ran and hid in the hills when the crowds wanted to make him king. Kingly rule was God's and it came about through mercy, poverty, self-giving to God and one's fellows. Even after death, Jesus went on suffering in his brethren. He would help them carry their cross; he would never approve any cruelty they did. Jesus' empire was of love and peace.

Christians were taken by the Romans to be a Jewish sect. They, too, were considered hostile to society. They were even accused of having their own king. Peter knew Christ was no rival to Caesar, nor were Christians traitors for worshipping him. Faith was distinct from citizenship; it made them better citizens.

Emperor Nero did not agree. He enjoyed persecuting these rebels. He made Christians play the part of Actaeon. Dressed in animal skins, they were torn to bits by dogs.

On 19 July 64, Rome burst into flames. The circumstances were suspicious. Nero was taking the sea air at Anzio; the *triumviri nocturni*, the military firewatchers, were off duty. The fire raged for a week, destroying ten of the fourteen regions of the city. When Nero returned, Poppaea his empress and the pantomimist Aliturus whispered in his ear: 'Christians.' Of course, *they* were responsible.

In his circus, built in the beautiful Quintillian meadows, Christians were appropriately punished. The circus, with the obelisk from Heliopolis in its spine, glowed night after night with lighted candles. Christians, men, women and children, fixed on crosses, burned very well. In fact they died magnificently, the first of many.

Not long after the fire, Peter was imprisoned. It was his own death he contemplated now, without fear. If only he could go to God as Jesus did.

He had his wish. One day, he was led up into fresh air that nearly choked him and blinding sunshine. Handed a cross, he was told to start walking. Word whipped round, and soon Linus was on the scene. The Big Fisherman was going to Jesus. From a discreet distance, they saw how thin and frail he was after his long confinement. But he was happy; they saw that, too.

When they reached the north side of the circus, Peter asked to be crucified upside down out of respect for his Master. The soldiers did not query it. A criminal's last wish should, if possible, be honoured. Death came quickly to the old man; the blood flowed to his head. He passed from unconsciousness to glory.

That night, his followers reclaimed the body and buried it close to the wall where victims of the circus were usually interred. The plot was by the first milestone on the Via Cornelia. Thirty years later, Anacletus was to build an oratory over it where three or four could pray together.

The Latin writer Tertullian said: 'Orientem fidem primus Nero cruentavit . . .', 'Nero was the first to stain the rising faith with blood. Peter, as Christ foretold, was girded by another when he was fastened to a cross; then did Paul attain, in the highest sense, the freedom of Rome. . . . How happy is this Church whose teaching the Apostles watered with their blood.'

The time is not far off when Peter's successors will be not the servants but the masters of the world. They will dress in purple like Nero and call themselves Pontifex Maximus. They will refer to the Fisherman as 'the first pope' and appeal not to the authority of love but to the power invested in him to act as Nero acted. In defiance of Jesus, Christians will do unto others what was done unto them, and worse will they do. The religion that prided itself on triumphing over persecution by suffering will become the most persecuting faith the world has ever seen. They will even persecute the race from which Peter – and Jesus – sprang. They will order in Christ's name all those who disagree with them to be tortured, and sometimes crucified over fire. They will make an alliance between throne and altar; they will insist that the throne is the guardian of the altar and the guarantor of faith. Their idea will be for the throne (the state) to impose the Christian religion on all its subjects. It will not trouble them that Peter fought against such an alliance and died because of it.

For three centuries after the apostle died on Vatican Hill, the church, in spite of persecution, grew in strength until the day came when it was tempted to throw in its lot with Caesar.

The Great Temptation

It was dawn, the sun's rosy fingers were twining round the hills. Before the sun itself was visible, there was a long deep silence broken only by the throbbing music of the lark and the barking of a dog somewhere in the desert of the Campagna. Just as the sun lifted above the horizon, there came a new sound: the tramp of a marching army. A cloud of dust rose on the great North Road. Out of the dust and haze crystallized the shape of rank on rank of armed men. On shield and banner, the army had a diagonal symbol standing for *Christos*, Christ.

Into view rode the commander-in-chief. Astride a magnificent steed, Constantine had come to take sole charge of the Empire. He did not rate his chances high. His rival, Maxentius, was holding all the cards. His forces were bigger, fresher. He had only to stay behind the walls of Rome and he was impregnable. Constantine marched on, none the less; he had no choice. Every inch a soldier, he had to fight to the end.

The day before, he had had a strange experience. No one was ever more devoted than he to the sun-god, Sol; Apollo, too, he frequently adored. So he was on his knees, face to the sun, worshipping this molten deity, when – was it a vision? an illusion due to dizziness? a dream? – he saw black rays leap diagonally out of the sun and heard in his head a name: *Christos*. His mother Helena was a Christian; she was always babbling on about *Christos*, but he had never given him a thought. Not till that moment. A voice from another world seemed to be saying: 'In this sign, you will conquer.' He was clutching at straws, no doubt, but he gave orders to his officers to substitute Christ's symbol for the Eagle Imperial. This Christ, he mused, was supposed to have risen from the dead. When he clashed with Maxentius, he might need a trick like that himself.

On the march, his scouts informed him that Maxentius had left the city and was making for Saxa Rubra, nine miles north of Rome. He knew he had a chance after all. There the road became a defile between two hills. He drew up plans to cut off Maxentius' rear. That night, he prayed fervently towards the sun, uttering the name of his new deity.

Next morning, 27 October 312, he waited for sunrise to be sure Jesus was with him, then ordered an attack. Surrounded, the enemy broke in confusion at the Milvian Bridge. Maxentius tried to escape by diving in the Tiber, but his armour dragged him down and he, like many of his soldiers, drowned. Constantine entered Rome in triumph, a new emperor with one more deity to guard him.

It was not long before he was dealing with the new pope, Sylvester, who succeeded the more cautious Miltiades as Bishop of Rome. Sylvester, like many prelates after him, saw nothing strange in a warrior coming to faith in a crucified Christ by slaughtering his enemies.

So began the fatal alliance between Caesar and Pope, Throne and Altar. In time, it was to be part of Catholic orthodoxy.

Emperor Constantine never relinquished his title Pontifex Maximus, head of the pagan state cult. When, in the year 315, his victory arch was completed, he attributed his victory to 'the inspiration of the deity', unspecified. His coinage still depicted the sun-god. He did not abolish the Vestal Virgins, or the Altar of Victory in the Senate House. At no time did he make Christianity the official religion.

Born in 274 to Constantius and a mere concubine, Helena, he should not have been eligible for imperial honours. He won his consecration by the sword. Twice married, he murdered Crispus, his son by his first wife, in 326. He had his second wife drowned in the bath; killed his eleven-year-old nephew, then his brother-in-law, after giving him assurances of safe-conduct under oath. He did not persecute Christians, only his family and friends.

Far from being the model of the Christian prince, he never ceased to be a hard-nosed politician with, according to Jacob Burckhardt, 'a cold and terrible lust for power'. He sponsored Christianity because it had proved itself useful in winning him a decisive battle. The church bowed to him, not too sensitive about his matrimonial entanglements, because he was useful to its cause.

Soon after this, Constantine made an agreement with his eastern rival Licinius known as the Edict of Milan.

> We have long considered that freedom of worship should not be denied. Rather, each man's thoughts and desire should be granted him, thus enabling him to have regard for spiritual things as he himself may choose. This is why we have given orders that everyone should be allowed to have his own beliefs and worship as he wishes.

It was an exemplary expression of the religious rights of all people without distinction. The tolerance it showed enabled Christians to come out of the catacombs into the full rights of citizenship. The tragedy was, this principle was never accepted by the Catholic church. Truth, she insisted, can never be compromised. Hence whenever she was in control, she denied freedom of religion to others. When the

Peace of Westphalia declared in 1648, 'Citizens whose religion differs from that of their sovereign are to have equal rights with his other citizens,' it was condemned by Innocent X. Similar statements of religious freedom were anathematized century after century by the Catholic church as un-Christian, pernicious, insane, no different from atheism.

It is ironic that no document in church history, not even from the Second Vatican Council, is as tolerant, generous or wise as the Edict of Milan, composed by two bloodthirsty warriors.

In the year 380 something happened to Christianity that would have astonished Jesus and Peter: it became the established religion of the Roman Empire. In Acton's words, the church became 'the gilded crutch of absolutism'. With the church's new prestige went ever-present dangers.

In the beginning, the state trespassed on the church's domain, trying to mould faith to its requirements of law and order. From then on, the church, which began as a movement of the masses and of spiritual liberation, became set in a pattern of conservatism right down to the present day. Only too often, prelates have sided with the rich against the poor; they have chosen from the right rather than from the left. They instinctively fear communism more than fascism.

In time, the church began to turn the tables, trespassing on the rights of princes. Popes appointed and sacked even emperors, demanded that they impose Christianity on their subjects under the threat of torture and death.

The end result was Christendom. In many ways, it was the greatest civilizing force the world has seen. The cost to the Gospel message was horrendous.

All this was in the future. In the early days after Constantine, the church, now respectable, was content to take advantage of the *Pax Romana*: a common language and system of law and straight roads to carry the message of Jesus across the Empire.

The church no longer had to fear persecution. It was Jews and 'unbelievers' who were now under threat. They were the ones who would be tortured, burned and crucified in the name of Jesus the Crucified Jew.

The Early Pontiffs

According to the German historian Gregorovius, 'Until the time of Leo I in the fifth century, the Chair of Peter had not been occupied by a single bishop of historical importance'. There were reasons for this. In the early days, the Christian community was intent on survival in a hostile environment. They were disliked by Jews and held in suspicion by the Romans for not honouring the local deities. Nor would Christians enlist in the army, thus casting doubt on their reliability as citizens. In spite of this, Christianity grew, especially among slaves and the poorer classes. These responded with glowing hearts to the Sermon on the Mount and the preaching of Jesus who was crucified like a slave and was raised by God from the dead as the forerunner of the Final Resurrection.

It was when the church emerged from the shadows, when the persecutions of Nero and Diocletian were becoming a bad memory, that things took a turn for the worse. The signs were there even before the conversion of Constantine.

For example, after the death of Marcellinus in 304, there was no bishop of Rome for four years because of a dispute in the Christian community about whether apostates who returned should do penance or not. Though it was a difficult time for the faith, and heresies were growing, the choice of a new bishop (pope) was not of overriding importance.

It was when the church became respectable after Emperor Constantine that vicious squabbles broke out. The community was granted lands and many privileges. The wrong sort of candidates came forward for the diaconate and priesthood. Mammon came into direct conflict with God in the church.

Bitter rivalries often showed themselves on the death of a pope. For example, when Liberius died in 366, two factions elected a successor. Ursinus was one pope, Damasus was the other. After a lot of street-fighting, Ursinus' followers locked themselves in the recently completed basilica of St Mary Major, known as 'Our Lady of the Snow'. Damasus' supporters climbed on the roof, made a hole in it and bombarded the occupants with tiles and stones. Others meanwhile were attacking the main door. When this caved in, a bloody fight ensued for three days. At the end of it, 137 bodies were carried out, all of them followers of Ursinus.

Ursinus was sent into exile by the emperor's representative, but the crime in Mary Major was a permanent blot on Damasus' copybook. To compensate, Damasus stressed his spiritual authority as 'successor to St Peter', a claim, as has been noted, not made by the Fathers of the Church. 'It was not until Damasus in 382,' writes Henry Chadwick, 'that this Petrine text ['Thou art Peter'] began to become important as providing a theological and scriptural foundation on which claims to primacy were based.'

By then the Bishop of Rome was a great landowner and civil leader. The paradox is that the popes became popes only when they took on, in addition to their religious role, completely secular functions. 'The combined result', says Jeffrey Richards, in his book *The Popes and the Papacy in the Early Middle Ages*, 'was a papacy whose power was enhanced beyond its wildest dreams.'

Damasus was a case in point. He came to office through blood. He thereby found himself a very rich and powerful man. When he asked the prefect of Rome, a pagan with many priestly titles, to convert, this gentleman replied: 'Willingly, if you make *me* Bishop of Rome.' The contemporary writer Ammianus Marcellinus suggested that there should be a lively contest for such a lucrative position. 'For if that post is once gained, a man enjoys in peace a fortune assured by the generosity of matrons; he can ride in a carriage, clothed in magnificent robes; he can give banquets, the luxury of which surpasses that of the emperor's table.'

Damasus' secretary, the ascetic St Jerome, described the kind of clerics surrounding Damasus; they looked more like bridegrooms, he said. And the pope, who had come to power with the help of the police, was constantly in need of police protection against Ursinus' followers.

This distasteful episode was not so rare. On other occasions there were two, even three rivals for the Bishopric. Sometimes the position was vacant for months and years because the Romans could not agree. Once two rival popes were toppled by a third who gave the exarch in Ravenna, the Emperor's representative, a hundred pounds in gold for his support.

The tradition of the Bishop of Rome being elected by the people of Rome went back to apostolic times. This, often led to confusion. In the eleventh century, matters were tidied up by making cardinals, as representatives of the local clergy, into the sole electors. The laity never did recover their right to have a say in the choice of their bishop. Even conclaves of cardinals did not solve the problem altogether, so that in the Middle Ages and after there was often more than one 'pope'. But in these early times the situation was sometimes chronic.

Gregorovius pointed out that in the sixth and seventh centuries most popes reigned for only two or three years. Were they chosen when close to death, or was their death hastened by rival factions? He did not know. According to Richards, most popes were chosen on the principle of a reward for services rendered, so that most were elderly and infirm. Pope Sisinnius, for example, was consecrated on 15 January 708. He was so crippled by arthritis, he could not even find his mouth to feed himself. He died twenty days later. Richards writes: 'In view of this interminable parade of infirmity and incapacity it is a wonder that the papacy achieved anything at all.'

So even elections that involved corruption, bribery and bloodshed only too often issued in giving the papacy to washed-out old men. Richards reports: 'The fire and spice of those times comes through to us in the surviving documents of the period. . . . This is the red, raw meat of papal history, and not the dessicated, pre-packed portions often served up in the guise of papal history.'

For all the chicanery and corruption, the time was not far off when those days would be looked on as innocent, almost the Golden Age of the Papacy.

An Astounding Document

Stephen III became pontiff in the year 752 after his predecessor Stephen II had lasted only four days, the shortest reign recorded. The new pontiff had been practically brought up in the papal court. He knew the pope was not merely a religious leader but, as a loyal vassal of the emperor, a civil governor, too, with extensive territories under his command.

The secularization of the church, started by Constantine, was well under way. He had seen the potential of the hierarchy as a governing class. They were as well organized as his own civil service, which they slowly replaced in the courts and in diplomacy. When, in the year 330, the emperor took his entourage to Constantinople, on the site of the ancient Greek city of Byzantium, the bishops of Rome became more and more involved in civil affairs. Two popes in particular are numbered among the greatest men who ever lived. Leo the Great (440–61), by an act of great daring, saved Rome from Attila the Hun. Gregory the Great (590–604) was effectively the civil leader as well as Patriarch of the West. With this dual role thrust upon them, there was an inevitable growth in bureaucracy. They worked heroically, but Christian simplicity was never again to be seen in Christian Rome.

When the Lombards, a barbarian tribe from the Baltic, settled in Italy after the year 568, the papacy had no peace. The newcomers took over most of the north. Gradually converted, the Lombards were never trusted by the Holy See. When the bond between popes and their liege lords, the emperors, weakened, the pontiffs had to forge a fresh military alliance if they were to hold on to Rome and the surrounding territories. It would perhaps have been better had they surrendered them, but to great landowners that has always been unthinkable.

One year into his pontificate, Stephen III travelled north in winter to see Pepin, king of the Franks. Never before had a pope sought aid from a Western sovereign; it was to be the first of many requests for military aid. In robes of black, his hair covered in ashes, the pope knelt at the king's feet, imploring him to use his armies to save the affairs of St Peter and St Paul and the community of Rome. There, at the Abbey of St Denis, he anointed Pepin and his son, Charlemagne, as 'patricians of the Romans'.

It was most likely at this meeting that Stephen showed his royal host a document of great antiquity. Dusty and crumbling, it had been preserved for centuries in the papal archives. Dated 30 March 315, it was called 'The Donation of Constantine'. It was a deed or gift from the first Christian emperor to Pope Sylvester.

The Donation tells the moving story of how Constantine contracted leprosy all over his body. Pagan priests erected a font on the Capitol and tried to persuade him to fill it with the blood of little children.

While the blood was warm, Constantine should bathe in it and be healed. Many children were herded together with their weeping mothers. The emperor, touched by their tears, sent them home loaded with gifts. That night, he had a dream. Peter and Paul told him to contact Pope Sylvester, then in hiding on Mount Soracte. The pope would show him the true 'pool of piety'. Once he recovered his health, he was to restore Christian churches throughout the world, give up praying to idols and worship the true God. Constantine did as he was told. 'When I was at the bottom of the font,' he said, 'I saw a hand from heaven touching me.' He came from his baptism healed. Sylvester preached to him the Trinity and repeated Jesus' words to Peter: 'Thou art Peter . . . and I will give to thee the Keys of the Kingdom.' Convinced he had been healed by the power of the Apostle, Constantine, in the name of the Senate and the entire Roman people, gave a gift to the Vicar of God's Son and to all his successors:

> Inasmuch as our imperial power is earthly, we have decreed that it shall venerate and honour his most holy Roman Church and that the sacred See of Blessed Peter shall be gloriously exalted even above our Empire and earthly throne. . . . He shall rule over the four principal Sees, Antioch, Alexandria, Constantinople and Jerusalem, as over all churches of God in all the world. . . .
>
> Finally, lo, we convey to Sylvester, universal Pope, both our palace and likewise all provinces and palaces and districts of the city of Rome and Italy and of the regions of the west.

Contantine also gave a hitherto unheard of explanation as to why he had taken himself to the East. He wished that Rome, where the Christian religion was founded by the Emperor of Heaven (Christ), should have no rival on earth. Pagan Rome had abdicated in favour of Christian Rome.

King Pepin was impressed. The document proved that the pope was successor to Peter *and* Constantine. The emperor had even acted as Sylvester's groom, inspiring many emperors and kings to imitate his humility at papal coronations in the centuries that followed.

When Pepin took to the field and routed the Lombards, he handed back to the pope all the lands that were rightly his by the Donation.

It was a surprising development of the gospels. Jesus possessed nothing but the clothes he stood up in. His chief disciples now not only had enormous territories to which they became excessively attached; they needed military alliances to keep them.

The Donation continued to be influential. For example, the only English pope, Adrian IV, appealed to it when he gave Ireland to

Henry II of England. Adrian was formerly Nicholas Breakspear, the son of a priest.

When Henry began the long and tragic occupation of Ireland in 1171, the Irish episcopate, assembled at Cashel, recognized him and his successors as lawful kings of Ireland. To this, the new pope, Alexander III, set his seal of approval, but not before insisting that he received his annual penny per household. This was the papacy's price for handing over this most Catholic and Celtic of lands to the Norman English.

What makes it harder to bear is that the Donation was a forgery.

The Donation was a fabrication, probably concocted by a Lateran priest just before Stephen III visited King Pepin. Such was the state of scholarship at that time, no one saw through it, though a schoolboy could do so today. It was not until a papal aide, Lorenzo Valla, took it apart line by line in 1440 that it was proved to be a fraud.

Valla showed that the pope at the alleged time of the Donation was not Sylvester but Miltiades. The text refers to 'Constantinople' whereas Constantine's city in the East still retained its original name of Byzantium. The Donation was written not in classical Latin but in a later bastardized form. Also, explanations are given, say, of Constantine's regalia, which would not have been needed in the fourth century but were necessary in the eighth. In a hundred irrefutable ways, Valla shot the document to pieces. He did so with trepidation, knowing that many Roman prelates would be out for his blood.

> Because I have attacked not the dead but the living, not merely any ruler but the highest ruler, namely, the Supreme Pontiff against whose excommunication the sword of no prince can afford protection. . . . The Pope has no right to bind me for defending the truth. . . . When there are many who will endure death for the defence of an earthly fatherland, should I not incur danger for the sake of my heavenly home?

It was not until 1517 that Valla's book was published. It was the critical year when Luther attacked indulgences. A copy of it came into Luther's hands, and he saw for the first time that many of his earlier beliefs about the papacy were founded on forgeries like the Donation.

Though every independent scholar was won over by Valla's arguments, Rome did not concede; she went on asserting the Donation's authenticity for centuries.

This was a pity in that the truth about it was far more incredible than the tissue of lies it contained.

* * *

The story of Constantine's leprosy and subsequent baptismal cure was a pious fifth-century invention. The fable is perpetuated in the baptistry of St John Lateran in Rome. An inscription relates how the emperor was baptized there by Pope Sylvester.

These are the facts: Constantine was a soldier at a time when shedding blood was unacceptable to the church. This may be why he delayed his baptism until he was on the point of death and he had no strength left to commit sin or kill anyone else. Not long before, his mother Helena had died, aged over eighty. Only then was the emperor enrolled among the catechumens, not in the church's headquarters but in distant Helenopolis, in the East. He was taken to the Villa Achyronia near Nicomedia. He was baptized there not by the pope, not even by a Catholic bishop or priest, but by a heretical Arian bishop named Eusebius. He died on the last day of the Whitsun holiday in the year 337.

This throws a murky light on many of the most significant events in the church's early history.

When Constantine called bishops his beloved brethren and styled himself 'Bishop of Bishops', which popes later appropriated, he was not a Christian, not even a catechumen. Yet no one remotely approached his stature and authority. Even the Bishop of Rome – not to be called '*the* pope' for many centuries – was, in comparison, a nonentity. In civic terms, he was vassal of the emperor; in spiritual terms, he was, compared with Constantine, a second-class bishop, with a title of honour over most other bishops because he held the Apostolic See where Peter and Paul had worked and lay buried. As Burckhardt stresses in *The Age of Constantine*, the emperor's title of ecumenical bishop 'was not merely a manner of speaking; actually the Church had no other central point'. Not the pope but he, like Charlemagne later, was the head of the church, its source of unity, before whom the Bishop of Rome had to prostrate himself and pledge his loyalty. All bishops agreed that he was 'the inspired oracle, the apostle of Church wisdom'.

To the end of his life, Constantine, while building magnificent churches in Palestine and elsewhere, was erecting equally magnificent pagan temples in Constantinople. This was clearly understood as part of the first settlement of 'the Roman Question'. The emperor was a sacred person, Pontifex Maximus, another title that the pope was later to assume. It followed that the emperor, and he alone, had authority to convoke religious assemblies like the Council of Arles in the year 314. As one contemporary bishop put it: 'The Church was part of the State. The Church was born into the Empire, not the Empire into the Church.' It was, therefore, Constantine, not the Bishop of Rome, who dictated the time and place of church synods and even how the votes were cast. Without his approval, they could not pass into law; he alone was legislator of the Empire.

It is another paradox of history that it was Constantine, a pagan, who invented the idea of a council of all Christian communities. Only in this way, his genius told him, would the church's faith be formulated incontestably and for ever. No bishop of the time would have asked the Bishop of Rome to decide thorny questions of belief.

After defeating Licinius in the east in 321, Constantine called the First General Council of the Church. It met in 325 in Bithynia, in a place called Nicaea, meaning 'Victory'. It was probably the most important Christian assembly in history. Arianism, a heresy that subordinated the Son to the Father, had spread all over the world. Controversy was not merely bitter, it was bloody. It was against the emperor's interests to have Christians fighting one another; they were meant to be the stabilizing force of Empire. He was dismayed to find that, after he had freed them from persecution, they were tearing each other to bits over the Holy Trinity.

At Nicaea, the Founding Father of Ecumenical Councils gathered 300 bishops, having laid on free transport. All but half a dozen were from the East. Sylvester, Bishop of Rome, did not attend; he sent two presbyters instead. Without a shred of doubt, Sylvester had no part in calling the Council or any say in running it. A pagan emperor had complete control. He held it in the big hall of his palace. According to the historian Eusebius, he was tall and slender, full of grace and majesty. To make his presence felt, he opened proceedings 'stiff with purple, gold and precious stones'.

It was soon clear that a majority of bishops were in favour of the Arian position. Constantine had no known theological preferences but he rose from his gold throne to end the discussion. Maybe he simply wanted to show he was in charge. He proposed what came to be called 'the orthodox view' of God's Son being 'of one substance' with the Father. All dissident bishops caved in, except for two whom Constantine promptly deposed and sent packing. Afterwards, he wrote to Alexandria where Arians still had a foothold: 'What has pleased three hundred bishops is nothing other than the will of God.'

The outcome was not what he had hoped. The Arian 'heresy' went on for generations. So did the complete immersion of the state in church affairs. Ecclesiastical politics replaced the priorities of the Gospel. Religion was unimportant, the church was all-important. The result, Burckhardt said, was a 'Church rapidly disintegrating in victory'.

The cost of Constantine's 'conversion' to Christianity was the loss of innocence. His cynical use of Christ, in which everyone, including the Bishop of Rome, acquiesced, meant a profound falsification of the Gospel message and the injection of standards alien to it. From then on, Catholicism flourished to the detriment of Christianity and of Jesus who wanted no part in the world of power and politics, who preferred to be crucified rather than to impose his views on anyone.

*　　*　　*

By the time Stephen III became pope, the church was thoroughly converted to the Roman Empire. From the Donation, it is plain that the Bishop of Rome looked like Constantine, lived like him, dressed like him, inhabited his palaces, ruled over his lands, had exactly the same imperial outlook. The pope, too, wanted to lord it over church and state.

Only seven hundred years after Peter died, popes had become obsessed with power and possessions. The pontiff strode the earth, a figure of worldliness and unworldliness. He, literally, wanted the best of both worlds, but certain Roman emperors kept a check on his ambition.

The Holy Roman Empire

Charlemagne was fifty-eight years old, huge for those days, with a round head and white hair, a long nose and big lively eyes. Intelligent and able to converse in Latin, founder of universities, he never could master reading, nor was he, in spite of having the best tutors, ever able to write his name.

In the fifty-three years since Stephen III, the papacy's need of military help had grown. The links between Rome and Constantinople, owing to distance and differences of outlook, were now almost completely severed. Charlemagne, king of the Franks, was man enough to step into the breach.

In the year 782, he had taken four and a half thousand Saxon prisoners and had them beheaded on the banks of the River Aller. He was perfectly capable of dealing with the Lombards who kept threatening the papacy.

The church's new defender was no more saintly than Constantine. He had divorced his first wife and had six children by the second. When he dispensed with the latter's services, he had two daughters by a third wife as well as another daughter by a concubine. Childless by his fourth wife, when she died he kept four concubines – twelve was his life-long tally – and had at least one child by each. Einhard, his frank biographer, who provides these details, insists he was always a considerate father.

Alcuin, an Englishman, the most learned monk of the day, had long pressurized Charlemagne into accepting the crown of the West. There were only three great men in the world, he told his master, of whom the pope and the emperor of Constantinople were two. 'The third is the royal dignity which by the dispensation of our Lord Jesus Christ is conferred on you as governor of the Christian people; and this is more excellent than the other dignities in power, more strong in wisdom, more sublime in rank.'

The reigning pope, Leo III, was desperate for Charlemagne to come to Rome. He needed protection from outsiders; he also wanted to have his name cleared at the highest level of a pressing charge of adultery. Not long before Charlemagne arrived, Leo was attacked by a hostile mob. They tore out his eyes and cut off his tongue. The result was that the coronation of 800 had none of the splendour and pageantry of Napoleon's when, in 1804, he crowned himself as 'Emperor of the French' in Notre Dame de Paris.

Charlemagne was kneeling in front of Peter's tomb when Leo, groping to find the head on which to place the crown, blubbered that Charlemagne was Emperor and Augustus, and knelt to adore him. According to Einhard, his master was black with wrath. Charlemagne later said in his hearing 'that he would not have gone to church that day, even though it was a solemn festival [Christmas], had he guessed the pontiff's plan'. He wanted the honour, of course, but not at the expense of being elevated by a vassal. Having taken the trouble to come to Rome to exculpate a miserable subject, he did not want to appear the recipient of his blessing.

Charlemagne sensed what historians would see only too clearly. By a master-stroke, Leo III was laying claim to a power that, in his successors, would triumph over the greatest temporal sovereigns on earth.

Charlemagne was not slow to act as supreme governor of the church, legislating, choosing bishops, archbishops and abbots from among his noblemen. He tried to stop monks fornicating and, worse, practising sodomy. He also punished by death any Saxon who, pretending to be a Christian, hid himself from baptism. In every way, Charlemagne fulfilled Alcuin's wishes. He acted as head of the Christian Commonwealth. There was logic in this, in that Leo's predecessor, Adrian I, had already given him, as a reward for enlarging the Papal States, the considerable privilege of choosing the Roman pontiff.

It so happens that the future of Europe was written into that moment of striking ambiguity when a pope, created by Charlemagne, crowned him as emperor. Which of them was the greater? For the moment, there was no doubt about it: Charlemagne. But in the years to come, by this *coup de théâtre*, Leo had assured the papacy of a fighting chance of supremacy.

This was how old St Peter's saw the beginning of the Holy Roman Empire which, as every schoolchild knows, was neither holy, nor Roman nor an empire. It was to last for a thousand years until, in 1806, Napoleon toppled a Habsburg monarch and dissolved it. By then, fifteen hundred years had passed in which the papacy, not content to trust in the power of God alone, had relied on armed princes to guard against the gates of hell.

But hell's fiercest attacks on the church came not from without; they came from within – in fact, *from the papacy itself*.

THREE

Papal Pornocracy

FIFTEEN MILES FROM ROME, high in the Alban Hills, there dwelt in the tenth century the famous *Conti*, the Counts Alberic of Tusculum. These war-lords took complete control of papal elections. Seven popes came from this one family, three in succession, and almost without exception, they helped shape *Roma Deplorabilis*, 'A Rome of Shame'.

History explodes the popular myth that Borgia was the one bad apple of the papacy. Not long after Charlemagne, for well over a century and a half the whole batch was rotten. They were less disciples of Christ than of Belial, the Prince of Darkness. Very many were libertines, murderers, adulterers, warmongers, tyrants, simoniacs who were prepared to sell everything holy. They were nearly all more wrapped up in money and intrigue than in religion.

By incessant political manoeuvres and an obsession with temporal matters, by an abuse of power and astounding wickedness, popes, supposedly the centre of unity, corrupted the whole of Christendom. It was not heresy but papacy that finally broke up the church.

There *is* a mystery in all this: how, in spite of the popes, the Western church held together for so long.

To begin with, it helps to examine any list of popes from about the year 880. In the next century and a half there were thirty-five pontiffs, reigning on average four years apiece. In the earlier period, there was the same sort of turnover; that is explained by the fact that popes were chosen *because* they were elderly and infirm. But in the ninth and tenth centuries, many popes were in their early twenties, several were teenagers. Some lasted twenty days, or a month, or three months. Six of them were dethroned, a number were murdered. It is actually impossible to be certain how many popes and antipopes (fakes) there were in this period, because there was still no fixed method of election and any number of pretenders.

When a pope suddenly disappeared, had he had his throat cut and been tossed into the Tiber? Had he been throttled in prison? Was he sleeping it off in a brothel? Had he had his ears and nose cut off like Stephen VIII in 930, who, understandably, never again showed his face in public? Or had he fled, like Benedict V in 964, who, after dishonouring a young girl, immediately took off for Constantinople

47

with the entire treasury of St Peter's, only to reappear when funds ran out and cause more havoc in Rome? The pious church historian Gerbert called Benedict 'the most iniquitous of all the monsters of ungodliness', but his judgement was premature. This pontiff was eventually slain by a jealous husband. His corpse, with a hundred dagger wounds in it, was dragged through the streets before being tossed into a cesspool.

Without question, these pontiffs constitute the most despicable body of leaders, clerical or lay, in history . They were, frankly, barbarians. Ancient Rome had nothing to rival them in rottenness.

One pope, Stephen VII, was completely mad. He dug up a Corsican predecessor, Pope Formosus (891–6) when he had been dead for over nine months. In what came to be known as the Cadaveric Synod, he dressed the stinking corpse in full pontificals, placed him on the throne in the Lateran and proceeded to interrogate him personally. Formosus was charged with becoming pope under false pretences; he was bishop of another place, hence ineligible for Rome. According to Pope Stephen, it made all his acts invalid, especially his ordinations. A chattering teenaged deacon replied on Formosus' behalf. After being found guilty, the corpse was condemned as an antipope, stripped of all but a hair-shirt clinging to the withered flesh and, minus the two fingers with which he had given his fake apostolic blessing, was thrown into the Tiber. The body, held together by the hair-shirt like a carcass of meat, was recovered by some of Formosus' admirers and given a quiet burial. Later, it was returned to its tomb in St Peter's. Stephen himself was soon strangled.

Popes maimed and were maimed, killed and were killed. Their lives bore no resemblance to the gospels. They had more in common with modern rich kids turned hooligans and junkies who haunt beach cafés and nightclubs than with Roman pontiffs as the world now sees them. Some owed their preferment to ambitious parents, some to the sword, some to the influence of high-born and beautiful mistresses in what became known as 'The Reign of the Harlots'.

Outstanding among the courtesans was Marozia of the Theophylact family. According to her contemporary, Bishop Liutprand of Cremona, she had been well coached by her mother, Theodora, who had a second daughter, also named Theodora, by Pope John X (914–29). Whoever says women have never had any influence on how the church is run have never come across these two incredibly determined ladies. In less than one decade, they created – and, when it suited them, destroyed – no less than eight popes. In his *Decline and Fall*, Gibbon suggests that it was these 'she-popes' who epitomized the politics of sex who gave rise to the legend, or satire, of Pope Joan. This female pontiff was believed in for several centuries, right up to the Reformation. It is some consolation to the English to know that the only female pope was a beautiful Anglo-Saxon girl. In full pontificals, so runs the story, she brought forth a son while travelling from the Colosseum to the Church of San Clemente and, alas, died on the spot.

This legend spawned legends of its own. In St John Lateran was a blood-red marble chair with a hole in the seat. On this chair, every newly elected pope sat to receive the obedience of his clergy. But rumour said, after Pope Joan, every pope was obliged to sit on this chair and undergo a kind of gynaecological examination to prevent a second woman ascending the papal throne. The examination – by female cardinals? – was accompanied by prayers in Latin. In fact, an entire ritual was written, and it was printed in many medieval manuscripts in all seriousness. Another more prosaic interpretation of this chair was that it truly was a commode, a visible symbol of the fact that the pope had been raised up by God like a beggar from the dunghill and set among princes.

There does not seem to be any theological bar to a woman becoming pope, even if, as John Paul says, women are forbidden by divine law to become priests. Many archbishops and popes were not ordained. For instance, Adrian V appears in the lists of pontiffs, though he only reigned six weeks, from 11 July to 18 August 1276. He was not a bishop, nor even a priest, but he was lawful pope.

The Beautiful Whore

Marozia, the chief source of the Pope Joan legend, was first intimately involved with the papacy in the person of Sergius III (904–11). Standing in his way to the throne had been Leo V, who reigned for one month before he was imprisoned by a usurper, Cardinal Christopher. Sergius cleaned up by slaughtering both.

Sergius once more exhumed Pope Formosus, now ten years dead, and had him condemned again. Sergius, having been ordained by Formosus, should really have considered himself irregular, but theological quibbles were alien to his nature. For good measure, he had Formosus' corpse beheaded; he also removed three more fingers before giving him to the Tiber. When the headless frame became entangled in a fisherman's net, his corpse once more led a charmed life, being returned a second time to St Peter's.

When Marozia became Sergius' mistress she was fifteen years old and he was forty-five. By him she had a son to whose career she was devoted. Sergius was to die five years later after a seven-year pontificate crammed with blood, intrigue and passion.

Marozia was never to forget her young love. Sleeping with the pope had given her a sense of purpose and an exhilaration that not even three marriages and numberless affairs could obliterate. The first time Pope Sergius had seduced her was in the Lateran Palace. Their paths had often crossed because much of her childhood had been spent there, her father being chief senator of Rome. But a moment came when Sergius realized this once stunning child had blossomed into a woman of breathtaking beauty. For Marozia's part, it was not so much pleasure she sought in his papal arms as the ecstasy of power.

Her mother, Theodora, had already made and unmade two popes when, in contravention of canon law, she took the hand of her favourite lover and led him from being Bishop of Bologna to being Archbishop of Ravenna and, finally, to Peter's Chair as Pope John X. Liutprand, Bishop of Cremona, wrote: 'Theodora, like a harlot, fearing she would have few opportunities of bedding with her sweetheart, forced him to abandon his bishopric and take for himself – oh, monstrous crime – the papacy of Rome.' This was in March 914 when Marozia was twenty-two. She did not mind too much; her son, Sergius' son, was only six, still too young for the papacy even for those impious times.

It was at this point, that the Alberics of Tuscany, originally northerners, burst on the scene. Pope John suggested to his bedfellow Theodora that a marriage between Marozia and Alberic might prove of benefit all round. Marozia recognized a rising star, and from the union came Alberic Junior. Alberic Senior, perhaps egged on by his wife, prematurely tried to seize control of Rome and was killed. Pope John forced the young widow to look upon his mutilated corpse. It was a mistake. A woman who had slept with Pope Sergius knew all about revenge.

When Theodora died in 928, Marozia had the pontiff imprisoned before issuing the order for him to be suffocated. Her first son was now seventeen. Soon, very soon, he would be experienced enough to take on the papacy. He had been groomed for it by a sensuous and totally immoral life. The next couple of popes had brief reigns, each of them disappearing in mysterious circumstances. Now, at the age of twenty, the son of Marozia and Pope Sergius became Pope John XI.

Marozia still had further ambitions. Guy, her second husband, having died, she married his half-brother, King Hugo of Provence. Hugo was already married, but his wife was easily diposed of. It was fortunate for Marozia that her son was pope; he was able to dispense the happy couple from all impediments, such as incest. What was to stop her new husband becoming emperor and herself empress? It was something Sergius would have wished. John XI officiated at his mother's wedding in Rome in the spring of 932.

Then everything fell apart because of Marozia's second son, the jealous eighteen-year-old Alberic Junior. He took over Rome to become the new pope-maker. Hugo of Provence abandoned his wife and fled in disgrace. Alberic put John XI, his half-brother and a pope's son, under permanent arrest in the Lateran – he died there four years later – and, the unkindest cut of all, he imprisoned his own mother.

Past her prime, Marozia remained a woman of distinction when she first set foot in Hadrian's Mausoleum, popularly known as the Castel

Sant'Angelo. She was to remain in that terrible place beside the Tiber, without one day's remission, for over fifty years.

She had turned sixty when news reached her in her dungeon that Alberic had died at forty and his son, her grandson, called Octavian, had foisted himself on the church as pope. The first pontiff to change his name, he called himself John XII. This was in the winter of 955. She promptly turned her grey old face to the wall and sank back into her reverie of past glories with her lover Sergius.

The new pope's youth may explain in part his irreligious behaviour, since he was only sixteen when he assumed the burdens of office. Whole monasteries spent their days and nights praying for his decease.

Even for a pope of that period he was so bad that the citizens were out for his blood. He had invented sins, they said, not known since the beginning of the world, including sleeping with his mother. He ran a harem in the Lateran Palace. He gambled with pilgrims' offerings. He kept a stud of two thousand horses which he fed on almonds and figs steeped in wine. He rewarded the companions of his nights of love with golden chalices from St Peter's. He did nothing for the most profitable tourist trade of the day, namely, pilgrimages. Women in particular were warned not to enter St John Lateran if they prized their honour; the pope was always on the prowl. In front of the high altar of the mother church of christendom, he even toasted the Devil.

Pope John aroused such wrath that, fearing for his life, he plundered St Peter's and fled to Tivoli.

When the fifty-year-old Otto of Saxony – he was crowned emperor in St Peter's in 961 – got wind of this, he ordered the young man to return home at once. It did not suit his plans to have an absentee pontiff; it was bad for the business of empire.

A synod was called to sort things out. Present were sixteen cardinals, all the numerous Italian bishops and many others who were conscripted from Germany. The Bishop of Cremona left a precise record of the charges brought against the pope. He had said mass without communicating. He had ordained a deacon in a stable. He had charged for ordinations. He had copulated with a long list of ladies, including his father's old flame and his own niece. He had blinded his spiritual director. He had castrated a cardinal, causing his death. All these accusations were confirmed under oath.

Otto then wrote John a letter that must rank among the great curiosities of all time.

> Everyone, clergy as well as laity, accuses you, Holiness, of homicide, perjury, sacrilege, incest with your relatives, including two of your sisters, and with having, like a pagan, invoked Jupiter, Venus and other demons.

John responded by dictating a letter, devoid of text and grammar, to the bishops. He warned them that if they deposed him he would excommunicate them all, so they would be unable to ordain or celebrate mass. He then jumped on a horse and went hunting.

When Otto finally grew tired of waiting and returned to Saxony, John's family raised an army to give him safe passage home. In Rome he resumed the Petrine office. Not satisfied with anything as mild as excommunication, he maimed or executed all who had contributed to his exile.

No pope ever went to God in a more embarrassing position. One night, a jealous husband, one of many, caught his Holiness with his wife *in flagrante delicto* and gave him the last rites with one hammer blow on the back of the head. He was twenty-four. The Romans, noted for their savage wit, said that this was the climax of his career. At least he was lucky to die in bed, even if it was someone else's.

Cardinal Bellarmine, in his book on the papacy, *De Romano Pontifice*, in the seventeenth century, was to say: 'The Pope is the supreme judge in deciding disputed questions of faith and morals.' This great defender of the papacy wrote in the same book: 'If the Pope were to err by imposing sins and forbidding virtues, the Church would still have to consider sins as good and virtues as vices, or else she would sin against conscience.' Small wonder the teenaged pontiffs got away with so much. Yet even Bellarmine, who knew all about the Borgias, had to agree that John XII 'was the dregs'. *Fuerit fieri omnium deterrimus.*

With one monster out of the way, the Romans chose Benedict V as a replacement. Otto, outsmarted, was furious. 'No one can be pope without the emperor's consent,' he declared. 'This is how it has always been.' His choice rested on Leo VIII.

Cardinal Baronius, in his sixteenth-century *Ecclesiastical Annals*, which Acton called 'the greatest history of the Church ever written', maintained that Benedict was true pope and Leo the antipope. It is hard to dispute this. Yet Benedict grovelled at Otto's feet and declared himself an imposter. To prove it, he stripped himself of his regalia and confessed on his knees before Leo that he was the lawful successor of St Peter.

It is not clear if a genuine pope's assertion that he is not genuine is an exercise in infallibility, though it must carry a message to the whole church concerning faith and morals.

When both Leo and Benedict died, Otto put John XIII on the throne. It was not a wise choice. The Romans promptly sent him packing. Otto brought him back, only to realize that the local instinct was correct. The new pope performed acts of incredible cruelty. According to Liutprand in his chronicles, he tore out his enemies' eyes and put half the population to the sword.

Soon after John XIII came Benedict VII, another to die in the act of adultery at the hands of an enraged husband.

Cardinal Baronius was understandably embarrassed by events he records with remarkable honesty. The pontiffs of this period he calls 'invaders of the Holy See, less apostles than apostates' (*non aposto-licos sed apostaticos*). He trembles badly, he admits, to have to write about them. On the Chair of St Peter sat not men but monsters in the shape of men. 'Vainglorious Messalinas filled with fleshly lusts and cunning in all forms of wickedness governed Rome and prostituted the Chair of St Peter for their minions and paramours.'

In view of the decrees of the First Vatican Council in 1870, his conclusion is startling:

> The chief lesson of these times is that the Church can get along very well without popes. What is vital to the Church's survival is not the pope but Jesus Christ. *He* is the head of the Church, *not* the pope.

A few centuries later, Baronius would have been branded a heretic. The Catholic faith now is: the pope is the head of the church on earth, Vicar of Christ, Rock on which the church is built, bond of unity, preserver of faith and morals. But the long period under review shows an entirely different picture. Not only Baronius but also the people of Rome would have laughed at such theological tomfoolery. For them, the Gates of Hell had visibly prevailed. If this was not the victory of the Prince of Darkness, what was? The only question that puzzled them was not 'How can the pope save the church?' but 'How can the pope save his own soul?'

During all these tempestuous events and others that followed, Marozia remained in her prison cell. Once the most ravishing creature of her day, she was reduced to a withered stringy heap of bones wrapped up in rags. Now in her mid-nineties, the memory of having slept with one pope and given him a son whom she made pope in his turn must have inspired her to survive. Neglected, she was never entirely forgotten in high places.

In the spring of 986, Pope Gregory V, aged twenty-three, and his cousin, Emperor Otto III, aged fifteen, decided the poor old woman had languished in prison long enough. The pope sent a tame bishop to exorcize her of her demons and lift her sentence of excommunication. She was absolved from her sins. Then she was executed.

The Boy-Pope

Nearly fifty years later, in 1032, Pope John XIX of the House of Tusculum died. Count Alberic III paid a fortune to keep the job in the family. Who better to fill the vacancy than his own son Theophylactus? Raoul Glaber, a monk from Cluny, reports that at his election in October of 1032 his Holiness Benedict IX was eleven years old. According to Monsignor Louis Duchesne, Benedict was 'a mere urchin . . . who was before long to become actively offensive'.

It was an odd spectacle: a boy not yet in his teens, his voice not yet broken, was chief legislator and ruler of the Catholic church, called upon to wear the tiara, celebrate high mass in St Peter's, grant livings, appoint bishops and excommunicate heretics. His Holiness's exploits with the ladies prove that the boy-pope reached the age of puberty very early. By the time he was fourteen, a chronicler said, he had surpassed in profligacy and extravagance all who had preceded him.

St Peter Damian, a fine judge of sin, exclaimed: 'That wretch, from the beginning of his pontificate to the end of his life, feasted on immorality.' Another observer wrote: 'A demon from hell in the disguise of a priest has occupied the Chair of Peter.'

He often had to leave Rome in a hurry. The first time, on the Feast of St Peter and St Paul 1033, an eclipse of the sun that turned the interior of St Peter's into an eerie saffron was sufficient pretext for ejecting him. On his return, a few nobles tried to cut him down during mass. They failed. When Benedict was next swept out of Rome, the army of Emperor Conrad swept him back in. In 1046, having been driven out once more for plunder, murder and oppression, he went home to his native Tusculum. In his absence, the Romans chose another pontiff, Sylvester III, a man from the Sabine Hills. Far better, they decided, to break canon law and offend the deity than put up with Benedict IX. After fifty blissful days, the boy-pope was restored by his family, who persuaded Sylvester to go elsewhere.

Eventually, Benedict wanted to resign. He had fixed his eye on his beautiful cousin, daughter of Girard de Saxo. Girard gave his consent on condition that the pope abdicated. In a surprising attack of scruples, Benedict decided to check that he was within his rights to do so. He consulted his godfather, John Gratian, Archpriest of St John *ad Portam Latinam*. Gratian was a remarkable man; a complete illiterate, he lived chastely, like a lily among thorns. Gratian assured him he was entitled to give up. More, he had a successor lined up for him. He touched his own breast.

Happy to resign, Benedict demanded a golden handshake of one to two thousand pounds (in weight). After a bout of hard bargaining, he settled for the whole of Peter's Pence from England. No collection by English Catholics was ever put to better use.

Amid scenes of jubilation, Benedict, having dispensed himself from the obligation of celibacy, abdicated on May Day 1045. 'Devoted to pleasure,' Pope Victor II was to write, 'he preferred to live more like Epicurus than a bishop. . . . He left the city and betook himself to one of his castles in the country.'

*　　　*　　　*

John Gratian, now Gregory VI, came in for severe criticism. Many popes had bought the papacy; none but he had ever bought it back. Gregory argued that he had done the church a favour. And Benedict pointed out that he had not been 'bought off'; he had simply recovered his father's original expenditure.

Gregory might have got away with it had not Benedict, now plain Theophylactus of Tusculum, been turned down by his lady-love. He was keen to make a comeback. With Sylvester still in the wings, there were now three claimants to the throne: Sylvester in St Peter's, Gregory in the Lateran, and Benedict biding his time in the Alban Hills.

In Rome, meanwhile, the coffers were empty; everyone from popes to the lowliest doorman was a simoniac; every cleric had one mistress at least; and the churches were falling down.

At this critical moment, enter Henry of Germany. He was noted for two things: he hated simony and wanted to be emperor more than anything in the world. Muscle succeeded where moral exhortation had failed.

At Sutria, on the way to Rome, he called a synod. At his direction, Sylvester was judged to be an imposter; he was reduced to the lay state and condemned to spend the rest of his days in a very harsh monastery if one could be found. Benedict had resigned and, according to Henry, had burned his papal boats. As to Gregory VI, Henry thanked him for ridding the church of a pest but he should not have employed simony to do it. This was a resigning matter.

Confronted, literally, by the temporal sword, Gregory declared: 'I, Gregory, bishop, Servant of the servants of God, on account of the simony which, by the cunning of the devil, entered into my election, decide that I must be deposed from the Roman bishopric.'

Present at his fall was his young chaplain, the monk Hildebrand, the future Gregory VII. He saw the tail strike the head and never was he to forget or forgive.

Henry chose as the new pontiff Clement II. On the day of his appointment, he crowned Henry as emperor, after which Henry, anticipating Napoleon, placed on his own head the circlet which of old the Romans used to crown their patricians. With this gesture, Henry showed that he was the head of Christendom; the Bishop of Rome was nothing but his private chaplain.

He took the old pope back to Germany with him to ensure that he did not make a nuisance of himself. Gregory soon died in exile and, when Clement also joined his Maker, Benedict jumped on the papal throne for another eight months.

Henry was too busy to deal with him but he ordered Count Boniface of Tusculum to make Theophylactus toe the line once and for all. The new pope, Damasus II, soon yielded up his spirit – poisoned, it was rumoured, by Benedict. It was probably nothing more than the climate.

With his passing, the road was clear once more for Benedict, but he decided to call it a day. He retired to the monastery of Grotta Ferrata where, it was said with a certain ambiguity, his life was an example to the rest of the community.

In this dark moment for the papacy, it seemed as if God took pity on the church. He sent two pontiffs considered by many catholic historians to have been the greatest the church ever produced: Gregory VII and Innocent III.

FOUR

The Papacy at
Its Height

HE WAS THE ONLY POPE ever to canonize himself but he is best remembered as a man haunted by a single memory. It pursued him for close on forty years until he came to die, probably the most revered and power-crazed pontiff in history.

The memory that practically rotted the brain of Hildebrand, who took the name of Gregory VII, was of his namesake, Gregory VI, being deposed and humiliated in 1046. The sinner who did it was Emperor Henry III, who put a puppet on the papal throne instead.

It troubled Hildebrand's soul as a young man when he accompanied Gregory VI into exile in Germany; also when, having joined the Benedictine abbey of Cluny, he rose by degrees to be prior. It still pained him when, summoned to Rome, he was adviser over eighteen years to four pontiffs and finally their chancellor. Above all, the bitter memory surfaced when, in the Lateran basilica, packed for the funeral of Alexander II in 1073, the congregation cried out spontaneously: 'Hildebrand is pope. St Peter has chosen him.' Ordinarily, Hildebrand would have spurned such a crude way of choosing the pontiff. He had persuaded a previous pope to leave the choice exclusively to the College of Cardinals. But he now accepted 'the will of St Peter'.

Without delay, the pope-elect, a midget, *homuncio*, sent word to the young Emperor Henry IV, begging for recognition.

In all his life, nothing went more against the grain than petitioning his godless inferior when he, Hildebrand, was the greatest man on earth. Why do it, when it went against his principles? Because he wanted no subsequent doubt to be cast on his legitimacy. The day of reckoning was not far off when the lamb would turn into a lion.

Henry's advisers warned him that Hildebrand was dangerous. An ascetic, he would treat others as he treated himself – abominably. The inexperienced emperor took no notice. Had not his father deposed a pope and appointed the next three in succession? How was he to grasp that here was a pontiff whose hands would grow ever longer and who would walk on stilts? Gregory VII was the last pope whose election had to be confirmed by the emperor and whose consecration took place in the presence of imperial legates.

Having gained the approval he despised, Gregory was bent on breaking princes once and for all. To him, all were corrupt. They were entitled to less respect than the meanest exorcist who at least cast out devils and did not give them princely hospitality. Monarchs only desire to dominate, said this most lordly of pontiffs. It would need an indecent magnanimity on God's part to save even one of them from the eternal flames. Everything they do is rooted in pride, yet what have they to offer? A dying king will come to the humblest country priest to be shrived. When did even a lay woman come to an emperor to ask for God's pardon? Where is the emperor who can grant salvation or make Christ's Body and Blood with a movement of his lips? A man with no brains can see priests are superior to kings. Then, how far above them all is the pope, successor to Peter? Was it not his duty to cut princes down to size, to offer them a lesson in humility?

That never-fading memory made this man of inflexible will hold all civil authority in contempt and one day, he was resolved on it, he would have his revenge.

Gregory VII and His School of Forgers

Ever since he was a boy in Tuscany, Hildebrand, son of a village carpenter, had had a passionate devotion to St Peter. As Prince of the Apostles, there was no end to Peter's powers. He was Chief Shepherd, he could bind and loose in heaven and on earth. When Hildebrand became pope, he drew up a *Dictatus*, or list, of twenty-seven theses outlining his powers as Peter's vicar. Among them were these:

> The pope can be judged by no one on earth.
> The Roman church has never erred, nor can it err
>   until the end of time.
> The pope alone can depose bishops.
> He alone is entitled to imperial insignia.
> He can dethrone emperors and kings and absolve
>   their subjects from allegiance.
> All princes are obliged to kiss his feet.
> His legates, even when not priests, have prece-
>   dence over all bishops.
> A rightly elected pope is, without question, a saint,
>   made so by the merits of Peter.

This sanctity he claimed to have experienced overwhelmingly at his election. It was, incidentally, an idea that his successors dropped like a burning coal. It was very odd in that Hildebrand had met the boy-pope Benedict IX.

It is hard to know whether he was aware that most of his theses were based on forged documents. The least that can be said is that his credulity was alarming, especially in view of what the New Testament reports about St Peter's mistakes. These forgeries made it seem that his absolutist claims were based on ancient records zealously kept in the Rome archives. For seven centuries, the Greeks had called Rome the home of forgeries. Whenever they tried talking with Rome, the popes brought out forged documents, even papal additions to Council documents, which the Greeks, naturally, had never seen.

Gregory went way beyond the Donation of Constantine. He had a whole school of forgers under his very nose, turning out document after document, with the papal seal of approval, to cater for his every need.

The leaders of the school were Anselm of Lucca, nephew of the previous pontiff, Cardinal Deusdedit and, after them, Cardinal Gregory of Pavia. Pope Gregory (and, later, Urban II) might require justification for some action against a prince or bishop. Very well, these prelates literally produced the appropriate document. No need for research; it was all done on the premises.

Many earlier documents were touched up to make them say the opposite of what they said originally. Some of these earlier documents were themselves forgeries. Hildebrand's school treated all papers, forged or genuine, with a completely impartial dishonesty. Orwell's *1984* was anticipated by nine centuries, not in some godless state at the behest of Big Brother, but in the heart of Roman Catholicism in favour of the pope.

This instant method of inventing history was marvellously successful, especially as the forgeries were at once inserted into canon law. By innumerable subtle changes, they made Catholicism seem changeless. They turned 'today' into 'always was and always will be', which even now, contrary to the findings of history, is the peculiar stamp of Catholicism.↙

Thus was accomplished the quietest and longest-lasting of all revolutions: it was all done on paper. It would not have worked in an era of universal literacy, printing, photocopying and carbon dating; it worked without a hitch in an age of rare manuscripts, inept scholarship, and when even some emperors could not read and write.

Gregory was not above a deception of his own.

The most influential of all forgeries was the ninth-century Pseudo-Isidorian Decretals, of French origin, which Rome seized on avidly and which Gregory, who 'could not err', took to be authentic. It consisted of 115 documents, purportedly written by early bishops of Rome, beginning with Clement (88–97). A further 125 documents had forged additions which increased the power and prestige of the papacy. According to the forger, the early popes forbade all commerce with an excommunicated person.

In 1078, Gregory, knowing there was no precedent for it, extended this principle *to emperors and kings*. If a pope excommunicated an emperor and his subjects were forbidden to deal with him, what good was he? He was fit only to be dethroned, which Gregory was pleased to do. Even the most ardent papalists have found this hard to forgive. For Gregory deliberately confused two codes of law, canon and civil, and turned a spiritual principle of excommunication into a political weapon. In his hands, it was devastating. He deposed the Greek emperor as well as Boleslaus, the Polish king, forbidding Poland ever again to call itself a kingdom. In country after country, he sowed civil unrest; there were rebellions and civil wars.

Looking ahead for a moment, the documents forged in Rome at this time were systematized in the mid-1100s at Bologna by Gratian, a Benedictine monk. His *Decretum*, or Code of Canon Law, was easily the most influential book ever written by a Catholic. It was peppered with three centuries of forgeries and conclusions drawn from them, with his own fictional additions. Of the 324 passages he quotes from popes of the first four centuries, only eleven are genuine.

Among his personal additions was a series of canons treating all excommunicated persons as heretics. This was alarming in view of the way heretics were treated. Urban II had decreed at the end of the eleventh century that they were to be tortured and killed.

Gratian remarkably invented a way of extending papal power. The pope, he declared to Rome's approval, is superior to and the source of all laws *without qualification*. He must, therefore, stand on an equality with the Son of God. This apotheosis became the inspiration of the Curia which acted in the pope's name. Every pen-pusher was, in some sense, a god.

Looking further ahead to the thirteenth century, the *Decretum* was Thomas Aquinas' source-book for quotes from the Fathers and the popes when he came to write his masterly *Summa Theologica*, the second most renowned work by a Catholic. Aquinas, who knew little or no Greek, was led astray by Gratian, especially in regard to the papacy. Aquinas, of course, had immense influence on the church, especially during the First Vatican Council when papal infallibility was defined.

One small irony: in his *Summa*, Aquinas says heretics should be executed on the same basis as forgers. Heretics forge not currency but something far more precious: the faith. He did not ask what penalties were appropriate to criminals who forged documents that misled the church, himself included, for generation after generation.

Gregory's forgeries had the advantage of being both original and sacrosanct, novel and yet ancient. A prince was unwise to oppose the pope when previous pontiffs like Innocent I and Gregory the Great had deposed an emperor and a king. Not that they had done any such thing, though Gregory VII had a document to prove they had. The forgers themselves believed with all their hearts that Gregory had the power to depose monarchs, and if they could, with a pen-stroke here and there, assist an impious world to believe the same where was the harm in that?

History became a minor branch of theology where it has remained ever since. After all, even history cannot contradict infallible truth. Hence in the formative years of Roman Catholic Christianity, all discussion was stifled by recourse to 'authorities' that were instantly fabricated. Development came not spontaneously but was forced into pre-established patterns. The traditional subjection of popes to General Councils in matters of faith and morals was reversed. Disputed and sometimes ludicrous views became established dogmas; partial views were consecrated as timeless and irreversible Catholic teaching.

It is no small thing to manufacture history.

No sooner was he elected than Gregory VII set about reforming everything. First, in order to ensure that church property was never given away, he tried to eliminate the universal 'fornication', that is, the marriage of the clergy. The law of clerical celibacy had been virtually forgotten, except by Gregory. If priests did not mend their ways, they were to be suspended and the laity were not to accept ministry from them. It was as if sinful priests were no longer priests. One critic asked: 'Would the pope say a sinful man is no longer a man?'

The effect of his legislation, according to Ray C. Petry, was 'to make virtual prostitutes by the thousands out of innocent wives of bewildered and angry little clergymen'. Lecky says: 'When the wives of priests were separated in vast numbers from their husbands by Hildebrand and driven blasted, heart-broken and helpless, not a few of them shortened their agony by suicide.' The German clergy wanted to know, when Gregory had driven men out of the priesthood, where he would find the angels to replace them. A group of Italian bishops met in council in Pavia in 1076 and excommunicated the pope for separating husbands and wives, and for preferring licentiousness among the clergy to honourable marriage.

Had Gregory carried out his threat of suspending incontinent priests, he would practically have wiped Catholicism off the map. Fortunately or unfortunately, his campaign met with no long-lasting success. Celibacy he might enforce but not chastity. Still, through celibacy, he guaranteed the perpetual *apartheid* system in Catholicism between clerics who have rights and the laity, men and women, who have not. Curiously, more laymen separated from their wives than priests, being perhaps more impressed by Gregory's ascetic ideals. Priests, after a lull, continued to take the line that what they did in bed was their own affair.

Next, Gregory turned to simony, the buying and selling of sacred things. Excommunication for this seemed excessive to cardinals who knew that everything from the papacy down had its price as a matter of course.

Against a centuries-old practice, Gregory excommunicated any cleric who received a living from a layman, be he a duke or prince. This was part of his quest for absolute power. No one in the church should owe anyone loyalty but to him. Against a thousand-year-old tradition, he made all bishops take a personal oath of loyalty to him. From now on, they were bishops 'by favour of the Apostolic See'. At a stroke, diocesan bishops, successors of the apostles, lost their independence, which not even Vatican II could restore to them. From Gregory VII on, in spite of denials, the pope is the real bishop in every diocese. *Any* cleric who conflicts on any issue with the pope can be dismissed as easily as he was appointed. If that is not to be the real bishop, it is hard to know what is.

The Great Clash

Gregory had been awaiting a chance to challenge the emperor for over thirty years. Finally, he accused Henry IV of interfering in the affairs of the church and of simony. Henry was genuinely astonished. He did meddle, of course, but he was doing nothing more than emperors since Constantine had always done. Had he not been asked and given his consent to Gregory's election? What made this pope think he could tell him what to do?

In a fit of pique, Henry called a council at Worms and declared the election void. He, as emperor, had not been consulted in advance.

Gregory responded by anathematizing Henry and followed it up with a circular letter.

> On the part of God the omnipotent, I forbid Henry
> to govern the kingdoms of Italy and Germany. I
> absolve all his subjects from every oath they have
> taken or may take; and I excommunicate every
> person who shall serve him as king.

It was the papal bombshell of the time. Emperors had deposed any number of popes: Gregory had witnessed one such sacrilege. Never before had a pope dared depose an emperor. How would things turn out?

The omens were good. Henry's mother, Empress Agnes, sided with the pope, as did his cousin, the formidable Matilda, Countess of Tuscany. To Henry's dismay, the madman in Rome was actually having an effect in Germany itself. Princes started withdrawing allegiance. To press home his advantage, Gregory backed Rodolph, Duke of Swabia and Henry's vassal, as next in line to the throne.

Henry, now twenty-one, realized he had his back to the wall. The anniversary of his excommunication was approaching when he would lose his kingdom officially and for good unless he made his peace with the pope.

With a small retinue, he passed through Burgundy and spent a pleasant if apprehensive family Christmas at Besançon. Then, in mid-winter 1077, he crossed the Alps. With him went his wife and baby son Conrad. Peasant guides had to gouge a passage through snow-drifts and drag the queen through on her ox-hide sledge. They tumbled down ravines and lost most of their horses. Once in Italy, they were joined by the huge Lombard army who hoped he had come to put the pope in his place. He disappointed them.

Gregory was sheltering from the Lombards in Matilda's triple-walled fortress at Canossa. It was built on the summit of a craggy red-hued hill on a spur of the Apennines. Twenty miles to the north-west was Parma, invisible in the mists of that particularly severe winter. At Canossa, Henry sued for peace.

Through intermediaries, Gregory laid down the ground-rules. Henry was to send his crown and all other royal ornaments to be disposed of by his Holiness. He must publicly confess his unworthiness to be emperor after his disgraceful behaviour at Worms. Finally, he must promise to do whatever penance the pope imposed.

Having indicated his agreement, Henry climbed up the white slope to the fortress, fearful and alone. Passing through the first portal, he was stopped in the next enclosure. High above him, the pope appeared in full pontificals to savour his humiliation.

With an east wind whistling around him, Henry was stripped of his royal ensigns and made to remove his clothes. A woollen tunic was thrown to him, rough as a hair-shirt.

Put it on. Gregory, his own hair-shirt close to his well-flogged back and hidden by his clothing, gestured without deigning to speak to one who was out of communion with God and the church.

Henry, teeth chattering, flesh blue with cold, obeyed. With bare head and bare feet, he stood ankle-deep in snow in the hair-cloth of beggary and penitence. He held a besom broom in one hand and a pair of shears in the other, tokens of his willingness to be whipped and shorn.

The emperor of the Holy Roman Empire, heir to Charlemagne, stood there for three days and nights, fasting from daybreak till long after the glittering stars came out, a sight so wretched his relatives on the battlements wept noisily, unable to look any more. Hour after hour, Henry, his hair and eyebrows stiff with frost, prayed with deep shuddering sighs to God and the pope for mercy.

Gregory gave an account of his own actions in a letter to the German princes later that year:

The persons who interceded for Henry murmured at the Pope's great heartlessness. Some even dared say that such behaviour was more like the barbarous cruelty of a tyrant than the just severity of an ecclesiastical judge.

What hardened Gregory was the distant memory of what Henry's father had done to his predecessor. As the Italians say, revenge tastes better cold.

Only when his hostess Matilda pleaded on the fourth day that her cousin would die if he stayed any longer in the snow did the pope relent.

Henry was dragged in, a lump of frozen flesh, to stand in rags before the tiara'd pontiff. Tall and handsome, he towered over this ugly swarthy Tuscan dwarf with his large nose and cold unblinking eyes.

Henry had to swear to submit to the pope's judgement in the time and place to be announced. Meanwhile, he was not to exercise sovereignty until the pope spoke the word. As Machiavelli remarked in his *History of Florence*, 'Henry was the first prince to have the honour of feeling the sharp thrust of spiritual weapons'.

But Henry, too, had his pride. He asked nothing of the pope except to have his censure lifted.

Once home, he took to the field against Rodolph, causing Gregory to impose the censures all over again. In a long-distance battle, Henry called a council to depose the pope. Bishop Berno of Osnabrück hid under the altar-cloth of Brixen Cathedral until the proceedings against Gregory were over, then reappeared as if by magic. Henry chose Guibert of Ravenna as Pope Clement III. For this, Gregory prophesied Henry would die within the year. Instead, after a couple of resounding victories, Henry marched on Rome and put Clement on the throne.

Gregory fled, old, tired and abandoned by his cardinals, to Salerno in the kingdom of Naples. He had been pope for twelve years. It was a typical Neapolitan summer, but he had not felt so cold since he stood on the battlements of Canossa. Imperious to the end, he gave absolution to the human race, 'save for Henry so-called King', whom, to make sure, he excommunicated for the fourth time. Even a pontiff with divine powers could not redeem *him*.

Contrary to known facts, he murmured: 'I have loved justice and hated iniquity, therefore I die in exile.' The lack of logic did not escape an episcopal aide. 'How in exile, Holiness, when the whole world is thine?'

Gregory died on 25 May 1085.

He is held in high regard by Catholics. His prestige rests on his asceticism, his fulminations against simony and priestly fornication, his attempt to turn back the tide of centuries of papal immorality, his ability, *by force of an idea alone,* to dethrone monarchs. He is also the classical exponent of Roman Catholicism, which he virtually invented. He never had a doubt or an opinion; he was always quite certain of everything.

Yet, leaving aside the forgeries which buttressed his shaky claims, even his admirers have to admit that before him Throne and Altar were allies. Popes and princes never ceased sizing each other up and, at times, they fought like tigers. First, one encroached on the other's province, then the roles were reversed. But, as God's anointed representatives, they never doubted that they were in some deep and holy sense bound up together.

Gregory set out to shatter that fragile harmony. He had seen an emperor dethrone a pope; he would dethrone an emperor *regardless.*

Had he put an emperor in his place, he would have been beyond reproach. He did far more. By introducing a mischievous and heretical doctrine, he put himself in place of the emperor. In the name of the Poor Man of Nazareth who renounced all kingship, he claimed to be not only Bishop of bishops but King of kings. In a parody of the gospels, the devil took him up to a very high mountain and showed him all the kingdoms of the world, and Gregory VII exclaimed: These are all mine.

As that most objective of historians, Henry Charles Lea, wrote in *The Inquisition in the Middle Ages*: 'To the realization of this ideal [of papal supremacy], he devoted his life with a fiery zeal and unshaken purpose that shrank from no obstacle, and to it he was ready to sacrifice not only the men who stood in his path but also the immutable principles of truth and justice.'

In this way, Gregory sowed broadside seeds that, when they bloomed, brought about not only the end of Christendom but the Reformation, too. The Bishop of Trier saw the danger. He charged Gregory with destroying the unity of the church. The Bishop of Verdun said the pope was mistaken in his unheard-of arrogance. Belief belongs to one's church, the heart belongs to one's country. The pope, he said, must not filch the heart's allegiance. This was precisely what Gregory did. He wanted all; he left emperors and princes nothing. The papacy, as he fashioned it, by undermining patriotism, undermined the authority of secular rulers; they felt threatened by the Altar. At the Reformation, in England and elsewhere, rulers felt obliged to exclude Catholicism from their lands *in order to feel secure.*

Another legacy of Gregory VII was the imposition of Romanism on the church. After him, a genuine Catholicism, a Catholicism rooted in and enriched by every locality and every culture, was impossible. Every church had to conform to the Roman pattern, however alien that pattern was to its origins and experience. Latin, celibacy, scholastic theology, all were imposed to such a degree that unanimity was replaced by uniformity based on Rome.

The changes Gregory brought about were reflected in language. Before him, the pope's traditional title was Vicar of St Peter. After him, it was Vicar of Christ. Only 'Vicar of Christ' could justify his absolutist pretensions, which his successors inherited in reality not from Peter or from Jesus but from *him*.

He set a trend. In the hundred years after him, popes excommunicated no fewer than eight emperors, deposing several of them, and each time disturbing the Christian commonwealth. Historians have traced seventy-five bloody battles directly to Gregory's feuding with the emperor.

A final paradoxical result of the reforms of the ascetic Gregory. His absolutist claims paved the way for popes as sensuous as Alexander Borgia. Even when there was a Satan on the papal throne, who dared question the Vicar of Christ?

Gregory VII had to wait five centuries before he was canonized officially by a pope other than himself. That pope, Pius V, also had a penchant for deposing sovereigns, with equally disastrous results.

But of all the post-mortem accolades he received Gregory would have treasured most the one given him not by a fellow-pontiff but by the church's greatest nineteenth-century foe. 'If I were not me, I would like to be Gregory VII.' The speaker was Napoleon, after the battle of Austerlitz.

If Napoleon chose Gregory rather than Innocent III, it was probably the result of tossing a coin.

Innocent III, Lord of the World

It was the most extraordinary meeting between two men since Jesus stood before Pilate in the Praetorium. The one in royal robes on the purple throne was the most powerful man in the world; the twenty-seven-year-old who knelt before him in the patched rags of a beggar had staked his claim to be the poorest.

It was the summer of 1209. Pope Innocent III had finally agreed to see this tiny unkempt fellow who had a reputation for holiness. The skinny petitioner had dark hair and level eyebrows, white teeth, small but jutting ears. His beard was sparse and straggly. His black twitching eyes sparkled, his voice was strong and musical, and he radiated a peculiar joy. He was a poet, people said. He spoke of Brother Sun and Brother Wind. Moon, Water, Earth, even Death were his Sisters. He was reputed to preach to birds and wild animals, and they listened to him. His great love was Poverty, whom he called the richest and most bounteous Lady in the world.

Innocent would not remember it, but he had met this strange little man once before. Francis of Assisi had found his way into the Lateran

Palace. His aim was to go straight to the top to get approval for the religious brotherhood he wanted to found. By chance he ran into Innocent in a corridor. Francis had come from St Peter's where he had exchanged clothes with a beggar whose rags were tattier and smellier than his own. The pontiff sniffed and ordered him out.

He was only prevailed on to give Francis an audience by Ugolino, Cardinal of Ostia. Ugolino, the future Gregory IX, did not understand Francis, either, but he thought he had something to offer the church. He was never to understand him, not even when he canonized him, with reservations, in 1228.

The interview with Innocent III was brief. The pope neither approved nor disapproved of Francis and his love of poverty. He had more important things on his mind. Like ruling the world.

Cardinal Lothaire had been elected unanimously on 8 January 1198. Innocent, like the boy-pope Benedict IX, was from the Alberics of Tusculum, a family that was to boast, in time, thirteen popes, three antipopes and forty cardinals.

At thirty-eight, Innocent was the youngest member of the Sacred College. He was short, stocky, handsome, eloquent, with steely grey eyes and firm chin. He had studied at the best universities of Paris and Bologna. Of fiery temperament, with greatness stamped all over him, he was born to rule, whatever the cost.

After his consecration in St Peter's, Innocent was crowned on a platform outside. The Cardinal Archdeacon removed his mitre and replaced it with the princely *Regnum*. Originally made of white peacock feathers, it was now a jewelled diadem, topped by a carbuncle.

'Take this tiara,' the Archdeacon intoned, in a ritual that would have surprised St Peter, 'and know that thou art Father of princes and kings, Ruler of the World, the Vicar on earth of our Saviour Jesus Christ, whose honour and glory shall endure through all eternity.'

The pontiff, disciple of Gregory VII, never doubted that this blasphemy was his due.

He was Constantine reincarnate. Thomas Hobbes's famous jibe in *Leviathan*, seems justified: 'The Papacy is no other than the ghost of the deceased Roman Empire, sitting crowned upon the grave thereof.' His garments shining with gold and jewels, Innocent mounted a scarlet-covered white horse and joined in the cavalcade through the garlanded city along the Via Papae. It wound its way under the old imperial arches.

At the Tower of Stephen Petri, an old rabbi, his shoulders wrapped in the scroll of the Pentateuch, came forward to do obeisance. 'We acknowledge', Innocent formally declared, 'the Law but we condemn the principles of Judaism; for the Law is already fulfilled through Christ, whom the blind people of Judah still expect as their Messiah.'

The rabbi, eyes downcast, thanked the pontiff for his kind words and retired before he got a beating.

Across the Forum the procession went. Rome, as Innocent inherited it, was nothing but a vast uncultivated field surrounded by the gaping moss-covered Aurelian wall.

The pontiff made a resolution to clean the place up and build his family a tower there, Torre de' Conti, to dominate the entire city. Past piles of rubble from temples, baths and broken aqueducts, Innocent skirted the Colosseum on his way to the Lateran.

There he received the oath of allegiance from the Roman Senate, had his foot kissed by prelates and princes, and then, having distributed largesse to the poor and not so poor, invited the nobles to a banquet.

The pontiff sat alone, as befits a deity. The vessels were of the costliest. The senior prince present served him his first dish before taking his place at table with the cardinals.

Innocent did not eat much; his health was never very good. He made up for a feeble body with the most iron will any pontiff ever had. He was already planning to make his most cherished title 'Ruler of the World' a reality.

The papacy was virtually impotent in Rome at his accession. His first aim, like that of many popes before and after him, was to restore his temporal domains. Before long, he had turned Rome into a clerical state. A critic in the Senate complained: 'He has plucked Rome as the hawk plucks a hen.' Within two years, he, not the emperor, was master of Rome and Italy. Not that he had everything his own way.

In early May 1203, during a brief rising of Roman citizens, he was forced to flee to Palestrina. He was too ill next year to take in the tales of how the knights of the Fourth Crusade had committed the most barbaric of medieval crimes: they had sacked Constantinople. In the grand old cathedral of Santa Sophia, the tombs of emperors had been desecrated, relics had been stolen, women, including nuns, raped and murdered. The most prestigious city in the world was levelled by Catholic soldiers who seemed to think schismatics had no rights in this world or the next.

This, the first great example of civil vandalism within Christendom, has never been forgotten by the Greeks. Innocent did not help matters by appointing a Venetian as Latin patriarch of Byzantium.

After two years, Innocent made his peace with the city of Rome and returned to take charge. Exile had only increased his ardour for domination. Earlier popes were not unhappy to be styled 'Vicar of St Peter'. He *repudiated* the title. 'We are the successors of Peter but not his vicar nor any man's nor any apostle's. We are the Vicar of Jesus Christ before whom *every* knee shall bow.' Even – no, *especially* – the knees of kings and emperors.

The church, he said, is the soul, the Empire only the body of the world. The church is the sun, the Empire a dead moon reflecting light from the great Orb, Christ's church.

Innocent's teaching on society contradicted the Bible. For him, princely power is a form of usurpation; only priestly rule is from God. This was Manicheeism applied to relations between church and state. The church, spiritual, was good; the state, material, was essentially the work of the devil. This naked political absolutism undermined the authority of kings. Taken seriously, his theories would lead to anarchy.

Innocent did not think so, of course, because he felt able to rule both church and state. This was his expressed aim. But on what pretext could he govern *secular* society? The answer was: Sin. Wherever there was sin, there the pope was omnipotent. And where, in church and state, was there no sin? It paid him to paint sovereigns in the darkest colours. It gave him the right, as he saw it, to legislate for the whole world.

He needed pliant instruments. He chose Otto IV as emperor because he promised to do whatever the pope told him. Otto was the first 'King of the Romans' to be called 'elect by the grace of God and of the pope'.

Within a year, Otto rebelled, claiming, correctly, his promise had no legal basis. Innocent excommunicated him and chose another. He was also to crown Peter of Aragon and the king of England. Even Gregory VII had not been able to bring to heel the king of England. William the Conqueror refused to be his fief, saying: 'I owe my kingdom to God and my sword.' John, who was crowned when Richard the Lionheart died in 1199, was of a different calibre.

John Lackland, only five feet five inches tall, was, in the words of a chronicler, 'a crooked king'. Spoiled as a child, he grew up wild, moody and unpredictable. He had slanting eyes like an oriental and a permanently sallow complexion on a vulpine face. Only in matters of personal hygiene was he beyond reproach; he was known to take eight baths in one year.

His lack of balance showed at his coronation. Contrary to protocol, he refused the sacrament. At solemn moments, he cracked lewd jokes and laughed his loud cackling laugh.

His contempt for the church was evident ten years before when he married his cousin Isabel of Gloucester without a dispensation. Within a year of becoming king, he fell for the young, beautiful and already betrothed Isabel of Angoulême. Having filed his own decree of nullity, he married his second Isabel and made her his queen. When Innocent expressed displeasure, John atoned by sending a thousand men on the Crusades and building a Cistercian abbey with stolen money. Innocent tacitly consented to the second union.

The pope finally fell out with John not over marriage but over money. The king was interfering in the liberties of the church – a way of saying he was taxing the clergy to pay for his wars with France.

When John nominated his own candidate to the see of Canterbury, the pope had had enough. He nominated Stephen Langton, whom John refused to recognize. Innocent gave him three months to change his mind or he would feel the full force of canon law. Far from giving in, John expelled the monks of Canterbury from his realm. All but one bishop sided with Innocent and went into exile. A seven-year quarrel between king and pope had begun.

Innocent showed how ruthless he could be by putting the whole of England under an interdict. It was a punishment of incredible severity. He had already practised on France, which he had put under interdict for eight months soon after his election.

John swore 'by God's teeth' that if any bishop spread this penalty in England he would send all the clergy to the pope with their eyes plucked out and their noses slit. When it was published on Palm Sunday 1208, John's first reaction was to confiscate church property with the help of greedy barons. He, its intended victim, enjoyed himself enormously. He levied taxes on the clergy, remitting nothing to Rome. His favourite prank was to raid parsonages at night and remove uncanonical wives – the *focariae*, or hearth-mates – from the parsons' beds. If these tonsured gentlemen wanted their women back, they had to pay a heavy ransom. This differed little from the antics of the archdeacon's summoner, that most hated of officials. When he rooted out a priest's mistress – and his success rate was phenomenally high – he charged a 'sin-rent' of two pounds per annum.

Most of England suffered. Children were victimized as well as adults. Religion, the people's entertainment and solace, was outlawed. Churches, the only meeting-places, were bolted and barred against all but bats in the towers and peregrines that nested in cathedral spires. Silenced by this censure was the loveliest sound in all England: the bells. No more pealed out over town and country of this 'ringing isle' the sound of funeral bells or the Gabriel bell of Angelus, no more the bronze but subtle music from the belfry that drowned out gulls' cries and crows' cries and punctured, according to popular belief, the pneumatic power of the storm.

The dying were anointed, penitents absolved, babies baptized. For the rest, England became a pagan land.

With eight thousand cathedral and parish churches closed, thousands of priests and lesser clerics were jobless. No services were held at Christmas and Easter, no masses said even in convents and monasteries, no communion given, no marriages celebrated, no sermons preached or instruction given; there were no processions, no pilgrimages to shrines like Ely, Walsingham or Canterbury, no beating of the parish bounds. The dead were placed in their shrouds and buried like dogs.

Summer passed into winter and returned without a single Christian celebration. This long Good Friday imposed by the pope in his mercy was to last in England for six years, three months and fourteen days.

In October 1209 the interdict was followed by the king's excommunication. Three years later, the pope deposed John and suggested to Philip of France that he prepare to expel him and take over the throne of England. Whoever obeyed the pope was promised the same indulgences as Crusaders.

England looked forward to getting rid of a tyrant. He slept at whim with any man's wife. He pulled out the teeth, one by one, of rich Jews who did not come up with the money. He took hostages and, when there was a rising in Wales, hanged twenty-eight boys, sons of Welsh chieftains, in Nottingham Castle in the summer of 1212.

As Philip armed his forces at the mouth of the Seine, John played his strongest card: he asked Rome to send a legate to make peace.

The pontiff, overjoyed, sent Cardinal Pandulf. On 13 May 1213, before an assembly of barons and people at Dover, John capitulated. He promised full restitution of church funds and lands.

Two days later, he gladly signed a second document, giving England itself 'to God and to our Lord Pope Innocent and his Catholic successors'. He affixed to it not the usual wax seal but a seal of gold. Thenceforward, John promised, he and his heirs would hold their dominions as vassals of the pope and pay an annual rent of a thousand marks for the privilege, over and above Peter's Pence.

Innocent's victory gave him immense pleasure, but it was another example of papal overkill. Papal suzerainty over England effectively ended in 1333, the year that Edward III refused to pay the pope any more rent. When Pope Urban V insensitively asked for thirty-three years' arrears, Edward, after consulting with his officials, concluded that John's donation of England to the Holy See was against his coronation oath, hence invalid. The popes did not agree, and this issue was to contribute directly to the secession of England from the Catholic faith in the reign of Elizabeth I. She did not much care to be called the pope's fief or to think she only rented England from a foreign potentate.

Philip of France was furious with Innocent III. He had poured sixty thousand pounds into the Channel, though he dared not set foot on English, now *papal*, soil.

Though John was absolved from excommunication, the interdict remained until June 1214 when he paid the last of the money. Only then were the church doors flung open, *Te Deum* sung and the bells rung again. And, by kind permission of Pope Innocent III, Christ was able to enter England again.

Meanwhile, the barons' hatred of John reached such a pitch that they drew up Magna Carta, guaranteeing the rights of church and people, especially the barons, and forced John to attach his seal to it.

By the terms of the charter, the king, like all free men, was subject to law; and the body of law had to be not secret but *known*.

John, now a pious Catholic, naturally informed his Holiness. Innocent exclaimed when he heard: 'By St Peter, we cannot pass over this insult without punishing it.' This document, often called the foundation of English liberties, was formally condemned by the pope as 'contrary to the moral law'. The king, he explained, was in no way subject to barons and people. He was only under God and the pope. Consequently, those barons who had wrongly squeezed concessions from a papal vassal had to be punished. In a Bull, Innocent, 'From the plenitude of his unlimited power and authority which God has committed to him to bind and destroy kingdoms, to plant and uproot', annulled the charter; he absolved the king from having to observe it. He excommunicated 'anyone who should continue to maintain such treasonable and iniquitous pretensions'. All English people, it must be presumed, are still excommunicated.

Stephen Langton, Archbishop of Canterbury, refused to publish this sentence. The pope's rule, he said, was not unlimited. 'Natural law is binding on princes and bishops alike: there is no escape from it. It is beyond the reach of the pope himself.' Langton was suspended from office.

Having conquered kings, Innocent found bishops easy meat. He called himself 'Universal Bishop', a title repudiated by many early pontiffs. With Innocent, the church achieved the ideal of Gregory; it became a single diocese. More laws were passed by Innocent than by any fifty popes before him; he himself was subject to no law at all. Six thousand of his letters have so far been published. The scope of them is extraordinary. He deposes and replaces bishops and abbots. He imposes penances for a wide range of offences. For example, a man named Robert had been captured by the Saracens with his wife and daughter. The Saracen chief issued an order that, owing to famine, prisoners with children should kill and eat them. 'This wicked man,' wrote Innocent, 'urged on by the pangs of hunger, killed and ate his daughter. And when, on a second occasion, another order went out, he killed his own wife; but when her flesh was cooked and served up to him, he could not bring himself to eat it.' Part of his penance was that he should never eat meat again. Nor should he remarry.

Innocent completed his dominance of the church at the Fourth Lateran Council in 1215. A massive gathering of fifteen hundred prelates listened politely to his decrees and passed them without a question being asked or a word of debate. One law they passed was that every Catholic had to confess his sins to his local priest and communicate at least once a year. In this way, the laity were made subject to the clergy, the clergy to their bishops, the bishops to the pope.

The only dissenters were the heretics. The second part of this book will deal with the crowning glory of Innocent's reign, namely, the crushing of the Albigensians in the south of France. Hundreds of thousands of them were put to death, by fire and sword, at his bidding. Being the sole depository of truth, Innocent felt free to eradicate heresy by every means at his disposal. It was he who gave a fresh impetus to the Inquisition and injected a special kind of intolerance into Catholicism that was to last for centuries.

Innocent III, statesman of genius, pontiff of 'an appalling force of will', ruled the world in tranquil majesty for close on twenty years. For most of the time, he encompassed Christendom with terror. He crowned and deposed sovereigns, put nations under interdict, virtually created the Papal States across central Italy from the Mediterranean to the Adriatic. He had not lost a single battle.

In pursuit of his aims, he shed more blood than any other pontiff. He profoundly misunderstood the Gospel, the church, the papacy, even the distinction between good and evil. His marvellous perversion of all these is evidenced in a single breathtaking statement: 'Every cleric must obey the Pope, even if he commands what is evil; for no one may judge the Pope.'

He was in Perugia when the end came in the hot July of 1216. News reached him that the French had once more dared assault his realm of England. As if to bow out in blood, he made a final address against Louis and Philip Augustus: 'Sword, sword, spring from thy scabbard. Sword, sword, sharpen thyself and then exterminate.'

Dying, he must have looked with trembling lids over the vast quilt of the Umbrian Plain towards the sleepy little town of Assisi, nestling on the side of a hill. Maybe some distant memory stirred in him. There was that day when a bright-eyed beggar came to him, asking recognition of a brotherhood he wanted to found. Did he give it or didn't he? In the grand scale of things it cannot have been important.

The beggar he threw out of the Lateran Palace, who threatened no one, who would have died rather than deprive anyone of the consolations of religion, was soon to experience in his body the wounds of the crucified Christ. Of him, Dante said in the *Paradiso*: 'Nacque al mondo un Sole', 'To the world was born a Sun'.

Innocent III, the true 'Augustus of the papacy', is now known only to historians. There is no one who has not heard, with joy and affection, of Francis of Assisi.

Innocent's successors repeated his absolutist claims, even enlarging on them. Gregory IX (1227–41), who canonized the Poor Little Man of Assisi, solemnly declared the pope is lord and master of the universe, *things as well as people*. Innocent IV (1243–54) decided that the

Donation of Constantine was misnamed. Constantine did not *give* secular power to the popes; they had supreme secular power already from Christ.

It only needed the pope whom Dante called the Black Beast, Boniface VIII, to put the seal on papal absolutism.

FIVE

Power in Decline

BENEDICT GAETANI was crowned Pope Boniface VIII in 1294. Jacopone da Todi, the poet who wrote the famous hymn *Stabat Mater*, remarked that no name suited him less. His was no 'bonny face'.

Tall and stout, he had, at eighty, the coldest eye ever seen on a man. Llanduff, a curial cardinal, strikingly said of him: 'He is all tongue and eyes, and the rest of him is all rotten.' Once, he refused to confirm the appointment of a metropolitan, simply because he did not like the look of his face, and told him so. Even a cardinal with a disability, such as an arthritic leg or a humped back, was likely to be ridiculed unmercifully. He said mass with ardour and tears, as though he were standing on Calvary and could see Jesus crucified. Immediately mass was over, he was likely to throw the ashes of penitence in the face of any archbishop who displeased him. According to F M Powicke, 'He was admired by many, feared by all, loved by none'.

Boniface was bald, and his ears shot out of an oval face that was aflame with the arrogance of a man who knows he has no equal on the earth. 'The breast of the Roman pontiff', he decreed, 'is the repository and fount of all law. This is why blind submission to his authority is essential to salvation.' In the Jubilee of 1300, he was found sitting on his throne, Constantine's crown on his head, a sword in his hand, chanting remorselessly: 'I am pontiff, I am emperor.'

His clothes were the costliest, from England and the East, and he dripped with furs and gems. When he spoke, he spat the words through the gap where two teeth were missing in his upper jaw. His predecessor, Celestine V, had said of him: 'You leaped on the throne like a fox, you will reign like a lion, you will die like a dog.'

Few popes ever enriched their kin as Boniface did. A Spanish diplomat said: 'This Pope cares for only three things: a long life, a rich life, a well-endowed family around him.' Known as 'The Great-Hearted Sinner', *Magnanimus Peccator*, he lost no time in making three of his nephews cardinals and bestowing vast lands and possessions on them. According to Dante, he turned Peter's burial-place into a sewer.

A libertine, he once had a married woman and her daughter as his mistresses. In one of those off-the-cuff remarks for which he was renowned, he said: 'Having sex is like rubbing one hand against the other.' Now, as he aged, his only hobby other than making money was making enemies. The Spanish physician who saved his life became the second most hated man in Rome.

For all his surface assurance, Boniface had one perpetual worry. Too many prelates suspected that he had tricked his predecessor into resigning. It is one of the weirdest stories in the history of the Catholic church, and it began in the year 1292 on the death of Pope Nicholas IV.

The conclave, held in Perugia, could not agree on a successor. The eleven electors were divided between the Colonnas and the Orsinis so that discussions went on fruitlessly for weeks, then months. Benedict Gaetani stood apart from it all, hoping maybe he would be chosen as a compromise. After two years of stalemate, Gaetani pretended to receive 'a letter of flame' from an old hermit. Peter of Morone, who hid out in a cave in the Abruzzi, had a reputation for holiness. He demanded that the cardinals give the orphaned church a pope. Instead of proposing Gaetani, the Dean successfully proposed Peter of Morone himself.

A papal party left Perugia in the hot summer of 1294. After a 150-mile journey and a thousand-foot climb, they came across the new pope. Lean, scraggy, unwashed, he was peering through the bars of his home-made cell like a bewildered monkey. The odour of sanctity was not pleasant. The papal party, headed by Cardinal Peter Colonna, went down on their knees with 'Your Holiness'. Once he grasped it was not a joke and he was not just an old man dreaming dreams, Peter of Morone accepted. He took the name of Celestine V.

The new pontiff did not approve of the licentious ways of Rome, so he insisted on setting up his seat in Naples. Gaetani, to gain his confidence, built him a wooden cell in one of the enormous rooms of the Castello Nuovo, the five-towered castle that overlooks the sea. There, as a contemporary put it, his Holiness hoped to hide like a pheasant in the undergrowth. This was not his scene, and these worldly princes were complete strangers to him. He could not understand the polished Latin phrases they used. He emptied his stables and travelled, when he had to, like Jesus, on a donkey.

The church had changed so much since the early days that Jesus himself would not have fitted into it. The cardinals soon realized their mistake. Celestine was giving away church possessions to unworthy people, like the poor, and the impoverished monks with whom he had always associated. He had no flair for simony. He would bankrupt the church in no time at all. He even kept away from banquets, preferring to nibble a crust of bread and sip water in seclusion.

Something had to be done, and who better to do it than Benedict Gaetani? He bored a hole into the wall of the pope's cell and put a speaking-tube in it. In the middle of the night, he whispered down the

76

tube: 'Celestine, Celestine, lay down your office. It is too great a burden for you to bear.' After several nights of listening to the voice of the Holy Ghost, the simple monk decided to abdicate. Only fifteen weeks after his coronation, he summoned his cardinals, begging them, with little hope of success, to send their mistresses to nunneries and live in poverty like Jesus. He exchanged his papal robes for his rough hermit's garb, resigned and left.

Gaetani, a lawyer, had engineered this successful outcome; he, the antithesis of Celestine, now claimed the throne by right. He took over in December 1294 and immediately returned to Rome. But, fearing that Celestine might reappear with spiritual fanatics like Jacopone da Todi, he took the precaution of locking him up in the castle of Fumone; the old hermit died there a few months later of starvation and neglect.

The Colonna family got to know how Gaetani had forced Celestine out of office and used this knowledge to question his legitimacy. Boniface VIII, for all his power, was never to feel secure on the papal throne.

The Colonnas were descended from the Counts of Tusculum. Apart from Boniface usurping the throne, *their* throne, they objected to him swallowing up their lands around Rome and donating them to members of his family. When the Colonnas ambushed a papal convoy laden with gold, Boniface treated them like Turks by preaching a crusade, with indulgences, against them. When they took the precaution of slipping out of Rome, he accused them of plotting with the French to overthrow him. In retaliation, he sent armies to destroy their citadels in the hills around Rome, killing the peasants on their lands or selling them into slavery. Soon, only the rock walls of Palestrina afforded the Colonnas sanctuary.

The two Colonna cardinals had no choice but to beg for mercy. Rushing to Rieti where the pope was in residence, they prostrated themselves before him, with cords round their necks and clothed in the black robes of penitence.

Boniface, his eyes brighter than his tiara, gave them their lives and took from them something they valued more: their honour. He expelled them from the Sacred College and broke their seals with a hammer. Then he travelled to Anagni, his favourite town, above the broad valley of the Sacco forty miles east of Rome. There on the lower ridge of Monte San Giorgio he had been born and bred.

He crossed to the window in the upper room of the papal palace where he had a thrilling view across the spring vegetation. Palestrina one of the seven pillars of the Roman church, was perched on the side of a hill, surrounded by olives and laurel. Horace wrote one of his loveliest *Carmina* in praise of Palestrina, and there, in the third century, the boy-martyr Agapitus was slain for Christ's sake.

After muttering a prayer, the pontiff raised and dropped his hand like an avenging deity. Immediately, a flag was lowered on the palace battlements, the sign for the pope's forces to begin storming Palestrina.

Nothing was spared. There were reports of six thousand dead, though many of the inhabitants must have fled to the surrounding countryside. Palaces, including the home of Julius Caesar, antiques and glorious mosaics, a circular temple to the Virgin Mary atop a marble staircase of a hundred steps, all met the same fate. Only the cathedral was spared. The rest was flattened as ruthlessly as Carthage of old. It was ploughed in and salt was sown into its furrows to make the desolation complete. There would be another town, Boniface promised, a *Civitas Papalis*, one that knew how to be loyal to his Holiness.

For this monstrous act in the spring of 1299 Dante buried Boniface VIII in the Eighth Circle of Hell, head down in the fissures of the rock.

Three years later, on a cold mid-November day in the year 1302, Boniface was back at Anagni. So foul was his mood, even the sight of a levelled Palestrina could not lift his spirit. What was Christendom coming to when he could not rely on his oldest son? His dispute with Philip the Fair of France had dragged on and on. The king was furious with the pontiff for not making him emperor as he had promised. In revenge, he had levied taxes on the clergy to finance his military campaigns.

Boniface had retaliated six long years ago with his Bull *Clericis Laicos*. He took it out and read it again. He still marvelled at his own intransigence. Gregory VII could not have improved on it. 'The laity have always felt hostile to the clergy.' So true, he sighed, with his usual sibilance. Philip exemplified the principle perfectly. Boniface had issued excommunications against any cleric who paid one farthing to a layman, be he king or emperor. In fact he decreed that if a greedy monarch laid a finger on a single piece of church plate he would instantly cut him off from Jesus Christ, and if he did not repent he would lose his kingdom.

Was Philip cured of his madness? By no means. He had forbidden the export of gold and silver; the thief was pocketing all church revenues; he had, most wickedly of all, imprisoned a bishop. Trembling with rage, Boniface took out his pen. A new Bull. This was to be addressed to the universal church. After him, many Catholics, including some popes, would wish he had not written it.

'Unam Sanctam' and the Clash of Swords

The pontiff sat absorbed at his desk, the only sound being his goosequill scratching the paper. His first words were to go round the world: *Unam Sanctam*. 'There is but one holy, Catholic and Apostolic Church outside of which there is no salvation or remission of sins.'

It was best to stake his claims loud and clear. He, pope, was the one head, with Christ and Peter, of the church. This church is the Ark of Salvation; anyone outside it is doomed to drown for ever, especially Greek Christians who refuse to admit the pope is Shepherd of the whole flock.

A less pastoral image sprang to his mind. His eyes lit up: the Two Swords. 'The apostles said to Jesus, Here are two swords. The Lord does not answer, Too many, but, Enough!' Medieval exegesis seldom rose above this level.

By now the quill was racing.

> He who denies that the temporal sword is in the power of Peter wrongly interprets the Lord's words, 'Put up thy sword into its scabbard'. Both swords, the spiritual and the material, are in the power of the Church. The spiritual is wielded *by* the Church; the material *for* the Church. The one by the hand of the priest; the other by the hand of kings and knights at the will and sufferance of the priest. One sword has to be under the other; the material under the spiritual, as the temporal authority in general is under the spiritual.

Boniface paused to gaze at the ruins of Palestrina. What better proof of the right ordering of things in a spiritual commonwealth? 'The spiritual power', he continued, 'has to establish the earthly power and judge whether it be good or not. As Jeremiah said, "See, I have set thee this day over the nations and over kingdoms."' He hoped that Philip and all monarchs would heed his words this time.

A final authoritative touch so there would be no mistaking his meaning: 'We declare, announce and define that it is altogether necessary for salvation for every creature to be subject to the Roman Pontiff.'

To stress its authority, he signed the Bull as from his palace of the Lateran, in the eighth of his pontificate. Calling his secretary, a bishop, he handed him *Unam Sanctam* for copying and distribution throughout the church.

In France, reaction was not favourable. A king's aide commented: 'The Pope's sword is merely made of words; my Master's is of steel.'

Philip spread the rumour that Boniface forced his predecessor to resign, then locked him up and murdered him. Boniface is a tyrant, he declared, a heretic, a prey to every vice.

The king knew words were not enough. He had to act forcefully and with speed before he was excommunicated. He summoned his chancellor, William Nogaret. Together they hatched a daring plot. A squad of armed men was to be trained, the aim to snatch the pope and carry him back to France. There he would stand trial before a General Council which, without doubt, would depose him.

Nogaret bowed to his Majesty and, within weeks, the expedition was ready to set off.

In Rome, Boniface was feeling jubilant. *Unam Sanctam* had brought him more pleasure than sacking Palestrina, more even than the sight of 2 million pilgrims flocking to Rome to enrich him during the Holy Year two years before. God had, as it were, authenticated his Bull by seeing to it that Philip had been defeated in battle by the Flemish forces at Courtrai.

Now the whole church knew that God's things are God's; and Caesar's things are – well, they are God's, too. Obviously. Even if some popes hadn't the stomach to say so. After all, everything is God's, because he created them, and the pope represents God. The pope as Chief Shepherd is duty-bound to feed all the flock, including the biggest sheep of all: kings and emperors.

He savoured again his favourite line from *Unam Sanctam*: No one can be saved unless he obeys the Roman pontiff. Not even Philip would dare oppose him now.

It was not Philip but the Colonna family that worried him. After he had demoted their cardinals, they had shown him no gratitude for sparing their lives but fled the city. He had no idea where they were, but they were doubtless plotting something somewhere. He kicked himself for not having had them executed on the spot.

A year passed. Boniface was once more in his favourite retreat at Anagni. He was putting the final touches to a Bull excommunicating Philip and ousting him from his throne. Yes, he would sack him like a stable-boy. The glorious feeling this gave him was only marred by a peculiar story coming out of Florence. Some while before, he had donated to that city a full-grown male lion. The Florentines had kept it chained up in a *cortile* in the heart of the city. One day, an ass had found its way into the courtyard and – he could hardly believe it – kicked the king of beasts to death. The Florentines were saying it portended the last days of Boniface VIII.

Where would such a calamity come from? Not a whisper had reached him that Nogaret had joined forces with Sciarra Colonna, nephew and brother of the former cardinals. Sciarra, a bloodthirsty headstrong young man, had been at Rieti, also dressed in the black of penitence, when his relatives' seals of office were broken, bringing shame to the whole Colonna clan. Sciarra was never to forget kneeling before that monster and hearing the sentence of excommunication. By it, the pope banished him from the fellowship of Christians and forced him into perpetual exile. It was virtually a death-sentence, and he had spent four years in the galleys until a member of his family rescued him. This alliance with the French would enable Sciarra to pay off all his debts – at a stroke.

On Saturday, 7 October, Anagni's gates were treacherously opened at dawn by the pope's captain of the guard. Into the narrow streets poured six hundred horsemen and a thousand cavalry. This city of dark steep alleys rang with the sound of horses' hoofs and tramping feet. Soon even this was drowned out by the clang of the alarm bells. The invaders quickly removed the hastily erected barriers and sacked the palaces of cardinals loyal to the pope.

The pope's own palace was well fortified on the crest of the hill and defended by the Gaetanis. From there, at six in the morning, he sent a messenger asking for a truce.

In secret, he begged the chief citizens to come to his aid. He promised them wealth untold in return for their allegiance in his hour of need. They turned him down.

For hour after hour he sat in his throne room, thinking, praying, casting his eye again over *Unam Sanctam*, astonished that a temporal prince dared raise his sword against God's Anointed, the Lord of the World. At the hour of vespers, the terms of the truce were conveyed to him. He must restore the Colonna cardinals to the Sacred College, resign the papacy and surrender unconditionally to Sciarra Colonna.

For Boniface VIII, proud member of the Gaetanis, this meant a fight to the death.

The invaders began by burning down the main doors of the cathedral to gain entry into the palace beyond. The clergy in long white albs fled like seagulls. Sciarra's men plundered the cathedral as they went, murdering all inside. They then advanced on the palace itself, smashing windows and breaking down doors. The pope's bodyguards, outnumbered, surrendered, offering to show them the layout of the building. Cheering wildly, the troops, with Sciarra leading them, made their way up the broad staircase to the pope's private apartments.

Sciarra had not bothered to count how many he had killed in the last few hours. He remembered running through an archbishop, but the rest was hazy. Blood, smelling of rust, spattered his breastplate; his sword and dagger were crimson to the hilt. When he threw open the door of the huge high-ceilinged audience-chamber, a tremendous silence engulfed him and his men.

The eighty-six-year-old pope was seated in majesty on his throne, alone save for a cardinal-aide cowering in the corner. Unstirring, he was clad in full pontificals: tiara, symbolizing he was Lord of the World; on his fingers, besides a great flashing oval sapphire, was the

Fisherman's Ring. The ultimate source of his power was in his hand, a gold cross.

Sciarra was so stricken with awe, at first he found it hard to move. As he slowly advanced towards Boniface with drawn sword, the pontiff haughtily kissed the cross. This gesture, the loud smack of the lips might have stopped a devout Catholic but not Sciarra Colonna. He slapped the Vicar of Christ across his veined and mottled face so that the audience-chamber echoed with it, making even Sciarra's men recoil, crossing themselves. This was sacrilege. What if God, in revenge, were to strike them down? Swearing, to keep his courage up, Sciarra shouted that this man was not pope but an imposter, Satan's son. 'Resign.' he demanded.

Boniface kissed the cross again. 'Sooner die,' he muttered.

Too proud to beg for mercy of this excommunicated cur, he lowered his head. Then, in that familiar rasping tone, 'Ec le col, ec le cape' – 'Here, my neck; here, my head'.

He had been born in Anagni; he did not mind dying there. This pontiff who claimed that the temporal sword was at his service now had that same sword pressed against his scraggy neck. Nowhere in church history is there a more symbolic moment. This was proof that the alliance of church and state had reached breaking-point.

Even Sciarra, with blood-lust in his belly, hesitated. Could he bring himself to cut off the Head of the Church? Having sworn an oath of *vendetta*, he had no choice. In an ecstasy of sadistic joy, he raised his sword on high and took careful aim.

That was when Nogaret burst in, screaming that the King of France wanted the pontiff back in Lyons to face deposition before an ecumenical council. Sciarra, his face all shades of purple, sheathed his sword. To compensate in part, he began stripping Boniface of his dignity. He knocked the tiara off, revealing an egg-bald head, then enjoyed himself by removing, sometimes with his dagger, one costly papal garment after another. His men, relieved not to be party to killing a pope, ransacked the rooms. They were amazed that even a pope in a long and greedy lifetime could have amassed such treasures.

Boniface, on his feet, statuesque, apparently oblivious of humiliation, kept tetchily repeating Job's lament, 'Dominus dedit, Dominus abstulit' – 'The Lord has given, the Lord has taken'. Finally, he stood in that cavernous chamber practically naked. His body, yellow and wrinkled and racked by the stone, was jumping with lice. When medievals pictured the torments of hell, it was not the fire but the lice everlasting they feared most. The chronicler said coolly: 'The pontiff had a bad night.'

Relief came unexpectedly. Many of Sciarra's men were mercenaries and had left with their spoils. The townsfolk were afraid that Anagni would come under an interdict; mass might never be said there again. It might even be obliterated like Palestrina. Three days later, arming themselves, they forced the enemy to withdraw and released the pope from his dungeon.

He was a changed man. Contrary to the habits of a lifetime, he blubbered, so that tears ran down his black-ribbed cheeks. He had risen miraculously on the third day like his Master, Christ. 'Thank you,' he whined, over and over. 'Thank you.' Perhaps senility had swooped down on him; through pride or fear of being poisoned, he had refused all food and drink in confinement. Hunger and thirst, nights of loneliness in the dark with rats running over him, the proximity of death had unhinged him. Led back under armed guard to Rome, he stayed in his locked room in the Lateran for thirty-five days. According to rumours, probably fanciful, he kept banging his head against a wall and nibbled his arm incessantly like a dog worrying a bone. There, in solitude and totally unloved – 'Morieris ut canis' was Celestine's prophecy – he died.

A colossal storm was raging at his funeral, so he was buried with the minimum of pageantry in the immense tomb he had prepared for himself in old St Peter's.

There is a curious footnote to the story of Dante's Black Beast, an irreligious pontiff who claimed he had as much chance of surviving death as a roasted chicken.

When, at the completion of the new St Peter's in 1605, his tomb had to be moved, it cracked open. To everyone's consternation, the pontiff's body, after three centuries, was incorrupt. Only his nose and lips had been slightly nibbled away. They measured him: five feet ten inches; he still wore his oval sapphire ring; he looked at peace.

Boniface had given final form to the heresy of papal power. He was in other respects, too, no ornament to a church which was at least spared, courtesy of Nogaret, the final indignity: having to honour him as St Boniface, pope and martyr.

The Babylonian Exile

The papacy's problems did not end with Boniface VIII. Philip of France, not content to see his great enemy go to his Maker, was determined to desecrate his memory. Benedict XI, who succeeded as pontiff, tried to appease his Majesty, absolving him from any blame for the sacrilege done to his predecessor. When Benedict died a year later, a scandalous intrigue in conclave led to the election of Bertrand de Grot, Archbishop of Bordeaux, as Clement V. Philip had his wish at last: a French pope whom he could mould according to his will.

Clement immediately announced to his astonished aides that they were to accompany him beyond the Alps. Anagni was setback enough, but this was the final humiliation of the papacy: to leave the seat of ancient empire and the tombs of St Peter and St Paul. Clement feared, as he put it, 'to cause pain to our dear son, the King of France'. He soon settled in the king's domain, under the king's watchful eye, in Avignon, a small Provençal city on the east bank of the Rhône. With Philip threatening to try Boniface posthumously for being a fraud and a heretic, the pope yielded to his Majesty at every point. Philip was praised for his godly zeal against Boniface, and Celestine V, whom Boniface had tricked out of the papacy, was canonized as St Peter Morone.

The prestige of the papacy suffered an almost fatal blow, and a succession of sensuous and greedy pontiffs brought the office of Peter to the lowest ebb since the Reign of the Harlots.

Papal Paradise in Provence

The Avignon popes were neither uniformly good nor bad. A fair representative was Clement VI, elected in the year 1342. A man without malice or moral principle, he had the merit of being a good pagan.

Clement was once plain Pierre Roger de Beaufort, Benedictine monk, Archbishop of Rouen, chancellor to his Majesty the King of France. The king afforded him the protection his Holiness needed if he was to live *comme il faut*. The fact was that Clement liked neither Italy nor the Italians.

Forty-five years had passed since Clement V made this inspired exchange: Rhône for Tiber; sweet-smelling Provence for the malarial, cholera- and typhus-ridden marshes of Rome where everyone seemed intent on killing someone else.

Before his time, several popes – Celestine V, for instance – had never seen Rome; Clement VI himself had never set foot in Italy. Nor had his immediate predecessors, John XXII and Benedict XII. Clement was determined to keep up this fine French tradition. It explained his vast expenditure on his new palace on the Rocher des Doms, next to the Rhône.

Unlike Benedict XII, who was a regular killjoy, Clement knew how to *spend*. 'Before me, no one had any idea how to be pope,' he often jested. 'If the King of England wants his ass made a bishop, he has only to ask.' On one occasion, a donkey made its way into a consistory with a placard round its neck: 'Please make me a bishop, too.' Clement took it in good part, as he did when he received a letter while enthroned in full consistory. It read: 'From the Devil to his brother Clement.' He and 'the little devils', the cardinals, roared with laughter.

Clement's one aim was to make his subjects happy. He achieved this by lavishing on the greediest petitioner more than he dared ask for. Some cardinals had between four and five hundred of the richest livings. It meant they could afford the handsomest little boys, if they were so inclined, or the most beautiful ladies-in-waiting. Everyone in Avignon was well off: the musicians, the craftsmen, the bankers, goldsmiths, astrologers, pickpockets and the spectacular whores. Few complained that Bacchus and Venus were more honoured than Jesus Christ in Avignon.

One who did complain was Petrarch, the great scholar and Poet Laureate of the Empire. One reason he became soured was that Benedict XII had wanted his sister. He even refused a cardinal's hat as part of the deal. Benedict still got her; he bribed the poet's brother, Gerardo. After staying in Avignon, Petrarch described – anonymously, since he did not want to be burned – the papal court as 'the shame of mankind, a sink of vice, a sewer where is gathered all the filth of the world. There God is held in contempt, money alone is worshipped and the laws of God and men are trampled under foot. Everything there breathes a lie: the air, the earth, the houses and above all the bedrooms.'

Pope Clement suffered from an 'ailment', diagnosed officially as a kidney complaint but which had been caught in his bedroom. He had not been discreet in his amours, everyone knew, but that was part of his largesse. He never could withhold his favours, even in bed. 'Sessions of plenary indulgence,' they were called. But, lately, he *had* legitimized all his children.

Much of his palace was given up to the Inquisition. The torture chamber was vast, solid and open at the top, with irregular walls off which the screams and shrieks of prisoners bounced back and forth into silence. Once or twice, to encourage the friars, Clement had climbed the winding staircase from La Salle de Torture to the gloomy dungeon above with a hole in the middle of the floor. A fastidious man, he did not like to see mangled bodies being shoved through that hole and tumbling down into the torture chamber but, he reasoned, heresy had to be stamped out somehow.

Froissart, the French diarist, was to call the Avignon palace 'the finest and strongest building in the world'. Seven towers soared to the sky and, at eye-level, thick white walls with beautifully corbelled machicolations reflected the sun. From its summit, Clement was able to look down on the Rhône as it flowed under the great bridge of St-Bénézet. That bridge, with its nineteen arches, took twelve years to build, and some arches rested on the island in the river. Young men in spring used to dance and sing under it and make love on the greensward. 'Sous le pont d'Avignon, L'on y danse tout en rond.'

His Holiness admired beauty in everything. First of all in a woman, that purest architecture of the flesh, but in stone buildings, too. His tapestries came from Spain and Flanders, cloth of gold from Damascus in Syria, silk from Tuscany, woollen fabrics from Carcassonne. His gold and silver plate, weighing in the region of four hundred and fifty pounds, was very dear to him. He desperately wanted to win the

Italian wars and reconquer the Holy Land for Christ, but not if it meant selling his plate. Far cheaper to get his thirty chaplains to pray for miracles.

He suspected Petrarch wrote that wicked line about how in Avignon the horses' hoofs are shod with gold. The pontiff knew such slander did his reputation no harm. Only the horses' bits were golden. He *was* pope; he had to put on a good show. The cardinals, in particular, were appreciative of his openhandedness. Their grand abodes in Villeneuve across the Rhône were not built or maintained with a staff of a hundred and fifty with pennies.

Clement's own favourite haunt was a small room in the tower with a double divan, redolent of the perfume of the Countess of Turenne. In Clement V's time, those who sought the pontiff's blessings laid their petitions on the silky white bosom of the lovely Perigord, daughter of the comte de Foix. But Clement VI considered his own countess to be beyond compare. Of all the laps his noble head had rested in, by far the sweetest was Cécile's.

Though he had made the Curia into the most efficient financial machine in history, he was always short of cash. Buying the entire town in 1348 had cost him eighty thousand florins. He thought it the best investment a pope ever made, but some were saying the church would never recover from his improvidence.

In 1350 the district of Avignon was bustling with pilgrims on the way to Rome. Thousands arrived in the traditional traveller's mantle or national dress. Some were on horseback, others in carts piled high with their belongings; most were walking, staff in hand. Clement appreciated their simple piety. It took them many weeks to get to Rome for the Jubilee, trudging through grim Alpine gorges edged with everlasting snows before they reached the cypresses and vine-clad slopes of Italy and started the long hot journey south. Many never made it; they died of old age or disease, were robbed or murdered. The more fortunate laid their offerings at Peter's tomb for the clergy to rake it in like hay and send to Peter's successor in Avignon.

Boniface VIII had decreed a Jubilee every century. To Clement that seemed mean. He had reduced it to fifty years. The results surprised even him, but most pilgrims were wanting to thank God for escaping the Black Death. In three years, it decimated a third of Christendom, including Rome. Avignon had lost over half its people. When the plague first struck, and no one stirred inside the Carmelite monastery, a brave soul broke in to find all 166 monks dead. One day the tally in the city was 1,312. Victims usually died within forty-eight hours. Some towns had been wiped out. Livestock in meadows and on hills perished of neglect. Ships at sea, their crews all dead, foundered on rocks. Many blamed the Jews, burning, hanging and drowning thousands of them in a pious effort to rid themselves of plague. In Avignon, Clement had protected the Jews. So it did not please him when someone said it was not Jews but the Pope's riotous living that had brought on this calamity. If he had discovered who said this, he would have had him tortured and burned like those so-called spirituals, monks and friars, who insisted, against all evidence, that Jesus had lived in poverty and not like the 'whores of the New Babylon', as Avignon was called.

There were many in Rome who wished the pontiff would return to his diocese. Queen Bridget of Sweden was one of them, the young Catherine of Siena another. These two, later to be canonized, spent their days praying and writing Clement long letters. They pleaded with him to end this scandal and come home.

Bridget, nearly fifty years old, was famed for her visions and dreams. Sometimes, when she recounted the more disturbing of them, the citizens surrounded her home in Rome's Piazza Farnese, crying out that the *Principessa*, as they called her, should be burned like a witch.

Jesus had first spoken to her when she was a little girl. She never forgot that vision of her love stretched on the wood like a bird of prey nailed to a barn door. On her wedding night, she begged of her spouse Ulf but one favour: that theirs should be a virginal marriage. And so it was for two years. After that, she had eight children in rapid succession.

One dream shook even this austere lady. St Lawrence the Deacon appeared. 'This Bishop', he said, unwilling to mention the pope by name, 'permits the fornication of his priests. He gives the possessions of the Church to the rich.' The saint vanished to be replaced by a tall knight in shining armour. Bridget approached him and, in one swift movement, took off his helmet, but it was no human form that met her eyes. Only a malodorous carcass of marrowless bones and squirming maggots. This, she knew, was the pox-ridden and dying pope already evidencing corruption. If you could take off his head and look into his soul, this is what you would see. That smelly mass had ears in its forehead for flattery spoken to his face; eyes in the back of its head so it could see nothing but filth; and in its heart was a huge burrowing worm.

Even Bridget could not foresee that Clement's noble head, cradled by the loveliest ladies of Provence, would one day be used as a football by Huguenots or that his skull would end up as a drinking-cup on the table of the marquis de Courton.

On 3 December 1352 an unseasonal sirocco from the deserts of Africa hit Rome. The heat was unbearable, a thunderstorm was brewing fast. The glowering dark was suddenly rent by lightning; at one and the same moment, there was a vivid crackling sound and a weird metallic peal. Bridget sensed that the bolt had struck nearby. Leaving her house in the pitch dark and pouring rain, she made her way by instinct to St

Peter's. The basilica had suffered a direct hit, and the bells *had melted*. In the market, everyone started celebrating. 'He's dead. Yes, the pope is dead and buried deep in hell.'

Three days later, the bells of Avignon were tolling to tell the world officially that the Bishop of Rome, Clement VI of happy memory, was no more. For nine successive days in that enormous and now freezing chapel, fifty priests said mass for the repose of his soul.

The merciful said: It is not enough. The unmerciful said: There can never be enough.

SIX

The Papacy's Descent
into Hell

THERE HAVE BEEN MANY GENERATIONS of Catholics who said: 'The papacy is now at its lowest ebb.' Dante said that of Boniface VIII. Petrarch said it of the Babylonian Exile in the Avignon period. Both eminent poets were wrong. The darkest days were still ahead.

The rot set in when Catherine of Siena went to Avignon to put pressure on the reigning pontiff, Gregory XI, to return to Rome. The year was 1377. Seven French popes in a row had made their corner of Provence the wonder of the world.

The spiteful women of the papal court had no pity on Catherine, this pale raw Tuscan nun who seemed to cast a spell on his Holiness. Perhaps he was impressed by her ecstasy at communion. If she became too influential, they might have to close down their *salons* where gorgeous young men, sons of dukes and princes, came in search of ecclesiastical preferments. In chapel they took turns at pricking and pinching her insensate body to see whether her trance was genuine or not. One vicious woman pierced her foot with a long needle, so that Catherine could not walk on it for days.

In the end, she won. Gregory went home, minus six cardinals who could not tear themselves away from their very desirable residences, their Provençal women and their Burgundy wines. An ultimatum from the Romans that unless he returned they would elect another pope may also have influenced him.

In the 278 years since 1100, the popes had spent only eighty-two of them in Rome. A massive 196 years these papal nomads had spent elsewhere. It was not a good record; and the example was not lost on the church.

The Eternal City soon finished Gregory off. Then the real tragedy of Avignon was revealed.

One Pope, Two Popes

On Gregory's death the conclave convened to appoint a successor divided into two cliques, French and Italian. During the exile, seven Avignon popes had made 134 cardinals, all but twenty-two of them French. The French were, naturally, determined to keep the papacy to themselves. Since the Lateran had been burned down, the conclave met that April in the Vatican.

Outside, a mob said to number thirty thousand roared for them to pick a Roman at last. 'Romano lo volemo.' If not a Roman, then an Italian. The choice was rather limited. There were only four Italian cardinals, and none of them *papabile*. To make their point, the mob piled the room above the meeting-place with firewood and, from below, banged on the floorboards with pikes and halberds all through the night. If that was not enough, the bell on the Capitol rang out and the bells of St Peter's joined in. In the morning, the crowd lost patience altogether and broke down the conclave door.

Of the sixteen cardinals present, all hungry and sleepless, thirteen voted for an outsider, Bartolomeo Prignano, the small, stout, yellow-faced Archbishop of Bari. He was not a Roman. A Neapolitan was the best they could manage. Doubting if it were good enough, they dressed a protesting Roman octogenarian, Cardinal Tebaldeschi, in papal robes and put him on display. A courier rushed off to Pisa where Tebaldeschi's election was celebrated with fireworks. Meanwhile, the French cardinals showed a clean pair of heels. For two days, no one bothered to tell Prignano or pay him the customary homage. When he finally got word, he settled on the name of Urban VI.

The low-born Archbishop of Bari had been a quiet, obedient if fussy curial official for fifteen years. The noble French cardinals took it for granted he would continue doing as he was told and take the court back home to the fleshpots of Avignon. They gravely misread their man.

Urban VI turned out to be one of the most spiteful and vile-tempered of pontiffs. His doctor revealed that he hardly ever touched food but could not leave alcohol alone. At his coronation meal, according to the Cardinal of Brittany, he drank eight times as much as any member of the Sacred College – though some have said this was not humanly possible. Drink, religion, revenge – and all to excess – proved a potent mixture.

Born and bred in the stinking alleys of Naples, he could not stomach the effete pretentious French cardinals. He preached to them, it was reported, like Jeremiah with bellyache. He would reform them at any cost. He spoke openly in his high-pitched eunuch voice of Cardinal Orsini as *sotus*, or 'dopey'. Once, his face black with wrath, he was only prevented from striking the Cardinal of Limoges by Robert of Geneva holding on to his arm. 'Holy Father, what are you *doing*?' When he was on the point of excommunicating another member of the Sacred College for simony and Geneva intervened again, Urban barked like a dog: 'I can do anything, absolutely anything I like.'

A handful of cardinals judged his rages to be a symptom of madness. They consulted a respected jurist: Were there any circumstances in which cardinals could take over from an incapacitated pope? Urban got wind of it and proved he still had his wits about him.

First, he excommunicated an old foe, King Charles of Naples, whom he accused of being behind this 'rebellion'. The king responded by blockading his Holiness in his fortress at Nocera near Pompeii. Urban climbed on to the battlements four times a day and serenely, with bell, book and candle, excommunicated the entire army ranged against him. He seemed oblivious of the arrows falling around him.

Rescued by the Genoese, he took the five rebel cardinals into custody. He was next seen in Genoa, possibly in an alcoholic stupor, walking up and down the garden reciting the breviary at the top of his voice. In a nearby chamber, the rebels were being tortured. Their screams in no way disturbed his peace with God.

The old Cardinal of Venice, trussed up, was being raised and lowered on a pulley. With his head pressed against the ceiling, he was able to see the pope through the bars of the window and each time croaked in agony: 'Holy Father, Christ died for our sins.' Then he was lowered to the ground. Not one of the prisoners was seen again.

A number of French cardinals singly slipped away to reassemble at Anagni where they prepared a *Declaratio* against Prignano. He was *not* pope. They had only elected him, they claimed, out of fear of the mob. They chose another pontiff: Robert of Geneva, cousin of the King of France, who called himself Clement VII. Urban counter-attacked by appointing twenty-six new cardinals who owed allegiance to him.

On numerous occasions before there had been two popes, but the present crisis was unique. These two popes had been elected by more or less the same group of cardinals. Thus, when they said they had not genuinely chosen Urban they spoke with authority, even if they lied.

In England, Wyclif got the quips off to a good start: 'I always knew the pope had cloven feet. Now he has a cloven head.'

Christendom was forced to take sides. If Urban *was* chosen under duress, the election was invalid. But, if they were so frightened, why had they not picked a Roman – say old Tebaldeschi – and immediately retired to Anagni to register an official complaint? The choice of a healthy Neapolitan and a three-months delay were suspicious. As Catherine of Siena shrewdly pointed out, they already had one fake pope in Tebaldeschi, why did they need another? It did look as if the French wanted to ditch someone who had proved impossible to live with.

Chaos followed. An absentee pope was painful enough; now the very Seat of Unity was becoming the source of disunity. By the election decree of 1059, an uncanonically elected Roman pontiff was called 'the Destroyer of Christendom'. It proved to be the case. If Christians could not identify the real pope, what good was the papacy? The King of England championed Urban, the King of France backed Clement. There was no consensus at the universities.

The lame squint-eyed Clement VII predictably took his French following back to Avignon where his conduct was so bad as to make him indistinguishable from a genuine Avignon pope. He had already proved he was papal material when, in 1377, he had acted as the pope's legate to Cesena on the Adriatic. The locals had objected to his mercenaries raping their women and killed some of the guilty men. After parleying with town officials, he persuaded them to lay down their arms. Then he sent in a mixed English and Breton force to slaughter all eight thousand inhabitants, including the children.

Two Popes, Three Popes

In October 1389, Urban, the pope no one wanted, performed the only kind act of his life: he died. The fourteen cardinals left in Rome chose as his replacement Boniface IX, a murderer and probably the greatest simoniac in history. He sold every living to the highest bidder with the result that Germany and France swarmed with Italian clerics on the make, often retired soldiers, who could not speak a word of the language. Boniface's brothers, his nephews, above all his mother, benefited from his largesse. No one, it was said, ever made more money out of the canonization of a saint. He never put his name to any document without immediately stretching out his hand, demanding: 'One ducat.' The only thing he did not charge for was excommunicating Clement of Avignon. Clement returned the compliment.

And so it went on. When a pope or antipope died, instead of calling a halt, the respective groups of cardinals chose a successor. What are cardinals without a pope of their own?

By this time, Christendom had had enough. Who, after all, wants to buy a bishopric or an abbey from a pontiff who turns out to be an imposter? What if an expensive indulgence or the authentication of relics like the Saviour's foreskin or his navel are not worth the parchment they are written on? There was even confusion in heaven. Bridget of Sweden was to be canonized a record three times to make absolutely certain *she* was a saint.

Schism was also bad for business. Bankers with hearts of stone were praying fervently for it to end. The whole life of the Empire was being disrupted. Who on earth would crown the next emperor?

From the universities came the suggestion that since church unity was a higher priority than the papacy and Christ is the ultimate Head of the Church, not the Roman pontiff, it was better to withdraw support from *both* popes. Historians invited the emperor to depose them on the solid grounds that many emperors had done so before, and his intervention would be universally applauded. However, since, the boy-pope in the eleventh century, the papacy had become more powerful than any emperor. And now, in spite of the confusion, one of the popes was authentic. What if the emperor deposed the wrong one? Would that not be like removing the Bible from the church and substituting the Koran? The same dilemma would face a Council. If a Council met to depose both claimants, one of the depositions would be invalid, but which one? Another problem was that jurists of the time claimed that only the pope – the genuine article – could call a Council.

The catastrophic state of the church meant something had to be done in spite of the canonical fog.

In 1409 a Council was convoked in the marvellous walled town of Pisa, whose tower, like the church itself, was already leaning over.

In the black and white marbled Duomo, under Cimabue's majestic portrait of Christ, the mitred fathers met. They solemnly decreed that the contending popes, Gregory XII of Rome and Benedict XIII of Avignon, were both heretics and schismatics. That was a clever move: popes who fell into heresy in a sense deposed themselves.

In mid-June they chose as a replacement Cardinal Filargi of Milan, a pious toothless seventy-year-old Franciscan of unknown parentage, vowed to poverty. He had three defects it was difficult to hide. Though small and spare, he spent half his day at the meal table; he kept a palace with four hundred servants, all female and all clad in his livery; he distributed livings with so free a hand even cardinals were astonished.

Filargi accepted the name of Alexander V. To the sound of bells, he rode through the streets of Pisa in full pontificals, from red slippers to tiara, on a white mule.

The prelates cheered in relief. After thirty bewildering years, the Great Schism was at an end.

Except that Gregory and Benedict did not agree, so that the astonished world woke up one morning when the news reached them to say: Yesterday we only had *two* popes, now we have *three*.

One wag suggested that the triple tiara should be divided since the church now had three heads to put it on. A new version of the Creed was popular: 'I believe in three holy Catholic churches.' The faithful had put up with generations of absentee popes, with periods of two to three years when there was no pope at all because cardinals could not agree. The present scenario was the worst of all.

The one certainty to emerge from Pisa should have been that the man they chose was *not* pope. Now followed a spectacle never seen before: three infallible popes, all claiming supreme authority over the church, all solemnly excommunicating the other two, all threatening to call a council of their own in different places.

The *dramatis personae* in this theatre of the absurd were as follows: (1) Angelo Corrario, Gregory XII, a Venetian, approaching ninety, with many 'nephews', direct in line from bad-tempered Urban VI. He had been chosen by the Roman obedience because, as the Cardinal of Florence frankly admitted, 'He is too old and frail to be corrupt'. Another fatal mistake. The old man's first pontifical act was to pawn his tiara for six thousand florins to pay his gambling debts. He went to Rimini. From there, he sold off everything in Rome that was portable and some things that weren't, such as Rome itself, to the King of Naples.

(2) Piedro da Luna, a hysterical Spaniard, representing the revived Avignon obedience. He counted the least. Dropped by the King of France and all but three of his cardinals, he was soon to return to his native Spain where he insisted to the end he was true pope and practically excommunicated the entire church.

(3) Baldassare Cossa, John XXIII. Alexander V had died after only ten months, and it was Cossa, a suave, charming, ruthless pontiff, who now represented the Pisan obedience. He was rumoured never to have confessed his sins or taken the sacrament. Nor did he believe in the soul's immortality or the resurrection of the dead. It was doubted by some if he believed in God.

He was noted as a former pirate, pope-poisoner (poor Filargi), mass-murderer, mass-fornicator with a partiality for nuns, adulterer on a scale unknown outside fables, simoniac *par excellence*, blackmailer, pimp, master of dirty tricks.

On his election to the papacy in Bologna, Cossa was a deacon. Ordained priest one day, he was crowned pope the next.

This charlatan was recognized by most Catholics as their sovereign lord who held the church together by his rock-like faith. When another Pope John XXIII was elected in 1958, several Catholic cathedrals had hastily to remove the fifteenth-century John XXIII from their list of pontiffs.

A Most Embarrassing Council

The tide of Cossa's fortune turned when Sigismund, emperor-elect, prevailed on him to call a Council in order 'to reduce the number of popes consistent with the Gospel'. The site was to be the walled city of Constance in southern Germany on the border with Switzerland. Within months, its population was to rise from six thousand to sixty thousand, then to double again.

When the clergy met in large numbers, it was always wise to choose a town near water – lake or river – for disposing of the bodies. Lake Constance received over five hundred while the Council was in session; the Rhine, too, hid many secrets. Another requirement was that the meeting-place had to be large enough to accommodate the vast number of prostitutes who found the clergy required their services more urgently than the military and paid keener prices. At the height of the Council, there were reckoned to be over twelve hundred whores in Constance working round the clock.

On All Saints' Day 1414, John XXIII, a forty-eight-year-old gout-ridden pirate draped in gold, celebrated and preached at the formal opening of the General Council. It was a massive gathering, including three hundred bishops, three hundred top theologians and the cardinals of all three obediences.

Huss, rector of Prague University, to whom Sigismund had granted safe conduct, was promptly arrested at Cossa's command and imprisoned. It was a lesson to everyone, especially to Pope Benedictus (called *Benefictus*, or 'Fake') and Pope Gregorius (called *Errorius*, or 'Mistake').

John XXIII had taken a risk in crossing the Alps into imperial territory, but he had enough votes in his pocket to feel safe. There were then, as later, more Italian bishops than all other nationalities combined. What defeated him was the decision of the Council to vote not as individuals but by nations. His majority was instantly wiped out, and he found there were three to one against him. Next Sigismund arrived early on Christmas morning and ordered him to resign.

Cossa saw the indictment, a huge catalogue of his misdemeanours drawn up with wicked accuracy. The madams in charge of every whorehouse in Christendom must have testified against him. When he heard the growing demands, especially from the English, that they should burn him and be done with it, he agreed to resign, provided the other two popes followed suit. Then, disguising himself as a groom, he left Constance by night. No pope no Council, he must have reasoned. Among the handful of cardinals who joined him at his hideout thirty miles away in Schaffhausen was Oddo Colonna. Imperial guards brought the pontiff back to face the music.

The Council had meanwhile assumed full authority. In its Fourth and Fifth sessions it made a unanimous declaration of faith that has haunted the Roman church ever since.

> The holy Council of Constance . . . declares, first, that it is lawfully assembled in the Holy Spirit, that it constitutes a General Council representing the Catholic church, and that, therefore, it has its authority immediately from Christ; and that all men of every rank and condition, including the pope himself, are bound to obey it in matters of faith, the ending of schism and the reformation of the church of God in its head and members.

Aeneas Sylvius, one day to become Pope Pius II, wrote: 'Hardly anyone doubts that a Council is above a pope.' Why should anyone doubt? The church's ancient teaching was that a General Council is supreme in faith and discipline. On the basis of this teaching, more than one pope had been condemned by Councils for heresy, as will he shown in Part 2 of this book.

The consequences of Constance were momentous. If the pope is bound to obey the church in matters of faith, he cannot of himself and without the church's consent be infallible. In fact, when he speaks independently of the Council, the pope may well err in faith. This teaching was obscured by medieval popes such as Gregory VII and Innocent III by dubious means.

Constance, having asserted its authority over the pope, now proceeded to use that authority, first, to depose Benedict, who was already in flight to Peñiscola.

John XXIII was next. He steadfastly refused to resign. The fathers of the Council agreed he was the legitimate pope, but the church was more important than the papacy. The charges against him were reduced from fifty-four to five. As Gibbon characteristically remarked in *The Decline and Fall*: 'The most scandalous charges were suppressed; the Vicar of Christ was only accused of piracy, murder, rape, sodomy and incest.' It was well known that since becoming Vicar of Christ the only exercise he took was in bed. It is significant that John XXIII was absolved from heresy, probably because he had never evinced sufficient interest in religion to be classed as heterodox. Till then, the only charge judged serious enough to depose a pope was heresy. Cossa was deposed simply because he did not behave as a pope should.

On 29 May 1415, John XXIII's seals of office were solemnly smashed with a hammer. But an ex-pope, like an ex-president, is entitled to consideration. In spite of his heroic promiscuity, he was given only a three-year prison sentence.

Huss, brave, chaste, incorruptible, stern opponent of simony and clerical concubinage, met a harsher fate. Forbidden counsel, tried on a trumped-up charge, interrogated by Dominicans who had not read his books even in translation, he was sentenced to death. Wearing a high hat with three dancing devils on it, flanked by Count Palatine's swordsmen, he was led out of prison on a glorious summer's day in 1415. Practically the entire town followed as the procession made its way past the cemetery where Huss's books were being burned into a bright green meadow. He prayed for his persecutors as the fire was lit. Three times he was heard to say, 'Christ, Thou Son of the living God, have mercy on me,' before the wind blew flames into his face. His lips were still moving in prayer as he expired without a groan. To prevent him being honoured as a martyr, his ashes were scattered on the Rhine. It was clearly more sinful to say, as did Huss and the New Testament, that after the blessing the Eucharist should still be called 'bread' than to be a greedy, murderous, incestuous pope who misled the church on almost everything.

Finally, Gregory XII, now in his ninetieth year and weary, solemnly convoked the Council which had been in session for months, and then resigned. With these formalities complete, all three popes were taken care of. Christendom could breathe again.

Sigismund, a libertine himself, was keen to reform the church *before* a new pontiff was elected, reasoning that no pope ever could be trusted to reform the church. For centuries, he argued, the papacy was not up to the task. At this time, chaste clerics were so few that those who had no woman were accused of having less creditable vices.

Unfortunately, Sigismund was not supported by the King of France, nor by Henry V of England, fresh from his victory at Agincourt.

Cardinal Oddo Colonna, who had pledged John XXIII his loyalty when he fled to Schaffhausen, was chosen without delay, naming himself Martin V. In his mid-fifties, he was an ecclesiastic born and bred, being the son of one of Urban VI's cardinals, Agapito Colonna. The church had a single pope again. Now there was no hope of reform, though much thought was given to the cut of clerical sleeves.

Two days after his election, Colonna, a deacon, was ordained priest. It was 13 November 1417. Next day he was consecrated bishop. A week after that, having been crowned pope, he set his feet on the altar to be kissed before being paraded through town on horseback. Sigismund and Frederick of Brandenburg held the bridle to right and left.

Like John XXIII, Martin's one aim was to get out of Constance fast. He had no wish to reform the Curia or the papacy. In fact, when Cossa was released from his comfortable prison in Heidelberg and went to Florence, Martin reinstated this self-confessed murderer and rapist, making him Bishop of Frascati and Cardinal of Tusculum.

Martin's anxiety for a quick getaway was understandable. The biggest Council the West had ever seen had decreed that General Councils derive their authority immediately from Christ. Everyone, pope included, is subject to it in matters of faith, the healing of schism and church reform. What made his position delicate was that this was carried unanimously. He had voted for it himself as a cardinal. But history shows that the papacy almost invariably transforms a man as soon as he gains office. He wanted to return to Rome where he would assert his superiority over a Council. In other words, he wanted to deny the very basis of his election. For, if the pope is supreme in the church, not he but John XXIII was pope.

This tension was not to be resolved for another 450 years. That was when the First Vatican Council said it was necessary for salvation to believe in papal supremacy and infallibility. The cost of resolution was high. Vatican I, contradicted everything implied in the earliest church Councils and explicitly asserted by Constance. For example, according to Vatican I, when a pope speaks *ex cathedra*, his definitions 'are irreformable of themselves and not because of the consent of the Church'. Constance said the pope himself 'is bound to obey it [the

Council] in matters of faith'. This is why Thomas More, the best-informed layman of his day, wrote to Thomas Cromwell in 1534 saying that while he believed the primacy of Rome was instituted by God, 'yet never thought I the Pope above the General Council'.

What if the Vatican I dogma of papal absolutism, had been in operation *before* Constance? In that case, Constance would not have felt competent to depose a pope and the church might have been plagued by a papal trinity for centuries. Only by flatly denying what was to become the central dogma of Roman Catholicism was the General Council of Constance able to save the church.

Whispers of the Storm

Not that Constance had really saved the church. It broke up without a single major reform being passed. Within weeks of returning to Rome, Martin V had given his blessing to the curial system that had brought the church to its knees in the first place.

A mood of despair settled on Christendom. In the tenth century, for all its adolescent, adulterous and murderous popes, the papacy was a local phenomenon. The head of a powerful Roman family put his cherished teenaged son on the throne; the lad made hay for a few frantic months or years and was ambushed by members of a rival family whose hour had come.

But since the eleventh century Gregory VII had put his stamp upon the papacy. It had grown in stature and prestige; it was able to control the entire church, from the simplest country curate to the most powerful archbishop. What emerged was the most appalling corruption that Christianity has ever seen or is likely to see.

It began at the top. The papacy was auctioned off in conclave to the highest bidder, irrespective of a candidate's worth. A nineteenth-century historian, T. A. Trollope, in his book *The Papal Conclaves* (1876), estimated: 'Few papal elections, if any, have been other than simoniacal. . . . The invention of the Sacred College has been, on the whole, perhaps the most fertile source of corruption in the Church.' Many cardinals went to Rome for the conclave with their bankers. They took into conclave their valuables, especially their silver plate; if they were elected pope, the Roman mob invariably sacked their palace, even removing the doors and windows.

Cardinals were seldom chosen for their services to religion. They owed their position to graft and intrigue. In Renaissance times they nearly all had their 'female companions'. Once appointed from among such men, the new pope, with fresh funds to draw on, lost no time in promoting his relatives – sons, nephews, great-nephews – quite shamelessly on the Italian principle, 'Bisogna far' per la famiglia', 'You have to do well by your family'. Time was of the essence since the papacy is not hereditary and he might have only a few months or years to establish an entire dynasty. Hence so many pontiffs, as soon as they donned the tiara, looked around for means of lining their pockets. A good example of this was the thirteenth-century Clement IV, a widower. He sold millions of southern Italians to Charles of Anjou for a yearly tribute of eight hundred ounces of gold. According to the terms of the contract, if the duke fell behind in his payment, he would be excommunicated. A further delay meant the whole of his territories would be put under an interdict. It did not strike a pope as sinful to deprive entire districts of mass and the sacraments simply because princes did not pay him his dues.

The cardinals had huge palaces with countless servants. One papal aide reported that he never went to see a cardinal without finding him counting his gold coins.

The Curia was made up of men who had bought office and were desperate to recoup their enormous outlay. Every office in every department had its price. These courtiers wielded day-to-day power with tremendous sanctions at their command. They could excommunicate anyone. Bishops and archbishops trembled before them.

It was the Curia that drew up the tariff of simony. For every benefice of see, abbey and parish, for every indulgence there was a set fee. The pallium, the two-inch-wide woollen band with crosses embroidered on it in black silk, was paid for by every bishop. These modest woollen trimmings brought in over the years hundreds of millions of gold florins to the papal coffers, so that the Council of Basle in 1432 was to call it 'the most usurious contrivance ever invented by the papacy'. By the sixteenth century, in Germany, whole dioceses were farmed out to bankers like the Fuggers and to joint-stock companies who retailed church livings to the highest bidder.

Dispensations were another source of papal revenue. Extremely severe even impossible laws were passed so that the Curia could grow rich by selling dispensations. Payment was demanded for dispensations from fasting during Lent. Also for allowing a sick or aged monk to stay in bed instead of rising in the night to recite his office. Marriage in particular was a rich source of income. Consanguinity was alleged to hold between couples who had never dreamed they were related. Dispensations from consanguinity in order to marry amounted to a million gold florins a year.

During the Renaissance, it was presumed that the top clerics had the loveliest women, and whole dioceses had open clerical concubinage. The Roman clergy, under the very noses of the Curia, were the worst of all. None of this is surprising. Offices and livings were bought and sold like any other piece of merchandise. The clergy had no training in self-discipline. They simply wanted a sinecure and an idle life. Many could not read and write; they stood at the altar muttering unintelligible drivel because they could not even parrot the Latin. The worst insult to be offered a layman at this time was to call him a priest.

After Constance, protests arose on every side. Martin V himself admitted that many religious houses were dens of vice. Bishops, universities, monasteries cried out for a Council to reform the abuses. The Curia, outwitted and outvoted at Constance, persuaded the pope that a Council would not be in his best interest.

At Constance, however, a solemn undertaking had been given that there would be a Council within ten years and thereafter at regular intervals. In spite of curial efforts to scupper it, a Council met at Basle in 1432. The bishops showed they were in earnest.

> From now on, all ecclesiastical appointments shall be made according to the canons of the Church; all simony shall cease. From now on, all priests whether of the highest or lowest rank, shall put away their concubines, and whoever within two months of this decree neglects its demands shall be deprived of his office, though he be the Bishop of Rome. From now on, the ecclesiastical administration of each country shall cease to depend on papal caprice. . . . The abuse of ban and anathema by the popes shall cease. . . . From now on, the Roman Curia, that is, the popes shall neither demand nor receive any fees for ecclesiastical offices. From now on, a pope should think not of this world's treasures but only of those of the world to come.

This was strong meat. Too strong. The ruling pope, Eugene IV, summoned his own Council at Florence. Basle he labelled 'a beggarly mob, mere vulgar fellows from the lowest dregs of the clergy, apostates, blaspheming rebels, men guilty of sacrilege, gaolbirds, men who without exception deserve only to be hunted back to the devil whence they came.'

The papacy had squandered its chances; there were to be no more. The same century that saw Eugene IV censuring the best efforts of Basle at reform was to end with the pope who, above all, had come from the devil: Alexander Borgia.

The Gathering Storm

In the fifteenth century, there was not one voice raised in defence of the papacy. With men like Francesco de la Rovere on the throne it is not hard to see why.

Francesco became Sixtus IV in 1471. He had several sons, called according to the custom of the day 'the pope's nephews'. Sixtus gave three nephews and six other relatives the red hat. Among the beneficiaries was Giuliano de la Rovere, the future Julius II.

Sixtus' favourite was Pietro Riario, whom the historian Theodor Griesinger believed was his son by his own sister. Certainly, the new pope had an alarming fondness for the boy. He made him Bishop of Treviso, Cardinal Archbishop of Seville, Patriarch of Constantinople, Archbishop of Valencia and Archbishop of Florence. Pietro, till then, had been a Franciscan. Each year he had baked his habit to kill off the vermin. On becoming a cardinal, he changed. He became a spender on a massive scale, entertaining visiting ladies and providing them with chamberpots made of gold. The diarists of the time complain of the base use to which the church's treasures were being put. Riario was to die young, completely burned out.

Sixtus IV built the chapel named after himself in which all popes are now elected. It has seen pomp and ignominy. Cardinals have picnicked, bivouacked, slept and often come to blows there. Under its vault, Napoleon stabled his horses. The Sistine Chapel is but one ornament in a Vatican that rapidly grew splendid in art and architecture while there was corruption within.

Sixtus was the first pope to license the brothels of Rome; they brought him in thirty thousand ducats a year. He also gained considerably from a tax imposed on priests who kept a mistress. Another source of income was granting privileges to rich men 'to enable them to solace certain matrons in the absence of their husbands'.

It was in the area of indulgences that Sixtus showed a touch of genius. He was the first pontiff to decide that they could be applied *to the dead*. Even he was overwhelmed by their popularity. Here was an infinite source of revenue that even his greediest predecessors had not dreamed of. It was breathtaking in its implications: the pope, creature of flesh and blood, had power over the regions of the dead. Souls in torment for their misdemeanours could be released by his word, provided their pious relatives dipped into their pockets. And which of them wouldn't if they had a spark of Christian decency? Widows and widowers, bereaved parents spent their all trying to get their loved ones out of Purgatory, painted in ever more lurid colours.

Praying for the dead was one thing, paying for them another. Simple folk were led to believe that the pope, or those who came to their village and sold the pope's pardon, guaranteed their dead would go to heaven on the wings of indulgences. The potential for abuse was considerable. The sale of relics from the tenth century had been bad enough. In fact, for a long time, Rome's biggest export trade had been in corpses, whole or in part. They were sold to pilgrims for big sums. T. H. Dyer said: 'The toe or finger of a martyr might be a morsel for a man of modest means but princes and bishops could afford to purchase a whole skeleton.' With the catacombs as a kind of papal El Dorado, many pontiffs bestowed the bones of martyrs on cities where they wanted to curry favour. Sixtus' talent consisted in this: he gave nothing away, except intangibles. Martyr's bones, like oil, were not a renewable commodity, but indulgences were limitless *and* could be priced to suit every pocket. Nothing was required of the donor or recipient, not love or compassion or prayer or repentance – only money. No practice was ever more irreligious than this. The pope grew rich in the measure that the poor were duped.

Purgatory had no justification, whether in Scripture or in logic. Its real basis was papal avarice. An Englishman, Simon Fish, in *A Supplicacyion for the Beggars*, written in the year 1529, was to point that out irrefutably.

> There is not one word spoken of it in all holy Scripture, and also if the Pope with his pardons may for money deliver one soul hence, he may deliver him as well without money: if he may deliver one, he may deliver a thousand: if he may deliver a thousand, he may deliver them all; and so destroy purgatory: and then he is a cruel tyrant, without all charity, if he keep them there in prison and in pain, till men will give him money.

In 1478, Sixtus published a Bull that did even more harm to the church. He sanctioned the Inquisition in Castile. It spread, literally, like fire. In 1482 two thousand heretics were burned in Andalusia alone.

Of Sixtus it was said that he 'waded mitre-deep in crime and bloodshed', plunging Italy into endless wars. When he died at a relatively pacific time for the papacy, one wit suggested that this warlord had been 'slain by peace'. He was reckoned to have 'embodied the utmost possible concentration of human wickedness'. In Bishop Creighton's words, 'he lowered the moral tone of Europe'.

In death, he was washed by his meticulous German chaplain John Burchard. The rooms had been ransacked, so that the chaplain had nothing with which to dry the corpse. He removed Sixtus' shirt and used that. Finally, he clothed him in a short cassock and a pair of borrowed slippers.

Eight years later, in 1492, Burchard was steeling himself to perform the same duties for Sixtus' successor, sixty-year-old Innocent VIII. Thin and anaemic, the pontiff was in bed, propped up with pillows. Dribbling from the corners of his mouth was mother's milk, his only sustenance for several weeks. Looking back, he felt he had things to be proud of.

He had married his favourite son Franceschetto into the great de'

Medicis of Florence, thus bringing that family into line for the papacy, with disastrous results.

Innocent also made an edict against the Jews in Spain. Those who refused to embrace Christianity were banished from the peninsula. There was a wave of emigration not matched until the 1930s in Nazi Germany. A hundred thousand fled, a similar number stayed, pretending to be converts. 'This' *The Catholic Dictionary* says, with unintentional irony, 'gave employment to the Inquisition for centuries'.

There were one or two blemishes on his record. For example, he had done nothing to clean up the city. His vicar had come to him, saying: 'We really ought to stop priests keeping women, Holiness.' Innocent had replied, on the record: 'A waste of time. It is so widespread among priests, even among the Curia, you will hardly find one without his concubine.' When this leaked out, someone said: 'His Holiness rises from the bed of harlots to bolt and unbolt the gates of Purgatory and Heaven.'

In the next room, as his life was coming to a close, his physician was examining three handsome youths. He was telling them that they could perform a great service for the Vicar of Christ. The pope's blood was old and tired; if they were to spare him some of theirs, he might continue to inspire the church. Burchard added his encouragement with a ducat apiece.

The doctor was a Jew. Innocent believed that the Jews' very wickedness gave them access to an arcane wisdom that Christian physicians lacked.

The doctor informed Burchard he was ready to begin. He bowed and scraped his way into the papal bedchamber and, with trembling hands, bled the pontiff.

The first youth was brought in and, by a direct transfer, blood passed from him to the pope. It was not an exact science. The room reeked with the smell; blood flowed over the bedclothes and down to the rugs on the floor. The young man was carried out semi-conscious. The second youth was called, then the third. Soon, all three of them were dead in the anteroom. Burchard unclasped their sticky hands and took back the money.

The sacrifice of the youths was in vain. Innocent confessed his sins and, his mind at rest, died with a pun on his lips: 'I come to You, Lord, in my Innocence.' Buried in his tomb, someone said, was 'filth, gluttony, avarice and sloth'.

Once more, it seemed as if the papacy could sink no lower. Then came Borgia.

The Eye of the Storm

Rodrigo Borgia, a Catalan, was reputed to have committed his first murder when he was twelve years old. He repeatedly drove his scabbard into another boy's belly. As a young man, his amorous propensities were not the best-kept secret in the world. His misfortune was to have a pope, Callistus III, for an uncle.

In 1456, Callistus made Rodrigo, then twenty-five, Archbishop of Valencia, the chief see in Spain. Rodrigo was already famous for having made impartial love to a widow and her two beautiful daughters, one of whom was his ever-beloved Vannozza Catanei. Summoned to Rome to become a cardinal at twenty-six and Vice-Chancellor of the church one year later, he could not bear to be too far from his mistress, so he installed her in style in that most stylish of cities, Venice.

When his uncle died, the new pope, Pius II, was not so tolerant towards him. He got wind of a Borgian orgy in Siena from which husbands, fathers, brothers and kinsmen had been excluded to allow lust a free rein. 'Is it fitting', Pius II asked with tact, since he himself had fathered two children, 'for you to have nothing in your head all day except thoughts of voluptuous pleasure?'

When Rodrigo became pope, he took the name of Alexander VI, not seeming to mind that Alexander V was excluded from the lists as the antipope of Pisa. Borgia, on his election, rapidly deteriorated. He was not deposed, nor even challenged. The system did not allow it.

Luther was nine years old when Borgia came to power. Everything in Rome was for sale, from livings and indulgences to cardinal's hats and the papacy itself. According to John Burchard, who acted as the conclave's Master of Ceremonies, Borgia won the votes of the Sacred College after a particularly expensive campaign. It is instructive to see, by way of Burchard's diaries, how the Holy Spirit goes about choosing St Peter's successor.

Money poured into Rome from all over Europe, being channelled into conclave by bankers. Borgia had stiff opposition. Resting on Cardinal de la Rovere were 200,000 gold ducats from the King of France and another hundred thousand from the Republic of Genoa. Only five votes were not bought. Borgia, being Vice-Chancellor, happened to be the richest of the cardinals. He was able to offer villas, towns and abbeys. He gave four mule-loads of silver to his greatest rival, Cardinal Sforza, to induce him to step down. Practically penniless, he was dismayed to find himself still one vote short.

Cardinal Gherardo of Venice clinched it for him, though he was in no way to blame. There are sound reasons for thinking he was senile. He was in his ninety-sixth year and, more tellingly, he did not insist on a bribe.

Having elected Borgia, the cardinals serenaded the Holy Spirit, thanking him for choosing a successor to St Peter. But Giovanni de Medici said afterwards to Cardinal Cibò: 'We are now in the clutches of perhaps the most savage wolf the world has ever seen. Either we flee or he will, without a doubt, devour us.' Cardinal de la Rovere, the future Julius II, took the hint and fled for his life, only to return ten years later when Pharaoh, the Borgia pope, was dead.

For the moment, 'the wolf' was very much alive. In a frenzy of joy, he exclaimed: 'I am pope, pontiff, Vicar of Christ.'

In the Borgia apartments of the Apostolic Palace there is a full-length portrait of Alexander VI by Pinturicchio. It shows him swathed in a brocaded and bejewelled cope; only his head and hands are visible. A tall man, he has a narrow forehead, fat cheeks and jowls and a big fleshy nose. His neck is monstrous, his lips sensual, his eyes penetrating. His puffy beringed fingers are tapered in prayer.

This man whom Gibbon called 'the Tiberius of Christian Rome' was wicked even for a Renaissance pope. His eye for a pretty woman was said to be infallible, even in old age. He had ten known illegitimate children, four of them, including the notorious Cesare and Lucrezia, by Vanozza. When she became faded, the pope, aged fifty-eight, took another mistress.

Giulia Farnese was fifteen and recently married to Orsino Orsini. He was a good husband: blind in one eye, he knew when to wink the other. That is why Giulia became known throughout Italy as 'the Pope's Whore' and 'the Bride of Christ'. A dazzling beauty, she was, as one diplomat put it, 'the heart and eyes' of the pontiff, without whom he could not live. With her papal connections, she had no difficulty gaining a red hat for her brother, the future Paul III, thus earning him the title of 'The Petticoat Cardinal'.

By Giulia, the pope had a daughter named Laura. Usually an honest man, he had followed Innocent VIII's example and openly acknowledged his children in what was called the Golden Age of Bastards. Pius II had even said that Rome was the only city in the world to be run by bastards. But Borgia tried to make out that Laura was an Orsini; in other words, that Giulia's husband was the father of Giulia's child. This was hard to believe. Further, as Lorenzo Pucci, an ambassador at the Vatican, wrote to his master in Florence: 'The child's resemblance to the pope is such she just has to be his.'

Giulia's child Juan, known as *Infans Romanus*, the mysterious Roman Child, was also his. Alexander must have repeated right to the end St Augustine's prayer, 'Lord, make me chaste, but not yet,' because La Bella Giulia gave him a last child, his namesake Rodrigo, as a going-away present when he died.

Life in the Vatican in those days was never dull nor wholly evangelical. There were reliable tales of drunken and sexual orgies. Alexander was reputed to have had incestuous relations with his daughter, the gorgeous Lucrezia. If so, and it is not certain, it was a record even for a Renaissance pope to have had sex with three generations of women: his daughter, her mother and her grandmother.

Cesare, his son, was Machiavelli's model for the utterly ruthless Prince. Even his father feared him. Lord Acton wrote of him: 'Having no preference for right or wrong, he weighed with an equal and dispassionate mind whether it was better to spare a man or cut his throat.' The Florentine statesman, Francesco Guicciardini, who became lieutenant-colonel of the papal armies, confided to his secret notebook, *I Ricordi*, that Cesare was born so that 'there might be in the world one man vile enough to carry out the designs of his father, Alexander VI'. In impressive Spanish style, Cesare once slew five bulls with a lance in St Peter's Square, then beheaded a sixth with a single stroke of the sword. He thought nothing of stealing a man's wife, raping her and tossing her into the Tiber.

Early in his reign, the pope nostalgically gave Cesare his old see of Valencia. His son was then a handsome seventeen-year-old with a high-bridged nose, black brooding eyes and dark hair tinged with red. A year later, in the consistory in which Alexander promoted his mistress's brother and fifteen-year-old Ippolito d'Este, Cesare became a cardinal.

This was a tricky business, because cardinals are supposed to be born on the right side of the bed. Alexander solved the problem brilliantly. On 20 September 1493 he signed two Bulls, both sworn to by the trustiest witnesses at his court. The first proved conclusively that Cesare was the son of Vanozza and her husband. In the second, published in secret, the pope acknowledged Cesare as his own.

In those days, there was an average of fourteen murders a day in Rome. When the culprit was caught, Alexander did not scruple to let him off, for a consideration. As he remarked, with the winning smile he had: 'The Lord requires not the death of a sinner but rather that he should pay and live.'

One of his less endearing habits was to appoint cardinals for a fat fee, then have them poisoned to increase the turnover. He favoured cantarella, a concoction made up mostly of white arsenic. The church, he decreed, could inherit the cardinal's goods and chattels. He, of course, as Christ's Vicar, *was* the church.

One of the few to protest openly at the scandal of the papal court was the Dominican Prior of San Marco in Florence. The greatest preacher of his age, Savonarola was declared by a later pontiff, Benedict XIV, to be worthy of canonization. That was not Alexander's view. He tried to silence the friar by promising him a cardinal's hat *for nothing*. When, to his astonishment, that failed, there was no alternative but to have him tried, hanged and burned instead – though, it was said, there was no rancour on the pope's part.

Three turbulent years passed before one of the most grotesque events in Vatican history occurred on the last night of October 1501. It was written up in his usual pedantic style by Burchard, personal aide to four successive pontiffs, in diaries that only came to light by chance.

Cesare invited his favourite sister Lucrezia and the pope, the only other male present, to a festival called 'The Joust of the Whores'. Fifty of Rome's finest danced in increasingly scanty attire before finally disporting themselves naked around the pope's table. They would have heard the rumour circulating in Rome that the pope preferred an orgy to a high mass. In a frenzied finale, the whores fell on their knees, scrambling in the rugs for chestnuts which the Borgias threw to them like hogs.

The pope did have his good side. He was a patron of the arts. He encouraged a penniless young monk by the name of Copernicus. He had a sharp nose for business and was, in fact, one of the few pontiffs of the age to balance his books. No hypocrite, he never pretended to be a sincere Christian, let alone a saint. Yet, like most pontiffs, he was intensely devoted to the Virgin Mary. He revived the ancient custom of ringing the Angelus bell thrice a day. He had commissioned a painting of a superb Madonna, with the face of Giulia Farnese to deepen his love. Nor was he one to forget the services of his former mistresses. Hence, when Vanozza died a few years after him, aged seventy-six, she was treated as the pope's widow. She was buried, with greater pomp than Borgia himself, in the church of Santa Maria del Popolo in the presence of the entire papal court 'almost as though she were a cardinal'.

It must also be said in the pope's defence that he was a proud and fond father. He baptized his children and gave them the best education that simony could buy. He officiated at their weddings in the Vatican to the best families of the age, but had not Innocent VIII done the same? When he married Lucrezia in the Salla Reale, she was escorted by Pope Innocent's grand-daughter and followed by the Pope's Whore and another 150 excited Roman ladies. For Lucrezia, on the occasion of her third marriage, he even delayed the beginning of Lent so that the people of Ferrara whither she was bound could celebrate her espousal with meat and dancing.

The pope's parental affection was never more evident than when he mourned the death of his son, the Duke of Gandia, assassinated, most probably by his other son, the pitiless Cesare. When Gandia was dragged out of the Tiber and deposited at the pope's feet, the cynics said: 'At last! A fisher of men!' He must have brought tears to the eyes of the consistory when he told them he would have given seven tiaras to have his son restored to life. They wept even more when, for the few days he was grieving, he called for an end to nepotism and threatened to reform the Curia. All clerical concubines, he decreed, were to be dismissed within ten days; even cardinals were to become frugal and chaste. Giulia must have ruined his best intentions since she bore him a son the following year.

Historians have suggested that his fondness for Cesare was misplaced. Cesare, he knew, carried poison on his person in case an enemy required it. Then, after the trouble he had gone to to have him made a cardinal, Cesare wanted to give up his hat. Alexander risked the wrath of the Sacred College by allowing him to leave 'the Purpled Ones', as Corro called them. The salvation of Cesare's soul was at stake, the pope pleaded. By now, his son's face was covered with dark spots and vivid wheals, signs of secondary syphilis. Their Eminences should, perhaps, have been relieved by his departure, but as one aide remarked soberly, if cardinals were allowed to resign for so trivial a reason, there would be none left. When Cesare's pox became severe, he took to wearing a black silk mask in public.

Having doffed his red hat at the age of twenty-two, he was free to marry and, his greatest ambition, to take over from Gandia as commander-in-chief of the papal armies. His father should have known he was not even to be trusted with a knife.

Once, Cesare had hacked to pieces a young Spaniard named Perroto, Alexander's favourite chamberlain, for making love to his sister. It was not the sin but the folly of it that he objected to. It was vital to family interests, and especially Cesare's, that Lucrezia's former marriage to Giovanni Sforza should be terminated to allow her to marry into Neapolitan royalty. The grounds of annulment were non-consummation. A commission testified to her virginity after three years of marriage and, by implication, accused her husband of impotence. All Rome rocked with laughter when the news leaked out. Lucrezia was known as 'the greatest whore that ever was in Rome'. Her husband, Sforza, refused to co-operate with the commission, stressing there had been an abundance of consummation. He swore he had 'known her carnally on countless occasions'. His uncle, Ludovico of Milan, drily suggested he should demonstrate his prowess before witnesses.

This was not the only divorce granted by Alexander while pretending to annul a marriage. Not that it helped Lucrezia's new husband. In 1500, when he had served his turn, Cesare had him strangled.

Perroto was an earlier victim. In Cesare's eyes, he was guilty of compromising his sister's reputation at a delicate moment and had to be dealt with.

The pope, his rheumy eyes blinking, tried to shield his chamberlain under his cape, shrieking in Spanish: 'No, Cesare, for the love of God, no.' Cesare went on with the knife, so that blood spurted up in the pope's face. Afterwards, the corpse was given the usual treatment; it was dumped in the Tiber. For days, the pontiff heard the boy's screams, smelt the blood that drenched his soutane right through to his wobbly breast, felt Perroto recoil with every fresh lunge until he shivered in death.

Alexander's own death, presaged by an owl flying through his window in daylight and expiring at his feet, was tailor-made. Most likely,

Cesare poisoned himself and his father by mistake. The cantarella in the wine was meant for a few rich and eminently disposable cardinals.

Cesare recovered. He was to die bravely three years later on the battlefield in Viana, Spain, taking on an army single-handedly. When his body was stripped, it had twenty-three wounds in it. The pope, seventy-three years old, succumbed to the poison. Burchard in his diaries, ambassadors in their despatches recorded in detail what happened.

The white arsenic created a fireball in his belly. For hours, he lay on his bed with bloodshot eyes and yellow complexion, unable to swallow. His face at first was mulberry-coloured and his lips puffy. His skin, flecked like a tiger's, started to peel off. The fat on his belly turned liquid. His stomach and bowels bled.

Doctors tried emetics and a phlebotomy but it was no use. Having received the last rites, this man in whom, according to Guicciardini, there was no religion, breathed his last in the Borgia Tower, in an apartment decorated by Pinturicchio.

Cesare, still confined to bed and devastated that his pope-father and patron was no more, ordered the papal rooms sealed so that his own men and not lackeys of greedy cardinals could ransack them.

The corpse was laid on a trestle between two lighted tapers. It was black as cloth now and beginning to putrefy. Burchard remembered the mouth foaming like a kettle over a fire. The tongue grew so big it completely filled the mouth and kept it agape. His frame was shapeless and started to swell frog-like until it was as broad as it was long. Giustiniani, the Venetian ambassador, wrote in a despatch that Borgia's was 'the ugliest, most monstrous and horrible dead body that was ever seen, without any form or likeness of humanity'.

Cesare's henchmen were tugging rings off the corpse's fingers, carting off candlesticks, ornaments, vestments, gold, silver, even the rugs on the floor. Against this background, the chaplain went on quietly washing the body.

By the time the room was bare, it was exploding and, from every orifice, giving off sulphurous fumes. Six porters and a couple of carpenters, pegging their noses, tried laughing their way through a terrible ordeal. Their chief problem was how to get that huge fetid lump into a narrow coffin. Reluctant to touch such a source of contagion, they tied a cord round the sacred foot, so often kissed by princes, prelates and pretty women, and dragged it off the trestle. The corpulent body hissed as it hit the cold floor. They knocked his mitre off and with ropes raised him just enough to let him plop down into the coffin.

By now, according to Burchard, 'there were neither tapers, lights, nor priests, nor anyone else to watch over the dead pontiff'. Like the mercy of God, the corpse was pressed down yet still overflowing. It needed all Burchard's strength to slap and bang it into the right shape for the coffin. Finally, since there was nothing else, he covered the Servant of the servants of God with a piece of old carpet.

The Palace porters had to fight the clergy of the basilica who were refusing entry to the corpse for burial. The funeral was attended by only four prelates. The coffin was permitted the briefest stay in the crypt of St Peter's. Pope Julius later affirmed it was a blasphemy to pray for the damned. Therefore, any mass said for the repose of Alexander's soul would be a sacrilege.

In 1610 the body was expelled from the basilica altogether and now rests in the Spanish Church in the Via di Monserrato awaiting, in trepidation, the Final Judgement.

SEVEN

The Inevitable Reformation

SOON AFTER BORGIA one of the most remarkable men in history ascended the papal throne, Julius II. A Franciscan from Genoa, tall, handsome and syphilitic, he bribed his way to the papacy with hundreds of thousands of ducats. Afterwards he decreed that anyone thenceforward who bribed a conclave should be deposed. An athletic man, he always carried a stick with which to hit anyone who annoyed him. In this storm of a man, religion was not even a hobby. His Lenten fare consisted of prawns, tunny, lampreys from Flanders and the best caviare.

He is best remembered as a patron of the arts. One day he led a thirty-one-year-old sculptor into the Sistine Chapel. The young man was broad-shouldered, lean, of medium height, with thick black hair and a broken nose, the prize for scrapping with a boy bigger than himself when he was an apprentice.

Pope Julius pointed with his stick to the ceiling. 'That. I want you to paint that for me.'

Michelangelo looked up and stifled a groan. The ceiling was sixty-feet high and concave. How would he, how would anyone, be able to work out perspectives? Besides, he was no painter. So far, he had only covered a few canvases and was none to proud of them. He preferred working in stone. Stone lasts. No, he would refuse. Giving no warning, he went home to his native Florence where he had been raised on the pure air of the Arezzo countryside and imbibed his sculptor's trade with the milk of his wet-nurse.

Two years later, in 1508, Julius forced him back to Rome without his hammer and chisel. So began the painting that would lift this young man from obscurity to the pinnacle of greatness. Defiant as ever, he wrote on his first pay-cheque: 'I, Michelangelo Buonarotti, *sculptor*, have received 500 ducats on account . . . for *painting* the vault of the Sistine Chapel.'

Julius was to strike him more than once in his anger at finding a man as tempestuous as himself. Once, Michelangelo had to appear before him in a halter in token of submission.

In four years, he was to fill 5,800 square feet of ceiling with 300 figures. In a poem, he confided his memories of those years. So long on his back, he grew a goitre that slopped around like a bucket that animals drank from. His back became bent like a bowman's. His beard was pointed heavenwards, so that chin and belly practically fused into one. His brush was forever dropping a mosaic of paint on his face. This is no place to paint on, he groaned, and I'm not even a painter.

On All Saints' Day 1512 this non-painter threw open the chapel door. High on that impossible surface was more than a work of art. It was an encyclopaedia of humanity. The Old Testament themes depicted every man's journey from birth to death. As the exultant Julius sang mass at the altar, he did so in the knowledge that he had commissioned the greatest work of art the world had ever seen.

Through Michelangelo, the pope began to create a new Vatican that has endured as a wonder to this day. He had no similar concern for the Christian faith. This is one of the ironies of the Vatican: outwardly, in terms of culture, art and architecture, the church had never been in finer shape; Bramante was alive, then Michelangelo and Raphael. Within, there was only corruption.

Julius' chief and abiding passion was not art but war. As a military strategist, he had few equals. Aged sixty at his election, he grew an impressive white beard which he tucked in his helmet. Then, breaking canon law, decked in armour, he mounted his charger and rode northwards to fight for God and the Papal States. He succeeded, too. He actually wanted them for the church, not for his family like most popes of his time. He was to establish territories that were to last virtually unchanged until they were swallowed up in the new Italy in the late nineteenth century.

He did conduct the occasional service in St Peter's. There were difficulties. A great womanizer, even when a cardinal he had sired three daughters. Hence on Good Friday 1508 his Master of Ceremonies reported that his Holiness could not allow his foot to be kissed, 'quia totus erat ex morbo gallico ulcerosus', 'it was completely riddled with syphilis'.

It did not stop him riding his horse. No scene was more representative of the Renaissance than Julius II, in full armour, sliding over frozen ditches to climb through the breached walls of Mirandola, then in French hands, and claim them for Christ. In that terrible winter the River Po had iced over. The pontiff put a white cloak over his armour, and his head was covered with sheepskin so he looked like a bear as he yelled: 'Let's see who has the bigger balls, the King of France or the pope.' The Italian makes it plain he was not referring to cannonballs.

When Michelangelo carved a statue of him, Julius examined it with a puzzled expression. 'What's that under my arm?' 'A book, Holiness.' 'What do I know of books?' roared the Pope. 'Give me a sword instead.'

His Holiness's preference of sword to Bible, of saddle to St Peter's Chair, had its effect in Rome. Michelangelo, who knew the Eternal

City better than most, left his impressions of popes he had known in a poem:

> Of chalices they make helmet and sword
> And sell by the bucket the blood of the Lord.
> His cross, his thorns are blades in poison dipped
> And even Christ himself is of all patience stripped.

Julius was so angry with Louis XII of France for not supporting his military campaigns that he drew up a Bull depriving him of his kingdom. Pious Henry VIII of England, whose favourite author was Thomas Aquinas, should have it, provided he showed himself a good Catholic by helping him fight his wars.

Julius died before the Bull was published. But for that, France, like England, might have become Protestant at the Reformation now drawing ineluctably nearer.

The Court of Leo X

On Julius' death, Cardinal Farnese rushed out of conclave into St Peter's Square yelling: 'Balls! Balls!' This reference to the *Palli* on the de' Medici coat of arms was immediately picked up by the crowd. They were astonished.

Giovanni de' Medici was only thirty-eight years old. Having had the famous Lorenzo the Magnificent as father and an Orsini as mother was no disadvantage. He had been brought up in luxury in their ancestral palace in the Via Larga in Florence and other equally opulent settings. At seven he was made an abbot for his first communion. When he was eight, the King of France wanted him made Archbishop of Aix en Provence; fortunately someone checked and found in the nick of time that there already was an archbishop of that see whom no one had seen for years. To compensate, the king gave the lad a priory near Chartres and made him a canon of every cathedral in Tuscany. When he was eleven, Giovanni received the historic abbey of Monte Cassino. At thirteen he became the youngest cardinal ever, even if it did not quite match Benedict IX's feat of becoming pope at eleven. Even broad-minded Innocent VIII seems to have had scruples about raising a teenager to the Sacred College; he insisted on three probationary years to give the boy every chance to master theology and canon law.

At his election to the papacy, pasty-faced Giovanni was fat, short-sighted, pop-eyed and, for reasons not at first understood, chaste. That is, he had no mistresses and no 'nephews' (or bastards). The reason was probably that he was an adventurous homosexual. Guicciardini said the new pope was excessively devoted to the flesh, 'especially those pleasures which cannot, with decency, be mentioned'.

He was ill when the conclave began, and he had to be carried in on a stretcher. Such an entry boosted his prospects. The electors thought highly of him for another reason: he was known to suffer from chronic ulcers on his backside. Surgery would surely bring about a fresh election. In spite of all this, Giovanni, who took the name of Leo X, was an ebullient character. His first words as pope were addressed to his illegitimate cousin Giulio de' Medici: 'Now I can really enjoy myself.' Keen to try on his tiara, he removed his red hat and handed it to Giulio. 'For you, cousin.' Giulio made good use of it. He was to become one of the most disastrous of all popes, Clement VII.

Leo was crowned in a temporary pavilion in front of St Peter's. Only the façade of the famous church remained, the rest was gutted in readiness for its replacement. The empty shell of old St Peter's was to appear in retrospect an omen of the dark days coming. Constantine's basilica had stood for nearly twelve hundred years when Julius II took it into his head to tear it down and build another. His cardinals had tried to dissuade him. The cost would be too high; they would lose the glorious mosaics and irreplaceable relics that linked all the ages with the Church of the Catacombs. While the new basilica was a-building, there would be an enormous gap in the faith and devotion of the Christian world. Julius would not listen. For the basilica he planned, the biggest in the world, he was willing to make any sacrifice. Under Leo, the new St Peter's was to cost the unity of Christendom.

Instead of giving up everything to follow Christ, Leo grabbed all he could in Christ's name for himself. A gambler and a big spender, he was said to obey Jesus in only one thing: he took no thought for the morrow. He was the only kind of pope the Romans felt relaxed with. He gave money to them, instead of squandering it like Julius on expensive wars.

It was an age of lavish entertainment. A certain Cardinal Cornaro gave dinners of sixty-five courses, each course consisting of three different dishes. Leo's dinners matched them. On the menu were sweetmeats such as peacocks' tongues. Nightingales flew out of pies; naked little boys jumped out of puddings. His chief jester, a midget Dominican friar, Fra Mariano, entertained him by eating forty eggs or twenty chickens at one sitting. At Carnival time, whole days were spent in the enjoyment of bullfights, followed by banquets and rounded off with masked balls at which Leo entertained his cardinals and their ladies.

He had 683 courtiers on his payroll. He also employed many jesters, an orchestra, a permanent theatre that specialized in Rabelaisian plays, and several wild animals. His favourite was a white elephant, the gift of King Emanuel of Portugal.

On 12 March 1514 there was a parade through Rome to the

Sant'Angelo Bridge where Leo was on a podium taking the salute. After a procession of exotic Indian poultry, Persian horses, a panther and two leopards came Hanno the White Elephant with a silver castle on its back. Three times, according to strict court etiquette, it bent the knee to a delighted pontiff. As a finale, it was given a bucket of water with which to asperse the crowd.

This elephant, housed in the Belvedere, became a celebrity and spawned an entire literature. Hundreds of poems were written in its honour. Many fine woodcuts of it still exist. On the lower cupola of the Vatican, Raphael painted its picture, though it was to be lost in renovations. In the Vatican Library, there exists a secret diary of the elephant's many engagements, ending with a death mourned more than many a pope's: 'Lundi XVI Juin, 1516, mourut l'éléphant.'

Contrary to canon law, Leo hunted for weeks at a time at Magliana, his spectacular retreat almost as beautiful as Castelgandolfo. Magliana was five miles from Rome on the road to Porto. He invariably rode side-saddle because of his 'complaint', the odour from which his courtiers pretended not to notice.

Like so many Renaissance popes, Leo was an enthusiastic builder and patron of the arts. The contemporary historian Sarpi said of him: 'He would have been a perfect pope, if to these [artistic] accomplishments he had added even the slightest knowledge of religion.'

None of Leo's interests came cheap, and he had to borrow prodigious sums from bankers at 40 per cent interest. The brothels simply did not bring in enough money even though there were seven thousand registered prostitutes in a population of less than fifty thousand. Syphilis was rife – 'a kind of illness', the syphilitic Benvenuto Cellini said, with genuine compassion, 'very common among priests'.

To bolster his income, Leo invented offices around the palace. These posts brought power and prestige and proved to be popular. Sixtus IV had had only 650 offices for sale; Leo had 2,150. He auctioned them. Most in demand were cardinal's hats, which went, on average, for thirty thousand ducats. Their Eminences recovered their money by corrupt sales of their own.

In spite of Leo's amazing liberality, several younger cardinals accused him of not living up to the promises he made them in conclave. Alfonso Petrucci of Siena, at twenty-seven a man of deep impiety and unshakeable atheism, was particularly indignant. With four other members of the Sacred College, he decided to assassinate the pope. His plan was to attack his Holiness at his weakest point, and it had the merit of originality. He bribed a Florentine doctor, Battista de Vercelli, to treat the pope for piles and, while operating, insert poison directly into his back passage. It made a change from figs.

Twice Leo turned down Battista's offer before his secret service intercepted a letter from him to Petrucci. Both conspirators were locked up, the cardinal in the Marocco, the lowest and foulest dungeon in the Castel Sant'Angelo.

Under torture, the doctor confessed. He was publicly hanged, drawn and quartered by a surgeon far less skilful than himself.

Leo forgave four of the rebel cardinals, though reparations were huge. Petrucci, as ringleader, was dealt with in the secrecy of the Marocco. His Holiness could not allow a Christian to lay a finger on a former prince of the church, so he employed a Moor as executioner. The Moor placed a noose of appropriate crimson silk around Petrucci's neck and slowly strangled him.

Leo's gravest danger came from a quarter he was too short-sighted to recognize, not in the papal court, not even in Rome, but in far-off Germany.

Luther and the Scandal of Indulgences

More than most countries, Germany was already reeling under the impact of a hundred papal abuses. It suffered from heavy taxes; the paying of annates, that is, one year's income from a living; tithes imposed on benefices for Crusades against the Turks that never materialized. By means of the terrible weapon of excommunication, clerics amassed immense wealth. Many men became clerics to gain immunity from civil courts. The Roman Chancery published a book with precise sums to be paid for various absolutions. A deacon guilty of murder could be absolved for twenty crowns. A bishop or abbot who had assassinated a foe could be absolved for three hundred livres. The wickedest crime had its price-tag. These 'anointed malefactors', as they were known in Germany, were exempt from civil jurisdiction. Instead, they brought into the ecclesiastical net for trial every form of litigation, including wills, legitimacy and usury. Any civil magistrate who tried to stop them was excommunicated, which meant he lost all rights as a citizen and a man. The church's possessions, since they belonged to God, were inalienable. In every country the church had immense wealth but in Germany it was estimated that half was in the hands of the clergy. They were exempt from all taxes and all obligations such as national defence.

The spark that set these dry lands ablaze was ignited by Prince Albert of Hohenzollern. At twenty-two, he already held the rich sees of Magdeburg and Halberstadt, but his ambition was to become Archbishop of Mainz and Primate of All Germany. For this he was prepared to pay. Pope Leo happened to be short of funds for the new St Peter's and was ready to do a deal. He would give Albert the see of Mainz *and* allow him, contrary to canon law, to keep his other two dioceses, for ten thousand ducats. This was in addition to the pallium fee, in this case twenty thousand ducats.

Since Albert did not have ready cash, Leo disregarded the church's condemnation of usury. He arranged for Albert to borrow the necessary from the Fuggers at an exorbitant rate of interest. How was Albert to repay his debt? Leo had thought about that. Taking his cue from Sixtus IV and Julius II, he provided him with a lucrative indulgence which he could hawk over eight years, even though, prior to his election, he had made a solemn vow to revoke all such indulgences. Of the revenue raised, half would go to the bankers and half to the Vicar of Christ for St Peter's.

The friar chosen to preach the indulgence in Germany was the Dominican Tetzel. A smart operator with a big booming voice, he was well paid for his services. His salary, apart from expenses, was twenty times that of a university professor. As the pope's representative, Tetzel always made a solemn entry into a town, surrounded by civil and church dignitaries. He was preceded by an acolyte carrying the cross blazoned with the papal arms. The Bull of Indulgence was borne on a velvet cushion trimmed with gold. With the cross planted in the market-place, business began. On sale were letters of safe-conduct to Paradise. An agent of the Fuggers was on hand to place the proceeds in a strongbox.

Tetzel was marvellous at depicting the sufferings of the souls in Purgatory. How they writhed in the flames, clamouring ceaselessly to their relatives on earth: 'Pity us! Pity us!' Twelve pence would enable a son to win his father's release from agony. Tetzel's most popular refrain was:

> As soon as the coin in the coffers rings
> A soul from Purgatory springs.

One of Tetzel's associates promised an indulgence so potent it would remit the sin of someone who, perish the thought, had raped the Virgin Mary.

Tetzel might have continued untroubled but for a thirty-four-year-old lean Augustinian monk. Of peasant stock, with smouldering eyes and friendly open face, Martin Luther looked as if he were rooted like a tree in the earth. His passion was the Bible, and there he saw no justification for these papal abuses. It made him furious to see the pope's ministers selling off indulgences at knockdown prices, even using them as gambling-counters in inns and taverns. The abuse had gone on for a long time. In 1491, Innocent VIII had granted the twenty-year *Butterbriefe* indulgence. For one-twentieth of a Rhenish guilder, Germans were given the annual privilege of eating milk-foods even on fast days. It meant they were able to indulge their favourite dishes while meriting from fasting. The proceeds of the indulgence went to build a bridge over the River Elbe at Torgau. In the year 1509, Julius II renewed the indulgence for another twenty years. What angered Luther most was the hoodwinking of simple people who were led to believe they could buy their way into heaven.

On the Feast of All Saints 1517, he took a hammer and nailed his Ninety-Five Theses Upon Indulgences on the great door of Albert's castle church at Wittenberg. Inside were relics, including a lock of the Virgin's hair, that bestowed 2 million years of indulgences. One of Luther's theses read: 'The Pope's wealth far exceeds that of all other men. Why does he not build the Church of St Peter with his own money instead of the money of poor Christians?'

According to this fractious monk, the Keys of the Kingdom were unlocking every treasure-chest in Christendom; papal avarice was turning Christ himself into an abetter of thieves whose one aim was to rob the poor. No wonder Luther threatened to knock a hole in Tetzel's drum.

For a long time, the papacy had betrayed ordinary devout Christians in cities, towns and hamlets. Pope after pope had turned his back on Christ. Not only did the papacy err; it was itself the major error, for truth is not primarily about *saying* but about *being* and *doing*. Its betrayal of the people is still embodied in the bricks and marbles of St Peter's. The cost of that basilica was the break-up of the church that has lasted for four centuries; it will last many more.

The Irreformable Papacy

Martin Luther was not the first to take onions to Rome and bring back garlic. In fact, the severest critics of the papacy have always been not enemies but friends, including many saints – and some popes! Their witness goes back a long way.

One of the most intriguing conversations ever recorded in Rome was between the English pope, Adrian IV (1154–9), and his plain-spoken compatriot John of Salisbury, later Bishop of Chartres. 'What', the pope whispered, 'do people really think of the Pope and the Church?' 'People are saying', John answered boldly, 'that the Church behaves more like a stepmother than a mother; that in it is a fatal vein of avarice, scribes and Pharisees laying grievous burdens on men's shoulders, accumulating precious furniture, covetous to a degree. And', he added, 'that the Holy Father himself is burdensome and scarcely to be borne.'

Pope Innocent IV (1243–54), owing to a dispute with Emperor Frederick II, was forced to leave Rome. He intimated he would like to be exiled in England. The peers of the realm refused to have him. They said that green sweet-smelling England could not bear the stench of the papal court. Innocent took the Curia to Lyons, instead. When Frederick II died, Innocent was able to return to Rome. Cardinal Hugo, in the pope's name, wrote to the people of Lyons a letter of gratitude. The document, dated 1250, is one of the most infamous in papal history.

> During our residence in your city, we [the Roman Curia] have been of very charitable assistance to you. On our arrival, we found scarcely three or four purchasable sisters of love, whilst at our departure we leave you, so to say, one brothel that extends from the western to the eastern gate.

In that same century, St Bonaventure, cardinal and general of the Franciscans, likened Rome to the harlot of the Apocalypse, thus anticipating Luther by three centuries. This harlot, he said, makes kings and nations drunk with the wine of her whoredoms. In Rome, he claimed to have found nothing but lust and simony, even in the top ranks of the church. Rome corrupts the prelates, they corrupt their clergy, the clergy corrupt the people.

Dante, a devout Catholic, not only gave hell to pope after pope, he dealt just as firmly with the Curia. Cardinals, who, according to a devout Durham monk, were once 'glittering like prostitutes', are stripped naked in the Fourth Circle of the *Inferno*. Teams of these hitherto indolent prelates are forced eternally to push big boulders, representing riches, against boulders pushed by other avaricious men.

The English poet William Langland, wrote:

> The country is the curseder that cardinals come in,
> And where they lie and linger most, lechery there reigneth.

Bishop Alvaro Pelayo, a papal aide in Avignon, suggested that the Holy See had infected the whole church with the poison of avarice. 'If the pope behaves like this, people say, why shouldn't we?' On a quite ordinary day, Pelayo's master, John XXII, excommunicated one patriarch, five archbishops, thirty bishops and forty-six abbots. Their only crime: they were behind in paying the pope his taxes.

Petrarch's friend Machiavelli wrote: 'The Italians owe a great debt to the Roman church and its clergy. Through their example, we have lost all true religion and become complete unbelievers. Take it as a rule, the nearer a nation dwells to the Roman Curia, the less religion it has.'

Catherine of Siena told Gregory XI that she did not need to visit the papal court to smell it. 'The stink of the Curia, Holiness, has long ago reached my city.'

In the fifteenth century, Saint Antonino, Archbishop of Florence, disapproved of his city selling bonds at a profit; this was usury. When his critics said, 'The Roman church allows it', Antonino replied:

'Members of the Curia have concubines. Does that prove that concubinage is lawful?' The sheer ordinariness of his argument is striking.

One reason for there being more prostitutes in Rome than in any other capital city was the large number of celibates. The convents were often brothels. Women sometimes took a dagger with them to confession to protect themselves against their confessor. Chroniclers tell of clerics spending their days in taverns, their nights in the soft arms of their mistresses. 'The holiest hermit has his whore.' As St Bridget said to Pope Gregory: 'The clergy are less priests of God than pimps of the devil.' The finest Roman choirs sang at mass songs so lascivious that a commission of cardinals debated whether to forbid all singing in church.

The sixteenth-century scholar Erasmus, one of the wittiest men of his or any age, said the tyranny of Rome was worse than the Turks'. He wrote a sketch in which Pope Julius is trying to bluster his way past St Peter at the heavenly gates. Peters screws up his eyes, unable to recognize a successor in this bearded warrior. Julius removes his helmet and dons his tiara. Peter is even more suspicious. Finally, an exasperated Julius holds up his keys in front of Peter's nose. The apostle having examined them, slowly shakes his head. 'Sorry, but they will not fit anything in this Kingdom.'

The Dutchman, Pope Adrian VI, confessed to the Diet of Nuremberg in 1522 that all evils in the church proceeded from the Roman Curia. 'For many years, abominable things have taken place in the Chair of Peter, abuses in spiritual matters, transgressions of the Commandments, so that everything here has been wickedly perverted.'

The Jesuit Cardinal Bellarmine was later to admit: 'For some years before Luther and Calvin there was in the church almost no religion left.' The papacy, he said, had almost eliminated Christianity.

In 1518, singing his 'Fool's Song', Luther wrote to the German nobility complaining of papal avarice. The Holy See he described as 'more corrupt than any Babylon or Sodom ever was. . . . It is a distressing and terrible thing to see the Head of Christendom, who boasts of being the Vicar of Christ and successor to St Peter, living in a worldly pomp that no King or Emperor can equal; so that in him who calls himself most holy and most spiritual there is more worldiness than in the world itself.'

Two years later, Luther was excommunicated by Pope Leo. Luther appealed to a General Council. For twenty-five critical years, popes and Curia refused the appeal to the only forum capable of settling the grave issues in the church.

Things by then were so bad that Contarini told Pope Paul III (1539–49) that the entire papal court was heretical; it was contrary to the essence of the Gospel. Christ's law brings freedom; the papacy,

Contarini said frankly, brings only serfdom and caprice. 'No greater slavery, Holiness, than this could be imposed on Christ's faithful.'

Paul III, the Petticoat Cardinal, whose only claim to eminence had been the irresistible charms of his sister Giulia, was not cut out to be a reformer.

Paul's Council – it was to last on and off for twenty years – got under way in Trent in December 1545. Edmund Campion, the saintly Jesuit who was martyred in London in 1580, said proudly of Trent: 'Good God! What variety of nations! What choice of bishops of the whole world!' The truth was that at Trent, 187 bishops, well over half, were Italians. It was hardly a 'catholic' gathering. In any event, it came far too late to undo the damage the papacy had caused. The fathers were astonished to hear themselves described in an open session as a worthless tribe, wolves not shepherds, the authors of the world's corruption in Italy and elsewhere.

How was it that Rome, far from being the champion of the Gospel, became in Contarini's phrase the embodiment of heresy?

Power was at the root of it. As if to endorse Acton's famous phrase, absolute power made not only the office-holders but also the papal office corrupt. This is why men like Borgia, far from being out of place in Peter's Chair, fitted it so snugly.

The Reformation came not when the church deteriorated further but when real holiness appeared. The Reformers saved the papacy, which had sunk too low to save either itself or the church. Jacob Burckhardt said: 'The moral salvation of the papacy is due to its mortal enemies.' But the cost was high. Trent consecrated medieval theology, thus ensuring that Catholicism would be narrow and backward-looking for centuries to come. It was the beginning of a religious Cold War. Father Paulo Sarpi wrote of Trent: 'This Council, desired and brought about by pious men in order to reunite the Church which was trying to break apart, has, on the contrary, so confirmed the schism and hardened attitudes as to make disagreements unresolvable.'

Trent, in his view, was responsible for the greatest 'Deformation in the ecclesiastical order ever seen, with the result that the name of Christianity is now hated'. After Trent, Rome's enormous power was confirmed, bishops so lost their independence that no Council was held for more than three hundred years. A Council was only called then to express formally and finally papal absolutism. The Roman church, divided in the West from the Protestants, was henceforward less a Catholic church than an inward-looking and frightened sect over which the pope held sway.

The curious thing is that Luther had no intention of leaving the church. Until it dawned on him that a divided Christendom was better than one over which the pope rules in denial of the Gospel. Better by far to be ruled by the open Bible than by a corrupt and apparently irreformable papacy. Western Christians still debate the wisdom of Luther's judgement. His analysis did not differ from Dante's. What was wrong with the church was the papacy's *libido dominandi*, its insatiable lust for power.

Leo X was obtuse enough to excommunicate Luther even for saying 'Burning heretics is against the will of the Holy Spirit'. The next few popes were no more perceptive.

The storm, long brewing, broke at last. The lightning flashed, the thunder rolled – and still they remained infallibly convinced that the world, *their* world, would continue as pacifically as ever.

Calvin introduced the Reformation in Geneva in 1541. Slowly, remorselessly, it spread to France, Holland, Scotland. And still no sign of recognition in the Vatican that its own influence was waning.

In the year 1555 a new pontiff appeared. Luther had already been dead for nearly a decade, Christendom was virtually exploding, a divided church was no longer willing to listen to the ravings of an ineffectual pope. Nor, above all, were the princes.

The new pontiff was blinder and deafer than any before him, though by no means dumb. He tried to outshout the storm and behaved as though he were Gregory VII returned to life.

EIGHT

The Twilight of
Absolute Power

THE ROMANS SAID OF HIM that had his mother foreseen his career she would have strangled him at birth. The man in question was John Peter Carafa, God's Wrath incarnate, who became Paul IV (1555–9).

Tall, bald, spare, elected at seventy-nine when he was tormented by rheumatism, Paul IV still had an elastic stride. His gestures, sudden and fierce, often knocked nearby aides to the ground. The Florentine ambassador described him as a man of iron who struck sparks off the very stones he walked on. His massive head was shaped like Vesuvius in whose shadow he was born. He, too, erupted without warning, spewing out destruction and death. His shaggy beard and craggy brow gave him a savage look; his cratered eyes, red and blotchy, shone like burning lava. His cracked voice, seldom free from catarrh, rolled and thundered, demanding instant, blind obedience.

Even the papal historian Pastor found it hard to say anything charitable about Paul IV. A foul-mouthed southerner, he was 'so carried away', Pastor remarked, 'as to make use of expressions which would seem incredible if they were not vouched for by witnesses above suspicion'.

Completely catholic in his execrations, he was as likely to dress down a cardinal as a lackey. He kept ambassadors waiting from four to seven hours, as though this was becoming in Peter's successor. He never admitted them without shouting in their ears that he was superior to all princes. As Christ's Vicar, he was able, he claimed, by wagging a finger, to change all earthly sovereigns.

In the year 1557, Paul published the Bull *Cum ex Apostolatus officio*. He claimed to be Pontifex Maximus, God's representative on earth. As such, he had unlimited power to depose every monarch, hand over every country to foreign invasion, deprive everyone of his possessions without legal process. Anyone offering help to one deposed – even basic human kindness – would be excommunicated.

A New Queen for England

In early 1559 the English ambassador Edward Carne appeared before this papal volcano. He informed his Holiness that Elizabeth Tudor, daughter of Henry VIII and Anne Boleyn, had followed Mary on the throne of England.

Paul hated all women with an inflexible theological ferocity and never allowed one of the species anywhere near him. He disagreed violently with Plato who said women were equal to men. Aquinas was right: women are men who have not quite come off. Their souls were simply not potent enough to fashion the male figure or the superior male intellect. For all that, he had warmed a little towards Mary Tudor from the moment he heard how she had dealt with the remains of Henry, her father. She had disinterred his heretical corpse and burned it. Then, in a few years, she had also burned over two hundred living Protestants.

Elizabeth was a different matter. Did not this female upstart know, the pontiff enquired of Carne, that England, since King John, was a fief of the Holy See? Nor that illegitimates cannot inherit? Had she not read his latest Bull? It was sheer audacity on her part to presume to govern England when it belonged to *him*. No, he could not let her get away with this. She was a usurper, a bastard, a heretic. If she renounced her ridiculous pretensions and came to him penitent *at once*, he would see what he could do for her. Otherwise. . . .

Within a couple of months, Elizabeth broke off diplomatic links with Rome.

The arrogant male chauvinist in the Vatican did not understand the twenty-five-year-old woman he was dealing with. She had, for all her faults, a heart of English oak.

Elizabeth had been born in a magnificent French bed at Greenwich Palace. As soon as Henry heard it was a girl, he left Greenwich in a tantrum that lasted for three days, screaming that Anne Boleyn, his second wife, was as stupid as his first, and was it for this he had risked excommunication by the pope and the loss of his realm? Anne knew then that she was doomed. She was only thirty when she was found guilty of having lovers and plotting to murder her rivals. She was executed with a heavy French two-handed sword, leaving Elizabeth, aged three, all alone. The little girl had the huge haunted eyes of her mother and the thin Plantagenet nose of her father. She lived by her wits, it is true. She had to. When she grew up, she was declared, by turns, legitimate and illegitimate, heir to the throne and, after her father died, one queenly nod away from execution.

Historians disagree as to whether Elizabeth was already committed at her accession to reintroducing Protestantism into England. When Mary, her half-sister had become queen, the first woman ever to rule England, Elizabeth instantly had mass celebrated in her household, reckoning, 'a life was well worth a mass'. Paul IV's gratuitous insults sealed the fate of English Catholics. If he thought he was supreme in England, she would make herself supreme in the church. Two could play at this deposing game, especially in the troubled time of Reformation. If history was anything to go by, more sovereigns had deposed popes than popes sovereigns.

Once again, by misreading events and overreaching himself, a pope was to see another country withdraw its allegiance from the Holy See.

Paul could not help himself. Heresy blinded him to all facts and consequences. It was a plague. In a plague, you set fire to clothes, even houses. In this plague of soul, the pope had no choice but to burn the body, the soul's dwelling. That way, others remained uncontaminated. This explains why, though he absented himself from numerous functions, he never missed a single Thursday meeting of the Holy Office. Even when he was dying, he invited the inquisitors to his room. Set up to deal with heresy, the inquisitors were now sentencing to death fornicators, sodomites, actors, buffoons, lay folk who failed to keep the Lenten fast, even a sculptor who had carved a crucifix judged to be unworthy of Christ.

When Paul came to die in the summer of 1559, the Romans burned down the prison of the Inquisition on the Via Ripetta. A mob tore down his statue on the Capitol, and Jews, whom he had persecuted more than any other pontiff, put a yellow hat on its severed head. Urchins spat on it and kicked it around before it was dragged through the streets and thrown into the Tiber. They were only sad they could not tear his corpse limb from limb with their bare hands. After gauging public opinion, the authorities buried the body deep in St Peter's in the middle of the night of 19 August and mounted a guard.

Paul IV had never doubted that, in similar circumstances, Jesus, a loyal Jew done to death for heresy, would have done exactly as *he* did. He was not loved. One was to follow soon who was loved no better.

The Last Sovereign to Be Deposed

Paul IV knew what he was about when he chose an excessively scrupulous Dominican, Michele Ghislieri, to be his Grand Inquisitor. After his election in 1566 as Pius V, he continued to live a monkish life in a cell in the Vatican. He ate little and threatened his cook with excommunication if he put forbidden ingredients in his soup on days of abstinence. His chief aim was to turn Rome into a monastery. He spoke with and listened to no one but God.

To look at, Pius was a bundle of yellow skin and shaking bones. Bald and with a big white beard, his waxen forehead was high and narrow over an eagle's beak of a nose. His eyes were pinpoints, his lips curved like a scimitar.

His first act as pontiff was to expel all prostitutes from Rome. The number of loose women in his diocese embarrassed him. The Roman Senate resisted for, they said, licentiousness always flourished where there were celibates. If the prostitutes left, not only would house-rents plummet, but no decent woman would be safe from the clergy.

Pius forbade residents of Rome to go inside taverns. He came within a whisker of making adultery a capital offence. Does he not know, complained a member of the Curia, *anything* about papal history? Pius next brought out what the English community called the Last Bull; it abolished bull-fighting throughout Christendom. It was published everywhere except in the Iberian peninsula, which somewhat diminished its impact. The Spanish hierarchy excused themselves on the grounds that they did not want to bring the church into disrepute.

It did not take Pius long to turn his attention to England. Behind the scenes, he encouraged civil disobedience to Elizabeth. He contributed twelve thousand crowns to a rising in the north. He was willing, he said, if necessary, to go in person to assist in it 'and engage in that service all the goods of the Apostolic See'. The rising failed. That was when Pius made a fatal, if predictable, blunder.

In the first week of Lent 1570, in a Rome court of inquiry, Elizabeth was pronounced guilty of infidelity on seventeen counts. The pope's own verdict was embodied in the Bull *Regnans in Excelsis* on 25 February. He described Elizabeth as the servant of vice and the pretended Queen of England. 'This same woman, having acquired the kingdom and outrageously usurped for herself the place of Supreme Head of the Church in all England', had to be punished.

This last attempt by a pope to overthrow a sovereign was the most sweeping and damaging of all.

> We declare the aforesaid Elizabeth to be a heretic and abettor of heretics and We declare her and her supporters to have incurred the sentence of excommunication. . . . We declare her to be deprived of her pretended claim to the aforesaid kingdom and of all lordship, dignity and privilege whatsoever. Also, We declare that the lords, subjects and peoples of the said kingdom and all others who have sworn allegiance to her are perpetually absolved from any oath of fidelity and obedience. Consequently, We absolve them and We deprive the same Elizabeth of her pretended claim to the kingdom. . . . And We command and forbid her lords, subjects and peoples to obey her. . . . We shall bind those who do the contrary with a similar sentence of excommunication.

The pope who wrote this was to die in his bed within two years. Others were to pay on the gallows for his mistakes.

For twelve years prior to *Regnans in Excelsis*, English Catholics under Elizabeth had been subject to fines for non-attendance at the Anglican church. Not one had been executed. The effect of the Bull was to turn English Catholics into traitors. Between 1577 and 1603, 120 priests were put to death with sixty of the laity who harboured them. These courageous men and women had to wait 250 years longer for canonization than did Pius V.

Long after his pontificate, Catholics found themselves caught between their loyalty to church and to country. The pope it was who decided 'out of the plenitude of his apostolic power' that a twin loyalty was impossible. He did a dangerous thing when he tried to undermine the patriotism of Englishmen.

The weapon forged by Gregory VII, which gave him such satisfaction at Canossa, was honed to perfection by Innocent III. It was now claiming its final victims.

Gregory had made excommunication into a political sword to strike down emperors and kings. That error was responsible for Catholics being hated and outlawed in country after country.

Christians, since theirs is a religion of faith not of race, should be citizens of the world. They belong to the Christ who claimed to suffer in all who suffer. A Christian, wherever he is was meant to be a sign of that catholic all-embracing love. But Rome, through its tendency to absolutism, its lust for power, turned Catholicism into Romanism. Heretical popes of heroic personal asceticism demanded of Catholics not merely a spiritual but a political obedience. As a result, Catholics seemed to owe and sometimes did owe political loyalty to a foreign power masquerading as vicars of Christ. Far from being universal people, they were seen as less than patriots.

In England, Rome absolved Catholics from having to try to overthrow Elizabeth. None the less, they were warned that, should England be attacked, they had to help the invader depose the queen. From then on, Catholics became for centuries not quite English.

As Trevelyan wrote in *A Shortened History of England*. 'Until the Roman Church throughout the world ceased to use the methods of the Inquisition, the Massacre of St Bartholomew, the deposition and assassination of Princes, the States which she placed under her formidable ban did not dare to grant toleration to her missionaries.'

In the sixteenth century Christendom disintegrated. Protestantism was an established fact. The Reformation had taken so firm a hold in Europe that some countries once solidly Catholic, like England, were under the sway of 'heretical' monarchs. Even in France, Protestantism was a force destined to endure through the fiercest persecutions.

The Catholic church withdrew into itself in the period which came to be known as the Counter-Reformation. It was as sectarian as the Lutheranism and Calvinism opposed to it. Polemics marred all its thinking. Originality was anathema. It was time to close ranks. Survival was the best that could be hoped for; and the papacy was the greatest survivor in history.

The French Revolution in 1789 shattered further the church's peace of mind. A new spirit was abroad, the spirit of 'unrestrained liberty'. It seemed intent on destroying not only the old absolutist monarchies, the *anciens régimes*, but religion and moral decency, too. This, in the eyes of the popes, was the devil's work. To an institution that stood above all else for order, this was anarchy. It was inevitable that the Catholic church should retreat even further into itself and feed on its ancient heritage. How could it possibly be expected to accommodate itself to 'liberty' in the guise of atheism?

In the next few years, Napoleon gave the papacy another great blow. He humiliated two pontiffs in succession. Pius VI was deposed and forced into exile in Valence where he died in exile in the last year of the eighteenth century. His obituary in the local registry read: 'Name: Citizen John Braschi. Trade: pontiff.' Pius VII, too, after an unsuccessful concordat in 1801, was exiled and made to officiate at Napoleon's coronation in Notre-Dame. At the solemn moment, Napoleon had snubbed the pope by crowning himself and Josephine, then proceeded to annex the Papal States. But, Pius IX (1846–78) must have thought, had not these precious lands been returned to their rightful owner, God, by the Congress of Vienna (1814–15)? The same would happen again, in God's good time. Or was King Victor Emmanuel mightier than Napoleon? It was merely a matter of patience.

Pius IX, a man of fortitude, failed to see what was staring in him the face.

Papacy: End or New Beginning?

The little old man with the white hair and round red face was woken from sleep by the sound of cannon-fire. The windows rattled, his iron bed rocked slightly on the marble floor. The shutters were still up, but since it was a dark morning in late September he could not see his clock anyway. Breathing heavily and wincing, the old man struggled up on to his pillow. His lumbago made his every move a torment; his hips in particular hurt. Once on the pillow, he made the sign of the cross.

At that moment, the door was flung open. A gaunt figure in a dressing-gown, carrying a lighted lamp, bowed before entering and dropping to his knees. The man in bed grunted: 'Che ora?' 'Just after five, Holiness.' 'So, Leonardo, it has begun.' Cardinal Antonelli, Pius IX's long-serving Secretary of State, bowed his head. 'And Kanzler?' asked the pontiff. 'The general is acting on your orders, Holiness. He will put up token resistance to prove the enemy is not welcome here. But. . . .' Antonelli's long bony fingers butterflied to indicate that the city was bound to fall, and very soon.

Having dressed with the aid of a manservant, Pius walked on crutches to his small chapel to celebrate mass. His fervent intention was never in doubt. That God would preserve the Eternal City from these Piedmontese vandals who had allied themselves with Satan.

The crump and whine of shells was clearly audible as his Holiness attended to his devotions. Shells were landing less than a mile away. It was plainly a two-pronged attack. As he was making his thanksgiving, he was informed that the main force under General Cadorna was concentrated at the Porta Pia. Twenty defenders had been killed and fifty wounded. 'Requiescant in pace,' the Pope murmured, signing himself. These young men, cut down futilely in the spring of their years were the last victims of the papacy's temporal ambitions.

Pius asked Antonelli to arrange a meeting of the diplomatic corps as soon as possible. The ambassadors assembled at mid-morning in an audience chamber in sight of the Castel Sant'Angelo. The pope, pointing, said nothing. They looked to where a white flag was flying over the castle. Surrender.

It was 1870. Exactly three centuries after *Regnans in Excelsis*, the pope was being knocked off his throne by an earthly monarch. Great institutions are the victims of great ironies. But in all the fifteen hundred years of the papacy's temporal power no moment was more galling than this.

Yet it was predictable; in fact, for at least two decades, it had been inevitable. But Pius IX was convinced that the future would always be like the past.

He had been pope for twenty-four years. Metternich, the Austrian chancellor who dominated Europe for forty years, made a snap judgement about him which was not far off the mark: 'Warm of heart, weak of head, and lacking utterly in common sense.'

He began in 1846 with the reputation of a liberal. In his ancestral home, it was said, even the cats were nationalists. No sooner was he on the throne than he granted amnesty to political prisoners. Throughout the peninsula, all kinds of people sensed that perhaps at last the Almighty had taken pity on them. Had He worked a miracle and sent them a liberal pope, one who would lead the eight disparate regions of Italy into the unity everyone was yearning for? Please God, someone remarked, the pontiff will not disappoint his family cat. Italians had long complained that God had not been kind to their otherwise lovely sea-lapped land: unpassable mountains in the north, two volcanoes in the south, and, most menacing of all, a pope in the middle.

Two years into Pius' reign and the office took over the man. A republican rising in Rome forced him to flee, in black cassock and tinted glasses, to Gaeta in the Kingdom of Naples. That was when he was converted to the reactionary cause. In a two-year exile, he repented all his left-wing sympathies to become the hardest of hard-liners. His sole adviser in those decisive years was Antonelli, son of a Neapolitan bandit, and notorious for his amours. This prelate who would sooner break than bend, kill than forgive, was to die laden with riches of which, to this day, no one knows the origin.

When, a few years after his first bitter experience, Pius was asked to head a federation of Italy, he flatly refused. He was opposed to every form of freedom and constitutional change. His one aim was to hold on to the states which he ruled as absolute monarch, without interference from anyone.

These states, which popes had treasured like the dogma of the Trinity, were, at this time, twice the size of the Holy Land, with a population of nearly 3 million. Ever since the church had begun acquiring them after Constantine left for Byzantium, their net effect was to corrupt and hamstring her spiritual mission. In the fourteenth century, Giovanni de' Mussi had written: 'Since Sylvester's time the consequences of the temporal power had been innumerable wars. . . . How is it possible that there has never been any good pope to remedy such evils and that so many wars have been waged for these transient possessions?'

None had fought so fiercely for them as Julius II. They were more or less intact when Clement VII, dazed by the sack of Rome in 1527, met with the Venetian ambassador, Contarini, soon to be a cardinal. Contarini tried to console the pope.

> Your Holiness must not imagine that the welfare of the Church of Christ rests in this little State of the Church: on the contrary, the Church existed before she possessed the State, and was the better for it. The Church is the community of Christians; the temporal State is like any other province of Italy and therefore your Holiness must seek above all to promote the welfare of the true Church which consists in the peace of Christendom.

By 1870 only tsarist Russia was more wickedly run than the Papal States. In them there was no freedom of thought or expression, and no elections. Books and papers were censored. Jews were locked up in ghettos. Justice was a blind and hungry lion. It was frankly a police state flying the papal flag, with spies, inquisitors, reprisals, secret police, and executions for minor offences a commonplace. A small, corrupt, lascivious, tight-knit clerical oligarchy ruled, in his Holiness's name, with a rod of iron.

The situation had only deteriorated since Lord Macaulay visited Italy in 1838. He tried then to imagine what England would be like if all Members of Parliament, ministers, judges, ambassadors, commanders-in-chief and lords of the Admiralty were bishops or priests. Worse than that, *celibate* bishops or priests. In order to gain promotion, the most lascivious men were obliged to become clerics and take a vow of celibacy. The result was, according to Macaulay, in his *Letters*, 'corruption infects all the public offices. . . . The States of the Pope are, I suppose, the worst governed in the civilized world; and the imbecility of the police, the venality of public servants, the desolation of the country, force themselves on the observation of the most heedless traveller.'

Thirty or so years later, the Papal States were ripe for rebellion.

Many overtures were made to Pius, begging him to save Italy and the papacy. It was respectfully pointed out to him that Herod was king in Judaea, not Jesus; and there was no mention of 'temporal power' in the gospels. On the contrary, Jesus said firmly: 'My kingdom is not of this world.' The Donation of Constantine notwithstanding, the popes never owned a single town outside Rome until the King of the Lombards gave them Sutria in 728. The pope was asked to remember that when the papacy was at its zenith, in the Renaissance, it was so disedifying it lost the allegiance of half of Christendom. He was given guarantees of complete independence as head of the church. In fact, his leadership in morals and religion would shine forth brighter than ever.

To all these pleas, the pope turned a stone ear. Modern civilization was of the devil, he reckoned, and he refused to parley with the Prince of Darkness.

Now the unifying movement was gathering strength in Piedmont under King Victor Emmanuel II. Cavour, its architect, was proclaiming the ideal of a free church in a free state. Like Moses, he was not to enter the Promised Land, but even on his deathbed he cried out to the priest sent to anoint him: 'Friar! Friar! A free church in a free state.' Pius IX stamped this testament of faith with the seal of heresy.

In 1862 he received a petition signed by twelve thousand priests. They implored his Holiness to read the signs of the times. Rome *had* to be the capital of the new Italy. Would he not 'say a word of peace'? Pius' reaction was to discipline these rebels, every one.

Even in the fateful year of 1870, when the French troops which had defended him for so long were withdrawn to fight the Prussians, leaving him with a Gilbert and Sullivan army, Pius held his ground. As he told the diplomatic corps on that morning of 20 September, he was not free to part with a forty-thousand-square-mile inheritance that was vital to his spiritual autonomy.

So, when Cadorna's guns breached the Aurelian Wall at the Porta Pia, the plumed Bersaglieri, part of a 60,000-strong force, swept into the City. On every building, they lowered the yellow and white papal flag and hoisted the tricolour. The crowds in the streets went wild. For them the pope was not so much the head of the church as a civil tyrant. This was their liberation day. A plebiscite showed they were a thousand to one against the pope and in favour of the king.

Cadorna had given strict instructions not to bombard the Vatican. Pius was left in peace. But when Victor Emmanuel asked for an audience, his Holiness refused. He had only one word for the king, and it was of excommunication, once more misusing a spiritual weapon. He renewed the censure on a kind of biennial basis, so that the king was excommunicated four times before he died in 1878, when he was allowed to make his peace with God if not with His chief representative on earth. Pius also forbade Catholics to engage in the democratic processes of the new Italy, whether as electors or as candidates.

In the eight years remaining to him after the invasion, the pontiff stayed at home, dubbing himself, somewhat dramatically, 'the Prisoner of the Vatican'. Holy pictures circulated everywhere, especially in Ireland and Germany, showing Pius lying on a bed of straw in a fetid dungeon. Contributions to Peter's Pence, the gift of the poor, rocketed as a result. His prison was rather comfortable, not at all like Peter's in the Mamertine. To be truthful, he had more living-space than all the Jews in Rome had had in centuries. He possessed a splendid garden and countless rooms in which to lay his head or play the occasional game of billiards with Cardinal Antonelli. A Jacobin poet said, more prosaically than Pius: 'The pope is a prisoner of himself.'

By the 1870 Law of Guarantees, the king of Italy proposed a very generous settlement. To every offer, even financial ones, Pius replied, 'Non possumus', 'We cannot', as though he had been invited to eat roast beef on Good Friday. To the very end and beyond, as the Vatican had done for centuries, he kept turning a political issue into a key matter of religion. Though he claimed to serve a Master who had nothing, he insisted he could not serve him except as a monarch. Pius VII had said the same to Napoleon when he stole papal territory. 'We demand the restoration of our states, for they are not our personal inheritance but the inheritance of St Peter who received them from Christ.' To believe that Peter – a Galilean fisherman who probably never owned more than an old timber boat – had received from Christ a big slab of central Italy without which he could not preach the Gospel of Jesus crucified was not lacking in a certain audacity. But Pius IX did not shrink from such a belief. Which is why the papacy had to be dragged by a secular state kicking and screaming into the New Testament.

Non-Catholics were delighted that the papacy had at last been cut down to something like New Testament size. The more foolish of them prophesied its demise. They underestimated the office and the man.

Theology was not Pius' forte. His private secretary, Monsignor

Talbot, admitted in a letter to W. G. Ward: 'As the Pope is no great theologian, I feel convinced that when he writes [his encyclicals] he is inspired by God.' Complete ignorance was no bar to infallibility, he said, since God can point out the right road even by the mouth of a talking ass. Talbot, without meaning it, had reached the heights of Voltaire.

What Pius lacked in intellect, he more than made up for by animal cunning. He had already prepared for an otherwise bleak future by a move whose daring Gregory VII himself would have applauded.

Two months before the invasion of Rome, Pius had presided over the final session of the Vatican Council. In contrast to the opening a year before, St Peter's was almost deserted. In the royal box, there were two ladies, one of them the Infanta of Portugal, as well as a decrepit officer with the Order of St Januarius blazoned across his chest. The diplomatic box, too, had many vacant seats. The Great Powers had instructed their ambassadors to boycott a function in which there was no mileage for them.

The weather was foul. A storm had been threatening all night. For a Roman morning in mid-July, the light was exceedingly dim.

There were 532 bishops, old men vested in white chasubles topped by white mitres, seated in the north transept of the basilica. For many, like Manning of Westminster, the only convert at the Council, this was the greatest day of their lives. Only through the transept's main door were outsiders able to glimpse the proceedings. The pope came hobbling in almost unnoticed; he vested and intoned the *Veni Creator Spiritus*. Then, in steamy heat, a bishop with the voice of a bass singer in a Verdi opera read out the new Constitution, *Pastor aeternus*, 'Eternal Shepherd'. The roll-call followed.

Now the most famous storm ever recorded broke like the wrath of God over St Peter's. In the intervals between each *placet* of the Council fathers, there was a peal of thunder. The timing was liturgically precise. Lightning flashed in every window and flickered round the dome and every smaller cupola, turning the bronze of Bernini's *baldacchino* into shiny gold.

For an hour and a half the storm went on raging until the roll was complete. Only two bishops voted *non-placet*: Riccio of Cajazzo in Naples and Fitzgerald of Little Rock, Arkansas. But 140 bishops had absented themselves. Voting *placet* would have offended their consciences; voting *non-placet* would have offended the Holy Father in front of the world.

A breakdown of the voting pattern is instructive. Three hundred of the five hundred bishops supporting the pope were titular bishops, or else they were Vatican officials who lived in Rome at Pius' expense. Most of the dissidents had dioceses whose beliefs and feelings they were representing in Council. At least two-thirds of the American bishops, led by Kenrick of St Louis, were opposed to the definition, believing it would make conversions more difficult.

The sheer size of the opposition proved that the church was not ready for so momentous a decision; it was passed, but it did not adequately mirror the mind of the Western church. A very important truth was at stake and the decree was felt by many to be defective. As the outspoken Bishop Strossmayer said in one session:

> This Council lacks both liberty and truth. . . . A Council which disregards the old rule of the necessity of moral unanimity, and begins to decide propositions of faith and morals by a majority vote will, according to my inmost conviction, forfeit the right to bind the conscience of the Catholic world as a condition of eternal life and death.

Pius IX refused to listen to the opposition, claiming he was 'merely the mouthpiece of the Holy Ghost'.

By passing the decree without concern for the Orthodox Church or the Protestants, Pius seemed to be making the centuries-old rift between Rome and the other great Christian communions perpetual.

The divisions at Pius' Council contrasted starkly with the fifteenth-century Council of Constance when it was decreed that the entire church, pope included, is subject to a General Council. Constance, it will be remembered, passed this *unanimously*. Not even the Curia, nor the pope-to-be, Martin V, raised the slightest objection.

The Vatican Council was to prove another pyrrhic victory for the papacy, even more terrible in its consequences than Gregory VII's at Canossa. It showed once more that it is not unholy popes like Benedict IX and Alexander VI who have done the most lasting damage to the church but holy ones like Gregory VII, Pius V and Pius IX. For Acton's dictum about absolute power corrupting absolutely applies, without qualification, to sinners *and* saints. In this case, Pius IX had triumphed; but he had sown the wind.

When the voting results were brought to him in St Peter's, the gloom was so thick that he could not see them. A candle was lit so that he could give his approval of the Constitution in his light musical voice: 'Nosque sacro approbante Concilio', 'With the approval of the Sacred Council, We thus decree, decide and sanction what has been read'.

The fathers clapped, the crowd in the body of the basilica waved handkerchiefs like the wings of ghostly doves. What was it his Holiness had just given the force of law? The crowd's cries provided the answer: 'Viva il Papa infallibile.' Pius, whom Montalembert called 'the idol in the Vatican', had invested himself with the powers of a god; he had infallibly decreed his own infallibility.

Those two brave bishops, who, a moment ago, denied it, now

confessed on their knees to Pius IX – 'Modo credo, Sancte Pater' – that they believed it as sincerely and unreservedly as they believed in God and Jesus' divinity. Theirs was the quickest conversion in history.

The bishops who had left Rome to avoid hurting the Holy Father by voting according to their conscience also came round, sooner rather than later, to accepting *Pastor aeternus*. It was either accept it or leave the church, and that, too, would undoubtedly have hurt the Holy Father. They returned home to tell the faithful that the Vatican decrees were unanimous, which was rather less than the whole truth. Some even found the courage to sack and excommunicate learned theology professors, men of international repute like Döllinger of Munich, for still daring to say what they themselves had said before and during the Council.

Henceforward, authority is to ride roughshod over reason and conscience, for Vatican I had set a precedent. Any Catholic scholar who promotes democracy or religious freedom or scientific research into man's origins has to be ready to take a hammering – or, at least, hide his head in a corner.

For what was decided in Council was this: When the pope exercises the fullness of his office and defines a doctrine for the whole church, his definitions are infallible of themselves and not from the consent of the church. The distinct impression was given that, far from the pope getting his faith from the church, the church gets its faith from the pope. The pontiff is on his own; there are no checks and balances, no cabinets, no parliamentary opposition. The world may become increasingly democratic, one man (or woman) one vote; the church, never. In Catholicism, one man one vote has a very different ring.

The Curia was delighted. They had dreaded a Council and, three centuries having passed since Trent, they sincerely believed Councils were not necessary. But now the bishops had generously and once and for all handed over the running of the church to *them*. They had given their consent to the pope, who never needed their consent again. Catholic episcopacy was finally the spent force that Gregory VII had wished it to be; bishops had abdicated before the world. By a wonderful metamorphosis, shepherds had turned themselves into sheep.

The Council went into recess in an atmosphere of international upheaval. Few thought it would reconvene, but why bother anyway? This, many curalists confidently predicted, would be the last Council of the Church. To call another, a pope would have to be a complete fool. Or, begging the Curia's pardon, a saint.

Sympathetic non-Catholics looked on, stunned. In the eyes of many of them, such as the British Prime Minister, Gladstone, it was a Giant Step Backwards for mankind into the Dark Ages. Many were genuinely puzzled. How was it that, eighteen centuries after Peter, it took weeks of agonizing debate to decide, on a majority vote in a fragment of the church, that this teaching, hotly contested up to the last minute, was suddenly evangelical and vital for salvation?

The theologically inclined, with a neat sense of irony, were pleased to find there was at least one Protestant exercising private judgement in the Catholic church: the pope. This was an astute criticism. Vatican I had turned the pope from being 'the Catholic of Catholics' into the church's only Protestant.

The more philosophical critics enquired how, if God is ineffable and dwells in inaccessible light, the pope can speak infallibly about Him.

But the wisest observers of all suggested: This is not so much a religious as a political statement. About to lose his states, the pope was determined to be absolute monarch in a land which not even the most powerful monarch can ever wrest from him.

The quest of absolute power had not halted; it was to go on in the area of truth.

Alas, as with power, so with truth, the record of the papacy was not good.

PART TWO

Truth

'The popes were not only murderers in the great style, but they also made murder a legal basis of the Christian Church and a condition of salvation.'
LORD ACTON

NINE

The Crushing
of Dissent

The Pope's House on the Corner

Though it always called itself Holy, Catholic and Apostolic, few if any pilgrims go to see it. Few guidebooks bother to mention it. This is strange in view of its history, for some would say that this building holds the key to understanding the Roman church. It is stranger still in that it stands within spitting distance of the sacristy of St Peter's, in a quiet street, left of the basilica behind Bernini's quadruple colonnade. A large corner house, this Casa Santa, with its great gateway, is known locally as the Palace of the Inquisition.

In recent years, having had a bad press, the Holy, Catholic and Apostolic Inquisition, like the Soviet secret police, has been renamed more than once. In 1908 this oldest of Rome's Sacred Congregations became the Holy Office; from 1967, it changed to the Congregation for the Doctrine of the Faith. The present secretary and chief executive – the Grand Inquisitor of old – is the Bavarian Cardinal Ratzinger, but the president has ever been the reigning pontiff.

Emile Zola, in his brilliant if bitter novel, *Rome*, written in the last years of the nineteenth century, describes the impression made on him by the Palace of the Inquisition:

> It is in a solitary silent district, which the footfall of pedestrians or the rumble of wheels but seldom disturbs. The sun alone lives there, in sheets of light which spread slowly over the small, white paving. You divine the vicinity of the basilica, for there is the smell of incense, a cloistral quiescence as of the slumber of the centuries. And at one corner the Palace of the Holy Office rises up with heavy, disquieting bareness, only a single row of windows piercing its lofty, yellow front. The wall which skirts this side street looks yet more suspicious with its row of even smaller casements, mere peep-holes with glaucous panes. In the bright sunlight this huge cube and mud-coloured masonry seems to be asleep, mysterious, and closed like a prison, with

scarcely any aperture for communication with the
outside world.

The apparent sleepiness is an illusion. An immense amount of reading
goes on in this place and from it comes an endless stream of warnings,
guidelines, censures. The dungeons, where so many were tortured in
the not so distant past, are no more. Fortunately, a secular state
wrenched temporal power from the fierce grip of Pius XI.

Since 1870 the dungeons and cells of the Inquisition have been
turned into offices and archives where the work continues as methodi-
cally as of old, though far less brutally.

Catholics go about their lives in the world without giving a thought
to the Inquisition. They have a reputation for devotion and normality.
Cranks and fanatics among them are few. Not for them a shrill and
showy proselytism. Catholic missionaries – priests, nuns, lay people –
are self-effacing. Many leave their homeland to dedicate their lives to
the service of the needy. In so far as the Holy Office crosses their mind,
they assume it is an essential arm of orthodoxy, a way of preserving the
apostolic faith. They would be shocked to discover the abuses that
have originated in this building in the Via del Sant'Ufficio.

Pope John Paul II

Where does the present pontiff stand? He is not without apparent
contradictions. In the first place, he is plainly a kind and compassionate man. In 1987, he gave permission to Mother Teresa of
Calcutta to build a hospice for the homeless within the walls of the
Vatican. He has a deep love for children and the sick. Wherever he
goes he pleads eloquently for the rights and dignity of man. On the
other hand, he frequently comes across as the sternest pope in living
memory. One would have to go back to Pius X at the turn of the
century to find a pope who listens less and demands more instant
obedience. The reason for this is clear. The pontiff is by nature and
training a Platonist. He believes that truth is eternal and unchange-
able. He, as Vicar of Christ, has a privileged, spirit-inspired view of
these truths which he is bound to present to the church and from
which no Catholic may be allowed to deviate by so much as one
iota.

Again, John Paul repeatedly says that clerics must stay outside
politics. But when he worked in Poland as priest, bishop and
cardinal, he continually engaged in what the communists at least
referred to as 'right-wing political activity'. Besides, his Holiness
must know that his visits to his homeland cannot but be interpreted
as playing politics. This in fact is entirely in the Vatican tradition.

For century after century, the Catholic church was the foremost political force in Europe. It meddled in the workings of every country as and when it pleased. Popes, almost at will, deposed emperors and kings. Pius X, in his first consistory on 9 November 1903, said:

> We shall offend many people in saying We must of necessity concern ourselves with politics. But whoever judges the question fairly must recognize that the Sovereign Pontiff, invested by God with the Supreme Magistracy, has not the right to separate political matters from the domain of faith and morals.

Many clerics and sisters in South Africa, faced with *apartheid*, have been perplexed to hear a Polish pope telling them that involvement in politics is contrary to their religious mission.

Finally, the Catholic church is the only religious body in existence that is both church *and* political organization. This is why it alone among churches exchanges diplomatic representatives and claims recognition as an independent member of the community of nations. It does this not as a small state (the Vatican) but as a worldwide religious organization.

Most commentators now agree that John Paul has gone round the Vatican closing the windows and pulling down the blinds. Even after the Second Vatican Council, he had the church's code of canon law revised in 1983 and did not bother to ask the world's bishops for their approval. Unlike his predecessor, Paul VI, he is in no way the victim of doubt or hesitation. This explains why he has dealt vigorously with any theologian who dares question his decisions, even non-infallible decisions.

As early as 1979, he revoked the licence of the world's best-known Catholic writer, Hans Küng. As a result, Küng was no longer considered a Catholic theologian and so lost his post in the Catholic faculty of the University of Tübingen. Had not the rector offered him a post outside the Catholic faculty, Küng would be out of a job. Rome seems satisfied that he has been muzzled and other potential dissidents in Europe and North America have been warned.

The Dutch theologian, Edward Schillebeeckx, has frequently been carpeted by the Holy Office; Father Leonardo Boff of Brazil, an expert at harmonizing Catholic and Marxist thinking, has also been rebuked. Both are on probation on the promise of good behaviour. John Paul has made his point: in line with Gregory VII and Pius IX, he is content with nothing less than total submission, even on matters that are hotly contested.

Target: The Jesuits

A bigger target than individual theologians has been the Jesuit Order. John Paul soon showed he was not happy with the traditional champions of the papacy. The then General of the Order, Father Pedro Aruppe, had a reputation for being a liberal. He was merely trying to put the forward-looking decrees of Vatican II into effect among his brethren. When he became ill, Father Vincent O'Keefe was appointed Vicar-General in charge. O'Keefe, an American, had been head of Fordham, the Jesuit university in New York. John Paul found him unacceptable. In 1981 he imposed on the Order Father Paolo Dezza, aged seventy-nine and nearly blind, as his personal delegate. No pope had ever acted like this before.

Karl Rahner, the most distinguished theologian of the day, combined with seventeen other leading Jesuits in West Germany to petition the pope: 'Holy Father, permit us to elect our future Superior General in the freedom that, from the beginning of the church, has always represented one of the basic rules of all Orders.'

The pope was irritated. If he could not demand blind obedience from Jesuits, from whom could he demand it? Had not the Order's founder, Ignatius Loyola said to his followers in his *Spiritual Exercises*: 'To arrive at the truth in all things, we ought always to be ready to believe that what seems to us white is black, if the hierarchical church so defines'? No, before they could have a new general, Jesuits had to stop dissenting from papal pronouncements. Only when he was assured that they had changed their ways and would vote for a general acceptable to him did he let them proceed. Even then, he took no chances. He personally opened the Thirty-Third General Congregation, the first pope to do so, in the Jesuit House on the Borgo Santo Spirito, near the Holy Office. His presence was less an honour than a threat. On the first ballot, they chose a moderate, the Dutchman, Father Piet Hans Kolvenbach.

Having sorted out the Jesuits, the Holy Father turned his attention to the biggest target of all.

Target: The Church in the United States of America

Apart from Holland, where there is almost total opposition to Catholic moral teaching and where ordinations to the priesthood have practically dried up, nowhere is the crisis more palpable than in the United States. The crisis, it should be noted, concerns structures not the spirit of the community which remains vibrant and hopeful.

In 1974, six years after Paul VI outlawed contraceptives, only 13 per cent of American Catholics agreed with him. All that Archbishop Bernadin, then head of the Bishops' Conference, could say was: 'Ethical values cannot be arrived at by counting noses.' There were signs, however, that Bernadin was not altogether happy at the prospect of an army made up of generals.

In 1986, Bishop James Malone of Youngstown, Ohio, outgoing president of the Bishops' Conference, admitted to 'a growing and dangerous disaffection between the Vatican and the US church'.

When, late in 1987, the Holy Father visited America for the second time, Archbishop Weakland of Milwaukee told him that from 1958 to 1987, church attendance in the States dropped from 75 per cent to 53 per cent.

Latest polls show that massive majorities of American Catholics actively favour contraception and remarriage after divorce. Only 14 per cent believe abortion should be illegal in all cases and 93 per cent believe they can be good Catholics while disagreeing with the pontiff on basic moral issues. The outlook for the American church remains stormy, and the squalls really began when John Paul disciplined Archbishop Hunthausen of Seattle. The archbishop was told in secret by the papal pro-nuncio, Pio Laghi, that he was being stripped of his authority in five key areas: moral teaching, laicization of priests, marriage annulments, liturgy and seminary training. An auxiliary, Donald Wuerl, ordained in Rome by John Paul II, was given plenary powers in his stead. Yet Hunthausen was no papal employee but as much successor of the apostles as the pontiff himself. Hence the Vatican's need to resort to these underhand tactics to contain him. John Paul acts as if *he* is Bishop of Seattle and Hunthausen is his deputy. Should the deputy displease him, he can be replaced. If and when the deputy gives proof of good behaviour, that is, of obeying every Vatican decree to the letter, he might be reinstated. There is little scope for local initiative.

In all this, the pope seems to be not only Bishop of Rome but also Bishop of the World. Benedict XIV said as much: 'The Pope is the principal priest in the whole Church who can take any local church from the jurisdiction of its bishop whenever he wishes.' There is logic to this; bishops take an oath not to serve the Church and religion but 'to maintain, defend, increase and advance the rights, honours, privileges and authority of their Lord the Pope'.

Most of Hunthausen's fellow-bishops sympathized with him but, as usual, they felt they had no choice but to line up behind the pope, even when he acted unjustly towards one of their number. Order is Catholicism's first priority.

Hunthausen was reinstated at the end of May 1987, and Wuerl was transferred to another post. This was after a United States Bishop's Commission, ordered by the Vatican, vouched for Hunthausen's orthodoxy, even though, 'unintentionally', their report said, others got the impression that he approved of 'a climate of permissiveness'. So the archbishop of a great diocese was disciplined by Rome because of wrong impressions taken by Catholic 'freewheelers'. In future, bishops are warned, they had better be careful not only about their orthodoxy but even about the impressions they give to people ill disposed.

It was also in 1986, in mid-March, that Ratzinger, the pope's right-hand man, deprived Father Charles E. Curran of his teaching licence. For John Paul, a theologian's job is simply to hand on decisions taken on high. Curran is candid in a profession where candour can endanger the species. He believes that a theologian has a sacred duty to 'evaluate and interpret' hierarchical decisions in the light of God's Word. Curran lost his teaching post at the Catholic University of Washington in 1987. Pope John XXIII laid it down at the start of Vatican II that the days of condemnation were over. And no theologian had been dismissed over an ethical issue since the Council. Ratzinger's claim that Curran is 'neither suitable nor eligible' to teach in a Catholic establishment was another warning shot to thinkers of an independent mind.

Ratzinger has also put it on record that loyal Catholics must obey not only defined teaching but also the entire ordinary magisterial teaching as expressed by pope and bishops. For practical purposes, this means as expressed by the pope. The case of Archbishop Hunthausen proves bishops have no independence. In plain English: Bishops and theologians can only serve truth by obeying the pope. Tragically, loyal dissent, in the Vatican as in the Kremlin, is a contradiction in terms.

Another American 'first' was the case of forty-one-year-old Father Terence Sweeney, a Jesuit from Los Angeles. With his superior's encouragement, he polled the 312 American Catholic bishops on four questions relating to priestly celibacy and women priests. Of the 145 who replied, thirty-five were in favour of priests marrying in view of the shortage of vocations. Eleven said they would like to see women ordained.

Sweeney was told more than once by Ratzinger and the Jesuit General in Rome: burn your researches or leave the Order. Sweeney, twenty-four years a Jesuit, felt his only option was to leave. How could he burn the truth? What value was obedience without reason or truth to back it up? That sort of obedience, he claimed, 'is not consonant with human dignity'.

It is hard to see why a distinguished Jesuit should be forced out not for doctrinal or moral deviation but for making public the attitudes of bishops who had freely responded to his enquiries. The pope seems terrified of anyone knowing what bishops, *his* bishops, really think. This image springs to mind: the pope thinks of bishops as top civil servants. They do not make policy; they carry it out. Whatever personal opinions they have, they should keep to themselves. He *alone* speaks for the church.

The impression was received that one bishop disagreeing with the pope is bad enough but thirty-five in one country is intolerable. Such a revelation shatters the façade of total agreement which is the pride of Catholicism. The Church of Silence exists this side of the Iron Curtain, too, and it includes prelates who do not wish to go the way of Hunthausen.

It is hard to escape this conclusion: bishops are too frightened of the pope to say what they really believe is best for the church and their dioceses. No means exist to express dissent, anyway. The same situation exists at parish level. Pastors counsel their flock in liberal attitudes but only in the confessional. Not for them the role of public martyrs. Better, they believe, to be quiet and survive. But where is the witness to Gospel truth? And what is becoming of this great institution that, at so many levels of responsibility, is living a lie?

Two Giant Systems Clash Head-On

The chief reason the pope has targeted the American church for his missiles is this: an absolute monarchy of the Vatican variety is in direct conflict with the basic ideals of the first and greatest republic in the world. America prides itself on being the land of the free; and certain forms of freedom are alien to the pontiff's notion of Christian faith. For him, Catholic truth is absolute and obedience to it a vital necessity. He, as God's Anointed Spokesman, is obliged to demand instant and unwavering obedience of all, from the humblest parishioner to the most astute theologian.

History reveals a stark contrast between the Catholic and the American ideal of freedom. It is this contrast that underlies the Vatican's deep distrust of the American church.

First, the church.

In 1520, Leo X condemned Luther for daring to say that burning heretics is against the will of God. Gregory XIII commemorated with joy the Massacre of St Bartholomew on the night of 24 August 1572 when thousands of Huguenot Protestants died. Clement VIII attacked the Edict of Nantes in 1598 because it gave equality of citizenship to all, regardless of their religion. The Edict was revoked in 1685 to the church's delight: within three years, fifty thousand Protestant families left France, scattered further abroad, said Voltaire, than even the Jews. Innocent X had meanwhile condemned the Peace of Westphalia for daring to grant toleration to all citizens, regardless of their religion or lack of it. In every instance and over centuries, the Catholic church proudly proclaimed its dogma of religious intolerance.

In the nineteenth century, politics in Europe altered profoundly, but not Catholic teaching. Church and state, the popes said, were indissolubly united as in a Christian consummated marriage. Liberty was un-Christian; law and order was the overriding aim. Pontiff after pontiff attacked freedom with the vehemence that twentieth-century popes have reserved for contraception. They seemed afraid that government of the people by the people for the people would lead to similar demands in the church.

Gregory XVI, in *Mirari vos* of August 1832, described liberty of conscience as a mad opinion. Religious liberty was said to flow from 'the most fetid fount of indifferentism'. He condemned freedoms of worship, the press, assembly and education as a filthy sewer full of 'heretical vomit'.

Pius IX kept up the onslaught. In *Quanta Cura* in 1864, he attacked freedom of religion and equated it with the liberty of death. Among the propositions condemned in his Syllabus of Errors was this: 'In the present day it is no longer expedient that the Catholic religion should be the only religion of the state, to the exclusion of all other forms of worship.'

Leo XIII who followed him realized that the world was changing. Yet in encyclical after encyclical he defined liberty of religion entirely in medieval terms. The church has a right to a *monopoly* of religion in any Catholic state. Therefore, error must not be granted freedom to spread itself. Freedom and truth are incompatible. Truth must be enforced by the state at the church's command wherever possible. Each state, he insisted, must still profess the true faith as its official policy and tolerate the least possible liberty of conscience for the least possible length of time.

This opportunism, this grudging approach to freedom of religion, is at the exact opposite pole to the American experience.

In 1492, owing to a navigational error, Columbus landed on the Bahamas before journeying south. Had he sailed due west and discovered the North American mainland, the United States might have had a religious history similar to that of Mexico, Brazil and Argentina. As it was, the first immigrants to North America, themselves victims of persecution in the Old World, brought with them traditional European notions of the relations of church and state. They, too, believed intolerance was a very great virtue. Hence, in New England, there was a single establishment; religion and government were almost indistinguishable. Strict religious orthodoxy was imposed, and church attendance was compulsory. It was a situation that could not last. The subjects of the colonies were too disparate in belief for any one system, usually right-wing Protestant, to prevail. The religious minorities, hounded in Europe, were determined to build not just a new earth but a new heaven in which all men were equal. In the New World, even religion was democratized, something that Europe had not known since the more enlightened days of the Roman Empire.

Providence, later Rhode Island, and Maryland started the break-up of the ancient religious intolerance. In Rhode Island, for the first time in modern history, there was a complete separation of church and state and freedom of speech for everyone. This extraordinary experiment was not only bold, it succeeded. Maryland, founded by Lord Baltimore as a refuge for Catholics, also opened its doors to all comers, in spite of Jesuits attempting to make his Lordship toe the medieval line.

By 1660 the liberalizing tendencies were strong in most of the colonies; a distinctively American approach was discernible. In the eighteenth century, with national independence came complete religious freedom. For example, in 1786, Jefferson drew up for Virginia a statute of religious freedom, the first ever passed by a popular assembly. It said:

> *Be it therefore enacted by the General Assembly,* That no man shall be compelled to frequent or support any religious worship, place or ministry . . . but that all men shall be free to profess, and by arguments to maintain their opinions in matters of religion and that the same shall in no wise diminish, enlarge or affect their civil capability.

In 1787 this freedom was built into article VI of the Federal Constitution: 'No religious test shall ever be required as a qualification to any office or public trust under the United States.' In 1791 came the First Amendment: 'Congress may not interfere with freedom of religion, speech, meeting, and petition. Congress shall make no law respecting an establishment of religion or prohibiting the free exercise thereof.'

These historic declarations mark the final break with the religious attitudes of the Old World. The United States expressed unhappiness with the notion of 'toleration'; it desired religious liberty and equality for all its citizens. Tolerance was judged a form of hypocrisy; it is an insult to those said to be tolerated. It implies they are something less than equal. Besides, what is tolerated today might not be tolerated tomorrow. Above all, the Constitution, in Jefferson's words, built 'a wall of separation between church and state'. Anyone, be he Catholic or Protestant, who attempted to make holes in that wall or smash it altogether had no right to call himself an American.

To Rome's amazement, the Catholic church flourished under a regime judged by Rome to be hostile to the most basic tenets of the faith. Gregory XVI (1831–46) said: 'In no part of the world do I feel myself so much the pope as in the United States.' And Pius IX, in whose reign Catholics in the United States numbered 6½ million, delivered the famous line: 'America is the only country in the world where I could be king.' It seems he had not noticed that the Americans had lost the taste for monarchy way back in 1776 with the Declaration of Independence.

Around Pius IX was woven the most intriguing might-have-been in papal history. When menaced in the Vatican by the growth of Italian nationalism, Pio Nono received two incredibly generous offers of help.

In the year 1863, the British Prime Minister, Lord John Russell, wrote to Cardinal Antonelli, suggesting that in an emergency the island of Malta might be a suitable haven for his Holiness. There he 'might be surrounded by his chief cardinals and most trustworthy counsellors. He would not be asked to subscribe to any conditions repugnant to his conscience.' The British government would guarantee him complete protection.

There is no proof that the pontiff gave this offer serious consideration.

Not long afterwards, when the heavens turned darker still, a top Vatican aide approached Rufus King, the American minister accredited to the Papal States. The one place, the aide said, where his Holiness would feel safe was in 'the great Republic of America'. The reply, when it came, was magnanimous. 'Our country is the home of civil and religious liberty as well as the refuge to all who have fled from political and other troubles in the Old World. His Holiness, should he see fit to go to the United States, would, no doubt, meet that kind of welcome and be left to pursue, unquestioned and unmolested, his great work as Head of the Catholic Church.'

Two American destroyers set sail from Lisbon to Civitavecchia and stood by to convey his Holiness to America. Alas, he never went aboard.

In 1867, with Garibaldi's small force in premature action only fifteen miles from the Vatican, the pope, still defiant, said: 'Yes, I hear them coming.' Pointing to the Crucifix: 'This will be my artillery.'

Mankind was, therefore, not to see a pope living in a republic, a second Avignon in the New World. The States lost the most potentially lucrative tourist attraction ever but, more than that, the papacy lost its chance to function in a modern democracy.

Back in the Old World, it still stood out for a strict medieval theocracy, the union of church and state under which the state guaranteed the Catholic church dominion in the religious field.

This was *always* a problem for American Catholics. For instance, Cardinal James Gibbons of Baltimore had no hesitation in condemning the Spanish Inquisition. He claimed to speak for all American Catholics when he wrote: 'Our Catholic forefathers suffered so much during the last three centuries for the sake of liberty of conscience that they would rise to condemn us if we made ourselves the advocates or defenders of religious persecution.'

These republican sentiments did not go down well in Rome. They were against traditional Catholicism. Cardinal Gibbons tried to clear himself of the charge of heresy by means of a distinction invented by a French bishop some years before. In a perfect world (thesis), the church's traditional teaching of church–state relations would apply. In an imperfect world (hypothesis), as in modern America, the church was reconciled to accepting, under sufferance, the *status quo*. Maybe, by this subterfuge, the cardinal stopped the Vatican condemning the American Constitution, as it had condemned all the European constitutions, though the latter were far less radical.

The cardinal's distinction may have been accepted in the Vatican; it did not please Americans. They did not look on the American way of life as inferior to the European. For them, it was a distinct improvement. As Emerson said, America had a special mission: 'To liberate, to abolish Kingcraft, priestcraft, caste, monopoly; to pull down the gallows, to burn up the bloody statute book.' Further, the implication of the cardinal's words was frightening: if conversions multiplied in the United States, his Eminence or his successor would have to try to impose a medieval regime on America in violation of its Constitution. The myth grew of the ineligibility of Catholics for high office. This myth sank the presidential ambitions of Al Smith, Democratic Governor of New York State, in 1928. It nearly destroyed the hopes of John F. Kennedy thirty years later.

Kennedy was accused of wanting to demolish the wall separating church and state. He was accused, sometimes sincerely, of being as much a prisoner of a religious system as Khrushchev was of a political system. Kennedy seemed to be facing a clear choice between being a 'good' Catholic, as it was traditionally understood, and a good American. Thirty years ago, when all hung in the balance, he declared:

> I believe in an America where the separation of Church and State is absolute – where no Catholic prelate would tell the President (should he be a Catholic) how to act and no Protestant minister would tell his parishioners for whom to vote . . . an America that is officially neither Catholic, Protestant nor Jewish – where no public official either requests or accepts instruction in public policy from . . . any ecclesiastical source . . . where there is no Catholic vote, no anti-Catholic vote, no *bloc* voting of any kind . . . and where religious liberty is so indivisible that an attack against one Church is treated as an attack against all. . . . I am not the Catholic candidate for President, I am the Democratic Party's candidate for President who happens to be a Catholic. I do not speak for my Church on public matters and my Church does not speak for me.

It was a fine expression of the American ideal. Kennedy had the best theological advice. He was no doubt told that the Christian state was a fourth-century product engineered by Constantine. The early church knew nothing of it, nor did the Bible. Still, Kennedy was probably not fully aware that he was contradicting centuries of Catholic teaching. Even that wise and far-seeing Pope, Leo XIII, said that politically 'it is always urgent, indeed, the chief preoccupation, to think best how to serve the interests of Catholicism'. In every election, he went on, Catholics are obliged to vote for those 'who pledge themselves to the Catholic cause and never prefer to them anyone hostile to [the Catholic] religion . . . which is the only true religion'. So, according to the pope, there *is* a *bloc* vote, the Catholic *bloc* vote for Catholic candidates; and an attack on Catholicism is *only* an attack on Catholicism. After the Second World War, Pius XII was ready to excommunicate any Catholic who gave his vote to a communist candidate instead of to a Catholic.

In view of this, Kennedy's election was a triumph not for the Catholic church but for American democracy. He had still to prove both before and after his election that he was not in the pope's pocket and he was quite prepared to say No to the entire Catholic episcopate of America.

Kennedy was fortunate to be campaigning for the presidency during the pontificate of John XXIII, the least bigoted and most truly catholic pope in history.

The Dilemma of Catholics Today

The dilemma of American Catholics today is simply the dilemma of most Catholics writ large. They live under two conflicting ideologies. Patriotism and religion have little in common. At the time of the Second Vatican Council, Catholics ceased to feel this. The Council was a second spring, a chance for liberty and free discussion to blossom and enrich the church as they enriched the state. But with Paul VI and John Paul II the second spring died out.

In the state, a Catholic rejoices in openness, complete freedom of worship, democracy. He takes it for granted that freedom leads to a deepening of the truth. He is used to his leaders having to present themselves for his approval. He can vote them in, he can vote them out. He demands press conferences, freedom of information, an unfettered press that is like a second government.

In the church, a Catholic has to put up with total secrecy and lack of accountability. There are no choices, no elections. No bishop or pope is, as far he is concerned, voted in or out. He has to accept what he is given. In the church, there are no press conferences, no checks and balances, no explanations. The control from the top is absolute. The impression given is that freedom and discussion lead to the dilution of truth.

It would be foolish to look on the pope and the Curia as the villains of the piece. They, too, are victims of a past unknown or, at least, unacknowledged.

John Paul sees himself as the great champion of Catholic truth. It is absolute. He can no more doubt it in all its ramifications than he can doubt the existence of God. He feels he *has* to be harsh to dissidents in order to be kind to the mass of Catholics who have a right to the fullness of truth. This is why he is prepared to plead for freedom everywhere *except* in his own church. *Every* form of dissent on the part of theologians, like Küng and Curran, even of bishops, like Hunthausen, must be suppressed. A scholar is as likely to be silenced for proposing that priests should be allowed to marry or women be ordained as for denying the divinity of Christ.

In his travels, John Paul presents the papacy as the champion of truth and the rights of man. He takes it for granted that popes have never contradicted one another on essentials or deviated from Gospel truth.

This part on truth aims to show by numerous illustrations that these assumptions are false. Apart from the fact that the tenth- and fifteenth-century papacy was *the* heresy, *the* denial of everything Jesus stood for, many popes have made astonishing errors. They have repeatedly contradicted one another and the Gospel. Far from championing the dignity of man, they have times without number withheld from Catholics and non-Catholics the most elementary rights. The pope's House on the Corner is proof of that.

History explodes the myth of a papacy lily-white in the matter of truth. In an age of barbarism, the popes led the pack; in an age of enlightenment, they trailed the field. And their record was worst when, contrary to the Gospel, they tried to impose the truth by force.

TEN

The Imposition
of Truth

POPE INNOCENT III was seated in his throne room, a mixture of excitement and wrath. In front of him, an aide was holding up a white Cistercian habit. It was rent, front and back, with a lance and was stained with blood. 'This, Holiness, is the habit of Brother Peter of Castelnau.' The pontiff corrected his aide solemnly: '*Saint* Peter of Castelnau.'

That tenth day of March 1208 when Innocent canonized Brother Peter, he also delivered his Bull of Anathema against the heretics of Languedoc. It was they, he decided, who had murdered his saintly ambassador. Rising to his feet, he intoned: 'Death to the heretics.'

A Bloody Crusade

Things, of course, were not as simple as the pope made out. There can be no doubt that he used Peter's death as a pretext for doing something he had wanted to do for a long time.

For a century, heresy had flourished in the beautiful feudal land known as Languedoc, that south-east corner of France between the Rhône and the mountains, with its capital Toulouse. Innocent was well aware that the aberration of these Catharists or Albigensians, named after their stronghold of Albi, was due to the corruption of the clergy. He even wrote:

> Throughout this region, the prelates are the laughing stock of the laity. But the root of all this evil lies in the Archbishop of Narbonne. This man knows no other God but money and keeps a purse where his heart should be. During the ten years that he has held office he has not once visited his diocese . . . where one may observe Regular monks and canons who have cast aside their habits, taken wives or mistresses and are living on usury.

Contemporary accounts agree that in Languedoc, as in many other places, abbots and bishops lived dissolutely. They gambled and swore;

they heard matins in bed, gossiped during the divine office on the rare occasions they went to chapel, excommunicated at whim anyone who crossed them, charged a fee for everything from holy orders to illicit marriages and cancelled legitimate wills in order to pocket the proceeds. In contrast, the Albigensians had many holy men and women. These *perfecti* shunned marriage and all worldly pleasures. Lean, pale, long-haired, clad in black, they were greeted with joy wherever they went for the sheer goodness of their lives. Mighty orators, closer to their flocks than were priests, their moral authority was immense. From them the believers, the *credentes*, received only one sacrament the *consolamentum*, or laying on of hands, in reconcilation, on the point of death.

They denied the dogmas and sacraments of Holy Mother Church, despised priests, called Rome the Whore of Babylon and its Bishop the Antichrist. They preached the equality of the sexes which Innocent said was contrary to the Bible. They also had their own vernacular version of the Scriptures which they actually read. For this alone, the pope called them heretics worthy of death.

The Albigensians seem to have preached a dualism. The evil God of the Old Testament was responsible for the material world which was the source of corruption and death. Jesus was the God of the world of the spirit. This is why they hated Catholic ritual. Images, relics, holy communion, the cross itself reeked of the dying world of matter. The body was evil, and sex by which bodies were multiplied was evil, too. The forbidden fruit of the Garden of Eden was sexual pleasure. Pregnancy was a sin; a pregnant woman had a devil inside her, and should she die before giving birth she inevitably perished. Marriage was a state of sin; sex in marriage was no better than incest. So great was their hatred of the body that suicide, the *endura*, was a heroic act of virtue, the way to heaven.

It is difficult to be sure what the Albigensians really believed since they left almost no documentary evidence behind. We have only the word of biased inquisitors who, like the pope, wished them all dead. It is possible they were reacting against priests who pretended to be celibate while living unchastely and making a fortune out of relics.

Innocent, who thought of himself as 'the Foundation of All Christianity', ordered the new saint's blood-stained habit to be shown in every church in Languedoc to promote a new Crusade. It was directed not against the Turks who held the Holy Land but against disciples of Christ who had the gall to deny the pope's authority. Do they not know, he asked, that without me there is no church, no Rock, no faith, no salvation? The new Crusaders would enjoy all the privileges of knights who went to Jerusalem. Innocent, like Muhammed, combined religion and war. By killing Albigensians, he promised, they would have the highest place in heaven.

The real Crusades had aroused enthusiasm ever since Peter the Hermit answered Urban II's call in 1096. A Frenchman from Amiens, small, lean, raven-haired, with a grey beard that fell to the clasp of his belt, Peter preached the Crusade to the poor. Walter the Penniless, a knight straight out of *Don Quixote*, joined him and they went by donkey at the head of a vast army that travelled on foot or on horseback or in donkey carts, as well armed as grasshoppers.

The journey from Cologne, through Hungary and Belgrade, to Constantinople took one hundred days. It was an epic march, full of hardship and horror; there were tales of babies being cooked and eaten. At every town, the children asked: 'Is this Jerusalem, Daddy?' Though ten thousand fell in one battle on the way, thirty thousand reached the Bosporus in July. There, on 21 October, they were hacked to pieces by the Turks. Peter the Hermit was one of the few survivors. When the army of Christian knights arrived in the following spring, they found, on the outskirts of Nicomedia and Civitol, nothing but mountains of bleached bones. 'Oh, with what severed heads and bones the borders of the sea were lined.' The French mixed the bones with lime, so that Peter the Hermit's pilgrims ended up in the very walls of the Crusaders' castles.

Over a century had passed when, in response to Innocent III's fresh appeal, whole towns and villages in Germany, unable to take the Cross, stripped themselves naked and ran in silence around the streets. It was a time of madness. Four years hence, in 1212, thousands of French boys and girls were to be inspired by a shepherd lad, Stephen of Vendôme. They left their homes without maps, guides or food, to travel to Marseilles. When asked where they were heading, they replied: 'Jerusalem.' Parents did their best to lock up their little ones, but they ran away. Unfortunately, the waters of the Mediterranean did not part like the Red Sea. Many, invited on board boats, were sold as slaves off the coast of Sardinia to the Saracens.

About this time, twenty thousand German children were enlisted by a boy named Nicholas. They began the journey to the Holy Land by crossing the Alps into Italy. Many dropped dead on the way; a few returned to tell the tale that became the legend of the Pied Piper of Hamelin.

No madness of this period matched the pope's. True, he had tried for four years to get rid of the Albigensians by more Christian means. In 1205 he had sent them Dominic, soon to found the Order of Preachers. 'I have preached to you,' Dominic said, after much effort. 'I begged you with tears. But, as we say in Spain, "Where a blessing fails, a big stick will do the trick". Now we shall arouse princes and prelates against you.' From then on, he promised, Christ would give them nothing but slavery and death.

Innocent had also sent to Languedoc Peter of Castelnau and Brother Raoul. Brother Peter had accused the lord of this vast land, Raymond IV, Count of Toulouse, of aiding and abetting the heretics. He was ordered to root them out. This was no small task, seeing that heresy had thrived on clerical corruption for four generations. Albigensians made up half of the population of the Midi. Was Raymond expected to burn them in their thousands? Brother Peter, soon to be canonized, believed so. He excommunicated Raymond for dereliction of duty and encouraged the *seigneurs de Provence* to rebel against their lord. 'He who deposes you', Brother Peter declared in his interdict, 'will be accounted holy; he who strikes you dead will earn a blessing from God.' Raymond hastened to assure his Holiness of his wholehearted support.

Next day, as the papal party was about to cross the Rhône at Saint-Gilles, one of Raymond's officers ran Brother Peter through with a lance. This soldier was never tried or sentenced. It was to the pope's advantage to blame the entire district for the crime.

Innocent's 'Crusade' was a landmark in the history of Christianity. The head of the church ordered and masterminded a war against fellow-Christians in a traditionally Christian land. Conversion was replaced by extermination. Yet orthodox and unorthodox lived so closely together that it was impossible to separate them. In striking opposition to Jesus' parables, wheat and tares were to be burned together.

Violence in Christian Tradition

In Catholic tradition, violence has had a chequered career. In fact, nowhere is there clearer evidence of the church changing its mind than in its teaching on war.

From the beginning, the church had a profound sense of the sanctity of human life. Shedding blood was a grievous sin. This was why Christians opposed gladiatorial combat. The army, too, was a forbidden calling. Christians like Maximilian preferred to die rather than to kill. 'I cannot fight in war,' he said simply. 'I cannot do wrong. I am a Christian.' While war and the use of force were necessary to preserve Rome, Christians felt unable to join in. 'The world', said Tertullian, 'may need its Caesars, but the Emperor can never be a Christian, nor a Christian ever be the Emperor.'

Christians considered themselves, like Jesus, messengers of peace; in no circumstances could they be agents of death. Even when they joined the army, or soldiers were converted, they were forbidden by their faith to fight, except by prayer and sacrifice.

Then Constantine defeated Maxentius at the Milvian Bridge under the sign of the cross. Being converted, he had the nails that crucified

Christ built into his helmet and his horse's bit. To Christians of an earlier age, no greater blasphemy could have been imagined; now Christians were part of the establishment with property and a position to defend. A bloodthirsty warrior was their chief bishop and commander-in-chief. They ceased being pacifists and beat their ploughshares into swords.

It is true that emperors and generals had to do penance if their hands were stained with blood, even in a just cause. But the old principles were relaxed. The same relaxation was to be seen in the enforcement of religion. The church was originally against the use of force to make converts or repress heresy. But Leo the Great (440–61) was to commend an emperor for torturing and executing heretics on behalf of the church. By then, even Augustine had approved not killing or torturing heretics but helping them find the right path with a good stout blow or two. Soon Christians were openly pleased that theirs was the only religion *not* persecuted. Only the abhorrence of bloodshed prevented them killing heretics.

This abhorrence gradually weakened. More and more Christians joined the army, now prepared to fight and die. Whereas up to the year 175 there was not a single Christian soldier, in 416, by an edict of Theodosius, only Christians were allowed to enlist. It was left to the clergy – bishops and priests who ministered at the altar of the Crucified – to uphold the church's ancient aversion to the shedding of blood. The clergy alone created a kind of zone and witness of peace in the midst of war.

Though violence was now, as it were, in the bloodstream of Christianity, after the barbarian hordes were converted and more or less civilized, a period of peace followed. In what are called the Dark Ages, religious intolerance seems to have been forgotten, perhaps through disinterest. Until Christianity came under the influence of its deadliest rival, Islam.

The speed with which the new creed spread was even faster than the alleged miraculous spread of Christianity. It blasted its way through the ancient Christian lands of Africa, Asia and Spain. It proclaimed a sensuous heaven and a horrible hell. Its fatalism – 'What is written, is written' – encouraged bravery on the battlefield. From there, a devout follower of Allah was transported, drenched with his enemy's blood, to heaven. 'The sword', Mohammed said, 'is the key of heaven and hell.' One drop of blood shed in God's cause was better than prayer and fasting. As Gibbon summarized it, 'whoever falls in battle, his sins are forgiven; at the day of judgement his wounds shall be resplendent as vermilion, and odoriferous as musk; and the loss of his limbs shall be supplied by the wings of angels and cherubim'.

In Paradise, as Santayana wrote in his *Little Essays on Religion*, the warrior sits 'in well-watered gardens with Mohamed, clad in green silks, drinking delicious sherbets, and transfixed by the gazelle-like glance of some young girl, all innocence and fire'. Gibbon's picture in the eighth volume of *Decline and Fall* is far less puritanical.

> Seventy-two *Houris*, or black-eyed girls of resplendent beauty, blooming youth, virgin purity, and exquisite sensitivity, will be created for the use of the meanest believer; a moment of pleasure will be prolonged to a thousand years, and his faculties will be increased a hundred-fold to render him worthy of felicity.

The Prophet was silent about how many magnificent male attendants would be created for the women fortunate enough to enter Paradise. Maybe he feared the envy of their husbands in a male chauvinist world.

Islam's advance in the West was only broken at Poitiers by Charlemagne's grandfather, Charles Martel. From then on, the martial spirit of Islam passed into Christianity. Muhammad replaced Christ as 'hero'. The Prophet had been a head of state, a commander of armies, an administrator of justice; Jesus had done nothing but preach and die on a cross. The ideal Christian was no longer the lonely ascetic monk but the warrior with the bloodied sword, taking revenge on the infidel who had dared capture and desecrate the Holy Land. Now, in mockery of the Gospel, Christian knights were incited to kill for Jesus' sake. Papal indulgences matched exactly Islam's guarantee of perpetual bliss for the dying warrior. Christianity, by a kind of perverse miracle, had inherited the concept of *Jihad*, the Holy War.

For two centuries, pulpits thundered out not the peace of Christ but the duty of war against the infidel. And so, on hill and battlefield, the Crusader dug his cross-shaped sword in the earth and prayed Christ to be with him in the slaughter of his enemies. If he died, the pope had assured him a high place in an, unfortunately, foodless, cheerless and angelically chaste heaven. That, at any rate, was where Islam scored.

On the way to the Holy Land, Crusaders turned their attention to infidels nearer home. The Jews had been the first to desecrate the Holy Land by torturing and crucifying Christ. The Crusaders offered them baptism or death. They would have known by heart the phrases of St John Chrysostom, the fourth-century Golden-Mouthed Doctor of the Church. 'I hate the Jews,' he said, over and over. No pardon is possible for the odious assassinators of the Lord. 'God hates the Jews and always did.' Hence, Jews, old and young, male and female, fell to the Crusader's sword. One thrust and heaven was already promised the killer.

In the year 1096 half of the Jews of Worms were slaughtered as the Crusaders passed through the town. The rest fled to the bishop's residence for protection. He agreed to save them, on condition that they asked to be baptized. The Jews retired to consider their decision. When the doors of the audience chamber were opened, all eight hundred Jews inside were dead. Some were decapitated; fathers had killed their babes before turning their knives on their wives and themselves; a groom had slain his bride. The first century tragedy of Masada was repeated everywhere in Germany and, later, throughout France. When the Crusaders took the great prize, Jerusalem, one of their first acts was to set the synagogue alight with all the Jews inside.

Lecky, in his two-volume classic *History of European Morals* (1911) wrote: 'It would be impossible to conceive a more complete transformation than Christianity had thus undergone, and it is melancholy to contrast with its aspect during the Crusades the impression it had once more justly made upon the world, as the spirit of gentleness and of peace encountering the spirit of violence and war.' The church was fully converted to the Roman Empire. The ministers – pope, bishops, priests – denied the beatitudes by proclaiming bloodshed as its official teaching. The ancient creed that upheld the sanctity of life was abandoned.

In spite of these cruel precedents, Innocent's Crusade against the Albigensians was in a class of its own. Under the banner of the cross, this was to be the bloodiest campaign of the Middle Ages. His soldiers virtually invented the scorched-earth policy. For the first time, they went in for indiscriminate slaughter. And as each crime was reported back to him Innocent urged them on to more strenuous efforts in Christ's name. The end was sublime; it justified *all* means. It was so much easier to murder heretics than to convert the clergy to a blameless life.

Let Murder Commence

When the King of France refused to lead the Crusade, Innocent made his legate, Arnald-Amalric, Cistercian General of Cîteaux, its commander-in-chief. Knights and retainers, peasants and burghers, as well as mobs of mercenaries, responded to the call to arms. On offer was a special indulgence for a mere forty-day service and, possibly, some valuable land in Languedoc besides. There were twenty thousand cavalry and almost ten times that number of foot-soldiers. There were feudal bishops and nobles, dukes and counts, including Raymond Count of Toulouse.

Only a week before, the Count had made his peace with the church. At the great door of Saint-Gilles Cathedral, he was stripped, this lord of the lands, to the waist like a penitent and made to swear on holy relics to obey the church in everything. To prove his orthodoxy, he pledged himself to slaughter all the heretics around.

From Montpellier, the army marched to Béziers, an Albigensian stronghold. The town was well fortified, though water was in short supply in that hot dry summer.

The twenty-second day of July, the Feast of Mary Magdalene, was a providential day, according to the legate, to begin the siege. He called on the Catholics in the town to hand over the two hundred or so known heretics; if they did, they would be spared. The townsfolk decided to stand together against these foreigners.

They might have held out for months had not a group of daredevils left the security of the walls to taunt some mercenaries lazing in a field. Too late, the youngsters realized they had strayed into danger. They raced back to town with the mercenaries right behind them.

The townsfolk retreated in confusion to the cathedral and the great churches of St Jude and St Mary Magdalene. The invading knights joined the mercenaries and they swept along, looting and murdering as they went. The command went out from Arnald: 'Kill them all; the Lord will look after His own.'

Behind locked doors of St Mary Magdalene's, the clergy tolled the bell while celebrants vested in black for a requiem. The churches, places of sanctuary from time immemorial, were crammed. In Mary Magdalene alone there were seven thousand women, children and the elderly. To the sound of priests chanting mass was added that of axes splitting the timber of the doors. When the doors gave way, the only noise in church was the Latin of the liturgy and the babbling of babies in their mother's arms.

The invaders, singing lustily *Veni Sancte Spiritus*, spared no one, not even the babies. The last to be cut down were two priests in the sanctuary. One held on high a crucifix, the other the chalice. With a clang, the chalice hit the stone floor, and Christ's blood mingled with that of the people of Béziers. It was, said Lea, in his book *The Inquisition in the Middle Ages*, 'a massacre almost without parallel in European history'.

When it was over, the mercenaries were told by those in command that the loot had to be handed over to finance the Crusade. They took revenge by firing the town. Everything went up in flames. The famous cathedral of Master Gervais cracked down the middle with the heat. All that was left of Béziers was a smouldering heap under which all the citizens lay dead.

In the cool of evening, the monk Arnald settled down to write to his superior. 'Today, your Highness, twenty thousand citizens were put to the sword, regardless of age or sex.' That was unusual. After a siege, women and children were spared, and especially the clergy who had immunity. Slaughtering babies was bad enough, but it was an unspeakable crime to cut priests down as they celebrated the ritual sacrifice of Calvary. Blood-lust had taken hold of the pope's Crusaders and was never to relax its grip. It has been reckoned that in the last and most savage persecution under Emperor Diocletian about two thousand

Christians perished, worldwide. In the first vicious incident of Pope Innocent's Crusade ten times that number of people were slaughtered. Not all were Albigensians, by any means. It comes as a shock to discover that, at a stroke, a pope killed far more Christians than Diocletian.

Innocent was deeply moved by Arnald's letter. He thanked God for His great mercy. Never once did he question the legitimacy of a monk slaughtering heretics and the Catholics who harboured them. It seemed right to defend Christ's truth by methods that led to Christ's crucifixion.

From Béziers, the Crusaders marched to Carcassonne. It took them only a couple of weeks to take the fortress, because its commander walked into a trap when suing for peace. Arnald simply imprisoned him. In writing to the pope about this second victory, the legate apologized profusely for the fact that no lives had been taken. Another town going up in flames, he explained, would have deprived the expeditionary force of funds. He allowed the inhabitants to leave – 'Naked but for the sins they wore' – with one day's safe conduct. If they were recaptured, they would be killed.

In place of the Count of Carcassonne, the legate chose a Norman knight, Simon de Montfort. Middle-aged, de Montfort had fought gallantly in the Fourth Crusade in 1199. His new job of keeping the peace was formidable. Most troops were leaving him after completing their regulation forty days. They went with their minds at rest, knowing that all their sins had been forgiven and they were guaranteed entry into Paradise. Behind them were two great victories but not a single convert.

With a depleted but closer-knit force, de Montfort felt forced to treat the entire land as heretical. On Catholic principles, he was free to exterminate as many people as he could. The legate discouraged him from taking prisoners.

At Bram in 1210, de Montfort having captured the castle, did not slay the prisoners. Dead men make bad messengers. He ordered his soldiers to lop off their noses and gouge out their eyes. One man was allowed to keep one eye to guide the rest. Each of them put a hand on the shoulder of the fellow in front and, like a giant bloodied whining insect, they wended their way to Cabaret to put the fear of God into the encampment there.

In June of the same year, de Montfort laid siege to Minerve. When it surrendered, de Montfort ordered 140 *perfecti* out of town into a meadow. No charge was read out; there was no trial or sentence. Wood had been gathered; it was lit. Soldiers made ready to force the heretics into the flames like infected swine. But as the obtuse Cistercian chronicler Vaux de Cernay remarked: 'There was no need for our men to cast them in; nay, all were so obstinate in their wickedness as to cast

themselves in of their own free will.' The heretics went calmly, prayer-
fully, to their deaths. The air was thick with the odour of burning flesh,
but from the victims not a scream or a cry.

This, the first great burning of heretics, was done under the church's
eyes and with her blessing.

After this, the Crusaders moved to Lavaur. The count, Roger, was
hanged and eighty of his knights were burned. The count's sister,
noted for her charity, was tossed alive into a well and buried under
stones. Afterwards, 400 *perfecti* were led out of town and burned on a
vast funeral pyre. Vaux de Cernay put on record for the pope's benefit:
'Cum ingenti gaudio combusserunt', 'They set them alight with
immense joy'. They were relaxed, knowing they had his Holiness's
blessing.

Only one of the *perfecti* renounced his faith. They were pacifists.
They died with dignity, without complaining. The Lavaur massacre
was the most brutal of this long Crusade.

The pope was kept informed at every stage. He opened one letter to
de Montfort with 'praise and thanks to God for that which He hath
mercifully wrought through thee and through these others whom zeal
for the orthodox faith hath kindled to this work against His most
pestilential enemies'.

It is beyond doubt that Innocent sanctioned in advance everything
done by this soldier whom he was to call in the Fourth Lateran Council
in the year 1215 'this gallant Christian gentleman'.

The Lesson of the Crusade

Innocent and de Montfort died within months of each other in the
following year. In 1226, after eighteen years in which hundreds of
thousands perished, the Crusade was over. In a profound sense, it was
never over. For all the fine words at the Lateran Council, the church
had suffered her most terrible defeat.

Under Innocent, disobedience to any aspect of the papal system was
unforgivable. The lust-filled Archbishop of Narbonne was a paragon
compared with the *perfecti* who lived selflessly and died in the spirit of
Christ. Their chief crime was that they did not show the pope the
respect due to him as Vicar of Christ.

Innocent's Crusade reveals how deeply the church feels about
heresy and the lengths to which it will go to deal with it.

Another lesson of that period is that in Catholic tradition truth is
primarily verbal; its main concern is with orthodox formulas.
Innocent, in particular, never seemed to grasp that the deepest and
wickedest of heresies is the denial of the Gospel, the practical renunciation of the Sermon on the Mount. He had no qualms about using
Christ's name to do everything Christ objected to. In Innocent's view,

it was more wicked for the Albigensians to call him the Antichrist than for him to prove it by burning them, men, women and children in their thousands.

Innocent's achievements were illusory. Languedoc ended up a wasteland; the picturesque traditions of Provence were irrevocably destroyed. But heresy did not die; it went underground. So that the church not only lost her innocence; she lost the battle for the minds and hearts of the people.

Instead of asking God's forgiveness for unparalleled crimes, the papacy was now set firmly on the path of violence. In rooting out heresy in future, the church would need not one big army but small groups of equally ruthless men to travel over Christendom in search of unbelief, real or imagined. These men were called inquisitors. In the pope's name, they were responsible for the most savage and sustained onslaught on human decency in the history of the race.

The Long Reign of Terror

The terror began in earnest with Gregory IX, who ascended the papal throne in the year 1227. Count of Segni, member of Innocent III's Conti family, he was then over eighty years of age.

Two years later, at the Council of Toulouse in Languedoc, Gregory decreed that heretics had to be handed over to the secular arm for punishment. 'It is the duty of every Catholic', he said, 'to persecute heretics.'

Emperor Frederick, an unbeliever, became the ferocious advocate of orthodoxy to please the pope. Gregory approved all his anti-heretic legislation, adding cruel touches of his own. In the year 1232 he made his decisive move.

The Inquisition Is Born

He published a Bull establishing the Inquisition. Bishops were too lax and, in any case, they lacked the time and talent to do a thorough job. Heretics, that is, all opposed to any papal pronouncement, were to be handed over to the civil authorities for burning. If they repented, they were to be imprisoned for life. No pope ever took up the torch of terror with more enthusiasm.

In April 1233 he restricted inquisitors to members of the mendicant orders; soon, the Dominicans had the honour to themselves. The twenty-seventh day of July 1233 was a red-letter day for the pontiff: the first two full-time inquisitors were appointed – Peter Seila and William Arnald. They were the first in a long line of serene untroubled persecutors of the human race. As a curtain-raiser, in 1239, two years before Gregory died, the Dominican Robert le Bougre went to Champagne to investigate a bishop named Moranis. He was accused of allowing heretics to live and spread in his diocese. In one week Father Robert had put the whole town on trial. On 29 May he sent 180 people, including the bishop, to the stake.

This was a return to barbarism. As early as the year 384, a synod in Rome denounced the use of torture, and Gregory the Great in the sixth century ordered judges to ignore testimony given under duress. Even in the Dark Ages, Nicholas I had condemned torture as a violation of divine law.

Since Gregory VII, however, fanaticism had crept into the papacy. Since the pope cannot make a mistake, he must be blindly obeyed in all things, however trivial. Between 1200 and 1500 a series of papal laws did away with every shade of difference in belief and discipline. Innocent IV's contribution in his Bull *Ad extirpanda* was to allow the Inquisition to use torture. From then on, any disobedience *even in thought* was punishable. Bad thoughts threatened church unity which was built on loyalty to the Vicar of Christ.

History does not support the view that the Catholic church has always championed the rights of man. In the thirteenth century, it went so far as to teach what the early church condemned: *heretics have no rights*. They can be tortured without scruple. Like traitors to the state, heretics have put themselves outside the mercy of the law. They must be put to death.

Not one pope for over three centuries opposed this teaching which should therefore by rights be a permanent part of Catholic doctrine. By means of it, the Inquisition achieved unprecedented power. The result was wholesale intimidation of those who had no protection against the charge or even slightest suspicion of heresy.

Everything Is Permitted

To the medieval Inquisition, everything was permitted. The Dominican Inquisitors, being the pope's appointees, were subject to no one but God and his Holiness. They were outside the jurisdiction of bishops and of civil law. In the Papal States they were a law unto themselves, acting as prosecutors and judges. Their guiding principle was: 'Better for a hundred innocent people to die than for one heretic to go free.'

They operated arbitrarily and in total secrecy. Anyone present at the interrogation – victim, scribe, executioner – who broke his silence incurred a censure that only the pope could lift. The inquisitors, like the pope, could make no mistake and do no wrong.

By papal command, they were explicitly forbidden to have mercy on their victims. Pity was un-Christian where heresy was concerned. They were told that his Holiness would take on himself any guilt they incurred if they overstepped the mark inadvertently. Like the Nazi SS in the twentieth century, they were able to torture and destroy with a quiet mind because their superior officer – in this case, the pope – assured them that heretics were a dirty, diseased and contagious foe that must be purged at all costs and by all means.

Torture was freely used. Only a hundred years ago, there was on display in the pope's House on the Corner the Black Book, or *Libro Nero*, for the guidance of inquisitors. This manuscript in folio form was the charge of the Grand Inquisitor. Its popular name was the Book of the Dead. This is part of what it said:

> Either the person confesses and he is proved guilty from his own confession, or he does not confess and is equally guilty on the evidence of witnesses. If a person confesses the whole of what he is accused of, he is unquestionably guilty of the whole; but if he confesses only a part, he ought still to be regarded as guilty of the whole, since what he has confesses proves him to be capable of guilt as to the other points of the accusation. . . . Bodily torture has ever been found the most salutary and efficient means of leading to spiritual repentance. Therefore, the choice of the most befitting mode of torture is left to the Judge of the Inquisition, who determines according to the age, the sex, and the constitution of the party. . . . If, notwithstanding all the means employed, the unfortunate wretch still denies his guilt, he is to be considered as a victim of the devil: and, as such, deserves no compassion from the servants of God, nor the pity and indulgence of Holy Mother Church: he is a son of perdition. Let him perish among the damned.

It would be hard to find any document so contrary to the principles of natural justice. According to the Black Book, a child must betray his parents, a mother must betray her child. Not to do so is a 'sin against the Holy Office' and merits excommunication, that is, exclusion from the sacraments and, if there is no amendment, exclusion from heaven.

When applying torture, medieval inquisitors were forbidden to mutilate or kill. Naturally, accidents happened. Arms and legs were often broken, fingers and toes wrenched off. One victim lost two fingers; this was not sufficient grounds for interrupting the investigation.

The rule, as specified by papal decree, was: Torture may only be used once. Since no time-limit was specified, no one knew what 'once' was. A victim who did not confess was left for a few days until he stiffened up, physically and mentally. He had been kept in solitary confinement, manacled in the cold and dark in his own filth, fed on meagre amounts of bread and water, hence the torture was judged, correctly perhaps, to have been continuous.

One remarkable aspect of the medieval Inquisition was that witnesses could be tortured. Boy witnesses under fourteen and girls under twelve were exempted.

Whoever refused to testify, whoever complained at having to testify was held to have heretical leanings. There were instances of entire families being tortured to make them incriminate one of their number.

One ghoulish feature of the tribunal was that it even tried the dead. The Sixth General Council in the year 680 had declared that the church can anathematize heretics, living *and* dead. As we saw, Pope Formosus was twice dug up and excommunicated. It started a fashion. Inquisitors disinterred corpses and put them on trial. If they could not find the corpses they were looking for, they tried them in effigy. After sentence was passed on the deceased, there was a big bonfire of bones. Hundreds of the dead were tried in this way. Some had passed on thirty or forty years before; one had been in his grave for seventy-five years.

It showed no one should underestimate the church's readiness to pursue heretics to the death and, if need be, beyond. This practice also enabled inquisitors to acquire the goods and chattels of the dead. When a corpse was pronounced guilty, his former assets were seized. His heirs lost their inheritance. A blameless Catholic son often found, after his father's post-mortem conviction, that he was deprived not only of his property but also of all civil rights. He was lucky to be left with his life as a special act of papal clemency.

The inquisitors were paid out of the proceeds of confiscation. The rich feared them, therefore, even more than the poor. There were various methods of dividing the spoils but, when the expenses of scribes and executioners had been paid, usually half of the remainder went into the pope's treasury and half to the inquisitors. Some popes, like Nicholas III (1277–80), amassed a fortune.

The most frightening of the inquisitors were the incorruptible ones; they tortured purely and simply for the love of God. They had no financial interest; as with Himmler and Heydrich at a later date, they acted solely for the good of the cause. The very ascetism of most of these pious God-fearing Dominicans made them pathologically harsh. Used to pain themselves, they had a spiritual yearning to inflict pain on others. The screams of their victims were a kind of theological music to their ears, a proof that Satan was taking a pasting. They also rejoiced like children at the pope's benevolence towards them; he gave them the same indulgences he gave the knights who went on the Crusades.

The inquisitors never lost a single case. There is no record of an acquittal. When, rarely, the verdict was Not Proven, no one was declared innocent. If the accused was not actually guilty of heresy, no matter. Inquisitors believed that only one in every hundred thousand souls would escape damnation anyway.

The Victims

The victims' Kafka-esque ordeal began with a knock on the door in the night. A family man in, say, France, Italy or Germany, rose from bed to find at the door the Chief of Police, armed guards and a Dominican. From that moment, he had no hope.

Taken to the *Casa Santa*, he was accused of heresy. His guilt was presumed, though it was policy never to tell him what the charges were and he was forbidden to ask. At no stage was he allowed to ask a question. He soon learned that every semblance of justice was to be denied him.

Alone and friendless, he was refused legal representation. No lawyer dared take him on, in any case. Since acquittals were unknown, an unsuccessful lawyer risked being tainted with heresy himself. He, too, was likely to be excommunicated and dealt with by the secular arm.

Defence witnesses were not allowed. All prosecution witnesses – their identities were kept secret from the prisoner – were given equal status. Among them might be the accused's servants whom he had dismissed for theft or incompetence. They might be persons who were refused a hearing in civil courts: convicted perjurers, the excommunicated, heretics. Some testimony was nothing more than hearsay or idle gossip. Cranks, perverts, maniacs, those with a grudge or a vendetta were acceptable. Saddest of all, the witnesses were often members of the accused's own family, who were told that, while he had no hope, complete frankness would ease the lot of the rest of the family.

No appeal against sentence was permitted. What higher tribunal could there be than one acting in the pope's name?

To the catholicity of witnesses corresponded a catholicity of charges. Heresy was a fluid concept. Anything in the slightest degree opposed to the papal system was 'against the faith'.

The utterances of medieval pontiffs created this oppressive climate. It began, of course, with Gregory VII's 'The pope cannot make a mistake'. Paschal II (1073–85), quoting a forged letter of St Ambrose, said: 'Whoever does not agree with the Apostolic See is without doubt a heretic.' Lucius III (1181–5) decided that all differences among Catholics must be grave sins because they deny the pope's authority which underpins the entire system. Innocent III (1198–1216) said those who take literally Jesus' word and limit their speech to Yes and No are heretics and worthy of death. Innocent IV (1243–54), as a kind of climax to this apotheosis, described himself as 'praesentia corporalis Christi', 'the bodily presence of Christ', presumably by a kind of transubstantiation at his election. Anyone who showed disrespect to him or his decrees was, naturally, a heretic. Boniface VIII (1294–1303), not to be outdone, defined it as Catholic doctrine that 'every human being must do as the pope tells him'.

Armed with this elastic notion of what contradicted the faith, inquisitors arrested people for eating meat on Friday, omitting their Easter duties, reading the Bible, saying it is a sin to persecute for conscience's sake, speaking ill of a cleric – priest or bishop. Any jibe against his Holiness was an indictable offence, even when uttered by a man in his cups. Any departure from the life of the community was proof of heresy meriting death. It is clear from this that the aim of the Inquisition was to defend not the faith but the papal system. As one victim of the Inquisition concluded: 'It is safer to discuss the power of God than the power of the pope.'

Other charges dealt with as heretical were sacrilege, blasphemy, sorcery, sodomy, non-payment of taxes to the pope and the clergy, saying that usury is not a sin. Any baptized person who did not light a fire on a cold Sabbath was presumed to be a covert Jew and merited death at the stake.

The ultimate injustice was being accused of *thinking* heresy. For the Inquisition, orthodoxy was not only speaking and acting in an orthodox (that is, papal) manner; it was also thinking as the pontiff would have a person think. If under torture a prisoner proved he had never said or done anything heretical, he could still be punished for his inmost thoughts, his doubts, his temptations.

The Process

As soon as the inquisitors reached a town, they met the civil authorities to present their credentials. In the pope's name, they ordered the governor to co-operate with them, accept their verdict on the accused and execute judgement.

The local clergy were made to gather their people in church where the inquisitors preached against the sin of heresy. The panic-stricken congregation were given a period of grace – a week or longer – to step forward and accuse themselves of their crimes. It might be heresy or associating with heretics, such as their misguided parents or children. If they confessed voluntarily, they received a mild canonical penance. After the sermon, the Dominicans went to their lodgings and waited. Sometimes no one came; at others, as in Toulon in 1245–6, eight to ten thousand confessed. Extra notaries were hired to cope with them.

Usually, informers approached the Dominicans' place under cover of night. On being guaranteed anonymity in the pope's name, every bigot and villain was free to lie as he wished.

The tribunal consisted of one or two inquisitors, two or more witnesses, and members of the inquisitors' staff. All of them were hidden under hoods.

The phrase constantly on the judge's lips was 'Tell the truth'. Whenever the prisoner asked for enlightenment, the inquisitor replied coolly and calmly: 'Tell the truth.'

Once it was clear that the accused was not going to confess spontaneously, he was carried to the dungeon where the executioner had his instruments ready. The sentence of heresy was read out under a crucifix, after which the executioner stripped the prisoner and tied him to a trestle. 'Tell the truth for the love of God,' the inquisitor intoned ritually, 'as inquisitors do not wish to see you suffer.'

With every part of the body accessible, cords were tied around thighs and arms. A belt was put around the waist with cords passing from it over the shoulders from front to back. Each time the cords were tightened, the Dominican interrupted his recitation of the rosary in honour of the Virgin to say: 'Tell the truth.' If the prisoner was stubborn, sticks were put inside the cords to make a garrotte. The effect was like a tourniquet on several limbs at once. Often the *strappado* was used. The victim was placed on a pulley and hoisted off the ground, sometimes as far as the ceiling. There was one torture that was worse than the rest.

The Water-Torture

A mild case of water-torture was described in detail by Henry Charles Lea in his unsurpassed four-volume *History of the Inquisition in Spain* (1907).

Elvira del Campo came before the Tribunal of Toledo in the year 1568. A young woman, she had been pregnant when she was arrested in July the year before. Her baby was born in prison at the end of August, though it was not known what happened to it. The charge against her was that she never ate pork and she put on clean underclothes on Saturdays. The presumption was that she was a crypto-Jewess.

Elvira was a Christian married to a Christian. Her father was a Christian, too, though her mother had Jewish ancestry. When Elvira was eleven, her mother instilled in her a dislike of pork; afterwards, when she tried to eat it, it made her sick. Her mother also taught her to change her underclothes on Saturdays. For the young girl, none of this had religious significance.

Two workmen who lodged in her house reported on her 'Jewish habits' to the Inquisition. There was probably no malice in this. They were afraid of being automatically excommunicated if they failed to report suspicious behaviour. By speaking up, they even gained three years' indulgence. The witnesses agreed Elvira was charitable to everyone and went regularly to mass and confession.

Official proceedings opened on 6 April. Confronting her were two Dominicans and an episcopal vicar. She was warned she would be tortured unless she came out with the whole truth. She insisted she knew nothing. Falling on her knees, she begged to be told what they wanted her to say and she would gladly say it. The inquisitors repeated that she *knew* the wrong she had done. 'Tell the truth.'

Protesting her innocence, she was carried to the torture-chamber and stripped naked. She was handed *zaraguelles* or *panos de la verguenza*, a small pair of trunks to cover her shame.

'Señores,' she shrieked, 'I have done all that is said of me and I bear false witness against myself.'

This did not satisfy the judges. 'Tell the truth.'

Her arms were tied, and the cords twisted painfully.

'I have done all that they say,' Elvira declared.

'We want details.'

'I did not eat pork because it made me sick, señores. I have done everything; loosen me and I will tell the truth. . . . Only tell me what to say.'

The cords were tightened until she cried out that they were breaking her arms. On the sixteenth turn, the cords snapped. At a nod from an inquisitor, the executioner transferred her to the *potro*, a trestle with sharp-edged rungs across it like a ladder. The trestle was slanted so that her head was lower than her feet. While she was fixed in that position, the garrottes on her limbs were tightened.

'Señores,' she pleaded, 'remind me of what I did not know. . . . They are tearing out my soul.'

'Tell the truth.'

'I broke the law,' Elvira said in desperation.

'Which law?'

'I don't know, señor. *You* tell me.'

Another nod and the executioner prised open the prisoner's mouth with a *bostezo*, an iron prong. A *toca*, a piece of linen, was thrust down her throat. 'Take it away,' she screamed. 'I am strangling and am sick in the stomach.'

Slowly, the executioner poured water from a quart jar on to the *toca*, allowing it to drip down her throat. Some prisoners had six to eight jars poured down them and suffocated as a result. Elvira tried to say she was dying. When the *toca* was removed, she was silent, either because she had nothing to say or because she was unable to speak. The torture was suspended for four days.

By then, Elvira had stiffened in every limb. In solitary confinement, her terror had grown as she anticipated the next session. No sooner was she back in the torture-chamber than she broke down, begging to have her nakedness covered. From then on, her speech was mostly incoherent.

In the end, the inquisitors managed to elicit from her that her refusal to eat pork and her Saturday change of clothes were proof of her Judaism. Once she realized what was required of her, she was relieved to admit her apostasy and plead for mercy.

One judge was for burning her. This was the ultimate penalty. Clerics were able to sanction burning whereas they steered clear of the sword because of the biblical ban on shedding blood. Prisoners who repented had their possessions confiscated and were imprisoned. If for life in the dungeons of the Inquisition, owing to conditions there it was usually brief. Sometimes imprisonment was for a specified duration. The minimum penalty was the 'Cross of Infamy'. Two crosses of yellow felt were attached back and front to every garment the accused wore. This guaranteed that they were treated as pariahs.

Elvira was not burned. Most of the judges were for leniency. She had spent over a year in gaol. Her property was confiscated; she was ordered to wear the robe of shame; she was sentenced to serve three more years in prison. For some reason, perhaps insanity, she was released after six months. The case was closed.

Elvira del Campo must stand as representative of many thousands of victims. A devout Christian, she was imprisoned and tortured without mercy by the pope's representatives in the pope's name. Her one crime was that she did what Jesus did throughout his life.

The Spanish Inquisition

The Inquisition at whose hands Elvira suffered was authorized in Spain by Sixtus IV in the year 1480. When Ferdinand and Isabella conquered the Moors, many Moors and Jews, to escape punishment, converted to Christianity. The monarchs feared that they were not true Christians and presented a threat to the state. They therefore asked the pope for permission to establish the Inquisition in their territories. The most famous of all Grand Inquisitors was the Dominican friar Thomas of Torquemada. Appointed in 1483, he ruled tyrannically for fifteen years. His victims numbered over 114,000 of whom 10,220 were burned. Many others were sentenced to life imprisonment.

Prior of the convent of Santa Cruz in Segovia, Torquemada, confessor to Queen Isabella, lived a holy life. He fasted frequently, never ate meat, and turned down the lucrative see of Seville. He lived in a palace with 250 servants and kept fifty horsemen. These were probably his bodyguards, and he had need of them.

He was no sadist. He burned thousands of people but seldom

watched his victims suffer. His was a strictly theological *odium*; he acted completely out of love for Christ and devotion to the pope. Once when he suspected that Ferdinand and Isabella were about to let some rich Jews remain in the kingdom for a price, he burst into their presence brandishing a crucifix. 'Judas sold Jesus for thirty pieces of silver,' he roared. 'Will you sell him for more?'

The curious thing is that, had this scourge of the Jews lived in the twentieth century, the Nazis would have put him in the gas-chamber. For Brother Thomas of Torquemada had a Jewish grandmother.

Llorente, Secretary to the Inquisition in Madrid from 1790 until 1792, estimated in his *History of the Inquisition* that up to his time thirty thousand had been put to death in Spain. During the reign of Philip II, Bloody Mary's Spanish husband, it is reckoned that the victims of the Inquisition exceeded by many thousands all the Christians who had suffered under the Roman emperors.

A few Catholic historians like de Maistre have suggested that the Spanish Inquisition was a purely political institution. The basis for this is that the popes were never entirely happy with it. But this was chiefly because they wanted absolute control, without which their revenues diminished. For, as Pastor remarked in his *History of the Popes*, it was 'a mixed but primarily ecclesiastical institution'. Those condemned were handed over to the secular arm; there would have been no need had the Inquisition been a church tribunal. A proof of this was that in the great *autos-da-fé* the Inquisitor sat on a throne higher than the monarch's. These 'Acts of Faith' were very much enjoyed by Spaniards. An interesting account of one of them was given by Charles Lewis, Baron de Pollnitz, in his memoirs, published in 1738.

Lewis had been a top official at the court of the King of Prussia. A Calvinist, he had converted to Catholicism, which meant he lost his job. Well connected, he tried to cheer himself up with a world tour of which he kept a detailed diary.

One Easter, he chanced to be in Madrid during an *auto-da-fé*. He saw several people 'convicted of Judaism' being burned. Among them was a girl aged eighteen to twenty. He saw no lovelier in all his travels. 'She went to her execution', he wrote, 'with joy imprinted on her face and died with the courage for which our own martyrs are so famous.'

Later during his visit, forty people were taken in one night, among them a famous surgeon whom Lewis had met named Peralte. It seems he was fated to die at the hands of the Inquisition. His mother had given birth to him in prison and was immediately taken out and burned for being Jewish. When he was thirty, he was accused of secretly following his mother's religion. He was put in prison for three years. On his release, he was captured a second time. After leaving Madrid, Lewis heard that Peralte had been burned. It was as if his mother's prayer had been answered, for the story was that on the funeral pyre she had begged God that one day her son would die the same death as she.

This is how Lewis concludes: 'I was very glad I was not at Madrid at the time of Peralte's execution, for I had some knowledge of him, and though he was a real bigot as far as Judaism went, I thought him one of the most civil men in the world.'

When Napoleon conquered Spain in 1808, a Polish officer in his army, Colonel Lemanouski, reported that the Dominicans blockaded themselves in their monastery in Madrid. When Lemanouski's troops forced an entry, the inquisitors denied the existence of any torture-chambers. The soldiers searched the monastery and discovered them under the floors. The chambers were full of prisoners, all naked, many insane. The French troops, used to cruelty and blood, could not stomach the sight. They emptied the torture-chambers, laid gunpowder to the monastery and blew the place up.

The Roman Inquisition

The Roman Inquisition, distinct from the medieval Inquisition which had flourished for centuries, was set up by Paul III on 21 July 1542. This was the first of the Sacred Roman Congregations. It was composed of cardinals, one of whom had dreamed up the idea, the volcanic John Peter Carafa, later Paul IV. As one of the inquisitors-general, he was entitled to imprison anyone on suspicion of heresy, confiscate his property and execute the guilty.

At his own expense, he immediately bought and equipped a house with instruments of torture that were state-of-the-art. 'No man', he said, 'may demean himself by tolerating heretics.' Another of his dicta was: 'If my own father were a heretic, I would personally gather the wood to burn him.'

Elected pope in May 1555, he was free to spread his own brand of fanaticism. An ascetic like Torquemada, he hated Jews and shut them in ghettos, hated sodomites whom he burned, hated women whom he forbade to darken the doors of the Vatican. Ranke said of him that at the end of his long life 'he lived and moved in his reforms and his Inquisitions, gave laws, imprisoned, excommunicated and held his *autos-da-fé*; these occupations filled his life'.

One of Paul's passionate interests was stifling freedom of thought. As a cardinal, he had burned all books he considered pernicious. As pope, he introduced in 1559 the Index of Forbidden Books. On the list went all the works of Erasmus, Rabelais, even Henry VIII whose *Seven Sacraments* had been greeted by Leo X in full consistory as if it had fallen from heaven. Also proscribed was Boccaccio's *Decameron*, so dear to Chaucer, 'until it should be expurgated'. This was like saying a book on honey cannot be published until all references to bees are removed.

Suppressing free thought had become more difficult after 1450 when books started pouring off the new printing presses. Printing was the greatest aid to democracy the world had yet seen. The papacy failed then, and later, to come to terms with it.

Even in the area of censorship fun surfaced. In the first place, Paul IV did the heroic thing by putting himself on the Index. It is an odd story.

A few years before, Paul III had appointed half a dozen cardinals, led by Carafa, to investigate all who were wandering from orthodox faith and morals. 'The guilty and the suspects', Paul stated, 'are to be imprisoned and proceeded against up to the final sentence [death].' Carafa had carried out the order to the letter. The pope was not disturbed, though he was a prime candidate for investigation, with his mistress, his illegitimate children, his gifts of red hats to his grandson and two nephews aged fourteen and sixteen.

In the final *Consilium*, or Advice, given Pope Paul, there was in fact outspoken criticism of papal absolutism, simony, abuses in the bestowal of bishoprics on unworthy candidates and much besides. Unfortunately for the Vatican, this document was leaked. Protestants read it with delight as confirming everything they had ever said about the papacy.

When Carafa became pope, he had no choice but to put this *Consilium* which he had written on the Index.

Another bit of unintended humour centred on the *Decameron*. Cosimo de' Medici, founder of his family's monarchy, later pointed out that this was a rare prose classic in Italian. He asked the reigning pontiff if some way could be found of having it taken off the Index. The result was that the impossible happened. An expurgated version appeared in the reign of Gregory XIII in 1573. Gregory, having a son, Giovanni Buoncompagni, to whom he was deeply attached and whom he made a cardinal, was more broad-minded than Paul IV. The new version of Boccaccio's masterpiece must rank as easily the oddest and most highly recommended 'dirty' book in history. It was prefaced by a papal Bull; it had two *Imprimaturs*, one from the supreme court of the Inquisition, the other from the Inquisitor-General of Florence, and tributes from several heads of state, including the kings of France and Spain.

How to account for such acclaim? The answer is that the censor, Vincenzo Borghini, was something of a genius. Apart from using scissors here and there, he cleaned up the entire book by a very simple device: any cleric compromised in Boccaccio's text was replaced by a layman.

The less amusing side to the Index was that in Paul IV's time there was such a blaze of books that publishers feared for their livelihood.

Authors, valuing their skins, stopped writing altogether. Free thought and expression came to an end in papal Italy, never to return. The effect of this on the Curia, and via the Curia on the Catholic church was incalculable.

A more comprehensive Index was prepared by the Council of Trent in 1564. Works were condemned under ten headings. Seven years later, a Congregation of the Index was set up in Rome that for centuries regularly issued new editions of forbidden works. Hardly a classic escaped. Thus the Counter-Reformation was guided by a narrow-minded censorship, relics of which are still to be seen in Catholic books bearing an *Imprimatur*. A book by a member of a religious order is likely to have five censors named on the fly-leaf. In this situation, a powerful self-censorship comes into operation. This apparatus of repression, so dear to totalitarian regimes, has done great harm to the spirit of free enquiry in the church. It explains why in so many areas – theology, the Bible, even science – contributions from Catholics have lagged behind the rest of the academic world. Scholarship withers in a climate of fear. Generations of students, scholars, bishops, too, were forbidden to read seminal books because they were on the Index. The forgeries which had contributed to creating the papal system, such as the Pseudo-Isidorian Decretals, the fabricated texts that fooled Gratian and Thomas Aquinas, were protected by the Index, at least until 1660 when a French scholar started telling the truth about them. Naturally, he, too, was put on the Index. It was not until 1789 that Pius VI, in response to an enquiry from the German bishops, admitted that the Decretals were a forgery. The admission was nine centuries overdue. As Lea wrote in his *Studies in Church History* (1883):

> It is not the least of the troubles of an infallible Church that it cannot decently abandon any position once assumed. Having received the false decretals as genuine, and having based upon them its claims to universal temporal supremacy, when it was obliged to abandon the defence of the forgeries it was placed in a shockingly false position. To have endorsed a lie, from the ninth to the eighteenth century, was bad enough, but to give up the fruits of that lie, so industriously turned to profitable account, was more than could be reasonably expected of human nature.

J. H. Ignaz von Döllinger was Professor of Church History at Munich in the middle of the nineteenth century. Just prior to Vatican I, he published *The Pope and the Council* in which he tried to show how false and exaggerated were papal claims to infallibility. He was put on the Index less than two weeks before the Council had its first session. Rome had always found it easier to stifle arguments than to answer them.

The Index was finally discontinued after more than four centuries by Paul VI. The year was 1966.

The Roman Inquisition continued its frankly barbarous activities well into the nineteenth century. In the year 1814, after his release from French captivity, Pius VII reintroduced the Sacred Inquisition for 'blasphemy, immorality, disrespectful attitude towards the church, non-participation in its festivals, neglect of its fasts, and especially abandonment of the true faith'. In 1829, anyone in the Papal States who kept a book written by a heretic was to be treated as a heretic. So said Pius VIII, who decreed that whoever heard a word of blame against the Holy Office and did not report it was as guilty as the offender and to be treated as such.

However, by this time, things were getting easier. The Inquisition was suppressed in Spain in 1813. Three years later, Pius VII forbade the use of torture in the tribunals of the Inquisition, though it did continue for another twenty years. Nearly six centuries late, his Holiness, 'teacher of absolute moral values', had seen the light.

Though burnings were now unlawful, Pius IX, by an edict dated 1856, still permitted 'excommunication, confiscation, banishment, imprisonment for life, as well as secret execution in heinous cases'. Nor did the Inquisition cease excommunicating boys and girls who did not denounce their parents for consuming meat or milk on fast days or for reading a book on the Index. In the Papal States these were *crimes* meriting imprisonment.

Right up to 1870, political offenders were tried by a special court, the Santa Consulta. Only priests sat in judgement, and their power was absolute. In the best traditions of the Inquisition, the accused were never confronted by witnesses, nor were they allowed a defence lawyer. Whenever one of the Papal States fell to the armies of the new Italy and the prisons were opened, the prisoners' conditions were said to be indescribable. The bad habits of the Inquisition died hard.

Judgement of the Popes

The record of the Inquisition would be embarrassing for any organization; for the Catholic church, it is devastating. Today, it prides itself, and with much justification, on being the defender of natural law and the rights of man. The papacy in particular likes to see itself as the champion of morality. What history shows is that, for more than six centuries without a break, the papacy was the sworn enemy of elementary justice. Of eighty popes in a line from the thirteenth century on, not one of them disapproved of the theology and apparatus of Inquisition. On the contrary, one after another added his own cruel touches to the workings of this deadly machine.

The mystery is: how could popes continue in this practical heresy for generation after generation? How could they deny at every point the Gospel of Jesus, who himself received an unjust trial and, though innocent, was crucified for heresy?

The answer seems to be: once a pope like Gregory IX had initiated the Inquisition, pontiffs preferred to contradict the Gospel than an 'inerrant' predecessor, for that would bring down the papacy itself.

Catholic historians point out that Europe at the time was a Christendom, a unity of church and state. Heresy was as much a civil crime as a sin. In fact, all princes regarded it as *lèse majesté*; a heretic endangered the unity of the kingdom and was therefore a traitor.

All that this proves is that the alliance of church and state, to which popes were so attached, had disastrous side-effects. From that alliance, the cruelties of the Inquisition sprang. Even this does not fully explain the special evils of the Tribunal which made it a paradigm of injustice: the presumption that the accused was guilty; the torture of the accused and witnesses and so on.

Some historians have attempted to absolve the popes for the crimes of the Inquisition. This is hard to do, for the root of the inquisitors' power was the knowledge that they were papal appointees and acted entirely on papal orders. Further, the extension of 'heresy' to cover every departure from the common life was due entirely to the popes. As Döllinger remarked: 'Both the initiation and carrying out of this new principle must be ascribed to the popes alone. There was nothing in the literature of the time to pave the way for it.'

Also to the popes alone was due the reintroduction of torture into the law courts. It took papal prestige to overturn a long civilized tradition that torture was very wrong. Lea wrote in *The Inquisition in the Middle Ages*:

> It [the Inquisition] introduced a system of jurisprudence which infected the criminal law of all the lands subjected to its influence, and rendered the administration of papal justice a cruel mockery for centuries. It furnished the Holy See with a powerful weapon in aid of political aggrandizement, it tempted secular sovereigns to imitate the example, and it prostituted the name of religion to the vilest temporal ends. . . . The judgement of impartial history must be that the Inquisition was the monstrous offspring of mistaken zeal, utilized by the selfish greed and lust of power to smother the higher aspirations of humanity and stimulate the baser appetites.

Catholic apologists like de Maistre have argued that the church did not kill anyone. The inquisitors handed over the guilty to the secular arm with a plea for mercy.

While this is so, it merely added hypocrisy to wickedness. It is ironic, too, in that when Jews throughout the ages were accused of killing Jesus no theologian ever suggested that the Jews did not kill Jesus but merely handed him over to the secular arm.

There is no known case of a secular prince or magistrate refusing to punish anyone convicted of heresy by the friars of the Inquisition. Popes made no bones about it: any prince who did not burn heretics as charged by the Inquisition would be excommunicated himself and go before the same tribunal for heresy. Far from being guiltless, the inquisitors were still guiltier by implicating the civil power in their crimes. What made the sufferings of Catholics at the hands of the Inquisition so poignant was that they were being tortured and burned, not by the church's enemies but by her holiest defenders acting on the orders of the Vicar of Christ. *Vicar of Satan*

Apologists would seem to be on safer ground when they argue that the Inquisition must be judged by the standards of its time, not by those of the twentieth century.

However, the Inquisition was not only evil compared with the twentieth century, it was evil compared with the tenth and eleventh when torture was outlawed and men and women were guaranteed a fair trial. It was evil compared with the age of Diocletian, for no one was then tortured and killed *in the name of Jesus crucified.*

It is also worth comparing countries that went along with the Inquisition with others, such as England, that did not. Ever since William the Conqueror, the common law of England had maintained a healthy disrespect for theocracy. A person was innocent until found guilty. The common law guaranteed basic elements of justice denied to the accused in the Inquisition: a man was judged by his peers, allowed witnesses to speak on his behalf, had the right to legal counsel and a public trial. The law forbade torture, knowing that it would only lead to hypocrisy and perjury.

It is noteworthy that one of the few prelates big enough to stand up to Innocent III was Stephen Langton, an Englishman versed in the common law. In splendid defiance of papal absolutism, he wrote: 'Natural law is binding on princes and bishops alike; there is no escape from it. It is beyond the reach of the Pope himself.'

Such was the intimidation by the Inquisition that no theologian, except 'heretics' like Marsilio of Padua and Martin Luther, raised his voice against it. Had anyone spoken out he would have been immediately silenced. Had he written against it, he would have been censored in advance. Tyranny continued unopposed. Not a single bishop in all those centuries raised his voice in protest at the way his flock was being ravaged, further proof that bishops in those days were puppets of the Holy See. Yet Protestants like Balthasar Hubmaier had clearer heads and braver hearts. Hubmaier wrote a whole tract against the burning of heretics in 1524. In a haunting series of propositions, he wrote:

> Thirteen: The inquisitors are the greatest heretics of all, since, against the doctrine and example of Christ, they condemn heretics to the fire.

> Fourteen: For Christ did not come to butcher, destroy and burn but that those who live might live more abundantly. . . .

> Twenty-eight: To burn heretics is in appearance to profess Christ, but in reality to deny him. . . .

> Thirty-six: It is clear to everyone, even the blind, that a law to burn heretics is an invention of the devil. 'Truth is immortal.'

Trying to excuse the papacy for the Inquisition by referring to contemporary standards fails for another reason. The papacy went on with its bad ways long after every civilized country in Europe had abandoned them. Just as the sixteenth-century Reformation helped purify some aspects of the papacy, nineteenth-century liberalism heartily condemned by Rome, eventually swept away the cruel tyranny to which popes and Curia were excessively attached.

There is one final flaw in appealing to earlier standards of behaviour in an attempt to exonerate the papacy. The whole emphasis of Roman Catholic moral teaching today is that it is above temporal and relativizing considerations. Others may vacillate about the wrongness of contraception or abortion but not Roman Catholics guided by the pope. John Paul II, for example, claims to teach an absolute morality, one based on natural law; not he, not even God himself can change it, since it is rooted in and springs from the nature of man himself.

If this is so, how can popes excuse the false, strident, even pernicious moral judgements of their many predecessors by referring to 'the standards of the time'?

The Catholic church is faced with a harsh choice: either its teaching is as relative as anyone else's, in which case it has no special claim to be heard. Or its teaching is absolute, in which case the behaviour of popes and their Inquisition is totally inexcusable. What it cannot do is claim *both* absolute wisdom *and* freedom from historic guilt.

The Judgement of Historians

In general, historians have not been kind to the Inquisition. Lea, a Quaker who spent many years of his life examining its operations, speaks of an 'infinite series of atrocities'.

Lord Acton, a Catholic, asserts it was nothing short of 'religious assassination. . . . The principle of the Inquisition was murderous.' As to the popes, they 'were not only murderers in the great style, but they made murder a legal basis of the Christian Church and the condition of salvation'.

Even after the Second World War, G. G. Coulton was able to say the Inquisition was responsible for 'the most elaborate, widespread and continuous legal barbarities recorded in all civilized history'. Nothing that the Roman emperors did to Christians can compare with its systematic wickedness in extent or duration.

The Egyptian occultist, Rollo Ahmed, in *The Black Art* (1971), described the Inquisition as 'the most pitiless and ferocious institution the world has ever known. . . . The atrocities the Inquisition committed constitute the most blasphemous irony in religious history, defiling the Catholic Church with the deaths of innocent victims who were burnt to avoid breaking the maxim, *Ecclesia non novit sanguinem*, The Church has never shed blood.'

A more poignant testimony was given by a devout English Catholic 140 years ago. Robert Richard Madden paid a visit to Avignon with a friend. He left his impressions in his book *Galileo and the Inquisition*. He was shaken to find how much of the great palace of the popes was taken up with the courts, cells and dungeons of the Inquisition.

He saw the torture-chamber with its acoustical device of irregular walls for absorbing the screams of the victims. He stood in the judgement hall where the prisoners had stood and noted above his head 'several circular apertures in the ceiling, about five or six inches in diameter, communicating with an upper chamber, where the prosecutors, it is said, and those who took down in writing the proceedings and answers of the prisoners, were stationed, unseen by him; and yet by whom every word he uttered was recorded'.

It struck Madden as wicked that someone on trial for his life was not allowed to see either the prosecutor or the hostile witnesses, nor to be told what he was accused of.

> Could any innocence, however boldly maintained, with any confidence stand up against the procedure of a secret tribunal of this kind, however fairly administered? . . . Is it not our bounden duty to acknowledge the scandals our own ministers have brought upon our Church, and to see rather with pity than anger the separation of our Christian brethren . . . when they attempted to get rid of the flagrant abuses into which the discipline of the Church had fallen?

Madden passed to the most appalling place in Avignon, where alleged heretics were burned. By means of a narrow passage, he entered a vast circular chamber, 'exactly like the furnace of a glass house or chimney', shaped like a funnel. It was about two hundred feet high with rings and bars to which the prisoners were chained. They had to put on sulphur shirts to make them burn better. The blackness of the walls testified to how many men and women had suffered in that terrible place.

Above, popes, like John XXII, had amassed a fortune by duping the poor, by selling livings, indulgences and dispensations. Others, like Clement VI, had sported themselves naked on bedlinen lined with ermine with their many mistresses. Below them, countless victims, also naked, screamed in agony as they were tortured and burned, sometimes for merely eating meat during Lent.

As they came out into bright sunlight, Madden's friend, David Wire, a Baptist, asked: 'Well, Madden, what do you think of your religion *now*?'

Madden thought hard before replying, 'I feel persuaded, Wire, that it must be a true religion, for if it had not a divine and vital principle in it, it never could have survived the crimes that have been committed in its name.'

An anonymous Catholic once said: 'It would be better to be an atheist than believe in the God of the Inquisition.' Another pointed out that Jesus himself would have suffered and died at the hands of the pope's inquisitors. He talked with heretics like the Samaritan woman; he dined with publicans and prostitutes; he attacked the ministers of religion, the scribes and Pharisees; he even broke the Sabbath by plucking and eating corn when he was hungry.

It is not surprising, therefore, that the pope's House on the Corner is still active. Cardinal Ratzinger picks up the phone and calls a priest in Los Angeles, telling him either to suppress his researches into the views of bishops on celibacy or to pack his bags and leave within the hour. It is not surprising that theologians are removed from their teaching posts, priests are suspended from office for opposing non-infallible teaching. It is not surprising that a bishop is disciplined for acting as Jesus acted, ministering to the downcast, refusing to excommunicate anyone who has sincerity and love in his heart. In view of six centuries of the Inquisition, it would be more surprising if these things were not happening.

But it was not only heretics that the church persecuted. She also went for two other classes of people, held to be equally obnoxious: witches and Jews.

ELEVEN

Persecuting Witches
and Jews

SUPERSTITION in the form of sorcery and magic has been a constant in man's journey from ignorance to enlightenment. In the Christian era, church and state had long combined to stamp out belief in witches and the harm they could do.

God, the church argued, is the absolute Lord and Master of the universe, and His dominion is total. Satan is a reality, of course. But Jesus had bound the 'strong man', so that Satan had no power over man or beast, except in so far as he could tempt humans to do wrong, or infect their minds with darkness and deceit.

This wise approach went back a long time. There was never anything in the church's rituals against witches. The church's canons said the faithful were to be instructed in the falseness and folly of witchcraft. Of those who practised it, some were wicked, some disordered, all deluded. It was held to be un-Christian superstition to think of witches possessing superhuman powers which they used to harm humans. The canonists referred back to the Council of Ancyra in the year 314 to buttress their arguments. Ancyra, they believed, had taught that witchcraft is merely a diabolical illusion without any basis in reality.

All the early collections of the canonists, Regino, Burchard and Ivo, take the same line. So did the most influential of them all, Gratian, in his Decretals, section 364. Those witches are crazy, he said, who 'believe and openly profess that in the dead of night they ride on certain beasts with the pagan goddess Diana and a countless horde of women, and that in these silent hours they fly over vast tracts of country and obey her as their mistress'.

Ordinary people were not so sophisticated. They were fascinated then, as now, by tales of sorcery, astrology and horoscopes. They bought love-philtres and amulets at fairs, charmed rings and magic mirrors. Christianity never completely uprooted rituals of ancient paganism. Hence the faithful feared comets and signs in the night sky, paid strange-looking persons to find them water or buried treasure with a hazel twig. Most of all, they feared witches.

These mainly ancient crones sometimes blessed, mostly cursed the village, creating havoc. If when they begged for alms they were refused, their curses did unimaginable harm to humans and their animals and lands. They were blamed for the loss of a cow or a child's death or a plague of caterpillars. These witches were not the tame emblems of a modern Hallowe'en, though even ugly-masked children with black pointed caps, broomsticks and papier-maché cats can still cause an involuntary shudder on a dark night. The real witches of the Dark Ages, dirty and wild-haired, were a source of infinite terror, even to the clergy who looked on them as rivals for the souls of their people.

For all that, orthodoxy had for centuries poured scorn on the idea that witches 'have the power to change human beings for better or worse, ay, even to turn them into another shape'.

Then came a great change.

The Inquisition Steps In

Gregory IX, who founded the Inquisition in 1231, was chiefly responsible. He was soon receiving sworn reports from his inquisitors to the effect that witches had started multiplying alarmingly. Whereas there had always been the occasional witch, in town, village or hamlet, now a new and terrible curse had settled down on mankind. If his information was correct – and he never doubted it – the church was not only fighting for its life; it was fighting for the survival of the world.

Under interrogation, women in large numbers were confessing to be witches and indulging in the most odious practices he had ever heard of. One of his chief informants was the sadistic secular priest Conrad who came from the small German town of Marburg. An ascetic, after watching a Cistercian being burned for heresy he conceived the idea that salvation can only come through pain. His most famous convert was Elizabeth, widow of the Margrave of Thuringia. She was eighteen, with three children to care for, when Conrad persuaded her to abandon her babies and work among lepers and the destitute. To make her more spiritual, he ordered her to strip and he flogged her till the blood flowed to the ground. She was to tell her confessor: 'If I fear a man like this, what must God be like?'

Pope Gregory personally chose Conrad to investigate a group of heretics called Luciferians. By torture, he forced confessions from them of such gruesomeness that all Germany was worried. The ravings of tormented lunatics were accepted by Conrad as Gospel truth and relayed to the pope. Gregory took the line that these monsters must be wiped off the face of the earth, regardless of age or sex. They must have made a pact with Lucifer, the Prince of Darkness, he decided; they were polluting the earth.

Conrad worked hard to eliminate as many heretics as he could. In Strasbourg, he burned eighty men, women and children. No one was spared, not even bishops. For six years, he waged a campaign of terror until he was assassinated. His work lived on after him in the mind and legislation of Gregory IX.

The pontiff accepted without reservation that the devil was appearing at the witches' sabbats, transformed into a toad, a pale spectre and a black tom-cat. There he incited his followers to indulge in the most obscene practices.

As soon as Innocent IV approved torture the confessions of witches became ever more incredible. Old women were being regularly burned at the stake for admitting to having had sex with Satan and borne him children whom no one had seen. This lack of visibility of Satan's offspring made them all the more menacing.

Pope Clement V (1305–14) was persuaded by the King of France to investigate the Knights Templars, an Order founded to protect the Holy Sepulchre against the Saracens. The king sorely wanted their lands and possessions. The Templars were tortured by the Inquisition for heresy, one of them in fear of the flames crying, 'I would gladly admit that I killed God'. What emerged was another mass of abominations. They confessed to worshipping a huge idol in the shape of a goat called Baphomet. They said the devil had appeared to them as a black tom-cat and they had fornicated with demons in the shape of women. Fifty-nine Knights Templars were burned in one holocaust.

Through the gullibility of popes and the terrors of the Inquisition, the teaching on witchcraft changed. It was no longer an illusion of crazy old women. And with the changed perception came an ever growing panic. Antichrist was in process of taking over the earth. No one could be sure who were witches or where they might turn up. As in a modern science-fiction novel, men awoke in the night to find that their wives whom they had known and loved for years were secret witches. Their children were not really theirs but the devil's. In some places, it was reckoned there were more witches than non-witches, proof that the end of the world was drawing nigh.

An Orgy of Destruction

However hideous the persecution of witches from the thirteenth to the fifteenth century, according to Lea it was only the prelude to 'blind and senseless orgies of destruction which disgraced the next century and a half. Christendom seemed to have grown delirious.' The prolongation of winter or a delay in the harvest meant another mass burning of these unfortunate women.

What set off this new outbreak of fanaticism? The answer is a Bull by Pope Innocent VIII entitled *Summis desiderantes affectibus* of December 1484. It went against the previous long tradition of the church. The outpourings of insane old women under torture were accepted as part of the Christian faith.

> Men and women straying from the Catholic faith
> have abandoned themselves to devils, *incubi* and
> *succubi* [male and female sexual partners], and by
> their incantations, spells, conjurations, and other
> accursed offences, have slain infants yet in the
> mother's womb, as also the offspring of cattle, have
> blasted the produce of the earth . . . they hinder men
> from performing the sexual act and women from
> conceiving, whence husbands cannot know their
> wives nor wives receive their husbands.

This was the clearest authentication of witchcraft. From 1484, anyone who denied it, be he bishop or theologian, was classed as a heretic. The pope had spoken; the matter was settled.

Witches now confessed under torture to acquiring a sacred Host, feeding it to a toad, burning the toad, mixing the ashes with the blood of a baby, preferably unbaptized, adding this to the powdered bones of a man who had been hanged, with a final pinch of herbs. The whole concoction was smeared over the witch's body. By putting a stick between her legs, she was carried immediately to the witches' meeting-place.

However fantastic the evidence, these women had to be wiped out. Did not the Book of Exodus declare: 'Thou shalt not suffer a witch to live'?

To mastermind the massacre, Innocent gave his own 'supreme authority' to two Dominicans. These inquisitors, Heinrich Kramer (or Institoris) and James Sprenger (known as the Apostle of the Rosary), operated in Germany, the first in the north, the second along the borders of the Rhine. They jointly wrote *Malleus Maleficarum, The Witches' Hammer*, in 1486. It led, according to historians, to more misery and deaths than any other book.

It is actually a handbook for the discovery and punishment of witches. It contains a complete theology of witchcraft that is unsurpassed in nonsense posing as scientific analysis. For three centuries, it was on the bench of every judge, on the desk of every magistrate. The preface to the numerous editions of this doom-laden book was the Bull of Innocent VIII.

'The Witches' Hammer'

The authors state their basic Manichaean conviction early on: Satan directly influences human beings, even to the point of changing their shape and doing them permanent harm. 'In this way,' they conclude, 'they could destroy the whole world and bring it to utter confusion.'

One of the first questions in the book is: Can children be begotten by the devil? The answer is affirmative.

To the witches' sabbats, the participants are transported through the air or astride a stick or stool or mounted on a demon in the shape of a dog or a goat. They meet up with the devil, who is present as a horned animal – stag, goat or bull. After the most hellish rites and sexual licence, the witches copulate with Satan himself.

How is such copulation possible? Kramer and Sprenger have the answer: artificial insemination.

> The devils take part in generation not as the essential cause, but as secondary artificial cause, since they busy themselves by interfering with the process of normal copulation and conception, by obtaining human seed, and themselves transporting it.

The *incubus* devil acts the part of the male, the *succubus* devil the part of the female in coition with humans. In the case of the *incubus*, 'the semen does not so much spring from him, as it is another man's semen collected by him for this purpose'. Not that the child born of satanic intercourse is strictly speaking the devil's; he only artificially inseminates the woman. His aim is to pollute humans through the already polluted portal of sex. For is it not through sex that original sin is handed on from one generation to the next, the sin that alienates the race from God? Nowhere is the medieval clergy's loathing of sexuality more evident than in *The Witches' Hammer*. The devil, powerless to affect other spheres of human activity, casts a spell on sex and the sex act. The reason is: 'The power of the devil lies in the privy parts of men.'

In a display of pseudo-science, they explain how it is that devils carry male seed over huge distances without it losing its procreative heat. They move too fast for evaporation to occur.

Devils have another marvellous talent: they can make males lose their sex. But for the fact that these passages are found in the most bloodthirsty book ever written, they would rank with the funniest in Rabelais. The first is about

> a venerable Father from the Dominican House of Spires, well known for the honesty of his life and for his learning. 'One day,' he says, 'while I was hearing confessions, a young man came to me and, in the course of his confession, woefully said that he had lost his member. Being astonished at this, and not being willing to give it easy credence, since in the opinion of the wise it is a mark of light-heartedness

to believe too easily, I obtained proof of it when I saw nothing on the young man's removing his clothes and showing the place. Then, using the wisest counsel, I asked whether he suspected anyone of having so bewitched him. And the young man said that he did suspect someone but that she was absent and living in Worms. Then I said: 'I advise you to go to her as soon as possible and try your utmost to soften her with gentle words and promises'; and he did so. For he came back after a few days and thanked me, saying that he was whole and had recovered everything. And I believed his words, but again proved them by the evidence of my eyes.

Confessions must have been quite interesting in those days.

Scholastic theology – defined by St Thomas More as 'milking a billygoat into a sieve' – is next used to clarify this phenomenon. According to Kramer and Sprenger, the young man, in spite of appearances, had not lost his member. The devil would not lightly remove it, for sex is his chief source of control over men. Rather, the devil, by some sleight of hand, makes it so that the male member is not seen or felt. The devil would not be able to delude a chaste man – not as to his own member, at any rate – though if this chaste man, like the holy confessor at Spires, looked at someone else's he might not be able to see *that*.

The devil *could* tear off the male member if he so chose, and this would be very painful. But, for theological reasons already given, he is loth to go to such extremes.

By means of torture, inquisitors had made witches own up to collecting sex organs, presumably male only.

What is to be thought of those witches who . . . collect male organs in great numbers, as many as twenty or thirty members together, and put them in a bird's nest, or shut them up in a box, where they move themselves like living members, and eat oats and corn? . . . It is all done by devil's work and illusion. . . . For a certain man tells me that, when he had lost his member, he approached a known witch to ask her to restore it to him. She told the afflicted man to climb a certain tree and take that which he liked out of a nest in which there were several members. And when he tried to take a big one, the witch said: 'You must not take that;' adding, 'because it belongs to a parish priest.'

To the authors' dread of sex was added an inbred hatred of women. They accepted with ease the idea of women removing male sex organs. Sprenger put his own views on record in another work: 'I would rather have a lion or a dragon loose in my house than a woman. . . . Feeble in mind and body, it is not surprising that women so often become witches. . . . A woman is carnal lust personified. . . . If a woman cannot get a man, she will consort with the devil himself.'

The Great New Purge

Armed with unassailable power from the pope, the two inquisitors 'traversed the land', writes Lea, 'leaving behind them a trail of blood and fire, and awakening in all hearts the cruel dread inspired by the absolute belief thus inculcated in all the horrors of witchcraft'. The authors of *The Witches' Hammer* laid down the basic principle that a witch must be convicted out of her own mouth. If not voluntarily, then by any other means.

Since witches were presumed to be possessed by the devil, they had no rights. They could be lied to, maltreated, tortured, killed. They were treated as aliens, non-human enemies of Christ and mankind. It is often said by popes, including the present pontiff, that not to believe in Satan is dangerous to morality. Opposed to this is the appalling injustice that resulted from believing in Satan during the persecutions of witches.

The tortures used were various. Thumbs, toes and legs were squeezed in vices. The victims were flogged until they bled. Curiously, whippings, thumbscrews, even the rack were considered only part of the preliminaries. They were not classed as 'real torture'.

The Archbishop of Cologne drew up a Tariff of Torture that included forty-nine measures and the related charges, to be paid to the torturer by the victim's family. For example, cutting out the victim's tongue and pouring red-hot iron into the mouth cost five times as much as a simple flogging in gaol. It was a kind of supermarket chamber of horrors. If the witch suffered the ultimate penalty, the torturers celebrated by having a banquet for which the victim's family also had to pay. If a 'witch' confessed, she not only saved her family a great deal of expense, she also gained for herself a less painful passage out of this world: she was strangled before being burned.

The records show one woman being tortured fifty-six times, and still she did not confess. In Germany, in the year 1629, a woman had alcohol poured over her hair which was then set alight. After that, her hands were tied behind her back and she was left hanging from the ceiling for three hours before the 'real torture' began.

The Witches' Hammer was followed by other manuals. One of these was the early seventeenth-century *Discourses on Sorcery* by a

Frenchman, Henri Boguet. In his view, children should be made to witness against their parents. Even small children had to be tortured to get at the truth. If they were witches themselves, they, too, were to be killed, though with more compassion – say, by hanging.

The witch-hunters never seemed to grasp that *they* were creating witches. Under torture, their victims said whatever was expected of them. Yes, they had made a pact with the devil at the midnight hour and exchanged their soul for gold. Yes, they had turned themselves into cats and other beasts like werewolves. Yes, with a glance of their Evil Eye, they had poisoned wells and, with a curse, brought hail-storms and unseasonable frosts. Yes, they had copulated with Satan in their old age – his penis was thin and frozen like an icicle, and his seed, how cold! And Yes, they had borne him a son, a monster with a wolf's head and a serpent's tail, whom for two years they fed on the flesh of newborn babies, before the child vanished into thin air.

Witches confessed to putting spells on people making them void from every orifice – mouth, penis, vagina – the most curious objects: locks of hair, needles, stones, pig's bristles, balls of paper with demonic characters written on them. According to Peel and Southern, 'one writer, at the limit of his warped imagination, equipped the devil with a long bifurcated penis so that he could enjoy sex and sodomy simultaneously'.

Under investigation, by inquisitors, whole convents of nuns cheerfully confessed to fornicating on a regular basis with the devil. The more outrageous their inventions, the more the inquisitors' eyes lit up. Their worst nightmares were being confirmed. They never suspected the accused simply wanted their tortures to end.

By a perversity still not fully understood, innocent people came forward and accused themselves of the most heinous crimes. It was as if they wanted brief notoriety, even if it meant that they burned at the stake for it.

These bizarre confessions forced the authors of the manuals to add hitherto unknown species of sexual deviation to the lists. Sodomy now included a male copulating with a male devil. Adultery included a witch having sex with Satan.

As a result of ravings under torture, one of the most honoured of professions became the most vilified. In one of the most extraordinary statements in any book, Kramer and Sprenger assert: 'No one does more harm to the Catholic faith than midwives.' What was their crime? Sometimes they killed babies in the womb or soon after birth by sticking needles into their fontanelle, so that the infants, unbaptized, went directly to Satan's fiery abode. At other times, they dedicated babes from birth to their Lord and Master, the devil. In the devil's efforts to ape God and take over the world, midwives were his closest allies. Thus the band of evil ones was growing day by day.

For a century and a half, everyone from king to commoner feared this secret organization that was undermining the foundations of the world. There were stories of witches' sabbats attracting crowds of over twenty-five thousand, all holding candles so that night turned to day, all worshipping Satan in mock enactment of rites sacred to Christians. After Innocent VIII's Bull, necromancy multiplied, the black mass became a commonplace. Many an apostate priest officiated. This was partly a social protest against the oppressive authority of the church, partly a desire to dabble in the occult. Often when a consecrated Host was used it was stamped with obscene invocations in letters of blood.

On moorlands or in moonlit glades, in Friday covens of thirteen or in huge seasonal sabbat assemblies, witches went through their masquerade of worshipping Satan with a goat's head. Every ritual of the mass was inverted. They trampled on the cross; they prayed with their back to the sky and their face to the earth; they even danced backwards. The devil preached to them, assuring them they had no souls and there was no afterlife. The ceremony ended, so it was said, with kissing the devil's backside, forging a compact with him in blood, and, finally, wild indiscriminate sexual orgies.

The church used its own forms of magic to counter those of the Black Art. There was holy water, blessed candles, church bells, medals, the rosary, invocation of the saints, relics, exorcisms and sacraments.

In spite of these safeguards, the church seemed to be losing the battle. Witchcraft continued growing by the very methods popes had devised to stamp it out. Under torture, witches named accomplices who named others in their turn. The world which not long ago had the odd witch in village or hamlet with her familiar cat, dog, raven or crow was now filled with witches. Witches, it was said, had more devotees than the Virgin Mary. They constituted an anti-church in which many cardinals were alleged to be active. Satan's power almost matched God's.

The situation was desperate and called for desperate remedies. According to The Witches' Hammer, any device for dealing with Satan was permissible. This was the book's advice to inquisitors investigating witches: Promise them a minor penance if they plead guilty. On conviction, give them a minor penance before burning them. Promise not to condemn any witch who incriminates others. Afterwards, get another inquisitor to condemn her. Many witches went to the stake complaining that they had been promised pardon in exchange for naming names or confessing their guilt.

Not even Kramer and Sprenger were able to explain why they gave credence to witches who were mouthpieces of 'The Father of Lies' nor how witches, apparently so formidable, allowed themselves to be captured without a struggle, tortured and burned. Not one single instance is on record of a witch successfully cursing an inquisitor, blinding a torturer, remaining alive after being burned at the stake.

Executions multiplied. Before, there had been one or two, now there were mass burnings. Among the damned were girls of six years old. 'A bishop of Geneva', writes Lea in *The Inquisition in the Middle Ages*, 'is said to have burned five hundred within three months, a bishop of Bamburg six hundred, a bishop of Wurzburg nine hundred.' So it went on. In the year 1586, the Archbishop of Trèves had 118 women burned and two men for incantations that prolonged the winter.

Papal Responsibility

It would be foolish to suggest that the papacy created witchcraft. It was there before Christianity appeared, and the church never stamped it out completely. There can be no doubt, however, that the papacy had a critical role in the fresh emergence and cruel treatment of witches.

Döllinger wrote in *The Pope and the Council*: 'The whole treatment of witches was partly the direct, partly the indirect result of the irrefragable authority of the Pope.' Lea agrees: 'The Church lent its overpowering authority to enforce belief on the souls of men. The malignant powers of the witches were repeatedly set forth in the Bulls of succeeding popes for the implicit credence of the faithful.'

Before Innocent VIII, to assert that witches had these powers was contrary to the faith; after Innocent, to deny it was heresy, punishable by fire. The contradiction of earlier teaching was so blatant, theologians had to resort to subterfuge to deal with it. Inquisitors argued that the witches that Ancyra and Gratian referred to, the harmless ones, *had died out*. A new and tougher breed had replaced them; these were the ones in league with the devil to carry out a kind of Satanic AIDS campaign to infect the social body. Papal authority – in the person of Innocent VIII, Alexander VI, Leo X, Julius II, Adrian VI and many others – guaranteed the existence of witches and their preternatural powers, especially in the realm of sex. As late as 1623, Gregory XVI decreed that anyone making a pact with Satan to produce impotence in animals or to harm the fruits of the earth was to be imprisoned for life by the Inquisition.

Then in 1657, without warning or explanation, an instruction from the Roman Inquisition said that not a single process for a very long time had been rightly conducted. Inquisitors had erred by reckless application of torture and other irregularities. Not a word was said about the popes' role in sanctioning torture and lies, nor about why so many popes had contradicted the tradition by affirming the reality of witches. Above all, not a word of regret was expressed about the many thousands who had perished in one of the most nightmarish periods in European history.

Over several centuries, the popes had orchestrated a practical Manichaeism whereby the devil had claimed dominion over half of Christendom. Now, without a word of explanation, this entire teaching was abandoned, as if no pontiff had ever been so foolish as to hold it. It is never easy to apologize for mistakes. For an authority which proclaims it cannot err, it would appear to be almost impossible.

One very worrying aspect of witchcraft was that the sabbath commenced on a Friday night. Could it be that the Inquisitors suggested this to their victims because it coincided with another demonic ceremony, the Jewish Sabbath?

YAHWEH'S SABBATH

Persecution of the Jews

Pope Paul IV, who hated Jews, had worked on the document for hours at a time, ceaselessly sipping the black thick-as-molasses wine of his beloved Naples. Soon it was finished. On 17 July 1555, a mere two months after his election, he published *Cum nimis absurdum*, a Bull which never appears in pious anthologies of papal documents. For this was to prove a landmark in the history of anti-Semitism.

Papal Anti-Semitism

By reason of this Bull, Paul was to merit an accolade he himself had offered his favourite nephew, Cardinal Carlo Carafa: 'His arm is dyed in blood to the elbow.' It is no surprise that during Paul's brief pontificate the population of Rome was almost halved. Jews, who had nowhere to run to, took the brunt of his bigotry.

He knew by heart all the church's edicts against Judaism. The onslaught on the Jews had begun very early.

In the Roman Empire, Jews had overcome initial hostility to win for themselves full citizenship by the Edict of Caracalla in the year 212. A century later, when Constantine became a Christian, persecution of Jews began.

They were excluded from all civil and administrative posts, forbidden to employ Christians, or give to and receive from them medical aid. Intermarriage between Christians and Jews was classed as adultery and made a capital offence. In a lawsuit between Christians and Jews, only Christian witnesses were acceptable to the court. Fathers of the church, such as Ambrose in the West and Chrysostom in the East, provided a theological basis for despising Jews which has the power to shock even today.

The very kindest of popes, Gregory the Great, while forbidding torture and persecution of Jews, was not above bribing them into baptism. Any Jew in Rome who converted had his rent reduced by one-third. He wrote:

> For even if they themselves come with little faith, there will certainly be more faith in their children who are baptized, so that if we do not gain the parents, we shall gain the children. Therefore, any reduction of rent for Christ's sake is not to be considered a loss.

Innocent III and the Fourth Council of the Lateran in 1215 took up the cause of anti-Semitism with a will. And Paul IV, who hated every form of dissent, was determined to carry on, with impeccable cruelty, the work of the great Innocent.

Cum nimis absurdum stressed that the Christ-killers, the Jews, were by nature slaves and should be treated as such. For the first time in the Papal States, they were to be confined to a particular area called, after the Venetian Foundry, a 'ghetto'. Each ghetto was to have but one entrance. Jews were obliged to sell all their property to Christians at knockdown prices; at best they realized 20 per cent of value, at worst a house went for a donkey, a vineyard for a suit of clothes. Forbidden to engage in commercial activity or deal in corn, they could otherwise sell food and secondhand clothes (*strazzaria*); thus was their status reduced to that of rag-pickers. They were allowed one synagogue in each city. Seven out of eight in Rome were destroyed, and in the Campagna eighteen out of nineteen. They were already without books; when he was a cardinal, Paul IV had burned them all, including the Talmud. They were obliged to wear, as a distinguishing mark, a yellow hat in public. They were to use only Italian and Latin in speech, in their calendars and accounts. They were never to employ Christians in any capacity, even to light their Sabbath fires in winter. They were not to give medical treatment to Christians, nor receive from them so much as the services of a wet-nurse. They were not to be called *signor*, 'sir', even by beggars. A House for Catechumens, that is, for convert Jews, was to be built and paid for by Jews. Censors of Jewish books had to be paid for by Jews, as was the Gentile gate-keeper whose job it was to lock them in at night.

Since Roman times, Jews had tended to live in the same districts. There they could build their ritual slaughterhouse and baths, their synagogues, their study-places, their courts, their own burial-grounds. They felt safer *af der yiddisher gas*, on their own Jewish street, where at least they would be left alone. But to be forced to live in one place like cattle, to have to return by nightfall, to own neither the land nor their homes – this was something menacingly different.

Roman Jews suffered specially in that their ghetto was a stretch along the right bank of the Tiber, malarial and frequently as waterlogged as Venice. Within a circuit of five hundred yards were crammed four to five thousand people. According to one Jewish writer, they were 'clothed in rags, living on rags, thriving on rags'. Only with Friday night did they get out of their rags, as the old crier called out, 'The Sabbath has begun,' for now, with the Sabbath, every Jew was king in Israel.

The impact of Paul's Bull was immediate. Within days, there was a ghetto in Venice, another in Bologna called the Inferno. Paul's aim was to convert Jews *en masse*. Many did cross over to Christianity; most did not. Atrocities resulted everywhere. In Ancona, Marranos, converted Jews from Portugal, had settled, with assurances from previous pontiffs that, though they had been forcibly baptized, they would be left in peace to practise their ancient faith. Paul IV withdrew these promises on the last day of April 1556. The Marranos rapidly dispersed, but twenty-four men and one woman were burned alive in successive 'Acts of Faith' in the spring and early summer of that year. Away from the fires, the Jews said the *Kaddish: Yiskaddal veyiskaddash*, their immemorial prayer.

Paul died in 1559, but his Bull had set a pattern that was to last for three centuries. In June 1566, Pius V personally baptized two Jewish adults and their three children; five cardinals acted as godfathers. In 1581, Gregory XIII reached the astounding conclusion that the guilt of Jews in rejecting and crucifying Christ 'only grows deeper with successive generations, entailing perpetual slavery'.

In the Romagna, two priests, ex-Jews, were delegated to force their way into synagogues on the Sabbath. In an act of desecration, they placed a crucifix in front of the Ark and preached Jesus as God and Messiah. Everywhere, synagogues were closed for months on end on the pretext that a single unauthorized book had been found there. Many books were obviously planted. Homes were broken into, searched and destroyed. Any excuse was good enough for sending the head of a Jewish family to the House of Catechumens for brainwashing. A Jew who approached the building without permission – say, a rabbi seeking to dissuade his fellows from converting – was savagely beaten. In the year 1604, Rabbi Joshua Ascarelli, his wife and four children were sent to the *Casa*. Father and mother, after a long detention, still refused to give in; they were dismissed. The children were kept behind. Without their parents, they eventually succumbed and were baptized. When the parents came to take them home, they were told to go away before they were flogged.

In 1639 a Jew in Rome was chatting amicably with a Dominican priest when as a joke he offered to have his child baptized, provided the pope acted as godfather. His flippancy cost him both his boys, one still in the cradle. This insult to their race caused a riot in the ghetto; it was ruthlessly repressed.

Between 1634 and 1790, 2,030 Jews in Rome 'converted'. Benedict XIII (1724–30) baptized twenty-six as a sign of his favour. Conversions were attended by fireworks displays and processions in the neighbourhood of ghettos where Jews, mostly reduced to silence, seethed. When they were forced to go to church and listen to sermons they were pelted with filth by Gentiles. Inside the church, beadles went round with rods to keep them awake. Sometimes they were medically examined to make sure that these 'crafty Jews' were not chosen by their community because they were deaf. Hardly a single humiliating detail was overlooked. They were forbidden to carry lighted tapers at funerals or erect stones over the graves of their dead, thus violating the Roman rule from which Christians themselves had benefited: a burial-ground is as sacred as a temple.

One Christian superstition of the time was that whoever was responsible for baptizing an infidel gained free passage to Paradise. Ruffians roamed the city, pouncing on Jewish children and christening them with rainwater. In the eighteenth century, Benedict XIV decided that a child baptized against his or her parents' wishes and contrary to the procedures of canon law was none the less a Christian and had to live as one. If he did not, he was labelled a heretic, with the dire penalties that entailed. The ghettos were loud in mourning when such crimes occurred. They grieved, too, when a Jew, converted to Christianity, did as the priest told him and snatched his children from the ghetto. Once they were baptized, the mother was never allowed to see them again.

In the worst days of papal oppression in Rome, Jews lived in a space confined by high walls. Naturally, they had to build upwards. As a result, houses collapsed, sometimes during wedding celebrations. Fires spread rapidly. Hygiene was practically nonexistent, supporting the myth that Jews had a vile smell that only disappeared at baptism.

Ramazzini, known as the father of occupational diseases, studied Italian Jews and published his findings in his book, *De Morbis Artificum* in 1700. They showed, he said, all the symptoms of a sedentary life. Their women, in particular, suffered from early blindness. They were victims far above the average, of headaches, toothaches, sore throats and pulmonary diseases. The popes were responsible for generations of pains that are not recorded in the history books.

The French Revolution ushered in the age of enlightenment. The light did not reach the Vatican. A succession of popes reinforced the ancient prejudices against Jews, treating them as lepers unworthy of the protection of the law. Pius VII was followed by Leo XII, Pius VIII, Gregory XVI, Pius IX – all good pupils of Paul IV.

If Jews bought or sold anything employed in Catholic worship – a chalice, rosary, crucifix – they were fined 200 scudi. The same fine was levied for leaving Rome without permission of the Inquisitor. If a

Christian doctor was called to treat a patient in the ghetto, he had first to try to convert him to Christ. If he failed, he was to leave at once. Three or four Jewish children were taken every Monday for baptism and turned into Christians. Whoever objected, even the parents, was hauled before the Inquisition. If two Christians testified that a Jew by word or deed had insulted a Catholic priest or the true religion, he was put to death.

Leo XII (1823–9) decided Christians were getting lax. He again locked Jews inside ghettos. He also forbade vaccination against small-pox during an epidemic because it was 'against the natural law'. But the real disappointment was Pius IX.

A disillusioned liberal, he issued even stricter laws against the Jewish community. Cecil Roth in his *History of the Jews in Italy* (1946), tells of a Jew of good standing being sent to prison under Pius IX for employing an elderly Christian lady to look after his linen. By this time, Jews in most places in the world had achieved freedom and dignity. Not in Rome and the Papal States. The House of Catechumens was still open for business. In the year 1858 it was the scene of perhaps the worst abuse of all.

A girl in Bologna told her confessor under the seal that six years before she had worked illegally as maid to a Jewish family named Mortara. They had a boy, one year old, whom this girl thought was dying, so she baptized him. Her confessor told her she had a duty to inform the authorities. Acting under clerical orders, the police seized the seven-year-old Edgardo and sent him to Rome to be brought up as a Christian. This *cause célèbre* raised a storm throughout Europe. Franz Joseph of Austria and Napoleon III of France both warned the pope that he was antagonizing world opinion. A mass meeting was held in the Mansion House in London. The distinguished British Jew, Sir Moses Montefiore, travelled to Rome to plead personally with the pontiff. Pius IX remained adamant.

After a triumphal parade through the Roman ghetto, Edgardo Mortara was given the solemn ceremonies of baptism. He was brought up as a Christian and, in time, became a distinguished missionary priest.

Once more, a pope, personally devout, was found devoid of all sense of natural justice towards Jews.

In September 1870, Italian troops took Rome. They were greeted by scenes of jubilation only matched when the Allies recaptured the city after the Nazi occupation in the Second World War. Eleven days after Rome fell, on 2 October 1870, the Jews, by a royal decree, were given the freedom which the papacy had denied them for over fifteen hundred years. The last ghetto in Europe was dismantled. When that happened, Jews must have felt that their trials were over at last. How could they know that their darkest hour was still to come?

Pius XII and the Great Silence

Christianity had prepared for it by persecuting them for their religion; fascism would persecute them for their race. Popes, for all their cruelty, had hoped to convert Jews; Hitler, with his reluctant ally Mussolini, made plans to wipe them out.

In spite of the vast differences, the similarities between the decrees of Innocent III and Paul IV, on the one hand, and the Nuremberg Laws of 1935, on the other, are beyond dispute. Christians had targeted the Jews: as pariahs, polluters of the earth, perpetrators *as a race* of the greatest crime ever known to man, namely, killing God. Christians invented the idea of dispossessing Jews of their houses, lands and cemeteries, forced emigration, forced confinement. When the Nazis named the Jewish living-spaces 'ghettos', they were aiming expressly to give their policies continuity with that of the popes and a species of respectability.

Pius XI, who died in 1939, was aware that Jesus, Mary and Joseph were Jews. He opposed a crude racism in Germany and wrote an anti-fascist encyclical which was unpublished at his death. His successor was more cautious.

Eugenio Pacelli, Pius XII, was born of patrician stock in 1876. Owing to ill health, he studied for the priesthood at home. Ordained in 1899, he was immediately drafted into the Vatican Secretariat of State. Sixteen years later, he was made a bishop, without having had a day's pastoral experience. He was born and bred a bureaucrat.

His grandfather, Marcantonio, had been a lay canon lawyer, operating in the Roman Rota. His father, Filippo, also a canonist, was dean of the College of Consistorial Advocates, and of such repute that he was the only layman to work on the new code of canon law that came into effect in 1918. Eugenio, a lawyer in the family tradition, was the right-hand man of Cardinal Gasparri whose idea it was to restructure the code and who guided the work at every stage.

Towards the end of the First World War, Pacelli was papal nuncio in Munich. After the war, he was transferred to Berlin where he witnessed the rise of the Brown Shirts. In 1929 he was recalled to Rome where he was made cardinal and Secretary of State. He was accompanied by Sister Pasqualina, a German Franciscan nun, who was his housekeeper.

In spite of seeing Nazism at close quarters, he always feared communism more.

Cardinal Pacelli became pope on 2 March 1939. He was sixty-three years old. Cold, distant, expressionless except when he reacted to the cheers of the crowd, he had brown weak eyes and, in profile, the face of an eagle.

When Mussolini began putting pressure on the Jewish community,

Pius initiated his habit of saying nothing. On 4 June 1940, Italy entered the war on Hitler's side. By the end of 1941, three-quarters of Italian Jews had lost their livelihood. The scene was set for what many, Catholics included, consider the most shameful of all papal encyclicals, more terrible by far than Paul IV's *Cum nimis absurdum*. It was the one that was never written.

Throughout Italy and the Reich, Jews were being systematically victimized and, in many well known cases, killed. Not one unequivocal word of condemnation issued from the Vatican. This silence, many say, was worse than any heresy. Usually so swift to correct and condemn the slightest deviation from faith, any 'mistake' in, say, sexual morality, Rome's lips were firmly and, it turned out, permanently sealed.

Long before the end of 1942, the mass extermination of Jews was common knowledge. On 1 July the BBC broadcast in French accounts of the massacre of 700,000 Polish Jews. A week later, Cardinal Hinsley of Westminster repeated this figure on the BBC, adding: 'This innocent blood cries out for vengeance.' In that summer, Vichy France showed itself keen to deport Jewish children, even before the Nazis in the Occupied Zone were ready to receive them. From 21 July to 9 September, a paediatrician counted 5,500 children who had passed through Drancy on their way to extermination. Over a thousand were under six years old. Their parents had been dispatched already. They were given Jewish guardians to hide the fact that they were orphans. George Wellers, a Parisian lawyer, was one such guardian. He described the scene of the transit camp near Paris in his book, *Drancy*. The children, six of whom in his contingent were under two, were 'like a frightened flock of lambs'. His description of their plight is haunting. Small children, who did not know their own name, waiting on the landing for an adult to take them to the toilet, lying in their own filth as a result of diarrhoea, perpetually crying in the night.

On 17 August, 530 children with a few adult companions were packed in cattle-trucks and locked in. The heat and stench were appalling. Two days later they were in Auschwitz and, by the evening, were dead. Just after this, an SS doctor at the camp confided in his diary: 'Compared with what I saw, Dante's *Inferno* seems to one a quasi-comedy.' Hitler's hell was to consume a million children.

The papal nuncio in Paris, Valerio Valeri, had reported on 5 August to the Cardinal Secretary of State in Rome that the children being shipped out of France were headed for Poland not Germany. Seven weeks later, Myron C. Taylor, the American ambassador, sent details of the mass exterminations of Polish and western Jews in Poland to the same Secretary of State, Cardinal Maglione.

The French hierarchy made what was described as a platonic protest to the Quisling government. Laval was able to say to Suhard, Cardinal of Paris, that he should keep out of politics and be silent like his Holiness. When further arrests were made, Suhard did indeed keep silent. But in January 1943 he went to Rome for an audience with Pius XII. He had brought with him good news in the form of Pétain's financial support for the church. Not one word was said between them about the Jews.

The mass exterminations of Jews were now common knowledge. A month before Suhard went to Rome, on 5 December 1942, the Archbishop of Canterbury wrote to *The Times* to comment on its previous day's report. 'It is', his Grace said, 'a horror beyond what imagination can grasp.' He expressed on his own behalf and that of the Church of England and the Free Churches 'our burning indignation at this atrocity, to which the records of barbarous ages scarcely supply a parallel'. There was one man in the world whose witness Hitler feared, since many in his armies were Catholics. That one man did not speak. In the face of what Winston Churchill was to call 'probably the greatest and most horrible single crime ever committed in the whole history of the world' he chose to stay neutral.

In the summer of 1943, Mussolini was dismissed and, that September, the Germans occupied Rome. An SS detachment arrived. They demanded 50 kilograms of gold from the Jewish community. If it was not paid within thirty-six hours, two hundred Jews would be deported. Pius XII offered to make up any shortfall. Even so, not one person was saved.

In October a squad of SS paratroopers, armed with submachine-guns, stationed themselves on the boundaries of the Vatican. They were there ostensibly to protect his Holiness but really to intimidate him. It seems they succeeded. He was not concerned for his own safety but, rightly or wrongly, he went into an even deeper silence, fearing that to break it would make the Jews' situation worse.

On the night of 15–16 October, Jews were at home observing the Sabbath. A thousand were rounded up, among them pregnant women and the elderly. One woman driven off in an army truck was in labour. A couple with ten children were among those taken to the Military Academy. On the first night there, two women gave birth. Two days later, on Monday 18 October, the whole complement of over a thousand was transported to a railway siding and put in sealed cattle-trucks. The train started at 2.05 p.m. North they went, through Orte, Chiusi, Florence, Bologna and across the German border. They were heading for Auschwitz.

Bishop Hurdal, head of the German church in Rome, recognizing that the round-up of Jews in Rome was a key moment, informed the German command that the arrests must stop. Otherwise, the pope would 'have to make an open stand which will serve the anti-German propaganda as a weapon against us'. The German ambassador, too, was deeply concerned. Jews, he reported to Berlin, were being snatched practically under the pope's window. He, like many French bishops, would have no alternative but to protest against German policy.

These fears proved groundless. Pius XII said nothing at all. When the American diplomat Harold Tittman was received in audience three days later, the pope did not mention Jews. His concern was for the small communist cells scattered around Rome.

The Nazis were amazed; they could not believe their luck. It encouraged them to carry out similar measures in Florence, Venice, Ferrara, Genoa and Fiume. Within six weeks, ten thousand Jews were rounded up and taken to Auschwitz where 7,550 of them perished. Italians gave shelter to as many Jews as they could. This was easier in that Jews were not so different from them to look at. Encouraged by the Holy See, churches, convents monasteries, all played their part; a few Jews sheltered in the Vatican.

In December 1943, Jews were deprived formally of Italian citzenship. In one round-up, 650 Roman Jews were captured, in another 244. There were seventy Jews among the 335 hostages shot in the Ardeatine Caves in March 1944. This number represented a ten-to-one reprisal for German police shot and killed in ambush by the Resistance, with five victims added almost by mistake.

Among the first hostages shot in the back of the head was Dominico Rici, a thirty-one-year-old Catholic clerk, father of five. Found in his pocket afterwards was a note scribbled in block letters: 'My dear God, we pray that You may protect the Jews from the barbarous persecutions. One Paternoster, ten Ave Marias, one Gloria Patri.' With Rici died six Jews named Di Consiglio: three brothers, their father, grandfather and uncle. Robert Katz wrote in his book, *Death in Rome*:

> A miracle was not necessary to save the 335 men doomed to die in the Ardeatine caves. There was one man who could have, should have, and must be held to account for not having acted to at least delay the German slaughter. He is Pope Pius XII.

The pope knew from Dollman, head of the SS in Rome, via the German Salvatorian Father Pancrazio that there was going to be a bloodbath. However, the pope's sympathies were mixed. He believed that the attack on the German forces by the Resistance was the greater crime because it was unprovoked. The day of the massacre found him in audience with the cardinals of the Holy Office and the Congregation of Rites, and preparing for his Lenten exercises.

The massacre was not recorded on independent Vatican radio.

If only the pope had risked arrest by wearing a star of David, or had spoken, if only once, to tell the Jewish people they were not alone in their agony.

Far away, one of the leaders of the Polish Uprising was lamenting the silence of all the world leaders. It was to him 'astonishing and horrible'. His message was: 'The world is silent. the world knows, it is not possible that it does not know, but the world is silent. God's representative in the Vatican is silent.'

The Roman horror ended on 5 June 1944 when the Allies delivered the city. The military chaplain removed the seals, including Pius XII's, from the gates of the Great Synagogue. Jews were free again. They emerged from hiding to find over two thousand of their number missing.

Cecil Roth expressed in 1946 sincere gratitude to the church for the help it gave to his people during the war. 'Thus, in the twentieth century, the great wrong of the Italian Ghetto was atoned for.' Pinchas E. Lapide praised Pius XII for his quiet work behind the scenes. Many observers are less charitable. For them, the question is: Why did the pope not raise his voice?

His defenders say he wanted to preserve the Vatican's neutrality as mediator; he was afraid to put an intolerable burden on the consciences of German Catholics. His critics reply: Can there be neutrality between right and such tremendous wrong? Besides, what about the burden on Jews whom Germans, Catholics and non-Catholics, were slaughtering by the million?

Hochhuth's picture of Pius in his play *The Representative* as a kind of super-capitalist, fearing only for the devaluation of his stocks and shares, is ridiculous. In his entire life, Pius probably never thought of personal possessions, Hochhuth was nearer the knuckle when he asked 'how, in this so-called Christian Europe, the murder of an entire people could occur without the highest moral authority on this earth having a word to say about it'.

Differences of opinion surfaced in the Vatican itself. After the war, Paul VI was to defend his one-time chief by saying that to have protested at German atrocities 'would have been not only futile but harmful'. Whereas Cardinal Tisserant, later Dean of the Sacred College, said, while the war was on:

> I fear that history will reproach the Holy See with having practised a policy of selfish convenience and not much else. This is extremely sad, especially for those [of us] who have lived under Pius XI. Everyone [in Rome] is confident that, after Rome has been declared an open city, members of the Curia will not have to suffer any harm; that is a disgrace.

The days of deposing rulers was long past. Catholics like Hitler and Goebbels would not have been worried by excommunication, nor would they have stopped persecuting Jews because the pope asked them to. But some have asked: Could not his Holiness, who declared infallibly in 1950 that a Jewess was taken up body and soul into heaven, have said authoritatively in 1942 that her race was not to be annihilated for being Jewish? What prevented him, as Cardinal Tisserant urged on him, from saying publicly that Catholics cannot participate in mass murder or that there are occasions when lawful leaders must be disobeyed, whatever the cost?

The only satisfactory explanation for Pius XII's silence is that he was first and foremost a Catholic; a Catholic before he was a Christian or a human being, even though he was a fine Christian and a deeply compassionate human being. His Jewish admirer, Lapide, wrote: 'A single papal edict, telling Christians that the Jewish law which Christ taught to his disciples – "Love thy neighbour as thyself" – must also apply to Jews, would have been more satisfying than long lists of prohibitions and restrictions. But such a simple letter never came from Rome.' If only Pius XII had cared for Jews as much as Pius IX had cared for his Papal States.

The great John XXIII followed Pius, aged seventy-seven, the quintessential human being. He immediately expunged 'perfidious', the adjective used of Jews in the Good Friday liturgy. He knew that Good Friday should rather be a kind of Catholic Yom Kippur, in atonement for the church's sin of crucifying Jesus in his Jewish brethren over the ages. Once, when he received the American leaders of the United Jewish Appeal, the pope said, with a smile: 'I am Joseph your brother', 'Son'io Giuseppe il fratello vostro'. Joseph was the youngest brother.

Under John's direction, Cardinal Bea prepared a document on the Jews to be placed before the Second Vatican Council. John died before it was passed. In any case, altered almost out of recognition, it turned out to be too little too late. In it there is no real suggestion, as there is in John's great prayer for forgiveness, that the church's teaching and the behaviour of Catholics over the ages contributed to anti-Semitism. At the Council, in response to objections from some bishops, Jews were not even cleared of the charge of deicide. The new pope, Paul VI, championed a weaker text. His lack of sensitivity towards Jews came out later in a sermon he preached on Passion Sunday 1965. 'Jews', he said, 'were predestined to receive the Messiah and had been waiting for him for thousands of years. When Christ comes, the Jewish people not only do not recognize him, they oppose him, slander him and finally kill him.' After the Holocaust, after all the deliberations of the Council, the pope, a kind-hearted man, was back blaming the entire Jewish race for killing Jesus.

Monsignor John M. Oestereicher, who drafted the original Vatican II document on the Jews, admitted: 'The council fathers could have made St Peter's resound with the cry: "No more concentration camps! No more gas-chambers! No more attempts to slay an entire people! No more persecutions of Jews!"' They never even found it in their hearts to say Jews cannot be charged with killing God.

Pope John Paul's Longest Journey

They agreed to meet in springtime, just before Passover in the year 1986, according to the Christian calendar. Pope John Paul had travelled to every continent, but this was to be his longest journey. He drew a deep breath as he prepared to enter this ornate building which stands practically in view of his own palace in the Vatican. Maybe a thousand people were crammed into a space meant for a few hundred. The main door was wide open as he passed out of bright sunlight into the shade of the synagogue.

Jews are, in a sense, the pope's oldest parishioners. They were living on the streets of Lungotevere de' Cenci when a fisherman came from Galilee to lodge among them nearly two thousand years ago. Since then, Jews and pontiffs, sole survivors of imperial Rome, have always figured in one another's thoughts.

On this day, among the assembled Jews, there were forty who, like ghosts from a past age, had blue tattoo marks on their arms. These were survivors of the Nazi death-camps. John Paul was met by Chief Rabbi Elio Toaff, also in white apart from the black stripes down his prayer-shawl. The two representatives eyed each other nervously. The rabbi fingered his tufted white beard, the pontiff clasped his gold pectoral cross from which many in the congregation could not take their eyes. They had suffered much because of that cross. Both men knew this meeting would go down in history. Both also were aware that there were members of both their communions who would not take kindly to the Bishop and Chief Rabbi of Rome meeting at this solemn liturgical season in the synagogue that was the heart and soul of the last European ghetto prior to the rise of Hitler. Many Jews present knew what Pius X said in 1904, because Golda Meir reported it in her *Autobiography*: 'We cannot prevent Jews from going to Jerusalem, but We would never sanction it. . . . The Jews have not recognized Our Lord; We cannot recognize the Jews.' Toaff had an added problem. He was unable to forget that a predecessor of his, Chief Rabbi Israel Zolli, became a Catholic in 1945 and took the name of Eugenio in gratitude to Pius XII for harbouring Jews during the Second World War. Not since Constantine had there been such a surprising conversion.

The pontiff, smiling sadly, gazed on the congregation with deep respect before entering on an address in which he deplored the hatreds and persecutions of the past against Jews 'by anyone'. The last phrase he repeated. A sporadic burst of applause was taken up by the entire assembly so that the rafters rang. When he expressed his horror at Nazi genocide, many wept openly. They knew that he, a Pole who hails from Cracow, just a few miles from Auschwitz, had entered into their sorrow. Three million of those slaughtered there were as much Poles as they were Jews.

As cantor and choir sang *Ani Ma'amin*, the song of faith sung by Jews on their way to death, the thoughts of many on that spring day turned to Auschwitz and Bergen-Belsen, Dachau and Treblinka.

At the end of the eighty-minute ceremony in the synagogue beside the Tiber, there were overwhelming reasons both for and against joint prayers, so pontiff and rabbi prayed together – in silence. Then, forgetting protocol and the deep religious divide, mindful only of their common humanity, Jew and Gentile warmly embraced. The assembly broke into applause again. Not once had the pope mentioned the State of Israel; that, an aide subsequently explained, is a political question. A curious reserve in a pontiff whose predecessors hungered to get and retain the Papal States. But those few who, at this sacred moment, represented Jewry worldwide knew that John Paul, if only modestly and indirectly, had accepted some of the blame for the incessant tragedies of their people that culminated in the Holocaust.

The long harsh treatment of Jews by the popes was the result of a serious misunderstanding of Gospel truth. For, by the church's own interpretation of the Cross, it was not Jews alone, whether wholly or in part, who were responsible for the Crucifixion but the sin of the world, that is, the sins of the entire race. Christians, in persecuting Jews, were perhaps trying to escape their own guilt. If they made scapegoats of the Jews, it was perhaps because they have never managed to forgive Jews for giving them such a holy and demanding Saviour.

Most historians would agree with the prophetic indictment of Henry Charles Lea, penned in the last century, in the first volume of his *History of the Inquisition in Spain*:

> The Church taught that short of murder, no pun-
> ishment, no suffering, no obloquy was too severe
> for the descendants of those who had refused to
> recognize the Messiah. . . . It is not too much to say
> that for the infinite wrongs committed on the Jews
> during the Middle Ages, and for the prejudices that
> are even yet rife in many quarters, the Church is
> mainly if not wholly responsible.

Is it too harsh to characterize what many Roman pontiffs said about Jews and the way they treated them as *heresy*?

TWELVE

Papal Heretics

'MANY ROMAN PONTIFFS were heretics.' To Catholics this sounds like a quote from a bigoted Protestant. A heretical pope seems as contradictory as a square circle. The First Vatican Council said that the pope, without needing the consent of the church, is the infallible judge of orthodoxy. It is surely unthinkable that a pope like John Paul II could separate himself from the truth and, therefore, from the church by falling into heresy?

The quote is not in fact from a Protestant but from Pope Adrian VI in 1523.

> If by the Roman church you mean its head or pontiff, it is beyond question that he can err even in matters touching the faith. He does this when he teaches heresy by his own judgement or decretal. In truth, many Roman Pontiffs were heretics. The last of them was Pope John XXII [1316–1334].

The themes of papal heretics and popes excommunicated by the church used to be common in theology but little has been heard of them since 1870. Even the imperious Innocent III admitted: 'I can be judged by the church for a sin concerning matters of faith.' Innocent IV, though he claimed that every creature was subject to him as Vicar of the Creator, none the less conceded that any papal utterance that is heretical or tends to divide the church is not to be obeyed. 'Of course,' he said, 'a pope can err in matters of faith. Therefore, no one ought to say, I believe that because the Pope believes it, but because the Church believes it. If he follows the Church he will not err.' For some reason, these words which appeared in the original text of Innocent IV's *Commentary on the Decalogue* were expunged from later editions. It is hard to know why, since any number of popes said more or less the same.

Fallible Popes

So great is the aura surrounding the papacy today that few Catholics realize that it is against faith and tradition to say a pope cannot fall into heresy. The pope was fallible long before he was infallible. From the earliest times it was taken for granted that Roman pontiffs not only can err but have erred in fundamental matters of Christian doctrine. Nor did anyone hasten to add in those distant days: 'Of course, he only erred as a private teacher or theologian.' That suggests that in addition to his own convictions and his responses to his diocesans he also regulated the faith of the whole church. There is no evidence for this. What is known today as papal infallibility was not even hinted at in the early church, and any suggestion that a Bishop of Rome was himself infallible would have aroused at times a degree of mirth. The church's faith belonged to the church and was regulated by the successors of all the apostles, namely, the bishops. They testified to the faith of their communities, especially when they met together in a General Council. A pope who stepped out of line in matters of faith was condemned as a heretic. Peter made mistakes. So did the Bishop of Rome. When he did so, the church had the right and duty to correct or depose him. After all, the pope, too, was a member of the church, not some sort of divine oracle separate from it.

Not merely the idea of infallibility but even the germ of the idea was lacking in patristic times. Rome was by agreement the most eminent see in the West. Peter and Paul taught there and died there. Their bones made it a place of pilgrimage, of light and hope. In spite of this, in the first three centuries, only one of the Fathers, Irenaeus, connects Rome's primacy with doctrine. Not even he relates this personally to the *Bishop* of Rome.

In all the Greek Fathers there is not one word about the prerogatives of the Bishop of Rome, no suggestion he had jurisdiction over them. No one, Greek or Latin, appeals to the Bishop of Rome as final and universal arbiter in any single dispute about the faith. As a point of fact, no Bishop of Rome dared decide on his own a matter of faith for the church.

Roma locuta est, causa finita est. St Augustine's phrase, 'Rome has spoken, the dispute is at an end', is quoted endlessly by Catholic apologists. With reason. Out of ten huge folios of his work, that is the one phrase which proves that the Bishop of Rome has, on his own, the right to settle controversies in the church. But does it? The context shows Augustine arguing that after two synods, with the Bishop of Rome concurring, it is time to call a halt. Repeatedly Augustine calls on synods to settle disputes. When Pope Stephen tried to settle a baptismal controversy for the African church and his view was rejected, Augustine says they were right to do so. This was a matter for the church not for an individual.

Augustine spent a great deal of his life disputing with the rival church of the Donatists. Never once does he suggest that they have separated themselves from the centre of unity, Rome; he knows no such centre for the church as a whole. He never says, for instance, as modern popes say: 'Return to Rome, believe all that the pope teaches.'

In 434, Vincent of Lerins laid down the criteria of Catholic doctrine: it must be held always, everywhere, by everyone. He does not mention a role for Rome or its Bishop. The faith is formulated by a Council not by an individual bishop.

Pope Pelagius (556–60) talks of heretics separating themselves from the Apostolic Sees, that is, Rome, Jerusalem, Alexandria plus Constantinople. In all the early writings of the hierarchy there is no special mention of a role for the Bishop of Rome, nor yet the special name of 'Pope'. Patriarchs are mentioned, of which Rome was first because of Peter and Paul, archbishops, metropolitans and bishops. No mention of, no role for a pope, not even in Isidore of Seville, the great author of the seventh century.

Another astonishing omission in view of Vatican I: of the eighty or so heresies in the first six centuries, not one refers to the authority of the Bishop of Rome, not one is settled by the Bishop of Rome. Episcopacy in general sometimes comes under attack; no one attacks the authority of the Roman pontiff, *because no one has heard of it*.

After Peter, the centuries roll by, full of controversies, any one of which today would involve immediate recourse to Rome for a decision. In those days, no Bishop of Rome ventures to try to solve them and not one bishop asks him to do so. Pope Siricius (384–98) was no Gregory VII. When a certain Bishop Bonosius fell into heresy, he refused to pronounce against him because, he said, he had no right to do so. It would have to be settled by the province's bishops.

We already noted that not a single Father can find any hint of a Petrine office in the great biblical texts that refer to Peter. Papal supremacy and infallibility, so central to the Catholic church today, are simply not mentioned. Not a single creed, nor confession of faith, nor catechism, nor passage in patristic writings contains one syllable about the pope, still less about faith and doctrine being derived from him.

Every indicator suggests that the Bishop of Rome is fallible, not infallible. In fact, the first pope to appeal to anything like what we know today as papal authority was Agatho in 680. He did so for a very embarrassing reason: a predecessor of his, Pope Honorius, was about to be condemned by a General Council for heresy.

A Long Line of Papal Heretics

The tradition of heresy among Bishops of Rome went back way beyond Honorius. Take Liberius (352–66). He did his best, like other bishops, to sort out the Arian controversy. Arius believed the Son was less than the Father. The great champion of orthodoxy was Athanasius. Liberius had been forced into exile, and the condition of his return was to condemn Athanasius. This he did, thereby suggesting that the Son was lower than the Father. For this, he earned the malediction of a very important Father, Hilary of Poitiers, who accused him of apostasy. 'Anathema to thee, Liberius,' was Hilary's famous cry, and every orthodox bishop took it up. Liberius' error was an unassailable proof throughout the Middle Ages that popes can fall into heresy like anyone else.

Other popes made unfortunate pronouncements. Gregory the Great said that unbaptized babies go straight to hell and suffer there for all eternity. Some pontiffs went further. Innocent I (401–17) wrote to the Council of Milevis and Gelasius I (492–6) wrote to the Bishops of Picenum that babies were obliged to receive communion. If they died baptized but uncommunicated, they would go straight to hell. This view was condemned by the Council of Trent.

The most Hamlet-like of all popes was Vigilius (537–55), whose career reads like a theatrical farce.

Vigilius was a portly unscrupulous Roman official who was never popular. Pope Boniface II wanted him as his successor and wrote a letter nominating him as pope on his death. A crowd, furious that a pope dared to infringe their democratic rights as the clergy and people of Rome, forced him to burn it. It was an interesting moment. Had Boniface been allowed to get away with it, there might not have been any more papal elections. Certainly, after 1870, it would have been taken for granted that a pope appoint his successor. Who better than the Vicar of Christ, one with the plenitude of power, to elect the next successor to St Peter? But Romans in the sixth century insisted that Rome was their diocese and they had a right to choose who would rule over them.

Years later, Vigilius did manage to get himself elected pope. His was not a happy reign. Emperor Justinian forced him to join him in Constantinople and kept him there until the pontiff agreed with his own heterodox views about Jesus and the authority of the Council of Chalcedon. Vigilius changed his mind as often as the emperor put pressure on him.

Eventually, Justinian called the Fifth General Council. It met in May in the year 553 in the south gallery of the church of Saint Sophia in Constantinople. Only twenty-five Western bishops attended out of a complement of 165. Vigilius sent his apologies, pleading he was sick. His absence was not considered important enough to delay proceedings. The Council met and decided, among other things, that his Holiness was a heretic. He was, therefore, excommunicated.

When the pope got to hear of this, he condemned the Council's decision and all those who had excommunicated him. In a fury, Justinian banished him to Proconessus, a dreary rocky inlet near the western end of the Sea of Marmara. Rumours reached Vigilius there that a new election for pope was imminent back home and his own name was being struck out of the dyptichs, the liturgical lists of pontiffs. His health was bad; he suffered agonies from the stone. After six months of this, he could take no more.

On 8 December 553, he sent a letter to the new Patriarch of Constantinople in which he claimed that till now he had been deluded by 'the wiles of the devil'. Satan had divided him from his fellow-bishops but, through the penalty of excommunication, he had seen the light. His former opinions, he admitted, were mistaken and, like the great Augustine, he wanted to retract. He accepted all the decrees of the Fifth Council and proclaimed them true and binding on the West.

Now that the pope had come round to his way of thinking, the emperor was prepared to let the pope go home. Back in Italy, a frosty reception awaited him. He only escaped a lynching by dying in Syracuse on 7 June 555. He was refused burial in St Peter's.

So outraged was Italy at Vigilius' conduct and his frequent changes of mind over the critical issue of whether Jesus was one or two persons that it refused at first to accept the legitimacy of the Fifth Council. The Archbishop of Milan and the Patriarch of Aquileia withdrew from communion with the Holy See in protest. It was left to the next pope, Pelagius I, to clear up the mess, with help from the military.

The significance of this controversy does not lie in what was debated at the time. It lies in the fact that a Council believed itself to be above the pope, so much so that it excommunicated and deposed him for heresy. During the Middle Ages, this was one of those famous case-histories that proved to all theologians that a *Council was superior to a pope*. It was not until much later that forgeries altered this settled conviction. Before then, no one ever *presumed* popes were orthodox by some sort of divine prerogative; they had to prove their orthodoxy like everyone else.

The Heretical Pope Honorius

Honorius, who was pontiff from 625 to 638, is the classic case of a pope condemned by the church for heresy. He was a remarkable man, holy, a good leader and fine statesman. He was, in moral stature, comparable with Gregory the Great.

His one fatal flaw was that, being a man of action, he disliked controversies because they wasted time which was better spent on serving God and the poor.

The Council of Chalcedon had settled that Christ had two natures; he was divine and human. A supplementary question was now asked: Did Christ have one will or two? In a much-publicized letter, Honorius ridiculed those 'bombastic and time-wasting philosophers' who, in weighing up the two natures of Christ, 'croak at us like frogs'. He was opposed to the two wills, though it is not clear why. Maybe he was merely reacting against the idea of two *contradictory* wills in Christ. In any case, his words were seized on as being contrary to the faith. He was labelled a Monothelite or One-Will-ite. Honorius died before he could explain himself fully. But his letter brought about a heresy in the Eastern church. These heretics appealed to it as proof that the pope approved of Monothelitism.

Forty years after Honorius' death, the emperor wanted the matter cleared up. He suggested a General Council, which the new pope, Agatho, agreed to. He prepared for it by holding his own synods in Rome. The Easter synod of 680 condemned Monothelitism and claimed, for the very first time, that Rome had supremacy over the whole church. They informed the emperor that the Roman church was his mother, and no one should dare say that she had ever erred in matters of faith. Had the synod never heard of Vigilius? It was probably this proud and unprecedented claim that sealed Honorius' fate.

The Sixth General Council took place in the Imperial Palace in Constantinople; it lasted from 7 November 680 to 16 September 681. The Monothelites maintained that Pope Honorius was on their side. The Council agreed. In condemning the Monothelites, the fathers also condemned *him*.

The 174 delegates approved the decrees; the papal legates, without any objections, signed first. The new pontiff Leo II, elected in 682, confirmed the condemnation of his predecessor. He wrote: 'Honorius tried with profane treachery to subvert the immaculate faith.' It was not a matter of condemning some private opinion or theological quirk. Leo condemned him for publicly undermining the faith of the church. Why otherwise was a General Council involved? From this time on, all pontiffs were obliged at their consecration to endorse the council's decision by an oath condemning Pope Honorius' heresy.

Gregorovius, in his *Rome in the Middle Ages*, wrote: 'The unique instance of a Roman Pope being publicly anathematized on the charge of heresy by an Ecumenical Council constitutes one of the most remarkable facts in ecclesiastical history.' It matters little whether Honorius *was* a heretic or simply a plain blunt man who preferred deeds to words and tried to end a controversy with a letter tossed off in a hurry. The key point is that a General Council, approved by a long line of popes, testified that the church does not believe a pope is infallible. On the contrary, when he makes a mistake that misleads the church he has to be condemned, like anyone else, as a heretic. In matters of faith, the Bishop of Rome is as subject to a Council as any bishop is. Thus, nearly twelve centuries in advance, was denied papal infallibility as defined by a lesser Council of the fragmented Western church in 1870.

Rome's Sacramental Heresies

Rome's most persistent lack of orthodoxy was in the area of the sacraments. This is partly explained by the collapse of learning brought about by the barbarian invasions. The Greeks, mischievously, tended to look on Rome as full of simpletons.

From the eighth century on, certain popes annulled ordinations and reordained priests. It began with an antipope, Constantine II, in the year 769. But, as we saw, after Pope Formosus died in 896, not only was he distinterred and excommunicated for heresy, but his ordinations were also declared invalid. It raised the alarming question: Are there any valid sacraments in Italy of which the pope is patriarch? Popes Stephen VII and Sergius III, Marozia's lover, both taught that the ordinations of heretical popes were invalid.

This attack on the sacraments continued into the eleventh century. Popes decided that where simony – that is, payment – was involved in the ordination of a bishop the ordination was invalid. This prompted Leo IX (1049–54), probably prodded by Hildebrand, to reordain many priests. When Hildebrand became Gregory VII, he affirmed clearly that *all* ordinations involving money were invalid. Taken seriously this decision would have nullified most ordinations in the Western world. There would have been no valid masses or confessions or last rites in country after country. It would practically have wiped out the Apostolic Succession, a disaster that Leo XIII was to say happened to the Church of England after the Reformation.

Urban II (1088–99) went further than Hildebrand. Even if a bishop did not pay to be ordained, he said, the ordination would be invalid if the bishop who consecrates him paid for *his* ordination! This interpretation of the sacraments which flew in the face of the entire tradition found its way into the Decretals of Gratian. In spite of this immense authority of popes and canon law, for some inexplicable reason – the Holy Spirit? – this heresy did not gain currency in the West. The East held itself aloof from such heterodox opinions.

In 1557, Paul IV, in his Bull *Cum ex Apostolatus officio*, defined 'out of the plenitude of his power' that all the acts of previous heretically or schismatically inclined popes were null and void. It had a semblance of logic: a heretic pope was not even a Christian, let alone pontiff. But, put into operation, it would have exploded the whole Catholic sacramental system, which is of its nature hereditary. That is, it is handed on from one generation to the next. If one generation loses it – for instance, by using the wrong formulas or having the wrong intention – it is lost *for ever*. However peculiar this may sound, it is orthodox Catholic teaching. It is peculiar in that, of its nature, it must breed uncertainty. For example, a child invalidly baptized by a priest who, in a stupor, says the wrong words or uses some liquid other than water might become a priest – all his masses and confessions are invalid; or a bishop – all his ordinations are invalid; or pope – most of the workings of the church are invalid. Happily, even Rome, that most intellectually rigorous of churches, does not take these matters to their logical conclusion. This may explain why it even turned its back on Gregory VII and Gratian over the sacraments.

It was not merely in the matter of ordinations that Rome strayed from the path of orthodoxy.

Pope Pelagius had said, correctly according to tradition, that the Trinity must be invoked for a valid baptism. Nicholas I (858–67) said that calling on the name of Christ is enough. Worse than this, he decided that confirmation administered by priests was invalid. At a stroke, he practically wiped out confirmation in the Greek church. The latter had from time immemorial allowed priests to confirm children. Pope Nicholas said the practice was invalid and the Eastern bishops would have to reconfirm the children. Perhaps the bishops had to be reconfirmed themselves! Rome's decision to 'annul' centuries of confirmations in their church naturally antagonized the Greeks and helped prepare for a permanent rift between East and West.

Rome's teaching on marriage was not without errors either.

Stephen II (752) went against the mainstream of tradition when he said that a marriage between a free man and a slave girl, both Christians, can be dissolved, allowing the man to remarry. Urban III (1185–7) also suggested that there were circumstances in which a consummated marriage between Christians can be terminated. Celestine III (1191–8) spelled this out. A marriage between Christians, he said, can be dissolved if one of the parties chooses to become a heretic. For this, Pope Adrian VI pronounced Pope Celestine a heretic. Even Innocent III blundered on this topic. He insisted that Christians had to keep the Book of Deuteronomy *to the letter*. His Holiness had overlooked the fact that Deuteronomy allows a man to divorce his wife.

Popes have even erred on the Eucharist. Apart from the early popes who, as we have seen, said that actual reception was necessary for salvation, even for babies, Pope Nicholas II (1059–61) said that Christ's body can be sensibly touched by hands and bitten by the teeth. The church rejected this view. Nicholas had an entirely mistaken notion of the real presence – not sacramental, at all – and he seemed also to assert that, after his resurrection, Christ goes on suffering.

It was, however, an Avignon pope, John XXII, whom Adrian VI, in his book on the sacraments, singled out as a heretic of unusual proportions.

The Heresies of Pope John XXII

When Clement V died in the year 1314, the conclave tried for two years to agree on a successor. Finally, in despair, they chose Jacques

Duèse from Cahors. The date was 7 August; the place Lyons. The new pontiff took the name of John XXII.

He seemed right for the job. Aged seventy-two, small, delicate, sickly-looking, this cobbler's son was unlikely to live long. John XXII was to prove a harsh and durable pontiff, ambitious, full of avarice, more worldly than a pimp, and with a laugh that crackled with unimprovable malice. This fragile little monster was to last for eighteen tempestuous years more.

When he took over, the treasury was bare. Clement V had given away absolutely everything to his relatives. John set about rectifying matters. A financier of genius, he worked on the basis that what a pope can give a pope can sell. And he sold everything an imaginative Frenchman could think of. Forgiveness for every crime had its price. For example, Catholics could pay so much to be absolved from murder, so much from incest and sodomy. The worse Catholics behaved, the richer his Holiness became. When a pirated list of sins and rake-offs was published, it was thought to be a forgery concocted by the church's enemies. It was true, but the enemies were the pope and the Curia. By the weirdest alchemy, they were turning vices into gold. They were giving sinners the right to sin and break their vows, or at least the freedom to avoid the consequences of so doing.

John XXII needed money. He had a passion for war, especially the Italian wars. It was reckoned he spent 70 per cent of his income on armaments, which would have aroused wrath in St Peter and envy in Julius II. John's feuds with the Viscontis of Milan, in particular, proved costly. A contemporary said of him: 'The blood he shed would have incarnadined the waters of Lake Constance, and the bodies of the slain would have bridged it from shore to shore.'

This greediest of popes, who kept his brother and nephews in clover, contradicted several previous pontiffs on the subject of Christ's poverty.

Even during the lifetime of St Francis of Assisi, two sects had appeared among his brethren, one in favour of the strict observance, the other of moderation. In the year 1279, Nicholas III had patched up the quarrel by a Bull *Exiit qui seminat*. This passed into canon law. Nicholas said that poverty was not so much an individual as a communal thing. As such it was meritorious and holy. For this was the practice of Christ and his apostles.

Popes after him confirmed that Christ and the apostles lived in poverty; the gospels plainly said so. Honorius III, Innocent IV, Alexander IV, Nicholas III and Nicholas IV, Boniface VIII, Clement V – all were agreed.

Not John XXII. In a Bull *Cum inter nonnullos* of 12 November 1323, he maintained: To say that Christ and the apostles had no property is a perversion of scripture.

The spiritual Franciscans, till then praised by the Holy See, were now labelled heretics; princes were obliged to send them to the stake or else face excommunication themselves. It was a feature of the times that this doctrinal issue turned into a political football. The emperor, Louis of Bavaria, had already rowed with John XXII when the latter said that in an interregnum *he* became administrator of the Empire and the new emperor had to take an oath of loyalty to *him*. John wanted to turn history on its head. For his part, Louis was delighted to be able to charge the pope with heresy. He called him Antichrist, deposed him and appointed another.

The emperor's choice fell on Pier di Corbario, a decrepit Franciscan who called himself Nicholas V. Unfortunately, Louis had not done his homework. Before long, an elderly lady appeared, claiming to be Mrs di Corbario. This was bad news. Pier, it seemed, was married with children when, without his wife's permission, he had left home to join a monastery. In terms of canon law, he was irregular; he was not even a real monk, let alone a pontiff. It was true that John XXII had a son who was doing well for himself as a cardinal, but the pope had never committed the sin of matrimony. Faced with a choice between a heretic pope and a married and irregular antipope, Louis opted for the latter. Nicholas V's wife was paid off and he set about appointing cardinals and a Curia of his own. At least, the emperor mused, *my* pope is a Catholic.

In the end, Louis tired of playing games. He deserted Nicholas at Pisa and handed him over to the church's authorities. It was 18 June 1329.

John promised to be a kind father to this renegade, which was rather like a sparrow-hawk promising to love a sparrow. On the way to Avignon, Nicholas was maltreated in every possible way. People remembered John's Psalm-type curse on him: 'May his children be orphans and his wife a widow! May they be driven forth from their hearth to beggary.'

When Nicholas arrived in Provence as plain Pier di Corbario, John, contrary to all predictions, *was* kind to him. His life was spared, he was given rooms in the papal palace, though he was kept under house arrest. When he died four years later, he was buried in the Franciscan habit.

John XXII had triumphed. It was now official Catholic teaching: Christ and the apostles did not live a life of poverty.

The pope was eighty-seven-years-old when he created a fresh scandal on All Saints' Day 1331.

The first clue was when an English Dominican preached before the papal court that the souls of the just see God immediately. John had him tried by the Inquisition. To please his Holiness, the baffled inquisitors put the friar in gaol and nearly starved him to death.

In the church of Notre-Dame des Doms in Avignon the pope now preached a sermon that caused a sensation. The souls of the saints, he said, do not have the vision of God prior to the resurrection of the body. They are still *sub altare Dei*, that is, under the altar of God. Only at the Judgement will they be placed *on* the altar to contemplate the divine essence.

No one in his entourage had the courage to tell him he was talking heresy.

On 5 January 1332 he enlarged his views to encompass the damned. There was, he told his astonished congregation, as yet no one in hell. Only at the end of the world will the damned go to the place of torment.

Once again, a theological dispute was transformed into politics. The emperor, in this instance, was supported by the Franciscan General, whom John had excommunicated over the poverty issue, and the great Franciscan theologian William of Occam. For the second time, the pope was declared a heretic.

If the saints and the Blessed Virgin, the emperor argued, are not in heaven, how can they intercede for us? Why visit shrines of the saints who are not with God in heaven? Most pointedly, why should Christians pay the pope for pardon and indulgences if, when they die, they have to wait till Kingdom come to enter Paradise?

Just as a dead man is no longer a man, so the emperor concluded a heretical pope is no longer pope. Ex-Pope John XXII was now plain Jacques of Cahors.

Philippe de Valois supported Louis. He wrote to John telling him his views were heretical and if he did not withdraw them he would be burned. The University of Paris gave it as their opinion that the pope was sorely mistaken and should recant at once.

John, haughty as ever, offered rich benefices to anyone who could show him a passage in St Augustine that supported his view. No one could. Finally, it dawned on him that the whole church opposed him. Against every instinct, he wrote back to Paris, saying that he had never positively denied that the saints see God immediately after death, only that he had left it an open question. Even this lie was not good enough. European theologians replied to a man: it is *not* an open question. The church's mind could not be more closed.

At this point, the story becomes unclear. He changed his mind, some said, just before he died at the age of ninety. Others say he never changed his mind; he died as he had lived, a heretic. What is certain is this.

On 3 December 1234, sensing he was soon about to have his ideas tested in practice, he summoned his cardinals to his bedside. He urged them, when he was gone, to select 'a worthy successor to the Chair of Peter'. They in turn urged him to save his soul and the church's honour by withdrawing his heretical views about the beatific vision. He died the next day. A Bull was subsequently published in his name, revoking all he had said and done that conflicted with the church and submitting himself totally to its judgement.

Did the Bull genuinely reflect John's final state of mind? Even there, he maintains that separated souls 'see God and the divine essence face to face clearly, so far as the state and condition of a separated soul permits'. Such subtleties seem beyond the scope of a ninety-year-old on the brink of the grave. Pointless, too, in that it was still not acceptable to theologians.

Judged by the church's own teaching, this pope was a heretic, as Adrian VI admitted. He pertinaciously and over a period denied an important article of faith. When challenged, he publicly altered his position, only to leave open a doctrine that was officially closed. He still *doubted*, therefore was still a heretic. What his final position was is not clear; even if he was responsible for the final Bull, it was still heterodox.

His successor, Benedict XII, stood no nonsense on the matter. On 29 January 1336, in a public consistory, he said that after death the saints enjoy the beatific vision without any delay. Anyone holding a contrary opinion was to be punished as a heretic.

Even after he left the scene, John XXII remained a controversial figure. He, the scourge of heretics, was proclaimed a heretic himself. He had handed over to the Inquisition for burning a large number of holy Franciscans – they eventually numbered 114 – whose only crime was to say that Jesus and his disciples lived a life of utter poverty.

For the final irony is this: when he died, the treasury which was empty when he took over was overflowing. The Florentine bankers called in to deal with the hoard were astounded. Never had they seen anything remotely like it. They counted 25 million gold florins, and there was an equivalent amount in gems and precious objects.

The real heresy of John XXII, Christ's vicar and successor of St Peter, was that he burned the poorest of Christ's poor and died the richest man in the world.

The Pope Who Rewrote the Bible

When Gregory XIII became pope in the year 1572, the Franciscan Cardinal Montalto retired from public life. His retainers passed it around that his Eminence had one foot in the grave already and wanted no more of life than to prepare for death. At the rare meetings of the Sacred College which he was obliged to attend, he coughed continuously as if he were in the final stages of consumption. To whatever was proposed he meekly bowed his big tonsured head in assent. He was too weak to argue. When his colleagues protested that he was far too young to die, Felice Peretti da Montalto shrugged sadly and added eight years to his age in an effort to convince them of his imminent decease. An English visitor to Rome chanced to catch a rare glimpse of his Eminence bent over his fire and wrote home about this 'most crooching, humble cardinal that was ever lodged in an oven'.

Pope Gregory died in 1585. Montalto appeared at the conclave, hollow-cheeked, dull-eyed, with wrinkles carefully applied. His gait was snail-like, his voice scarcely audible. He walked on crutches, and so round-shouldered was he that his head nearly touched the ground. It was evident to all forty-two cardinal-electors as they cast their votes that Montalto was perfect for the papacy. They were immediately undeceived. As soon as Montalto won the vote, according to his biographer Leti, he straightened up, threw his crutches away with the cry, 'Now I am Caesar,' before intoning the *Te Deum* with a voice of thunder.

In five years, Sixtus V got through fifty years' work. He had teams of men labouring day and night to put the dome on St Peter's. He had the obelisk moved, inch by inch, by hundreds of workmen and mules, to its present central position in the piazza. He built the Vatican Library. He constructed an aqueduct over valleys and hills to bring water twenty miles into Rome. He well earned his nickname, 'The Consecrated Whirlwind'.

Allied to titanic energy was a fierce and clamorous egotism. He asserted his temporal jurisdiction over all kings and princes. When the Jesuit, Robert Bellarmine, the stoutest champion of the papacy since Aquinas, suggested in his book of *Controversies* that the pope only had indirect jurisdiction over temporal rulers, Sixtus resolved to censure him. He could for any reason, he said, and *whenever he pleased*, appoint or dismiss *anyone*, emperors included. He also disapproved of the theologian Vittorio for daring to write that it was lawful to disobey unjust orders of a pope. Yes, he, Sixtus, pontiff, would ban the books of both these renegades.

The cardinals of the Congregation of the Index were too terrified to tell his Holiness that these eminent authors based their views on the works of countless saints and scholars. Count Olivares, the Spanish ambassador in Rome, wrote to his master Philip II that the cardinals stayed silent 'for fear Sixtus might give them a taste of his sharp temper and perhaps put the saints themselves on the Index'.

Sixtus was particularly ungracious towards Bellarmine. The Jesuit had gallantly co-operated with him on editing the works of St Ambrose. It cannot have been easy. At every point, Sixtus had overruled his judgement. Afterwards, the pope made the order that his version was now the standard text. It was and it remains the most unreliable in existence.

The same high-handed approach he adopted to the Bible. The results were devastating.

* * *

The Latin version of the Bible, the Vulgate, was the work of St Jerome in the fourth century. By the Middle Ages it had pride of place. By then, many false readings had crept in, owing to sleepy copyists. With printing, editions multiplied, as did the errors. At the Reformation, Protestants had their own versions of the Bible; it was imperative for Catholics to have a reliable text of the Vulgate in all disputes.

The Council of Trent in 1546 had called the Vulgate the church's authentic version of the Bible. It alone was to be used in lectures, disputations, sermons. 'Authentic' means that Catholics can be sure it is free from doctrinal and moral error and substantially faithful to the originals. When the fathers of Trent commissioned a new edition of the Vulgate, they had no idea of the size of the task. Eleven popes lived and died, and nothing happened. Until Sixtus V.

Three years into his pontificate, at the end of 1588, the scholars he had appointed to edit the Vulgate presented him with their final text. There was too much scholarship in it for the pope's liking; and they had put in too many variant readings. He shouted the president of the commission, Cardinal Carafa, out of his room, screaming he could do far better on his own. This astounding claim he set about trying to prove. In a 300-word sentence, he declared in a Bull that he, the pope, was the only proper person to decide the question of an authentic Bible for the church.

Hour after hour he laboured, and night after night, for he was an insomniac. He had only one full-time secretary, who was almost driven to the grave. In the main, Sixtus kept to the Louvain text which he was familiar with. It was not particularly scholarly. Where it was obscure, he did not mind adding phrases and sentences to clarify. Often he translated according to whim. Another of his idiosyncrasies was to alter the references. A system of chapter and verse had been worked out in 1555 by Robert Stephanus. It was not perfect but it was convenient and was universally used. Sixtus discarded it in favour of his own scheme. All previous Bibles became instantly obsolete; all books in the schools, with their armouries of texts, had to be reprinted. Apart from changing the titles of the Psalms which were considered by many to be inspired, he omitted, probably through carelessness, entire verses.

After only eighteen months, his work was done. In 1590, the first folio copies appeared. 'Splendid,' he muttered, admiring the beautiful binding, until one glance at the text revealed many misprints. Then more and more. The printers, too, had been expected to operate, night and day, in whirlwind fashion.

So as not to waste time, Sixtus started patching things up on his own. He wrote corrections in ink on tiny bits of paper – squares, oblongs, triangles – and pasted them over the printer's errors. It took him six months, and he botched a lot of it. Publication kept getting deferred as the pope's nightmare continued. His Bull, *Aeternus Ille*, was long ready. Never was there a more authoritative document:

> By the fullness of Apostolical power, We decree and declare this edition . . . approved by the authority given Us by the Lord, is to be received and held as true, lawful, authentic and unquestioned in all public and private discussions, readings, preachings and explanations.

No printer, editor, bookseller was allowed to deviate by one jot from this final and authentic version of the Latin Bible. Anyone contravening the Bull was to be excommunicated, and only the pope could absolve him. Temporal punishments were threatened, too.

In mid-April copies were at last delivered to cardinals and ambassadors. They inspected it, boggle-eyed. Four months later, on 27 August, the bells of the Capitol announced the pope was dead. That night a storm arose so fierce it was as though Sixtus' departing spirit had whipped up the elements into a frenzy. Rome went wild with delight, but none was so elated as his enemies in the Sacred College.

The next pope died after a twelve-day pontificate. Gregory XIV (1590–1) was left to limit the damage. But how? A Bible had been imposed with the plenitude of papal power, complete with the trimmings of excommunication, on the whole church – and it was riddled with errors. The academic world was in turmoil; Protestants were deriving enormous pleasure and amusement from the predicament of the Roman church.

On 11 November 1590, Bellarmine returned to Rome from a mission abroad. Personally relieved that Sixtus, who had wanted him on the Index, was dead, he feared for the prestige of the papacy. He suggested to the new pope how he might deal with this dilemma. In his *Autobiography* he was to tell all.

> Some men, whose opinions had great weight, held that it should be publicly prohibited. I did not think so, and I showed the Holy Father that, instead of forbidding the edition of the Bible in question, it would be better to correct it in such manner that it could be published without detriment to the honour of Pope Sixtus. This result could be achieved by removing inadvisable changes as quickly as possible, and then issuing the volume with Sixtus' name upon it, and a preface stating that owing to haste some errors had crept into the first edition through the fault of printers and other persons.

In brief, Bellarmine advised the pope to lie. Some of his admirers have disputed this. Their task is formidable.

The options were plain: admit publicly that a pope had erred on a critical matter of the Bible *or* engage in a cover-up whose outcome was unpredictable. Bellarmine proposed the latter.

He may have been tempted to take this line because it was a selfless thing to do: he was defending the honour of a man who had impugned his own. He may also have meant to include Sixtus in that vague reference to the fault of printers 'and other persons'. Yet could any reader have possibly guessed that the pope was one of the other persons? Besides, the only damaging errors were the pope's, not the printers'.

The deceit did not stop there.

A thorough overhaul of Sixtus' Bible would take years. Years they did not have. A small band of scholars, including Bellarmine, went to work in a country house on a slope of the Sabine Hills eighteen miles from Rome. They did a remarkable job, completing their revision in mid-June 1591. The problem now was how to present it to the world. Bellarmine, asked by a new pontiff, developed the cover-up.

The new version should be printed at once. Sixtus' version was bound to fall into the hands of heretics. They would point to the changes, omissions, mistranslations and say: 'Look, popes think nothing of corrupting Bible texts to suit their own purposes.' With the new text should go a preface saying Sixtus had published a Bible revised according to his orders but, on examining it, he had discovered that many errors had crept into it owing to unseemly haste. This was not so unusual in first editions. Sixtus, therefore, decided that the work must be done all over again. At his death, his successors were keen to carry out his wishes. Hence the new edition.

This was very far from the truth. The only really disturbing errors were those of which Sixtus was unaware: his own. He never had the slightest intention of revising his own work, only that of the printers. The decision to revise and republish was taken after his death.

Uppermost in Bellarmine's mind was this: popes must never be seen to condemn the solemn decrees of their predecessors. That would reflect badly on papal authority itself. On the other hand, respect, was also due to the Bible; that, like the papacy, was inerrant. Out of the need to reconcile the irreconcilable came the cover-up.

Bellarmine suggested that the new version should not be the only one allowed. It had been done in a hurry and there were, no doubt, errors in it that time would reveal. Besides, he added, 'though the Pope has given us our commission, he could not give us the assistance of the Holy Spirit which is his exclusive prerogative'. There was in Bellarmine's mind, for all its greatness and subtlety, an almost childish strain when it came to the papacy. He did not care to explain what happened to the assistance of the Holy Spirit while Pope Sixtus was working on the Vulgate.

The Bible was ready for publication at the end of 1592, and Clement VIII agreed to it going out under the sole name of Sixtus. In

The Church and the Papacy (1944), Jalland says, tongue in cheek, that this affair

> serves to provide unique documentary evidence of the possibility that even the Roman See can change its mind. Yet the fact has subsequently been obscured, for when the new edition appeared in 1592 it was boldly and somewhat disingenuously presented to the world as the 'Sixtine' Bible. If the name of Clement was later introduced, it scarcely served to atone for a strange feat of literary dishonesty, nor to conceal the truth that the Roman See had so far yielded to popular clamour as to treat one of its earlier decisions as reversible.

After the lies, one problem remained: how to get back copies of the real Sixtus Bible. Bellarmine advised the pope to buy them back, regardless of cost, which was likely to be high. Not only were they magnificently produced, but a half-wit would see their curio value.

Instructions went out to the Inquisition in Venice and to the Jesuit General to scour printing houses and private homes, especially in Germany, to save the honour of the papacy. The search had elements of farce. At a time when Protestants were distributing free Bibles, the Catholic church was desperately trying to buy some back.

How many copies were recovered is not known, but at the most ten. One copy found its way into the Bodleian Library in Oxford. Its first librarian, Dr Thomas James, treated it like manna from heaven. In 1611 he wrote a book contrasting the two Bibles of Sixtus and Sixtus-Clement. He found 'that the two popes did notoriously differ amongst themselves, not only in the number of the verses [the later version went back to Stephanus' system of reference] but in the body of the text and in the Prefaces and Bulls themselves'.

James claimed to see a remarkable thing: two popes warring in open contradiction of each other. 'In this war, their Head hath been so soiled and their Church so deadly wounded that all the balme in Gilead will not cure them. We have here one Pope against another, Sixtus against Clement, Clement against Sixtus, disputing, writing and fighting about the Jerome Bible.' The Bible, as far as Catholics were concerned, said James, was a wax nose which popes bent into whatever shape suited them. 'If the Pope said what was white was black and black white no Catholic dared disagree.'

It was good polemics, and Sixtus thoroughly deserved it. But even Dr James did not find more than one or two fundamental differences between two popes or any real attempt by either to deceive the reader. Enormous stupidity was present but precious little malice.

What the affair revealed was something quite different.

In any other institution, mistakes such as those made by Sixtus would have been a mere passing embarrassment easily laughed off and soon forgotten. Only in the Roman church could it provoke what, in Bellarmine's view, was the greatest crisis of the Reformation. Reacting to this crisis, a man of Bellarmine's integrity felt compelled to tell lies and half-truths which more than one pope swallowed with relief. If a saintly person like Bellarmine was prepared to lie for the papacy, what will others not do? What have others not done? What are others not doing?

Bellarmine, selfless and poor, emerges as the sad victim of the papacy which he gave his life to defend. So large did it figure in his mind that in him Dr James's jibe was verified to the letter. He did, to please the pope, say that black was white and white black in a most dangerous area: ethics. He states in his book on the Roman pontiff that whatever the pope commands, however evil or ridiculous, has to be obeyed, as if it is virtue itself. Whatever the pope does, even when he deposes an emperor on the most frivolous pretext, has to be accepted by Catholics who henceforward have to obey the pope and *not* the emperor.

The affair of the pope who rewrote the Bible proves once more that the teaching that the pope cannot err creates its own version of history and leads even saintly men to lie on its behalf. But Bellarmine is chiefly remembered today not because he covered up for a pope, but because he helped ruin the career of a layman – one of the most famous who ever lived.

The Greatest Scandal in Christendom

Galileo was old now, in his mid-seventies, and completely blind. In the summer of 1640, he knew that his days were numbered.

Why did they go on persecuting him? In the village, there were still paid informers who told the Inquisition everything about him. They intercepted his mail, wrote memos on every visitor he received. His Holiness Urban VIII would never forgive him, he knew that. When he applied to Rome for permission to go into Florence for medical treatment, the Inquisition had replied: 'Sanctissimus [the Most Holy] refused to grant the request and ordered the said gentleman should be warned to desist from handing in supplications or he will be taken back to the gaols of the Holy Office.' That hurt the 'said gentleman', not only because he had always thought of the pope as a friend but also because the reply came on the day that his daughter, aged thirty-three, died of melancholy at her father's fate.

Ah, but it was good to be in his beloved villa of Il Gioiello (The Gem) with all its familiar sounds and smells. And its familiar sights on parade before his inner eyes. Walking out in the cool of evening, he could vividly imagine Florence, city of light, beneath his villa at Arcetri, the Babel-high, red-brick, flower-like cupola of the cathedral beneath Giotto's belfry, the Palazzo Vecchio with its soaring tower, the broad sweep of the River Arno. All around him, in the still air, he could hear the cicadas and smell the ash-grey olive trees and vines. Once, he had been an expert at grafting vines; the wine he drank was always the product of his own hands.

But more precious than this Tuscan villa, or Florence itself set in a gentle landscape, was the sky above: moon and stars. Was it pride on his part to feel that these celestial forms were more his than most men's, more his than even Il Gioiello?

Though blind as Homer, he kept on dictating his scientific works to his secretary. They were, curiously, among his best. The Inquisition had forbidden him to publish anything new or to reissue his old works. Banned for life, they said. But only in Italy, and not for ever. Inquisitors, though they disagreed, were not God.

Besides, though he was blind now, who could take from him the memory of what his eyes had seen? Those eyes of his had seen things hidden since the beginning of the world. They had opened up new Americas in the skies, and, one day, he never doubted it, his name would be as famous as – no, *more* famous than Columbus.

Galileo Galilei had been born in the year 1564, in the year Michelangelo died. His father Vincenzo, a cloth-merchant had hailed from Florence, but his first child was born in Pisa. Galileo started in university as a medical student but soon dropped out. His burning interest was mathematics, pure and applied. Mathematics, he was to say, provided him with wings to soar above the world and see the stars. In a humbler vein, it made him an inventor. He fashioned an instrument for finding the centre of gravity of bodies of varying shapes.

In 1589 he became professor of mathematics in Pisa. He did not get on well with his colleagues; he was constantly complaining about his salary and conditions of work. The more useless the professors, he said, the higher their salaries. He switched to Padua where pay was slightly better. He still had to take in students to cover his expenses. There he stayed for eighteen years.

In 1609 he was forty-five years old, with only one small publication to his name. A year later, as a result of a pamphlet he wrote, he became one of the most famous men in the world. Kepler praised his intellectual courage and called him the greatest philosopher of his time.

His change of fortune began with a piece of luck fertilized by genius. He heard of an optical device, a spyglass or *occhiale*, invented by a Dutchman. Instantly, he decided to make his own, basing it on the theory of refraction. He took a hollow tube of lead and fitted glass lenses at each end. The lenses were plain on one side while on the other they were convex and concave respectively. He put his eye to the concave lense and was amazed to find the object he was looking at three times nearer and nine times larger. Being an expert in grinding lenses, he made another spyglass which increased the object sixty times. Finally, after great effort and expense, he made an object thirty times nearer and enlarged by a thousand times.

He instantly applied the invention to a military purpose. In a public ceremony, he handed over a telescope to the Doge of Venice in the presence of the Senate. The Republic was delighted to have an instrument that could detect hostile armies and navies long before they were visible to the naked eye. They confirmed his professorship for life and doubled his salary in exchange for an instrument that, from now on, any craftsman could make.

Next, Galileo turned his telescope to the night sky. That was the moment when the whole history of man was altered. The scientific revolution was born.

The first thing he focused on was the moon. Those were more than shadows on its surface, he realized; they were mountains. He soon found out how to gauge their heights from the length of their shadows. He also saw vast plains he took for oceans and which have been called ever since the Seas of the Moon.

In a sensational extrapolation, he presumed that to an observer on the moon the earth would look exactly as the moon looked to an observer on earth. He even guessed that from the moon the earth would be divided up into dark zones (sea) and light zones (land). In a moment of instinctive poetry, he spoke of earthshine, 'the old moon in the new moon's arms', namely, sunlight reflected from the earth to the moon and back. He was able to work out why irregular surfaces reflect more light than smooth surfaces and why the edge of the moon looks smooth to the naked eye when it was not the perfect sphere it once appeared to be.

In a second spectacular moment of revelation, Galileo grasped that 'scientists' had been wrong for over two thousand years. Aristotle, followed by scholastics like Aquinas, took it for granted that the celestial world was totally different from the terrestrial. Up there and out there, no change, no decay, only eternal abiding. This implied a different kind of matter from 'down below' on earth. But through his telescope the moon looked suspiciously like the earth. What if the entire creation was one, a true . . . universe? What if the earth was not special but simply one lump of matter among other lumps? And if the moon, so earth-like, can revolve without harm around the earth, why cannot the earth itself revolve? What if the entire picture of creation conceived by the monk Copernicus was real and no mere mathematical hypothesis?

Over ten years before, Galileo had written to Kepler that he felt

Copernicus was right. The earth was not static; it went round the sun. But what if now he could set about making this conviction plausible? Not merely plausible but a fact?

From the moment that Galileo glanced at the moon through arranged pieces of glass, the earth experienced its greatest quake. It ceased to be a centre, *the* centre of the universe. And what of man? If he no longer stood on this central immobile plank of earth, what should be said of *him*? Even the mind of genius dared not look too hard at first for fear of shaking the foundations of his faith, his faith in the Bible and in the church.

Question followed question and he gave what answers he could. But he was quick to grasp that what mattered most was not that he had enlarged the perception of the universe a hundred or a thousand times. What kept ringing in his head, intoxicating him, was the thought that no one had ever seen *this way* before.

To his dismay, when he asked Aristotelians to look through his telescope to check his findings many refused. They knew already, they said, from calculations they had made on paper and by comparing texts that the moon is a smooth and polished surface. How could a tube with glass at the ends disprove Aristotle and an interpretation of Scripture that was centuries old? Of the few who dared take a peep, most suggested in all seriousness that what they were seeing was in the lenses, not in the stars. Galileo joked that, when they died, what he saw they, too, would see on their way to heaven.

Approaching fifty, with twenty penurious years behind him, he was at last a free man. *Nuncius Sidereus*, his book, known as *Messenger* [or *Message*] *from the Stars*, was an instant success.

At this time, Galileo had many clerical friends – indeed, supporters in Rome itself, like the eminent Jesuit mathematician Clavius. Clavius confirmed his discoveries and informed an aged Cardinal Bellarmine. This inspired Galileo to visit Rome in the spring of 1611. The Jesuit cardinal was friendly, as was Cardinal Barberini. Both of them warned him to express his ideas as hypotheses, to avoid trouble with theologians. He was made a member of the prestigious Lyncean Academy who first named his instrument a 'telescope'.

He returned to Florence naïvely convinced he had made lasting and influential friends in the Eternal City. Maybe that is why he became more outspoken. He attacked Aristotelians unmercifully, writing in Italian so as to appeal above the heads of dry academics to the general public.

In spite of his best intentions, he was raising questions of the relation between science and revelation, the Copernican system and the Bible. Were they compatible? In his defence, he quoted Cardinal Baronius' witticism: 'The aim of the Holy Ghost is to teach us how to go to heaven, not how heaven goes.' The Bible was not a scientific text, and there was no need to take its 'scientific statements' literally. There are many literary forms in the Scriptures. Most tellingly, if scientific theory is bad science, good science will correct it. It presents no challenge to faith. On the contrary, nature and the Bible are two divine texts that cannot contradict one another.

His arguments would convince churchmen a couple of centuries later; they left contemporary clerics cold. Galileo seemed to be contradicting the plain sense of Scripture. In putting forward the Copernican system as more than a mathematical theory, he had trespassed on their domain. A matter for the Inquisition, perhaps? The Bishop of Fiesole called out for Copernicus to be gaoled immediately. His Lordship was dismayed to be told that the heretical monk had been dead for seventy years. Ominously, one of Galileo's books did find its way into the dreaded *Casa Santa* of the Holy Office.

He had been warned that Bellarmine had never wavered in his view that Copernicus' system was contrary to Scripture if taken as a scientific fact. None the less, Galileo went to Rome and proceeded to demolish anyone who cast doubts on Copernicus. But even he, so naïve in the ways of the world, was beginning to catch a whiff of gunpowder.

A priest sympathizer sent him a copy of a letter he had received from Bellarmine. According to the cardinal, when the Fathers and all modern scripture scholars analyse the relevant Bible passages

> all agree in interpreting them literally as teaching that the sun is in the heavens and revolves around the Earth with immense speed and the Earth is very distant from the heavens, at the centre of the universe, and motionless. Consider, then, in your prudence, whether the Church can tolerate that the Scriptures should be interpreted in a manner contrary to that of the holy Fathers and of all modern commentators, both Latin and Greek. . . . Scripture says, 'The sun also *riseth* and the sun *goeth down*'.

Galileo read it a hundred times. He still could not believe it. Old Bellarmine was a good and wise man. How could he take so childish a view of the Old Testament? His Eminence went on to say that anyone, simply by consulting his senses, could know for sure that the earth is motionless. Did he expect to feel dizzy if the world was going round the sun? If he were on the moon, would he expect to *feel* it moving? Great theologian he might be, but Bellarmine was as clueless about astronomy as those people who seriously said that if the earth moved round the sun all the towers in Italy would fall down. 'Their senses told them' everything in the universe was moving *except the earth*!

Galileo became really worried. His Eminence was telling him not to meddle with Scripture while he was pontificating on science without any training at all. He knew now that Bellarmine would not scruple to silence him by summoning him before the Inquisition.

That is what happened. Pope Paul V, pious, fat, short-sighted, with a small beard and pointed moustache, known to everyone as a philistine, handed over his case to the Congregation of the Index. A decision was given in March 1616.

The view that the sun is the immovable centre of the universe was judged to be 'foolish and absurd, philosophically false and formally heretical'. The opinion that the earth is not the centre but revolves and rotates was judged at least 'erroneous in faith'.

Not Galileo but his Copernican beliefs were censured. None the less, the pope instructed Bellarmine to tell Galileo to abandon his opinion. If not, he had to give an undertaking not to teach or defend his views, nor even discuss them. Otherwise, he would be put in prison.

Though convinced of his own orthodoxy, Galileo gave the guarantees. He merely asked Bellarmine to write him a letter, which he did on 26 May 1616. The cardinal witnessed to the fact that he had not been compelled to recant or to undergo any penance. Nor was he forced to stop his researches, even into astronomy. He was simply told not to hold or teach *as if it were true* the system of Copernicus. The latter was put on the Index where he remained until 1822.

Galileo, in ill-health, was glad the ordeal was over. What upset him was that 'minds created free by God are compelled to submit slavishly to an outside will'. He was *the* expert on astronomy and he was being judged by persons without any competence. The pope had personally endorsed Bellarmine's view that to say the earth revolves is against the infallible teaching of the church. If the earth moves, heaven would not be 'up there' or hell 'down there'. The whole teaching on the Last Things would have to be revised. As one papal aide said, with a sigh: Now we are 'safely back on solid earth and we do not have to fly with it as so many ants crawling around a balloon'.

A few tranquil years passed and Galileo wrote *Il Saggiatore (The Assayer)*. It was 1623. That same year, his 'friend', fifty-five-year-old Cardinal Barberini, became Pope Urban VIII. In the eleven days of voting, there was a heatwave; malaria whipped through the conclave. Eight cardinals and forty aides died. Urban himself had contracted malaria but he survived. To him, Galileo dedicated his new book.

The pope appreciated the compliment. When, in the following year, Galileo, aged sixty, went to Rome, he presented his Holiness with a microscope. Urban peered down it and shook his head in wonderment. In gratitude, he gave the great scientist several Agnus Deis against acts of God and, of more value, advice against the acts of man. What he said was this: 'You may have irrefutable proof of the earth's motion. This does not prove the earth actually moves.' Galileo's eyes widened. 'God is above human reason; and what seems perfectly reasonable to men may prove folly to God.' Urban went on to say that he, as pope, was responsible for the salvation of souls. Sometimes scientific discussion imperilled souls. The Copernican system, unless taken as a pure mathematical device, might cast doubt on Scripture. Should that happen, he would have to take steps to stamp it out.

The pope's views on God and the relation between science and religion were so absurd that Galileo did not take in the excellent advice he was being given at the top level. In fact it was good of Urban to take time off from his great building projects: the Barberini palaces for which he cannibalized the Colosseum, the Bernini colonnade enclosing the piazza of St Peter's, the *baldacchino* under Michelangelo's dome for which he filched the bronze from the Pantheon. The Romans savagely said: 'What the Barbarians did not do, the Barberini did.'

Somewhat mystified, Galileo returned to Florence where he was soon at work on *The System of the World*. Since he cast it in the form of a Platonic dialogue, he no doubt thought this would enable him to hide his own convictions, while pasting the opposition. When it was finished in the year 1630, all that remained was to get a licence to publish and, as a precaution, a papal *Imprimatur*.

In good heart, he went back to Rome where once more Urban received him warmly. The pope re-emphasized the need to make everyone aware of the hypothetical nature of his opinions. As regards the book, Galileo ought perhaps to entitle it *Dialogue of the Two Chief Systems*. Yes, yes, the pope promised, he would write a preface himself, stressing the tentative nature of the enterprise.

When the censors received their copy, they were disturbed by its contents. But his Holiness had given the book his approval, had he not? And was he not going to write the preface?

There were unavoidable delays in publication, so that Galileo had it printed in Florence in February 1632. It created a sensation. The arguments for the earth moving were set out masterfully. The Aristotelian view in the dialogue was put in the mouth of Simplicius, a half-wit, whose ideas corresponded exactly with the pope's as he had expressed them in that interview with the author a few years before.

When Urban got wind of this seemingly studied insult, he was furious. He told the Holy Office to take over and order the author to report to Rome at once. When Galileo, nearing seventy, wrote back pleading, honestly, ill-health, Urban bade him come freely or in chains.

When he arrived in Rome after twenty-three days on the road, he had to wait two months for his ordeal to begin. Time passed slowly. Two nights in succession, he was heard crying out with the pain of his sciatica.

His childlikeness never left him. He actually expected to be allowed to defend himself, even to discuss sensibly with the inquisitors, as though these clerical gentlemen were interested in finding out the truth. In fact they in no way resembled his fellow-professors with whom he had argued in the salons of rich Roman ladies. He did have a kind of insurance policy in his pocket. For years, he had kept Bellarmine's letter under lock and key for just such an emergency as this.

When the trial began in April 1633 he was moved from the Tuscan embassy into the *Casa* of the Holy Office. The hearing was held in the upper room of a Dominican convent. He was immediately told that the Inquisition was not there to listen to him but to judge him. Evidence he was not allowed to see, witnesses he was not allowed to hear.

His chief offence was in violating the injunction of 1616, namely, not to discuss or write about the Copernican system. He begged their Eminences' pardon but he had a letter from the late Cardinal Bellarmine proving he was only forbidden to hold Copernicus' views as if they were a true picture of the world. This he had never done. He had merely discussed it and, as his recent book showed, in a hypothetical way. He pointed out that the dialogue ended without any conclusions.

The inquisitors countered his letter with an unsigned unofficial minute found in their files, dated 1616, in which he was forbidden even to discuss Copernicus' theories. Galileo was never shown this document. Further, their Eminences argued, in spite of the dialogue form of his recent book, no reader could possibly doubt his own position, and this was contrary to the faith of the church. He was guilty of contumacy and heresy. He could expect leniency only if he submitted unconditionally and declared his appreciation of the Inquisition's kindness towards him.

After four sessions, the verdict was given in late June 1633. The pope had intervened to say that his old friend was to be tortured if he did not conform.

> The said Galileo [is] . . . in the judgement of the Holy Office vehemently suspected of heresy, namely, of having believed and held the doctrine which is false and contrary to the Sacred and Divine Scriptures, that the sun is the centre of the world and does not move from the east to the west and that the earth moves and is not the centre of the world. . . .

His books were banned; he was to be imprisoned by the Inquisition; he was required to say the seven penitential Psalms each week for three years. The document was signed by seven cardinal judges of the Holy Office.

Galileo had made up his mind to acquiesce but, for his honour's sake, he asked for two of the charges to be withdrawn. He wanted it stated that he had not denied the Catholic faith, nor had he knowingly contradicted a previous decision of the Holy Office. The judges accepted these marginal alterations. Galileo had conceded that he was wrong about astronomy and they were right.

So, on that Wednesday in late June, Galileo Galilei knelt on the cool stone floor of the Dominican convent of Santa Maria sopra Minerva to make his confession: 'I, Galileo, son of the late Vincenzo Galilei, Florentine, aged seventy years . . . must altogether abandon the false opinion that the sun is the centre of the world and immobile.'

Outwardly, by denying his deepest convictions, he perjured himself. In his heart, at least, he must have said of the earth: 'All the same, it does move', 'Eppur si muove'.

When Galileo touched the Gospels and admitted his 'heretical depravity' in the heart of Rome, it was a solemn moment in the history of the church. Only the trial of Jesus before Pilate can surpass it in gravity.

The Founder of Modern Science, at the behest of the Roman Inquisition, was forced to affirm, in accordance with the Catholic faith, that the earth is the motionless centre of the universe. A scholar who, in any list of the world's great men, would figure in the first twenty, was condemned by a group of clerics, none of whom would figure in the first million.

With Copernicus on the Index and Galileo condemned by the Inquisition, Catholic astronomers now had to choose between being good Catholics and being good members of their profession. By all the normal criteria, the immobility of the earth was *Catholic doctrine*. It was held by every pope, bishop and theologian for centuries. Nor was it merely implicit. When the teaching was tested, when Copernicus and Galileo cast doubt upon it, the reigning pope and popes for centuries afterwards explicitly confirmed it with the plenitude of their power. And they were *wrong*. The earth does move, however many popes denied it, saying it contradicts Scripture and the faith. If Catholics today claim this was never really Catholic doctrine, can one ever be sure of *any* Catholic doctrine?

In 1686, Newton's law of gravitation made it impossible for any scientist to believe that the huge sun revolved around a midget earth as its centre. In the year 1725 this theoretical proof was confirmed by Bradley's meticulous observation. It took another hundred years before Copernicus was removed from the Index. In the early 1980s, John Paul II was heard to say something about 'rehabilitating Galileo', though to date nothing has come of it. After three and a half centuries, Rome is in no hurry to apologize.

Rome refused to publish the documents on the Galileo affair. Then Napoleon, in a huge operation, removed the Vatican archives to Paris.

When they were eventually returned, the documents relating to the affair were missing. The most strenuous investigations failed to find them. Critics of the church presumed the great man had been tortured. Without any warning or any explanation, the documents resurfaced. It was clear from them that Galileo had been threatened but not tortured. Nor was his imprisonment so severe. After ten days of the trial, he was allowed to return to a house belonging to the de' Medici. He was eventually to retire to his own villa at Arcetri. This was mild treatment considering that Urban VIII condemned bigamists to the galleys for life.

What wounded Galileo most was the disgrace. It had been visited on him for no reason he could understand. He thought of himself as a devoted Catholic. How could anyone insist on taking Genesis literally when there were overwhelming reasons for it being a myth! He was convinced that scientific problems could not be solved by a clerical police force. Ranged against him, he saw only ignorance, malice and impiety posing as Christian faith and virtue. Small-minded Vatican clerics had humiliated him but they could not stop the progress of science. His was the classic case of truth being crushed by power, genius being silenced by petty bureaucracy. It showed Rome's fear and hatred of the enquiring mind which was to be repeated time after time in the centuries ahead. The church's backward march into the future meant that its war with science and progress was to go on. It warred against liberty and the democratic process at and after the French Revolution. It made war on Darwin and Freud, on biblical scholarship, on attempts to understand the world on its own terms, free from divine 'interventions from outside'. Today, it wages war against birth control and the equality of women. On each and every occasion, the Catholic church at the highest level refers to the Bible and natural law as it tries, with the best intentions, to halt the forward march of the world. It is a melancholy fact that it would be hard to find in the last four centuries one instance in which Rome greeted with unqualified joy a decisive advance of the human spirit. Any theologian who is censured today can at least take comfort in the fact that he is not treated as harshly as the Father of Modern Science.

After eight years of house arrest, Galileo Galilei died in January 1642, the year of Newton's birth. The Grand Duke of Florence wanted to erect a monument over his grave in the church of Santa Croce, next to the grave of Michelangelo. Pope Urban VIII was not yet finished with his friend. He warned the duke that Galileo had pertinaciously held a doctrine opposed to the Scriptures. He repeated that it is against the faith to say the earth moves. He would therefore take any such memorial as a personal insult to his authority. So it was that the body of the greatest scientist of his age was interred for almost a hundred years in the cellar of the bell tower in Santa Croce.

Urban, wrong on almost everything, was at least right in the reason he gave for refusing him decent exequies: Galileo by his sins had given rise to 'the greatest scandal in Christendom'.

Clement XI's Great Mistake

Clement XI held court in his palace on Monte Cavallo. It was cooler there than in the Vatican, the air less full of pestilence. On Wednesday of Holy Week in the year 1715, he journeyed in state to St Peter's.

Next day, after mass in St Peter's, Clement ascended his *sedia* and was carried on to the loggia. The crowd filled the piazza of St Peter's and stretched down every side-street. As soon as he appeared, kettle drums sounded, trumpets blew. In the deep silence that followed, a cardinal read the Holy Thursday Bull of excommunication against all heretics, schismatics, pagans, Mediterranean pirates and all who did not render the Holy Father obedience or pay him their taxes when due.

This Bull, *In Coena Domini*, dated back in broad outline to 1372. Pius V in 1568 said it was to remain an eternal law in Christendom, and it was confirmed by pope after pope until it was finally dropped without explanation in the reign of Clement XIV (1769–74). Some explanation would have been welcome, since the Bull expressed the most full-blown of all papal heresies: that the pope has dominion over the entire Christian world, religious *and* secular. This belief has never been explicitly abandoned by the Vatican.

During the reading of the Bull, the pope, his long lean close-shaven face full of melancholy, held a lighted torch in his hand. When the reading was over, his eight bearers lifted the pontiff up in his chair and, with a loud voice, he pronounced excommunication on practically the entire world before tossing his torch over the balcony. It sparked and looped in the air before hitting the crowd below, a sign of the church's vengeance on her enemies.

Clement XI was an exemplary thunderer. Yet his endless anathemas, which his contemporaries took for great holiness, hid a dreadful insecurity. On his election fifteen years before on 20 November 1700, Gian Francisco Albani was fifty-one years old. Ordained but two years and feeling unequal to the task, he refused the crown at first. He only yielded when four learned religious told him that not to accept the unanimous decision of conclave would be to resist the manifest will of God. Oddly, he accepted *their* decision immediately.

Those four religious were never to know that, had they given Cardinal Albani the opposite advice, the entire face of Catholicism, literally, might have been different.

Clement seemed a good choice for pontiff: a disciplinarian, learned, chaste, he slept and ate little, he even said mass daily – which, in a pope, was unusual. But – a further clue to an essential weakness – he also made daily confession of his sins. His was a small scrupulous world of personal piety.

In his constitution *Unigenitus* of 1713, for instance, this chronically insecure pontiff, after consulting two cardinals of like mind, roundly condemned Jansenism in France. Some of his condemnations seemed to be sensible; others were to cause in the years ahead laughter and embarrassment.

'The reading of the Holy Scriptures is for all men.' Condemned. The banning of God's word, at first surprising, was consistent with the Catholic approach since the Reformation. Some people were reading the Bible unwisely. Instead of helping them read it wisely, how much less troublesome to forbid them to read it at all? Besides, this approach made it clear that Rome is superior to the Bible and has God's authority to interpret it.

'Christians are to sanctify the Lord's Day with reading godly books, more particularly the Holy Scriptures.' Condemned.

'To pull the New Testament out of the hands of Christians is to shut the mouth of Christ against them.' Condemned.

'To forbid Christians the reading of the Holy Scripture and especially the Gospel is to forbid the use of the Light by the children of Light and to punish them with a kind of excommunication.' Condemned.

'The fear of an *unjust* excommunication ought not to deter us from doing our duty.' Condemned. According to Voltaire, this meant that God commands us never to do our duty if we fear injustice. Clement's view was that there is no higher duty than obedience to the pope. Obey him and there can be no question of condemnation from God.

Once his vacillating mind was made up, Clement left the church in no doubt where he stood.

> We declare, condemn and disallow all and each of these Propositions as false, captious, ill-sounding, offensive to pious ears, scandalous, pernicious, rash, injurious to the Church and its practices, not only outrageous against the Church but even against the secular powers, seditious, impious, blasphemous, suspected of heresy and savouring of heresy itself, as also encouraging heretics and heresies and even schism, erroneous, often condemned, and lastly also heretical, containing divers heresies manifestly tending to innovation.

The pontiff, one gathers, does not much care for these propositions.

Clement, like most pontiffs, assumed that discussion leads not to truth but to further falsehood or, at best, to a little truth and great falsehood. It is not worth the risk. As with Bible-reading, it is better to forbid discussion of important issues altogether. Rome has spoken and Rome knows best.

Two years later, Clement was to publish the Bull *Ex Illa Die*, with far more devastating effects. To understand it, one has to go back over a century and a half.

In 1552, the noblest of Jesuits, Francis Xavier had died on an island off the Chinese mainland. He had worked himself into an early grave. As he lay dying, his only regret was that across that stretch of water was a vast land full of pagans who, because they were unbaptized, would roast in hell eternally.

Thirty years later, a fellow-Jesuit, Matthew Ricci, entered the Imperial Court at Peking. With his knowledge of mathematics, he was honoured as a 'wise man from the west', but he was a great and original missioner, too. His method was to become Chinese in order to win the Chinese. He and his Jesuit assistants grasped that it was vital to present a church in sympathy with the traditions of China. Nowhere in the world was there a greater sense of filial piety, of respect for lawful authority and ancestral traditions. When Ricci died after nearly thirty years of labour, he left behind him three hundred churches, one in Peking itself. He was followed by other Jesuits, the only Order entrusted by Gregory XIII with this mission.

In 1631 the Dominicans were allowed to join them. Before long, Father Morales, OP, accused the Jesuits of gaining converts at the cost of allowing the Chinese to keep their ancient 'idolatries'. Jesuits since Ricci had taken a tolerant line with the Chinese rites. They said that reverence done to the wooden tablets of the ancestors, the candles, incense, food and money offered them were simply a matter of courtesy and gratitude. Respect offered by mandarins to Confucius, the Teacher of Wisdom, also seemed harmless, a part of their culture worth preserving.

In 1643, Morales, sent seventeen Jesuit propositions to Rome, asking for them to be condemned. The Inquisition headed as always by Dominicans, supported him; Innocent X agreed that the Jesuits should back off until the matter was examined further. The Jesuit Martini argued that the practices were purely civil; condemning them would make conversions impossible. Scholarly investigation showed, he said, that the Chinese had a concept of the one God that, in its purity, had no parallel among pagans.

The controversy raged for many years. The Jesuits on the spot were continually reported to Rome.

The year 1692 was momentous. The Jesuits achieved the break-through that had eluded them for over a century. Emperor Kang Hi gave them permission to preach the Christian Gospel all over his kingdom and to convert whomsoever they wished. The Jesuits were convinced that Kang Hi, with his immense power and prestige, would be the Chinese Constantine; he was able to bring the whole empire to the feet of Christ. Unfortunately, by this time, the Jesuits were obliged to take orders from vicars apostolic hostile to their mission.

The fated Clement XI ascended the papal throne. For a long time, he could not make up his mind what to do. He put aside one day a week to study the problem of the Chinese rites. He noted the emperor's conviction that there was not the least superstition in them. 'No one', Kang Hi declared, 'really believes the souls of the dead are present in the tablets of their ancestors.'

Clement sent a bishop to Peking as his personal representative to make enquiries. His lordship, very foolishly, condemned the rites in public as idolatrous. The emperor, annoyed and puzzled that Christians were not only divided but hated one another, put the bishop in prison. Clement responded by making him a cardinal just before he died bravely in Macao in 1710. Clement took the imprisonment of his legate as a personal insult. His indecision came to an abrupt end. In his considerable anger, he approved all the decrees of the Inquisition against the Jesuit approach. Now, in the year 1715, every missionary in China had to swear detestation of the Chinese rites and promise never to tolerate them.

This very intolerance, Clement declared, will clear the weeds away and make Chinese soil more fruitful for Christianity. The church had to be Roman, even in Peking.

It was a paper solution, given thousands of miles from the scene of the action. Probably no more disastrous error was ever made by a pontiff. From the publication of *Ex Illa Die*, the Christian mission to China was doomed.

In that same year, 1715, Giuseppe Castiglione, a twenty-seven-year-old Jesuit, was sent by his superior to Peking. He was honoured by the Chinese as one of the most wise and revolutionary foreigners ever to go there. His fame was due not to his preaching but to his artistic gifts.

On 16 April 1717, the Nine Highest, counsellors to the emperor, heard of *Ex Illa Die*. They advised his Majesty that, owing to the insults offered China by Christians and their total lack of respect for the ancestors, all missionaries should be banished, their churches destroyed, their converts forced to renounce their new faith. Reluctantly, the emperor confirmed their sentence. 'What would the pope say', he asked, 'if the Emperor of China told him how he should worship in Rome? He reserved to himself the right to grant a *piao*, or special licence, to Europeans useful to his kingdom.

Among those granted a *piao* was Castiglione, who became official painter to the Imperial Court. Only top painters and watchmakers were allowed to roam freely in the Summer Palace. Castiglione was given a palace of his own to paint in. Almost every day the emperor visited him, marvelling at the naturalness of his work, especially the horses in which the Jesuit, now named Lang Shining, excelled. Most of his work was done indoors. When he wanted to paint from life, he was escorted by Imperial eunuchs as he walked on tiptoe, like a burglar, out of respect for the emperor. Thus Lang Shining lived for fifty years. If only in that time he had been allowed to teach the gracious Chinese something more than a technique for painting horses.

Two centuries passed. In the year 1939, when the mission to China was dead and buried, the Sacred Congregation of Propaganda declared that times had changed. They had been assured by the Chinese that there was now nothing religious in their rites. Christian converts need not give up reverencing their ancestors.

Without admitting it, Propaganda was reversing Clement's decision. Since papal decisions are never 'reversed', they had to find a pretext for this volte-face. Emperor Kang Hi, the Asian Constantine that might have been, had already made it plain that there was nothing blasphemous or un-Christian in the rites; the Jesuits had been right all along. If Kang Hi had been told by unsympathetic spies that, in Rome, Catholics kissed the pontiff's feet, even the feet of statues, he might have been tempted to think of Catholics as idolaters. Clement's mistake was of that order.

The consequences of *Ex Illa Die* are unfathomable. China might today have been as Catholic as Ireland or Poland.

In view of the church's opposition to birth control, instead of a billion Chinese communists there might be now 2–3 billion Catholics in China. Two out of every three Catholics over the globe might have Chinese faces and speak Chinese. But then the problems of mankind – famine, stress, lack of living-space and natural resources – would long ago have become completely insoluble. By depriving China of Catholicism, Pope Clement XI arguably saved the world from catastrophe.

Conclusions

This brief survey shows that all popes are fallible, that many made very bad mistakes, and that several were heretical. They contradicted the teaching of the church, contradicted each other and, not infrequently, contradicted themselves on essential Christian doctrine.

As a result, the tradition was that any pope, including the reigning pontiff, can be as mistaken as anyone else. He has no special grace to prevent him falling into heresy.

Further, there can be no question of a pope being right and the church wrong. If the pope distances himself from the church – perhaps by not listening to it – the pope, not the church, has to change his mind. If he refuses to listen and falls into heresy, he is pope no longer, for, having abandoned the faith, he is not even a Christian.

Theologians tend to say that a distinction has to be made here. A pope, like any Christian, can err in private matters of faith. What the Spirit promises is that he will not mislead the church when he makes an *ex cathedra* definition concerning faith and morals.

The distinction of the pope speaking (1) as pope and (2) with some other hat on – either as a private theologian or diocesan bishop or a pastoral preacher – has one serious defect: it was unheard of in the early church. No one ever said when a pope was convicted of heresy: 'He is a heretic but fortunately for us he was not speaking *ex cathedra*.' Why? Because no one thought he was able to define the faith of the church. That was for General Councils to do. That is what General Councils did. A pope could endanger the faith of the church, as did Honorius, but no pope on his own ever formulated the faith for the church. There were occasions when such a gift would have been a boon – say, during the Arian controversy or when the divinity of the Spirit was questioned. Today, all Catholics would turn to Rome for a decision in even small matters; then, no one turned to Rome for a 'final word' even when the foundations of the faith were tottering.

Papal infallibility runs into an even bigger difficulty. If papal heresies of the past do not come under the heading of *ex cathedra* statements, which papal teachings do? When did popes first speak to and for the whole church in a definitive way? Certainly not in the first millennium. Some would say not till 1302, others not until 1854. If this is so, Roman pontiffs as such did not err simply because they did not exercise this function at all.

Papal infallibility is supposed to be crucial to the church's faith and a way of *regulating* it. How can this be when it was not exercised for most of church history? One can understand the *church* being infallible, either in Council or through its normal episcopal teaching worldwide. But it is hard to make sense of a critical role for the pope that was never exercised until he was actually proclaimed infallible by a Council and that has been exercised only once in the last century.

This analysis is not quite accurate. One pope certainly did exercise infallibility before Vatican I. Pius IX is so central to an understanding of the modern papacy that he requires a chapter to himself.

THIRTEEN

The First
Infallible Pope

On the eighth day of December 1854, Pope Pius IX defined the immaculate conception of the Virgin Mary in *Ineffabilis Deus*:

> We declare, pronounce and define that the doctrine which holds that the most blessed Virgin Mary, in the first instant of her conception, by a singular grace and privilege granted by Almighty God, in view of the merits of Jesus Christ, the Saviour of the human race, was preserved free from all stain of original sin, is a doctrine revealed by God and therefore to be believed firmly and constantly by all the faithful.

This act of devotion towards the Mother of Jesus was also the most contrived political decision of any pontiff in recent times. It is worthy of comparison with Gregory VII's deposition and utter humiliation of the emperor in the winds and snows of Canossa.

The Immaculate Conception

Until the twelfth century, Christians took it for granted that Mary was conceived in original sin. Pope Gregory the Great said emphatically: 'Christ alone was conceived without sin.' Again and again, he said all human beings are sinful, even the holiest, with the sole exception of Christ. His reasoning and that of all the Fathers leaves no doubt in the matter. The sex act *always* involved sin. Mary was conceived normally, *therefore* in sin; Jesus was conceived virginally, *therefore* without original sin.

Whereas Ambrose and Augustine took the line that Mary did no actual sin, many Fathers disagreed. Tertullian, Irenaeus, Chrysostom, Origen, Basil, Cyril of Alexandria and others accused Mary of many sins, arguing from biblical texts. She was conceived in sin, she committed actual sin; the New Testament said so.

So firm was the tradition that Mary was conceived in sin that the only problem for a great medieval saint-scholar like Anselm was how the sinless Christ could be born of a sinner. Anselm praised Mary in many ways: her spiritual plenty made 'all creatures green again'. Yet he steadfastly followed Pope Gregory and the great tradition: 'The Virgin herself was conceived in iniquity, and in sin did her mother conceive her, and with original sin was she born because she too sinned in Adam in whom all sinned.'

The Greek and Russian Orthodox churches have kept to this tradition. To suggest Mary was conceived sinlessly is to rob her of her grandeur and achievements which are those of a human being like us in every way.

In the West, by contrast, the cult of the Virgin developed apace in the Middle Ages. Catholics tended to lose sight of the humanness of Christ. As a result, he appeared remote, not so much the Mediator between God and men as God Himself. This created the need for a mediator with the Mediator, someone holy and powerful. The rise of Mariology coincided with the decline in Christology.

Mary was Christ's mother, she had held him in her arms. Her virtues had always been extolled. In Patristic times, she was seen as the model of virginity. Now she had a more important role to play.

In the middle of the twelfth century, in Lyons, a new feast was celebrated in honour of the conception of the Virgin.

St Bernard of Clairvaux was horrified. He wrote to the canons of Lyons, warning them that their argument for Mary's sinless conception would apply to all Mary's ancestors, male and female. They would be forced to postulate a whole line – a kind of infinite regress – of ancestors of Mary who were conceived immaculate. The nightmare would not end there. If they were all conceived immaculate, they must all have been virginally born. Bernard followed the Fathers in his views of sexual intercourse. It always involved sin. Hence he asks the prelates of Lyons: 'Was the Holy Spirit a partner to the sin of concupiscence [of Mary's parents]? Or are we to assume there was no sin of lust present?' Bernard is simply repeating Gregory's argument: sex means lust. Mary came of sexual intercourse, she was conceived in sin. He held that Mary was *born* sanctified. A feast of Mary's nativity was in order, not of her conception.

Peter Lombard, the most influential medieval theologian before Aquinas, followed the Greek Father, John of Damascus. Mary was conceived in original sin and was not cleansed of it until she consented to bear the Saviour. Innocent III approved of this view. Even this did not stop the new cult spreading, though not to Rome itself.

Bonaventure, the thirteenth century Seraphic Doctor, denied that Mary was free from inherited sin. His contemporary Thomas Aquinas, the Angelic Doctor, agreed. He followed Aristotle, who claimed that animation of the foetus is a gradual process. Initially, the *conceptus* is vegetative. Thus, for Aquinas the idea of the immaculate conception was about as intelligible as a sinless carrot. He did believe that the Virgin Mary was sanctified at some, unspecified, time before birth.

Dominicans agreed with their hero Aquinas, as did the Franciscans for a while. In the fourteenth century, Bishop Pelayo, the Franciscan penitentiary to John XXII, had no doubts that Mary was conceived in original sin.

Still the cult grew and for the first time a theologian of stature, the Franciscan Duns Scotus, supported it. The Subtle Doctor's problem was to know how Mary could be among the saved if she had no original sin to be saved from. His solution was based on the principle that prevention is better than cure. Mary was not cured of sin but prevented by the foreseen merits of Christ from incurring sin. This scarcely stands up to examination. A young baby can be immunized against, say, diphtheria, tetanus, polio and so on. With advances in medicine, it is possible that some immunization procedures will precede birth when the child is still in the mother's womb. But how can a baby be immunized before *conception*? According to Scotus, Mary was 'immunized' against original sin before she was conceived. Probably nothing more would have been heard of this odd opinion had not Pius IX used it to underpin his infallible definition of Mary's immaculate conception.

After Scotus had taken the opposite line to Aquinas, sides were taken. Franciscans and Dominicans engaged in bloody battles, not all literary. Emperors joined in, as when Charles VI forced the Dominicans out of Paris and arrested anyone found on the streets who denied the immaculate conception.

For centuries, disputes and fisticuffs continued. Each party denounced the other as heretical. If ever a papal decision was needed to stop the fighting, it was now. There were good reasons why it was not forthcoming. Scripture was silent on the immaculate conception; the Fathers of the Church were all opposed; until Scotus not one theologian of note had accepted it and the greatest had denied it. Yet there was a powerful groundswell of popular opinion in its favour.

Sixtus IV ordered the Feast of the Conception to be kept in all churches; to it he gave, free of charge, a special indulgence. It provoked a still more bitter controversy between Dominicans and Franciscans. To stop it, he wrote another Bull. The Feast was honouring Mary's conception, he said, not her sanctification. The Dominicans must accept this or they will be excommunicated; but if the Franciscans gloat over the Dominicans *they* will be excommunicated.

This Bull was confirmed by Alexander VI. But Borgia, a realist, threatened to call in the army to keep the peace between the friars if they did not settle down.

The Dominicans remained unmoved. Their hero Aquinas had come out against the immaculate conception, and had not John XXII, delighted with his views on the papacy, said that to deny anything Aquinas said was tantamount to heresy? So, though the Dominicans spread the devotion of the rosary, they were mocked unmercifully by the Franciscans as 'maculists'.

Then came an event that seemed to tip the scales in the Dominicans' favour.

In the year 1507, in the Dominican convent in Berne, Mary appeared to a humble friar, Brother Letser. To Letser, she revealed her annoyance at the Franciscans for teaching her so-called immaculate conception. She confirmed to Letser that she had been conceived in original sin. It was not till three hours after conception that she was sanctified. The view of St Thomas Aquinas was, the Virgin confirmed, on this point as in all others, perfectly orthodox. To prove the reliability of the vision, Mary gave the friar a cross tinged with Jesus' blood, together with three of his tears shed over Jerusalem. She also handed him a letter addressed to the reigning pope, Julius II, who at the time was engaged, sword in hand, in the Italian wars.

The apparition was *the* sensation of the day. Crowds flocked to the convent in Berne. Brother Letser was a good subject for Marian revelations: he was chaste; he fasted; he scourged himself; he fell easily into ecstasy; he developed the stigmata, those wounds of the Crucified in hands and feet that have authenticated many a saint. In the convent chapel was an image of the Virgin that wept perpetually for the errors of Franciscans whom Mary implored to accept her Maculate Conception.

Then, out of the blue, something even more surprising happened. Brother Letser himself appeared. He put in an appearance, that is, before the magistrate in Berne, asking for asylum. His superiors, he claimed, were torturing him and trying to poison him. What he revealed was a Dominican plot.

The Order's superiors in chapter at Wimpffen had decided to prove the falsity of the immaculate conception by means of a home-made miracle. Berne was chosen as the site, since it had a large and credulous population. The four heads of the priory hit on John Letser, a tailor, recently admitted to the Order, as a suitable visionary. They prepared him by drugging him. Letser was completely taken in. Until one day he entered the room of the lector Bolshorst without knocking and found him clad in the female attire of the Blessed Virgin. This was far more of a shock to Letser than a real apparition of the Virgin. He wanted to withdraw his services but, under threats, he continued till he could take no more.

The matter came before the Inquisition. Torture was used on Letser and the four conspirators. The latter confessed that they had coloured a Host red, made the statue weep with wet sponges and painted the stigmata on Brother Letser with a brush.

Though the four were burned, the Dominican Order pronounced them martyrs for the cause. They fought back by publishing a manual of all the great thinkers in the church who had opposed the immaculate conception. It included most theologians of note and numerous popes. Many Franciscans were on the list, including St Anthony of Padua and St Bonaventure.

The official church still temporized. The Council of Trent could not decide the issue, and Paul IV banned all discussion of the matter. But the tide was running against the Dominicans. One contributory cause was the work of a Roman physician, Paulo Zacchia. He denied Aristotle's idea of a progressive animation of the foetus. Zacchia said in 1621 that a rational soul is infused at the very moment of conception. Applied to Mary: if she was not conceived first as a vegetable, it made slightly more sense to say she was conceived free of sin.

In 1622, Gregory XVI said that no one could disagree, even in private, with the Feast of the Conception, though he forbade the use of 'immaculate'.

In the year 1701, Clement XI made the immaculate conception a feast of obligation throughout the church, thus reinforcing Zacchia's view of instantaneous ensoulment.

Benedict XIV (1831–46), in his decree on Beatification, said the church *inclines* towards the immaculate conception but has never made it an article of faith.

His successor had no such reservations.

Pius IX, like Gregory VII, had a sharp nose for politics. The days of the Papal States were numbered, he knew. No sooner was he pope than a temporary republic was set up in Rome and he fled to Gaeta. There, he had time to reflect on the one area where he could reign supreme. He prepared the way for it with the encyclical *Ubi primum*, 2 February 1849, in which he painted this picture of Mary.

> The resplendent glory of her merits, far exceeding all the choirs of angels, elevates her to the very steps of the throne of God. Her foot has crushed the head of Satan. Set up between Christ and his Church, Mary, ever lovable and full of grace, always has delivered the Christian people from their greatest calamities and from the snares and assaults of all their enemies, ever rescuing them from ruin.

Pius IX's picture of Mary owed more to Murillo's dark-haired cherub-borne Beauty than to the gospels.

In Gaeta, with Jesuits as his mentors, Pius began 'consulting' the bishops on the expediency of defining the doctrine of the immaculate conception. He received almost unanimous support from the nearly five hundred Italian, Spanish and Portuguese. The rest were not enthusiastic.

A day or two before the definition in 1854, the pope's private secretary, Monsignor Talbot, said in confidence to a friend: 'You see, the most important thing is not the new dogma but the way it is proclaimed.' Frankly, the pope was slipping in, so to speak, his own infallibility.

Before 1870, this was far from being universally accepted. The French church, for example, was renowned for its opposition. The Fourth of the Gallican Articles of 1682, signed by the great Bishop Bossuet, said: 'The pope has the principal share in questions of faith . . . nevertheless his judgement is not irreformable without the consent of the church.' The decrees of the Council of Constance were still in force in France in the seventeenth century and, in spite of Rome, many still held them up to 1870.

The English-speaking world, too, was far from unanimous in accepting papal infallibility. In 1822, Bishop Barnes, the English Vicar Apostolic, said: 'Bellarmine and other divines, chiefly Italians, have believed the pope infallible when proposing *ex cathedra* an article of faith. But in England and Ireland I do not believe *any* Catholic maintains the infallibility of the pope.' Later still, Cardinal Wiseman, who in 1850 headed the restored hierarchy of England and Wales, said: 'The Catholic church holds a dogma often proclaimed that, in defining matters of faith, *she* (that is, the church, not the pope) is infallible.' He went on: 'All agree that infallibility resides in the unanimous suffrage of the church.' John Henry Newman, a convert and the greatest theologian of the nineteenth century, said two years before Vatican I: 'I hold the pope's infallibility, but as a theological opinion; that is, not as a certainty but as a probability.'

In the United States, prior to Vatican I, there was in print the Reverend Stephen Keenan's very popular *Controversial Catechism*. It bore the *Imprimatur* of Archbishop Hughes of New York. Here is one extract. 'Question: Must not Catholics believe the pope himself to be infallible? Answer: This is a Protestant invention, it is no article of the Catholic faith; no decision of his can bind on pain of heresy, unless it be received and enforced by the teaching body, that is, the bishops of the church.' It was somewhat embarrassing when, in 1870, a 'Protestant invention' became defined Catholic faith. The next edition of the *Catechism* withdrew this question and answer without a word of explanation.

Pius IX, by getting mostly Italian and other Latin bishops to support him in 1854, was already canonizing 'the Italian doctrine' of papal infallibility.

The manner of proclaiming the immaculate conception was unique. It did not come from a General Council; it was the pontiff's alone. Ten years later, the Jesuit theologian, Clemens Schrader, was to call the definition 'an act peculiar to the pontificate of Pius IX, and one to which no former pontificate can show any parallel'.

The strongly disputed doctrine of the immaculate conception was only the pilot balloon for the 1870 definition of papal infallibility. The unpalatable fact for all bishops opposed to the definition at Vatican I was that, only sixteen years before, Pius had already exercised that power before the whole world – and they had done nothing about it. Pius IX had turned the church's infallibility into a personal prerogative to be used independently of church or council.

After 1854 the Dominicans had to submit. No apparitions of the Blessed Virgin would help them any more.

Non-Catholic Christians were even more upset. The definition confirmed their worst fears about the papacy. The immaculate conception was no longer a pious belief that Catholics were free to accept or reject. They were now threatened with excommunication if they disbelieved it or simply withheld consent. Without an explicit act of faith in it, they were told by Pius IX, they *could not be saved*. Those who think otherwise 'are by their own judgement condemned, have made shipwreck concerning the faith and fallen away from the unity of the church'.

It was not necessary for Pope St Gregory the Great, the Fathers of the church, St Anselm, St Bernard, St Bonaventure, St Thomas Aquinas – who denied it. Nor for Irenaeus, Jerome, Chrysostom who, in common with St Peter and St Paul, never even thought about it. Over eighteen and a half centuries after Mary's conception, it was heretical to deny she was conceived immaculate. This marginal opinion was now as important for salvation as belief in the Trinity, the divinity of Christ, the Atonement and the Resurrection.

Absolute power had fashioned an absolute 'truth'; and other Christians found one more sky-high barrier between themselves and the Roman church. Some enquired where it would end. Maybe a future pontiff would define that Mary, too, was virginally conceived. The phenomenal progress of the immaculate conception from blank papal denial to a papal definition shows that nothing is impossible. For in this matter the pope contradicted basic principles: that the gospels provide the basis of belief; that no individual, not even the pope, can decide *Catholic* doctrine, it needs the entire episcopate in Council or in their general teaching representing the faith of their churches; that Catholicism cannot treat in this cavalier fashion a tradition dating back to patristic times. Against this, all that Pius IX could say was 'I am tradition'.

An amiable man, he was to prove the most autocratic pontiff since the Middle Ages.

The definition of the immaculate conception was not only extraordinary in its content and method of delivery. For all its apparent marginal significance, it has influenced almost the entire theology of the Catholic church. This is self-evident in regard to papal authority, especially in defining doctrine. But it also influenced the theology of original sin and sexuality.

Original sin: Pius reinforced the concept of original sin as a hand-on from a remote ancestor (Adam) who had sinned and transmitted this sin to the rest of the race. Pius IX was chiefly responsible for the Catholic church being unable to accept the findings of Darwin as, two centuries before, it had been unable to accept what Galileo said. The *Origin of Species* came out five years after the definition of the immaculate conception. In spite of the accumulating scientific evidence that man had evolved over millions of years from lower forms, Rome kept insisting and still does that there was orginally one pair only, perfect in body, mind and spirit, from whom the entire race sprang. Even on the ethical level, some theory like Darwin's would have helped the church out of a difficulty. For if there was a single pair at the origin of the race, in God's plan, mankind could only have begun to propagate itself by means of incest, which, according to Catholic moralists, is against the natural law and which God Himself cannot condone.

Sex: the doctrine of the immaculate conception has also affected Catholic teaching on sexuality and, in particular, on birth control, abortion and *in vitro* fertilization.

Since 1854, Catholics have more and more come round to believing that the soul is infused by God at the first moment of conception. Mary was a saint, according to Pius IX, in the first moment of her conception. That reinforces the idea that at conception a human being with all the rights of a human being is present in the womb. It follows that abortion at any stage is really murder. Contra-ception is the next worst evil to abortion, since it prevents the production of another human being. It shows that between Pius IX's 1854 decree and Paul VI's 1968 encyclical on birth control there is a firm connection.

These matters will be dealt with more fully in Part 3, where we shall see that celibacy too is connected with Rome's teaching on the immaculate conception. Celibates, who have vowed not to express themselves sexually, that is, not to propagate original sin, are held to live a more perfect life than married people.

The Syllabus of Errors

Ten years to the day after defining the immaculate conception, Pius IX published his Syllabus of Errors, together with an encyclical letter, *Quanta Cura*. For nineteen years, Pius had condemned everything new, good as well as bad. Out of sympathy with the ideals of the French Revolution, he was particularly hard on anything that smacked of freedom.

Pius believed that the Roman church has the fullest possible grasp of truth in the world, and is therefore divinely pledged to be intolerant. He exemplified this two years before he issued his Syllabus when he entered into a concordat with the President of Ecuador. This right-wing Catholic had come to power by means of a coup against liberal anticlerical elements. The concordat was one of the most unjust documents ever agreed to by two sovereign powers. Roman Catholicism was to be the only religion allowed in Ecuador. The church was granted complete control of education and a dominant role in the life of the country. This was Pius IX's idyll. He dreamed that one day the rest of the world, especially France and America, would follow suit. *Quanta Cura* is less a dream than a nightmare.

Full of fear and foreboding, Pius writes as one without hope. He stood for absolutism: church and state were to carve the world up between them as they had done for centuries; the state was to be subject to the church in moral matters and the church's protector even when she proposes complete intolerance towards other religions.

Pius IX's Syllabus of Errors too is reactionary throughout. Among the contemporary views which he condemned are these:

15. Every man is free to embrace and profess that religion which, guided by the light of reason, he shall consider true.

24. The church has not the power of using force nor has she any temporal power, direct or indirect.

30. The immunity of the church and of ecclesiastical persons derived its origins from civil law.

38. The Roman pontiffs have, by their too arbitrary conduct, contributed to the division of the church into Eastern and Western.

76. The abolition of the temporal power of which the Apostolic See is possessed would contribute in the greatest degree to the liberty and prosperity of the church.

77. In the present day it is no longer expedient that the Catholic religion should be held as the only religion of the state, to the exclusion of all other forms of worship.

79. Hence it has been wisely decided by law, in some Catholic countries, that persons coming to reside therein shall enjoy the public exercise of their own peculiar worship.

80. The Roman pontiff can and should reconcile himself, and come to terms with progress, liberalism and modern civilization.

In their chiefly Italian context of anticlericalism which Rome's intransigence had brought to the boil, these medieval teachings were bad enough. Taken out of context and strung together, they looked like a caricature of Catholicism. No enemy of the church could have harmed it half as much as Pius IX. Gladstone in England and Lincoln in America were scandalized to hear a pontiff condemning progress, liberalism and modern civilization.

The reaction of the world's press was predictable. Britain, in particular, expressed its incredulity.

The Syllabus came out in time for Christmas 1864. In its first number of the new year, *Punch* had a clown declaiming:

> I was prepared to swallow with unquestioning docility,
> The biggest things delivered by Superior Infallibility;
> To stretch my mouth from ear to ear I shouldn't have objected,
> Would willingly have opened it to any width directed.
>
> But really that Encyclical, so contrary to reason,
> Your Holiness had published just at this special season,
> Insisting on the divine right of priestly domination
> O'er civil power, the family, and public education;
>
> Against despotic government denouncing insurrection,
> Denying people's rights to choose their rulers by election,
> Proclaiming the Church bound to back the State in persecution,
> Condemning free press, conscience, free and liberal constitution. . . .

All of which was too much for even a big-mouthed clown to swallow.

The *Spectator* suggested that the pope should 'as soon pray against the first law of motion'. The Anglican *Church Times* saw the pope as the divider rather than uniter of Christendom and greeted the encyclical with 'disgust and derision'. The leader-writer pointed out that Pius had no sympathy with civilization, progress, science or intellect. He looked on these as 'deadly enemies of faith'.

The comment of *The Times* was the shrewdest: 'There is scarcely a political system in Europe, except the Papal Government, that does not rest on principles which are here declared to be damnable errors.'

This was true. Throughout the nineteenth century, the papacy, had been pressurizing governments to deny their citizens those rights which were denied citizens in the Papal States. From 1831 the popes attacked each new constitution – the Austrian, French, Belgian – as 'godless'. Why? Because they dared like atheists to grant freedom of conscience; freedom of the press; free parliamentary institutions for which all were entitled to vote, regardless of their religion or lack of it; complete equality of all citizens before the law. The papacy kept urging other Italian states to imitate its own repression. For example, in 1852, Pius IX persuaded Tuscany to forbid Jewish doctors to practise medicine.

The overriding impression given was: The one thing Rome cannot abide is freedom in any form.

All this while, the popes were fuelling anticlericalism throughout Italy. Pius IX might eventually be pitied and popular in the church; he was almost universally disliked in Italy. One consequence of the papacy's rejection of the new constitutions was that Catholic citizens of the emerging republics were seen as unpatriotic. When, for instance, the Austrian constitution was published, the Vatican said:

> We declare these laws and their consequences to have been, and to be for the future, null and void. We exhort and adjure their authors, especially those who call themselves Catholics and all who have dared to propose, accept, approve and execute them, to remember the censures and spiritual penalties incurred *ipso facto* according to the apostolic constitutions and decrees of the Ecumenical Councils, by those who violate the rights of the Church.

Pius IX went so far as to condemn this constitution for allowing Protestants and Jews to have their own schools and colleges.

In France, Bishop Dupanloup was so worried that he introduced a distinction which, we have seen, Cardinal Gibbons of Baltimore was to find useful. The pope's Syllabus applied to a perfect world (thesis); not to an imperfect world (hypothesis). Unfortunately, the pope's notion of perfection was not that of most Catholics, who were suspicious of a theocratic state. As a Parisian wit commented: 'The thesis is when the church condemns the Jews; the hypothesis is when the papal nuncio dines with Baron de Rothschild.'

The time was very near when the democracy which Pius IX unwearingly condemned freed Catholics themselves from the tyranny of the

Papal States and brought a whiff of freedom to the church which Pius IX, had he had the power, would have withheld from it for ever.

There could hardly have been a pontiff in history on whom the church could bestow the accolade of 'infallible' with more trepidation.

Papal Supremacy

Significantly, the date chosen for the opening of the First Vatican Council in 1869 was 8 December, the anniversary of the purely papal definition of the immaculate conception.

According to *Pastor aeternus*, the major decree of Vatican I, the pope is not merely a supervisor or top administrator of the church. He possesses 'full and supreme jurisdiction of the Church in those matters which concern discipline and direction of the Church dispersed throughout the world'. The pope's power is supreme; it extends directly and immediately to every church, every pastor, every lay person.

The Council maintains that in saying this it is 'resting on the plain testimonies of the Sacred Writings and adhering to the plain and express decrees of both our predecessors, the Roman pontiffs, and of the General Councils'. These assumptions do not stand up to scrutiny. To review the evidence briefly:

As to the Sacred Writings: not one of the early Fathers of the church saw in the Bible any reference to papal jurisdiction over the church. On the contrary, they take it for granted that bishops, especially metropolitans, have the full right to govern and administer their own territory without interference from *anyone*. The Eastern church *never* accepted papal supremacy; Rome's attempt to impose it led to the shism.

As to General Councils: the fifteenth-century Council of Constance put a Council in many important areas *above* the pope. That would be enough to undermine Vatican I's reliance on Councils. But matters are far worse than that.

The eight Councils of the undivided church were not called by the Bishop of Rome. Beginning with Nicaea in 325, Councils were summoned by the emperor who approved their decrees. The emperor ruled; he imposed the creeds. Canon 6 of Nicaea decided that all sees were to retain their ancient rights. Alexandria was to rule over Egypt, Libya and Pentapolis 'since there is a similar custom in the case of the Bishop of Rome. Likewise at Antioch.'

Fifty years later at the Council of Constantinople in 381, the Bishop of Constantinople was ranked next to the Bishop of Rome. Canon 3 of the Council explained why. 'Next to the Bishop of Rome, the Bishop of Constantinople shall have primacy of rank *because Constantinople is the new Rome.*'

This canon was repeated in 451 at the Council of Chalcedon. Pope

Leo the Great wanted greater recognition for his See of Rome. He did not get it. The Council simply said:

> The fathers properly gave the primacy to the Throne of the Elder Rome *because that was the Imperial City.* And the hundred and fifty most religious bishops, being moved with the same intention, gave equal privileges to the most holy Throne of the New Rome [Constantinople], judging with reason, that the city which was honoured with the sovereignty and senate, and which enjoyed *equal privileges with the elder Rome,* should also be magnified like her in ecclesiastical matters, being the second after her.

There is no reference to Scripture or the role of Peter which the Bishop of Rome inherited, no supremacy given 'the pope'. The pope is *honoured* because he is Bishop of the Imperial See of Old Rome.

Far from it being plain, as Vatican I declared, that Scripture and the Ecumenical Councils gave the pope universal jurisdiction, there is *no* such evidence for it. As Cardinal Manning of Westminster said: 'The dogma must overcome history.'

Even *papal* testimonies to the pope's jurisdiction only surfaced after Constantine left Sylvester marooned in Rome as his vassal. A tone of menace soon began to be heard in the Roman See. Then Leo I called himself Pontifex Maximus and deposed a bishop.

In spite of this, one looks in vain in the first millennium for a single doctrine or piece of legislation imposed by Rome *alone* on the rest of the church. The only general laws came out of Councils such as Nicaea. In any case, how *could* the Bishop of Rome have exercised universal jurisdiction in those early centuries when there was no Curia, when other bishops brooked no interference in their dioceses from *anyone*, when Rome issued no dispensations and demanded no tribute or taxation, when all bishops, not just the Bishop of Rome, had the power to bind and loose, when no bishop or church or individual was censured by Rome? Further, for centuries, the Bishop of Rome was chosen by the local citizens – clergy and laity. If he had jurisdiction over the universal church, would not the rest of the world want a say in his appointment? When he *was* believed to have supremacy the rest of the church *did* demand a say in his election. This came about only in the Middle Ages.

Vatican I, defined papal supremacy in terms that medieval pontiffs would have approved of but bear no relation to Scripture, tradition or the history of the Ecumenical Councils of the undivided church.

Papal Infallibility

The pope's infallibility was seen by Vatican I as part of the pope's supremacy over the whole church. These are the terms of the definition:

> The Roman Pontiff, when he speaks *ex cathedra*, that is, when in the exercise of his office as the pastor and teacher of all Christians, he defines by virtue of his supreme apostolic authority the doctrine concerning faith and morals to be held by the universal Church, is, by the divine assistance promised to him in the person of St Peter, possessed of that infallibility wherewith the divine Redeemer wished His Church should be endowed in defining doctrine concerning faith and morals; and that for this cause such definitions of the Roman Pontiff are irreformable of themselves and not because of the consent of the church.

To review briefly the evidence against papal infallibility: Peter was fallible, both before and after the crucifixion. Nor is there any hint in the New Testament that Peter had some kind of power that a successor would inherit. According to the Fathers, Peter as such had no successor. They see all bishops as succeeding to the apostles, not an individual bishop succeeding to an individual apostle, in this case Peter. They, therefore, could not possibly have accepted the claim that 'Peter's successor' had to rule the See of Rome.

We have seen, too, that all the great doctrinal statements, especially the creeds, came not from popes but from Councils. In the early centuries, it never occurred to the Bishops of Rome that they could define doctrine for the whole church. Vatican I really needed to explain why, if papal infallibility is crucial to the church, there is no mention of it in the creeds and Councils of the undivided church and why it was not imposed until 1870. Before then, papal infallibility was in no way demanded of Catholics. They could, and whole countries did, deny it without any suggestion that they were bad Catholics.

But if Catholics were not obliged to believe in papal infallibility before 1870 they were free to believe or not what any pope said. In the words of Cardinal Newman, it was a 'theological opinion . . . a probability'. Until 1870, Catholics never could *believe* a doctrine on the basis of a pope's definition; at best, they were free to hold it as probable. But, if this option existed, the pope cannot have *regulated* the faith of the church as a Council did. In a word, papal *ex cathedra* statements throughout history – even presuming, for the sake of argument, that there were some – were only imposed on the church from 1870 on. There might of course, be other grounds for the pope being infallible, and there *were*. He was a bishop teaching alongside other bishops in what is called the ordinary magisterium. But precisely in the terms set out by Vatican I the faithful could accept what he said *or reject it*. In other words, papal infallibility did not critically affect the church until 1870. The notion some Catholics have that they get their faith in God and Jesus and the church *from the pope as such* is mistaken. The church never had and never required *papal* infallibility for its Christian faith.

According to Vatican I, the pope is only infallible when he speaks *ex cathedra*. It would seem, then, more appropriate to say that the pope is *fallible*, except when, rarely, he makes *ex cathedra* pronouncements. As was pointed out by a bishop in the Council itself, to say 'The pope is infallible' is rather like saying 'Mr X is a drunkard because he got drunk once'; or, worse, 'Mr X is a drunkard because his great-great-grandfather got drunk once,' for *ex cathedra* statements are extremely rare. It would be hard to find one before the 1854 definition of the immaculate conception. And, as all agree, there has only been one since 1870. That was when Pius XII defined another Marian doctrine, the Assumption, in 1950. He declared that at the end of her life Mary was taken up body and soul into heaven. Even with his 'special divine assistance' he was unable to say for certain whether she had died or not. This did not stop him adding the usual anathema: 'If anyone, which God forbid, should dare wilfully to deny or call in doubt that which We have defined, let him know that he has fallen away completely from the divine and Catholic faith. . . .'

The rarity of *ex cathedra* statements makes John XXIII's remark something more than a jest: 'I am not infallible. I would only be infallible if I spoke *ex cathedra*, which I do not intend to do.' Even Paul VI did not invoke infallibility when condemning birth control in 1968.

The infrequency of infallible pronouncements would hardly satisfy those nineteenth-century Catholics who looked forward to a new dogma on their plate with *The Times* at every breakfast. But could not a pope at least provide a list of *ex cathedra* statements so far, or criteria for recognizing them? To be unsure which statements *are* infallible tends to undermine confidence in the system. Non-Catholics, too, would like to know what they would have to believe prior to reunion.

Catholic theologians are keen to point out that infallibility does not mean the pope is inspired, can see into the future, can decide any issue as and when the whim takes him, necessarily expresses the truth perfectly so it never needs revision or expansion. What almost all of them fail to point out is that even on Catholic principles popes by and large are not infallible at all. They do not speak infallibly even when the church and the world are crying out for light in darkness.

Since 1870 everyone would like to know the answers to many stupendous questions: Are there people or other planets and, if so, how does Christ's Incarnation affect them? Is nuclear warfare justifiable under any circumstances and may a Catholic engage in the research and development of such weapons? Hundreds of similar questions have been raised by science and technology. Not one infallible answer has emerged from Rome. It would have helped if a pope had defined, with the Bible's backing, 'Jesus, a poor Man is always on the side of the poor'. Or: 'He who has it in his power to feed the hungry and does not do so is starving Christ himself.' Pius IX and Pius XII chose to exercise their infallibility on Marian doctrines without basis in the Bible or in tradition. The harvest of infallibility is meagre.

Papal infallibility does nothing to enlighten the church. What, then, is its function?

It seems to have less to do with truth than with control. The pope's prestige rests not on infallibility but on what has been called 'creeping infallibility'. The pope is infallible, so to speak, even when he is not. This explains why the pope and the Holy Office feel free to impose silence even on issues that are not of faith. Discussion would ruin harmony which is the blessing the pope brings to the church. Alas, its cost is sometimes truth, for truth can only come from frank and open discussion. The lack of it is the reason why for centuries, since Galileo, Rome has tended to arrive breathless and late on the scene of every genuine human advance, whether it be freedom of expression, universal suffrage, the abolition of slavery, the role of women in society and in the ministry, the control of population by scientific means, and so on.

In the last hundred years, especially, the church has had to endure what Newman prophesied in his diaries: 'a stern nemesis for imperious acts ... a tyrannous use of his [Pius IX's] spiritual power. . . . He claimed, he exercised, larger power than any Pope ever did.'

Infallibility also gives the impression of ominiscience, or at least of a grasp of divine truth that is hardly reverent. God is the Unknown and the Unknowable. According to Joseph Pieper, Thomas Aquinas did not finish his *Summa Theologica*, not because death took him before he could complete it but because he had a sense of God that made all he had written so much straw. He went for months unable to write because of what he had seen and was unable to express. If only church leaders gave the impression that even their best efforts were so much straw, it would lead to less intolerance.

Pius IX and the Deposing Power

Soon after Vatican I, the Jesuit publication *Civiltà Cattolica* reported a sermon by Pius IX. He spoke angrily of the 'many malicious errors regarding infallibility'. The most malicious, he said, concerns the pope's right to depose sovereigns and to declare their subjects free from allegiance. This right, he agreed, was exercised 'at times by popes in extreme cases'. But this had 'nothing to do with infallibility'. It was a matter of authority, 'that authority, according to the public law then in force and by the agreement of Christian nations, which revered in the pope the supreme judge of Christendom, including the judging, even in temporal matters, of princes and states'.

Pius went on to say that times have changed utterly. 'And only malice could confuse things and times so different, as if an infallible judgement concerning a principle of revealed truth had any affinity with a right which the popes, solicited by the desire of the people, had to exercise when the common good demanded it.' Pius knew why currency was being given in 1871 'to such an absurd idea, that no one any more thinks of, least of all the Supreme Pontiff. They seek for pretexts, even the most frivolous and the most untrue, to stir up princes against the church.'

Even coming from Pius IX in the aftermath of Vatican I this is remarkable. Almost every pope from Gregory VII on claimed that their power to depose sovereigns *came from God*. The pope rules on earth, whether in the church or in politics, in the place of God; and God's power knows no limits.

On the other hand, not one pontiff ever attributed his power to the gift of the Christian commonwealth. If it were a gift, where is a single statement of pontiff, emperor or king to that effect, any law or code conceding him this right?

One eighteenth-century historian counted ninety-five popes who claimed to have divine power to depose kings. All their arguments were based – badly, it must be admitted – on Scripture. 'Whatsoever thou shalt bind on earth,' said Christ. This, the popes said, was unqualified. Christ gave popes the keys to heaven *and* earth; he feeds the whole flock, including the Chief Sheep, the emperor.

When Gregory VII deposed Henry IV, when Pius V deposed Elizabeth I, they claimed power from God to do so. When Bellarmine attempted to limit slightly the pope's deposing power, Sixtus V moved to put him on the Index.

It is not the malice of non-Catholics that makes a connection between papal authority to depose and papal infallibility. It is innumerable popes themselves whose teaching Pius IX has to distort or ignore because it does not suit his thesis.

Faced with this enormous weight of evidence, any other institution would say: Our predecessors made a mistake. They misread the gospels. Popes were as wrong to depose emperors as emperors were to depose popes. We ought not to judge them too harshly; they belonged to their time as we belong to ours. What we can and must do is to see that these things never happen again.

Unfortunately, an infallible church is not in a position to acknowledge one mistake of this sort. It cannot err or contradict itself. It is tempted, as was Pius IX, to say that its critics are either blind or malicious.

Thus infallibility tends to make history a minor branch of theology. Papal mistakes in the past are illusions. By a Catholic form of Orwellianism, history must be officially 'forgotten' – otherwise, rewritten to make it seem as if the entire course of the papacy, doctrine-wise, is unblemished. No error is possible even in popes who flagrantly contradicted one another.

Pius IX died in 1878. Twenty-five years later, another Pius ascended the throne of Peter. He, too, was convinced that no pope, himself included, could ever make a mistake.

FOURTEEN

The Great Purge

IT WAS EARLY AUGUST 1903, in the Sistine Chapel. In the shadow of Michelangelo's fresco of the Last Judgement, the voting seemed to be going according to plan when a crisis erupted. Cardinal Puszyna, the Polish Bishop of Cracow, then part of Austria, stood up to address his sixty-one colleagues in the conclave. Before the third vote for Leo XIII's successor, he had a message to deliver. He coughed in embarrassment. It was from Franz Joseph. By reason of his long-standing privilege as head of the Austro-Hungarian Empire, his Majesty was exercising a veto against one of their number: Cardinal Rampolla, Leo XIII's Secretary of State.

The temperature in the Sistine, high in spite of the tall ceilings, rose even higher. Their Eminences seethed. This was a blatant interference in the liberties of the church at the most sensitive of moments: a papal election. It was doubly insulting in that for thirty-three years the papacy had been deprived of temporal power. Now here was an earthly sovereign saying through this scarlet puppet who could and who could not wear the papal crown.

The Everlasting Father

Gioacchino Pecci, Leo XIII, had died on 19 July 1903. Rome was so hot they feared the body would decompose before their eyes. Leo and his predecessor, Pius IX, whose head he, as Camerlengo, had tapped in death with a silver hammer, had both reigned longer than any other pontiffs. They had counted together a massive fifty-seven years. Old when elected, Leo was ninety-four, with sixty encyclicals to his name, when he died. Often in his later years his aides were heard to mutter: 'In Pecci we sought a Holy Father, not an everlasting Father.'

Slight in build, with a huge beaky nose from which melted snuff dripped on to his cassock, with thin lips and white diaphanous complexion, he had dominated the church. The faithful would miss those huge eyes, like black diamonds, and those slender swan-like hands with which he blessed, with an old man's kindness, his subjects.

True, like Pius IX, he had been a 'prisoner' of the Vatican. He was never able to visit his own basilica, St John Lateran, or escape the dog-days by refreshing visits to his villa at Castelgandolfo on the edge of the Alban Lake. But he could still ride in his gardens, and smell the sweet odours of pine and eucalyptus and fresh orange blossom.

Leo had a reputation for being a liberal. He was scarcely that, though he did open up the Vatican archives, saying 'The church is not afraid of history'. He still demanded the sort of obedience he felt due to him as absolute monarch of God's truth. His friend and biographer, Julien de Narfon, reports a typical Vatican conversation of the time. '"What would you do," one of the Princes of the Church was asked, "if the Holy See tried to force you to admit that two and two make six?" "I would admit it at once," was the reply; "and before signing, I would ask, 'Wouldn't you like me to make it seven?'"'

In 1896 Leo decided that Anglican orders were invalid. This meant that this world-wide communion had no Christian clergymen and no sacraments except baptism. The head of the Anglican communion was a mere layman, baptized, hopefully, in a 'church' that had no apostolic foundation. This is why, until 1950, the Vatican newspaper, *Osservatore Romano*, referred to him thus: '"the archbishop of Canterbury"'. The word 'archbishop' was always lower-case and the title in inverted commas. It was a nicely judged literary insult.

For all that, Leo, unlike Pius IX, had begun to recognize political realities in Europe. He had insisted that French bishops should accept the Republic and cease harking back to the days of the absolute monarchy. So a breath of fresh air had slightly stirred some soutanes of the papal entourage.

A Peasant Pope

Leo's Secretary of State, Rampolla, had been favoured to succeed him. He went into conclave with high hopes in that fateful summer of 1903. In the first vote he polled twenty-four out of sixty-two. His closest rival was the balding Carmelite, Cardinal Gotti, with his strange haunted eyes. Gotti had seventeen votes, with five for Sarto, Patriarch of Venice.

Sarto, with his broad pleasant face and thick white hair, interpreted this, perhaps correctly, as a little joke on the part of his colleagues. He was not really papal material; he had not the brains or the experience for the job, not after Leo had set such standards. Besides, nearing seventy, he was too old a dog to learn new tricks.

In the second poll Rampolla rose to twenty-nine, there were sixteen for Gotti and ten for Sarto. One final push on Rampolla's behalf and the election would be over.

Then came the intervention of the Cardinal of Cracow. When the initial burst of anger had subsided, Rampolla stood up under his canopy. His long handsome face showed the strain of reining in his wrath. His dark intelligent eyes were blazing, the nostrils of his classically straight nose were aquiver. The whiteness of his face seemed to glow against the black of his straight hair and the purple of his robes.

'I thoroughly deplore', he managed to say, with the evenness of the skilled diplomat, 'this serious blow aimed by a civil power at the dignity of the Sacred College and at the liberty of the Church in choosing its head. That is why I protest with the utmost vehemence.' His voice softened considerably as he added: 'So far as I personally am concerned, nothing more agreeable could have happened to me.'

His Eminence sat down in a compelling silence.

A third poll was taken. Rampolla had not lost a single vote. It was Gotti who suffered from the veto. He was known to back the Austrian cause, as Rampolla was alleged to favour France. Gotti polled nine votes, whereas Sarto, the dark horse, shot up to twenty-one.

The next poll followed. Thirty for Rampolla. Gotti was out of the race with three. Sarto had risen to twenty-four.

When the cardinals went to bed on that second night, they knew, for all the indignity of it, that Cracow's intervention had altered the course of the election. He had revealed that the choice of Rampolla would lead to an antagonism between two traditionally Catholic powers. In the circumstances, it was vital to choose a middle-of-the-road candidate. The next round, they guessed, would be decisive. And so it proved.

From the moment that Sarto polled twenty-seven, three more than Rampolla, everyone knew who would be pope. If only he was willing.

Centuries before, canonists had worked out the criteria for making a pope. The problem was: if the pope alone has the plenitude of power, how can this be bestowed on him by the church, whether by cardinals or, more anciently, by the clergy and laity of Rome? The favourite answer was: the Sacred College, by their votes, merely pointed to the candidate. It needed the nominee's own acceptance for God to grant him the plenitude of power *directly*. The only question now was whether Sarto would accept or not.

Monsignor Merry del Val, the thirty-eight-year-old secretary of the conclave, English-born of Spanish extraction, was sent to ask Sarto to say yes. When he found him, the cardinal's face was bathed in tears; his reluctance had, if anything, intensified. But in the next poll, with thirty-five votes, he had more than double Rampolla's.

On the fourth morning, at the seventh poll, Sarto had fifty votes; he was pope, if only he would consent. Cardinal Gibbons of Baltimore, who had stunned Rome by arriving in a black suit with a straw hat over his scarlet skullcap, was among those urging him to do so. In agony of mind, Sarto acceded, and took the name of Pius X because he associated his predecessors of that name with suffering.

Merry del Val, soon to be made Secretary of State, was even then giving Cardinal Puszyna a dressing-down. It was said that never, not even in the halcyon days of Alexander VI, had the air of the Borgia rooms been so blue.

The new pontiff, being a prisoner of the Vatican, gave his blessing, not from the balcony overlooking the piazza, but form the inner loggia of St Peter's. The symbolism was to prove decisive: in the moment of assuming office, he turned his back on the world. As Cardinal della Chiesa, the future Benedict XV, at once observed, Pius X looked uncannily like Pius IX.

Humble Origins

Giuseppe Sarto was born, son of a labourer, in the small northern provincial town of Riese in 1834. He was the second of ten children. His father swept out the town hall. The little Giuseppe was to become infallible and sweep out the universal church.

The boy was pious, affectionate, slim, curly-haired and devoted to his mother. Feeling called to the priesthood at an early age, he entered the junior seminary at Castelfranco. He often walked the seven kilometres there and back in his big bare feet to save on shoe leather.

He never changed his simple attitude to life; he had a natural goodness. He went to the senior seminary in Padua where he followed the customary cut-down course of medieval philosophy and theology. He was ordained priest when he was twenty-three in the year 1858. After that, he was curate in Tombolo for nine years – he pawned his watch to feed the hungry. He was parish priest at Salzano for another nine – his door was never closed – until, at forty-one, he became diocesan chancellor at Treviso. He lived in the seminary, in one room overlooking the colourful plain. He was contented in his ministry. He was noted for his kind disposition and generosity to the poor. He worked hard for no other motive than the love of God and his fellow-men.

In 1884, Sarto was nominated Bishop of Mantua. He was astonished, thinking a bishopric beyond his capacity. He did his best to refuse, but Pope Leo insisted.

In June 1893, when he was fifty-nine, he was made Patriarch of Venice. For sixteen months he was unable to take over his see because an anticlerical government refused him an *Exsequatur*. It was another sign of the times. The church was exposed to danger on every side. One consolation he had was a three-day visit to his home in Riese where he was able to please his mother – bedridden and in her eighties – by dressing up in his cardinalate robes.

The *Exsequatur* finally came on 5 September 1894, and he celebrated by issuing his first pastoral letter. This kind warm-hearted man showed that, as a bishop, he could be as belligerent as his enemies.

'God', he wrote, 'has been driven out of public life by the separation of Church and State.' His attitude to the papacy was of the strictest sort. 'When we speak of the Vicar of Christ, we must not quibble, we must obey; we must not measure what he has said in order to restrict the extent of our obedience. . . . Society is sick. . . . The one hope, the one remedy, is the Pope.' Even for this holy and deeply unhappy man, the one hope was not Christ but the Pope.

No sooner was he patriarch than he was denouncing the 'perfidious plots' of liberalism, and especially Catholic liberals, whom he called 'wolves disguised as lambs'.

On 24 November he made his way by cardinal's gondola to the City of Gold. There were crowds on every bridge and parapet; they leaned through every window and perched perilously on narrow ledges over-looking the canal to receive his blessing. Up to the Quays the gondola glided, until Cardinal Sarto disembarked at the piazza of San Marco. Every building was decorated, except for the town hall. It was a snub from the anticlericals that he was never to forget or forgive.

So he entered into the life of what he called 'a poor country cardinal'. His two sisters attended to his needs, which were few. From five in the morning till midnight, he worked without respite. He did not mind being called Don Beppe. The income of the church, he said, as one who had never had any money, is the patrimony of the poor. He insisted on a liturgy worthy of God and not the usual casual Italian affair. It was to be graced with the Gregorian chant, the music of the angels; there was to be frequent reception of the Eucharist.

In this way, he passed nine relatively tranquil years until he set off to cast his vote for Leo XIII's successor. He bought a return railway ticket and promised his diocesans he would come back to them dead or alive. It was the one promise he ever made that he did not keep.

Stranger in the Vatican

He was a complete foreigner in Rome. All his life he had been used to unsophisticated people and simple problems that could be solved by hard work and personal kindness. His reign was not to be a happy one. His big luminous eyes were filled with perpetual sadness. Aides, such as Merry del Val and Cardinal de Lai, put before him not just facts but interpretations of fact that convinced him, if he were not convinced already, that mankind was sick. Chief among its woes was apostasy from God. He spoke, privately and publicly, of moral depravity, of a world falling apart. Most popes since the French Revolution have been incurable pessimists.

What Pius IX had seen as a disaster was the advent of democracy. What Pius X saw as a dying world was but a new world being born. Unprecedented advances were being made in science and technology.

Archaeology was revealing just how old the world is. Christians, following John Lightfoot, a seventeenth-century Cambridge scholar, supposed that creation had taken place on an autumn morning – in the Northern Hemisphere, that is – in the year 4004 BC. To be precise, God had said 'Let there be Light' on 23 October 4004 at 9 a.m. Scholars were now denying man was created perfect, as a literal reading of the Book of Genesis suggested; man, too, was part of the evolutionary process. Historians were revealing things till then unknown about the church's past, especially in the formative years. Most alarmingly of all, from Pius X's point of view, exegesis was calling into question a literal interpretation of the Old and New Testaments. Renan's *Vie de Jésus* had spawned countless works of 'infidelity', as Pius IX had prophesied.

Pius X was staggered at the size of the task God had set him, a peasant from Riese. Another example of God choosing the foolish things of the world to confound the wise. He was pontiff, the one hope and remedy of a sick world. From his exalted, near-divine elevation, he was prepared to demand for himself the blind obedience he had pledged to Leo XIII. He trusted that the Spirit would help save the church from grave dangers that threatened her *from within*. A conspiracy was afoot at the very heart of the church, he was convinced of it. Theologians, Scripture scholars were in league with all the anti-God forces in a post-Revolutionary world. Their one aim: to annihilate the church.

Pius X's second encyclical appeared on that magic date, 8 December 1904. It was the fiftieth anniversary of the definition of the immaculate conception. His Letter reveals the kind of mind he brought to bear on the problems mankind was grappling with at this, one of the most original and exciting moments in history.

> Adam wept in his punishment but he perceived Mary crushing the serpent's head. Noah in the safety of the Ark looked forward to her. So did Abraham as his hand was stayed. Likewise Jacob when he saw a ladder standing on the earth, with its top reaching up into heaven; a stairway for the angels of God to go up and come down. Moses saw her in the bush that was alight and did not burn. David sang of her as he danced before the ark of the covenant. Elias saw her in the little cloud rising up out of the sea. But why go on?

This misapplication of Scripture might have passed unnoticed in an obscure Italian village of the time; it did not bode well as the meditation of a pope in the post-Vatican I period. He had the plenitude of power. He was the supreme governor of the church. Personally infallible, he was expected, practically on his own, to answer all the difficulties against traditional Catholicism that science was raising. No wonder he was overwhelmed by problems which, after 1870, he was expected to solve *on his own*.

Bible Truth for Catholics

Even before Pius X, the church had got itself into a tangle over the Bible, in particular over a passage in the First Epistle of St John (5:7), known as the Johannine Comma.

> For there are three who give testimony in heaven: the Father, the Word and the Spirit, and these three are one. And there are three who give witness on earth: the Spirit, the water and the blood, and these three are one.

In 1897 the Holy Office took it upon itself to decide that this was all genuine Scripture. It forbade Catholic scholars to say otherwise. This was first in a long line of official errors.

The heavenly testimony does not figure in a single Greek manuscript. It was added to the Latin manuscripts, probably in North Africa, because Cyprian mentioned it in 258, as did Augustine about the year 400. In their text, the earthly witnesses came first. In the fourteenth century, the text was tampered with to put the heavenly witnesses in the first place. This was a purely academic discussion. The intervention of the Holy Office meant Catholic scholars were obliged to forget the evidence and bow to a foolish judgement on the basis of blind obedience. As a result, they had to pretend the Holy Office was right when any scholar worth his salt knew it was wrong.

From this time on, Bible scholarship in the Roman church was a hazardous occupation. The 1897 decree remained in effect for thirty years. Then, disregarding the truth, the Holy Office said it had simply been meant to curb the 'audacity' of private teachers who, instead of leaving things to the pope, took it on themselves to judge the authenticity of biblical texts. So, from 1927, Catholics were entitled to 'incline against the genuineness of the Comma, provided they profess themselves ready to stand by the judgement of the church to which Jesus Christ entrusted the office not only of interpreting the Sacred Scriptures but also of faithfully guarding them'.

The implication was that the church has no need of scholars. Their role is only to hand on decisions of popes who alone can tell the world the true meaning of Scripture. The papacy's long record of misinterpreting Scripture – even to the extent of making the emperor the pope's puppet – did not suggest scholars could place total confidence in its decisions.

Leo XIII realized there was something wrong with his theological watchdogs at the Holy Office pontificating on Scripture, so he established a Biblical Commission in the years before he died. He appointed forty-one consultors, many of them liberals.

Pius X immediately replaced the liberals by reactionaries, and between 1906 and 1914 they issued a series of fantastic decisions which all Catholic Bible scholars had to adhere to.

After Vatican I, everything in the church was centralized. Every biblical difficulty, every moral conundrum was referred, usually by ultra-conservative bishops and scholars, to Rome for a decision.

By conforming to the decrees of the Biblical Commission, Catholic scholars effectively put themselves outside reputable academic life. Against all the accumulating evidence, they had to accept that Moses wrote the whole of the Pentateuch (the first five books of the Bible), and that chapters 40–66 of Isaiah were from one hand. Fifty years after the *Origin of Species*, they had to hold and teach that the first three chapters of Genesis were strictly historical. The first woman was formed from the rib of Adam; the first sin was a transgression of a specific divine command at the temptation of the devil in the form of a serpent. In 1907, the Biblical Commission 'decided' that all four gospels were written by those whose names they bear, and Paul wrote all the pastoral epistles as well as the Epistle to the Hebrews.

Catholic Bible scholars scuttled for cover like startled crabs. They lived in dread of being reported to Rome by their students or fellow-professors. Haunted by the fear of excommunication for one false step, they could at best report the enlightened researches of their Protestant brethren with affected disapproval: it was one way of getting sensible views across. Only thus could they survive, hoping against hope for better days. Even the finest biblical scholar of the day, Père Lagrange, was forbidden to publish his Commentary on Genesis.

And yet for well over a hundred years, long before Darwin, no sophisticated person, religious or irreligious, had been able to take the early Chapters of Genesis literally. If the church had not put Voltaire on the Index, it might have learned from him. In his Homily on the Old Testament, he pointed out the errors and contradictions of the text of Genesis. The idea that all man's woes, even sickness and death, are due to the fault of a First Parent of the race is no more credible than Pandora's box. Only when the myth is accepted as a myth does it have beauty and meaning.

Voltaire was more satirical when he dealt with the Flood and Noah's ark:

> It is fruitless for people to object that in the wettest
> years we do not get thirty inches of rain . . . that the

animals could not reach the ark from America and southern lands; that seven pairs of clean animals and two pairs of unclean could not have been put in twenty arks. . . . There is no end to their difficulties. But the whole of them are solved by pointing out that this great event was a miracle – that puts an end to all dispute.

Over a hundred years before Voltaire, Galileo had offered church authorities virtually the same key to unlock the myths and mysteries of Genesis. Reason was centuries ahead of the church in what should have been the church's chief province: the Scriptures. Instead, in Voltaire's phrase, the church fed its children on 'a diet of acorns'.

In Pius X's time, Catholic scholars were subject to a terrible persecution. The immediate cause of it was Pius' understanding of what he called 'Modernism'.

The Attack on Modernism

Just as Pius IX issued his Syllabus of Errors against all liberal tendencies, so, in July 1907, Pius X wrote *Lamentabili*, an attack on 'novelties'. He came down particularly hard on the latest interpretation of dogmas and Scripture. Among the propositions he selected at random from the writings of theologians and exegetes to condemn were these:

2. The church's interpretation of the Sacred Books is by no means to be rejected; nevertheless, it is subject to the more accurate judgement and correction of exegetes.

5. Since the deposit of Faith contains only revealed truths, the church has no right to pass judgement on the assertions of science.

12. If he wishes to apply himself usefully to biblical studies, the exegete must first put aside all preconceived opinions about the supernatural origin of Sacred Scripture and interpret it the same as any other merely human document.

16. The narrations of John are not properly history, but a mystical contemplation of the Gospel. The discourses contained in the Gospel are theological meditations, lacking historical truth concerning the mystery of salvation.

13. Heterodox exegetes have expressed the true sense of the Scriptures more faithfully than Catholic exegetes.

22. The dogmas the church holds out as revealed are not truths which have fallen from heaven. They are interpretations of religious facts which the human mind has acquired by laborious effort.

33. Everyone who is not led by preconceived opinions can readily see that either Jesus professed an error concerning the immediate Messianic Coming or the greater part of his doctrine as contained in the gospels is destitute of authority.

53. The organic constitution of the church is not immutable. Like human society, Christian society is subject to perpetual evolution.

With a few qualifications, these propositions would stand today as an expression of what most scholars believe.

Lamentabili was a sad attempt to stamp out all progress as though it were a heretical sect. Often Pius X gives the impression of condemning his own fantasy. Much of what he censures is garbled, and it is doubtful if anyone ever held it. He tended to put in one heap everything he disapproved of, labelled it 'Modernism, a compendium of heresies', and warned Catholics to have nothing to do with it. *He*, the Vicar of Christ, would lead them to safety through the marshlands of the modern world. He was right, of course, to be worried. The church, backward for centuries, was now being shown such by history, science, palaeontology, exegesis. The church had to choose either to learn very quickly or to roll up in a ball. The encyclical *Pascendi* that soon followed on *Lamentabili* showed that Pius had chosen to roll up in a ball.

It is unfortunately full of the black rhetoric of papal pronouncements of the period. There are enemies of the Cross of Christ, Protestants in the church's own bosom, whose one aim is to destroy Christ's church and annul his work. These crypto-Protestants want to reduce Christ to the status of an ordinary man. These 'Modernists', he said, do not believe in revelation, nor in God, nor in the church as a divine institution. They are a closely knit organization; they are hiding in every sphere, philosophy, theology, Bible studies, politics.

None of this was remotely plausible. It is hard to believe that Catholics, with explicit Protestant convictions, were hiding in the bosom of the church with the one aim of destroying it by spreading their unbelief.

What was really happening was that the world was coming of age. A revolution was taking place in the mind of man that was the extension of what had taken place in the mind of Galileo. Science was beginning to provide answers to questions that previous generations had left to priests and prayers. Pius still lived mentally in a medieval world, where God intervened from 'out there' or 'up there' by means of miracles and propositions uttered in the ears of prophets and popes. He believed, for instance, that simply by looking at a Bible text a pope, himself for one, without any special competence in Scripture, could interpret its meaning now and for ever. Pius stood for the timelessness and absoluteness of all doctrines at a period of history when it was becoming ever more clear that relativity entered into all moral judgements and expressions of belief. Scholars were saying that everything had to be thought out anew.

Man is not a creature of the absolute, except in his reaching out to the Beyond; he is necessarily part and parcel of a changing world. Everything is changing, including his understanding of himself, God and revelation. The Old Testament provides examples of this. Gradually, a local Jewish God with limited powers and still more limited sympathies, develops into a God of Armies, until he is eventually perceived to be the God of creation and of history. The New Testament, too, shows that Jesus is not a creature from outside the world who irrupted into it but a human being, who in a sense, like all human beings, was always present. New Testament revelation is not the giving and receiving of divine propositions but a gradual grasp of the meaning of Jesus' life, death and resurrection, fashioned by preaching and teaching into a pedagogic tool, in different places and according to the diverse needs of differing communities, Greek and Jewish.

Man's historicity, which so excited scholars of the time, was anathema to Pius X. He felt it as a threat to the church and his position in it as the Voice of eternal truths.

Two Modernists

Almost the best way to judge a regime is to examine its treatment of intellectuals. In Pius X's time, Catholic intellectuals were treated very severely.

George Tyrrell was one of these. Born in Dublin in 1861, he was educated in the Church of Ireland but at eighteen went to England where he became a Catholic and a Jesuit. He was a fine writer and destined, so it seemed, to become one of the elite of the Society. That was until it struck him that St Thomas Aquinas did not provide all the answers to questions modern man was asking. It was absurd to think that, had Aquinas been able to read Galileo, Newton, Darwin, he would not have changed one of his ideas. On the contrary, he would have altered almost every line he wrote. Yet Pius X, in his encyclical on the priesthood, *Pieni l'anima* of 1906, said: 'Let the study of philosophy, of theology and of related subjects, especially Holy Scripture, be pursued in the spirit of papal documents and of St Thomas Aquinas.'

Feeling under threat, Tyrrell wrote books under various pseudonyms: A. R. Waller, Hilaire Bourdon, Dr Ernest Engels. He was found out and dismissed from the Society on the first day of January 1906. He was forbidden to celebrate mass, though he was never formally charged with heresy.

Archbishop Mercier of Malines was ready to receive him into his diocese. But Cardinal Ferrata, Prefect of the Sacred Congregation of Bishops and Regulars, laid down strict preconditions. The famous forty-five-year-old Tyrrell was 'to pledge himself formally neither to publish anything on religious questions nor to hold any correspondence without the previous approval of a competent person appointed by the Archbishop'.

Tyrrell could not bear the thought of having his letters censored. This, he said, is 'the treatment the Czar might mete out to an anarchist'. But, then, in the eyes of the church he *was* an anarchist, in league with other anarchists to undermine the foundations of the church.

He wrote a personal letter to the pope. 'We have a right to look to your Holiness for positive as well as negative guidance; for construction of truth as well as destruction of error.' He was never answered.

When Fr Tyrrell wrote in criticism of *Pascendi* on the last day of September 1907, he was forbidden to receive the sacraments. By now he was suffering badly from migraine and a kidney complaint.

He was tempted to return to the church of his childhood, but he had suffered so much for Catholicism and longed to be of use to his fellow-Catholics. He stayed on the cold doorstep of Mother Church, hoping for a kind word that never came.

On his deathbed, he was absolved from his sins, though he had made it clear he would not recant. This was in the village of Storrington on the edge of the South Downs. His old friend, the Abbé Bremond, had been summoned. In a lucid moment, Tyrrell was able to speak with him. The Abbé once more absolved him from his sins.

In spite of this, Tyrrell was forbidden a requiem mass. He had not submitted to the Holy See. He was refused burial in a Catholic plot, so his friends buried him in an Anglican cemetery. Over the grave, after a few simple prayers, Abbé Bremond gave a magnificent panegyric which must have reached the ears of the Bishop of Southwark. For, three days later, the Prior of Storrington received a telegram from him: 'Do not allow Bremond to say mass.'

Just before the end, Tyrrell had written to a friend: 'My own work – which I regard as done – has been to raise a question which I have failed to answer.' It will serve as the epitaph of a great and holy priest for whom Rome had no room.

Another priest to come under the papal hammer was Abbé Loisy. A pupil of the great Monsignor Louis Duchesne, he saw early on that Rome's attitude to the Scriptures could not be sustained. Even to pretend loyalty to it was ruinous of the Christian conscience. In 1903 he published his *L'Evangile et l'Eglise*. Pius X responded with an immediate censure. In March of the following year, Loisy wrote to the pope. It was an act of great humility in a man for whom humility did not come easy.

He began his letter: 'Most Holy Father, I well know your Holiness's goodness of heart and it is to your heart that I now address myself.'

He offered to denounce publicly his recent book, to give up his lectureship at the Ecole des Hautes Etudes, and to suspend scientific publications he had in hand.

Pius X did not answer him. Instead, he wrote to the conservative Cardinal Richard of Paris: 'I have received a letter from the Rev. Abbé Loisy in which he appeals to my heart, but this letter was not written from the heart.' He insisted on an absolute and unqualified submission from the Abbé. In particular, he must be urged 'to burn what he adored and to adore what he had burned'.

When this information was relayed to Loisy, he confessed that something snapped inside him. Was it the last thread binding him to his childhood faith? 'Pressed into my letter', he wrote, 'was the last drop of feeling left in my Catholic soul.'

Pius X had extinguished the smoking flax, and broken the bruisèd reed.

In March 1908, Pius X excommunicated Loisy, naming him *vitandus*, the severest form of censure known in canon law. It means that Catholics are forbidden, unless there is strict necessity, to have anything at all to do with him, not merely in church but out of church. As far as Pius was concerned, the Abbé Loisy had ceased to exist.

When Abbé Bremond, friend of Tyrrell and Loisy, was received into the Académie Française in 1924, he said in his address: 'I have lived under four pontiffs: Pius IX, Leo XIII, Benedict XV and Pius XI.' What was the implication? That neither he nor anyone else had *lived* under saintly Pius X? Or that Pius X had ceased to exist for *him*?

Of what use was it for Tyrrell or anyone else to raise a question, when Pius X had all the answers ready up his sleeve?

Aftermath

Tyrrell and Loisy were not the only victims. Pius X instigated such a purge of scholars that fifty years after his death the effects were still being felt. Lagrange in Scripture, Duchesne in history were made to toe the papal line or find themselves on the heap of discards. Duchesne was forced to give up his chair at the Institut Catholique in Paris; his seminal book on the origins of Christianity was put on the Index.

A vigorous censorship was imposed on all books and magazines prior to publication. Priests needed permission to write to or for newspapers. A council of vigilance was set up in every diocese. There was even a secret society, championed by the pope, to offset the workings of the alleged 'secret society' of Christ's enemies. Teachers in seminaries and universities were screened and, if found wanting in 'loyalty', replaced. Fortunately for the future of the Catholic church, one priest who came under suspicion was a young Italian; he was reported to Rome for examination as a possible 'Modernist'. His name was Angelo Roncalli, the future John XXIII.

Pius X drew up an anti-Modernist oath which all ministers and teachers were obliged to take. Not even the Inquisition in its heyday was more efficient in rooting out every sign of dissent. For many loyal Catholics even today, Pius X saved the church. For others, this holy and most tragic of popes only saved it from being influenced by the accelerating progress of the human race.

It is said that by 1910 Modernism was dead. It is truer to say that, as Pius X understood it, it never lived. None the less, among the propositions he condemned, there were elements destined to haunt the Roman church for generations to come.

The problems confronting the church in every field could not be put off for ever. Catholicism trailed the world. There was a danger that if it went on too long, intellectually speaking, the Catholic church would be a laughing-stock.

The next two popes, Benedict XV and Pius XI, were intellectually lightweight. They did little to help the church face up to the modern world.

Pius XI was very much a pontiff in the tradition of Pius IX. On ecumenism, he had this to say:

> This Apostolic See has never allowed its subjects to take part in the assemblies of non-Catholics. There is but one way in which the unity of Christians may be fostered, and that is by furthering the return to the one true Church of those who are separated from it.

Pius XII was, in comparison with Pius XI, an intellectual giant. It has been said that few advances made at Vatican II were not adumbrated in some way in his work. But few pontiffs in this century exemplified better than he the absolutism of the papacy. The impression he gave was that he and he alone had the solution to every problem. *As a church*, Catholicism was falling further and further behind the findings of science and the aspirations of modern man.

When Pius XII died in 1958, the Catholic world mourned the passing of a very great man whose place, it seemed, no one on the horizon could fill.

At that dark moment, a miracle occurred.

PART THREE

Love

'The devil never harmed the church so much as when
the church herself adopted the vow of celibacy.'
PETER COMESTOR, in the twelfth century

FIFTEEN

The Pope Who
Loved the World

IT DID NOT LOOK LIKE A MIRACLE when, in 1958, Angelo Roncalli shuffled out on to the loggia of St Peter's to give his blessing *Urbi et Orbi*, to the City and the World. He seemed less like the Supreme Pontiff than like a benign Italian grandmother.

Pius XII had accustomed Catholics to a majestic presence and evidence of a knife-sharp brain. Roncalli, it would appear, was a stopgap pope, an old man who would hold on for a few years until the cardinals could decide next time round who would replace the irreplaceable. It would probably be Montini of Milan, once Pius' confidant. If only Montini had been a cardinal when the 1958 conclave began, he might have succeeded there and then.

And the name of this amiable old fellow? John XXIII. There had not been a Pope John for over five hundred years. Before then, it had been easily the most popular name for pontiffs. After all, it was the name of the Baptist and the Beloved Disciple. The more learned in the crowd in St Peter's Square realized there already *was* a Pope John XXIII. In fact he was responsible for the blight descending on the name. He had been deposed by the Council of Constance in 1415. He lay buried in a tomb designed by Donatello in the octagonal baptistry of Florence Cathedral. His stone effigy bears the inscription, 'Here lies the body of Baldassare Cossa, John XXIII, who was pope'. In the stress of election, no pope since Cossa had dared assume the name of John. Why begin a pontificate with a puff of controversy? Roncalli was to explain that, as far as he knew, the Johns had not lived long, and he was in his late seventies. The situation was even stranger than probably Roncalli himself knew. Leaving aside Cossa ('John XXIII'), John XVI (997–8) was an antipope. Further, in the list there is no John XX. The pope who might have taken that name in 1276 called himself John XXI because he was convinced there had been an extra pope in the ninth century. This 'extra' was Pope John (alias Pope Joan)! While Roncalli puzzled many by not calling himself John XXIV, the truth is that he was only John XXI.

Angelo Roncalli was born on 25 November 1881 in the hamlet of Sotto il Monte, near Bergamo in northern Italy. His father, Giovanni Battista, was a poor farmer. Angelo was the third of thirteen, and the

273

eldest boy. The house he was born in had three rooms, counting the kitchen, though soon after Angelo was born the family moved into a slightly more spacious home.

Angelo was baptized on the day he was born. His zealous uncle Zaverio wrapped him up against the freezing cold and blinding rain and took him to the little church of Santa Maria in Brusico. That was in the early afternoon. The parish priest was out visiting, so they all had to return later that night. By then Giovanni Battista already had his newborn registered. The delay meant that his sturdy wife, Marianna, was also able to attend.

Angelo's memories of his early days remained vivid to the end. The house was always crowded with his brothers and sisters and numerous cousins. At times, theirs was a hand-to-mouth existence. He wrote:

> There was never any bread on our table, only *polenta* [made from maize flour]; no wine for the children and young people, and seldom meat; only at Christmas and Easter did we have a slice of home-made cake.... And yet when a beggar arrived at the door of our kitchen, when the children – twenty of them – were waiting impatiently for their bowl of *minestra* [vegetable soup], there was always room for him and my mother would hasten to seat that unknown person beside us.

The beggar was not really unknown, of course. It was in Marianna Roncalli's eyes Jesus himself. It was an insight she conveyed to all her children through this simple act of charity.

At the age of ten, Angelo decided he had a vocation to the priesthood. It meant a great sacrifice for the family but he was given a place in the Junior Seminary at Bergamo. By then he had already acquired the rudiments of Latin from his local parish priest.

In 1900 he entered the Collegio Cesarola in Rome. Ordained on 10 August 1904, he said his first mass at the Altar of the Confession in St Peter's. Having obtained his doctorate in theology, he was appointed secretary to the liberal Bishop of Bergamo, a post he held for nine years. During that time, he lectured on church history at the seminary.

During the First World War he was a medical orderly. For some reason, never explained, he grew a bushy black moustache. Maybe it was in the nature of an experiment.

In 1922, while researching in Milan Library, he ran into the director, Monsignor Achille Ratti, the future Pius XI, who took a liking to this wide-eyed eager priest. Three years later, on 19 March 1925, Angelo Roncalli was made a bishop. Once more he celebrated mass over the tomb of St Peter. Now, aged forty-four, he entered the church's diplomatic corps.

Those who think of Pope John as an unlearned man should remember that, apart from his native Italian, he was fluent in Latin, Greek, French and Bulgarian. He spoke quite a bit of Spanish, Turkish and Romanian. He read English, German and Russian. He had a long and distinguished career in the Balkans before being sent as nuncio to Paris at the end of the war. His task was to make the church there respectable again after its poor performance during the Nazi occupation, when some bishops collaborated with the enemy. He did a marvellous job of reconciliation.

As Dean of the Diplomatic Corps, it was his duty to represent it on official occasions. His speeches are on record. They betray an unusual spirit of intimacy and relaxation. The theme he stressed over and over was liberty and respect for the rights of everyone. In one address to President Auriol in 1947, he referred to the New Testament as the Magna Carta of the civilization that has made us great. 'Blessed are the meek for they shall inherit the earth; blessed are the peace-makers for they shall be called the children of God.'

In another New Year Address to the President he spoke of:

> liberty, liberty in all its fields in life . . .
> Among the memories of my boyhood I still cherish that of a powerful saying of Cicero's, which we were set to learn in our first Latin exercises; it is a noble expression of Roman wisdom: *Legum servi sumus, ut liberi esse possumus.* 'We are subject to law in order to be free.'

By now – it was 1947 – he was already saying in private correspondence that, though his health was good, he was 'getting old and I show the marks of age'. He was unmistakably the Pope John as history will remember him. Everything about him, except his height, was big: eyes, ears, mouth, nose, neck, heart. Above all, his heart. His face was like a jigsaw puzzle of borrowed pieces; his heart was one of God's masterpieces.

Though he was a man of the world, he never lost the vision of a child. He was at his best when talking to young people. When he addressed a youth congress at Angers in 1946, he revealed his own fundamental attitude to life:

> Your life, children, is directed towards the future. I beg you: do not waste time blaming the present, or sighing for the past, which has no interest for you except in so far as it may offer you useful lessons and warnings not to repeat those mistakes which were and still are fatal for men and for nations.

Like a child, Angelo Roncalli was entirely orientated to the future. It was this priceless gift he was to bring to the papacy. This, and his utter fearlessness. In his final address to President Auriol, after eight years as dean, he said: 'If we preserve a firm faith, an invincible optimism, and hearts sensitive to sincere appeals to human and Christian brotherhood, we all have the right to be fearless, and to trust in the help of God.' Love, friendliness, optimism, these were virtues he had in abundance. And his colleagues recognized it, as did his opponents, who refused to call him an enemy. Roncalli was outside such categories. At the farewell banquet given in his honour in Paris, Edouard Herriot, leader of the Radical Party, gave his own testimony. 'If all priests were like Nuncio Roncalli,' he said, 'there would be no anti-clericals left.'

It was time to take up his new appointment as Patriarch of Venice. In a ceremony in the Elysée Palace, his friend President Auriol insisted on his ancient privilege of bestowing the red hat on a man he had come to revere. In his speech, Roncalli had said there would be always a lamp lit in Venice for his friends. Beware, the Vice-Dean, the Canadian General Vanier, said in reply. 'We are all your friends, and when we go to Venice, the first thing we shall look for will be the lamp lit in front of the Patriarch's house. We know that we have only to knock and the door will be opened.'

After a brief stay in Rome for an audience with Pius XII, he took up his new appointment in Venice. The magnificence of the reception overwhelmed him. It was a week of palms, he said. He wrote to a former colleague in Paris: 'Oh! what enthusiasm! What a triumphal entry within the incomparable setting of the Lagoon, all decorated as if for a great feast.' He took possession of the ninth-century cathedral of St Mark to which the Turkish standards were brought after the battle of Lepanto in 1571. To this great diocese he said: 'I am the child of poor parents. Providence decreed that I should leave my home and go out into the world. . . . Think of your Archbishop not as a politician but as a pastor.' This was his constant and unvarying theme. He had no other role than that of Good Shepherd. 'I embrace with special fatherly protection', he said in his first message to his diocese, 'the children, the poor, the suffering and the workers.'

As patriarch, Roncalli had a handful of years of peace and contentment. His optimism was infectious. It seemed the climax of an amazing career. A peasant boy, he was able to say with Homer in his *Odyssey*: 'Many cities saw I, and many men.' Ten years in Sofia, Bulgaria, were behind him and another ten in Istanbul. Paris was his last foreign assignment. He was ready to take leave of a world he had done his best to serve. Each year, he returned to his old home in Sotto il Monte, to recover his energies, to be himself among his brothers and sisters. They were a long-lived family. His father had died at ninety-six and his mother at ninety-four. The pictures taken at this time show the patriarch with his brothers Giovanni, Zaverio, Alfredo and Giuseppe, in dark suits and with polished shoes, all but Angelo looking somewhat uncomfortable. On the face of Angelo, the only fat one, is nothing but pride in his brethren.

Like Giuseppe Sarto before him, Roncalli naturally expected to end his days in Venice. He, too, was mistaken.

There were fifty-one cardinals voting for the successor to Pius XII. The first vote was taken on 26 October 1958. It was not until the eleventh ballot that Roncalli was elected as a caretaker pope and Cardinal Canali presented him to the crowd of 300,000 in St Peter's Square.

It did not take long to realize that John XXIII was different from any pope they had ever seen or read about. He was first and foremost a human being. He was a humble Christian. He was a catholic Catholic. He was the world's pope. In fact it could be said of him that he was the first non-Italian pope in centuries. He did not for ever keep his eye on the Italian situation and compromise the church and the papacy by giving it priority. His aides were to complain bitterly that he had won communists many votes in the national elections. He had even given an interview to Khrushchev's son-in-law, editor of *Izvestia*, at a most delicate moment in Italian politics. He thus became the first pope ever to be attacked by the right-wing press of his native land. The truth was that he was not primarily concerned with saving Italy from communism; his priority was spreading the Gospel of Christ to all mankind and, above all to the church.

Whereas his predecessors had scolded the world, denounced it, warned it, condemned it, John XXIII loved it, encouraged it, smiled like a cherub upon it.

It was said of Giotto, the thirteenth-century artist, that he had 'sculpted with paint'. On canvas, he had given entirely new perspectives, so it seemed as if a new world had 'broken out' that was to become the Renaissance. John was the great artist of the Spirit. He gave a new dimension to Catholicism with the old materials, which is why men, even astute men like Cardinal Heenan of Westminster, failed to perceive his originality. Heenan said repeatedly: 'I have met the man. He is simply an old-fashioned Garden-of-the-Soul type of Catholic.' His Eminence was not alone in being blind to the real greatness of this extraordinary man who humanized the face of the Roman church. With John began the Renaissance, or so it seemed, of the papacy itself. In and through this most absolutist of offices he was in touch with the whole world because he never lost touch with the Gospel. He proved that it *was* possible to be a saint and yet be good at his job.

Stories abounded. The truth was better than many legends. He left the Vatican for the Regina Coeli prison on St Stephen's Day 1958. 'You cannot come to see me,' he told the inmates, 'so I have come to you.' A child wrote to him, saying he could not make his mind up whether to be a pope or a policeman. John wrote back: 'It would be safer for you to train for the police. Anyone can be pope, as you can see, since I became one.' He did not schedule his walks in the gardens too carefully, so that visitors to the cupola of St Peter's were being turned away at short notice on the plea that the pope was taking the air in the gardens, visible from the dome.

'But what's the trouble?' John asked a distressed official of the basilica.

'They will see you, Holiness.'

'Why not?' Pope John asked, genuinely puzzled. 'I'm not doing anything wrong, am I?'

One day, Monsignor Helm, a Swiss and his former secretary in Paris, brought him a new coat of arms he had designed for his Holiness. It showed a Lion of St Mark's, rampant with extended claws. John looked at it for some time. 'Don't you think', he asked kindly, 'he is too fierce for me?' Another look. 'A little Germanic?' Smiling he added: 'He would have suited Gregory VII, don't you agree? Do you think you could make him . . . more human?'

Helm took to the drawing-board again. He came up with a Venetian lion which, Pope John said, in an audience in April 1963, 'would not frighten anyone'.

There is a picture that embodies Pope John to perfection. He is talking to a little girl in a white First Communion dress that matches his own white cassock. Their heads are very close and they are lost in each other. The little girl, he knew, was dying of leukaemia; he himself was to die soon of cancer. The pope is gazing at this child with profound respect, a reverence of rare beauty. It is as if the pontiff is looking on the face of God.

The world liked what it saw. In John there was a primacy of love, a fatherhood that even Protestants were envious of. What was not possible with such a human being on the papal throne? Already there was talk of the tide of the Reformation turning at his feet. The Orthodox, bitter critics of papal absolutism, did not object to Rome's primacy of apostolic love, and here was a man who embodied it to perfection. The time of Vatican dirges was over; the music emerging from Rome was more like Stravinsky's *The Rite of Spring*.

How did John XXIII differ from Pius X? Both were of peasant origin. Both were intensely holy, selfless, God-filled men, on whose private life no stain ever appeared. They differed in the way they thought of the papacy and, therefore, in their role as pontiff.

Pius X, a man of immense humility, demanded for himself as pope a blind obedience, even a servile submission he would never have thought of asking for himself, Giuseppe Sarto. Even from the time he was bishop, and later Patriarch of Venice, he felt obliged to assert his authority as a representative of the pope and of Christ. It is clear he never overlooked the slight he received from the municipality of Venice on taking up his diocese. They were snubbing not him, but Christ in him. Pius X was equally hostile to anyone whom he considered an enemy of the Gospel of Christ, hence his harsh treatment of the 'Modernists', such as Tyrrell and Loisy.

John XXIII was altogether more relaxed. He had no fears of any kind, except not to act as Christ would act. There was no divorce in him between being a simple Christian and being pope. Nor did he think, as did Pius X, that as pope he had to sort out all the problems of the world. He was no extra-terrestrial, no Supreme Theologian. He was nothing but a Good Shepherd. His words on this, soon after his election, are perhaps the most remarkable of his career.

> Some people expect the Pope to be a statesman, a diplomat, a scholar and an administrator – a man who understands all forms of progress in human life, without exception. But such people make a great mistake, for they misunderstand the true function of the papacy. To Us, the function of the Pope is to be a Shepherd to the whole of his Flock.

This explains why John had none of the usual masterly coldness of a pontiff. It explains why he did not keep having to remind the church of his authority; he had the greatest and the only meaningful authority, that of love and service. His blessing embraced the whole world, and not just Catholics. He was simply the father of mankind. To be a good pope, he thought, he did not have to persecute anyone, terrorize theologians, issue dire warnings about the future, make ever more stringent laws; he simply had to be a good Christian. Part of this was *trusting* everyone. He did not have to do everything himself. He broke away entirely from Pius X's idea of the papacy which was Pius IX's and Innocent III's and Gregory VII's. This is why, though an 'ancient of ancients', he had the nerve to call a Council. After much thought and prayer, he announced his decision to eighteen cardinals at a ceremony at St Paul's-outside-the-Walls on 25 January 1959. They were utterly stunned. He was a caretaker pope – why was he behaving like this? John asked for their advice. They had none to give. He confessed on paper later: 'Humanly speaking, We could have expected that the cardinals, after hearing Our allocution, might have crowded round to express approval and good wishes. . . . Instead, there was a devout and impressive silence.'

Why should they show enthusiasm? The only Council in over four hundred years had proclaimed the pope infallible. What did Pope John need a Council for?

The inspiration to call a Council marked John out as something very special. He was the first pontiff to call a Council when there was no pressure on him to do so. The church was not in a state of revolt; there were no dogmatic questions outstanding. He went ahead because he believed a Council would be good for the church and the world. He wanted the church to 'bring itself up to date', the *aggiornamento*, and open its arms wide to the separated brethren. Symbolically, he threw open the windows in that last of all ghettos, the Vatican, to let the stale air out and the fresh air in. No wonder the Curia did their best to dissuade him.

It would take twenty years of preparation, they told him. Such things must not be rushed. And then the organization required to get 2,500 busy bishops from the four corners of the earth and accommodate them satisfactorily! Why, the expense of it? And why not a synod in Rome, Holiness, to prepare the ground, so to speak?

John jumped at the idea of a synod, but he opted for a Council, too. The synod, with its limited aims, was a success. His aides told him it was not *legally* satisfying. John knew that meant they would only have been content with laws and penalties. He would have none of it. The time of condemnations was long past. The church herself was in need of Christ's compassion. This compassion he extended to priests who had given up the ministry. Even the law of Italy was unjust to them, barring them from many jobs, because of the 1929 Concordat. He begged priests to greet their former colleagues with the love of Christ and, where necessary, with a few thousand lire.

The Council Begins

Pope John was eighty-one years of age when, on a marvellous October morning in 1962, he was carried on his *sedia gestatoria* into St Peter's. His face was wet with tears.

Never had the papacy been so high in public esteem. If all popes were like him, it was said, everyone would be lining up to be a Catholic. He personified the phrase of Horace: 'Nothing prevents one from telling the truth with a smile on one's face.' The Council showed that even a pope was prepared to listen and learn.

In his opening address, he made it plain the church was not to heed the prophets of doom. The church had to update herself radically, and without fear. The Cold War of the Churches, as far as Rome was concerned, was over. There were to be no anathemas; instead, a return to the Gospel of the Master, Jesus Christ. The presence of non-Catholic observers in the aula was a sign of the church's change of heart. John had reckoned it would be hard for bishops to talk small in the presence of distinguished male and female visitors. Some of his aides were already muttering, 'Communicatio in Sacris', a phrase that meant the pope was indulging in forbidden intercourse with heretics.

* * *

The notion of renewal did not come easily to some of the assembled prelates. Cardinals Spellman of New York, McIntyre of Los Angeles, Godfrey of Westminster did not see the need of any such thing. Catholicism was rushing along on the crest of a wave. Schools and churches were being completed every day and, from day one, were full to overflowing. Converts were coming in clouds to find a haven from the permissiveness of modern life. What was needed was more of the same, not things new and untried. And what was this distinction between ancient truths and their expression? Was not the truth inseparable from its expression? Was it not the strength of the church that the old expressions were always valid, thus giving continuity between today and every other day of the church's long march through history?

This reactionary spirit permeated the Curia. The original drafts of the Council's documents had been drawn up by Curial hands. The language was legalistic and confrontational, in the tradition of the Counter-Reformation. A well-founded story tells of Pope John receiving an old priest friend in the Vatican. He held an imaginary ruler to the most recent Curial offering. 'See, five inches of imperatives, seven of condemnations.' In the first meeting of the most important of the Council's commissions on doctrine, the old guard, led by bull-necked Cardinal Ottaviani, head of the Holy Office, spoke in turn for nearly two hours. They explained to the elected members why nothing in the preparatory documents should be changed. It was 'imperative' to stand firm against 'heretical trends'. According to Father Bernard Häring, a moral theologian present, Cardinal Léger of Montreal could finally take no more. 'You will have to do the job on your own,' he said, 'if your attitude is, you are orthodox and everyone else is heretical. Goodbye.'

The first defeat of the old guard was due to the courage of two cardinals, Frings of Cologne and Liénart of Lille, who in the first open session objected to the make-up of the commissions, all Curial appointees. Their rebellion was upheld by the majority of the Council. Watching on closed-circuit television, John must have smiled his Mona Lisa smile of approval. Already, a major lesson had been learned. The Curia who had for so long masterminded doctrine and policy did not begin to represent the church. There had been wisdom in the demand of the Council of Constance for frequent Councils to inform, teach and guide the church, a demand that had been thwarted by popes and curias over the ages. Rome's tsarist centralized bureaucracy was opposed to the true catholicity of the church. Many present at Vatican II were beginning to see this for the first time.

So the Council took heart, assured that it had the Spirit on its side as it debated urgent questions of the day. For the moment, Pope John was content.

The personnel of the commissions altered to take account of the appreciation bishops now had of their apostolic authority. Commissions began to reflect the more liberal ideas expressed on the floor of the Council. But there was another move of the pope's that created a kind of panic in the curial ranks. He established a small group or commission to advise him and the Council on birth control.

Why is he doing this? was the question most on curial lips. The church's mind was plain: all contraceptive acts are mortally sinful. No circumstances, however poignant, can make something which is essentially evil to be good and moral. There, they all agreed, the matter begins and ends. It is wrong, always wrong, grievously wrong. Pius XI had said this in 1930 in *Casti connubii*, reinforcing centuries of unwavering Catholic tradition. What was John XXIII up to? The pope's critics were even more enraged when it leaked out that the majority on the commission were laity. What did *they* know about birth control? This was a strictly theological matter, and theologians were not exactly in a state of disarray. Specialist lay persons could inform his Holiness about population growth, the attitudes of hostile governments and so on. But it should have been made crystal-clear from the start that there was not the slightest possibility of change. This was the eternal law of God.

No sooner was the Council under way than one man emerged as a prophetic figure. He was eighty-four-years-old and venerable. His days on earth were numbered; he was, in fact, to die soon after the Council ended. He was marked out from most other prelates even by his dress, for he was an Eastern patriarch. Maximos IV Saigh of Antioch, in his long dark robes and round hat and with his big grey beard, feared no one except his Lord. He was of the Melchites, the Greek Catholic church of Antioch, which submitted to the Holy See in the early eighteenth century. Its lower clergy were allowed to marry before ordination. It has members in Syria, Egypt and Galilee, as well as widespread communities in the United States of America.

Pope John must have been glued to his television set on 28 October when the patriarch stunned everyone by speaking not in Latin but in French. The Moderator of the day was Cardinal Spellman, who in 1932 had completed a seven-year stint in Rome. He was the first American to be officially attached to the Secretariat of State. Spellman was taken off guard, for he missed the challenge at the very opening of Maximos IV's address: 'Their Beatitudes.' Pope John must have chuckled at that. Maximos was paying tribute first of all, as he thought right, to his fellow-patriarchs. In his mind, cardinals were a lesser breed of cleric who had come to prominence late in the day. Patriarchs had once been next to the pope in importance; they had taken part in the early Councils of the undivided church. Where were cardinals at Nicaea? Even the Fourth Lateran Council in 1215 had noted the pre-eminence of patriarchs, and was not Maximos patriarch of the first see established by Peter himself?

But why the French? It was Maximos' way of stressing that Latin is not the language of the church which he represented. That is why he chose to speak a more catholic language. Through the use of French, Maximos made a veiled attack on the narrow thinking of the curialists who had organized the Council. He went on to criticize a draft document for treating the prerogatives of the head of the church 'in such an isolated way that the rest of the body seemed dwarfish in comparison'. As a non-Latin, he protested at this attempt by Rome to impose itself on his people.

He then laid into the tone of the schemas drawn up by the Curia. Far too legalistic, out of touch with life. Current presentation of the faith was altogether mistaken. The Middle Ages are past; man has grown up. It was futile imposing laws without explaining the reasons for them.

The patriarch went on to suggest that Catholic moral teaching needed updating, root and branch.

> Take, for instance, the catechism. We make it an obligation for the faithful to abstain on Fridays and to assist at Mass on Sundays *under pain of mortal sin*. Is this reasonable, and how many Catholics believe this? As for unbelievers, they merely have pity on us.

However simple the patriarch's comments, they had a dramatic effect on the fathers. Most of them had suspected since childhood that canon lawyers had rewritten the Sermon on the Mount, portraying a God Argus-eyed for the faults of men. Can one really imagine Jesus saying it is a mortal sin worthy of eternal fire to eat meat on Fridays or miss mass on Sundays?

Everything, Maximos continued, must be laid down for the sake of love. Not orders but guidelines prompted and inspired by love. 'A mother does not like having to chastise her child with a stick.'

Pope John, fluent in French after his years as nuncio in Paris, must have followed this discourse, nodding vigorously. Everyone knew that Catholic children over seven, 'the age of reason', were nourished on a diet of fear. Detailed rules were imposed on Christ's little ones with sanctions annexed that would have turned Christ white with wrath. Love was hard to find in the black labyrinth of law. Even holy communion, the receiving of Christ in the Eucharist, had not escaped. Catholics had to fast from food and drink before communion. But what constituted 'eating and drinking'? Did having a piece of toffee in your mouth, left over from the night before, constitute 'eating'? Did swallowing a drop of water when brushing your teeth constitute 'drinking'? As if they had never read Jesus' denunciation of pettifoggers who endlessly discussed the washing of cups and plates, moralists solemnly asked: 'Does chewing a match or swallowing a fly break the fast before communion?'

This worst sort of casuistry was applied to every detail of morality. It paralysed the life of the spirit. God did not come across as a God of love who had incarnated Himself in Jesus' life, death and resurrection, but as a legalistic judge trying to catch his creatures out and, when they did not conform to the letter, sending them, with very little provocation, to hell.

Hell was far more vivid than heaven, which seemed little better than a medieval monastery. There was no food and no sex. Why one needed a resurrected body was not clear. What did one do in heaven except engage in highly intellectual exercises, gazing uninterruptedly at the divine essence, as if death gave everyone an obsession with theology?

The longer the Council went on, the more conservatives found themselves fighting a rearguard action. They were having to retreat on all fronts. Pius IX's Syllabus of Errors, Pius X's *Lamentabili* were being discarded by the Council as if they had never been written. They *knew* John XXIII had made a mistake. Positions held by them as sacred and unrevisable Catholic teachings were being cheerfully abandoned by huge majorities of the fathers.

The Council was proving an education for most bishops. Ideas they had cherished in the secret of their hearts as perhaps idiosyncratic were coming into the open and winning acceptance. This lesson was crucial: far from being an immutable institution, the genius of the church was to change with the changing times. The church is so fond of tradition, one bishop said, she is constantly forging new ones.

But one worry kept surfacing in private discussions and was eventually to find expression in the final documents. Because of the myth of teaching eternal truths, the Council wanted to deny it was changing at the very moment it was changing for the better. There was talk of 'evolution' or 'development' of doctrine which in some cases was true and in others manifestly false. The metaphor did not explain change, merely obscured what was really happening. An acorn develops 'miraculously' into an oak, not into a boat. As one Catholic writer put it: 'The Church began with the principle of absolute toleration; it ended with the stake.' Was this true 'development'? Likewise, all the nineteenth-century pontiffs spoke of freedom or worship as insane, atheistical, an insult to God. Was it 'evolution' when the Second Vatican Council wanted to number freedom of worship among the rights of man?

Apart from this, another defect would show up in the near future. Instead of rethinking the constitution of the church entirely, the fathers took Vatican I as read and tacked on their own additions.

Vatican I had left the pope as virtually the only Protestant in the Catholic church. Vatican II simply added fine words about the episcopal office. In effect, the former council remained in force. It became inevitable that as soon as the Council ended the Curia would take charge and see that everything returned to the way it was before. There would be a promise of a synod of bishops, but this was only a consultative body.

But when the first session of the Council came to an end on 8 December 1962 no one, Catholic or non-Catholic, doubted that the Catholic church was beginning to move as a body into the twentieth century. John's closing address suggested he was not too happy with the speed of progress. He urged the bishops to continue with the *aggiornamento*, which one curial cardinal whispered was what Pius IX had condemned in the eightieth preposition of his Syllabus.

In March 1963, Pope John received the Balsan Peace Prize. The four Soviets on the committee were obviously told by Khrushchev to vote for him. Once more, members of the Curia criticized him for 'shaking blood-stained hands'. Besides, what is a pope, Vicar of Christ, doing, receiving third-rate prizes from secular committees? The man was a crypto-communist. No wonder *Izvestia* published his opening speech to the Council in full.

In that same spring of 1963, John published his encyclical *Pacem in Terris*. He welcomed progress. He proclaimed every man's right 'to worship God in accordance with the dictates of his own conscience and to profess his religion both in private and in public'. Here was a pontiff who did not ceaselessly look over his shoulder. As E. E. Hales wrote in *Pope John and His Revolution*:

> Pope John's position on the right dictates of a man's conscience represents a clear advance on the teaching of his nineteenth century predecessors, even involving a repudiation of much that they taught, and it is best that this simple fact should be openly acknowledged.

He broke away completely from the idea that error had no rights, a principle that had inspired the Inquisition. He replaced it by the principle that human beings have rights from God that no one can take from them.

By the time *Pacem in Terris* was published, John was showing symptoms of a fatal illness. At the end of May, he started suffering from internal bleeding, then peritonitis set in. He was given the last rites.

Before the end, three of his brothers arrived with his sister, Assunta. They knew him only as their beloved brother, not as pope or saint. He felt at home with them.

He suffered very much but with a glad heart for the church, especially his Council, and for the world he had looked on with unparalleled love.

June 3rd was a Monday, a bright shiny day. An evening mass was said for him in St Peter's Square. Later, just before eight in the evening, he died. In the great piazza, a crowd of ten thousand people knelt in the shadows. The curtains of his room were drawn back, a harsh light came on; they knew their beloved pope had gone to God.

His own image of himself was of one who wanted peace at any price. He really looked on himself as a coward afraid to take risks. A brief bewitching interlude was over. When he first appeared on the loggia of St Peter's, he was greeted with dismay; his passing left a gap in the world that no one else could fill. He had made goodness and holiness attractive; he had made the Roman church truly catholic.

He had given Catholicism a new spirit and a new heart. But the work was only begun. Not a single document had yet been passed by the Council. Who would be his successor and how would he fare?

The conclave met for its first session in the Sistine Chapel on 17 June. As was predicted, they chose Montini of Milan, who took the name of Paul VI.

SIXTEEN

The
New Galileo Affair

GIOVANNI BATTISTA MONTINI was born on 26 September 1897 in the north Italian town of Brescia. Like Pius XII, he was educated at home and ordained in 1920. Two years later he was sent to the Vatican Secretariat of State, where he served under two imperious pontiffs, Pius XI and Pius XII. In 1954, Pius XII sent him into exile as Archbishop of Milan, perhaps because of his sympathy with certain left-wing elements in the lay movement. Pius XII never did make him a cardinal.

As soon as John XXIII succeeded Pius XII he elevated Montini to the Sacred College, putting him at the head of the list. When Vatican II began, Montini was the only visiting prelate given accommodation in the Vatican Palace. It seemed that, though John described Montini as 'Amletico', a Hamlet-like figure, unable to make up his mind, he none the less realized that this was his probable successor.

The humourless Paul VI was of medium height and slight build, with the pale face and bluish eyes of a northerner – eyes that, as the years passed and anxieties crowded in upon him, became milky with pain.

One of his priorities was to enlarge the papal commission on birth control. By 1964 it had over sixty members, a third of them priests, the rest lay persons. It was to be increased later to include sixteen cardinals and bishops.

To the Curia's dismay, Paul did not dismiss the laity. Was he going to tread the same path as John XXIII? Their only consolation was that the bulk of the theologians he chose were ultra-conservative. Horror set in when the three liberal theologians began to make 'converts'. New solutions were freely discussed, old positions were abandoned. In an astonishingly brief while, all the laity were convinced – this was critical – that there is no moral difference between the calendar–thermometer method of the safe period and, say, a condom. If a couple had intercourse, planning it that seed and ovum would not meet, that, on traditional principles, was a grave sin. It meant a deliberate intention to express love and have pleasure for their own sake. Prior to Pius XII, this was considered a form of mutual masturbation. When Pius XII allowed the safe period as a method of controlling birth, he implicitly abandoned procreation as the sole purpose of each and every sex-act. Granted that current teaching was a muddle, the choice surely had to be: *either* condemn contraception and the infertile period together, one as a space-barrier, the other as a time-barrier to conception, *or* permit them both.

More surprising than the conversion of the laity was the fact that four-fifths of the theologians on the commission were won over. Far from change being impossible, they considered it imperative. Every field of research – theology, history, demography – was pointing them in one direction: radical change. As word of these trends whipped around the Vatican, a mood of despair settled on the old guard and enveloped his Holiness. He let it be known that he was withdrawing the matter of contraception from the competence of the Council. It was too divisive an issue to parade before the world, and too painful to debate with non-Catholics present. He would take the Commission's findings, deliberate on them and give the final word.

It was an amazing decision in the light of everything the Council had learned from Pope John about honesty and openness; about learning from one another; about the church being a *collegium* of love and brotherhood.

This was *the original sin* of the Council. From it stemmed all the ills that were to afflict the Catholic church in the years ahead. Even at the time, some prelates were perceptive enough to see that Vatican II had already returned to the basic stance of Vatican I. The pope was the only bishop in Christendom; the rest were at best his civil servants.

So, once more, the Catholic church adopted the post-1870 attitude of *'il Papa* knows best'. Catholicism, with a Council in the very middle of its deliberations, would have to wait – hopefully? apprehensively? – for the pope to tell them what to think. It was as absurd as if Nicaea or Chalcedon had met to discuss the divinity of Christ and, with all the bishops assembled, they were told the Pope was going to settle matters *on his own*.

Father F. X. Murphy, even before Paul gave his 1968 decision, wrote:

> The failure of the hierarchy to involve itself expli-
> citly in the argument [over contraception] is all but
> criminal. Leaving the burden solely in the hands of
> the Pope does not, under the present circumstances
> [of Vatican II], seem right and proper.

The bishops gave in. They accepted the papal and curial line that, even if the demands for contraception were turned down by the Council, the world would see that a very large group of bishops spoke in favour of it. This would be bad for the image of Catholicism.

Paul believed that he was superior to a Council. It was his prerogative to act as he thought fit. He forbade bishops, who had come from all over the world to pool their collective wisdom, to express their conviction and that of their flocks. Possibly the more progressive bishops, already knowing the trend within the birth control commission, believed that the pope would have no option but to yield. In the light of history, this was a massive mistake for which they must be held accountable. Their failure to protest must rank with the failure of dissident bishops at Vatican I to vote against papal infallibility, even when their conscience told them they should. But a handful of bishops did speak their mind and gave the world a glimpse of what might have been had not the pope put a veto on free discussion.

A Minor Revolt

The two most explosive days of the Council were 29–30 October 1964. The fathers were debating 'The Church in the Modern World' when the Council chamber was electrified by the contributions of three bishops.

First, Cardinal Léger of Montreal. His suggestion was that fruitfulness in marriage should not be related to each individual act of intercourse but to the marriage as a whole. Love, he insisted, must be seen as an end in itself and not merely the servant of some other end, such as fecundity. 'Otherwise, this fear with regard to conjugal love which has paralysed our theology for such a long time might persist.'

Any married lay person would take this for granted. But, coming from a prelate of the Roman church, the entire hierarchy of which is celibate, it sounded original.

Next came the Belgian Cardinal Suenens. He demanded a re-examination of the classical doctrine of contraception in the light of modern science. In words that have haunted the Roman church ever since, he said: 'I beg of you, my brother bishops, let us avoid a new "Galileo Affair". One is enough for the Church.'

Even Suenens had not the fire-power of the eighty-seven-year-old Patriarch Maximos IV Saigh. He voiced the concern of liberal prelates that the church he loved and had dedicated his life to was on the brink of disaster.

> It is an urgent problem because it lies at the root of a great crisis of the Catholic conscience. There is a question here of a gap between the official teaching of the Church and the contrary practice of the immense majority of Christian couples. The authority of the Church has been called into question on a vast scale. The faithful find themselves forced to live in conflict with the law of the Church, far from the sacraments, in constant anguish, unable to find a viable solution between two contra-

dictory imperatives: conscience and normal married life.

According to the patriarch, the Council simply *had* to come up with a practical answer; it was their duty as pastors. He must have known that, in the light of Pope Paul's veto on discussion, he was guilty of disobedience. But near the end of a long life he realized that his first duty was to God, his conscience and his flock. 'Venerable fathers,' he pleaded, 'be aware of the Lord who died and rose again for the salvation of men, of the really sad crisis of conscience of our faithful and have the courage to tackle the problem without prejudice.'

He called for a frank review of the official position in the light of theology and modern sciences. He brushed aside the distinction between the 'primary' purpose of marriage (procreation) and the secondary purposes (the love and fellowship of the partners). With all the bishops in the crammed aula now sitting on the edge of their seats, Maximos said:

> Are we not entitled to ask if certain positions are not the outcome of outmoded ideas and, perhaps, a bachelor psychosis on the part of those unacquainted with this section of life? Are we not perhaps unwittingly setting up a Manichaean conception of man and the world, in which the work of the flesh, vitiated in itself, is tolerated only in view of children? Is the external, biological rectitude of an act the only criterion of morality, independent of family life, of its moral, conjugal and family climate, and of the grave imperatives of prudence which must be the basic rule of all our human activity?

In these brief remarks, the patriarch raised every issue that was to dog the Catholic church for the next generation and probably into the next century. The distinction on which the church's opposition to birth control was based, the primary and secondary ends of marriage, is not biblical. It arose, he said, from a fear of the body, an almost Manichaean hatred of the flesh, which a bachelor psychosis had reinforced, making procreation the sole justification of sex. This celibate demand for more babies was made irrespective of the partners' existing family commitments. To accede to this demand, the patriarch suggested, would be to deny a cardinal virtue, namely, prudence, by which all morality is to be judged. There is no evidence that Jesus insists on imprudence. Next, Maximos said that a biological, instead of a moral criterion was being used as the basis of sexual morality.

He was not yet finished. Is it not obvious, he said, that for far too long the church had excluded *the* experts in the field of marriage, namely, outstanding married Christians? Moreover, why was the Council praising our separated brethren while writing off *their* experience both as married people and as churches? This is not a Catholic problem but the problem of mankind. He concluded:

> Let us open our eyes and be practical. Let us see things as they are and not as we would like them to be. Otherwise we risk speaking in a desert. What is at stake is the future of the Church's mission to the world.

On that dramatic note, the old man sat down to a burst of applause which the Moderator immediately stifled.

Another brave old man, Cardinal Alfredo Ottaviani, from Rome's Trastevere region, Grand Inquisitor in charge of the pope's House on the Corner, now had his turn to speak. He has been portrayed as a heartless man. He was far from that. He was simply an extreme conservative. From his brilliant youth, this conservatism had led him, paradoxically, to champion a liberal approach to the dissolution of marriage. Christ's Vicar, he maintained, had such tremendous power that he could dissolve far more marriages than had hitherto been believed. On this autumn morning, he was in a grim mood.

Something in the text of 'The Church in the Modern World' was bothering him. His was an impromptu effort that betrayed the depth of his concern. He was not alone in the Curia in thinking that the foundations of the faith were shifting. In a rising, trembling voice, he said: 'I am not pleased with the text where it says that married couples can decide for themselves the number of children to have. This has never been heard in the Church before.'

This was a startling admission from the seventy-four-year-old watchdog of the Catholic faith in view of what was finally passed by the Council. The fathers approved of 'responsible parenthood', with the first ever implication in Catholicism that having a child might be irresponsible, that is, a *sin*. Ottaviani, on the other hand, knew Pius XII had referred to 'planned parenthood' as if it were a device of the devil. An idea which, Ottaviani admitted, he had not heard of was thus to become an essential part of Catholic morality. His opposition, springing from 'ignorance', suggested that, had any moral theologian proposed the idea *before* the Council, he, as head of the Holy Office, would have condemned it. It raised the question, How far is the Holy Office representative of the mind of the church? What if the 'guardians of the faith' are out of touch with the rest of the church? And, if the pope relied on their advice, what hope was there of a catholic solution to the birth control problem?

There was much steam left in the debate on contraception when, after less than two days, at 11.15 on Friday, 30 October, Cardinal

Agagianian called for a standing vote to terminate. Some bishops were in the bar. An unusual number of them were in the chamber where they remained seated. Seemingly blind to this, Agagianian declared the motion carried.

This was the last time that Catholic bishops were allowed to engage in free debate on this, the most important issue affecting the church. Afterwards, bishops, like women, were told to 'keep silent in the church'. As far as is known, no challenge was made to the pope's decision to reserve the matter to himself. Even Cardinal Suenens said in a press conference: 'The methods to be followed in these [birth control] studies would have to be submitted to the pope and judged by his supreme authority.'

Many *periti*, theological experts, found this hard to follow. If the pope were to decide the matter *ex cathedra*, he would need first to examine in detail the mind of the church. He had not done this. On the contrary, he had suppressed an examination at the highest level of a Council. On the other hand, if he spoke but *not ex cathedra*, his decision, while authoritative, would not be able to impose the kind of assent that would settle the dispute once and for all. The final state might be worse than the first.

It is hard to deny that the bishops failed to accept the challenge made by Maximos IV. In the name of Christ crucified and risen, they should have come up with a practical solution; without it, the church's mission in the world was imperilled.

On 25 November, a month after the explosive debate that fizzled out, the pope sent five *modi* or amendments to the text on marriage in the document on 'The Church in the Modern World'. These would have altered the text *after* it had been approved by two-thirds of the Council. The Conciliar Commission was incensed. Cardinal Léger stood up to protest that this was an infringement of the rules laid down by John XXIII and Pope Paul himself. To this, the pope's theologian, the Irish Dominican Cardinal Michael Browne, said that the pope had spoken, the matter was at an end. He wanted a clear reaffirmation of *Casti connubii*. When the Commission refused, Ottaviani had to tell the astonished pontiff that a big majority of the Commission had said No. Another Cardinal, Garrone, informed the pope frankly that he was playing with fire. In the first place, he had vetoed the right of the fathers to discuss birth control; now he intended unilaterally to impose his own solution and dress it up as if it were conciliar! A compromise was worked out. The amendments were to be accepted but not verbatim, and there was to be no repetition of *Casti connubii*.

The trap was now set. And Paul VI, a selfless if indecisive man, was preparing to walk into it. Or, at least, wondering if he should.

Hamlet Goes to Work

Paul looked on the issue facing him as the gravest in the church's history. He said as much in a statement dated 23 June 1964. He would make the final decision. 'But meanwhile We say frankly that up to now We do not have sufficient motive to consider out of date and therefore not binding the norms given by Pope Pius XII in this regard. Therefore they must be considered valid, at least until We feel obliged in conscience to change them.' To many commentators, his mind seemed wavering rather than closed to change.

True, in his magnificent address on peace to the United Nations on 4 October 1965, he said: 'You must strive to multiply bread so that it suffices for the tables of mankind, and not rather favour an artificial control of birth, which would be irrational, in order to diminish the number of guests at the banquet of life.' The simplistic alternative – bread or birth control – boded ill for the church. On the other hand, that same day, the Italian newspaper *Corriere della Sera* published an interview with the pope in which his Hamleticism seemed to have got worse.

> The world is wondering what We think and We must give an answer. But what? The Church has never in her history confronted such a problem. This is a strange subject for men of the Church to be discussing, even humanly embarrassing. The commissions are in session and mountains of reports are piling up. There is a good deal of study going on; but We have to make a decision. This is Our responsibility alone. Deciding is not as easy as studying. But We must say something. What? . . . God must truly enlighten Us.

Humility before so momentous a task was understandable. He, like all clerics, was a life-long celibate without firsthand knowledge and little imaginative grasp of the topic he had to judge. Even he admits it was 'embarrassing'. He was approaching seventy, tired and worn, with a solicitude for the whole church. Every day he was asked to settle disputes, authorize thousands of documents, meet with foreign dignitaries and ambassadors. On top of this was the 'mountain' of reports on birth control, the most worrying question any modern pope had faced. To independent observers, the situation was bordering on farce. This great and enduring institution was in turmoil over an issue that most people inside and outside the church had settled for themselves ages ago. A communion of 700 million people was looking on this holy celibate cocooned old man as the concentration of wisdom on sex and marriage.

Paul was intellectually able, especially in his chosen field of diplomacy; but it would have taken genius to deal with a problem he had taken *upon himself* to solve. With the help of bishops in Council, he might have adopted a more progressive attitude, as had happened over Judaism, freedom of worship and so on. But he had dismissed the collective wisdom of the episcopate and, Atlas-like, taken the world on his shoulders. It was heroic but was it prudent? His only close advisers now were members of the Curia like Ottaviani and Browne, those whose views had been flatly turned down by the Council's commissions and by the fathers when it came to the vote. The Supreme Pontiff was in the hands of the old guard who, had it been in their power, would never have had a Council at all.

Paul did not increase confidence in his final decision when he addressed delegates of the Italian Society of Obstetrics and Gynaecology on 29 October 1966. In a performance worthy of Salvador Dali, he said:

> For Us, Woman is a reflection of a beauty which transcends her, it is the sign of a goodness which seems to Us infinite, it is the mirrored image of the ideal man such as God conceived him in His image and likeness. For Us, Woman is a vision of virginal purity which restores the highest moral and emotional sentiments of the human heart. . . . For Us, she is the creature most docile for formation. . . . Therefore, singing, praying, yearning, weeping, she seems to converge naturally towards a unique and supreme figure, immaculate and sorrowful, which a privileged Woman, blessed among all, was destined to become, the Virgin Mother of Christ, Mary.

It is not recorded whether the gynaecologists recognized in these words the average pregnant woman who came to their rooms for consultation. It is a fact that whenever a papal document mentions women and Mary together the cause of women in the modern world tends to suffer.

'You see, gentlemen,' Paul said, 'this is the plane on which We meet Woman. . . . Do not doubt it. It will provide you with food for new, noble and good thoughts, and you will add dignity and merit to your profession.'

Next, the pontiff turned to birth control. It did not help that the sale of contraceptives was then illegal in Italy and family law was in favour of large, indeed *very* large families. Two years had passed since the Council, and he was still studying, he said, scientific and demographic data, as well as doctrinal and pastoral implications. No pope was so enveloped in paper since Sixtus V revised the entire Bible on his own. Paul spoke of his commission being 'broad, varied and extremely skilled'.

'That commission . . . has completed its great work and has presented its conclusions to Us.' The admission of its extreme skill is followed by a typical Hamlet-like addition: 'It seems to Us nevertheless that these conclusions cannot be considered definitive.' There were grave implications of the report and it was his sole responsibility to resolve them. Meanwhile, he reminded them, the norm of behaviour taught by the church till then was still in force.

> It cannot be considered not binding as if the magisterium of the Church were in a state of doubt at the present time, whereas it is rather in a moment of study and reflection, concerning matters which have been before it as worthy of the most attentive consideration.

Commentators were puzzled. Several years had gone by since Pope John XXIII had established the commission. Paul had enlarged it and urged it to treat the matter promptly. If there was no doubt, why did he need a commission in the first place? And why not even at this late stage simply repeat his predecessors' teaching, as the Curia wished?

At the grass-roots level, a quiet and durable revolution, unknown in the history of Catholicism, was taking place. Many lay folk, encouraged by their priests, were starting to think for themselves. They presumed that there was no explanation of the pope's interminable delay but genuine doubt; meanwhile, they had resolved it in their own minds. The safe-period method – known as Vatican Roulette – was a nuisance and *really* artificial. It even upset the calculations of advanced mathematicians, assisted by computers, giving rise to certain witticisms: 'The safe period is only permitted because the pope knows it isn't safe', and 'The only safe period for some women is between sixty and ninety years of age'.

From the medical standpoint, the method worked well for those who needed it least. It is relatively easy for a single girl to plot her infertile periods. A woman with a family finds it virtually impossible. She is likely to spend her nights jumping out of bed to assist her children; she tends to catch their germs, which raises her temperature and interferes with her calculations. The method is no use, either, during lactation when menstruation ceases but when she can still conceive. Finally, the safe-period method is no use to a woman who is approaching the menopause, when her cycles become hopelessly wobbly.

The lack of confidence can bring its own anxieties, even a bitterness and sense of rebellion when, in spite of all precautions, the method fails. Some women find it so artificial, so contrary to true love, that they prefer total abstinence. Some, when the method fails and they become pregnant, rejoice over a miscarriage. Such are a few of the weird consequences of 'the natural method' of birth control.

For those women who must avoid pregnancy at all cost – owing to ill health in the family, their own, their husband's or that of a handicapped child – the safe period becomes a nightmare. This happens when they ovulate twice in a month or have gone for years without menstruating, owing to a pattern of confinement, followed by nursing, followed by the next pregnancy.

How can these women explain to their priests that, even granted that sex during the safe period is natural, the marriage itself is hopelessly artificial? Many married people in the early 1960s were already beginning to ask. Is it right to leave the clergy in their ignorance and their arrogance? Ignorance of the many facets of sex and the chaos of children, and arrogance that convinces them that ignorance is the best basis for pontificating on marriage. As one woman wrote in *The Experience of Marriage* (1964): 'Why does the clergy take such an unsympathetic view of the problems facing parents? Probably because they are not married. . . . Perhaps religious base many of their ideas of family life on memories of their families, in which they lived as children, not as adults who had to worry about the problems. The responsibilities of parenthood must be lived to be fully understood.'

In the immediate post-Vatican II years, many couples, anticipating change, made their own decisions. They were not prepared to risk over-burdening their families or being estranged from one another by not expressing their love or by having their love dictated by a calendar. Abstinence from sex prior to marriage was one thing: abstinence after marriage quite another. How explain to priests that sex was not crude passion but love-making, and sometimes essential in a family crisis or as a means of reconciliation when they had fallen out? To abstain as though they were celibates would undermine the physical basis of marriage and rob them of a fundamental right. Using contraceptives was scarcely more 'unnatural' than a marriage without sex or with sex ruined by anxieties. If clerics thought it was 'natural' for young couples in love to sleep together for years without expressing that love fully, they should try it.

A generation of married people arose as a kind of wedge separating Catholics before and after the setting up of the birth control commission. Even conservative clerics are inclined to point the finger of blame at Pope Paul for the chaos in the church since Vatican II.

In view of his attempt to impose *Casti connubii* on the Council, it is necessary to take Paul's words at their face value. He personally never doubted the 'traditional' teaching on contraception. All barrier methods were intrinsically wrong. There might be therapeutic reasons for taking the Pill – for instance, to regulate the menstrual cycle – but no justification for using it as a contraceptive. Perhaps he was hoping that the commission would support him in this, provide him with solid 'natural law' arguments that all men of goodwill could accept. His hopes were blighted.

An overwhelming majority on the Commission came out against him. Its four conservative theologians admitted they could not justify on the grounds of reason or natural law alone the old position. That needed the support of authority and revelation.

In brief: after several years of study by this learned body, the pope found himself way behind the starting-line. Not only did it fail to back him; its conservative members said there were no convincing arguments on which the prohibition was traditionally based.

Ottaviani, though joint president of the commission, refused to present the majority report to Pope Paul. The four diehard theologians submitted a private brief to the pontiff.

The Two Reports

According to the majority report, to say contraception is not always wrong is a 'development' of Catholic teaching in the light of changed circumstances. Since traditional teaching was that contraception is instrinsically wrong and no circumstances can alter that essential wrongness, it was asking a lot of an indecisive pope to accept what it said.

The way in which their report was couched in a personalist philosophy also made acceptance unlikely. The report spoke of 'the principle of totality'. The sex faculty must not be regarded as a person; it is part of a person. And the person was, in marriage, one of a couple and a member of a family. It follows that the morality of intercourse is gauged not by examining the workings of a faculty, nor on the basis of isolated acts of sex. Marriage must be looked at as a whole. It is marriage as such that is in accordance or not with God's law, that is, fruitful or unfruitful.

The majority also refer to the Council's teaching that couples have the right to decide for themselves under God how many children they should have. Responsible parenthood was a condition of conjugal chastity. How to achieve such parenthood today? By using modern methods, one of which, first permitted by Pius XII, is the use of the infertile period. The report repeats the Council's statement – it was never accepted by the church before – that prolonged absence of love-making in marriage can lead to infidelity.

The commission concluded that once sex is no longer seen primarily and invariably as procreative, when sexuality is seen, in the full context of marriage, as *love-making* and not always *baby-making*, there is no

297

moral objection to contraceptives. Moral and spiritual values should dictate behaviour and not biology.

The document, only summarized here, was well-argued, but for Pope Paul it had nowhere near the cogency of the minority report.

'Is contraception always evil?' The minority brief – it was never an official report – went straight for the jugular. With the deceptive lucidity of a scholastic text-book, the authors analyse each term of the question.

Contraception: any use of marriage in the exercise of which the act is deprived of its natural power for the procreation of life through human intervention. *Always evil*: something which can never be justified by any motive or any circumstance. It is always evil because it is intrinsically so, by reason of natural law. It is not evil because it is forbidden; it is forbidden because it is evil.

Next the brief asks: 'What answer has the Church given to this question up to now? A constant and perennial affirmative is found in the documents of the magisterium and in the whole history of teaching on this question.'

The brief quotes sources. Significantly, it goes no further back than Pius XI's encyclical *Casti connubii* of 1930. Was this sufficient for their purposes in that the encyclical spoke of 'the uninterrupted Christian tradition'? There was another reason for not digging back further into the past which will be mentioned later.

According to Pius XI, contraception is a 'criminal abuse'.

> No reason, however grave, may be put forward by which anything intrinsically against nature may become conformable to nature and morally good. Since, therefore, the conjugal act is destined by nature for the begetting of children, those who in exercising it deliberately frustrate its natural power and purpose, sin against nature and commit a deed which is shameful and intrinsically vicious.

'The Divine Majesty', Pius goes on, 'detests this unspeakable crime with the deepest hatred and has sometimes punished it with death.' The idea of a deity prepared to mete out death for contraception is daunting indeed.

Pius XI spoke next of the Catholic church 'standing erect in the midst of the moral ruin which surrounds her, in order that she may preserve the chastity of the nuptial union from being defiled by this foul stain'. Those who 'indulge' in contraception 'are guilty of grave sin'.

It was a virtuoso performance in the finest tradition of Italian opera. It had been occasioned by the Lambeth Conference which earlier in

1930 had sanctioned artificial birth control. In 1951, Pius XII was still opposed to what was known in Catholic circles as 'The Lambeth Walk from the Straight and Narrow'. 'This precept [against contraception]', said Pius XII, 'is as valid today as it was yesterday, and it will be the same tomorrow and always, because it does not imply a precept of human law but is the expression of a law which is natural and divine.'

Having quoted Pius XI and Pius XII, the authors of the brief now make their most compelling appeal to Pope Paul. For centuries, without a single exception, the church condemned contraception. If she changes her mind she will not only be denying herself and her claims to teach truth valid for all time; she will have to submit to something far more humiliating.

> If contraception were declared not intrinsically evil, in honesty it would have to be acknowledged that the Holy Spirit in 1930, in 1951 and 1958 [dates of papal pronouncements] assisted the Protestant churches and that for half a century Pius XI, Pius XII and a great part of the Catholic hierarchy did not protest against a very serious error, one most pernicious to souls; for it would thus be suggested that they condemned most imprudently under pain of eternal punishment, thousands upon thousands of human acts which are now approved.

It would be hard to find in Catholic literature a more brilliant argument. They were virtually daring Pope Paul to say that the Reformation was a good thing after all, that Protestants with private judgement had done better than Catholicism under the popes.

If the pope now permits contraception, it will mean the end of papal authority. He might just as well abdicate. He will have destroyed his own authority and that of his predecessors; he will have tacitly admitted that the Anglican church was more inspired than Romanism; he will have agreed that many Catholics were damned for doing what he, Paul VI, will be proclaiming is no sin at all – rather, an act of matrimonial virtue. All that anguish, all the sacrifices of loyal and obedient Catholics, all those lost souls, *because of a papal error?*

For all its brilliance, it should be added here, the argument is not entirely honest. While the authors stressed the constancy of tradition on birth control, they failed to point out that this 'tradition' was based on a view of sex that the church had decisively *rejected*. They went no further back than Pius XI for confirmation of their view because they could not. Beyond him, they would only find partial confirmation. For over fifteen hundred years, the church had approved a view of sex that was now *abandoned*.

For example, they had Pius XII on their side, to this extent: he said that contraception is always wrong. But he also said that sex in marriage is pure and holy. The first thesis is traditional, the second is totally against tradition. Had the authors pointed to this unpalatable fact, Pope Paul might have gone on his Hamlet-like way until he died.

The minority brief also suggested that, were the pope to give way on birth control, there would be a domino effect. There would be an instant clamour to legitimize sex before marriage, masturbation, sterilization, divorce, abortion. Once the primary purpose of marriage was repudiated, liberal theologians would start to argue that sex outside marriage is morally acceptable, provided contraceptives were used. It was, however, the minority's attitude to papal authority that impressed the pontiff most.

Having read both reports, he realized his position was intolerable. A great gloom came over him that was not to lift though he still had twelve years of life left.

His dilemma was: If he said No to contraception, he would stir up immense opposition to the papacy *within* the church; if he said Yes, there would be no papacy left. Not as he understood it. Unfortunately, having learned little from Pope John, he still clung to the medieval notion of the papacy that had prevailed since Gregory VII.

The whole world was intrigued by what was happening in the Vatican. Never was an encyclical awaited with such interest. Yet it took Paul another two years to finalize his thoughts. Hamlet had much reading still to do.

There was, to begin with, Pius XII's attack on planned parenthood in 1958 when he addressed the Italian Associations for Large Families. It seemed devout then, not in any way a parody. The pontiff said:

> Wherever you find large families in great numbers, they point to the physical and moral health of a Christian people. . . . Good common sense has always and everywhere looked upon large families as a sign, a proof and a source of physical health. . . . Virtues flourish spontaneously in homes where a baby's cries always echo from the crib. . . . The series of happy pilgrimages to the baptismal font is not yet finished when a new one to confirmation and first Communion begins. . . . More marriages, more baptisms, more first Communions follow each other like ever-new spring-times. . . . Their [the parents'] youth never seems to fade away, as long as the sweet fragrance of a crib remains in the home, as long as the walls of the house echo to the silvery voices of children and grandchildren.

The pontiff pointed out that saints have come from large families. Bellarmine was one of twelve, Pius X of ten, Catherine of Siena of twenty-five. Still, it is hard to believe that even in 1958 all 'pilgrimages' to the church by Italian parents were happy.

When Paul read further into Pius XII, he must have noted that one important prediction of his ten years earlier had proved false. The new sources of energy, he said, will guarantee 'prosperity to all who dwell on the earth for a long time to come'.

Paul knew that the world had changed profoundly since the optimism of Pius' day. Among the mountain of documents on his desk were some provided by demographers. They made grim reading. The biblical injunction, 'Multiply and fill the earth', had been amply fulfilled. Human fecundity is tremendous; it has to be to guarantee survival in times of plague, wars, high infant mortality, early deaths. Then came modern medicine, and the picture was instantly transformed. In developed nations, infant mortality approached zero, death in the elderly was more and more postponed. Even among developing nations, many were starving while medicine was keeping alive people who, in past ages, would have perished, a quarter of them before the first year and a third of the rest before the age of forty-five.

This entailed a radical rethink of procreation. This was true of nations and the families comprising them.

At national level, it was estimated that in France, if mortality had declined without a corresponding decline in the birth rate, France would now have a population of 500 million. The combined population of France and Britain might today equal that of China.

Pope Paul would have read the World Population Data Sheet, based on United Nations sources and published by the Population Reference Bureau of Washington. Statistics showed the world was growing by 1.9 per cent. Since 1958, when alarm bells first sounded, there were 500 million more people alive; the grand total was 3,520 million. India's 500 million was increasing by 2.7 per cent; Pakistan was leaping ahead at 3.1 per cent. Latin America was just behind with 3 per cent. The last increase meant the population would double in just over twenty-three years. Invariably slum areas grow faster than others; the poor become poorer, the hungry hungrier. By the early 1960s – long before the present debt crisis – there was absolutely no hope for nations with high growth rates ever having adequate food, education, health facilities, housing, leisure and, critically, jobs. Nor was there any dole money.

Contraception was never *the* answer to so vast and complex a problem; without it, no answer was possible. If all, including the poor, continued to procreate close to the biological maximum, whole nations would be reduced to beggary. Mankind, at or below subsistence level, would be faced with the traditional scourges: disease and war.

By the 1960s, when Paul was writing his encyclical, the peoples of South America were living in conditions worse than Europeans had had to put up with in the darkest days of the Industrial Revolution. One way to ameliorate conditions was abortion. It is known that Pope Paul had on his desk official reports on almost every country in South America. In Chile, according to a 1967 census, one out of every two to three pregnancies was terminated; for years, over a third of maternal mortalities were caused by abortion. In Colombia, 60 per cent of abortions occurred in women with seven or more pregnancies. Uruguay topped the list; studies showed a ratio of 750 abortions for every 1,000 pregnancies. A strict Catholic ethic was leading to uncontrolled fertility which, in its turn, led to a massive number of abortions entailing the death of many mothers.

India, the world's largest democracy, was already over-populated; curbs were vital. Close adherence to Catholic teaching would have soon destroyed democracy in India. If China alone were to adopt the Catholic approach, there would be no hope for mankind. In 1965 one person in four on earth was Chinese. Catholic prelates, like Cardinal Heenan of Westminster, were arguing that few Indians and virtually no Chinese were Catholics; they would not listen to the pope anyway. Which was to miss the point. Any doctrine which, if generally practised, would destroy the planet can scarcely be said to have reason on its side. Moreover, Catholic teaching is supposed to be part of the natural law written on men's hearts. The rest of the world could thank God that Chinese and Indians did not read it on *their* hearts.

The church's only solution to over-population was total sexual abstinence or restriction of sex to the 'safe period'. To beg governments, already verging on despair, to ban the Pill, intra-uterine devices, condoms, and replace them by thermometers and calendars, as well as provide a vast army of educators to see that the rhythm method is understood, was unrealistic. Besides, it is the poor, the badly housed, and under-nourished – those who need to curb their numbers most – who find sexual abstinence intolerable and the safe period impossible.

Moving from the national to the family level, Catholic teaching forbade contraception for any reason. God would, of course, understand that some people are tried to the limits of their endurance. But never *beyond*. With grace, all couples can abide by the natural law teaching. Sad cases make bad laws. While Pope Paul, owing to his lack of pastoral experience, would not have met many such cases personally, they were in the dossiers on his desk.

A husband is on the dole with no prospect of a job. He and his wife are forced to live with the wife's parents – or in wretched rented accommodation or in a top-floor flat of a high-rise block. They have three children. It is too many for their straitened circumstances. They are told to abstain from sex, which may amount to abstaining from

302

love and compassion, or use the safe period. All three children are products of that method. *Deus providebit*, God will provide.

After a motor accident, a man is disabled for life. His wife works to support them both; a pregnancy would leave them penniless. *Deus. . . .*

After her sixth pregnancy in seven years, a wife has just emerged from a mental hospital. She is desperately afraid of another pregnancy. *Deus. . . .*

A couple's last child was born mentally handicapped and requires all the mother's attention. *Deus. . . .*

A woman is warned by her doctor that another pregnancy would gravely affect her health, possibly kill her. She has eight children already. *Deus. . . .*

Many women today feel unable to risk a large family. They have neither the desire nor the spiritual and emotional equipment to cope with it. *Deus. . . .*

One woman produced triplets; another, on fertility drugs, produced sextuplets. Both are finding it very hard to manage. *Deus providebit*, God will provide.

In September 1967, President Carlos Lieras Restrepo of Colombia, a staunchly Catholic country, addressed the Inter-American Conference.

> I have visited the poorest slums of the republic and I recommend the same visit to the people who are examining population from the moral point of view. . . . What can we say of the frequent incest, of the primitive sexual experience, of the miserable treatment of children, of the terrible proliferation of prostitution of both sexes, of frequent abortion, of almost animal union because of alcoholic excesses?
>
> It is, in consequence, impossible for me to sit back and examine the morality or immorality of contraceptive practices without thinking at the same time of the immoral and frequently criminal conditions that a simple act of conception can produce in the course of time.

A year after this, Pope Paul's long study of birth control was ended. Its conclusions were as inevitable as a Greek tragedy. Its origins lay far back in the time of Pope Gregory VII and Pius IX. If only his Holiness had gone to live in the slums of Colombia while he was making up his mind.

A Bitter Pill

Humanae Vitae was given to the world on 25 July 1968. Its opening words set the tone for what was to come: 'The most serious *duty* of transmitting human life. . . .' The next sentence, too, contains the word 'duty'.

He pays lip-service to modern problems, such as that population is growing faster than available resources. He examines, briefly, the idea that the sex-life of married couples should be judged morally and in the round, and not just in terms of biological organs and their functions. What is required of him as pontiff, he suggests, is a new and deeper reflection of the basic moral principles underlying marriage.

This new and deeper reflection turns out to be: No change whatever in the church's teaching. He refers to it repeatedly as 'constant'. He is unaware of just how late this 'constant' teaching was arriving on the scene.

Paul sanctions the infertile period when couples feel they want no more children for the time being or for an indeterminate period. Abortion and sterilization are both condemned.

> Similarly condemned is any action, which either before, or at the moment of, or after sexual inter-course is specifically intended to prevent procre-ation – whether as an end or as a means. . . . It is never lawful, even for the gravest reasons, to do evil that good may come of it . . . even though the intention is to protect or promote the welfare of an individual, of the family or of society in general.

Let an individual, a family, a nation die, rather than use contraceptives. It matches Newman's famous saying:

> The Church holds that it were better for sun and moon to drop from heaven, for the earth to fail, and for all the many millions who are upon it to die of starvation in extreme agony, so far as temporal affliction goes, than that one soul, I will not say should be lost, but should commit one single venial sin, should tell one wilful untruth, though it harmed no one, or steal one poor farthing without excuse.

For Paul, any use of contraceptives is, in itself, no *venial* sin. While he does not talk of its gravity, he obviously was not softening Pius XI's teaching that contraception is always mortally sinful.

Therefore, to prevent the conception of a child who will be born to misery and starvation or who, the doctors say, is bound to be handi-capped is a mortal sin. To prevent conception when, as Pius XII admitted, it would lead to the probable injury or death of the mother, is a mortal sin. The only option is for a couple to lead a completely sexless life; God will give couples, through the grace of matrimony, the strength to lead a life of celibacy. However tough the family situation, however ill the mother, not one exception can be approved by the Catholic church.

This is an extreme doctrine. The only parallel – though it is by no means *so* extreme – is the Jehovah's Witnesses' refusing a blood transfusion to a dying child. To support his view the pope is unable to offer a single specific Bible text. The prohibition on divorce, the pope's power to dissolve certain marriages have *some* biblical justification. The ban on contraception has none.

Paul quotes the Second Vatican Council several times in *Humanae Vitae*, even though he forbade the Council to contribute to the discussion then raging in the church. Further, *Humanae Vitae* stands or falls by a distinction between primary and secondary ends of marriage which the Council expressly declined to use. The pope's attempt to include it through his *modi* was rejected by the theological commission.

'God', the pope continues, 'has wisely ordered the laws of nature and the incidence of fertility in such a way that successive births are already naturally spaced.' Even conservative Catholics find this difficult to follow. Apart from his usual identification of laws of nature (biological) and natural law (moral), what is this 'wise ordering', this 'natural spacing' of births? He cannot mean that if a woman conceives in March she cannot conceive in April, May, June etc., thus avoiding a conveyor-belt effect of babies coming out each month. Nor can he be unaware that, although ovulation only takes place once a month, births can happen regularly each year – unless precautions are taken.

The fact is that in animals the sexual urge is primarily related to the continuance of the species. This is why there are mating seasons. Paul *seems* to equate humans with animals; the prime purpose of human sexuality is also the continuance of the species, and everything must be subordinate to that. Humans in fact are rather less fortunate than animals because they do *not* have mating seasons, their births are *not* naturally spaced. This suggests that in humans sex has more than a procreative significance. Humans have sex when, say, the woman is pregnant or post-menopausal. In other words, sex has a far larger significance in humans than in animals, but what this is the pope is unable to say, because with his purely biological criterion of morality he equates humans with subhumans.

In fact, all the pope can mean by 'natural spacing' is that couples are free to guess when ovulation occurs, and hopefully outwit nature by thermometers and calendars. But if God has made it so difficult to outwit nature it can hardly be called a 'wise ordering' of nature on mankind's behalf.

The pope goes on to say: 'We believe that our contemporaries are particularly capable of seeing this teaching is in harmony with reason.' He writes this, knowing that some of the most senior cardinals at

Vatican II saw the opposite. Most cardinals on his commission did not see it, nor did any of its laity. The four diehard theologians on the commission said the teaching could not be seen by reason alone. Statistics proved that most ordinary Catholics did not see it, either. What Paul should have said was, Our contemporaries, with the best will in the world, will not be able to accept this. Catholics must accept it because I say so.

Since Paul's objection to contraceptives is based on an interference with the biological workings of nature, why did he not also condemn most of modern medicine? He is in favour of drugs, operations to cure infertility, heart bypass procedures, kidney transplants. Why, if interference in 'natural processes' is what leads him to condemn contraception? As one anguished Catholic put it: 'Will this pope let me keep my reading-glasses?' Certainly, it seems odd to say: 'Preventing a woman conceiving when she has six children already is a mortal sin; helping a barren woman conceive sextuplets artificially is in accord with nature and morally acceptable.

A picture of women emerges from *Humanae Vitae* in keeping with Paul's earlier talks on women and the Virgin Mary.

> A man who grows accustomed to the use of contraceptive methods may forget the reverence due to a woman, and, disregarding her physical and emotional equilibrium, reduce her to being a mere instrument for the satisfaction of his own desires.

Was he thinking of a woman living in a hovel in a Colombian slum with a dozen children already? Or a woman married to a 'Saturday-night drunk'? And what of men whose sole aim is to treat their wives as equal partners and not mere baby-making machines, men who want to decide with their spouses, responsibly under God, what is the right number of children for them *as a family*? In any poll taken in any country in the world, the vast majority of women would agree that contraceptives have improved their status, as well as their physical and emotional equilibrium.

Having condemned all forms of contraception, the pontiff is worried that public authorities will not take notice of his views. To governments he says: 'Do not tolerate any legislation which would introduce into the family those practices which are opposed to the natural law of God.' Some governments of South America did heed this plea from a pontiff who, within two years, was doing his best to stop *civil* divorce in Italy.

Towards the end of *Humanae Vitae*, the pope called on priests to give

> that sincere obedience, inward as well as outward, which is due to the magisterium of the Church. For,

as you know, the pastors of the Church enjoy a
special light of the Holy Spirit in teaching the truth.
And this, rather than the arguments they put forward, is why you are bound to such obedience.

Is this a hint that the Holy Father knows he has no natural-law
arguments for a natural-law morality to offer his priests? Since there is
no Bible proof, either, priests are told to obey him on the basis of
authority alone. To papal laws, no priest can be a 'conscientious
objector'. Though papal authority has had a very bad record on human
rights for centuries, priests must simply hand over their consciences to
the pope.

First Reactions

Newspaper reaction was predictable. Journalists had not been given
such an opportunity since the Syllabus of Errors in 1864 condemned
all human progress.

In England, the *Guardian* called *Humanae Vitae* 'one of the most
fateful blunders of modern times'. Surveys had shown that 'between
half and two thirds of Catholics in advanced countries neither agree
with nor adhere to their Church's teaching on contraception and the
protracted dither in the Vatican has further encouraged priests to
throw the decision open to individual choice.'

The Times said:

The endorsement with qualifications of the 'safe
period' or rhythm method of birth control further
confuses the position for it appears to admit that
sexual intercourse may be licitly practised other
than for the procreation of children.

The Economist pointed to South America which the pope was due to
visit that August. The 3 per cent growth rate foretold almost unimaginable misery. 'Although it will become the focus of bitter controversy,
the encyclical within days of its issue is intellectually deader than a
Dodo.'

Even the Catholic weekly, *The Tablet*, demanded to know 'where is
the new and deeper reflection' the church had been promised?

Naturally, some bishops were pleased. Bishop (soon Cardinal)
Wright of Pittsburg enthusiastically endorsed the encyclical. He was
delighted that the pope had 'not been swayed by statistics', as
though the millions of starving children and many aborting mothers
did not count in clerical circles. Cardinal Heenan of Westminster had
been joint president of the pope's commission. He wrote: 'Majority

opinions are notoriously unreliable. . . . A majority of Nazis decreed the sterilization of the unfit and the liquidation of the Jews.' The analogy did not endear him to readers, most of whom could not see any connection between them using a condom and Hitler putting millions in gas-chambers. Further, Heenan omitted to say that when the papal commission came to vote he abstained because he could not make his mind up; the pope had made it up for him. Archbishop Murphy of Cardiff said contraceptives were, for a man, 'a cheap way of controlling his instincts and avoiding his responsibilities'. In time to come, his Grace prophesied, 'this encyclical will be hailed as the Magna Carta, not merely of all women but of all men and all children'. His Grace was obviously not aware that Pope Innocent III had declared Magna Carta null and void.

Correspondence columns throughout the world were filled with mostly hostile contributions from Catholics. A leading English layman, the MP Norman St John Stevas, referred to 'the theological barrenness of the encyclical, to its lack of reality and its imprudence. To call upon public authorities in our contemporary pluralist society to place a ban on contraception shows the divorce from the facts of the contemporary world that is both incredible and alarming.'

To most Catholic correspondents, the pope's position seemed insensitive to the huge variety of human dilemmas. It was indifferent to the consequences of the ban. It did not even ask whether it is better to prevent a child coming into the world than having him starve or die when he is born. Many objected to the attack on the purity of most Catholic and virtually all non-Catholic marriages. Some said that Pope Paul had condemned more people to a life of misery and an ugly death than Hitler. The encyclical would create new ghettos and concentration-camps, especially in Catholic countries of the Third World.

Conservative Catholics were overjoyed. Paul had reaffirmed traditional teaching and preserved his role as teacher of absolute moral truth. Then fifty-seven-year-old Monsignor Ferdinando Lambruschini presented the document to the media. He said that attentive reading of it makes it plain that it does not have the theological note of infallibility. Conservatives were shattered. If *Humanae Vitae* expressed the unwavering tradition of the church, surely it was ripe for the pope's seal of infallible approval? If not on this, on *what*? It dawned on them that the long delay and the ensuing chaos and bitterness were not to be compensated for by an infallible pronouncement. Being fallible, it could not bind conscience absolutely. Discussion would go on, probably more divisively than before.

Liberal Catholics were hit far harder. The pope, repudiating all advice except that of the Curia, had acted like a Protestant. To modify a famous phrase, he had turned his back on the church, then claimed he had the church behind him. The hope they cherished, that sex and marriage would be seen morally and not in biological terms, was dashed. There was no hope any more of 'Christianizing' birth control, making people aware of its benefits and dangers in a Christian context of love and concern. The pope had said it had no benefits; it was only dangerous. With this decision, Catholics risked losing their moral influence in the world; they would henceforward be classed as back-woodsmen left over from the Middle Ages. Many felt that the pope had fought the wrong fight. He had opposed contraception without which abortion was inevitable. He should, they said, have condemned abortion not made it more likely.

Considered Reactions

Such was the state of fear and intimidation in the church that priests and theologians banded together for safety. In England fifty-five priests wrote to *The Times* respectfully dissenting from *Humanae Vitae*. In the United States of America a group of eighty-seven theologians led by Father Charles Curran demanded a more creative role for themselves than simply nodding the encyclical through. Papal documents in the past had caused tremendous harm – for example, to Jews, witches, ordinary Catholics who fell victim to the Inquisition. 'History shows', they said, 'that a number of statements of similar or even greater authoritative weight have subsequently been proven inadequate or even erroneous. Past authoritative statements on relig-ious liberty, interest-taking, the right to silence, and the ends of marriage have all been corrected at a later date.' Among the deficiencies in the encyclical, these theologians list 'over-emphasis on the bio-logical aspects of the conjugal relations as ethically normative; undue stress on sexual acts and on the faculty of sex viewed in itself apart from the whole person and the couple . . . an almost total disregard for the dignity of millions of human beings brought into the world with-out the slightest possibility of being fed and educated decently'.

Not even the Syllabus of Errors by Pius IX had occasioned such anger and dissent from Catholic priests and theologians worldwide. Why was this? It was because the memory of Pope John's Council was still fresh in everyone's mind. The Council had, with openness and courage, contradicted what most nineteenth-century popes had said on matters as far apart as Judaism and religious liberty. The church had moved on; it was now committed at the highest level to ideas that any number of popes had called insane and atheistic.

Paul's major mistake was going it alone. In all honesty, he could not see how something his predecessors had labelled a 'moral obscenity' could evolve into an 'act of grace'. For him, it was therefore a straight-forward choice between holding on to his infallibility and relieving the misery of millions. He had not minded giving his assent to an 'insanity' evolving into a 'right of man', namely, freedom of worship; but that was when he had the backing of the Council. What *Humanae Vitae* proved once more was that the exercise of papal supremacy, without the church's and especially episcopal approval, does not always unite the church; it sometimes divides. *Humanae Vitae*, at a stroke, undid a great deal of what the Council had achieved. The pope could no longer pose as the champion of human rights, as the focus of unity for all Christians. He had even divided his own church. Had the Council back in 1962 been given *Humanae Vitae* as a draft document, it would have rejected it at once with the rest of the curial draft documents as being archaic and as embodying one narrow theological standpoint. When Paul withdrew contraception from the Council's competence, he hoped his authority would ensure that the final outcome would gain unanimous consent. The opposite happened. This one purely papal decision rent the church asunder.

Another reason for the unprecedented revolt of Catholic theologians was that they knew *Humanae Vitae* would reinforce the casuistry of sex which had blackened the pages of moral theology for so long.

The matter is far too distasteful to go into it in too much detail, and even some moralists writing in English leave their discussion of sex in Latin. There are pages in respectable moralists cruder than Rabelais and as obscene as *The Witches' Hammer*. For Paul VI repeated that the morality of the act of intercourse is to be judged entirely from the biological point of view. There must be *penetratio* and *inseminatio*; the penis must deposit its seed in the vagina. The seed must not be trapped in a condom, nor held back from reaching its 'natural destination' by a pessary. *That*, the Pope says, with his recent predecessors, is moral; anything else is not. The consequences of this are printable only with care.

If, for example, a husband approaches his wife with a condom on, she must resist him, said the Sacred Penitentiary, 'as a virgin would a rapist'. If the wife cannot resist without grave personal injury or death, she is allowed to submit 'passively', that is, she may take no pleasure in the act of intercourse but hold herself rigidly resisting throughout.

In the case of a Catholic couple unable to have children, the gynaecologist is likely to find them less co-operative than other patients – that is, if they obey their church. For there are no exceptions to the rule that the only rightful place for a man's seed is his wife's vagina. How, then, would a doctor obtain seed from Catholics in order to examine its potency, the reality being that that seed has *never yet fertilized an ovum*? The man is not allowed to masturbate. That is always wrong, even when it is done for the sake of procreation. When a renowned moral theologian suggested that the seed might be immediately subtracted from the testes, since that did not involve pleasure, Rome said no, since seed must be acquired 'naturally', that is, by normal intercourse. Moralists suggest that husband and wife have intercourse just prior to the gynaecological examination, though doubtless the doctor would prefer the seed in a more readily accessible form. Besides, is he not compelled in any case to remove the seed for examination 'from its natural receptacle'? Indeed, answer the moralists, but the seed was initially deposited in the right place and enough remains *in situ* to fertilize the ovum, should that be Nature's and God's will. Some moralists came up with a daring idea approved by Rome: husband and wife could have condomistic intercourse, provided the condom was first *perforated*. They do not define the extent of the perforations, but presumably enough seed must be allowed to enter the wife to fertilize her, should that be God's will. The gynaecologist will then be given a perforated condom from which to begin his analysis of the husband's sperm count. The doctor no doubt prefers this to another of the moralist's solutions, using a cervical spoon after the couple have had intercourse just prior to entering his rooms.

These are but a couple of the many curious consequences of the papal ruling that the rightness or wrongness of the act of sex must be judged by its biological and not its moral pattern. Even so, for all its pedantry, there is no logic to the moralists' teaching. For, if 'correct biology' must be adhered to, the removal of *any* semen from the vagina or the retention of *any* semen in a condom must be immoral. While all water might be judged the same if it quenches thirst, not all semen is the same. On the contrary, each sperm is different. By removing some for examination, the doctor risks removing the one out of millions that might fertilize the ovum. It is almost as if moral theologians believe that the same child would result from whichever sperm fertilized a particular ovum. On their biological premises, it is surely always wrong to use a condom, whether it is as 'safe' as Fort Knox or holed like a sieve. In strict logic, they ought never to allow any semen to be sited anywhere except in the vagina. This would mean that all scientific examination of semen is immoral.

Bishops, like liberal theologians, also exhibited discomfort with *Humanae Vitae*. Of course, like their predecessors after Vatican I, they immediately closed ranks. But an examination of their statements shows the depth of the dilemma the pope had landed them in.

In South Africa, Bishop van Nielsen, member of the Secretariat for Christian Unity, said the pope's ban was 'a discipline rather than doctrine and leaves the door wide open for personal decision'. The pope had, in fact, deliberately slammed the door shut. Archbishop Hurley of Durban admitted the encyclical was 'the most painful of my life as a bishop. . . . I have never felt so torn in half.' As a result of the Council, he had left his life-long conservative position. The Council showed 'what magnificent results are achievable through full and open debate. . . . It was collegiality at its finest, or almost finest, for the method and scope of consultation can be widened to include more of God's people – his clergy, Religious and laity. . . . As brothers of Pope Paul in the episcopate, bishops cannot shrink from the issue of how they think the authority of their senior brother should be exercised. To discuss it with him is not disloyalty but speaking the truth in love.'

Joint pastoral letters show the same post-Vatican II embarrassment. In Holland, where a poll showed 80 per cent of Catholics were against *Humanae Vitae*, the bishops said coolly: 'May the discussion about this encyclical contribute to a clearer appreciation and functioning of authority inside the Church.'

The Canadian bishops also demurred, as did the Belgians led by Cardinal Suenens. In an unprecedented move, the Belgians stressed that Catholics were not bound to give unconditional obedience to this non-infallible document. Someone who is competent and conscientious in such matters 'is entitled to follow his own convictions'. Even the arguments used by the pope were said to be defective, so that those who disagree with him cannot be called selfish or hedonistic. The bishops continue:

> We must recognize, according to traditional teaching, that the ultimate practical norm of action is conscience which has been duly enlightened by all the factors presented in *Gaudium et Spes* [the Council document]. Furthermore, we must recognize that the ultimate decision on the timeliness of the transmission of new life rests with the parents and they must make this decision in the sight of God.

The more conservative hierarchies, such as the British and American, stressed obedience to his Holiness. They urged Catholics to continue receiving the sacraments. Since many of their flock were using the Pill, it was not easy to see how they could have a purpose of amendment, a prerequisite of sincere confession and holy communion. Catholics were being encouraged to see themselves not merely as sinners but as repentant sinners while actually using the Pill on a daily basis as a contraceptive. *Humanae Vitae* was about to cause a regress to the worst excesses of moral theology. Many women whose one intent was to avoid conception were taking the Pill on the plea that this helped regulate their menstrual cycle.

Most bishops, on orders from the Holy Office, carpeted dissident priests – those who, in Mill's phrase, were 'afflicted with the malady of thought'. Bishops said: 'Either be quiet or be sacked.' Did not the Pope insist in *Humanae Vitae* that priests had to give internal and external obedience to his teaching? Thoughtful priests found this incomprehensible. Was there to be no religious freedom even in disputed and corrigible matters?

The way they saw it was this: If *Humanae Vitae* is not infallible, it is fallible. If it is fallible, the pope might be mistaken. If he might be mistaken, it is dangerous to treat his teaching as if it cannot be mistaken. The only sensible attitude is to treat it with caution, the more so in that the happiness of millions of married people is at stake. Had Pope Paul VI said, 'This is infallible, that is, it is the faith of the church, therefore God demands internal and external obedience,' that would have made sense. But for him to say, 'This is not infallible but I, the pope, still insist on external *and* internal obedience to a pronouncement that is possibly mistaken,' is to ask too much. Some sincerely believe it was immoral. For the pope demanded assent to something that is not absolutely certain. Unless he could guarantee its truth, he should not have demanded unqualified obedience. In any case, if a priest was convinced that birth control is good, how could he give internal assent to the contrary view? Many bishops realized this and only demanded external obedience to the pope's ruling. Again, this was compassionate but it was two-faced and encouraged sycophancy. If bishops were not themselves going to obey the pope by demanding internal as well as external obedience, they should not have imposed *anything* on their priests.

In spite of strenuous efforts at damage control, it was as though a hurricane had hit the Catholic church. Polls taken after *Humanae Vitae* showed *more* Catholics were now in favour of contraception. It proved that in bed most Catholics turn Protestant.

The laity were becoming angry with the hierarchy. It was dawning on them that the clergy's only qualification, ignorance, was not enough in matters of sex. Any married man or woman has more sex-pertise than all the priests combined. Many lay persons were beginning to say that a celibate clergy, for all their sacrifices on the church's behalf, were a luxury they could no longer afford. The priests' attitude seemed to be, If you haven't the moral strength to be celibate like us, you have to take the consequences – including all the children God sends. One American Jesuit suggested that, while celibacy should be optional for priests, it should be obligatory for bishops, so they could acquire some sense.

As Archbishop Hurley intimated, not even in Council was the whole church represented. How can elderly celibates represent the *sensus fidelium* on matters where they have no competence, where even the free use of their imagination will land them in sin? It was as unreal as lay people telling monks and clerics how to lead *their* life of celibacy.

The wealth of wisdom which the laity possessed was simply not being fed into the common pool which should nourish the church. Twenty-five years after the Council, the clergy are still holding synods 'on the laity' without one lay person having a vote.

Women, in particular, felt *Humanae Vitae* had given them a raw deal. It portrayed a God who does not love women. In Christ there is neither male nor female, but in the Catholic church there is only male. For all Paul VI's fine words about the dignity of women, he was actually describing beings who never existed except in his imagination. For the first time, it was possible for women to be equal partners in marriage; the bias in evolution towards the male was being largely rectified by scientific advances. Catholic prelates could not see this. They preferred women to be permanently 'Doll's House' people, tied to home and procreation. Women saw things differently.

For them, birth control had not only helped equalize marriage relations; it had humanized sexuality. Sex was now a matter of joy for male and female, without the endless fear of conception. It had made child-bearing and child-rearing a matter of choice. Couples were at last able to have children when they were prepared for them, when it was best for all the family, so that every child was a wanted child.

The clergy, trained and steeped in solitude, could not be expected to understand women. For them, women represent temptation, a falling away from their vocation. This is why 'woman' in papal documents is really a portrayal of the Virgin Mary; she alone of all women does not constitute a danger to a priest's vocation.

In the nineteenth century, the popes constantly attacked civil and religious liberty; in the twentieth, their preoccupation is sex. They have, with the best of intentions, tried to stifle freedom in that most intimate and private area of love. Faced with the nuclear explosion of people – houses, even continents bursting with people – papal wisdom can only offer the highly unsafe 'safe period' method and matrimonial celibacy to control fertility. Both showed how out of touch the clergy were. They spoke as if sexual desire was something that could be turned on and off at will. The laity were disillusioned.

Priests were affected by *Humanae Vitae* in another way. The encyclical forced them to rethink their own sexuality. Many faced up to celibacy for the first time. The encyclical showed them that the pope was wrong about sex in marriage. What if he was wrong about sexuality altogether? Where did that leave them?

Whatever the reason, once the birth control question surfaced in 1962, Rome received a flood of applications from priests wanting to give up the ministry. The chief reason given was the inability to live up to the discipline of celibacy. History shows that celibacy was nearly always a disaster, but never before had so many priests been willing to own up to it and petition Rome for release.

One member of the papal commission was missing when the final vote was taken: Karol Wojtyla, Cardinal of Cracow. His absence has never been explained. Undoubtedly, he, like Paul VI, believed no change was possible. Perhaps he simply wanted to dissociate himself from what seemed impending disaster. On 12 November 1978, exactly three weeks after becoming pontiff, he reprinted two of his earlier articles in the *Osservatore Romano*. The first was entitled 'The Truth of the Encyclical *Humanae Vitae*'.

Twenty years have passed since *Humanae Vitae*, and nothing has changed fundamentally. If anything, positions have hardened. Strangely, the papacy itself has been the chief victim of its own decisions. America provides sound evidence of this.

Over the years, the work of Father Andrew Greely and his team of researchers has accumulated sociological data that helps explain why the Catholic church is at present in steep decline. The chief reason is not Vatican II, as theologians tend to presume. It is rather papal leadership in the area of sexual morality.

In 1977, in his book, *The American Catholic*, Greely was able to say:

> We could find no evidence to link the Council to the decline of Catholic belief and practice; we found substantial evidence linking that decline to a rejection of the Church's sexual ethic and erosion of the credibility of papal leadership. . . . One disagrees with the Church's sexual teaching, rejects the authority of the leader who attempts to reassert that teaching, and then becomes alienated from other dimensions of religious belief and practice.

The conclusion has to be: Vatican II without *Humanae Vitae* would have enabled the church to take an immense step forward into the modern world. *Humanae Vitae* without Vatican II would have been a total disaster, nothing short of a return to the Dark Ages of Catholicism. Vatican II and *Humanae Vitae* taken together constitute a mitigated disaster. The present pain is the result of the conflict of two mighty and irreconcilable forces in this remarkable institution.

The decline in papal leadership has led to a decline in priests, seminarians, sisters, those agreeing with the church's teaching on all moral matters. It has even led to a decline in funding, for church collections have gone down dramatically. Cold statistics show that, even if Paul VI and John Paul II are right, they have failed to convince more than a tiny minority of devout Catholics, and those chiefly in the older age-bracket.

One reason has to be that Catholics take a far less sanguine view than popes about world population. A glance at the population graph shows it took mankind from year zero to 1800 to reach a billion births. From 1800 to the 1920s there was another billion. The third billion was reached in 1958, the fourth in 1975 and the fifth in the summer of 1987. Out of all the babies ever born, close to four out of the five billion are alive today. Most live in the Third World. In spite of the Green Revolution, there are more hungry people today than ever before. Millions in Africa and South America eat little and badly; they never use a lavatory; they live and die in gutters running with human excrement, rubbish and polluted water. In 1920, Mexico had a population of 20 million. Today, Mexico City alone has almost that number. By the end of the century, Mexico will have at least 100 million people. Even today, in the capital, there exists a group known as *pepinadores*; it is a scavengers' union, apportioning the rights to feed off the local rubbish dump.

John Paul II refuses, as one Vatican official put it, to play the numbers game. In June 1987, one month before the United Nations announced the birth of the five billionth baby, he repeated once more: 'What is taught by the Church on contraception is not a matter that can be discussed freely by theologians.' When Catholic theologians meet to discuss contraception, they have to begin by presuming no change is possible. Since most of them presume change is inevitable, they are wiser to keep silent.

'Every act of sex must be open to the transmission of life,' says John Paul. The fact that such a teaching practised by one nation alone – say, India or China – would over-populate the world, lead to massive misery and starvation, civil and international conflicts does not disturb his faith. God will provide.

There appears no chance of change in the official line during this century. John Paul has filled the episcopate with men who either fully approve of *Humanae Vitae* or who have shown it no opposition, even when they are convinced it is wrong. Whole hierarchies, such as the Dutch and the American, are being stacked with bishops of one theological persuasion. This ensures, humanly speaking, that when John Paul goes his teaching will endure. In this highly charged atmosphere the slightest disagreement on the part of bishops and theologians leads to instant dismissal.

A peripheral teaching, without biblical basis, has become, for good or ill, the touchstone of orthodoxy. It is a situation to which only Voltaire or Jonathan Swift could do justice. Among many devout Catholics arises the haunting question: On this matter, is the pope a Catholic? Could it be he is acting as a Protestant in the church, exercising his own private judgement, contrary to the *sensus fidelium*, the real mind of Catholicism everywhere?

Since 1968, apart from massive population growth which was predictable, an entirely unforeseen factor has entered the debate. This is the AIDS pandemic. Pope Paul decreed that all artificial forms of birth control, including barrier methods, are intrinsically evil. But it is the opinion of doctors today that condoms are the best method of controlling infection. Without condoms, many innocent partners to a marriage and their children will be condemned to an appalling death.

Haemophiliacs, too, have become infected through blood transfusions. To their double calamity, does the Catholic church wish to add a third: celibacy? This is the logic of the Catholic position, set out by Pope Paul and reinforced repeatedly by the present pontiff. The use of condoms violates the biological integrity of the sex act and so is wrong even if it helps to prevent the spread of a disease which is probably the worst since the Black Death of 1348. Nothing can justify the use of something intrinsically wrong, not even the survival of the race. Newman's hypothetical situation has become a reality.

According to *Humanae Vitae*, the end can *never* justify the means. Catholics are forbidden to argue that contraception is only a secondary effect of using a condom. Clearly, condoms only prevent the spread of AIDS because they stop semen entering the woman's vagina, thus violating the biological integrity of the act of intercourse. The Catholic church, according to Paul VI, cannot look at any broader parameters than the sex faculties themselves. When the *primary purpose* of the faculties is blocked, as when condoms are used, the act is intrinsically evil, a mortal sin. This is so, even when a husband is infected, either because he went with a prostitute, or used an infected needle when taking drugs, or, as a haemophiliac, was given an infusion of infected blood. He and his wife must not use barrier methods of contraception. They must have sex without condoms or no sex at all.

With millions now AIDS carriers, the Catholic church's only options are: pray God for a quick antidote to the virus *or* preach virtual celibacy in marriage to millions of couples. To the rest of the world, this attitude is not rational but irresponsible and life-threatening.

It is time to ask, Was Pope Paul right when he said that his teaching in *Humanae Vitae* was 'constant' Catholic tradition? The question 'What is Catholic tradition on sexuality?' turns out to have some very surprising answers. To begin to look for them one has to go back a long way.

SEVENTEEN

An Unloving View
of Sex

A SMALL BIRD-LIKE MAN with big deep eyes, he was, at a guess, aged about thirty-six or thirty-seven when he arrived at the tiny bustling harbour-town. Clad in a rough grey tunic, he had walked northwards on the straight paved Roman road through a treeless land rich in grain. Known as the Great Sinner, he gloried in the title. Who had not heard of his slavery to lust, his sensuous hot-blooded student life at Carthage, his first mistress by whom he had a son, his second mistress whom he took while waiting for a chosen bride to come of age? Who had not heard of his passion for stage plays and gladiatorial combat, his fascination with every nasty heresy? Nine years of self-indulgence had left their mark on his face, in his heart.

The year wass 391, the place Hippo Regis in the Roman province of Numidia, now Algeria. The stranger was Augustine, former professor of rhetoric, the genius who was to teach Western Christianity to speak Latin and to impose a large part of his version of Christ's message for the next fifteen hundred years.

He was a convert. Within a while, phrases from his *Confessions* were to be on everyone's lips. 'Thou hast made us for Thyself, O God, and our hearts are restless till they rest in Thee.' 'Like water I boiled over, heated by my fornications.' Most famous of all: 'Too late have I come to love Thee, O thou Beauty, so ancient and so fair.'

The old Bishop Valerius agreed to make this stranger his assistant at the request of his congregation. Augustine went on to succeed him, and became the greatest theologian the West ever produced. Most of his ideas were formulated in sermons, which may be why they were so popular. He was a marvellous communicator.

His Fear of Sex

Sex, his congregation often complained, was his hobby-horse. He demanded the same standards of men as of women. He protested against men keeping concubines. But there were other, more questionable sides to his teaching; and the bad as well as the good were to become the norm of Christian belief.

His admirers say that after his conversion he was pure spirit. The truth is that he never shrugged off the flesh. He always harboured a deep distrust of it and a loathing he could never quite disguise. His experience of sex had been restricted to illicit loves from which he gained a sense of guilt and misery. Extrapolating in later life, he saddled all sex, even in marriage, with wickedness and sin.

'Nothing', he wrote in his *Soliloquies*, 'is so powerful in drawing the spirit of man downwards as the caresses of a woman and that physical intercourse which is part of marriage.' In fear, remembering his own falls, he never allowed women to set foot in his house or even speak with him except with witnesses present. He made no exceptions even for his elder sister. Continence was the beginning of the service of the Lord, but he understood it in a rigoristic way. The holy fountain of life, he said, was always dirtied by lust (*libido*) even in the tidy garden of marriage. His conviction that sexual appetite is of its nature evil became the great tradition of the church. Because of the Fall, man has been attacked at his most vulnerable point: sex. Even in marriage, it is vitiated by lust. That is the chief and inescapable penalty of Adam's fault. Lust can be justified only by the desire to procreate. Without that desire, the venial sin of lust within marriage is transformed into a mortal sin against marriage itself. The couple become 'whores'; their marriage systematic adultery.

In sermon after sermon he repeats: 'Husbands, love your wives but love them chastely. Insist on the work of the flesh only in such measure as is necessary for the procreation of children. Since you cannot beget children in any other way, you must descend to it against your will, for it is the punishment of Adam. . . . A man should yearn for that embrace in which there can be no more corruption.'

If only a couple could have children without the sordidness of sex, say, by praying on their knees together. According to Augustine, a man in his wife's arms should concentrate icily upon the child and look forward to heaven when he can embrace her like a statue.

This helps explain why he praised virginity. It is free from the lust that shames even the lawful use of marriage. A virgin is close to God because he or she has turned aside from the inevitable sins of matrimony. It is hard to know how he can call marriage good when the acts proper to marriage are *necessarily* evil.

During Augustine's time, there was a crude attempt to gauge 'the safe period'. Manichees, haters of the flesh, had worked this out and told their followers to restrict intercourse to it. This way, they would avoid the worst aspect of carnality, which was bringing a new body into the world. The body, product of an evil deity, was destined for corruption. Augustine had been a Manichee; he was the first saint ever to have used the safe period. It worked for him, too, in that over eleven years he and his mistress only had one child, the beautiful Adeodatus, who died in the spring of his youth. Like many a convert, Augustine was vehement against his former friends. He was appalled not merely by fornication but by the Manichees' approval of the safe period, too. When he heard that Catholics had started using the safe period to avoid conception, he said categorically it is a very grave sin. It is to take pleasure in sex while intending not to procreate. This view prevailed in the Catholic church until, in 1951, Pius XII made the safe period the only method approved by God.

The Good of Marriage

In the year 401, St Augustine wrote a treatise, *On the Good of Marriage* (*De Bono Conjugali*), which was to influence the entire Christian tradition. In it, he established the three *bona*, the goods, values, aims of marriage. These were: offspring, indissolubility and fidelity. Fifteen centuries later, in 1930, Pius XI used these categories as the basis of *Casti connubii*. These, he said, constitute a marriage; without any one of them, a couple would not be contracting a true marriage. This was somewhat tactless of him, in that he thereby nullified most marriages in the world.

In the twentieth century, Augustine's treatise is distasteful because of its coarseness and its profound misunderstanding of what sexuality is. His basic principle is: Sexual intercourse in marriage for the sake of children is good and lawful; for any other reason, it is a sin. Today, the consequences he drew from this principle seem somewhat peculiar.

Older people 'are better in proportion as they begin earlier to refrain from sexual intercourse'. When they can no longer have children, they should strive for chastity of soul, that is, to do without sex altogether.

For younger people, 'marital intercourse makes something good out of the evil of lust' – provided that while having sex they think of themselves not as husband and wife but as father and mother.

But suppose the wife cannot conceive. What would justify a man having sex with his wife? Well, it helps him avoid sleeping around. It is the choice of the lesser evil. Even on Augustine's own principles, this is hard to justify. It comes perilously close to the end (avoiding adultery) justifying the means (the matrimonial sin of lust).

Would not this make intercourse with a pregnant wife a sin of lust? Of course. He wrote: 'There are men incontinent to such a degree that they do not spare their wives when pregnant.' The conclusion should surely be that the wife ought to refuse her husband and not allow him to sin with her. On the contrary, Augustine argues, she must admit her husband because he has dominion over her. Besides, it is better for the wife if he sins with her rather than with another woman. Leaving male chauvinism aside, this, too, is illogical. Would it not be better for a man to sin with a willing prostitute than with an unwilling wife whose chastity he is violating? In the language of moral theology, should not his pregnant wife rebuff him as a virgin would a rapist?

Since partners sin, venially at least, even when they intend to have a child, other odd conclusions follow, which Augustine is happy to accept. 'Abstaining from all intercourse is certainly better than marital intercourse itself which takes place for the sake of having children.' The ideal marriage is a union of 'celibates'. St Paul has suffered greatly from commentators, but who would suppose he meant anything like this? According to Augustine, most couples have to settle for something less than the ideal. 'While continence [in marriage] is of greater merit, it is no sin to *render* the conjugal debt but to *exact* it beyond the need to generate is a venial sin.' Plainly, sex in marriage is only for people who cannot control themselves. The ideal is no sex now or in eternity. The Virgin is here the model he uses.

Mary was wholly continent, a virgin. But she also combined 'impossibles': virginity and motherhood. This was perfection: motherhood without sex, virginity with the blessing of a child. It is almost as if Augustine wished God had made virginal childbearing the norm. In fact, the only way he can absolve God from the guilt of instituting marriage is by saying the inevitable lust of sex is Adam's fault, not God's.

The child, as it were, justifies marriage as we know it. God brings good out of evil. However, frigidity (Augustine called it 'spirituality') is to be aimed at, not sexual pleasure (*libido*). The perfect marriage would follow this pattern: Husband and wife should find out prior to demanding the marriage debt if their partner is in a holy mood, that is, not sexually aroused *and* intending to procreate.

Augustine does not shirk the most paradoxical conclusion: the ideal marriage is made up of two virgins. If this became the norm, the City of God would soon be complete. The least couples can do is strive, as they get older, to become chaste, that is, sexually non-active and, hopefully, in the long run, impotent. But for the fact that St Paul wrote that a man does not sin by allowing a girl to marry, it would have been hard for Augustine, on his principles, to do so.

Sex with no thought of children – worse, sex during the safe period when there is an intention *not* to have children – is gravely sinful. 'For intercourse that goes beyond the necessity to procreate no longer obeys reason but passion.' Sexually active elderly couples or couples who have intercourse when the wife is pregnant or infertile are bound to run up a huge number of sins.

What about the Jewish patriarchs who, according to the Scriptures, had several wives? Augustine's answer is that they took extra wives not for the pleasure or variety of it, but out of the need to have more children. Presumably, these noble figures acted without passion and a deep sense of duty to the race while they were servicing their wives and concubines. It was selflessness on a heroic scale. It is also, incidentally, another example of the end (increasing the number of the chosen people) justifying the means (having sex outside marriage). Augustine was the model of a moralist: rigorist with a talent for justifying almost anything.

Augustine's emphasis on Mary's virginity encouraged celibacy in the church, regardless of the fact that Mary had a husband and, according to the gospels, children other than Jesus. With biblical criticism in its infancy, the Fathers failed to grasp that Mary's virginity had nothing to do with chastity. It was a theological device by which the evangelists expressed the fact that Jesus was God's Son, the fruit not of man and human power but of God and divine power. The Old Testament had similar devices: babies are born of women who are sterile, or who are, as in Sarah's case, practically centenarians. Sadly, Mary's 'virginity' has not merely inspired women to do great things for God and fellow human beings, it has helped down-grade Christian marriage. It reinforced the growing conviction that virginity was superior to marriage which was essentially flawed; it fostered the idea that ministers at the altar should be celibate. This preference later became an obligation; ministers had to be celibate, with often serious consequences for the church's good name.

The chief influence on Augustine, had he realized it, was not the Bible but the Stoics. In, say, the writings of Seneca, duty was paramount. In his austere philosophy, whenever reason gained the upper hand it killed emotions, which were nothing but a disease. The aim of life was to annihilate self-seeking; nothing should be done for the sake of a reward. In view of this, sex had a single aim: procreation. Joys, satisfaction, pleasure were proscribed and, as far as possible, extinguished. The ideal was a cold and passionless intercourse.

Augustine came to his own loathing of sex by a different route: he analysed the effects of original sin. What Stoics called *perturbatio*, he called concupiscence, but they were one and the same. Yet to keep a stiff upper lip while undergoing pain is one thing; it is scarcely appropriate for a couple in the throes of intercourse. A studied coldness, a stifling of human feelings in the marriage bed is, in the strict sense, unnatural, that is, contrary to human nature.

There would be no point in resurrecting this doctrine of a great if, in this instance, misguided teacher, had not the Catholic church accepted it *totally*. There was no pope, no theologian who did not follow Augustine's views on sex and marriage. Through them, he influenced lay people for generation after generation. The Stoical view that sex is exclusively procreative became Catholic orthodoxy for over a thousand years. What lay people inferred from this was that sex is indecent and ridiculous. An abiding sense of sin entered the bedroom, with the result that many Christians identified sin with unchastity. Not a few popes reinforced this impression by criticizing impurity above every other vice, such as greed and callousness.

In his time, Augustine was not the only Christian teacher with an anti-sex bias; he was simply the most influential. Emphasis on chastity and virginity meant marriage was looked on as the mildest and least objectionable form of lechery. For the married, as for the rich, entry into heaven, while not impossible, was difficult. Virginity, said John Chrysostom, is as superior to marriage as heaven is to earth or angels to men. 'Vocation' meant 'giving up sex'. Jerome said that St Peter himself only washed away the dirt of marriage by the blood of martyrdom. The aim of the saint, according to Jerome, 'is to cut down the wood of marriage with the axe of virginity'. Marriage's only justification is that it produces virgins.

In his *History of European Morals*, Lecky says he was able to find only two or three fine descriptions of marriage in a mass of patristic writings. 'It would be difficult to conceive anything more coarse and repulsive than the manner in which they regarded it.' Sex was seen as nothing but unbridled lust. Having intercourse when the wife is pregnant was held universally to be sinful; it was wasting life-giving seed on a field already sown. Even animals do not do such a 'filthy thing'. There was *not a single mention* in patristic times of the tender love married people have for one another, no sign that the Fathers realized the act of sex *was* an act of love. The proof of its turpitude was the pain of childbearing. The woman in particular – God, too, was a male chauvinist! – suffers in the place where she sinned. Even when a child comes into the world, God pointed the finger of blame.

'Edifying' stories abounded of husbands abandoning their wives and children to 'live a chaste life', of wives pleading to have their honour respected on the wedding night. The hero was the man who left his wife on the wedding night to spend his life in the wilderness. The ideal was asceticism, interpreted as liberation from sexuality. To this, all popes subscribed, including Gregory I.

Pope Gregory the Great

Gregory, who reigned from 590 to 604, was one of the wonders of his age. Only Leo I (440–61) could rival him as a pastoral bishop and theologian.

Gregory was of medium height with a huge bald head which many cities – Constance, Prague, Lisbon, Sens – were to claim they possessed as a relic. He had a broad forehead and tiny yellow-brown eyes. His nose was aquiline with flared nostrils, his lips were full and florid. Of noble senatorial family, he decided early on to become a monk. His health was never good, especially in the last fifteen years of his life. He ruined it by fasting and penance. He also suffered from indigestion and was a martyr to the gout. This may have been due to the wine he imported directly from Alexandria, flavoured with resin, called Cognidium.

Pope Gregory was one of the first pontiffs to put his seal of approval on the works of Augustine. Intercourse, he said, is sinful not only during pregnancy but during lactation, too. After a man has slept with his wife, he may not enter a church until he has purged himself by penance and washing, for his will remains evil. Marriage is not sinful, but sex between the partners assuredly is. Gregory also follows Augustine in making a close connection between sex and original sin.

Original sin is an innate corruption of the soul. It takes the form of lust or concupiscence, a rebellion of the flesh against the spirit. Ultimately, it derives from Adam, the human race's first representative. Because of Adam's sin, the very substance of humanity is tainted. It is as if Adam, the first man, contracted a spiritual disease that leads inevitably to death. This disease is handed on at birth to every member of the race. Adam acted in the name of mankind – there was no one else around at the time – hence what he did everyone did. Therefore, everyone is responsible for what he did.

In this, Gregory took St Paul literally: 'In Adam *all* have sinned.' This means that from the first moment of a person's existence there is guilt. This is not a personal taint, but a taint of nature and so unavoidable. The nature derives from the parents. From the beginning, the baby's soul is polluted by this original, this inherited sin.

Gregory was not blind to the problems this raised. For example, parents were cleansed from original sin in baptism. How could they hand on original sin to their babies? He answers: Though holy themselves, they handed on corrupt nature through sex, desire galvanized by lust. Babies are born as the damned fruit of the lust of their redeemed parents. From the first, they are the offspring of Gehenna or Hell; they are justly children of wrath because they are sinners. If they die unbaptized, they are condemned to everlasting torments for the guilt of their birth alone. Existence is itself a state of sin; to be born is to qualify for eternal punishment.

To prove that Gregory's views are not merely of interest to historians, it is enough to examine canon 747 of the church's 1917 code of law. This canon, though dropped from the revised code of 1983, still determines the practices imposed by moralists. There are fewer sadder passages in literature. If there is a danger of a baby dying in the womb, he must be baptized *before* birth. Christ's great clarion call, 'Go, baptize all nations,' is reduced to someone – a doctor, nurse, priest, husband – groping in the womb during a difficult delivery to baptize the *unborn* with water from a syringe. One can imagine the mother's twofold terror. Not even Swift with all his satirical inventiveness could have dreamed up such behaviour.

Gregory agrees with Augustine that sexual desire is sinful in itself. He wrote to the other Augustine, the apostle of England, 'Sexual desire is absolutely impossible without fault', so that every act of sex in marriage needs penance for its atonement.

'We come into the world', Gregory says grandly, 'from corruption and along with corruption, and we carry corruption with us.' He is convinced that 'the Prince of this world is involved in the action, the speech and thought of all those who are concerned with carnal delight'. Only Jesus managed to escape. 'He alone is truly born holy who, in order that he might conquer that same condition of a corrupt nature, was not conceived by carnal conjunction.' There is here, as we noted, a denial of Mary's immaculate conception.

Nothing said here is intended as a slight on Gregory's memory. His ideas were shared by many great men before and after him. The problem only arises because he was pope; and popes are now presumed to be infallible guides; they teach eternal doctrines and lay down moral absolutes. Gregory's views are only an embarrassment because of Catholic belief that popes cannot possibly have been wrong and gravely wrong about something as basic as sex and marriage.

Another enormous difficulty for Catholics should be mentioned here. If Paul VI felt, when he wrote *Humanae Vitae*, that he had to agree with his illustrious predecessors, such as Pius XI and Pius XII, why did he take no notice of Pope Gregory? He was no lightweight. In any list of pontiffs, he would have to be placed in the top six. He inherited a Rome in ruins, surrounded by barbarians. Within a decade, he had made it heir to the empire of the Caesars in the West. If the papacy really does teach moral absolutes, surely Paul VI should have been as concerned to teach what Gregory taught in the sixth century as he was to repeat the teaching of Pius XI in the twentieth. Or does it not matter that modern pontiffs solemnly contradict Gregory's teaching?

After Pope Gregory

Augustine's profound pessimism about sex, marriage and original sin found the supreme champion in Pope Gregory. His teaching passed unopposed into the Middle Ages. Married couples were warned not to have sex on their wedding night in case they desecrated the sacrament of matrimony. Why time should lessen the evil of something intrinsically sordid was never made clear. Lecky recalls the twelfth-century vision of St Alberic in which a lake of torment – resin, hot lead, burning pitch – is prepared in hell for married couples who had the temerity to sleep together on church festivals or fast days. At the centre of *The Witches' Hammer* by Kramer and Sprenger was the belief that sex is so irrevocably evil that it is the chief door through which Satan enters the world.

Distinguished theologians of the Middle Ages simply worked out, in a more scholastic way, Gregory's opinions. Century follows century, and the act of sex is described in terms of sin, and *never* in terms of love. Theologians, all celibate, failed to grasp the most basic point of sexual intercourse among humans, as opposed to animals: it is an act of love.

This negative attitude prevailed in moral theology in this century. In 1966, a book was published in England called *Birth Regulation and Catholic Beliefs*. It purported to be written by G. Egner and published originally in Munich. It has a German dedication and a preface thanking the translator. In fact, the book was written in English by a Durham priest with a very Irish name.

Father Egner selected interesting passages on sex from the most respected moral theologians of that period. They make dismal reading.

> Capello, talking about love-play, says that the spouses may perform any incomplete *lustful* actions. These include oral-genital contacts, for these are still lawful though *enormously obscene*. Génicot, for whom such actions are *most foul* and usually mortally sinful, speaks of *lewd* actions permitted to the spouses, the *foul* words and looks, the touches upon the *decent, less decent and indecent* parts of the body.

As Egner points out, the verdicts of these moralists is as lamentable as their language. Love-play is carried on 'in what can only be described as an atmosphere of tolerated venial sin', as though sin were 'a technical infringement of some trivial bye-law'. He was a brave man to rescue these and other observations from text-books and allow Catholics to see how their clergy were trained to understand their problems. For what Egner has revealed is that their moral guides had no idea what they were talking about. Totally lacking as a body in practical experience, they were like a group of congenitally blind people pontificating on 'colour in modern art'.

Against this background, Pius XI's *Casti connubii* of 1930 was enlightened. What is most intriguing about this encyclical is how the pontiff picks and chooses from the teachings of his predecessors.

In section 14, he follows Pope Gregory in saying that even holy parents cannot pass on holiness to their children. Birth is 'a way of death by which original sin is passed on to posterity'. The baby needs to be regenerated in the waters of baptism. Why does Pius XI not complete Gregory's teaching and insist that babies are the offspring of Hell and doomed, if they die unbaptized, to end up in everlasting torments? Why does Pius accept Gregory's principles and not his conclusions?

In section 23, Pius XI quotes St Augustine's phrase 'the faith of chastity'. He cites with approval Augustine's words, 'Matrimonial faith demands that husband and wife be joined in an especially holy and pure love, not as adulterers love each other'. What he omits to say is that Augustine intended to condemn by this something that he, Pius, allows. For, in section 59, Pius writes:

> Nor are those considered as acting against nature
> who in the married state use their right in the proper
> manner, although on account of natural reasons
> either of time or of certain defects new life cannot be
> brought forth. For in matrimony as well as the use
> of the matrimonial rights there are also secondary
> ends, such as mutual aid, the cultivating of mutual
> love, and the quieting of concupiscence which hus-
> band and wife are not forbidden so long as they are
> subordinated to the primary end and so long as the
> intrinsic nature of the act is preserved.

Although Pius had just spoken (in section 54) of the 'uninterrupted
Christian tradition', almost everything in this passage is *against
Christian tradition*. Augustine and Gregory expressly contradicted
everything in it. They did not distinguish between primary and
secondary ends of marriage. Marriage was for procreation; that was
not the primary end but the one end that could justify sexual intercourse. Any other purpose *added* to procreation was sin. So it is naïve
of Pius to say that provided nature is not interfered with there is no sin;
a couple may have sex to foster mutual love, quieten concupiscence
and so on. Pope Gregory would have said that sex is not for that, it is
not for anything *except* the child. Anything else must be sinful. *This*
was the uninterrupted Christian tradition, not Pius XI's opinion. Even
Innocent XI (1676–89) solemnly decreed that to have sex purely for
pleasure is a sin. This was logical. If sex was for the child, and sex
could not issue in a child, either because the wife was barren or
pregnant or post-menopausal, the act of sex *had to be a sin*.

It is one thing for Pius XI radically to alter a tradition, quite another
to say his teaching is in accordance with it. For by distinguishing
primary and secondary ends of marriage, and permitting the secondary on condition that the primary end is not obstructed, he introduced
an entirely new criterion for judging sexuality. What is this criterion?

The tradition was that the morality of sex is judged by one thing only,
namely, is it directed to the child? Pius substituted for this the natural
integrity of intercourse. If the sex act is fulfilled, that is, if there is
penetration and insemination, nothing else matters. Hence, if the wife
is already pregnant or sterile, provided there is penetration and
insemination, this is a virtuous act. There are two major defects in this
view. First, it contradicts over fifteen hundred years of Christian
tradition. Second, it replaces a moral criterion, however inadequate,
by a biological criterion. Pius began a new tradition of judging the
morality of sex not by looking at persons and what they do as persons
but by looking at the physical 'integrity' of an act. Obviously, if the
biological is the only consideration, nothing can justify contraception,
not the love of the partners, the health of the wife, the stability of the

family and so on. It has to be said therefore, that when Paul VI appealed to the 'constant' tradition of the church on contraception he was really appealing to a teaching that went back forty years to *Casti connubii* and was against the genuine tradition.

When Vatican II refused to use the distinction between primary and secondary ends of marriage, it was very wise. That distinction made any solution to the dilemma of contraception impossible.

In recent times, moralists had become aware of the many dimensions of sexuality. Freud had shown that sex is not primarily about genitals and genital contact but about human beings and relationships. The old teaching was an entirely genital approach to sexuality. Once it was recognized that sex is about persons and about love, then it was vital to integrate this into the Christian morality of sex. Instead of rethinking sexuality, moralists were forced by the Holy Office and *Casti connubii* simply to add the new findings to the old. The result was a hybrid. *Casti connubii* does have modern elements – mutual aid, mutual love – but these are tacked on to what is now called the primary end of marriage, namely, procreation.

But the new hybrid solution is as unacceptable as the traditional one, and far less logical. In fact the new is not a *moral* solution at all. It calls love 'secondary' and subordinates it to a biological criterion of sexuality. What really matters is correct copulation. Love, respect, compassion, concern for the children already born – all these moral elements take second place to the biological, namely, penetration and insemination. If these biological elements are present, the act of sex is in accordance with the 'natural law'. But the *really* natural-law elements, love and compassion, are not allowed to play the determining role in what is the most moral of all acts, sexual intercourse between husband and wife. Written into *Casti connubii* was the tragedy that was to unfold finally in *Humanae Vitae*.

It is not at all mischievous to say that today the Catholic church is plunged in tragedy because popes misunderstood their own tradition. Pius XI structured an encyclical on the basis of Augustine's teaching, then proceeded to say many things contrary to the entire tradition that Augustine influenced. Pius XII seemed unaware that he, too, denied the long tradition of the church.

In 1940 he gave an address to newlyweds. He said:

> The same Creator, Who in His goodness and wisdom desired the conservation and propagation of the human race to be served by the work of man and woman by uniting them in marriage, has also disposed that in that function, the couple should experience pleasure and happiness in body and soul. The couple, then, in seeking and enjoying this pleasure, do not do wrong.

The pontiff speaks of pleasure, unable, it seems, to bring himself to speak of intercourse as an act, *the* act of love. His choice of language is interesting for two reasons. First, it contradicts the teaching of most previous pontiffs who said that sex pleasure is *never* free from sin, and couples should not communicate the morning after intercourse. Second, by concentrating on pleasure and refusing to utter the word 'love', he puts procreation as the primary end of marriage. But, whereas 'pleasure' smacks of hedonism, what about 'love'? In the light of the Gospel, could Pius XII so easily have subordinated *love* to procreation? Surely not.

But Pius XII's major departure from tradition came when he spoke in 1951 to midwives. There, for the first time, a pontiff gave a limited welcome to the rhythm method of birth prevention.

Although there were attempts made in the nineteenth century to put this method on a scientific footing, it was too unreliable until Ogino and Knaus published their findings in the late 1920s. Whereas Rome had earlier pronounced *against* the morality of the rhythm method, Pius XII's address brought about a complete change in Catholic thinking.

According to him the use of the sterile period was legitimate because it did not vitiate the nature of the act. 'They do not prevent or jeopardize in any way the consummation of the natural act and its further natural consequences.' Husband and wife would need to have a good reason for using the safe period, but in itself it was not wrong. It is this teaching that Paul VI repeats in *Humanae Vitae*, section 11.

Neither pontiff seemed to notice that this was the first time in Catholic history that the act of sex was said to be virtuous in itself not merely when procreation could not occur, but *because* procreation could not occur.

Unfortunately, Pius XII, like Pius XI, made biology the criterion of morality. He broke the traditional link between sex and procreation. But while granting Catholics the right to regulate births for themselves and not leave it all to 'providence', he deprived them of satisfactory means of doing so. By this one decision, Pius XII set Catholics on a path littered with thermometers and calendars. It might have been kinder to leave Catholics with the one traditional alternative, namely, procreate or refrain entirely from sex.

For the foreseeable future the Catholic church is saddled with a birth control teaching that has cut all its links with its Christian past *and* the modern world. To cling to *ancient* principles in the face of contemporary hedonism is one thing; to produce a *new* principle that prevents couples regulating their families in the face of a population explosion is quite another.

A historical example already alluded to may help illuminate the present Catholic dilemma.

Original Sin and Birth Control

According to the age-long tradition, formulated by Augustine and sanctioned by Pope Gregory and all his successors, baptism was a prerequisite of salvation. Day-old babies born of Christian parents went to hell if they died unbaptized. So did catechumens if they died unexpectedly. Of course, the entire pagan world was doomed to damnation. According to Augustine, even the Good Thief was only saved because in some unspecified way he was baptized.

There is no better proof of the church's fallibility than this. It is not as if pontiffs and fathers said they did not know how babies could be saved; they said categorically it was impossible. They did not plead ignorance of the fate of the mass of mankind who had never heard of Christ; they affirmed without qualification that they all went to hell. There was no salvation outside the church; and by the church they meant the Catholic church wherein entry was gained *only* by baptism of water. These views were repeated century after century without one dissenting voice. It was Catholic teaching, taught always, everywhere, by everyone. We noticed that when Francis Xavier went to the Indies he was certain that unbaptized pagans, *however virtuous*, could not get to heaven.

The hard-heartedness of Christians of earlier generations astonishes everyone today but, whatever the reasons, it is a fact. Any Catholic who doubted it would have been burned by the Inquisition. According to Lecky, this teaching surpassed in atrocity any tenet adopted by pagans. It merited Tacitus' tag of a 'pernicious superstition'. Lecky writes:

> That a little child who lives but a few minutes after birth and dies before it has been sprinkled with the sacred water is in such a sense responsible for its ancestor having six thousand years before eaten a forbidden fruit, that it may with perfect justice be resuscitated and cast into an abyss of eternal fire in expiation of this ancestral crime, that an all-righteous and merciful Creator, in the full exercise of these attributes, deliberately calls into existence sentient beings whom He had from eternity irrevocably destined to endure unspeakable, unmitigated torture, are propositions which are at once so extravagantly absurd and so ineffably atrocious that their adoption might well lead men to doubt the universality of moral perception. Such teaching is, in fact, simply demonism, and demonism in its most extreme form.

Extreme demonism or not, it was Catholic orthodoxy until almost modern times. God's image never emerged more tarnished from a witch's manual. The most monstrous of human cruelties perpetrated by Attila the Hun or Adolf Hitler pale in comparison with the cruelties attributed by gentle Christian theologians and contemplative monks to God the Father of Our Lord Jesus Christ. In fact not even the devil has been painted in such lurid colours.

The real mystery is why Christians held these views for so long. There is only one answer: authority. The authority of the Bible, in the first instance, but the Bible as interpreted by the teachers of the church (the magisterium). St Paul's mystical words, 'In Adam all have sinned', were boneheadedly taken to imply that even newborn babies were responsible for original sin and doomed to hell if they died unbaptized.

Christians who would never have forgiven themselves if they had injured a child gratuitously were content to think that God would punish him with unspeakable and eternal torments for something which was not in his power to avoid. No Christian parent in his or her heart could possibly have believed that *ever*; but they assented to it. It is perhaps the best example in history of Catholic authority, without reason or humanity on its side, demanding obedience to a morally absurd doctrine. As Lecky also remarked:

> Christians esteem it a matter of duty and a commendable exercise of humility, to stifle the moral feelings of their nature, and they at last succeed in persuading themselves that their Divinity would be extremely offended if they hesitated to ascribe to Him the attributes of a fiend. . . . Their doctrine is accepted as a kind of moral miracle, and, as is customary with a certain school of theologians, when they enunciate a proposition that is palpably self-contradictory, they call it a mystery and an occasion of faith.

This parallels papal teaching on birth control. Just as Pope Gregory's God condemned infants to the eternal fires of hell, Pope Paul's God consigns millions of human beings to a hell on earth. The difference is that today ordinary Catholics are saying that they think Pope Paul was wrong.

There are no valid arguments to support Paul VI's view of morality or his idea of the Deity behind human nature. What remains a puzzle is why Pope Paul, who subscribed to the myth that all popes say the same, was so selective in the choice of his predecessors whom he did not like to contradict. Why did he not mind contradicting Pope Gregory whose view that sex is always sinful even when it issues in children was repeated by many popes including Gregory VII and

Innocent III? Why did he not mind contradicting the tradition that children who die unbaptized go straight to hell for all eternity? Why did he not mind contradicting any number of pontiffs who said sex and love are incompatible? And Sixtus V who said that contraception is a form of homicide? Why was Paul's over-riding concern not to contradict Pius XI and Pius XII?

Is the answer simply that Paul had lived under Pius XI and Pius XII? That this casual fact somehow made disagreeing with them more unpalatable than disagreeing with Gregory, Augustine and the great tradition? Or was he unaware that what he called 'constant tradition' was but forty confusing years old?

Whatever the reason for this inconsistency, the church was left trying to cope with a biological morality. A celibate ethic had put the laity on the rack. A couple living in a hovel with a dozen children must use the safe period or sleep back to back. Masturbation is always mortally sinful, even when the reason for it is to find out why the husband cannot impregnate his wife. According to logic, masturbation is more immoral than adultery, because less natural. A rapist who wears a condom sins more than one who does not. *In vitro* fertilization is banned automatically, whatever progress science makes in this field, for the only 'natural' way for a couple to have children is by intercourse; if it does not work for them, they have to be reconciled to being childless. At every stage, the Catholic morality of sex betrays its priestly origin. It is not a matter of celibates having a spite against men whom they envy or women whom they hate; they simply do not understand.

A last point: Pius XII grudgingly gave his *nihil obstat* for the use of the safe period. This has now become the standard Catholic method of avoiding conception. Official teaching is that it is morally right to copulate when intending *not* to procreate, to achieve sexual satisfaction without the inconveniences of pregnancy. It is curious that Marie Stopes in England and Margaret Sanger in America were once attacked by the Catholic church for advocating the same broad principles. The question arises: If Pius XII had really wanted to continue the great Catholic tradition, what should he have said?

Logically, he should have argued: sex is only for procreation. Everything else that enters into intercourse over and above the desire to procreate is sinful. Therefore, to use the safe period is, as Augustine plainly taught, as sinful as using a condom. Pius XII should in fact have gone further.

Since the tradition is that sex is exclusively for procreation, the church should welcome the discovery of the safe period for another reason altogether. Couples should make it their urgent duty to find out when sex is not safe for them and *restrict intercourse to those times only*. That way, they will not be wasting precious life-giving seed which *every Father of the church said was wrong*. This means that devout Catholics, far from restricting themselves to the safe period, will avoid it altogether. Once their families are complete, they will say goodbye to sex.

That Pius XII and his successors did not take this line does more credit to their kindness than to their sense of logic or grasp of church history.

Since recent pontiffs, for all the rhetoric about 'constancy', have mostly rejected their predecessors' views on sex and birth control, perhaps they have also departed from tradition in other matters. For example, abortion. And, first of all, divorce.

EIGHTEEN

The Popes,
Pioneers of Divorce

THE CATHOLIC CHURCH, it is repeatedly said, is against divorce. The ban spreads wide. The Vatican does not allow accreditation to ambassadors or lesser diplomats if they are divorced or married to divorcees. They may be Protestants, even atheists, but they and their spouse must, matrimonially speaking, be above reproach.

The view that the church never allows divorce is held by most people, including Catholics, though many behind their hands mutter that the church permits it under different names. Even divorced Catholics tend to believe that their church holds *all* marriages are for life and refuses divorce to anyone for any reason.

Catholics point with pride to Pope Clement VII's refusal to grant a divorce to so powerful a monarch as Henry VIII who wanted to abandon Catherine of Aragon for the young and beautiful Anne Boleyn. To be precise, Henry asked for an annulment of his first marriage, a favour Pope Alexander VI granted his daughter Lucrezia after three years of an abundantly consummated marriage. Henry's grounds were better than Lucrezia's. Catherine was first bedded then wedded by his brother Arthur, who died. Hence the papal dispensation permitting him to marry Catherine, he maintained, had been invalid. It was preying on his mind. Maybe the fact that Catherine had failed to provide him with a male heir and was getting old had something to do with his scruples. But his sister, Margaret, Queen of Scotland, had had her marriage recently annulled by Rome on a pretext flimsier than his.

Alas for Henry, Catherine's nephew, Emperor Charles V, had the Pope in his pocket at the time. At first, the pope had given the impression that Henry's suit would present no problems. But, when Charles threw his considerable weight around, Henry's petition to be classed as a bachelor after twenty years of marriage was finally turned down.

Everyone knows of worse predicaments than Henry VIII's. Spouses find themselves deserted, sometimes within weeks of marriage. Their partners may have set up home with someone else and started a new family in a different country, perhaps on a different continent. Wives are yoked to drunks and gamblers, to brutes who beat them and the children. In fairness, it must be added that some men are married to wives who beat *them* on a regular basis. Some spouses discover too late they are joined to someone who is homosexual or bisexual or suffering from venereal disease or who becomes insane or has a religious mania. The endless permutations of domestic drama provide the basic material for television soap operas. To all these complex situations the Catholic church has one solution: separation but no divorce. The bond of marriage, says one pontiff after another, is of its nature indissoluble. 'Marriages are made in heaven', even if they end in hell. No power on earth can break the bond. 'What God hath joined together, let no man put asunder.' Any relaxation of this rule would open the floodgates.

Has this not happened? In the Western world, there has been a tremendous increase in the incidence of divorce. In the United Kingdom prior to 1858, divorce was only granted by a special Act of Parliament. Between 1669 and 1858 there were only 229 divorces, of which a mere three or four were granted to women. Today, marriages last on average nine years, and the grounds of divorce is the irretrievable breakdown of marriage.

In the United States, where there was no divorce prior to the Revolution, divorce has become a business like any other – say, the sale of cars or peanuts. Divorces contribute to national productivity. In 1930, the year of *Casti connubii*, there were less than 200,000. By 1975 there were well over a million a year. Today, the divorce rate in the States is the highest in the world.

In seventeenth-century England, John Milton's was a lone voice protesting at the absence of divorce. Today, he speaks for multitudes. The poet, who had been deserted by his wife, commented in his *Tetrarchordon* on the words 'What God hath joined':

> Shall we say that God hath joined error, fraud, unfitness, wrath, contention, perpetual loneliness, perpetual discord; whatever lust, or wine, or witchery, threat or incontinence, avarice or ambition, hath joined together faithful and unfaithful, Christian with anti-Christian, hate with hate or hate with love – shall we say *this* is God's joining?

The Pope Alone Can Grant Divorce

Until recently, Catholics who divorced and remarried believed themselves to be 'bad Catholics'. Living in sin, they were on the road to hell. Recent surveys, apart from showing that divorce rates among Catholics are at best marginally below average, reveal that the divorced no longer consider themselves bad. Just as Catholics defy the pope and use contraceptives, so they divorce without a sense of sin or shame. True, divorce is usually a traumatic experience, but Catholic divorcees today do not have the added burden of their forefathers: they do not think themselves damned. Often they seem to feel not that they have failed marriage, but that marriage has failed them. In any case, once a marriage is over, it is over, even if they acknowledge their own responsibility, in part or in total, for the break-up. What is the point in pretending that some kind of bond – mystical, metaphysical – exists when they know it is ended between them? Love has died. Living without love is a sin. Not remarrying would be trying to live without love and only an added sin. Celibate clergy do not realize that trying to mend a broken marriage is often like trying to put a fractured spider's web together with bare hands.

Today, if the polls are correct, most Catholics believe their church should permit divorce. There *is* life after divorce, and many want that life for their own sake and for the sake of their children. Why does the church prefer children to be brought up with no *family* around them? Not that Catholics think change is likely.

As was shown in the case of *Humanae Vitae*, the church never changes. Its strength is in *not* changing. It demonstrates a firmness of purpose, a refusal to compromise on basic moral principles. If pressed, many Catholics in favour of divorce might agree that if the church did move with the times she could lose her moral authority and many members. She consoles her children by teaching eternal truths, instead of bending with the latest winds of fashion. The truths may not be believed any more, the morals may no longer be accepted, but *they are there*, and Catholics by and large are happy that the pope keeps the standards up, as ideals to aim for. It is as if beliefs are very important, even when they are not true.

This book has shown already a few of the many issues on which the church has changed, even while proclaiming change is impossible. The church's genius is in changing even in moments when she most loudly yells No Change. So-called 'traditions' often turn out on examination to be a generation old.

As John T. Noonan has shown in his scholarly book, *Power to Dissolve*, contrary to popular belief, the church has changed more on divorce than on most things. This is hardly surprising in view of the complexity of the human condition and the variety of social experience. If only the church did not hide behind the myth that she never allows divorce when the truth is almost the opposite.

She allows divorce – she prefers the term 'dissolution of the bond' – in every case but one: a consummated marriage between two Christians. Far from the pope being completely opposed to divorce in any shape or form, he thinks *he is the only person in the world who can grant it*. Pius XI said not even governments can be trusted with this power of God. They can legislate, judge, imprison, even execute, but they cannot be trusted with divorce. The astounding fact has to be faced that the papacy pioneered divorce in Europe as it pioneered torture. It was not governments but the papacy that in the sixteenth century reintroduced divorce into Christendom after it had been outlawed for several centuries, during which time ecclesiastical legislation prevailed even in civil courts.

Boniface VIII asserted that all creatures are subject to the Roman pontiff. This has been extended in the present century by popes to cover *all* marriages. Even marriages of unbelievers, infidels, Jews, Muhammadans. They are all subject to the Roman pontiff, and he can dissolve them for the salvation of souls. In practice, this means for the benefit of the Roman church. At any one time, there are millions of broken marriages caused by desertion, cruelty, incompatibility, child-battering, wife-battering, infidelity – they are found in obscure towns and villages in countries as far apart as Zaïre and Scotland, Finland and Canada. But only one person in the world, an elderly celibate who dwells in a palace in the Vatican, is empowered by God to dissolve them. This he never does unless they involve some Catholic interest, in which case he acts as God's Vicar to bring relief. This strains credulity a little. The natural bond is so strong – 'indissoluble' says Rome – that it is a grave wrong for a government in the United States or in Britain, in China or the Soviet Union to legislate to sunder it. But in the hands of the Roman pontiff this naturally indissoluble bond can be quietly snapped and the partners allowed to remarry.

In the 1940s and 1950s, Pius XII extended this power of dissolving marriages to a degree that was unthinkable to Christians of even a generation before. All the early Councils of the church would have deposed him for heresy.

Since, far from being opposed to divorce, the pope can dissolve all types of marriage save one, can he dissolve that one? Most Catholics wish he would dissolve a Christian consummated marriage and complete the cycle, but can he? History has something to say on this.

Briefly, in anticipation. Some popes by personal initiatives bordering on the quixotic have dissolved marriages. In so doing, they set in motion forces that accelerated almost out of control. There have been moments in history – ours is one of them – when popes have issued decrees that have implicitly questioned or rendered null and void most marriages in the world. Civil divorce, in this scenario, does not cause evil but helps put a stop to public concubinage.

So false is the picture of the Catholic church never changing its doctrines on marriage that a third-century Christian would have been astonished at medieval teaching; a medieval would have been even more astonished at twentieth-century teaching. Doubtless a Christian today would be astonished if he knew what the church will teach in the next century or the century after that. In the light of history, the only improbability is that today's teaching is the last word. Whatever popes think or say they think, Catholic tradition is not a mere repeat of the past, nor always a development out of the past. It is often a radical departure from everything that has preceded it.

Jesus' Teaching on Marriage

Jesus' teaching, as reported in Matthew's Gospel, seems clear.

> It was said [in the Jewish Bible], 'Whoever divorces his wife, let him give her a certificate of divorce.' But I say to you that everyone who divorces his wife, except on the ground of unchastity [Greek *porneia*], makes her an adulteress; and whoever marries a divorced woman commits adultery.

Later in Matthew, Jesus was asked why, then, did Moses allow divorce?

> He said to them, 'For your hardness of heart Moses allowed you to divorce your wives, but from the beginning it was not so. And I say to you: whoever divorces his wife, except for unchastity, and marries another, commits adultery.'

The differing interpretations of these passages over the ages prove things are not as simple as they seem.

The first problem centres on the phrase, 'except on the ground of unchastity'. What was meant by 'unchastity'? Was it used in the ritual sense of someone who had broken a rule and was not really married at all? Did it mean simply infidelity? Whatever the meaning, is it not obvious that Jesus himself envisaged some exceptions to the rule?

Many church Fathers and most Eastern Fathers, notably St Basil, took it for granted that divorce was permitted on the grounds of infidelity. This tradition, accepted by all the early synods of Gaul, Spain and the Kingdom of the Franks, has remained in force in the Eastern church. To say, therefore, that the church has always taught that no Christian marriage is dissoluble for any reason is historically false. Unless, that is, the Eastern church was not truly Catholic even before the Schism, that is, her formal break with Rome in 1054.

Since the Reformation in the sixteenth century, only the Catholic church has maintained that divorce is forbidden to all Christians whose marriage has been consummated. This hard word remains in force even when an innocent partner has been deserted. Other churches have at least found it possible to allow innocent and deserted spouses to remarry after divorce.

Contrary to popular belief, the Catholic church has never *defined* that Christian consummated marriages cannot be dissolved. The Council of Trent was on the point of doing so in 1563 when the ambassadors of the Venetian Republic politely reminded the fathers that the Eastern church granted divorce. This custom, they added, had never been condemned by any pope or Ecumenical Council. Thus cautioned, the bishops stepped back from the brink. They altered the text. Instead of condemning the Eastern practice unreservedly, they were content to say: 'If anyone says the [Catholic] Church errs when she teaches . . . that the bond of marriage cannot be dissolved, let him be anathema.' It left open the possibility of the church revaluating this position at some future date. Since Trent, this has not happened. The door has not been closed.

Scripture scholars have recently suggested that the church of East and West tackled the Scripture texts in the wrong way. Jesus was looked on primarily as a law-giver, rather like Moses. In fact he was looked on as a *canon* lawyer intent on laying down precise criteria for valid marriages and divorce. This is why, over the ages, the church turned this part of the Sermon on the Mount into a legal document. Since then canonists have worried over details like a dog worrying a bone. What are the conditions of a lawful and valid marriage? What are valid reasons for dispensing from impediments of consanguinity, of mixed marriage or of marriage with an unbaptized person? And so on.

Of course, marriage is part of church law and, as society changes, she has to respond by sometimes complex legislation. The mistake was in thinking that the Sermon on the Mount had anything to do with this sort of thing.

Jesus presented the ideal of marriage to his disciples. It is most unlikely that he had in mind any particular exception, whether of desertion or of infidelity. But laying down an ideal of marriage is one thing, legislating with what amounts to Talmudic complexity for divorce quite another. The context of Jesus' words makes this plain.

In the Sermon on the Mount, immediately before he spoke of marriage, Jesus said: 'If your right hand causes you to sin, cut it off and throw it away; it is better that you lose one of your members than that your whole body go to hell.' One of the Greek Fathers, Origen, obeyed to the letter, cutting off his offending member which was not his hand. This was a personal tragedy in that Origen, who excelled in mystical interpretations, took hardly anything else in the Bible literally.

The church disapproved of Origen's use of the knife, fearing he might start a fashion. Jesus did not want a follower of his to cut off his hand or anything else. It was different when popes, Fathers and theologians dealt with hellfire that never goes out. This, they said, had to be taken literally. This was a worse mistake than Origen's. It led them over several centuries to ask questions like this: What sort of fire is it that can burn endlessly and never go out? What sort of body do the dead rise with that enables it to burn for ever? *Where* is this fire? In the bowels of the earth? And how can a person feel the pain of burning before his body rises at the last day? There were unanswerable ethical questions as well. How can one justify eternal punishment for an act done in time? God is infinite, *therefore*, they argued superficially, an offence against Him is also infinite. Psychological questions surfaced. How can parents rejoice in heaven, knowing that their sons and daughters are roasting in hell? We saw how, through most of Christian history, the church condemned unbaptized babies to eternal fire, as God's just verdict upon them. This fact mysteriously does not diminish the parents' bliss when they reach Paradise. How is this possible? And theologians were off on another wild-goose chase.

To modern exegetes, the answer is simple. Jesus was not talking literally about 'the everlasting flames'. His reference was to the burial-ground of Gehenna on the edge of Jerusalem. It smoked all day and night, fed with the city's refuse and the corpses of crucified criminals. A literal interpretation trivializes what he was saying. The same applies to his teaching on marriage. He is speaking *prophetically*.

He holds up marriage as a lifelong commitment of one man and one woman. To sin against that commitment is adultery. Taking this seriously is not the same as taking it literally, which is the way, unfortunately, that the church has often treated it. It led to canonists chasing their tails exactly as theologians chased theirs over hell and hellfire. An ideal has no exceptions and Jesus was expressing an ideal. To misunderstand this is to turn an ideal of marriage into rules about divorce. Once that mistake is made, canonists start to ask: What is required for a lawful and valid marriage? What is a valid dispensation? And so on. Whether the church can or cannot permit divorce and, if she can, under what circumstances are matters in which Jesus had not the slightest interest. He was a prophet, not a canon lawyer.

The curious thing is this: the church maintains that in the Sermon on the Mount Jesus taught a rule which is universal and without exceptions. This rule the church is bound to uphold. Yet not one element in this rule can be found in the text.

In the first place, the Sermon on the Mount was addressed by Jesus, a Jew, to his fellow-Jews. They were not baptized and probably none of them ever would be. To them Jesus is said to have given 'the rule' that marriages of baptized Christians, once consummated, cannot be dissolved. In other words, Jesus is supposed to have forbidden divorce under any circumstances to the very class of people to whom popes regularly permitted divorce. There are records of Martin V (1417–31) allowing Jews to divorce and remarry according to their law. In fact, throughout the Papal States, Jews were allowed to divorce and re-marry with approval of the popes. They were potentates; they could have forbidden them with a stroke of the pen, but they did not. In modern times, popes have felt free to dissolve the marriages of Jews who want to convert to Catholicism. This means that in practice, though popes interpret Jesus' ideal as a rigorous law, they themselves allow exceptions to it. This was a strange development in the light of history.

Teaching of the Early Church on Divorce

The church came into being at the time of the Roman Empire. The Romans had a liberal approach to divorce. Cicero parted from his wife because he needed an extra dowry. Augustus forced Livia's husband to divorce her when she was pregnant, so he could marry her himself. Wives, according to one Roman writer, were like shoes: they pinched in places which other people could not see. If your shoes hurt, you change to another pair. St Jerome reports that in Rome in his day one woman was marrying for the twenty-third time. She was her husband's twenty-first. Plainly, marriage was nothing but a casual liaison that could be dissolved almost at will.

In contrast, the church insisted that acts of sex are forbidden except in the context of a permanent relationship. When Christianity became established, marriages were consecrated by a special religious ceremony. Until the tenth century, however, the church's blessing was not obligatory. The natural union of man and woman now came under the clergy's control. Yet it was not until the Council of Trent in 1563 that the form of marriage was finalized. From then on, marriage was no longer valid unless a couple exchanged consent before their parish priest (or his delegate) and two witnesses. Even this only became universal in the church with the publication of *Ne Temere* in the year 1908.

In the early centuries, marriage, whether blessed by the church or not, whether the state recognised it or not, was held by Christians to be indissoluble. 'What God hath joined, let no man put asunder.' Civil law continued to permit divorce for a long time. Attempts by emperors such as Constantine to limit it failed. The right to divorce was left unimpaired in the Justinian code which ruled the Empire. Thus for centuries, church and state went their own way. The church at most only allowed a deserted spouse to divorce and remarry, whereas the state allowed this privilege to everyone.

Charlemagne, as head of Christendom, did his best to harmonize the two codes. A divorcee himself, he declared divorce a crime, though, wisely, he attached no penalty to it. The church sometimes excommunicated divorcees, but certainly not anyone as important as Constantine or Charlemagne.

Not until the twelfth century, when Europe was a Christendom, did church and state combine to prohibit divorce. The church had won the day. All the stranger that it was the church not the state that started to undermine the institution of marriage.

*   *   *

Mixed marriages are one area in which phenomenal changes have occurred over the course of time. These are marriages between Christians and pagans.

From the beginning, the church forbade them as contrary to the Gospel. How could a Christian unite himself to someone who, he believed, was condemned by unbelief to hellfire? How could a Christian agree to his children being brought up under pagan influence, perhaps as pagans themselves, thus dooming them to torments everlasting? Before Christianity, differences in religion were not taken too seriously. Christianity alone was so exclusive as to look on all non-believers as combustible material. Incidentally, Christianity also brought in a fear of dying never known before.

The Fathers bluntly called the marriage of a Christian to a pagan 'adultery' or 'fornication'. It prostituted the very limbs of Christ by joining them to the limbs of a heretical harlot. As soon as the church became the religion of empire, the marriage of a Jew and a Christian became a capital offence. Council after council denounced all marriages between Christians and 'others' as a crime.

So common was this attitude that Gratian, in the twelfth century, described all marriages between believers and unbelievers as 'contrary to the ordinances of God and the church'. If a Christian had entered into such a liaison, he should separate immediately. His faith was in peril, he was corrupting his morals and endangering the salvation of his children. Most theologians, such as Peter Lombard, said mixed marriages were null and void.

This tradition allowed no exceptions. From the Council of Trent to the nineteenth century, the Inquisition saw to it that no Catholics married Protestants. Yet, though mixed marriages were against divine law, contrary customs arose in countries such as England and Germany. Being in a minority, Catholics often had no alternative to marrying Protestants if they married at all. Other exceptions were officially allowed by Rome. Clement VIII in the year 1604 permitted a Catholic prince to marry a Protestant princess 'for the common good'. It was never made clear how something contrary to divine law and intrinsically evil could be permitted for any good, common or otherwise. To minimize the harmful effects of mixed marriages, Rome insisted on certain guarantees. The Catholic had to do his best to convert his partner; the children, boys and girls, were to be brought up as Catholics. This had to be confirmed in writing.

In the nineteenth century, Catholics in England and Germany were forbidden any longer to marry Protestants without permission. To compensate, this permission was granted with ever increasing ease. What the church had condemned without reserve was becoming a commonplace. What had been banned as against divine law and intrinsically evil was now written into canon law.

While the language of the popes remained the same, practice had changed considerably. In the year 1748, Benedict XIV, in a letter sent to the Polish hierarchy, called a marriage between a Catholic and a Protestant 'a sacrilegious union'. On 25 March 1830, Pius VIII in *Litteris alto* referred to mixed marriages as 'grave crimes'. 'The Church', he said, 'has a horror of these unions which present so many deformities and spiritual dangers.' Such unions were 'direct sins against canon and divine law'. The early church said the same and banned them. From the eighteenth century on, the church dispensed from them. Was this really a development or a fundamental change of mind?

In 1858, Pius IX, with his usual bombast, said the Holy See only allows such 'pernicious and detestable' marriages for serious reasons. Without a just and serious reason, Propaganda added, dispensations would not be valid. But when in 1877 Propaganda gave a list of sixteen 'just and serious' reasons for granting a dispensation, many of them turned out to be trivial. For example, a dispensation is automatically given if the woman is over twenty-four years of age (*superadulta*). Or the Catholic party has a firm determination to marry anyway, if not in church then outside in a civil ceremony. A splendid example of disobedience being rewarded. Since 1970, even written guarantees are not demanded; the Catholic's word to do his or her best for future children suffices. Sometimes, a Catholic in a mixed marriage may even be wed in front of a Protestant minister. On this issue, it seems the church has come full circle.

The popes seemed to hope that identical language – as ferocious as that used by the Fathers – would obscure the fact that changes had occurred. Such is the magnitude of the changes that any Father of the church resurrected today would think that Satan had triumphed and Mother Church had given in to paganism.

The teaching on mixed marriages provides this lesson: when the Catholic church changes radically, she says unchanging principles are being benignly applied to changed circumstances; when she refuses to change – as up till now on contraception and divorce for Christians – she says her unchanging principles allow no change under any circumstances. An early Christian would have found any change for any reason in matters of contraception, mixed marriages or divorce equally incredible. The Church has changed on mixed marriages. What is her record on divorce?

Papal Divorce of Unconsummated Marriages

In the middle of the twelfth century, Pope Alexander III was presented by the English Bishop of Exeter with a conundrum. A nobleman in his diocese had, at his betrothal, sworn on oath to marry his fiancée. However, before the wedding, he experienced a call to the religious life.

There was a conflict between his oath to marry and his divine vocation to serve God as a monk. Alexander was the leading lawyer of his day. His solution had no precedent and no logic to it, and it started a canonical hare that is still running. Many other mad hares took up the chase.

According to the pope, the nobleman was obliged to keep his oath and marry his fiancée. Straight after the wedding, without any carnal coupling, he was to leave her and enter a monastery. His decision was influenced by stories of saints – men and women with a phobia about sex – who left their spouses on their wedding night.

Only an extreme celibate, soaked in a tradition antipathetic to marriage, could have thought up such a nasty little game. The nobleman's marriage, Alexander said, would be valid because, according to Gratian, it is consent not coupling that makes a marriage. Were not Mary and Joseph married, though theirs was a virginal union? More, their virginal union was not merely a genuine marriage, it was the *ideal* marriage. The nobleman of Exeter, having gone through with his wedding, could dissolve his unconsummated marriage by becoming a religious. It was a somewhat cavalier approach to the great sacrament of Christ and his Bride the church. And where was the justice to the bride? Her conjugal rights, her honour and that of her family were completely ignored. His Holiness took no notice of St Paul, who wrote: 'The husband does not have power over his own body, but the wife.'

The question asked by canonists was, How could the husband's unilateral decision break up the marriage? In his decree *Commissum*, Alexander answered that this was a special case. The good of religion overrode the lesser good of marriage, religious vows annulled the marriage vows. Popes claim to be able to interpret the Bible. Did Jesus really have this exception in mind when he said, 'What God hath joined, let no man put asunder'? Would St Augustine have agreed that the purposes of marriage – offspring, indissolubility, fidelity – had been safeguarded by his Holiness, who let a husband rush away immediately the wedding was over? Moreover, did not the pontiff's decision mean that the ideal marriage, the one between virgins like Mary and Joseph, was the only kind that was dissoluble? It had always been hard to understand how a virginal marriage can be the ideal when the chief end of marriage is procreation. Alexander's decision on dissolubility compounded the problem.

Because Alexander was pope, from his silly decision something momentous emerged. He had approved the idea that for a marriage to be absolutely indissoluble it required both consent *and* coupling, saying Yes *and* having sex.

One of his aides should have pointed out to his Holiness that two absurd consequences follow from this. In the first place, if coupling is necessary for indissolubility, anyone intending not to copulate would not be intending indissolubility, hence not intending to marry. The nobleman had gone through a ceremony but he was not really married. Far from keeping his oath to his fiancée he had broken it. Second, for centuries the church had taught that sex in marriages was invariably sinful. How could this *sinful* element make marriage so sacred as to be indissoluble? Or was one to say, not 'What God hath joined', but 'What lust hath joined, let no man put asunder'?

Since 'the pope cannot make mistakes', the church had to live with this piece of papal frivolity. Owing to Alexander, a new class of *dissoluble* Christian marriage had come into being. A man, on his own initiative, could divorce his wife! A church which says any exception opens the floodgates had made a big crack in the institution of marriage.

Alexander's view became, naturally, part of orthodoxy. In 1563 the Council of Trent decreed that religious profession dissolved marriage. How did it do so? The mystical notion arose that religious profession was a kind of spiritual death which, like bodily death, ended a marriage. It was not the pope who dissolved the marriage but the religious profession. But already ardent papalists were beginning to smell out new papal powers. If a mere spouse could dissolve his own marriage, perhaps the *pope* too could dissolve certain marriages for spiritual reasons. After all, he was God's vicar on earth. Who dared limit his authority in advance?

Three hundred years passed when, in the middle of the fifteenth century, Antonino, Archbishop of Florence and formerly a distinguished member of the Curia, claimed to have seen the Bulls of two popes that *dissolved* non-consummated marriages. In each case, the spouse was allowed to remarry. In spite of his credentials – he was the top moral theologian of the day – no one believed his Grace. Religious profession could dissolve a marriage, but a pope? Surely not. And a divorced spouse was allowed to remarry? Impossible! Jesus said: 'What God hath joined. . . .'

What came out much later was that the papal habit of dissolving such marriages, that is, granting divorce, went back beyond Antonino's contemporary Pope Martin V. What could justify this reversal of the clear teaching of the Master?

These were the cases in question. After marrying and before consummating, a man finds his wife is pregnant by someone else. He asks for the marriage to be dissolved so he can remarry a virgin. Another man was married by proxy. His wife was travelling to meet him when she was captured by pirates. Her husband never met her and was not likely to. Though married to her, he was allowed to remarry.

Canonists argued that the popes must have dissolved those marriages as vicars of Christ. Their motive was, presumably, mercy. But mercy as a reason for granting a divorce seems strange in a church that mercilessly refuses divorce to her children in circumstances quite as heart-breaking as those just mentioned. Furthermore, these exceptions can hardly be derived from the Sermon on the Mount which the church continues to interpret as an iron rule: No divorce. It has to be said that the church has not kept to absolute indissolubility. Popes breached it, to the initial incredulity of canonists.

Owing to Rome's passion for secrecy, these momentous documents on divorce did not see the light of day for five hundred years. Antonino's testimony could not, therefore, be checked.

Once the papal practice of divorce was established, however, the question in curial circles was: How can the pope do this, when no man can break a marriage asunder? The answer came loud and clear: The pope is *not* a man but God's vicar. He is using divine power to dissolve the indissoluble. In plain English, indissolubility has a variety of species, one of which is the dissoluble.

Had canonists taken Jesus' teaching as an ideal of marriage, all problems would have been resolved. But as a piece of legislation it had to be interpreted in ever more abstruse ways. Jesus plainly meant that what God has joined must always and in all circumstances remain joined. Rome, in practice, disagrees and, to justify its disagreement, resorts to very subtle distinctions.

The passage prohibiting divorce has, therefore, to be linked in the Catholic mind with other key Scriptural passages: 'Thou art Peter' and 'What you shall loose on earth shall be loosed in heaven'. Implied, too, is the belief that, in the Sermon on the Mount, Jesus desired to give this power to grant divorce not merely to Peter but to his successors, the Bishops of Rome. Not for nothing do the popes claim to be able to interpret Scripture.

There is another odd consequence of these first papal divorces. In church documents, the bond of marriage is said to be of natural and divine law. Such language is taken to mean that not even God can make exceptions to it. Yet in this case natural law *can* be broken. For some unexplained reason, the church claims to have power to modify or rescind the natural law on divorce but not on contraception.

When Rome goes on to say that the pope himself cannot sunder a consummated Christian marriage, people want to know why. Theologians point to the Scripture and say that a Christian marriage reflects the love of Christ and his church. But before the fifteenth century theologians also pointed to Scripture to prove the pope could not sunder unconsummated marriages, either.

But this is to leap too far ahead.

Alexander III's weird decision on the nobleman from Exeter spawned a large number of papal divorces. As a result, Martin V and other popes dissolved confirmed but unconsummated marriages. What perplexed Antonino in the mid-fifteenth century, and what the scholars of the day said was incredible, was by the seventeenth century standard practice. On the basis of his divine power, the pope was regularly dissolving unconsummated marriages.

Was he also able to dissolve any *consummated* marriages?

Papal Divorce of Consummated Marriages

With the exception of 'unchastity', the early church took it for granted that Jesus had forbidden *any* dissolution of marriage. But there was a passage in St Paul's First Letter to the Corinthians that appeared to allow other exceptions:

> I say, not the Lord, that if any brother has a wife who is an unbeliever, and she consents to live with him, he should not divorce her. If any woman has a husband who is an unbeliever, and he consents to live with her, she should not divorce him. For the unbelieving husband is consecrated through his wife, and the unbelieving wife is consecrated through her husband. Otherwise, your children would be unclean, but as it is they are holy. But if the unbelieving partner desires to separate, let it be so; in such case the brother or sister is not bound. For God has called us to peace.

St Paul was responding to questions put to him by his converts. Pagans had converted. The question underlying the above text may have been, Are newly baptised Christians allowed to stay married to their still pagan partners? Did they *have* to stay married? Paul, like a good diplomat, replies: If the marriage works, leave well alone. It is a real marriage; he speaks of unbelieving spouses as 'husbands and wives'. It is a *good* marriage, for the believer sanctifies the unbeliever. The children too are holy which means the marriage is now sanctified by God. However, if the unbeliever finds his partner's conversion to Christ intolerable and separates, so be it. The believer must not be the first to leave. Paul goes on to say that after a separation, the brother or sister 'is not bound'. Does this mean the deserted Christian has the right to *remarry*?

Augustine, the pioneer of Catholic teaching on marriage, said: Certainly not. Jesus' prohibition on divorce has no exceptions. Even among pagans, marriage forms a bond that no man can sunder. He implied that the deserted Christian must remain faithful to the marriage; should he or she remarry, they commit adultery. The alternative was to suggest that within a few years of the Crucifixion an apostle 'created' a special group of people whose marriage bond was dissoluble. If so, where would it end?

347

In spite of his authority, Augustine's opinion was rejected. In his day, a Roman lawyer, a convert from Judaism called Isaac, took a different line. The fact that Isaac's book on the subject was later attributed to Gregory the Great increased its prestige. Isaac interpreted the apostle's words like this: Paul had in mind a pagan who withdraws from marriage with a converted Christian *out of hatred of God*. The convert is not to blame. He or she simply chose to answer God's call, and if this meant the end of the marriage, so be it. In canonical language, the pagan refused to confirm the marriage after his spouse's conversion. It was contempt of God on the pagan's part that dissolved the marriage, leaving the Christian free to remarry. This came to be called 'The Pauline Privilege'.

Isaac's interpretation raised as many questions as it answered. The casuistry that followed, especially in the Middle Ages, was labyrinthine. What constituted 'hatred of God', of which, incidentally, there is not the slightest trace in St Paul? A deserted believer could remarry. Could a believer who deserted for the good of the faith also have the right to marry again?

The view prevailed that only the Christian who was deserted was entitled to remarry. This found its way into Gratian's *Decretals* to become church law in 1142. Innocent III sanctioned it in his decretal *Quanto te* in the year 1199.

Now *theologians* began to worry the bone. When and how was the original marriage dissolved? Was it dissolved as soon as the pagan walked out? The popular opinion was that it was dissolved only when the deserted partner remarried.

The crucial point was that a pope, the magisterial Innocent III, approved the idea that a *consummated marriage could be dissolved*. Nor was it dissolved by a pope or the hierarchy but by the Christian spouse. A fatal breach had been made in the belief that marriage was absolutely and in all circumstances indissoluble. The reason given was a good one: God's cause outweighed the value of a naturally valid and consummated marriage. But however merciful, it was surely a curious step for the church to take, seeing she still insisted on a *literal* interpretation of Jesus' words. Jesus had spoken without qualification of the irrefragable unity of marriage. If he was 'laying down the law', would it not be logical to say: The deserted convert must remain unmarried to demonstrate the indissolubility of the marriage bond as God envisaged it since time began?

Once the breach was made, new questions rose in an endless stream, not necessarily at once, but inevitably. For instance, if an unbeliever's hatred of God allows a Christian to withdraw from a marriage, why cannot a Christian withdraw from a *Christian* marriage if his spouse becomes an unbeliever and makes a truly Christian life impossible? The church itself was starting the dominoes turning.

It is a little-known fact that two twelfth-century popes before

Innocent III, namely, Urban III and Celestine III, even said that some consummated *Christian* marriages can be dissolved. Celestine took this example. A Christian wife is abandoned by her Christian husband who apostatizes and marries a pagan. She is free, says the pope, to marry again, with her priest's consent. If the husband has second thoughts and wants to return to his first wife, she is not obliged to take him back. Celestine quotes Isaac's book, which he believed was written by Pope Gregory, and argues that the husband's 'hatred of God' has *dissolved the marriage*. This is why the wife is completely free of him. It may come as a surprise to find two medieval popes saying that good reasons exist for dissolving a consummated Christian marriage. In fact they were not the first.

Gregory II was ahead of them. On 22 November 726 he wrote to St Boniface, the apostle of Germany, to decide the fate of a man whose wife was so seriously ill she could not live with him. He ought not to remarry, Gregory II decided, but he was *free* to do so, provided he maintained his first wife.

Catholic commentators from Gratian on have not been pleased to come across a pope who granted a man a divorce because his wife was incapable of having sex. A Jesuit author, Father G. H. Joyce, writes: 'It is reasonable to suppose that it [the pope's letter] concerned a marriage in which, previously to consummation, the bride had been attacked by a disease which made conjugal life impossible.' In other words, it is unthinkable that a pope contradicted the faith of the church, even when he has plainly done so. Gregory II, Joyce says, must have dissolved an unconsummated marriage. Joyce's splendid hypothesis that the wife contracted a disease between marriage and consummation is hard enough to accept. But he also fails to note that dissolution for non-consummation did not come in for another five centuries. Even when it came in, it was only for entry into religious life, not for re-entry into marriage.

It cannot be argued, either, as some have tried to do, that Gregory II was nullifying the marriage owing to the wife's impotence. For Gregory II always insisted that in cases of impotence spouses had to live together as brother and sister. In fact, impotence is another example of the popes, far from agreeing, being at sixes and sevens over several centuries. This is another area in which the idea of papal harmony in teaching is a myth.

Returning to Celestine III's 'heterodox' opinion about dissolving consummated Christian marriages, it is good to point out that his successor, Innocent III, was not perturbed by it. He says, quite evenly, 'Although one of our predecessors seems to have judged otherwise', the marriage of two Christians is life-long and cannot be dissolved by one of them lapsing into unbelief. When a union has been confirmed by intercourse, it cannot be sundered.

Canonists were more nervous than Innocent. To them it was so distasteful to find a pope contradicting the faith of the church that Celestine's views were edited out of the collection of papal decretals a quarter of a century later.

Cajetan, the sixteenth-century Dominican scholar-cardinal who came into direct conflict with Luther, had views similar to pope Celestine's. He taught that consummated Christian marriages can be dissolved because of adultery. Jesus said so. The Eastern church had always said so. If popes did not agree, it did not matter. The popes, Cajetan said, have made mistakes about marriage many times before.

Papal Divorce for the Missions

In the late fifteenth century, as Noonan shows in *Power to Dissolve*, the spread of the church in America began to create new problems. Indian chiefs with several wives were converting. Later, black slaves, who had left their wives behind in their homelands, were becoming Christians; they had no prospect of ever being united with their families. The Catholic church, which prides itself on never having changed its basic principles, certainly adapted them with genius and deep sympathy in this novel situation.

The main question was: Did these converts have to remain celibate, so to speak, and, if not, why not?

Rome's first response was a cautious negative: They must keep faith with their first wife. Then Pope Paul III, asked about chiefs who had several wives, replied that if the chief could not remember which wife came first he could choose whichever one he liked. His decision was of help to Indians with faulty memories.

Thirty years later, Pius V said a chief with several wives, after his conversion, was free to choose the wife who was baptized with him, even if she were not the first. Pius did cover himself by insisting that if the first wife could be found without great difficulty the chief had to stay married to *her*.

Then came Gregory XIII, who in the year 1585 extended papal authority over marriage in a remarkable way. He gave a blanket dispensation to married convert slaves to remarry. Their original unions were true marriages but not so *confirmed* after the slave's baptism as to be indissoluble in all circumstances. He, as pope, was judge of what circumstances permitted divorce. He freely delegated this power to bishops and priests.

This was a huge step forward. It meant that the pope felt able to dissolve a marriage between a believer and an unbeliever. On what grounds? Presumably, for the good of the faith. It was not a case of the Pauline Privilege, when an unbeliever walked out on a Christian. St Paul's text was turned on its head. A Christian was, in a sense, walking out on an unbeliever. This authority to dissolve the natural bond did not come from St Paul, therefore it had to be Christ's; and the pope was the Vicar of Christ. To some canonists, it seemed like Christmas. They greedily started to look for other cases where the pope could grant a divorce.

After 1585, however, the Curia drew in its horns. It was reflection time in the Vatican. They were left in tranquillity because not one of those three extraordinary papal documents on the missions was published. Popes, apparently, did not want the world to know that, behind the scenes, they were busily unmaking marriages, *especially as the state was not allowed to do so*. It is one of those startling facts a historian comes across from time to time. It was not governments but the papacy that reintroduced divorce after it had been outlawed for over four hundred years.

The potential for change was now enormous.

In the beginning, interest centred on converts deserted by their pagan partners: the Pauline Privilege. In the missionary era, Gregory XIII secretly dissolved marriages between pagans and newly converted Christians. What about Christians who had been deserted by their pagan partners? To this question, Rome gave a deafening No.

America's first notable moral theologian, Francis P. Kenrick, later Archbishop of Baltimore in the mid-nineteenth century, was undaunted. He believed that a Christian who had married a pagan and was deserted *was* entitled to remarry. No one shared his view. In response to questions, the Holy Office always said: If a Christian marries a pagan with a church dispensation, the marriage is indissoluble.

However, as the nineteenth century wore on, the secret decrees of Paul III, Pius V and Gregory XIII started to leak out. It began to dawn on canonists what the popes had been up to all this time. If they had power to dissolve unconsummated marriages and marriages between pagans and newly converted Christians, where did the popes' power end?

Divorces Granted by Modern Popes

Leo XIII often denounced divorce. It was born, he said, 'of the perverted morals of a people and leads . . . to vicious habits in public and private life. . . . Once divorce has been allowed, there will not be sufficient means of keeping it in check.' This makes it difficult to understand a decision he made in the year 1894. It was never published in the official *Acta* or *Acts of the Apostolic See*. This was the case.

Two Jews, Isaac and Rebecca, married and divorced. Rebecca became a Catholic, while Isaac married a Catholic named Antonia in a civil ceremony. Next, Isaac wanted to become a Catholic in order to regularize his union with Antonia in the eyes of her church. On 23 May 1894, Leo XIII, stern opponent of divorce, simply divorced Isaac and Rebecca. This astounding case was, wisely, kept under wraps for forty years.

In 1917 the three missionary documents of Paul III, Pius V and Gregory XIII, were printed as an appendix to the new code of canon law. These once private exceptions granted in view of an emergency in the New World suddenly were part of the general law of the church. Canonists found in them possibilities they had not dreamed of before. For example, could not the pope even dissolve the marriage of two non-Catholics, say of a Protestant and a Jew?

Out of the blue, a pope *did* dissolve a marriage between a Protestant and a Jew. The Protestant was already baptized when she married, so there was no question of appealing to the Pauline Privilege. She wanted to become a Catholic and marry a Catholic. Pope Pius IX, in a historic decision, dissolved her first marriage in April 1924. Three months later, with the bit between his teeth, he dissolved the marriage of a Protestant and a pagan. It was the third case that caused the most commotion.

In 1922, Gerard G. Marsh, unbaptized, petitioned the Bishop of Helena, Montana, John P. Carroll. Three years before, he had married an Anglican. Their marriage had ended in the divorce court, and his former wife had remarried. Marsh fell in love with a Catholic, with the Tennessee Williams-type name of Lulu La Hood, and expressed a desire to convert. Bishop Carroll, not up-to-date in canon law, applied to Rome to see if Marsh's first marriage could be *annulled* on the grounds of disparity of cult. The new 1917 code said plainly that in his case these were no longer grounds for annulment. The Holy Office, ignoring the reasoning in the bishop's plea, changed it to a petition to the pope to *dissolve* the marriage in favour of the faith.

On 6 November 1924, Pius XI gave Marsh a divorce. There was no mention in the rescript that it depended on Marsh becoming a Catholic. To the canonists' astonishment, the pope had simply broken up the first marriage. A valid, binding, naturally indissoluble marriage had simply been severed by the say-so of Pius XI.

Four years later, at the time of the Lateran Treaty, the same pontiff got Mussolini to pledge that civil divorce would be outlawed in Italy. The year after that, *Casti connubii* was published in which, apart from condemning contraception, Pius XI thundered against divorce.

> The advocates of neo-paganism today . . . continue
> by legislation to attack the indissolubility of the
> marriage bond, proclaiming that the lawfulness of
> divorce must be recognized and that the antiquated
> laws should give place to a new and more humane

legislation. . . . Opposed to all these reckless opinions stands the unaltered law of God, fully confirmed by Christ. . . . What God hath joined together let no man put asunder. . . . These words refer to every kind of marriage, even that which is natural and legitimate only; for . . . that indissolubility by which the loosening of the bond is once and for all removed from the whim of the parties and from every secular power, is a property of every true marriage.

This from a man who was in the divorce-granting business himself. His loftiness rivals that of medieval pontiffs like Gregory VII or Boniface VIII. No one on earth can sunder even the most intolerable marriage. But the pope can, for he, raised far above all secular governments, the only man in the world whom God can trust on such a sensitive issue, acts on God's behalf and for the good of God's church.

This pontiff, who disclaimed any power to alter the 'tradition' on birth control, had made a radical change in the nature of marriage and divorce. The code came out in 1917. Within four years, he went far beyond the code and, to a Catholic world totally unprepared for it, dissolved consummated marriages between Christians and non-Christians. No theologian had asked him to do this. For two hundred years the Holy Office had stolidly denied that a pontiff could do this. Pius XI – was it kindheartedness, a desire to flex his papal muscles, sheer ignorance? – simply did it.

To the Pauline Privilege was now added the Petrine Privilege. The latter was so broad in scope that it simply made the former redundant. Canonists, with their marvellous flair for hypotheses, were to say that St Paul must have checked with St Peter. Peter must have ratified Paul's privilege, since it was but part of a far more extensive power which he, Peter, and his pope-successors, have to dissolve marriages. One wonders whether Paul got it in writing.

Pius XI, like many a pope before him, had shown himself capable of squaring the circle. He had dissolved what he himself called the indissoluble, he had made the perpetual temporary, simply 'for the good of souls', very generously interpreted. Marsh, after all, was not a Catholic; the rescript dissolving his first marriage did not say he had to promise to convert. The 'good' the pope had in mind was that of his second (Catholic) wife.

Four years after *Casti connubii*, Pius XI agreed 'Norms for the Dissolution of Marriage in Favour of the Faith by the Supreme Authority of the Sovereign Pontiff'. The conditions for a papal divorce were simple. One party was unbaptized and the original couple had not had sex *after* the non-Christian was baptized. With these provisos, the pope

353

was prepared to nod through whole batches of divorce cases presented to him by a curial aide.

Not that Rome came clean on the matter. The norms were not made public. Only those in the know could benefit from them. It needed a whisper in the Vatican's best conspiratorial manner. The pope's fear, perfectly justified, was that he would seem to be far less opposed to divorce than the fulminations of his encyclical made out. Besides, Rome liked to keep up the pretence that the Holy Father only granted divorce as a favour (or privilege). Favours do not *have* to be granted. The popular view that palms in Rome are so greased they are positively slippery is almost completely false. Far worse than incidental graft and corruption is a system of favours only procurable through a wink and a nudge. A thousand favours are no substitute for one just *law*.

It has to be said that Pius XI's new norms worked for no other reason than that civil divorce was already in place. Christendom no longer existed. After eight hundred years, ecclesiastical and civil laws on marriage went their own way, apart from countries like Italy where Mussolini and Pius XI had a working relationship. Marriages were dissolved in civil courts in ever increasing numbers. In spite of protests to the contrary, the church herself benefited from this.

In the matter of divorce, the state had done the church's 'dirty work' for it. It had made divorce respectable. It had also taken care of legal details, such as property and inheritance. The church never had to take the initiative or grant a divorce in the first instance. She appeared to be simply sorting out the sacramental consequences, without encouraging or condoning divorce. In this, too, the church showed her usual genius at adaptation, even if an element of hypocrisy was present. Instead of thanking the state, popes uniformly accused governments of doing the devil's work. In the Vatican the pope went quietly on granting divorces of his own.

With the 1934 norms, there was a perceptible speeding up of divorce and remarriage within the church. In Rome, the conviction was growing that the pope's power was as wide as the Almighty's. All peoples, Christians as well as non-Christians, were subject to him in the realm of marriage.

Pius XII confirmed this two years after his election. In October 1941, he gave an allocution to the Rota, the Rome Marriage Tribunal. Over the normal consummated Christian marriage, he said, he exercised his fatherly protection. Every other form of marriage was 'intrinsically indissoluble'. Did that mean that no one could dissolve them? Not quite. *He* could. Was he not vicar of Christ on earth?

He developed this theme in his 1942 encyclical *Mystici Corporis*. He quoted the Bull *Unam Sanctam* to the effect that Christ and the pope are one as head of the church. It might be thought that Pius XII would have distanced himself from a monster like Boniface VIII. He does not claim to have two swords at his disposal; the temporal power had passed away, which, we have seen, numberless popes said was theologically impossible. Pius does, however, follow Boniface in claiming that *he rules the whole world*, at least to the extent of having dominion over *all marriages*. As Christ's vicar, he can, if need be, dissolve these marriages for the salvation of souls.

Seven years into his pontificate, Pius received a petition from the Bishop of Monterey-Fresno, California. This was the first of three epoch-making cases Bishop Willinger was to forward to Rome.

An unbaptized woman had married a Catholic. The latter had got a dispensation from disparity of cult. This was normal procedure and cost a trifle. The pair were married before a priest and two witnesses. Later the woman divorced her Catholic husband, but having, it seemed, a liking for Catholics she married another in a civil ceremony. Now *she* was hoping to become a Catholic. She did not appear to have a hope.

The serene Bishop Willinger asked Rome to regularize the second union. He offered as grounds that the first marriage could be nullified because it was not consummated. That lowered the odds considerably. Only, according to Rome's strict rules, non-consummation could not be proved. Again, it looked hopeless. That was until the Holy Office changed the Bishop's plea, recommending that the Holy Father *dissolve* the marriage in favour of the faith. This Pius XII did on 17 July 1947. He granted a divorce to the unbelieving partner of a marriage to a Catholic, a marriage celebrated with a dispensation and presumably consummated. Canon law had never contemplated such a thing.

Three years on, Bishop Willinger chanced his luck again. He enquired in a similar case if, on dissolution, not only the prospective convert could remarry but her original Catholic husband, too. On 4 May 1950 the reply came: Affirmative.

Willinger, convinced he was on a winning streak, proceeded to put a third case to Rome. He asked for a marriage between a Catholic and an unbaptized person to be dissolved on the petition of the *Catholic* party. This was quite new.

The Catholic was Alfred Cinelli of Bakersfield, California. He had married Elinor Robbins, first in a civil ceremony, then in church with the required dispensation. On returning from war service overseas, he found his wife had cooled towards him. In April 1946 she divorced him and remarried. Cinelli wanted to marry a would-be convert. Bishop Willinger supported him, pleading eloquently that the faith of a convert was at stake, and the faith of children to be born, and the said Cinelli was of good Catholic stock, Italian like the Holy Father, and no one would be scandalized in the slightest; on the contrary, everyone would applaud the church's great benignity. In brief, he paraded all the reasons that church Fathers, theologians and centuries of popes had unanimously turned down as grounds for divorce.

On 23 January 1955, Pius XII dissolved the first marriage. The Petrine Privilege had been exercised in a way unthinkable even one generation earlier.

In the late 1950s other dioceses jumped on the bandwagon set in motion by Monterey-Fresno. In countries like the United States of America, where there were many unbaptized people and divorce was reaching epidemic proportions, petitions rained in. So much so that the American hierarchy took fright and warned Rome that the wrong impression – or was it the right impression? – was being given that Rome actively favoured divorce, at least in certain circumstances. Rome told them not to worry. Meantime, the Petrine Privilege now had its own application form and, of course, its own (modest) fee.

For the first thousand years, no pope had endorsed the rare case of the Pauline Privilege. It took four more centuries for the pope to dissolve the marriages of Indians and American slaves. Another three and a half centuries passed before this power to dissolve marriages entered the code of canon law in 1917. Thirty years after that, the Bishop of Fresno waged his own campaign to increase the scope of papal divorces. And only three years after Cinelli got his divorce from the pope came the ultimate – or the penultimate, according to one's theological point of view – divorce.

No pope had ever divorced two complete unbelievers. In 1957 it happened. On 12 March in that year Pius XII dissolved the marriage of two Muhammadans. The girl, having divorced civilly, took custody of the child. Her husband went to France where he married in a register office, his bride being a Catholic. He was a prospective convert. The Holy Office, under the direction of Cardinal Ottaviani, recommended the Petrine Privilege – it took less time than the Pauline Privilege. Pius XII dissolved that marriage as he was later to dissolve five others that involved no Christian party. He really *did* walk in the footsteps of Boniface VIII.

John XXIII followed suit. By now it was established that the term 'in favour of the faith' was so broad that it included any spiritual benefit to be gained from divorce.

Paul VI took time off from writing *Humanae Vitae* to grant a divorce to two Jews from Chicago on 7 February 1964. The husband, having divorced his wife, had married a Catholic. He had no wish to convert; he was quite honest about that. He simply wanted to put his new wife's mind at rest. Archbishop Meyer backed his petition to regularize his union. The early church would have said that any marriage between a Catholic and a Jew was a crime and a sacrilege; as to a second marriage. . . . But Paul VI was moved to pity. He showed the Catholic girl the compassion he felt unable in conscience to extend to millions who were suffering from the ban on contraceptives. That, in granting a divorce, he was contradicting a hundred pontiffs did not worry him. If Pius XII said it was all right, it was all right by him. Once more, he selected carefully the popes whom he agreed with.

Through all these changes, the most momentous being the most recent, the church adapted to novel situations. Something had to be done about converts in the New World who had been nurtured in societal structures alien to Christianity, and she did it. In modern times, she adapted to the fact of widespread civil divorce by granting divorces of her own and on her own terms, usually in the form of 'carrots for converts' or solace for their Catholic partners. These practices prompt the question: Why is the church not more honest and consistent? If she still takes Jesus' teaching literally, why not insist that prospective converts previously married should remain celibate like, say, abandoned Catholic partners of a Christian and consummated marriage? Or, to turn the question on its head, why punish only born Catholics?

By continuing to treat the Sermon on the Mount as a piece of legislation, the church has only been tinkering with a problem of alarming magnitude. She keeps up the pretence that she is wholly against the dissolution of marriage, that she will not tolerate it under any circumstances, that governments are doing something unspeakably evil in allowing divorce. While she, meanwhile, is chipping away at her 'rules' in order to try without success to keep pace with secular society.

By failing to legislate sensibly, by making all divorces a 'favour' – worse, the favour of *one man* – she has bred a special class of curial lawyers, good minds engaged in trivial pursuits. Watching them at work is like seeing eels wrestling. Far from being biased in favour of the rich and powerful, as is often alleged, they are not really interested in human beings at all. It is principles and their applications that they care about. It is not their fault that the job they do is often preposterous.

They may be obliged to read the evidence of witnesses who claim to remember with angelic clarity incidents that occurred over thirty years ago. Witnesses' memories mature with the years like wine, for frequently they function better a decade after their first testimony. Curial officials have to read or listen politely as Italian petitioners assemble their entire *famiglia* – brothers, sisters, parents, grandparents, uncles, aunts, wet-nurse, cousins several times removed, former lovers, lovers of former lovers – all loyally perjuring themselves to help one of their own out of a matrimonial tangle. A petitioner, in true Dickensian style, has often begun a case when a young man, grown old in it, died out of it. Some cases, owing to retrials, have been before the Curia for twenty to thirty years.

And, as Noonan has pointed out, in no instance is it recorded that any marriage benefited from the labours of the Curia. No one petitioning for an annulment of his first marriage has ever gone back to his first wife. In the whole sorry process, the rules of marriage may have been clarified, but marriage itself has never benefited.

In opposition to the Gospel of Jesus, the rules dictate everything. No sooner did Rome grant dispensations than they, too, became integral to the crazy process. To disputes about valid marriages were added disputes about valid dispensations. Did the petitioners get the correct dispensation? If someone applied for it on their behalf without telling them, was it valid or not?

Today, a vast number of enquiries into marriage end up as enquiries into the parties' baptism! It makes a big difference whether a party was baptized a Catholic. Even if someone was brought up as a non-Catholic or an atheist, the mere fact of being baptized by a Catholic priest means he is subject to church legislation. If, therefore, this person did not marry before his parish priest and two witnesses, his marriage was invalid. Every little twist and turn of legislation opens up new fields of complexity.

The canonists who run this system in the name of the pontiff are more to be pitied than blamed. What makes their lot even sadder is that not so long ago lawyers worked for twenty or more years before getting a negative response to a case that a modern pope will dissolve with a nod.

Most if not all these time-wasting and capricious procedures could be discarded, if only the Catholic church accepted that some marriages break down. If, after counselling, it is as plain as St Peter's that they have broken down irreparably, divorce should be granted as the only decent and Christian solution.

Even Rome's divorces are subject to endless nit-picking. And the strange thing is that only Christians who marry and consummate their union cannot benefit from the church's new-found generosity.

Yet here, too, there have been great strides forward.

When a Divorce Is Not a Divorce

Modern popes, unlike Gregory II and Celestine III, have said over and over that no power in heaven or on earth can dissolve a consummated Christian marriage. The bodily union of two Christians has been sealed by a sacrament. It is the living embodiment of the love of Christ and his church. Without matrimony, the church could not continue to give witness to Christ and the unfailing character of his love.

It is a splendid ideal: children, indissolubility, fidelity. The church must always preach this, for failing to do so would be a grave loss to the church and mankind.

Unfortunately, everyone knows life does not always allow the realization of the ideal. Failure is often no one's fault.

A young couple, childhood sweethearts, marry, pledging one another lasting love. Within a year, the lad has tired of his wife and gone off to seek pastures new. The deserted girl has to make a life for herself. The church says she is still married to her departed husband. Most people, Catholics included, believe she should be encouraged to marry again.

Catholics, appreciating the church's discipline, do not seek a divorce when their marriages fail. Some, like Henry VIII, petition for an annulment. Here, too, the potential for casuistry is considerable.

Marriage, says the church, is primarily for children. What if one or other of the partners does not intend having children? That would seemingly nullify a marriage. But would that partner have to state *expressly* that he or she did not want children? Or would a marriage be null if one of them *privately* resolved to exclude children?

This issue has grown in importance with the spread of contraceptives. Does the use of them, or even the permanent use of the safe period, prove an unwillingness to have children contrary to the first aim of marriage? Consummation, moralists say, requires *penetratio* and *inseminatio*. If contraceptives have always been used, can the marriage be anulled, even after frequent intercourse, on the grounds of non-consummation?

Problems, too, with indissolubility. Maybe one of the partners never intended to marry 'till death us do part'. Would an express decision not to wed for life nullify the marriage? Would an *implied* decision have that effect?

Problems with fidelity. Would the church consider it a true marriage if one partner, at the time of the wedding, was having an affair with someone else? Or if a man said expressly to a friend that if his wife did not prove faithful he would divorce her?

The questions are endless, as are the possibilities of manipulating the rules, with the aid of a canon lawyer.

Apart from intention, there is the matter of consent. Not even God can supply consent if one of the parties internally withholds it or is coerced into it. But what constitutes coercion? Doesn't it depend on the person coerced?

In recent times, it is mostly the young and impressionable who plead coercion. A famous American case involved Consuela Vanderbilt, who wed Charles Spencer, Duke of Marlborough in 1916. After ten years of marriage, blessed by two children, she asked Rome to annul her union on the grounds that her mother had pressurized her into it. The public was astonished to hear of Pius XI annulling a marriage entered into by two Protestants before a Protestant bishop. Manning, Episcopal Bishop of New York, called Rome's decision an 'amazing and incredible' attack upon 'the sacredness and permanence of marriage'.

In parts of Italy and Spain today, matters are more contrived. It is not unknown for the well-to-do, prior to the wedding, to write letters, at their lawyer's dictation, alleging coercion or implying some defect in intention. These letters are kept in a safe just in case the marriage is not a success.

For centuries after Innocent III, the church took it for granted that everyone getting married gave proper consent and had the right intention. What were they doing, after all, but obeying the dictates of nature? Since the 1917 code, these presumptions have been questioned. Canonists have become increasingly aware that the prayers of the wedding ceremony are not matched by the mind and will of the parties. Until recently, a spouse applying for a nullity had to show that, in front of two reliable witnesses, he expressly denied that he was marrying for life. Today, this denial might be *inferred* from his beliefs, the beliefs of his family and community, his behaviour prior to marriage and immediately after.

It was a big step when the church began to accept, however cautiously, that in many cultures the parties probably do not have the right intention to contract a marriage. How many today, for example, pledge themselves to an exclusive and lifelong love? The old natural-law assumptions of the church are being exploded and on a global scale.

From the decretal *Gaudemus* of Innocent III in the year 1202, the church has balked at the inevitable consequences of her teaching, namely, that most weddings are *not* marriages in *her* sense. If she insists that every valid marriage must have the goods of offspring, indissolubility and fidelity, she should reconcile herself to the fact that most modern marriages are null and void.

Take China where there is a strict policy of family-limitation. Most couples are allowed only one child. It is undeniable that by strict Catholic principles there are virtually *no marriages in China*, and therefore no God-given graces for their unions. But one does not have to travel so far afield. In the West the express belief of most people is that it is wrong for couples to go on living together where there is no bond of affection. In their eyes, it is continuance in such a union, not divorce, that is the sin. This denial of tenets fundamental to Christian marriage *has* affected canonical practice both in Rome and in the dioceses that deal in the first instance with problem marriages.

Catholics are inevitably part and parcel of their culture. They share its presuppositions, its standards and aspirations. And these are inconsistent with the tradition of Christian marriage.

It takes little investigation to find that the church's norms, far from reflecting the beliefs of the world community, do not even reflect the *real* beliefs of most of her own children.

It is when divorced Catholics apply to Rome to have their marriages *annulled* that the suspicion arises that the church allows divorce *under another name*. It is well known that many Catholic couples are being granted ecclesiastical annulments after, say, twenty years together and half a dozen children. How to account for this phenomenon, especially when, prior to marrying, a priest took them carefully through what the church *means* by a true marriage?

On the face of it, it looks as if the marriage was real enough; it is the annulment that is a fiction. In order to be free of a partner whom they no longer love, they are obliged to pretend that they were never married at all, that they have lived in sin all this while and their children are all illegitimate in the eyes of God. How can an ecclesiastical court declare such a profound reality a *nullity*? It requires not a little subtlety and suggests some grave defect in the law that allows these almost clownish exceptions.

The reasons justifying annulments are many but they all have in common the discovery of some 'defect'. It may be a defect of consent: there was fear or force employed. Or a defect in intention in one or other of the parties, expressed openly or in only the most veiled and fragmentary way. Or a defect can be interpreted from their subsequent behaviour. In brief, Catholic marriages also yield to evidence of some vital element lacking at the time of the wedding but only showing up later, sometimes much later. In particular, the courts in Rome and in local dioceses, using a wide discretion, seem to agree that the necessary lifelong commitment, even for Catholics, is far from universal.

The Catholic church is now getting the worst of most worlds.

Having begun by transforming Jesus' teaching on the ideal of marriage into an iron law prohibiting divorce, then relaxing that iron rule for practically everyone but her own children, she is finding that even for them it is not satisfactory in the present fluid state of society. Catholics are themselves complaining bitterly that 'the church', meaning the celibate priesthood headed by the pope, does not understand them or their problems. The ideal of marriage, they say, should not be used to crush married people and make them into celibates, to turn the bond into a bondage, when the union is plainly and permanently over. Marriage was to put an end to loneliness not to perpetuate it by forbidding couples to remarry. How can the church force a man or woman to be forever alone, for the sake of marriage? This is to repeat Christ's words without Christ's spirit. If freedom is of the essence of marriage and compulsion would annul it, does not compulsion dissolve it? The purpose of marriage is for two helpmates to live in a communion of love. When it happens, often through no one's fault, that this communion is impossible, the marriage has ceased to exist. Without love, the couple would not be two in one flesh but, in Milton's phrase, 'two carcasses chained unnaturally together'. How could the celibate clergy know that marriage can divide and destroy as well as unite? The final question that springs straight from the Bible is: Was marriage made for man, or man for marriage?

As has been shown, the church *has* changed, and more radically in this century than in any other. But it has taken the form of tinkering with the system. She has refused to rethink it on the grand scale required by new understanding of the Bible, psychology, sociology, as well as moral theology.

The strains upon the Catholic system are now prodigious. Its norms of marriage are fast resembling the rules of English grammar: everything is an exception to the rule. More and more Catholic couples are pleading that they qualify as exceptions. Divorces among them are about average, as is to be expected. In past ages and under different social set-ups, marriages united whole families and clans. Today, marriages usually bond together two solitary people. Once they fall out, there is nothing left. With their break-up, the thing falls apart.

It has been estimated that the number of American Catholics involved in broken marriages exceeds 10 million. It would be absurd to try to treat even American cases as though they were all possible candidates for nullity, requiring endless research into reasons that might prove they never were marriages in the first place. Moreover, even in the church, the idea is growing that nullities are divorces by another name.

John Paul II himself seems to share this fear. In his solemn Address to the Rota on 5 February 1987, he said that marriages were being broken on the plea of nullity of which there was an 'exaggerated and almost automatic increase'. It was due, he said disparagingly, to the influence of psychological experts whose point of view is often irreconcilable with church teaching. Such leniency, he said, increases marriage break-up. 'The principle must remain clear that only incapacity and not just difficulty in agreeing to and realizing a real community of life and love can render a marriage null.' But who is to judge when a difficulty is an impossibility? Canonists? The pope himself?

Meanwhile, Catholics, loyal in every other respect, are outlawed by the church they love; and their children are left wondering why Daddy and Mummy do not receive communion with them. These Catholics are left pondering ruefully why they were so unfortunate as to be baptized in the church. If only they had converted *after* their first marriage, they might have been able to remarry in the church. Why does the church persecute its own? Above all, they demand a rationale for why they cannot be divorced by the church, when even some popes said they could. As with contraception, so with divorce, in the absence of satisfying reasons for the ban, why should they think of themselves as sinners?

The Final Papal Divorce

It is taken for granted in Catholic circles that Rome is irrevocably committed to never allowing Christians to divorce and remarry after a consummated marriage. History would suggest, on the contrary, that it is only a question of time before the change occurs, though *when* and the form it will take cannot be predicted. In any case, it is always dangerous with any institution, most of all one with the genius of Rome, to say Never.

We have seen already that by permitting the use of the safe period Rome has recently approved something completely opposed to tradition: the dissociation of sex and procreation. From Augustine and Pope Gregory onwards, this would have been called a mortal sin. Such authorities would also have judged it unthinkable that popes could allow mixed marriages, the divorce of non-consummated marriages, divorce of consummated marriages where one partner is not a Catholic. Pope John Paul II does not seem to be aware of how many of the things that *he* says would have been condemned by his predecessors at the beginning of *this* century.

For instance, in his regular Wednesday audiences between 5 August 1979 and 21 May 1980, the pontiff gave a series of addresses on love and sexuality. In one of them, he distinguished, in the Book of Genesis, two literary strands. In the first of them, called J, God is referred to as Yahweh; in the second, a later strand called E, God is referred to in the plural Hebrew word Elohim. Pius X would have condemned him and taken from him his title of Catholic theologian for that. The Holy Office insisted that Moses wrote the whole of the Pentateuch.

In another address, John Paul spoke in glowing terms of the propriety of 'sexual ecstasy', provided the marriage act was performed without contraceptives. Yet for over fifteen hundred years pope after pope, far from approving ecstasy in sex, said it was always in all circumstances a sin. If only the present pontiff would reflect more on the history of the papacy before he speaks of 'eternal truths' and the 'unalterable law of God' made known through the successors of St Peter.

In view of the tremendous changes made by the church in marriage even in this century, who is to say that one day the Catholic church, too, will not broaden her discipline to allow divorce between Christians? The Council of Trent left the question open, and no Council or pope has yet closed it. The Orthodox and other churches remain as a kind of beacon, pointing to a more biblical approach to the problem of marital breakdown.

It is clear that the present rumpus in the church of Rome is not going to subside. Things will get much worse before they get better. The piecemeal annulments of marriages, many of which by any standards were real marriages, is not only inadequate, it has had a harmful effect on the church's morale.

The rationale for divorce will take time to work out, as it took time to work out the rationale of mixed marriages and divorce for other kinds of marriages. As a first step, Catholics who have divorced and remarried in civil ceremonies might be allowed to follow their conscience and return to the sacraments. In fact, many priests world-wide are already advising divorced Catholics to receive communion without a sense of guilt. Bishops know it and say nothing. It is, in any case, in keeping with the spirit of Vatican II to leave couples free to make their own decision about the rightness or wrongness of their lifestyle. If they are aware of having sinned, they might be asked to do penance for a time before receiving communion, as was done in the early church. For their second marriage, the Tridentine law that demands an exchange of consent before a priest and two witnesses would have to be waived. This legislation is, in historical terms, of only recent origin anyway. The second marriage would be deemed to have dissolved the first officially, just as some popes said, with far less justification, that the vows of religion dissolved a monk's marriage. Another advantage of this approach is that the pope would not be asked to divorce individual Catholics – they run into many millions – who have divorced civilly and remarried. Besides, the clergy could not cope with the avalanche; they would be officiating at weddings all day for months on end.

Later on, when the Catholic church, like other churches, has grown accustomed to divorce, the matter can be made more canonically precise. The overriding consideration must be that the millions of Catholics worldwide now barred from the sacraments should be allowed to return, for their own sake and for the good example of their children. Why does the church risk millions of children giving up Catholicism by refusing to grant their parents what the Orthodox and other Christian churches grant their followers, with no noticeable disarray? Once the myth of 'unchangeableness' is exploded, and Catholics realize just how much the church has changed in response to social needs over the ages, the dissolution of Christian marriage will not seem so astonishing.

If the church has learned anything from the *Humanae Vitae* débâcle, it is that matters of great moment cannot be left in the hands of one man, however eminent. It is the task of the whole church, clergy and laity, freely and fearlessly discussing what they really believe.

It has to be said, with respect, that John Paul's record suggests that none of this will happen in his pontificate. For the time being, therefore, Catholic divorce will have to be bracketed with contraception as 'contrary to the eternal law of God'. In the same category will be found the thorniest subject of all: abortion.

NINETEEN

The Silent Holocaust

TWO IMAGES CRYSTALLIZE a violent clash of opinion. A Catholic doctor exhibits a developed foetus in a jar; the foetus shows all the features of a tiny but unmistakably human being. *This*, he says passionately, is what abortion is really about, the murder of this baby.

His opponent, a woman, no less passionate, holds up a metal coat-hanger. *This*, she says, is what killed a woman when abortion was a criminal offence. Do we want to return to the dark old days when women had to resort to backstreet butchers? And why? Simply to avail themselves of a basic woman's right *not* to become a mother.

Abortion is the subject of the most polarized and agonizing debate in modern times. Popes, representing the Catholic church, teach that abortion cannot be justified under any circumstances; it is always the direct killing of an innocent child in the womb. At the other extreme are those who say abortion is the arbitrary choice of the mother; there is *no* child in the womb, only a potential child.

Popes stress that all life, from conception, is a sacred gift of God; in the first miraculous moment a human being is present whom God creates and loves and has destined for eternal life. Those at the opposite pole retort that what is in the woman is nothing more than foetal tissue; she may rid herself of it as serenely as she would have plastic surgery to improve the shape of her nose. It is *her* body, after all. Who has the right to condemn her to nine months hard labour? As Stella Brown said back in 1915: 'Woman's right to abortion is an absolute right. Abortion should be available for any woman without insolent inquisitions or ruinous financial charges, for our bodies are our own.'

According to recent polls, most people who reflect on this topic seem to take up the middle ground. They reject absolutes, they dislike extremes. Abortion is not always wrong, for there are clear indications that would permit a woman to abort. On the other hand, the content of the woman's womb is nòt *just* tissue; it is in some sense sacred. It should not, therefore, be disposed of without great thought and moral anguish.

A New Feeling for Life

From the beginning, Christianity brought into the world a new respect and reverence for life in all its stages. The New Testament contributed to this with texts such as the child leaping for joy in Elizabeth's womb when Mary came to visit her.

For Greeks and Romans, abortion and infanticide were an everyday occurrence. The ancients, in general, had no deep feelings for the early stages of pregnancy. This is partly explained by the fact that many thought that a being was not human until he drew his first breath. Aristotle looked on abortion as a necessity when population exceeded reasonable limits.

Abortion manuals abounded, and there were professional practitioners. The embryo could be destroyed by purging the abdomen, by vigorous exercise, by bathing in various concoctions, by the woman being bled, by the use of suppositories, by deadly drugs, by sharp instruments. Women submitted to this for many reasons: because their life was in danger, to hide their adultery, because they did not want to lose their figure. The wrongness of abortion was never grievous.

Christianity, said Lecky, did mankind a great service when it 'definitely and dogmatically asserted the sinfulness of all destruction of human life as a matter of amusement or of simple convenience, and thereby formed a new standard, higher than any which then existed in the world'.

'Thou shalt love thy neighbour as thyself' applied first of all to the little neighbour next to the mother's heart.

The church's ban on abortion was reinforced by its teaching on original sin but not created by it. If salvation depended on baptism, it was obviously more than murder to kill a child in the womb; it was, in a sense, to kill it for ever. That is why abortion was considered an almost unforgivable sin. The penances imposed for it were severe, in some cases exclusion for life from the sacraments. It was considered more wicked to abort a foetus than to kill a child already born and baptized.

Modern popes look upon themselves as upholders of this great tradition. In *Casti connubii*, Pius XI said:

> We may pity the mother whose health and even life is gravely imperilled in the performance of the duty allotted to her by nature, nevertheless what could ever be sufficient reason for excusing in any way the direct murder of the innocent?

Twenty-one years later, in 1951, Pius XII said:

> Innocent human life, in whatever condition it may be, is from the first instant of its existence, to be

preserved from any direct voluntary attack. This is a fundamental right of the human person, of general value in the Christian conception of life; valid both for the life still hidden in the mother's womb and for the life that has already left it; equally so against the causing of abortion and the direct killing of the child before, during and after birth.

On his visits abroad, John Paul never loses the opportunity of repeating the same message. In the United States of America, where abortion has been declared the constitutional right of every woman, he insisted on the sacredness of life in the mother's womb; the foetal child has as much right to life as the mother or children already born. On his first American tour in 1979, in front of the Mall in Washington, he stressed one of the main themes of his pontificate: the sacredness of life 'from the first moment of conception and through all subsequent stages'. Because of Christ, all human life has been redeemed. Therefore, 'all human beings (those in the womb, too) . . . are called to be a brother or sister of Christ by reason of the Incarnation and the universal redemption'.

Since 1979, whenever John Paul has spoken about abortion, he has witnessed to a consuming fire within him. He believes with every fibre of his being that this is the issue that will decide whether our generation has the right to consider itself civilized or not. He constantly repeats an idea that he developed long before he became pontiff. Opponents of abortion are in the front line of the battle against the new paganism; they are fighting for the dignity of man and the sacredness of all life from the first speck in the womb to the last flickering breath of an aged and dying man. Wherever respect for life is breached, the Christian message is threatened in its entirety. That message is of God's love for everyone, however frail and sick and insignificant such a one may seem. This is why he shows a special love for children *and* the old and ailing. This is the domino theory applied at the most sacred level of life. Contraception leads to abortion leads to infanticide leads to euthanasia. It is all of a piece: wasting seed in sexual intercourse must lead, by a cruel logic, to killing with however merciful an intent the handicapped and the elderly who cannot 'contribute', who are a drain on resources. He thinks back to his earlier days in Cracow, so close to Auschwitz. He cannot but see that abortion clinics in New York and London, Paris and Amsterdam are nothing more or less than little death-camps, hygienically run – but, then, was not Auschwitz a model of efficiency?

A Radical Change of Attitude

Beyond doubt, present attitudes to abortion point to one of the most amazing ethical reversals in the history of morals. As late as 1939, there was not a single country in the world where a woman could freely choose to have an abortion, though certain exceptions did exist. For instance, in Catholic Poland a 1932 law allowed abortion to safeguard the woman's health after rape or incest. Lecky and other late-nineteenth-century moralists would not have believed the current transformation possible. Even prior to 1960, moralists would have found today's scene reminiscent of the Greco-Roman world before it was influenced by Christianity. Twenty centuries after Christ, women are once again being aborted because it will ruin their holiday or their figure. The popes are not alone in believing that this is the great scandal of the age.

From being a crime punishable by law, abortion is now a right enshrined in laws and constitutions. In some countries, it is subsidized by taxpayers' money. Gone is the stigma. Women who abort are doing the community a service, especially if they refuse to bring a handicapped baby into the world. The community is saved billions a year on medical services, schools, disability grants. The poor benefit most; they are not born. Hunger is eliminated by killing off the potentially hungry. Those who lobby for abortion on demand pose as philanthropists.

Many in our society are worried that the child, once seen as a blessing of God, is too often regarded as a menace, a blight on family happiness. Not so long ago, the state was willing to protect the unborn at almost any cost; now the unborn is freely disposable. 'If your foetus offend thee, pluck it out.' The great archetype of care and concern, a mother's love for her child, has been undermined and cheapened. Reverence has been replaced by hard-nosed calculations. There is a plague of death, a silent holocaust, a massacre of the innocents beyond Herod's wildest imaginings. There are 2 million aborted each year in Japan and America together, and perhaps as many as 800,000 in Italy. According to Colin Francome in *Abortion Freedom*, it is estimated that there are 55 million abortions a year worldwide.

Abortion is often used as a means of family planning. Vast numbers of women of all ages are going into hospital in order *not* to have a baby. The womb has become more dangerous than a war zone. In the United States of America more babies die in the womb annually than military personnel died in the Vietnam War, than are killed in road accidents. Annually a carnage equivalent to the battle of the Somme or the eight years of the Iran–Iraq conflict occurs in the quiet operating rooms of expensive clinics. In some cities, abortion is such big business that elementary mistakes are made. Women are 'aborted' who are not even pregnant. And doctors are becoming millionaires by dealing out death. Traditional guardians of life and health, they spend their entire careers killing. The prodigious change in feeling among ordinary people is due to the fact that it is no longer butchers who abort but surgeons in white coats and surgical masks. It is reported that, after aborting hundreds of foetuses a year, many of them suffer harmful psychological effects.

Aborted foetuses are sometimes sold for experimentation or for health and beauty products. This blackest of black markets reminds many of how, quite recently, Nazis were turning Jews into bars of soap. In some circles, reaction to this suffers from a lack of logic. The high-minded disapprove of experimenting on foetuses for medical research but have no qualms about destroying foetuses in the womb to the benefit of no one but perhaps a perfectly healthy mother. If the foetus is human, should it not be reverenced and held sacred? If it is subhuman, mere disposable tissue, why cannot it be bought and sold or experimented on or turned into face cream? The fact is that it is only useful for these purposes because it *is* specifically human.

Another anomaly: at a time when pregnant women are warned by the medical profession not to smoke, drink or take drugs, in case they harm their babies, they are given the legal freedom to destroy them, more or less as they please. At a time when those born handicapped are treated with great consideration, society allows those who will or might be born handicapped to be killed in the womb. An implicit message is delivered to the disadvantaged: 'If your condition had been diagnosed earlier, we would have disposed of *you*.' Of the handicapped, society seems to say what Jesus said of Judas: 'It were better if he had never been born.' It would probably be safer and make more medical sense if all foetuses were allowed to come to full term and the handicapped were *then* killed. Today, we do not execute criminals because they *might* be later proved innocent. Ought we not to refrain from killing the *possibly* handicapped – by rubella, for instance – just in case they turn out to be healthy? If not, *then* kill them. The reasons for justifying abortion would surely justify infanticide, would they not? Will that squeamishness also disappear in time? Will society not imitate the Romans in this, leaving babies to perish not on cold mountainsides but in stainless-steel buckets? Research shows that infanticide already does take place in abortion clinics. The foetus may turn out to be more developed than was estimated. To the physician's dismay, a perfectly healthy and viable baby is born. Instead of draining off the amniotic fluid, aspirating and warming this fellow human being, the doctor either puts a gloved finger down his throat or, with a cursory glance to see if the abortus is breathing – this to cover himself – drops the abortus in a bucket.

Anomalies multiply. In some places, kittens are put down with more consideration than is shown babies in the womb. In an age that finds capital punishment more and more abhorrent, babies are killed by the million in cold blood by modern medical lynch-law. Child murderers, rapists, sadists, spies are not put to death; only the innocent in their mother's womb or those who, annoyingly, emerge from it unexpectedly alive and are murdered. Those who batter babies are put in gaol;

those who maim and kill them before they take their first breath are paid handsomely and afforded professional status.

Whereas under Roman law the father had the right of life and death over his family, today it is the woman who decides which of her babies lives or dies. Following on recent court decisions in the United Kingdom and the United States of America, the father, it would appear, has no rights. He has contributed in the act of love to the child's conception, the child is genetically part of himself; but even he is not allowed to interfere in the woman's absolute right to abort his baby. The child in the womb has no advocate nor any rights at all.

To justify these attitudes, it is often argued that what is in the womb is in no sense a human being, only a potential human being. No person exists until there is actual and independent existence *after* birth. New phrases have been coined to express this new phenomenon.

Abortionists never kill babies; they terminate pregnancies, or dispose of foetal material. Abortions are classed as therapeutic, though not for the unborn for whom they are lethal. The emphasis is exclusively on the woman and her 'condition'. She is not even to be called a mother in this context; she is a mother-not-to-be. The pretence must be maintained that she is physically or mentally ill, even in cases where she plainly is not. Language itself is sterilized. Extruded are negative words that smack of destruction and death. Abortion is always positive and, since doctors are involved, it must be portrayed as of benefit to the world, a medical advance, a public amenity.

To the non-medics who never have to look into the stainless-steel bucket when the surgeon is finished, nor at the foetus writhing as the needle is plunged into it, this may seem humane. Pregnancy comes across as an illness and, in the early stages, a minor illness. Abortion is not really an operation; a mere scrape, perhaps or a minor suction job. After all, the baby was not planned, was it? The neuter case helps mask the human reality. Only babies who are wanted and loved should come into existence. This one was an accident, and accidents ought not to happen; the doctor provides insurance against accidents. No child is killed; at worst, a potential child. But in a sense each woman has up to a million potential children, ova awaiting development, inside her from the time she is born. Only a tiny fraction can become babies; one less will not matter. So what she is carrying, especially before she feels it move, is only tissue, a sort of benign tumour, like a lump in the breast, like tonsils or an appendix. No one is harmed; the woman is giving up an annoying part of herself. Besides, what doctor would do anything nasty like killing a human being?

It so happens that ordinary language as well as English common law is against such terminology. A woman carries a baby not a non-human foetus. 'How is my baby?' the pregnant mother asks her doctor. The law has hitherto protected the unborn child as its most precious charge; it even granted him right of inheritance, permitting him to sue for damages *after* birth, when the harm was done him or his parents in, say, a car accident while his mother was carrying him. Whenever a child was damaged in the womb and, after birth, died as a result, whoever did it was charged with murder.

This, it might be argued, was in the bad old days when we knew far less than we know now. The truth is the opposite.

Modern science reveals a strict continuity between the conceptus and all its later stages of development. Far from being part of the mother, the child is a unique individual from the beginning. The conceptus has its own genetic code that will evolve but never alter substantially. From the union of sperm and ovum results the distinctive being composed of forty-six chromosomes that distinguish the human karotype. What the woman carries is not an inert piece of matter, not a vegetable, not a sort of tadpole, not anything but a particular human male or female in embryo. This embryo is not a potential human being but a human being with potential. One day, he or she might think, dream, love, just like any other human being. It is only a question of time. So, as the days and weeks pass, it is a human heart (forty days), a human brain (seventy days) that a scan reveals, responding to stimuli, turning from pain and cold, sucking his thumb, breathing, crying his own tears. It is this human being, male or female, who is knifed, poisoned, soaked in acid in the womb, decapitated perhaps; and, who, after birth, should a doctor's calculation prove mistaken, is exposed to a hostile environment and left to choke or suffocate or freeze to death because his mother does not want him. And society, so it would appear, approves or at least condones that decision.

Extreme pro-abortionists do not have science on their side. Never was science more against the view that the foetus is part of the mother and that *therefore* she has the right, as was the case under Roman law, to remove what is 'part of herself'. The foetus creates, in a sense, its own environment within the womb; the placenta is a construct not of the mother but of the baby. The baby has his own blood which is sometimes incompatible with the mother's. At about four months, examination of the amniotic fluid – by amniocentesis – enables the physician to sex the child. It is a little boy or a little girl who dies when a foetus is killed or when, as they say, a pregnancy is terminated. These days, as everyone knows, a baby may be kept alive in the womb long after the mother is dead. It is not birth or the first breath, as modern Stoics maintain, that makes a foetus human. It was human from the beginning.

Changes in the Law

In view of this, legal changes in the 1960s came as something of a surprise. The law seems to take little or no cognizance of the fact that the embryo has its separate genetic constitution, its own independent circulatory, hormonal and nervous system.

In 1967, Britain passed an Abortion Act which legalized termination of pregnancy, provided it was performed by a doctor and approved in good faith by two registered medical practitioners who believed

(a) that the continuation of the pregnancy would involve risk to the life of the pregnant woman, or of injury to the physical and mental health of the pregnant woman or any existing children of her family, greater than if the pregnancy were not terminated; or

(b) that there is a substantial risk that if the child were born it would suffer from such physical or mental abnormalities as to be seriously handicapped.

This act was acclaimed by most people in Britain, and remains popular even though subsequent events showed it was open to abuse. Prior to 1967, three thousand women every year were being hospitalized with septic or perforated wombs, the result of backstreet abortions. The number of deaths was impossible to determine. The new Act would stop this maiming and killing by allowing modern suction techniques to be used. The termination, which took account of a woman's actual and foreseeable circumstances, had to be carried out in an approved hospital or clinic. This was certainly not abortion on demand; it involved clear medical indications and a moral choice. Commentators said this was not true of the American approach.

On 22 January 1973 the Supreme Court *seemed* to go back to pre-Christian times when it decided that human life begins at birth. This unqualified verdict was unprovoked by public clamour and was unprepared for by public debate. According to the court, the foetus is in no sense a person, it has no rights. It is not a subject but an object. It is not a citizen and therefore is not entitled to any protection from the law. It is a zero to which the state is totally indifferent. A mother may choose in complete freedom between child-birth and child-death. According to John T. Noonan, Jr, in his book, *A Private Choice*: 'The liberty of the pregnant woman, or gravida, was the liberty of an author over his manuscript, a farmer over his crop, or a girl over her doll. . . . The gravida was protected from shoddy surgery, but the unborn could be given no protection whatsoever.' Like a black slave in the Colonial and early post-Colonial period, like Jews under Nazism, the unborn had no legal existence.

Even communist states were astonished at such a liberalization in an ostensibly Christian country. The Vatican, naturally, was horrified. It may well be that a large part of John Paul's fear for American Catholicism stems from the United States' abortion laws. What better proof that the famed American freedom ends up in a barbaric anti-life mentality?

It comes as an even bigger shock to realize that as early as 1969 a

372

Harris poll for *Time* magazine showed that 60 per cent of American Catholics believed abortion was best left to parents and their doctors. The proportion of American Catholics favouring this approach has risen by twenty points since then.

No wonder his Holiness thinks America needs teaching a lesson. He thinks *all* abortions are wrong and the decision is up to *him*.

To readjust the balance, a further question has to be asked: Is it possible that the popes themselves have contributed to the slide into an abortion mentality? It sounds preposterous, and yet some Catholics are prepared to argue that the papacy's extremism led to Catholics abandoning the middle ground at a critical moment in the post-war years. Only on the middle ground can this battle be fought with even a moderate hope of success.

The Mind of John Paul

It might be thought that John Paul's opposition to abortion is due to his Polish right-wing background. Poland, it is presumed, is like Ireland, opposed tooth and nail to abortion.

Amazingly, this turns out to be false. As Daniel Callaghan says in his book, *Abortion: Law, Choice and Morality*: 'Despite Poland's strongly Catholic character (conservative, with high rates of observance) and repeated condemnation of abortion by the Polish hierarchy, the legal abortion rate and ratio are high and the birth-rate low.'

For instance, in 1962, when the pope was working as a bishop in Poland, the abortion rate was far higher than America's. It was even higher than America's is now after the Constitutional decision by the Supreme Court! There were 200,000 registered abortions in a population of around 30 million. Moreover, there was in operation a splendidly financed and run birth control programme to which Catholics did not take exception. One remarkable fact emerges: far from Poland not taking to contraceptives, it was the first country in the world where the careful use of contraceptives actually reduced the abortion rate. In 1968 the number of abortions dropped to 121,700. Even so, the ratio of abortions to live births remained very high.

It is plain that John Paul suffered no trauma when he moved from Cracow to the Vatican. In his homeland there was an abundance of contraception and abortion. His opposition to both these practices stems not from his sheltered Catholicism but from his convictions, which the Poles were betraying.

As we noted, history does not bear out the Vatican's view that its present opposition to contraception is 'constant'. Is its attitude to *abortion* quite as constant as it likes to make out?

In his addresses, John Paul takes certain things for granted: (1) the conceptus is human; (2) it is human from the very instant of fertilization; (3) this means the conceptus has exactly the same rights as any other human being – say, the mother or the children born already; (4) to kill the conceptus directly is always murder.

Even if he is right on every point, how much of this is constant Catholic teaching? The answer is: none of it. Every stage in his argument is untraditional, which makes it imperative that his reasoning on abortion, like Paul VI's on contraception, be subjected to close scrutiny.

Is the Soul Infused at Conception?

Most Catholics assume that the soul is infused at conception. They may take it as an article of faith. In fact it is not. Vatican II deliberately left the issue aside and for a very good reason. For fourteen hundred years until late in the nineteenth century, all Catholics, including the popes, took it for granted that the soul is *not* infused at conception. If the church was wholly opposed to abortion, as it was, it was not on the basis of the conceptus *starting* as a human being.

From the fifth century, the church accepted without question the primitive embryology of Aristotle. The embryo began as a non-human speck that was *progressively animated*. This speck had to evolve from vegetative, through animal to spiritual being. Only in its final stage was it a human being. This is why Gratian was able to say: 'He is not a murderer who brings about abortion before the soul is in the body.'

The characteristics of the foetus were attributed solely to the father. It (and it was correct to refer to the embryo as 'it') became human at forty days for the male and eighty days for the female. A female resulted, said Aquinas, from defective seed or from the fact that conception took place when a damp wind was blowing. It followed that to abort a foetus in the early stages of pregnancy was wrong, since it was the destruction of a potential human being. It was not murder, since it was not the killing of an actual human being.

In the fifteenth century, moralists began to ask whether it was not possible in certain circumstances to get rid of the foetus without fault. For example, when it results from rape or incest or even of adultery, thus threatening the husband's rights and the marriage itself. The same dilemma arose in the case of a mother whose health would be endangered if she had to bring a foetus to full term. Was it not a moral duty to save a human life at the expense of a non-human if potentially human life? Some of the best theologians answered Yes.

Some went further. They said it was permissible to save a mother's life even *after* the foetus was humanized, that is, after the soul was infused. For what reason? Because the foetus' life had no absolute value; its value had to be weighed with others. What, then, in the classical case, when it came to a straight choice between saving the mother or the child? Was not the mother's life more valuable than the child's? Many hesitated. They said it was always wrong to kill an ensouled foetus directly. They were content to say it is permissible to kill it indirectly, that is, when medical treatment to help the mother incidentally and without intending it also killed or expelled the foetus. The aim was solely to save the mother; the death of the foetus was a sad by-product of that virtuous act.

History shows that popes, far from being able to solve these difficult moral dilemmas once and for all, were as mystified as anyone else. They had no access to privileged information. They had to put forward arguments that were subject to rebuttal. For example, Gregory XIII (1572–85) said it was not homicide to kill an embryo of less than forty days since it was not human. Even after forty days, though it was homicide, it was not as serious as killing a person already born, since it was not done in hatred or revenge. His successor, the tempestuous Sixtus V, who rewrote the Bible, disagreed entirely. In his Bull *Effraenatum* of 1588, he said all abortions for whatever reason were homicide and were penalized by excommunication reserved to the Holy See. Immediately after Sixtus died, Gregory XIV realized that, in the current state of theological opinion, Sixtus' view was too severe. In an almost unique decision, he said Sixtus' censures were to be treated as if he had never issued them. Popes can be precipitate. They never did have answers up their sleeve to ongoing moral problems. Moral judgements depend on facts and circumstances, all of which must be kept under review. The nineteenth-century papacy forgot this basic principle on every issue related to liberty. Twentieth-century popes have forgotten it on every issue relating to sex. Paul VI was not alone in reissuing ancient teachings regardless of entirely changed circumstances and the findings of science. In particular, the morality of abortion depends on biological facts.

In 1621 a Roman doctor, Paulo Zacchia, suggested that there was no biological basis for Aristotle's view that ensoulment was delayed for some time after conception. Zacchia was the most honoured physician in the papal court, yet his view had no impact on papal or theological teaching. The Vatican issued a pastoral directive permitting but not enforcing the baptism of foetuses less than forty days. As late as the eighteenth century, the church's greatest moral theologian, St Alfonsus Liguori, was still denying that the soul was infused at conception. Like Aquinas before him, he did not say direct abortion was right, but his view allowed a flexibility of approach to abortion, especially when the mother's life was in danger. After 1750, this flexibility disappeared. For the first time in centuries, the church started to return to the intransigent attitude of the Fathers.

The Growing Rigidity of Rome

Far from repeating *the* tradition, Pius IX went against several centuries of constant teaching when he stated in 1869 that *any* destruction of *any* embryo was an abortion that merited excommunication. In other words, he adopted Sixtus V's extreme view that had been instantly reversed by Gregory XIV. The rationale for Pius' teaching was twofold. First, ensoulment takes place at conception. Second, the embryo and the mother are always of equal value. Neither of these positions could remotely be called traditional. In fact most theologians of the time disagreed with the first, which entailed a disagreement with the second. For if the soul is not immediately infused it is extremely hard to see how the embryo is *always* of equal value to the mother.

The following year, Vatican I acclaimed the pope infallible. From then on, bishops looked to Rome to answer all their problems for them. Now Zacchia's view that ensoulment takes place at conception, reinforced by Pius' definition of the immaculate conception of the Virgin Mary, began to win over theologians, especially Roman theologians, to the notion that a human being is present from conception. The embryo, being a human being, has all the absolute rights of a human being. By then, Karl Ernst von Baer had discovered the ovum in 1827. In 1875 it was proved that the joint action of sperm and ovum resulted immediately in a new organism that proceeded to evolve into the child.

The Vatican's pastoral approach firmed up to conform with this new thinking. The Holy Office closed off every possible avenue to abortion. Nothing was permitted that endangered the embryo in any way. It was held unsafe to teach that craniotomy was all right *even to save the mother's life*. In the year 1895, Leo XIII personally approved a still more reactionary decision of the Holy Office. The case submitted was this: A mother was in *certain* danger of death. Unless the foetus was removed, both would die. The reply was: Doctors were forbidden to remove the foetus, even though the consequence was *both mother and foetus would die*.

Further reactionary decisions followed. Doctors were refused permission to deal with ectopic pregnancies. This was fatalism of a corrosive kind. What nature has done, man must not undo. Taken to its logical conclusion, the principle would be catastrophic in every branch of medicine. It is clear what was happening in Rome. As society started approving of abortions for serious medical conditions, the Vatican became correspondingly more disapproving. In the 1917 code of canon law, for the first time the mother was included in the censure reserved for abortion.

Finally, as we saw, *Casti connubii* taught thirteen years later that 'Thou shalt not kill' extended to the foetus at *every* stage of its development. Not even extreme necessity could justify the direct killing of the innocent in the mother's womb, for that innocent had an absolute right to life. 'The lives of both are equally sacred,' said the pontiff, unaware, it seemed, of the moral dilemmas that ensued from embracing the extreme views of Sixtus V. Unfortunately for the church, this extreme approach became the new orthodoxy at the very moment when, owing to advanced medical techniques, it was never less acceptable. Surgery was becoming ever safer and doctors were beginning to predict with accuracy the hazards of bringing a pregnancy to full term.

Pius XI did not claim infallibility for *Casti connubii*, but it laid a heavy hand on Catholic moralists. The pope seemed even to ban indirect abortions. These are, say, the removal of a cancerous womb when the woman is pregnant, or the excision of a fallopian tube when the embryo is rooted there instead of in the womb. This was so extreme that a few moralists refused to accept it, thereby putting their jobs on the line. Their courage paid off, for the Vatican made a concession: it stopped condemning *indirect* abortions when the intention was not to kill the embryo but to save the mother's life. Pius XII was positively to approve this at last in 1951. It was then official: 'indirect killing' was permissible in certain cases.

Even so, this still strict teaching leads to unacceptable conclusions in medicine. Say, for example, the doctor opts to remove the embryo from the fallopian tube without excising the tube itself: this is a sin. In the eyes of the Vatican, it constitutes a *direct* and not an *indirect* killing of the embryo. This is why almost all moralists feel obliged to say it is better to remove the tube with the embryo in it than to remove the embryo and leave the tube intact – even though the latter procedure makes future pregnancies possible. This is one more area where women could help put Catholic male moralists on the right path.

One other bizarre result of Rome's strict approach. The church says it is a grave sin for a girl of twelve to have an abortion after she has been raped, even if the offender is her own father. A leading Catholic moral theologian, Father Bernard Häring, in *The Morality of Abortion*, writes of one tragic case of a rape in this way:

> If she has already yielded to the violent temptation to rid herself as completely as possible of the effects of her experience, we can leave the judgment of the degree of her sin to the merciful God and try to build up her willingness to integrate both her suffering and her fault with the sufferings and sins of the world that Christ took upon himself on the cross. . . . I would never go so far as to advise a person to abort. Neither would I say to the person involved that this is the right decision if she has made up her mind.

When the gentlest and wisest of Catholic teachers writes with such insensitivity, one can only wonder at the current state of Catholic ethics as moral theologians try to justify the papal stand on abortion. Father Häring speaks of the victim in terms more suited to the criminal.

The church's refusal to allow abortions to child rape victims and her slowness to allow indirect abortions for ectopic pregnancies are due to her fear that soon every case will be looked on as an exception. Though understandable, inflexibility cannot be defended. For, if circumstances demand moral reassessment, the refusal to take account of such circumstances, for whatever motive, is wrong.

While the papacy thinks of itself, therefore, as the moral champion of the age, there are not a few who credit it with immorality. It would indeed, be fairly easy to show that Rome's extremism created its mirror-image, the lobby for permissiveness. The Vatican's refusal to enter dialogue meant that the voice of the Catholic church was not heard at the critical moment when new legislation on abortion was coming before the courts. The church, owing to its intransigence, became an easy target; its official views were easily discredited, for polls showed that even most Catholics disagreed with them. In no country was this so plain as in the United States. The abortion lobby was able to point to the staunchest opponent of abortion as being obscurantist. Why, they said, in 1968 the pope banned contraception, an attitude which, as everyone knows, makes abortions necessary.

Subsequent events have proved what many theologians said at the time: Pope Paul fought the wrong fight in *Humanae Vitae*. He should have put his considerable energy into attacking the permissive attitude to abortion. And yet, even here, one has to enter a caveat. There is no doubt that he would have made no progress on abortion, either.

Pius XII said in his address to midwives in October 1951: 'A baby as yet unborn is a man [human being] in the same degree and for the same reason as the mother.' Vatican II followed this up in its decree *Gaudium et Spes* by condemning abortion, the first Council ever to do so. 'Life', it said, 'from its inception is to be guarded with the greatest care. Abortion and infanticide are horrible crimes.' The Council was wise not to bracket contraception and abortion; it was less wise in bracketing abortion and infanticide. They are often quite different things, as centuries of moral theology have shown. To speak with unqualified disapproval of both showed a weak grasp of Catholic history. John Paul, of course, has gone back to a pre-Vatican II approach by always bracketing contraception and abortion.

John Paul's Approach

Even the present pontiff's admirers are not unaware of the dangers he faces in continuing to condemn contraception and abortion in the

378

same breath. A reading of his addresses shows that, with almost Pavlovian consistency, having attacked one he attacks the other. He disregards the fact that recent researches into embryology show that a huge genetic change occurs at conception; the fertilized ovum is a distinct individual with its own genetic code. As George Hunston Williams writes: 'This genetic fact puts artificial contraception and wilful abortion on entirely different moral planes.' John Paul either does not see this or chooses to ignore it. But, for whatever reason, he too gives encouragement to the abortion lobby. 'Sure he condemns abortion,' they say. 'Doesn't he also condemn contraception? Even his own flock don't follow him on contraception; nor, if the polls are anything to go by, do they agree with him on abortion.'

Many Catholics now suspect that John Paul has not only confused two medically and ethically different things; he continues fighting the abortion battle in an unwise way. His approach is too extreme. Can he expect more than a handful of Catholics to agree with him that a girl who has been raped sins by having an abortion? Who is prepared to add to the outrage and physical abuse already done her the further outrage of obliging her to bear a rapist's child? When questioned on this, bishops reply: 'She has to bear his child; she does not have to rear it.' This is unacceptable even on Catholic principles. If a woman cannot rear a child, she ought not to have a child. Mothering is not just a biological fact, it is a continuing moral and spiritual commitment.

The official Catholic position is also hard to defend in certain grave medical conditions. Should a woman have to bring to term a child who, doctors assure her and even *show* her on a scan, is brain-damaged or who is without the central nervous system? The pope always says Yes. This seems to most people to be stressing only the biological aspect of the matter, as if the biological *is* the moral. It is to repeat the mistake Paul VI made over contraception. It is to turn an ideal of mothering into an inflexible law, even when it is known that mothering in the proper sense is impossible.

The pontiff is unlikely to succeed in converting women to his point of view. He may say the abortion issue is simple; they say it is complex and multi-faceted. The pope, through his ban on abortion, wants to take vital decisions into his own hands. But women are determined to decide these issues for themselves. They alone will say whether they feel able to be the mother of this child they are carrying, for they know that mothering involves more than giving birth. They also know that they are more than producers of this child; they are wives and mothers of children already born. Their decision will not be based on biology alone but on a whole range of moral issues, of which bringing a foetus to full term is one and, in normal circumstances, the overriding one. Catholics do not want to elude the challenge of the Gospel; they simply do not want to hand over their moral responsibility by submitting totally to a rigid loveless and basically biological law.

Many Catholics, believing the pope's view is extreme, are beginning to ask with deep respect: Where has he gone wrong? Which among his assumptions are correct and which are questionable?

Against a long Catholic tradition, the pope takes it for granted that the conceptus is a complete human being from the moment of fertilization. Modern genetics do suggest that a fertilized ovum is *human*. It has an individual genetic code. Does it follow that the fertilized ovum is a human being in the full sense, that is, that it has exactly the same rights as the mother? That it must be treated with exactly the same respect as a child already born? That it, too, has an absolute value that outweighs all other values? If these questions can be answered affirmatively, the pope is correct; abortion is always wrong.

However, medical science itself makes it extremely difficult to identify conception as the moment when a human being starts to exist with all the rights of a person. Experts have estimated that at least one out of every three fertilized ova is naturally aborted without the woman being aware of it. Is one to conclude that, literally, a third or more of *human beings* are washed down the drain? (The church has an added problem in that, because of its teaching on original sin, Hell or Limbo must be heavily populated with unbaptized embryonic beings.)

Further, when in the course of *in vitro* fertilization, say, half a dozen ova are fertilized by male sperm, are Catholics really committed to believing there are six human beings in that dish, with the same rights as half a dozen babies in their cots? Another complication: if the soul is infused at conception, how can the cell divide at a later stage, as happens in the case of twins? Has the soul – an immaterial reality – been divided?

There are many Catholic philosophers today who do not see how a fertilized ovum can be called an ensouled being or person, since in Thomistic tradition ensoulment can only take place when there is a body sufficiently evolved to be informed by the soul. Even though the fertilized ovum has its own specifically human genetic code, this is not enough to make it a human *being* or person. For that, it needs to develop limbs and a human brain. In their view, the great tradition of ensoulment taking place at a *later* phase of development remains intellectually more respectable.

At a lower level, an acorn has programmed into it all that is required for the final evolution of an oak. But an acorn, though different from every other form of life, is *not* an oak. People quite happily crunch acorns under foot or feed them to pigs, whereas they tend to treat oak trees, even oak saplings, with respect.

According to some Catholic philosophers, hominization (or humanization) for the individual, as for the race, is a gradual process. It follows that the *traditional* arguments in favour of limited abortion are still valid. The mother is a person in the full sense of the word; the embryo is only developing into personhood. This is not to say one should not respect the embryo. On the contrary, the entire Christian tradition is one of reverence for the embryo at every stage as the gift of God. The whole bias is in favour of protecting nascent life. The extremes of the abortion lobby contradict the basic feelings of Christians, and abortion as a means of family planning, as in Japan, is utterly repugnant to them. In normal circumstances, the embryo is to be nurtured and cherished and brought to full term. But not all circumstances are normal. Sometimes, a very sad decision to abort has to be made. This is a *moral* decision. It is unfair to suggest that all who favour abortion for certain cases are hedonists or woolly thinkers or malicious. As we saw, most people who reject the pope's viewpoint do so on *moral* grounds. It seems to them unethical to treat an evolving being on a par with a fully fledged person who has a range of relationships and responsibilities. While abortion practice has gone too far and led to the trivialization of life and motherhood, the papacy has not helped by propagating a scarcely less acceptable extremism.

Even if John Paul is correct and the embryo is a person in the first instant of fertilization, would it follow that the conceptus has exactly the same rights as the mother or children born already?

The pontiff repeatedly argues: The right to life is the most basic of human rights and no other right – say, the mother's right to health – can take precedence over it. But to say that life is the most basic of rights is ambiguous. If it means it is the first right without which a person cannot have other rights, such as the right to education or to marry, the pope is correct but he has merely stated the obvious. He seems to mean more than this. He believes that it is the *only* right one should ever consider; it is a value that always and in every circumstance outweighs all other values. But this is surely false.

If the right to life were always the paramount consideration, war would be outlawed, for it leads inevitably to the loss of life. But there is another consideration that often outweighs the loss of life, namely, justice. Equally, if the pontiff were correct, no one would be allowed to climb mountains, become a racing driver, be rocketed into outer space; all *that* is risking life for, in his view, lesser considerations. But, clearly, at this level, the right to life is one value to be weighed with others: life with knowledge, life with the joy of conquering heights, speeds, of opening up new frontiers in space. To say that life is the basic human right cannot possibly mean that it is a value that may *never* be allowed to yield to other values, whether one's own or other people's.

Whereas the pope starts from a basic principle and concludes that all abortions are wrong, the man or woman in the street starts from the opposite end. They know there are cases, such as those involving rape, incest, brain-damaged foetuses, when abortion is a truly moral option. They then have to ask: What is wrong with the pope's argument? Has he overlooked something very obvious?

Could it be he has failed to take into account that, human or not, a person or not, the embryo is within the mother? It is not a part of the mother but it cannot survive without her. This shows that the embryo, the child in process of becoming, has not the absolute rights the pope claims for it but qualified rights. These rights, like *all* rights, are conditioned by the circumstances in which they are exercised.

The pope's opinion rests on the child in the womb being no different from the child in the crib. This can hardly be sustained. The child in the womb has rights but they are conditional upon and subject to the mother's rights as a fully developed person. In cases of conflict, most people take it for granted that the mother takes precedence. She is the host and, speaking purely medically, the child is parasitic. Should the rights conflict, she is entitled to demand her rights, both for her own sake and for her husband's and children's sakes. Many say it is immoral to insist she should risk her life and the well-being of her family for the life of the unborn. Her decision to abort is critical when the embryo is known to be severely damaged. Nature frequently aborts these foetuses anyway. She may consider that Nature, the bounteous Mother, is worth imitating in this situation. Popes speak in terms of biology as destiny, one suspects, because, for all their goodness, they speak, as male celibates, abstractly and without experience. Fathers of families and especially mothers disagree with them.

A Catholic priest, in championing the papal view, has unwittingly indicated the strange logic of it: it is better for both mother and child to die than for a doctor to abort a foetus. 'Two natural deaths', writes David Granfield, 'are a lesser evil than one murder.' Because mother and child have an equal right to live, they both must die. If any statement revealed the ethical bankruptcy of a biological morality, this is it.

To take life is not always the consequence of disrespect for life. The church should know this. In times past, she approved of capital punishment and she still sanctions 'just wars' in which the innocent are bound to die. In the case that Granfield mentions, a conceptus is in the process of destroying the mother's life and, in some sense, her family's life. The decision to terminate the pregnancy is for the sake of *life*, not of death. If only such awesome decisions did not have to be made by human beings.

An example may clarify further. A woman is shipwrecked. She manages to clamber on to a raft that will only support one person. Someone else in the water tries to clamber on. She is in possession; she knows that if that other person gets aboard they will both drown. She is within her rights in a tragic situation to keep that person off the raft, even if she has to use force. The case of the child in the womb who endangers a mother's life seems even easier to solve. The child, like the person in the water, has a right to life. But no rights are absolute; they are subject to circumstances. Sadly, for this is a grievous moral dilemma, the unborn is unable to exercise that right.

The reduction of morality to a rigid biological law imposed on all women in all circumstances has its drawbacks. As Callaghan wrote in *Abortion: Law, Choice and Morality*:

> The good it would accomplish is at the expense of other goods; the price exacted for the protection of fetal life is too high a price. A reading of the 'sanctity of life' which establishes fixed moral entailments, rigid hierarchies of values and rights, and a rigid exclusion of experience and social data is an untenable position.

Should Abortion Be a Crime?

Even those who sympathize with the pope and believe with him that society is sliding into permissiveness would not necessarily agree that all abortions should be criminalized.

It is even possible to interpret modern legislation on abortion as simply allowing women to make a decision that, in the nature of things, primarily concerns them.

In the United States, the influential Dean at the Boston Law College and a member of Congress was Robert Drinan, a Jesuit priest. Totally opposed to abortion, he was also initially opposed to abortion law reform. Then, in 1967, he came to the conclusion that there was a good case for total *repeal* of the abortion law. This way, he argued, the law would not differentiate between those entitled and those not entitled to to be born, which, as a lawyer, he considered a dangerous form of discrimination. In a paper delivered at the International Conference of Abortion in Washington, DC, in September 1967, 'The Right of the Fetus to Be Born', he said he preferred the withdrawal of legal 'protection from *all* foetuses during the first twenty-six weeks of their existence'. His change of mind split the Catholic opposition and eventually Rome asked him to step down from Congress. But what Drinan proved was that it made good sense even for people opposed to abortion to accept the repeal of abortion laws.

In fact, such a liberalization is in keeping with contemporary attitudes towards civil rights. To permit abortion is not to approve of it or to say it is morally right in every case. Only that it is more prudent for society to permit it than to prohibit it. Prohibition never has and never will stamp out abortion; it can only drive it underground. It would make hundreds of thousands of abortions dangerous. Prohibition of alcohol was bad enough; prohibition of abortions would be a catastrophe, especially in the present social climate. Who wants states to pass unenforceable laws? Who wants women to resort once more to coat-hangers, sharp knives, meat-skewers, purgatives and poisons? Of course, the pope would not want any of this, but he seems to be prepared to risk it. In this, he is probably in a small minority. Most people today would say that even if it is wrong for a woman to abort her child it is even more wrong for society to force her to continue in an unwanted pregnancy.

When John Paul goes on to demand that governments pass stricter and stricter legislation against abortion, he shows that he has little idea of the democratic process. It is hardly surprising. In the Poland of his youth and early manhood, he was subject to totalitarian regimes. In the church the pope's word was law. He, therefore, does not see that in a democracy those who rule have to be responsive to the wishes of the electorate, otherwise they will soon cease to rule. As regards abortion, any government that tried to repeal its legislation would be voted out next time round.

The papal approach to abortion is out of keeping with the times. Scolding in solemn addresses, even before huge ecstatic gatherings of the faithful, is *counter-productive*. It impresses no one in the long run.

As Maximos IV Saigh said in the early days of Vatican II, Catholic moral teaching is far too legalistic. His words apply particularly to sex. Moral teaching often suffers from a shallowness, a sense of unreality. It is a Euclidian ethic that simply steps back from the real situations in which human beings find themselves. So-called natural-law morality is often most unnatural. It takes no account of those specific situations and personal differences by which individuals come to their own decisions as to what is right and wrong for them. It is an imperialist morality. It offers no choices, only a fixed order of rights and duties, irrespective of changed circumstances and fresh moral insights. People's instincts tell them something is wrong with this kind of imposition from above. The church continues to deal with persons in an impersonal way.

The same high-handed treatment meted out to those who use contraceptives, who divorce and have abortions for serious medical reasons is meted out to homosexuals. It is significant that the only modern pontiff to admit that he had a sexual life was Pope Paul when, to the consternation of his aides, in a public audience he denied he was homosexual. The Italian press was full of 'scandalous rumours' which he wished to scotch once and for all.

Homosexuals obviously do not conform to the rigid biological pattern of sexual behaviour which alone Rome approves of. This is why John Paul, though undoubtedly a kind man, feels obliged to condemn them all as sinners who do what is 'unnatural'. As G. H. Williams reported with regret:

> For one class of adults, homosexuals, he [John Paul]
> has been consistently severe as to the overt expres-
> sion of the proclivity, although one gathers he

would be pastorally benign with all who exercised restraint over their 'unnatural' inclination.

Homosexuals are not a homogeneous group. There are many varieties. Some are bisexual, some have no attraction to any but their own sex; some were born homosexual, others become so by the circumstances of their life. A born homosexual is surely entitled to ask: 'Who can tell *me* what is "natural"? The law of *my* nature is not the same as yours. I did not choose to be like this. I did not systematically "pervert" my nature. God made me like this. Nor did he grant me or any other gay the gift of celibacy.'

In the Gospel story, Jesus showed a special love and concern for outcasts. He did not pillory them. On the contrary, he enjoyed being in their company, even when he was despised for it. He was surrounded, day and night, by publicans and prostitutes, the lame, the sick, the lepers; and he touched them all with his healing hands. His closeness to these marginal people was the great parable of his mission. He was the Saviour.

By contrast, the Catholic church as part of official policy distances herself from all marginal people, such as divorcees and homosexuals, and refuses to let them near Christ. The crusade against homosexuals obscures the message of Jesus, who calls everyone to himself, especially those who once were and often still are the outcasts of society. The Catholic church, in this instance, seems to prefer respectability to preaching the Gospel of Christ to the sinner.

As a matter of principle, it is surely a mistake for the pope to tell a homosexual or any other person how to lead his life. His task is to preach the Gospel, to explain the principles of love, the ideals that spring from the life, death and resurrection of Jesus. It is for the individual to embody these ideals as best he can in the circumstances of his life. There seems to be no justification, for the pope or anyone else who does not know a person or his circumstances to dictate to him in detail how he should live. Unfortunately, natural-law morality in Catholicism has come to mean just that: dictating to everyone how they should behave and the censures that they will incur if they fail to comply. Sadly, Roman Catholicism has become the most punitive religion ever known to man: those who break the rules, called the natural law, are labelled sinners, *mortal sinners*, whose unrepentance leads to exclusion from heaven and to eternal flames. Millions of honest sincere Catholics all over the world are so judged. They may be using contraceptives – each act of sex is a mortal sin; or are remarried after divorce – they are 'living in sin'; or they have, with the utmost faith and moral anguish, had an abortion – they are excommunicated for 'a wicked act'; or they are homosexuals who crave to give and receive love according to the dictates of their inmost being – they are living an 'unnatural and perverted life'. All are barred from the sacraments. They are excommunicated in the deepest sense, excluded from the banquet of Christ's body and blood. In the name of Christ, they are denied access to him.

The pontiff adopts the same approach to other modern dilemmas. For instance, in the spring of 1987 he personally endorsed a document of the Holy Office on the subject of surrogate motherhood and test-tube babies. Most people today are perturbed by aspects of surrogate motherhood as in the case of a middle-aged South African lady who became host-mother to her daughter's and son-in-law's triplets. She literally gave birth to her own grandchildren. The public are concerned, too, about the ramifications of *in vitro* fertilization. An *a priori* negative approach from the Vatican when the whole scene is shifting month by month is scarcely *aggiornamento*. Queen Elizabeth in the New Year's Honours List 1988, decorated Edwards and Steptoe, pioneers of the test-tube baby technique which has so far brought 5,000 children into the world. The Vatican, by contrast, has condemned this technique as a grievous sin.

Conclusion

Ask an Irish mother if her little Paddy likes chocolate, and she is likely to reply: 'Is the pope a Catholic?' The implication is, it is unthinkable that the pope is *not* a Catholic. The second part of this book showed this presumption to be false. Far from it being unthinkable, many popes were not Catholics; they were heretics and acknowledged to be such by the church, including their successors.

Today, there is some doubt as to whether all papal moral teaching is really catholic. What if much of it is merely papalism or Vaticanism? To be catholic, a teaching must reflect and spring from the *sensus fidelium*. Before polls became common, the Vatican could always claim the number of those dissenting from papal teaching was minimal. That can no longer be maintained. The polls not only reveal that most Catholics disagree with the pope; each new poll increases the number of dissidents. They find that they are not alone in what they previously took to be rebellion.

What are the sources of the present enormous malaise in the church?

The first is the papacy itself, or, rather, the way the popes have come to look upon their role since pontiffs like Gregory VII and Pius IX. They believe they are called upon to decide matters in which they have no competence. The result is that they feel they have to legislate in detail for everyone, especially in the matter of sexual mores and medical ethics, where boundaries are shifting all the time. Pope after pope falls into the same trap, victims of their own titles. They are Infallible Teachers and 'vicars of Christ'; they and they alone should know the answers to the most complex dilemmas. In reality, they know no more than anyone else.

In the light of history, both ancient and modern, Catholics would do well to scrutinize every piece of legislation coming from the Vatican which poses to be *the* answer to their problem. The papacy just as solemnly declared that heretics and witches were to be hounded to death, and Jews treated with barbarity in Christ's name. The papacy flatly denied basic human rights to Catholics in the long night of the Inquisition, reintroducing torture to assist it in its operations. The papacy denied all civil rights to its subjects in the Papal States including freedom of religion and freedom of the press. It is not encouraging rebellion to suggest that, in view of its record, instant obedience of the laity to a celibate institution on sexual issues would be incautious.

Since Vatican I the papacy's chief mistake would seem to be preaching natural law instead of the Sermon on the Mount. Or, rather, popes have interpreted the Sermon on the Mount in the light of their own theory of natural law. This natural law, in sexual and related matters, turns out to be a strictly biological law. Popes, in a quite untraditional way, have accepted one biological criterion of the rectitude of sexual activity. In intercourse there must be penetration and insemination of the wife by the husband. Any contravention of that criterion is 'unnatural', a mortal sin. Once an ovum is fertilized by male seed, it is a human being with all the absolute and inalienable rights of a human being.

From these simple biological principles, understood as 'the moral law' of sexuality, a whole series of 'natural laws' is derived. These laws are imposed on everyone in an inflexible way. Circumstances, individual differences, all those things which enter into a person's calculations when he tries to decide what is right and wrong for him do not count. The pope, through his interpretation of natural law, has decided for every individual what he or she must do or not do, now and for ever. The individual has no right to make up his own mind; the pope has made it up for him. The great challenge of the Sermon on the Mount has been institutionalized; ethical bureaucrats, called moral theologians, interpret the will of Christ for the individual. These bureaucrats determine the minutiae of behaviour with rabbinic complexity, but always in accord with the great biological patterns established by the papacy.

On the basis of a very few principles, an entire legislation is imposed on Catholics. Whenever there is an innovation in medicine, popes simply take another look at their biological criteria of moral rectitude and decide instantly what is right and wrong. These are grave matters; violation of papal decrees is a mortal sin. By its own standards, the popes are accusing most Catholics of sinning mortally by using contraceptives and millions more of living in sin through remarriage after divorce. Mortal sin entails separation from Christ. Catholics are forbidden to approach Christ in communion until they propose to amend their lives. They must stop using the Pill or the condom, stop having sex in their second marriage and seek reconciliation with the church. Only then will the church allow them to come to Christ their Saviour in holy communion. This is a curious consequence of Catholic morality: a person may not communicate with Christ while he is a sinner, only after he agrees to abide by the rules of the church. The church, of course, says she did not make the rules; God did. She said exactly the same to justify persecutions in the past. The present persecutions, though bloodless, are hardly less tragic. To force whole groups of people to live their lives with a sense of sin and the threat of eternal damnation hanging over them is very cruel.

The critical question has to be: Has the papacy understood Jesus aright in his Sermon on the Mount? For instance, can his ideal of marriage justify the church's harsh treatment of the divorced? Are the beatitudes reducible to inflexible commands inferred by popes from biological laws? All the polls suggest that Catholics no longer believe, even if once they did, that the popes know what is right and wrong for them.

What, then, is the role of the popes? One answer worth considering runs like this: If they really want to live up to the title Vicar of Christ, they should, like Christ, lay down the challenge of the Gospel, without frills or equivocation. The law of the Gospel is a law of love; and love is absolute. It is harsh as well as tender. It is all-embracing, and its demands are unpredictable because they come to each follower of Christ differently. For as long as the popes think their role is to *legislate* for everyone in every possible circumstance, so long will their teaching fall on death ears.

The sacraments belong to the church not to the popes. The sacraments are, as it were, special means whereby Christ meets people today. They are not the reward for good behaviour; it is not for *anyone*, not even the pope, to bar a person from such communion with Christ. What will bar a man is his own conscience. As St Paul wrote to the Corinthians: 'Whoever eats the bread and drinks the cup of the Lord in an unworthy manner will be guilty of profaning the body and blood of the Lord. Let a man examine himself and so eat of the bread and drink of the cup. . . . But if we judged ourselves truly, we should not be judged.' A man must examine *himself*; the church in the person of bishops or popes is not to examine him. We must judge ourselves. And in the light of the Gospel the examination and the judgement might be far harsher than any other person would impose on us.

Only the individual can say whether he is acting in an un-Christ-like way by having or not having more children. He will be judged not by the rectitude of a biological pattern of sex, but by all the demands of the Gospel upon him in the light of his total situation.

Only the individual woman knows whether her decision to continue a pregnancy or terminate it is made in the light of her own selfishness or of God's love as evidenced in Christ.

Only an individual homosexual can say whether he or she is acting in accordance with the Gospel or in violation of it by pursuing a particular lifestyle.

Only an individual couple can say whether their overriding desire for a child can justify resorting to the *in vitro* method of fertilization or another method, or whether, on the contrary, they should accept the lack of children as God's will for them.

The papacy, by considering itself the moral referee of the world, the instant legislator for every aspect of sexuality, has got itself into an appalling mess. Most Vatican decrees are rabbinical in the worst sense of the word, negative and condemnatory. The pontiff may, if he wishes, put Catholic opposition down to permissiveness. But might it not be that the chief problem lies not with the laity but with the clergy who make all the rules for the laity? Many Catholics are beginning to think that Margaret Sanger was right when she questioned the eligibility of chaste infertile clerics to lecture women on matters like contraception. What, indeed, if celibacy, far from giving clerics a clear insight into matrimonial matters, blinds them to what marriage is about? In brief, what if, contrary to the Vatican's belief, celibacy is not the solution but a very big part of the problem?

TWENTY

Unchaste Celibates

IN RECENT YEARS, the Catholic priest has had, on the whole, a sympathetic press. He has been portrayed in films and novels as a lonely and heroic figure, a man who has turned from the path of family life to serve Christ and the community. The faithful respect him for his self-sacrifice on their behalf, a sacrifice that entitles him to be their leader and guide. Only from the 1960s onwards have the public been able to glimpse the tremendous burden this band of men are obliged to bear. This came about through a relaxation of discipline in the reign of Paul VI. Before then, any priest asking to marry was treated as curtly as Catholics wanting to divorce. The rule allowed no exceptions, not even for the most poignant cases. The story is told of a telegram begging the pope to dispense a priest from his vows. 'Either he marries or he burns.' The reply was even briefer: 'Let him burn.'

The Mitre and the Coronet

One story exemplifies Rome's tough stance to perfection. It is told by Con Costello in his book, *In Quest of an Heir*.

John Butler was the Catholic Bishop of Cork. As a youth, he lost an eye in an accident. In spite of the fact that Roman clerics should have two eyes, he was dispensed from this impediment and ordained at the age of twenty-seven. Five years later, he was consecrated bishop. He was thirty-two and the year was 1763. 'All Ireland rejoices at his coming,' sang one bard. It was otherwise at his going.

After twenty-three years of undistinguished service, the bishop inherited from his deceased nephew one of the ancient peerages of Ireland. Since the twelfth century, there were Lords of Dunboyne. Butler had now a mitre and a coronet; he was a bishop and a baron. It entered his head that he had a duty to perpetuate the line. But how was this possible? Was he not a cleric committed to life-long celibacy?

Aged fifty-five, he was of forbidding appearance. Tall and thin, with a black wig and a black eye-patch over his empty left socket, he was not exactly marriageable, anyway. But he did live in Ireland where it was not uncommon for farmers to wed at an age without parallel in the rest of Europe; and he did have a title, lands and castles to offer a prospective bride.

The lady he set his heart on was a cousin of his, Miss Maria Butler from Wilford in County Tipperary. She was a *Protestant* cousin. Presumably, he took it for granted that no Catholic woman would be willing to compromise herself by marrying a bishop. Maria's other advantage was her age: she was only twenty-three. Plenty of time to produce a son and heir. It was sad that she was in love with a young man whom she was keen to marry. But her father was a sensible fellow and persuaded Maria that a lord was a better bet.

Bishop Butler was naïve enough to think that Rome would grant him a dispensation, seeing the continuance of his house had need of it. The first clue that his diocese had as to their bishop's intentions was when he failed to turn up at the Ursuline convent in January 1787 to profess a nun.

At the end of April he was married in St Mary's Church, Clonmell, by the Protestant curate. The dispensation, he hoped, would come soon to validate his marriage.

As the news leaked out, it was a sensation in Ireland. A Catholic bishop marrying a Protestant in a Protestant church before a Protestant minister! He had divorced his diocese and married a woman. He had removed his episcopal ring in favour of a wedding ring. He had swapped a bishopric for a bride. Many expected the sun to drop out of the sky. He has done, one paper said, what 'the poorest peasant in his humblest hut would shudder to mention'. His fellow-bishops were said to be dying of grief.

When Pope Pius VI read Butler's letter of resignation 'he wept openly'. His Holiness replied through the Archbishop of Cashel, telling him 'he must use every means to convert the apostate from his sinful life of concubinage'. The pope's own letter to Dunboyne was handed to him by Cashel on 11 August. There was to be no dispensation. What he read was this:

> It is not to be believed, venerable brother, with what consternation and anguish of mind We have been seized and overwhelmed, ever since We have received authoritative information that such was the height of infatuation which your misconduct had reached, that you intended to espouse a Protestant female; and dare, even now, to live with her in a state of most disgraceful concubinage. . . . In Our bosom is a truly paternal commiseration for yourself, and an ardent longing to rescue you, if possible, from such an abyss of profligacy and wretchedness.

After these kind words came the threats. If Butler remained deaf and persisted 'in the mire and turpitude of so opprobrious a life', he would be excommunicated, bishop or no bishop.

Dunboyne put the letter down in disbelief. The pope simply did not understand him, he said to Cashel. He had not married out of a desire for pleasure. It was a real burden for him at his advanced age to abandon the sweet life of celibacy and share bed and board with a woman less than half his age. He was acting simply out of a sense of duty. He refused to open his eye to disaster.

'Rome can grant a dispensation,' he said. 'Many of the apostles and Fathers of the church were married. . . . Even today some of the Eastern rites in communion with Rome permit married clergy.'

Cashel withdrew. The 'shameless concubinarian' was determined to defy the Holy Father. He should have been more intent on his coffin than on the marriage bed. He was clearly firm in his perversion – Rome's word for conversion to the Church of Ireland.

A week after that interview, on Sunday 19 August 1787, in the same church where he was married, the ex-Bishop of Cork denied his ancestral faith on a Protestant Bible and took heretical communion before administering it to the congregation that included his bride. He then signed the Roll of Allegiance and Supremacy plus a declaration against popery. He was officially a Protestant. Now he had several marks of distinction. He was the only one-eyed Irish bishop and the first member of the Irish hierarchy to apostatize.

Catholics were not pleased. With evangelical fervour, they pelted his carriage with turf, potatoes and lumps of dung. His Lordship took himself off to Dunboyne castle in County Meath. The old place was in ruins, but a fine new building had been erected. There, on the couple's first night in the bridal bed, the locals serenaded them with lewd noises and catcalls under their window. The bride complained, what with one thing and another, she got little sleep. The balladeers, those composers whose songs were more feared than excommunications, got to work:

> Think not of scandals, scandals there must be,
> Or why a Judas, or a sot like thee?

And a less felicitous ending:

> But oh! Keep Judas in your mental eye
> Lest Judas-like you hang yourself high.

In spite of this, Dunboyne was happy, for his wife was pregnant. But the baby was born with hydrocephalus and it was a girl, anyway. The little one with the large head died within the hour and was secretly buried without either parent being present.

The pregnancy had seemed to Dunboyne the sign of God's favour;

the birth seemed to him a sign of His wrath. His conscience troubled him from then until his death.

When he was sixty-nine, childless, lonely, on the verge of the grave, he wrote to the pontiff again. The letter was dated 2 May 1800. He made no excuses for his weakness; he had wanted, too much, a child. He asked to be allowed to return to his ancient faith and to be absolved from his sins. 'With my spouse', he wrote, conveying in a few words all the misery of his later life, 'I have had no cohabitation, except at table, for more than five years.'

An old priest friend was sent to see him in his home in Leeson Street, Dublin. Dunboyne confessed his sins and was reconciled to the church. He had never attended the Protestant church after his apostasy. When he died soon afterwards, he was buried in a secret place. His burial was as low-key as his wedding. His wife Maria, who remarried, survived him by sixty years, dying in August 1860, aged ninety-five.

It was not until the mid-1930s that two lead coffins were found in the Augustinian Abbey of Fethard, County Tipperary. One was of Dunboyne; the other, next to it, was his baby daughter's. The custom was to bury baptized babies and priests with their heads towards the altar; for the priest it symbolized he was, as herald of the Gospel, facing eastwards to the rising sun. The baby was so buried; but Dunboyne was buried with his feet towards the altar. Even in death, he was not altogether forgiven by the church he had betrayed.

On the day before Dunboyne wrote his final letter to the pope, he made his will. In it, he left his estate in County Meath to the Roman Catholic College of Maynooth. There was a protracted legal battle over this, but none the less the national seminary of Ireland was endowed with moneys from the inheritance of Ireland's solitary apostate bishop. Those who live in Dunboyne House in Maynooth are known as 'Dunboyners'. The lesson of the baron's life is doubtless not lost on them.

A Touch of Mercy

It was against this background that Paul VI began giving dispensations from celibacy in what were termed 'hard cases'. It had not been an easy decision to make. In a Holy Thursday sermon in 1966, Paul spoke, in the language used by Irish balladeers, of apostate priests as 'new Judases' who besmirch the name of Mother Church. But he knew the reality was not always like that. These Judases were sometimes old men who had left the priesthood forty to fifty years before; they had children and grandchildren and wanted simply to regularize their situation in the eyes of a church they had never ceased to love. The Judases were often young men who had been educated in a junior seminary since their early teens; they were chosen for the priesthood before they even realized what sex was, let alone life-long celibacy. There were priests applying who had become promiscuous, a menace to themselves and their parishioners; psychiatrists testified they simply had not the capacity to remain celibate. There were others who were broken by drink as a way of escaping an ever increasing loneliness.

Paul knew that John Butler, Bishop of Cork, was right. Celibacy in the Roman church was a matter of discipline not of faith. Parish clergy had *never* taken a vow of celibacy. They were simply unable, according to the laws of the church, to contract a valid marriage. Paul was pope; he could suspend this discipline. He considered it right for him to do so, especially after Vatican II when mercy and generosity of spirit had invaded the church.

The method of dispensing was not perfect. The petitioner had to accept full blame for his defection. He had to acknowledge all his sexual faults and peccadilloes before and after ordination. He was forbidden ever again to celebrate mass, preach or administer the sacraments. This was a hard condition, especially for middle-aged clerics trained exclusively for the institution. Even so, the prospect of being able to marry with relative dignity within the church they had loved and had served sometimes for years was very welcome. They did not mind moving far away from places where they had ministered, nor being married secretly in church cloisters or sacristies. They obeyed the regulations without bitterness – if anything, with an increased affection for the community which had sympathized with them in their difficulties. Dunboyne would have been more than content to have been treated so.

The trickle of applicants grew to a flood. Paul's touch of mercy was revealing a problem whose magnitude was breathtaking. Hundreds, then thousands of priests started to apply for dispensation. Often the applications were granted with a minimum of fuss. Priests were being dispensed to marry dispensed nuns. Many priests were dispensed to marry divorcees with children whose marriages had been anulled. After centuries in which it was anathema to release a priest from celibacy, priests were being released within a month of applying.

The numbers involved are impossible to verify. No one questions they were unparalleled in the history of the church.

After Paul VI, the mood in the Vatican changed abruptly. John Paul put all applications on the back burner. He was not at all sure that swift dispensations were good for the image of the priesthood or the church. Mercy was all very well; but the old discipline was best, and merciful in its own way. Priests, in particular, knew where they stood. The irrevocableness of their commitment meant it was wrong for them to doubt the grace of God, which is why so few *had* doubted in the past. There was no trial they could not overcome with God's grace.

John Paul's approach is consistent with his classical ideas. The priest is, he believes, a man of destiny and ultimate commitment in a world of changes and shadows. He is a living sign of the eternal in the midst of time; he is a beacon in a dark world. If Catholic moral teaching is hard – and John Paul would be the first to admit it – it needs priests of tough moral fibre to promote it. Only celibates can do this because only they fully testify to the Crucifixion of Christ, a voluntary act of self-immolation. Others suffer; priests suffer freely. When married couples run into difficulties, when they are tempted to use contraceptives, sue for divorce, have an abortion, they can turn to the priest and learn from him that, with the grace of God, they can overcome their temptations.

In spite of John Paul's tough policy, there has been no decline in the number of priests leaving the ministry, only a slow-down in the number asking to be dispensed. Not all petitions are refused, but it is no longer a matter of course. To qualify, priests must have left some time ago and be in a situation that makes it virtually impossible for them to return to the ministry. They may have a wife and children, a home and domestic responsibilities. Rome *will* dispense them, but it is typical of Roman procedures that the applicant never knows when his release will come. The Vatican does not seem to mind that the priest and the woman he loves have to marry first in a register office, hoping that some day the pope will allow them to regularize their union in the sight of God and the church.

Some Catholics think this is a small price to pay for holding the line on celibacy in a permissive age. Others think that John Paul has simply driven the problem underground. Priests are continuing in the ministry who, for the church's own sake, should not be there, should never have been there. It is impossible to quantify this, except on the basis of past history, but the flood of applications in Pope Paul's time suggests that the Roman church has a monumental, if as yet partly hidden, crisis on its hands.

This is nothing new. The Catholic church has nearly always been in crisis over clerical celibacy.

Just as Catholics presume that all popes have been models of rectitude on the pattern of Paul VI and John Paul II, so they presume that most priests have been chaste on the pattern of their parochial clergy today. The fact is that priestly celibacy has hardly ever worked. In the view of some historians, it has probably done more harm to morals than any other institution in the West, including prostitution. For everyone is on his guard against women of the streets, whereas ministers of the Gospel, even when unfaithful, are given respect and personal confidences. The proof of the harm done by celibacy comes not from bigoted anti-Catholic sources; on the contrary, it includes papal and conciliar documents and letters of reforming saints. They all point in one direction: far from being a candle in a naughty world, priestly celibacy has been more often than not a stain on the name of Christianity.

Paul VI went some way to accepting this in his encyclical *Sacerdotalis Caelibatus* of 20 June 1967. It may well be that his acquaintance with the history of celibacy persuaded him that it was disastrous keeping priests in the ministry when they were unable to live up to its demands. The encyclical begins with a sentence that is contradicted by almost every page of church history: 'Priestly celibacy has been guarded by the Church for centuries as a brilliant jewel.' But he comes closer to the truth when he says in section 36 that popes

> promoted, defended and restored clerical celibacy in successive eras of history, even when they met opposition from the clergy itself and when the practices of a decadent society did not favour the heroic demands of virtue. The obligation of celibacy was then solemnly sanctioned by the Sacred Ecumenical Council of Trent (in the sixteenth century) and finally included in the Code of Canon Law (1917).

It takes some reading between the lines to see that the clergy have never been happy with the discipline of celibacy ('opposition from the clergy') and they failed to live up to it ('when the practices of a decadent society did not favour the heroic demands of virtue'). Why did the popes have to restore celibacy over and over ('in successive eras of history'), except the clergy showed themselves unable or unwilling to live up to its demands?

In the light of the past, those thousands of priests who asked Pope Paul to be dispensed were simply more honest than their predecessors in accepting that celibacy was not for them. It was far better to admit this and leave the ministry than harm both themselves and the church by pretending to live chastely when they could not.

The history of celibacy makes for reading so black that not even the sexiest novel today can rival it.

The classical exposition was written by Lea in 1867. Lecky, the European expert on the period, said that no work on the Middle Ages since Dean Milman's was so impressive. 'This subject', Lecky wrote, 'has recently been treated with very great learning and with admirable impartiality by an American author, Mr Henry C. Lea in his *History of Sacerdotal Celibacy* (Philadelphia 1867), which is certainly one of the most valuable works that America has produced.'

It is strange that neither Lecky nor Lea knew that the ground had already been covered by two German brothers, J. A. and A. Theiner. Their book, *Die Einführung*, had come out in 1828 and was reissued in 1845. The elder, Anton, turned Protestant; the younger, Augustin, was to become the first non-Italian Prefect of the Vatican Archives.

Their work, less objective than Lea's masterly treatise, none the less confirms it. Their aim was to expose 'the terrible immoralities which accompanied celibacy, on the evidence of testimonies persisting all through the centuries and which it still brings in its train'. As G. G. Coulton wrote: 'No student of the Middle Ages can be excused for ignoring Lea and the Theiners.'

The long line of popes who were libertines before and sometimes after ascending the throne of Peter suggests that celibacy was not honoured by the rank and file of the clergy, either. As we noted in Part One, a list of popes who misbehaved would include, among others, Benedict V, Sergius III, John X, John XII, Benedict VII, Benedict IX, Clement V, Clement VI, 'John XXIII', Sixtus IV, Pius II, Innocent VIII, Alexander VI, Julius II, Paul III, Julius III, Gregory XIII, Gregory XV, Urban VIII, Innocent X, Alexander VII. When popes had mistresses of fifteen years of age, were guilty of incest and sexual perversions of every sort, had innumerable children, were murdered in the very act of adultery, there can be no doubt that celibacy among the clergy as a whole was more honoured in the breach than in the observance. In the old Catholic phrase, why be holier than the pope?

A Cautionary Tale

The celibate is pledged to renounce the most satisfying of his natural rights: to marry and have children of his own. No one knew this better than a pious Catholic layman who was born in Siena in the early years of the fifteenth century. He was an outstanding writer, destined like Petrarch to become Poet Laureate; he was also a skilled diplomat, and his name was Aeneas Sylvius Piccolomini.

On one mission, he strayed from the path of diplomacy by siring a boy by a Scottish lass, though to his deep distress the baby died. Later, he was sent on an embassy by the last antipope, Felix IV. Piccolomini was staying in Strasbourg in early February 1442. He was nearing forty but, in his own words, always objectively expressed, 'he grew hot and burned for a woman there'. The woman was a Breton named Elizabeth. She was married and had with her her five-year-old daughter. Her husband had left her briefly on business.

Piccolomini found her witty and charming, and she spoke to him in his native Tuscan. She was vivacious; he was lonely. He fell head over heels in love with her. He begged her to go to bed with him. For three days, she resisted him, until, the night before her departure to meet her husband, he implored her to leave her bedroom door unbolted. On the night of 13–14 February, he slept with her. It was a source of great joy to him that his child was conceived on St Valentine's Day and born in Florence the following 13 November. It was a boy. On hearing the news, he enthusiastically wrote to his father. His father must have replied somewhat coldly, for Piccolomini sent him another letter.

> You write that you do not know whether to be glad or sorry, Father, that the Lord has given me a child. . . . But I see only cause for gladness and none for sorrow. For what is sweeter to mankind than to beget in one's own likeness, and, as it were, continue one's stock and leave someone after one's own death? What on earth is more blessed than to see your children's children? For my part, I am delighted that my seed has borne fruit and that some part of me will survive when I die: and I thank God who has made this woman's child a boy, so that another little Aeneas will play about my father and mother, and give to his grandparents the comfort which his father should have supplied. For if my birth was a pleasure to you, who begat me, why should not my son be a joy to me? And will not my baby's face rejoice your heart, when you see me in him? Will it not make you happy when the little one hangs about your neck and charms you with his baby's ways? But perhaps you will say it is my offence you mourn, because I have begotten a child in sin. I do not know what idea you have of me. Certainly you, who are flesh, did not beget a son of stone or iron. You know what a cock you were and I am no eunuch nor to be put in the category of the cold-blooded. Nor yet am I a hypocrite who wants to seem better than he is. I firmly confess my error, for I am no holier than David the King, nor wiser than Solomon.

The writer of this wise and moving letter was to see his mistress Elizabeth once more in Basle, but his little Aeneas died only fourteen months later. With the death of Piccolomini's two sons, the church lost the virtual certainty of two cardinals, for he entered the church and fifteen years later was elected pope, taking the name of Pius II.

The Most Ancient Tradition of Ministry

Theologians have tried to prove that clerical celibacy goes back to the Bible and apostolic times. In vain. As far as the early church was concerned, the gospels revealed one massive fact: Jesus chose as his chief disciple Peter, a married man. How could anyone argue that

Jesus or Paul believed that small-time clerics in rural areas had to be celibate when the 'first pope' chosen by the Lord himself was married? If Jesus had wanted only celibates to be his ministers, he was very short-sighted in choosing Peter, whatever his talents.

The Fathers of the church took it for granted that not only Peter but Paul, too, was married. There *were* grounds in the New Testament for honouring celibacy. They were flimsy enough, seeing that even Jesus' mother was married. Jesus spoke in mystical terms of those who have castrated themselves for the Kingdom of God. Paul, also in the light of the imminent Coming of Jesus on the clouds of heaven, proposed waiting in the state in which a person found himself: if married, so be it; if not, stay unwed. The unwed person could keep his mind constantly on the Coming.

When the Coming was delayed, or frankly did not happen, it was possible, with casuistry, to turn this temporary and provisional celibacy in view of an event that never materialized into a life-long commitment for itself alone. But, it should be noted, Paul never made any connection between celibacy and *ministry*; he was no advocate of celibate priests. In fact, when he deals with the ministry, he assumes the *opposite*. A bishop, he says, should have only one wife. This was taken, probably in error, by celibate theologians to mean that a bishop should only have been married once. More likely, Paul meant that any Christian who continues the Jewish patriarchal tradition of having several wives *at the same time* could not be a bishop.

Paul's word was authoritative: there was nothing incompatible between marriage and ministry. This is why many married men became priests.

The earliest Apostolic Constitution dates from the end of the third or beginning of the fourth century. This laid down the rule that married men, far from giving up their wives when they were ordained, *had to keep them*. If, however, a bachelor entered the ministry, he was obliged to remain celibate. The Greek church has more or less retained this discipline. As with divorce, so with celibacy, it was the West that departed from the earliest tradition.

The two greatest medieval authors admitted this. Gratian, the canonist, said in 1150 that the Greeks were keeping the church's 'most ancient practice'. Aquinas, the theologian, said that Jesus did not separate Peter from his wife because he did not wish to sever the bond of matrimony which was of God's making.

The question is: What lies behind the change to a harsher discipline?

The Change to a Harsher Discipline

An ascetic movement grew up in the church in opposition to heresies with an anti-sex bias. Orthodoxy itself started disparaging marriage.

Purity became identified with sexual abstinence; chastity replaced charity as the central virtue of the Gospel. Religion, as a consequence, became sombre and joyless. Happiness was reserved for the Hereafter where, incidentally, there would be no sex, no marrying and giving in marriage.

The sordidness of sex was accentuated, we noted, because of its connection with original sin. Sexual pleasure (*libido*) was the first and bitterest fruit of original sin without which that sin could not spread in the world. Even second marriages after the death of one spouse were looked on with suspicion, hence no one twice married was allowed to become a priest or bishop.

In those early days, virginity was honoured but it was a state which people were free to enter and free to leave. It was not institutionalized. Virginity's popularity was inspired by Mary, not by Christ. The title 'the Virgin Mary' was in fact in no way biblical. To honour Mary's *chastity* would have perplexed the apostles, as it perplexes Jews to this day. In biblical tradition, New Testament as well as Old, 'virginity' was not a word expressive of honour. A virgin was not 'a pure girl' but an unwed girl, someone as yet empty and impoverished. To the first Christians the virgin birth meant not that God's Son was born of someone chaste but that he was born of someone poor and impotent. The Magnificat is explicit on this. Mary praises God for looking, not on her purity but on her lowliness, her nothingness. It was her hunger he filled, her poverty he endowed. The virgin birth expressed God's capacity to bring life from an unsown womb. It corresponds in the Jewish tradition to those Bible stories of elderly and sometimes barren women having babies by the power of God who alone can bring new life and salvation.

This basic mistake about Mary led to a further disparagement of sex and marriage. Mary was blessed *because* she had given up sex. The salvation of the world began with a vow of virginity.

This led to local synods, like that of Elvira in Spain, trying to make all ministers of the Gospel live without sex; sex was becoming *the* enemy that prevented Christ the Son of God coming into the world. Another idea was that hands that touch the (virginal) body of Christ should not touch the body of a woman, even if she is his wife. Ritual purity was of pre-Christian origin, but this pagan idea soon spread in the church and, in the end, became part of orthodoxy.

The rule forbidding priests to marry *after* ordination became general. It became official at the Council of Nicaea in the year 325; clergy ordained as bachelors who afterwards married or kept a concubine were solemnly condemned. The Bishop of Rome wanted to go further; he wanted to forbid even married priests to keep their wives. The Council decided against him. Unmarried priests must not marry; married priests must not give up their wives. This dual standard led to problems. Bachelor priests saw their married colleagues sleeping with their wives while they were compelled to live like angels, without sex or the comforting presence of a woman.

When Christianity became the religion of empire under Constantine, not only clerics but consecrated virgins were given legal privileges. For the first time, scandals arose. Many men on the make took advantage of whatever benefits, including tax-relief, were going. Celibacy made good economic sense even for men and women who were dedicated to free love. The church found she had to lay down stricter rules for celibates. Meanwhile, the blessing of priests who had wives legitimately was held to be somehow less potent than that of celibates.

Things became still worse at the end of the fourth century. The church was then respectable, with rich endowments and plenty of real estate. She did not want a married priest bequeathing it to his wife and children. Further, the ascetic ideal became more demanding at the very moment when the wrong kind of candidates, greedy and ambitious, were taking up the ministry as a career. Celibacy without chastity became the norm.

Damasus, who became pontiff in the year 366, exemplified a different sort of abuse. He renounced his wife and family. In those days, women had to be careful whom they married. Adrian II was another who, in 867, gave up his wife Stefania and his daughter when he ascended Peter's Chair.

It was probably Siricius, Bishop of Rome in 385, who first told married priests they must give up sleeping in a double bed. He was grieved, he said, to hear that clerics in Spain were still maintaining marital relations with their wives. Bishops, priests and deacons should not indulge 'in such immorality'. If they continued in it, they were to be expelled from the ministry. If they had 'sinned through ignorance', they were pardoned but were never to be promoted. Sex with their wives had, as it were, soiled them for ever. This great burst of puritanism, totally alien to the Gospel, was very unjust to priests' wives. It was a very clear signal of what women were to expect in the centuries ahead from a celibate hierarchy.

Even Siricius must have doubted if his discipline would take hold. In 386 he wrote to the African church, presuming that clerical celibacy was not a regular custom in Africa and he had no power to impose his views on a church outside his jurisdiction. He cites not one canon of a Council, no letters of earlier popes, no biblical or patristic text. The reason is that none such existed. But the discipline that had seen the church through three centuries of persecution was being modified, codified irrespective of the individual priests subject to it. This was to lead to moral disaster.

Innocent I (401–17) reinforced Siricius' views. Any violation of priestly celibacy and a priest was out of office. If only this had been enforced. Celibacy would then have gone hand-in-hand with chastity.

For example, if a priest fornicated or slept with a married woman or a whore, he would have been thrown out of office. But this never became the law of the Roman church. Even today, a priest can fornicate and commit adultery on a regular basis, and, however much his behaviour is frowned on, he is allowed to continue in office. If sinning priests had been ejected from the ministry, it might have led to a public acknowledgement of the clergy's problems under a puritanical regime. The numbers of priests would have been decimated or, in an age of miracles, the clergy might have led decent lives. But to insist on clerical celibacy without proper legal sanctions against unchastity led to many priests in every age professing one thing while practising another, proclaiming celibacy while living as libertines.

The next seven centuries witnessed an incredible see-saw of harshness and relaxation of discipline. Pope Leo I said married bishops and priests were to treat 'their wives as sisters'. Meanwhile, Italy was full of clerics with very large families, most of whom went unpunished. The truth is that the priesthood itself was practically hereditary. Many popes were the sons of priests and bishops. Among them were Boniface I (418–22), Gelasius (492–6), Agapitus (535–6), Sylverius (536–7) and Theodore (642–9). Sylverius rocketed to stardom since he was only a subdeacon when he was chosen as pontiff but, it was admitted, he had a head start: his father was Pope Hormisdas (514–23).

Everywhere, the rule of celibacy triumphed at the expense of chastity. The efforts of Jerome, Ambrose and Augustine were to produce ever more bitter fruit. Jerome was not afraid to admit that he regularly saw clerics who passed their entire lives in female company, surrounded by beautiful girl slaves and living a life that differed from marriage only in name and lack of respectability. His observations were to be repeated throughout church history. Many an honest bishop became so worried at the promiscuousness of his priests that he turned a blind eye if they had wives. It kept them out of worse mischief. For their part, priests were forced to choose between having a wife and having a career. The middle course was to choose a concubine.

What confuses the whole history of clerical celibacy is one fact that is little understood: all priests' marriages were held by the church to be valid. If men married after ordination, their marriages, though unlawful, were valid. Why? Because a man has a natural right to marry, and no one, *not even the church*, can deprive him of it.

There is an astounding consequence of this principle about which the early church had no doubts: Rome's present discipline of invalidating priests' attempts to marry is immoral. There can be no law, not even papal law, that deprives a person of that with which God the Creator endowed his inmost being. When, therefore, Lord Dunboyne, Bishop of Cork, asked Pius VI to dispense him so he could marry, he may have been naïve but he was doing nothing more than wanting to exercise his natural right to marry.

Unfortunately, while the fifth-century church did not take away a priest's right to marry, she did something equally harmful. She deprived him of his right to have sex with his wife. His marriage may have been valid, but because it was unlawful it was considered an adulterous union. Women found themselves validly married to clerics who sinned mortally by taking them to bed. It was obviously not just priests but their wives too whose basic rights were infringed. Wives in name only, they were looked on as lower than whores.

Rome never should have permitted married men to be ordained if one of the conditions was depriving their wives of marital rights. Such legislation shows the depth of fear and abhorrence of sex from which the discipline of celibacy sprang. No wonder it brought about so much immorality.

This theological confusion in an age of depravity led the clergy, in fifth-century Rome in particular, to become a byword for everything that was gross and perverted. They behaved far worse than the Barbarians. The Teutons especially had a great respect for womankind. When Pope Sixtus III (432–40) was put on trial for seducing a nun, he ably defended himself by quoting Christ's words, 'Let him who is without fault among you throw the first stone'.

The Eastern church kept all the while to its own discipline which was shaped by the Council of Nicaea and the Apostolic Constitution. Papal demands that married men should renounce their wives seemed to the Greeks an outrage against humanity. The Eastern church had its own problems. It failed to stop bishops having numerous children or ordained ministers from marrying. Often the latter were told they had to leave their wives and put them in distant nunneries. But those married in good faith prior to ordination were told to be faithful to their wives. In the ninth century, the East finalized this as its discipline.

The Farce of Celibacy

In the West in the fifth century, roving monks were proving to be a social menace. They were the worst of vagabonds, the consecrated sort. It took the genius of St Benedict to provide a rule for those who were sincere in wanting to lead a monastic life. Even so, there were long periods when many monasteries were nothing but houses of ill repute.

During the barbarian invasions, clerical celibacy was a bad joke. Bishoprics, with civil as well as religious responsibilities, were given to powerful chieftains. Many could not read a line of the mass. Telling such men they were not to have 'improper relations with their wives' naturally had little effect. Where was the sense in not going to bed with their beloved? It was like tipping good wine into a ditch.

The second Council of Tours in the year 567 decided that any cleric found in bed with his wife would be excommunicated for a year, and reduced to the lay state. Since the Council publicly admitted there was hardly a cleric anywhere without his wife or mistress, the results were negligible. Bishops and priests lived shamelessly with their wives and concubines. If anyone was punished, it was the wives. Many received a hundred lashes from the state for the sin of gaining access to their husbands.

Pope Pelagius II in the year 580 was more or less content if married clerics did not hand over church property to their wives and children. Priests had to make an inventory of church possessions on taking office and account for the same on their departure. Even Gregory the Great's efforts to clean up the clergy came to nothing. For one lapse, he superbly said, priests would be barred from office. He had to give up, or else there would have been no masses said.

In the eighth century, St Boniface went to Germany. He found such depravity among bishops and priests that he begged Pope Gregory III to let him wash his hands of the whole crowd. Once in Germany, he sent a frightened SOS to the new pope, Zachary. *All* the clergy were promiscuous – what was he to do? Young men who spent their youth in rape and adultery were rising in the ranks of the clergy. They were spending their nights in bed *with four or five women*, then getting up in the morning – in what state, he leaves to the imagination – to celebrate mass. This was the quality of candidates who were eventually promoted to the episcopate. What was the answer? The obvious one, abolition of the discipline that led to such defilement, did not occur to him. In Boniface's letters there are frequent references to 'adulterous bishops' and one who was 'propugnator et fornicator', a fine mixture of a fighting and fornicating man. To dismiss all who had lapsed from common decency would have meant the demise of Catholic worship.

St Boniface spent all his days dealing with wicked clerics. His labours raised the question: Was it the clergy who were to blame or the discipline imposed on them?

A large part of the history of celibacy is the story of the degradation of women and – an invariable consequence – frequent abortions and infanticide.

In the ninth century, many monasteries were the haunts of homosexuals, many convents were brothels in which babies were killed and buried. Since the end of the Roman Empire, historians say that infanticide was probably not practised in the West on any great scale – except in convents. The Council of Aix-la-Chapelle in the year 836 openly admitted it. As to the sex-starved secular clergy, they were so often accused of incest that they were at length forbidden even to have mothers, aunts or sisters living in their house. Children, the fruits of incest, were killed by the clergy, as many a French prelate put on record.

Some priests of the time acknowledged they preferred not to marry. It made it easier to keep their escapades secret. The church more easily condoned concubinage than marriage for the usual practical reason: concubines could not claim church property as a right for themselves and their offspring when their priest-lovers died.

Still, whole dioceses were filled with priests who took a more moral attitude and married. Increasingly, the priesthood, including bishoprics, became hereditary. A father handed on his living to his eldest son. Some regions allowed the priest one wife; any more and he was likely to be excommunicated. Bishops readily conceded that allowing priests to marry and keep their wives was the only way to purify the church from the worst excesses of celibacy. One holy bishop, St Ulric, argued for married priests on the basis of the Bible and common sense. Some prelates, he claimed, were pressing the breasts of Scripture to make them yield blood not milk.

The appalling behaviour of tenth-century Roman pontiffs was matched, so to speak, in the provinces. Bishop Segenfried of Le Mans was married to Hildeberga for thirty-three years, insisting gallantly that she should be called 'Episcopissa'. Grown old, he handed over his diocese with all its rich pickings to his son Alberic.

Another Alberic, Bishop of Marsico, was less of a gentleman. Being married, he gave up his see in favour of his son. Later on, being bored and wanting a challenge, he set his heart on the famous abbey of Monte Cassino. He entered into a pact with the abbey's arch enemies. Part of the deal was that the abbot's eyes were to be brought to him, without the abbot. Alberic handed over half the agreed sum in advance, the rest to be paid on delivery of the eyes. Alberic's own eyes were closed for ever at about the time the abbot lost his. The authority of this story was St Peter Damian. His written testimony to the evils caused by enforced celibacy was so horrendous that the pope pretended to borrow it and would not give it back, much to the saint's annoyance. Fortunately, it was preserved in the papal archives. It proves that profligacy among the clergy of the time was universal. After six centuries of strenuous efforts to impose celibacy, the clergy were a menace to the wives and young women of the parishes to which they were sent.

One celebrated offender was Rainbaldo, Bishop of Fiesole. After a heroic number of concubines, he took a wife who gave him many children to extend his empire. The Italians took it in good part, even crediting his Lordship with being a wonder-worker, as indeed he must have been.

Another Italian bishop, Rathurio, said sourly that if he excommunicated unchaste priests there would be none left to administer the sacraments, except boys. If he excluded bastards, as canon law demanded, not even boys.

Of this period, which included the abominable boy-pope Benedict IX, Pope Victor III (1086–7) had to admit that throughout Italy clerics from bishops down, without shame or concealment, were married, lived with their wives as openly as laymen and generously provided for their offspring in their wills. The scandals were often greatest in Rome itself, with popes setting a hot pace.

John, a disciple of Peter Damian, reported that clerical marriages were so common in the West that it was no longer punished by canon law. Bishops did not bother to administer a reprimand. Provided priests married, behaved themselves and did not marry a second or third time, they made no objections. Marriage was far less of a scandal than concubinage. Nicholas II (1059–61), prompted by Peter Damian, did implore bishops to give some sort of a lead. They replied defiantly that they were unequal to the task of preserving chastity and indifferent to any punishment the pontiff meted out.

Rome went on insisting it was more sinful to marry than to keep a concubine because it savoured of heresy and was a transgression of the law of the church. This explains some surprising decisions of Alexander II.

A priest of Orange in France committed adultery with his father's second wife. In the year 1064, Pope Alexander, instead of dismissing him, refused even to deprive him of holy communion. Leniency was called for because *he had not committed matrimony*. Two years later, a priest from Padua confessed to incest with his mother. The pope dealt very kindly with him and left it to his bishop to decide whether he should continue in the ministry or not. For Pope Alexander, adultery, even incest was preferable to a priest marrying.

When Peter Damian tried personally to impose celibacy on the clergy of Milan, he was fortunate to escape with all his faculties. It was hard for the Milanese priests to see that having sexual intercourse with their wives was adultery. Damian was also embarrassed to find that the clergy of Piedmont, all married, were 'a chorus of angels' in their ministry. If only, he moaned, they were not having improper relations with their wives they would be perfect. It never struck him that perhaps they were good priests because they were good husbands.

Damian, like Gregory VII, was not slow to call in the civil arm to impose celibacy on priests – an odd thing for prelates opposed to civil interference in church affairs to do.

It was Gregory who decided that in future no one could be ordained without first pledging himself to celibacy. With the power of his personality, he succeeded in throwing whole crowds of wives on the rubbish tip, many of whom, we noted, committed suicide. His purpose was clearly set out: 'Non liberari potest Ecclesia a servitute laicorum nisi liberentur prius clerici ab uxoribus', 'The church cannot escape from the clutches of the laity unless priests first escape from the clutches of their wives'. This was an open admission that celibacy is not principally about *holy living* but about the independence of the 'church' from lay interference. Above all, it was about keeping church possessions intact. In the eyes of this autocrat, the clergy *are* the church. This is why the nepotism of the medieval and Renaissance popes was doubly outrageous. For, though celibate, they gave away immense amounts of church property to their relatives, thus making celibacy void of *any* purpose. Boniface VIII, for example, was reckoned to have given 25 per cent of all church revenues to his family. Some popes bequeathed everything to their relatives, leaving their successors with no alternative but to sell spiritual goods in order to make ends meet.

Gregory VII did not have it all his own way. For instance, the Bishop of Pavia excommunicated him for preferring clerics to have mistresses instead of wives. The Archbishop of Mainz joined the other German bishops in saying Gregory had forfeited all claims to the papacy. Gregory, naturally, retaliated by excommunicating him. The rogue Council of Brixen in the year 1080 condemned Gregory for 'sowing divorce among legitimate spouses', and causing priests' children to be abandoned. The Patriarch of Constantinople rubbed his bit of salt in the wound by saying, tongue-in-cheek: 'In the Western churches there is a vast multitude of children but no one knows who the fathers are.'

Some priests said they would give up their ministry rather than their wives and denounced the pope as a heretic and a madman who expected creatures of flesh and blood to live like disembodied beings. When they were driven out, they asked, where would Gregory find the angels to replace them? Bishops did their best to carry out Gregory's wishes, sometimes at the risk of their lives. But the pope's trump card was the laity.

Against the entire tradition of the church, he excommunicated lay folk who accepted the sacraments from non-celibate priests. This led to many lay people treading the Eucharist of 'unchaste priests' in the dust and baptizing their own children. In many dioceses, religion virtually disappeared – because of celibacy. It was a paradox that was to be repeated down to the present day.

The matter was finally settled by Urban II at Piacenza in the year 1095. A council of 400 clerics and 30,000 laity condemned clerical marriages once and for all. To prove the evangelical impulse of this measure, they sold priests' wives into slavery.

Getting celibacy on to the statute-book was only the beginning. Without the civil arm, it would have been a dead letter. When Gregory VII's arch-foe Henry IV was deposed by his more orthodox son, celibacy was enforced in Germany and throughout the Empire. But shaving a man's head and putting him in mass vestments did not change his nature. Priests continued calling their wives *presbytera*. In fact, whenever canons were promulgated, they were forgotten with amazing speed. Bishops, like the Archbishop of Rouen, were driven out by their clergy for promulgating celibacy and told never to come back.

There also crept in the infamous *cullagium*, a charge for keeping concubines. Clergy were able to show their bishops the royal seal of approval on their domestic arrangements. Sometimes, bishops and archdeacons themselves benefited from this sex-tax; in Rome, it was the pope.

Norman priests not only had wives; they made solemn contracts with their wives' families to keep them in the style to which they were accustomed and to bestow church endowments on all boys *and* girls born of the union. In many places, livings were handed on from father to son to grandson to great-grandson. In Brittany, the Bishops of Dol, Rennes and Nantes were married; their wives had the courtesy title of countess. This was a recurring pattern. Strict laws were issued which authorities, even when they were willing, were unable to enforce. Human nature proved too strong for them. Archdeacons, pledged to see the canons obeyed, were often the worst offenders.

Such was Aldebert of Le Mans. He kept a public harem and delighted in his numerous progeny. He shocked people so little, he was made a bishop.

Promiscuity was rife in monasteries and convents. The great Ivo of Chartres (1040–1115) tells of whole convents with inmates who were nuns only in name. They had often been abandoned by their families and were really prostitutes.

A Momentous Change

Even Catholics are sometimes under the illusion that clerical celibacy was introduced in the twelfth century. This is a common mistake. Celibacy, however badly kept is several hundred years older than that. But something momentous did occur under Pope Callistus II. He summoned the first General Council of the West in the year 1123, known as the First Lateran. A thousand prelates decreed that clerical marriages should be broken up and the spouses made to do penance *because these marriages were invalid*. For the first time, celibacy was proclaimed to be the strongest spiritual reality. By it, a priest was marked in his soul as a man set so far apart from the laity that he could not even validly contract the sacrament of matrimony. This teaching was new; it went against centuries of tradition. One has only to quote St Gregory the Great who, in 602, made it plain that a priest's marriage was valid but he had to choose between keeping his wife or his ministry. Callistus withdrew this option. A priest's marriage was invalidated by his ordination.

No more than other Councils did the First Lateran alter priests' behaviour. This is why the Second Lateran in 1139 repeated its teaching. A union contracted in opposition to the church's rule on celibacy was not a true marriage. Though Pope Eugene IV confirmed this at the Council of Rheims in the year 1148, it was still hotly contested even in Rome. The great canonist Gratian, who wrote under the auspices of Eugene, clearly had difficulties with it. He continued to teach that a deacon can marry if he chooses to leave the ministry, and the sacrament of matrimony is so potent that *no antecedent vow can render it null and void*. In Gratian's view, the new law of the church – it has survived into our day – lacks all scriptural and patristic support and cannot be justified by any theological or ethical argument. As we saw, it seems to violate a person's natural right to marry.

Untraditional or not, unjust or not, the popes went on insisting from 1123 that marriages of priests were invalid because the ecclesiastical system demanded it. It made no obvious impact. Priests still married; their wives kept house for them; their children ministered at the altar.

Alexander III (1159–81) repeated the teaching of the Lateran Councils, but the sheer scope of priestly concubinage overwhelmed him. Discouraged, he was on the point of switching to the Greek tradition and allowing married men to be ordained. His Curia backed him up with one exception: the Chancellor, an ascetic abbot named Albert, who was to become Gregory VIII for one year in 1187. His intervention proved critical. The Western church was about to capitulate in the face of the massive disobedience of the clergy. It had reached the stage where bishops were pleading with their priests at least to abstain from sex three days and nights prior to touching the body of Christ.

So frightful were the abuses that another understandable error is to attribute the present discipline of celibacy to Innocent III at the Fourth Lateran Council in 1215. What Innocent did was simply use his tremendous authority to win acceptance for a discipline that had tradition against it. He never achieved the semblance of clerical chastity. All contemporary sources agreed on this. Priests, without the discipline of the bond of matrimony, became almost completely promiscuous. It has to be said that chastity of priests was not Innocent's prime concern, any more than it had been Gregory VII's. He wanted an unmarried priesthood to operate Gregory's clerical and absolutist system. Priests, however holy, who married were not so loyal to the system as celibate priests who were fornicators and adulterers on a grand scale.

The discipline of celibacy now in place actually led to unchastity. Proof of this comes in the writing of one of the great reforming saints, Bernard of Clairvaux. In the year 1135 he was responding to the Albigensian claim that marriage is sordid. Bernard said: 'Take from the Church an honourable marriage and an immaculate marriage bed, and do you not fill it with concubinage, incest, homosexuality and every kind of uncleanness?'

This argument applied with equal force to priestly celibacy. Orthodoxy, no less than heresy, by a false and forced asceticism, encouraged every kind of clerical abuse. Concubines were actually the least harmful method of restraining the priests' sexual appetites.

The evidence for this exists on an alarming scale. Impeccable Catholic sources, papal documents, letters of reforming saints, all paint the same depressing picture. Monasteries full of women; every friar had his 'Martha', every nun her lover. Bishops, in every sense the fathers of their people, kept harems and the few brave souls who tried to enforce the discipline risked being poisoned or beaten to death. Alexander IV, in a Bull dated 1259, bemoans the fact that the laity were not reformed but corrupted by the clergy. In Avignon, the avaricious John XXII allowed priests to keep their mistresses on payment of a tax. Even the few chaste priests had to pay up just in case they, too, fell into the arms of a woman. It was a cynical acceptance of the fact that even offences against God could benefit the system, only disobedience to canon law undermined it. 'The subject', says the fastidious Lea, 'is too repulsive to be presented in all its loathsome details.' The clergy did not scruple to use the sacrament of penance for beginning and continuing their immoral liaisons. Petrarch, Boccaccio, Chaucer, all give witness to the sheer size of the scandal. They satirized the situation but in no way exaggerated it.

An Italian diarist, the wandering thirteenth-century Franciscan friar Salimbene, wrote:

> I have seen priests keeping taverns . . . and their whole house full of bastard children, and spending their nights in sin and celebrating Mass next day. . . . One day, when a Franciscan friar had to celebrate Mass in a certain priest's church on a feast day, he had no stole but the girdle of the priest's concubine, with the bunch of keys attached; and when the friar, whom I know well, turned round to say, *Dominus Vobiscum*, the people heard the jangling of the keys.

Celibacy in the British Isles

English priests found celibacy difficult from the moment that Augustine of Canterbury first set foot on their soil. The church already there knew nothing of the Roman discipline, so that Pope Gregory was forced to recognize there were clerics in Britain who do 'not wish to remain single'. He authorized Augustine to let them marry and draw their stipends separately.

Later, Rome's best efforts at reform proved fruitless. The old custom of bishops turning a blind eye to clergy marrying continued. Priests thought of their 'shrift-shire' as family property to be handed on to their sons and grandsons.

The parlous state of the clergy is easily explained. There were times when a third of the male population were in holy orders. Most of the richer clergy were pluralists; they had several livings. They farmed them out to stipendiary chaplains who had to survive on starvation wages. The benefice might be worth fifty marks a year. The rector looked around for a curate who would take it over for five marks, pocketing the remainder himself. In such circumstances, the parson needed a wife to help him make ends meet. He grazed his sheep, the woolly sort, in the churchyard. He spent his days up to his waist in stream-water fishing and many a night in a tavern, drinking and brawling. Chaucer's Miller boasted his wife was a priest's daughter, but the clergy did not always have a good reputation. They were quick with their fists, and, when they were refused the living of their fathers, were quite likely to take possession of it with incense and the sword.

'Priests know full well', went one tenth-century statute, 'that they have no right to marry. . . . But some are guilty of a worse practice in having two or more wives, and others, though they forsake their former wives, afterwards take others while these are still alive, a thing which no Christian man ought to do, let alone a priest.' As usual, the attempt to impose celibacy meant clergy were more promiscuous then the laity.

One priest justified his rape of a parishioner by saying 'he must needs have his pleasure of her'. His idle hands had to have something to do.

Lanfranc, the Norman who became Archbishop of Canterbury in 1070, permitted many priests who had married with a clear conscience to keep their wives, telling them not to do it again, and warning bishops that future ordinands must give an undertaking not to marry. This was a realistic move in a land where even bishops were married.

In this, England was no different from the rest of Christendom. In the West, from the fourth century to the eleventh, celibacy was sunk in oblivion. It is an illusion to suggest that the Catholic church survived because of the ministry of chaste and celibate priests. She survived, in fact, through the ministry of unchaste and mostly married priests. The discipline of celibacy was breached as often by clerics as the discipline of birth control is today breached by the laity.

Anselm, who succeeded Lanfranc as Archbishop of Canterbury, was more severe. Wives were sent away; their priest-husbands were not allowed to see them except in the open air and in the presence of chaperons. Many priests rebelled; they locked up their churches and refused to say mass or administer the sacraments. Even in Canterbury, the clergy kept wives. When Anselm excommunicated them, they took no notice. The times were such that Pope Paschal II agreed to waive the canons and let the sons of priests be ordained, otherwise there would have been no candidates for the ministry.

When, at Rome's bidding, bishops got tougher, many priests indulged in incest, or felt that, being deprived of lawful wives, they were entitled to their mistresses.

When Pope Honorius II got wind of the hot-blooded English, he sent John, Cardinal of Crema to reform them. His Eminence gathered the senior clerics together and, during mass, bitterly denounced the clergy's evil ways. So magnificent was his oration that the priests gave a banquet in his honour. The cardinal, wisely leaving them to their revels, retired for the night. Not long afterwards, representatives of the English clergy crashed into his room to find the cardinal was not saying his prayers. On the contrary, in the most glorious Chaucerian tradition, he was abed in the arms of a woman, without his vestments on, or, as a contemporary wrote, 'nudatus usque ad unguem', naked to his finger-nails. It was a clear case of medieval entrapment. Having toasted the prelate of the Scarlet Skin and the 'fayre ladye' beside him on the pillow, the intruders left him in peace for the night. He soon slipped quietly out of England.

When in the year 1171 the monk Clarembald was made abbot-elect of St Augustine's in Canterbury, the most prestigious monastic post in England, Pope Alexander III, who had for some while been fruitlessly trying to make the English chaste, decided to play it safe. He appointed three prelates to enquire into his suitability. They discovered that Clarembald had seventeen bastards in one village alone. His reputation was no secret, yet no one around him doubted that he was the best candidate for the job.

It was in the reign of Alexander III that church documents stopped referring to a priest's 'wife', using 'concubine' and 'focaria', or hearthmate, instead. These were the ladies whom King John snatched out of the parson's bed at dead of night during his conflict with Innocent III, demanding a high tax for their return.

Whatever the labels, these *focariae* were true and loyal wives to the clergy, most priests in England having hearthmates. No matter what penalties the church imposed – and sometimes these women were denied Christian burial – she never did prevent priests having companions of their bed and board. It was not until about the year 1250, after general and local Councils, that the clergy finally accepted the reality of celibacy. From then on, promiscuity took over.

Records show that many men became celibate because they could not be chaste. One wife was one wife. A priest could have as many women as he wished, and many priests did.

In the year 1250, Bishop Grosseteste of Lincoln wrote to Pope Innocent IV. Of priests, he said: 'They are in truth teachers of heresy, inasmuch as the word of action is mightier than the word of speech.'

He was blunt enough to blame the Roman Curia for all the troubles that ensued.

Later, Pope Innocent tried to foist his own nephew on Lincoln as a pretend. Grosseteste was an extreme papalist but he found this unseemly, hateful to Christ and a menace to the human race. In a marvellous act of defiance, he wrote to the pontiff: 'As an obedient son I disobey, I contradict, I rebel. You cannot take action against me, for my every word and act is not really rebellious but the filial honour due by God's command to one's father and mother.' In the opinion of the Bishop of Lincoln, loyalty to the pope was not the same as loyalty to the Gospel of Christ. It is significant that the diocese of Lincoln was one of the few in which priests behaved themselves. The bishop emptied presbyteries of suspicious-looking females. When he visited convents, he insisted that all the sisters had their breasts squeezed. He needed visible proof that they had not done anything naughty since his last visitation.

In the next century and a half, things deteriorated further. In the year 1414, King Henry V asked the University of Oxford to prepare articles for the reform of the church. Article 39 began: 'Because the carnal and sinful life of priests today scandalizes the entire church and their public fornication goes completely unpunished. . . .'

In the parish of St John Zachary in London, there was a church service of a very remarkable kind. It provided a brothel exclusively for priests and friars. Only men with a tonsure, the shaven circle representing Christ's crown of thorns, were admitted. No doubt the women selected for this place felt they had a special vocation. It was at this time that a call came from the gentlemen of Kent to deal firmly with lascivious clerics. The rite of ordination, it was suggested, should include enforced castration.

It was not canon but civil law which made the clergy more discreet, if not more holy, in their behaviour. Henry VII was prompt to imprison any priest found guilty of unchastity.

Pope Innocent VIII authorized Morton, Archbishop of Canterbury, to enquire into the state of religious houses in the year 1489. As a result, Innocent said, all the houses were sunk in iniquity. St Alban's Abbey, for instance, was nothing but a den of prostitutes serving the local monks. Nuns were regularly raped therein and the entire place, in a phrase worthy of Shakespeare, was 'a riot of seed and blood'.

Henry VIII, Defender of the Faith, husband of six wives, was also a stout champion of priestly chastity. This may have been due to the fact that, had not his brother Arthur died, Henry might have become a priest. Hence his frequent attendance at five masses daily and his poring over scholastic theology. Who knows, he might have ended up as a distinguished Archbishop of Canterbury.

In the year 1535, Henry, now furious with the pope, ordered Thomas Cromwell to look into life in the cloister. One of Cromwell's men, Dr Leighton, visited the abbey of Langdon in Kent. Breaking down the abbot's door, Leighton found him in bed with his mistress. The woman's male attire, a disguise, was hanging up in a cupboard. The overall report said that 144 religious houses were equal in viciousness to Sodom; countless convents, served by 'lewd confessors', were full of children; clergy – abbots, monks and friars – were carrying on not merely with whores but with married women. Nothing had changed since Archbishop Morton's inquiry half a century before. After receiving Cromwell's dossier and in the wake of Henry's excommunication by Pope Paul III, Parliament began to suppress the monasteries.

Even then, the king cruelly insisted that monks, without monastery or livelihood, were still bound by their vow of celibacy. He sent one priest to the scaffold without benefit of clergy for not abandoning his wife. It is not clear what St Peter would have made of that. Cranmer, Henry's Archbishop of Canterbury, who had secretly married for the second time, sent his wife home to Germany, just in case the king cut up rough.

Henry VIII's enthusiasm for celibacy was handed on to both his daughters.

For Bloody Mary, the Catholic, married priests smacked of heresy. Summarily dismissed and forbidden to cohabit with their lawful wives, they were reduced once more to secret concubinage and promiscuity.

When Mary died in November 1558, Elizabeth the Virgin Queen and a Protestant found married priests not to her liking, either. Though she made her married tutor, Parker, Archbishop of Canterbury, she went out of her way to make it known she did not wish to speak with his lady.

In the end she was forced, barely, to tolerate clerical marriages for the sake of the Reformation but she attributed them to the weakness of the flesh. Moreover, the clergy's fiancées had to be thoroughly examined by a bishop and two justices of the peace to guarantee they were suited to gentlemen of the cloth. In the Thirty-Nine Articles, the clergy of the Church of England finally achieved respectability. 'Therefore it is lawful for them as for all other Christian men to marry at their own discretion, as they shall judge the same to serve better to godliness.' Not that Elizabeth, even in death, could bear being ministered to by a married priest. Many a cleric probably found it no less onerous having a woman as Supreme Governor of the Church of England.

England was not alone in a strenuous grass-roots opposition to clerical celibacy. St Patrick found great obstinacy in Celtic Ireland. He was content if a bishop had one wife and one child. This was his interpretation of St Paul. One child, he seems to have surmised, a bishop can keep under control, thus giving his diocesans a good example of family discipline. Patrick did not find it in the least embarrassing that he himself came from a very religious family. In his *Confessions* he tells that his great-grandfather had been a deacon, his grandfather a priest, and his father, Calpornius, a deacon. But for the fact that Patrick's clerical forebears had had intercourse with their wives, there would have been no St Patrick and no conversion of Ireland.

After Patrick, there were married *bishops* in Ireland until the twelfth century when St Malachy was ordained by Celsus, Archbishop of Armagh. According to St Bernard, Malachy's biographer, Celsus' eight predecessors in the primatial see had all been married men.

The Welsh went one better than the Irish. Welsh authors take pride in the fact that celibacy *never* took root in Wales. As J. M. Willis Bund wrote in *The Celtic Church in Wales*: 'The Welsh clergy are the only clerical body who have, from first to last, in spite of all opposition, asserted and maintained their right to marry. . . . When the rest of Europe were pledged, as a matter of principle, to celibacy, but tempered it in practice by fornication, the Welsh clergy remained alone the defenders of the right, the absolute right, of the clergy to marry.'

Gerard, the thirteenth-century Archdeacon of Brecon, is the chief historian of the period. As a confidant of Innocent III and a man hungry for promotion, he always refers to clerical wives as concubines. All the canons of St David's, he says, were public fornicators and given to concubinage, even within the cathedral precincts. They made strict provisions for their sons to take over from them when they retired. As James Conway Davis wrote: 'This system of succession prevailed not only in cathedrals but throughout the whole clergy and people of Wales. Nor was it an abuse in Wales alone. All the clergy, English and Welsh, who went to Ireland were incontinent.'

According to Gerard, abbeys were full of happy women and laughing children. Most parishes belonged to families, so that one parish might have two rectors, one a priest and one a layman. Bishops were buried with their wives. As to presbyteries, they were not exactly havens of peace and solitude. 'The houses and homes of parish priests', Gerard wrote, 'are full of bossy mistresses, creaking cradles, new-born babes and squawling brats.'

For all his apparent sourness, Gerard questioned the wisdom of celibacy. He pointed out that marriage was not originally forbidden to priests. But was not a priest married to the church? he was asked. How could he be married to a woman? *Nonsense*, he replied. The church is the Bride of Christ, not the bride of a clergyman. In Gerard's book, *Gemma Ecclesiastica*, occurs a superb aphorism which he attributes to Pope Alexander III: 'The pope deprived the clergy of sons and the devil sent them nephews!'

The Welsh clergy continued to marry until the Reformation when their lifestyle was no longer dictated to them by Rome.

*   *   *

The Scots were far less honourable than the Welsh in their opposition to the rule of celibacy. The behaviour of the Scottish clergy prior to the Reformation was outrageous. The rot had set in a long time before.

King James IV had received permission from Rome to appoint whom he wished to the see of St Andrews. He first appointed his brother as archbishop, but when he died he replaced him with his nine-year-old bastard son, Alexander Stewart.

When the king died on Flodden Field on 9 September 1513, he left a year-old son who succeeded him as King James V. When he reached the age of twenty, James V wrote to Pope Clement VII. The Scottish king already had three illegitimate children. He enquired of his Holiness if his bastards might be dispensed from illegitimacy so as to hold future office in the church. Clement agreed, provided none of the boys was made a bishop or archbishop before he was aged twenty. James thanked the pontiff and proceeded to distribute among his bastards some of the prime abbeys of Scotland, including Kelso and Melrose, St Andrews and Holyrood.

A measure of the clergy's decadence can be gauged by an examination of the Register of the Great Seal in the thirty-year span between 1529 and 1559. It was the custom for gentlemen to have their bastards legitimated to allow them to succeed. Every class of cleric was represented in the Register from cardinal to curate. There were ten bishops on it, even more vicars and still more chaplains.

One amazing statistic emerges: in a country of 900,000 people, there were 3,000 clergy; and yet two out of five bastards were born to the clergy. The picture of the priest as a 'drunken Sir John Latinless' was very accurate.

The most notorious cleric of all was David, Cardinal Beaton. He was Chancellor of Scotland and, from 1538, Archbishop of St Andrews and Scottish Primate. He was a widower, and everyone knew he had never lost 'the talent God gave him'.

At Beaton's enthronement in the late summer of 1539, Archbishop Hay gave a brave address, *Panegyricus*:

> I often wonder what bishops were thinking about when they admitted such men to the handling of the Lord's holy body, when they hardly knew the order of the alphabet. Priests come to that heavenly table who have not slept off yesterday's debauch. . . . I will not treat of the riotous living of those who, professing chastity, have invented new kinds of lusts, which I prefer to be left unknown rather than be told by me.

His Eminence, as he listened to this, must have remembered that, seven years before, three of his children had been legitimated: David, Elizabeth and Margaret. He was already planning to have his sovereign, James V, legitimate other productions of his, including James, Alexander and John. There were all described in the official lists as 'bastards of the Archbishop of St Andrews'. Historians are not sure how many of these bastards he had, but possibly eleven sons and four daughters.

John Knox, the Reformer, called him this 'carnal Cardinal' and spoke of the 'Cardinal's graceless Grace'. This prelate with his prodigious brood married off one of his daughters with great *éclat* to the Earl of Crawford in 1546, calling her 'my daughter' at the wedding. The same man was prepared to burn a heretic for eating an egg during Lent.

It is no surprise that Calvinism was greeted in Scotland as a breath of fresh air. The Scots had had enough of 'pestilent Papists and Mass-mongers', 'adulterous whoremongers', 'insolent shavelings'. When a Calvinist minister was sacked for adultery, he stayed sacked.

On Continental Europe

Over the sea in France, bishops found it hard enough to get their clergy to wear vestments at the altar; they were scarcely likely to get them to obey regulations in bed. Gerson, a mystic, Chancellor of the University of Paris, recommended clerical concubinage as the lesser of two evils. It was a counsel of despair in the face of overwhelming odds.

Across the border in Belgium lived Henry, Bishop of Liège. The man was a legend in and beyond his lifetime. Henry was finally deposed by Gregory X at the Council of Lyons in 1274 'for deflowering virgins and other mighty deeds'. His children by many concubines, several of them nuns, numbered sixty-five, which was a trifle excessive for a prelate even in those days. He ended up murdered by a Flemish knight who was outraged at what the bishop had done to his daughter.

In Germany, where the Reformation was first to take root, the evidence for clerical abuse is embarrassing. In the fifteenth century, Busch, a monk, was appointed papal visitor to clergy houses and monasteries. He found abbots who could not read or write and who had no sense of right and wrong. When Busch tried to rid parishes of unworthy priests, he realized that it would mean the end of sacramental life. One knight came to Busch and said:

> You have decreed that the parsons must dismiss
> their maidservants or concubines. But there are two
> or three parishes on my estates in Meissen whence
> the parsons have departed with their concubines,
> leaving their churches without pastors: therefore
> the parishioners have neither mass nor sermon nor

other services, but walk like pagans, almost without God. It were better that you should suffer them to retain their concubines than that the people should become as heathens.

Ever since celibacy was imposed, the church has had to make a stark choice between an 'immoral' clergy and none at all. As Peter Comestor said: 'The devil never harmed the church so much as when the church herself adopted the vow of celibacy.' Three centuries later, Martin Luther agreed with him, and not just because the clergy were misbehaving on a grand scale. Luther saw the danger of saying that celibacy is 'the way of perfection'. It meant that marriage is a state of imperfection. This was a fundamental denial of the Gospel. All men and women, he said, were called to be perfect, not just celibates. All were called to be Christians, not half-Christians and half-pagans. His evangelical claim seemed revolutionary at the time: in whatever state of life a person found himself, he was called to be perfect, whether he was a potter or priest. The humblest carpenter was called to be as perfect as the pope.

Luther's rebellion was an attack not only on the abuses of celibacy but on celibacy itself as an institution that distorted the Gospel and demoted the laity. The abuses were the inevitable consequence of this misconception. The benefits of Luther's intervention were immediate. According to Owen Chadwick: 'To turn the mistress into an honourable wife, to turn the bastards into honourable children, was the momentous single gift bestowed upon the clergy by Protestantism. Apart from higher considerations it was said that, before his marriage to Catherine von Bora, Luther's bed had not been made for a year.'

Spain's record on celibacy was no better than Germany's. Since it was off the beaten track of Europe, divided internally and subject to Moorish invasions, the papacy tended to treat Spain as a special case. Up to the year 1130, there is only one reference in papal documents to celibacy there, and that was to say the clergy were to be left in peace with their wives. The case of the abbot of Santo Pelayo de Antealtaria was proof that Spanish clerics were hard to handle. Openly criticized by his archbishop on at least seven occasions for his immorality, he was finally brought to trial in 1130. Sound witnesses testified that he had seventy concubines. For this truly Solomonic hoard of femininity, the abbot was deposed and, as punishment, was given a benefice in abbey lands to support himself, his good ladies and his, doubtless, numerous progeny. To Spain in 1322 can be traced the sensible custom of the laity insisting that their priests take a female consort *before* taking up residence.

Of course, Rome's example, as was seen in Part 1, was the worst of all.

The Unholy See

The papacy, which imposed celibacy against the wisdom of the early church and against natural justice, was often the worst offender. The tenth-century Reign of the Harlots, the complete corruption of the papacy during the Avignon exile, the sheer misery of the Great Schism were matched in all periods. The record is absolutely consistent. Even reforming popes could not clean up their own Curia. We noted how in 1250 Cardinal Hugo thanked Lyons for its hospitality to the Curia. But the Curia had been generous, too. They found only three or four prostitutes when they came to Lyons but they left it one big brothel.

It was not merely the extravagant lives of libertines like Sixtus IV, Innocent VIII and Alexander Borgia that did the damage. The church suffered from the refusal of more chaste popes to reform the church according to the demands of the Councils of Constance and Basle.

The clergy were quite as prolific as the laity, but the popes said they could do nothing about it. Innocent VIII dissuaded his vicar from attempting to clean up Rome because immorality among the clergy was endemic. During Borgia's reign, the Florentine friar Savonarola said that nuns were worse than harlots. As to the clergy, 'one priest spends the night with his concubine, another with a little boy, and in the morning they proceed to the altar to celebrate Mass. What do you think of that? What do you make of such a Mass?'

Pope Paul III's commission of nine prelates, headed by Cardinal Carafa, reported in 1535:

> In this Rome, harlots go about in the city like married women, or ride on their mules, followed from the heart of the city by nobles and clerics of the Cardinal's household. In no city have we seen this corruption, except in this [which should be] an example to all.

The evil was too deep to be uprooted; the last opportunities of reform were long past. Guicciardini, in his unpublished works, said: 'One cannot speak badly enough of the Roman Curia but it deserves more, for it is infamous, an example of all that is vicious and nasty in the world.' With the Reformation looming, a bishop of the Papal States like Chiari of Foligno found that only two priests in his diocese knew the words of absolution. It did not matter; no one would go to them for confession because their lives were so unchaste. 'The fault', Chiari said, 'lies with bishops and parish priests, for our whole life is a continuous preaching of unbelief.' A proverb passed from mouth to mouth: 'The profession of the priest is the surest road to hell.' An honest man like Pope Adrian VI freely admitted this.

When the Reformation struck, it was the celibacy of the clergy that provoked it as much as the scandal of indulgences. In Germany, many priests realized that only through marrying could they gain the evangelic, even the human freedom that the system was denying them. By marrying, the Reformers believed they were not acting dissolutely. They were simply restoring the ancient tradition and giving marriage the honour due to it. Celibacy, they decided, had done too much harm to the church to let it continue. The laity agreed with them.

In desperation, but far too late, the papacy tried spiritual measures.

The Council of Trent finally met in November 1542. Hardly any bishops turned up, so it broke up and reassembled two and a half years later. It continued on and off for over twenty years.

By the year 1560 the Emperor Ferdinand was begging the pope to permit the clergy to marry as the only way to get them to behave. 'For although all flesh was corrupted,' he wrote, 'none the less, the corruption of the priesthood is worst of all.'

The Duke of Cleves, sovereign of three populous duchies, reported that there were not five priests in all his territory living without a concubine.

The emperor joined with the staunchly Catholic Duke of Bavaria, begging Trent to rid the church of imposed celibacy *for the laity's sake*. The scandals were now unendurable. Many patrons of livings, they told the Council, were flatly refusing to accept clerics without wives because it was *too dangerous for their flocks*. The church might suffer the loss of some property as a result of clerics bequeathing things to their children; this had to be weighed against the bigger loss of souls under the prevailing discipline.

None of this had any effect. The Council was completely under the thumb of Rome. As Father Sarpi said, the Holy Spirit came to Trent in a suitcase packed in Rome.

The chief reason for maintaining the discipline was the one dearest to the heart of Gregory VII: a celibate priest owed total allegiance not to wife and children but to the institution. He was a creature of the institution. The Roman system was absolutist and hierarchical. For such a system to work, it needed operatives completely at the beck and call of superiors. The conservatives at Trent were quite frank about this. They actually said that without celibacy the pope would be nothing more than the Bishop of Rome. In brief, the papal system would collapse without the unqualified allegiance of the clergy; celibacy alone could guarantee that sort of allegiance. Celibacy, on Trent's own admission, was not and never was primarily a matter of chastity but of *control*. Clergy are the worker bees that enable the hive to function. Far from being first and foremost a way of serving God in freedom, Trent said it was a way of serving the institution through compulsion. Once a priest was ordained, he was a prisoner of the system. If he proved disloyal, he was unable to function even as a normal human being by marrying. The church took that natural right away from him when she said to him: 'Thou art a priest for ever according to the order of Melchisedech.'

Trent, contrary to the first thousand years and more of tradition, said it is *against the faith* to say priests, monks and nuns could contract a valid marriage. God would not deny the gift of chastity to those who asked. Further, the celibate state was higher than the married state. On 11 November 1563 the Council solemnly decreed:

> If anyone says the married state is to be placed above the state of virginity or of celibacy and that it is not better and more blessed to remain in virginity and celibacy than to be united in matrimony, let him be anathema.

This was the final hammer-blow against the sanctity of marriage dealt by a celibate clergy. At a time when priestly celibacy was such a scandal that it made people ashamed to be Catholic, the Council proclaimed celibacy the jewel in the crown. When the wounds of Christendom needed balm, the bishops, urged on by Rome, poured in vinegar. Trent made it plain that it stood for confrontation not conciliation.

So, strangely, celibacy, which had to a large degree provoked the Reformation, now became the standard-bearer of the Catholic Counter-Reformation, the proof that Catholicism was not going to yield an inch to Protestants. The latter were outsiders, heretics, not true reformers at all. What Rome demanded of them was instant obedience to the Holy See and a renunciation of their foolish plea for a married clergy.

Trent gave no reason for saying celibates could not contract a valid marriage. The Council did not explain why it was prepared to condemn not merely Protestants but most generations of Catholics who took it for granted that any marriage between two people was valid by natural law, even if they were in orders.

Above all, Trent had sown the wind by defining that celibacy was superior to marriage. The Council declared that only celibates had chosen the better part and were in 'the state of perfection'. It was some consolation to men who were celibates by compulsion to be told that they were the only real Christians in the church. But what would St Peter have made of it? And what would priests in years to come make of it?

Trent's major contribution to improving the behaviour of priests was issuing strict rules for their education. Seminaries not only consolidated the church's teaching; they also helped bring about a semblance of propriety among the clergy. For the first time clerics were trained in 'priest-factories'. This was two-edged. They could no longer get by without a knowledge of the alphabet; they received a minimum theological formation and a regimen that fitted them for the ministry. On the other hand, they were more than ever isolated from the life and concerns of the laity. Better-fitted to serve the institution, they were aliens to the life of the people.

Apart from the benefits of seminaries, the advent of the secular state meant that clergy were forced, externally at least, to conform to the standards of society. They were no longer a law unto themselves, endowed with the privilege of clergy. Not any more were their crimes withdrawn from civil to ecclesiastical courts which knew how to protect their own and conceal their misdemeanours. Civil penalties helped check the clergy's improprieties which canon law had failed to do for over a thousand years.

Not that Trent was effective immediately. As late as the year 1616, the Archbishop of Salzburg expressed himself happy enough if his priests kept their concubines and brats outside a six-mile exclusion zone. More surprising still, popes with dubious reputations continued to be elected well into the seventeenth century.

Gregory XV, who became pontiff in 1621, was credited with remaining faithful to the lady whose affections he had possessed as cardinal.

Innocent X, during an eleven-year reign beginning in 1644, could not have been closer to his brother's widow, Donna Olympia. She entertained on his behalf. She signed papal decrees and was First Lady in everything but name. She even sold benefices and granted promotions in the church. The period became known as 'the Pontificate of Donna Olympia'. A medal was struck in Florence. It shows Olympia on one side, in papal robes. On the reverse is Innocent X in a coif, sitting next to a spinning-wheel. When his aide, Cardinal Pencirillo alerted his Holiness to the scandal he was causing, Innocent did his best to do without her but found her indispensable. In the last few weeks of his life, she never left his side. In 1655, in his eightieth year, he expired on her bosom.

Sins of the Confessional

Did the rule of celibacy finally succeed in producing a chaste clergy? In view of the post-Reformation secretiveness of the Roman church, is there any possibility of finding out the state of clerical morals?

By a remarkable piece of research, Lea managed to cast some light on one of the murkiest of celibate preserves: the confessional.

The Fourth Council of the Lateran in 1215 made it obligatory for lay people to confess annually to their parish priests. This was the same Council at which Innocent III gave celibacy its final form. The combination of these two rules was to prove harmful to the morals of both clergy and laity. It led to the sin known in canon law as 'solicitation', that is, a priest using the confession for immoral purposes. Of course, penalties were imposed by the church. They became increasingly severe, but there is no evidence that they diminished the number of times priests took advantage of their position to make passes at their penitents.

So widespread was confessional abuse that the laity were told that if their priest was of evil repute they were dispensed from the need to confess their carnal sins to him. The privacy of the confessional provided the clergy with ready access to women at their most vulnerable, that is, when they were obliged by canon law to confess every impure thought, deed and desire. If, say, a woman confessed to fornication or adultery, the priest made matters far worse if he solicited her. But she was not keen to take this outside the seal of confession. She did not want to risk losing her reputation.

It has to be remembered that for centuries after Innocent III penitents confessed either sitting next to the priest or kneeling at his feet. The confessional box or stall, now a fixture in churches, was not invented until the middle of the sixteenth century. Only from 1614 was it made compulsory by the Roman Ritual. Even then it was not widely used. In Spain any number of *ad hoc* substitutes were employed. It might be a grating that separated priest and penitent, or a handkerchief, a sieve, twigs or a fan. Soliciting under these circumstances in a dark and lonely church remained prevalent. Confession was thus often a means by which the clergy corrupted women and eluded the demands of celibacy.

Whenever a parish priest was denounced by a penitent, the ecclesiastical court bent over backwards to be lenient to him. In February 1535 the parish priest of Almodovar was accused of numerous sexual offences, including frequenting brothels and soliciting in the confessional. He had refused to give a young woman absolution until she consented to have sex with him. He was given a small fine and confined to his house for thirty days. Afterwards he was doubtless free to continue as before.

So lax had the Bishops' Tribunals become that the Inquisition was keen to take over from them. Paul IV decided that soliciting implied heresy; this enabled him to grant the Inquisition what it wanted. This was a decision that proved the church was more interested in the integrity of confession than in the integrity of women. Through all the subsequent violations of the sacrament, the chief concern of the interrogators was not that women but the sacrament had been abused. For example, if a priest was able to show that, though he had seduced a penitent, it was in his room and in no way related to confession, he walked away without penalty.

Moralists made things worse by casuistry. What, they asked, did soliciting consist in? Would touching hands, or playing footsie, or fondling a woman's breasts, or passing love-letters? And how lewd did language have to be before it constituted grave matter? Some Spanish moralists came to the conclusion that if a woman fainted while confessing and the priest took the opportunity to rape her this did not *technically* amount to soliciting. The woman was clearly in no condition to respond. Books on moral theology were consulted by priests, not to make them better confessors, but to teach them how to manipulate women in confession without incurring the penalties of canon law.

Pope after pope tightened up the legislation, making penalties more severe. For example, a priest's 'accomplice' was forbidden to confess to him. If he absolved her from sins committed with him, he was automatically excommunicated and his absolution declared invalid. The number of priests denounced in no way diminished.

Popes enlisted the cleverest canon lawyers to close the loopholes that priests kept finding in the rules. The penitent, for example, was obliged to denounce any confessor who solicited him or her. But proof was difficult; it was the penitent's word against the confessor's, and there were no witnesses. The church had provided the clergy with an almost foolproof way of tempting those who were under an obligation to confess their unchastity to them. Aggrieved penitents had little hope of seeing justice done. The catch was that they often had to accuse themselves and before two male interrogators who belonged to the same élite group as the priest they were denouncing. Anyway, in a small town or village, could anything be kept secret?

Lea gained access to the diocesan archives of Spain. By painstaking research of Inquisitorial documents, kept with customary thoroughness, he made a number of discoveries. Between 1723 and 1820, when the Inquisition finally folded, 3,775 cases came to the attention of the authorities. Of these, all but 981 involved priests of religious orders, that is, monks and friars. Another unexpected item: a large proportion of those indicted held high office. They were provincials, guardians of houses, ministers, priors or rectors. It was a perk of office, it seems, to be in a position to solicit women.

The figures are not merely high, they are staggering for other reasons.

In the first place, on 1 June 1741, Benedict XIV had issued a Constitution, *Sacramentum Poenitentiae*. It contained the stiffest ever penalties for the crime of soliciting. A priest found guilty was suspended from saying mass and hearing confessions; he was stripped of his titles and deprived of his living. This and the holiness of the confessional should have made soliciting taboo. It clearly did not. In view of the vast numbers of cases reported, the amount of misbehaviour inside and outside the confessional beggars the imagination. Lay women often visited the clergy in their presbyteries; priests were able to visit lay women in their homes while the husbands were at work. Why did priests *need* to risk their livelihood in the confessional, except that the temptation proved too much for them? The reason more religious solicited than secular priests is attributed by Lea to an economic fact. Secular priests had more cash available to pay for female consolation outside the danger area; religious had to take their pickings when and where they could.

Another reason that makes the number of reported solicitings amazing is that Spanish women must have found it very hard to point the finger of blame at a priest. He was a professionally holy man. Who were they to challenge his integrity publicly? Besides, they must have thought their case was unique. After all, the authorities always hushed up the sins of the clergy; it was bad for morale. This also explains in part the leniency of the sentences imposed on priests. Whereas the Inquisition treated Jews and Protestants with unswerving severity, they tended to show mercy to their own. A young woman who had been solicited, thinking her case was unique, was tempted to tell no one, not even her husband or lover. If she did denounce her confessor, her own reputation was bound to suffer. Far better to put the priest's indecency down to a regrettable lapse that he would not dare to repeat. Until recently, Western women adopted the same attitude when they were raped. They were reluctant to report it to the police in case they were not believed or would be accused of *wanting* to be raped.

The cases recorded in scrupulous detail by the church's own teams of investigators show every form of sexual deviance. Some priests solicited on a grand scale. Interfering with ten penitents was not uncommon. Nuns were solicited, as were small children, men and boys.

There were numerous instances of a confessor acting as a *flagellante*; he would order the female penitent to remove her clothes so he could whip her as she deserved. Sometimes priest and penitent undressed and flogged each other. Priests were sometimes accused of being 'solicitante y flagellante'. One priest of Yepes had had sex with nine sisters of the Bernardine convent; they lashed themselves under his gaze, applying the whip to their peccant parts. That which travelling businessmen pay handsomely for today, some Spanish priests had for nothing in the sanctuary of the confessional. One intriguing detail: though the clergy were frequently found guilty of soliciting in the confessional, there is no recorded instance of a church being reconsecrated, as was demanded by canon law when sexual misdemeanours occurred and seed was spilt. If the canons were heeded, there would have been some churches in need of regular blessing by the bishop.

Of the clergy indicted for sex-offences some were of advanced years. One priest from Toledo, denounced in 1734, was aged seventy-eight. Another from Cuenca in 1786 was eighty. They were probably coming to the end of a very long soliciting career.

*   *   *

It would be unfair to suggest that Spanish priests, in spite of their record, were worse than the clergy of other countries. Such a studied abuse of the sacrament is, however, proof, if proof were needed, that too many clerics were forced to lead an unnatural life. They were probably well intentioned when they offered themselves for ordination. If they became corrupt, it was because an enforced celibacy corrupted them. They were the first victims of a papal system that ignored the apostle's warning: 'It is better to marry than to burn [with passion].'

According to Lea, 'only a small proportion of offenders were denounced, and of these but a fraction were brought to trial. . . . The strain of the confessional is too great for average human nature, and the most that the church can do, in its most recent regulations, is to keep their lapses of the flesh from the knowledge of the faithful.'

Priests are trained from eighteen and sometimes ten years of age in a seminary, away from all contact with girls and women. They are forbidden to indulge in sex even in their thoughts and imaginings. Every sexual impulse has to be suppressed as a danger to their celibacy. No sooner are they ordained than these young and mostly innocent men are forced to listen, in the secrecy of the confessional, to the most lurid descriptions of sexual activity and deviance. Every sin of sex has to be spoken into their ears, as to number and species. Young women tell them of their innermost thoughts, deeds and longings, sometimes in situations of physical proximity. Through the confessional, a priest with homosexual leanings can discover who are the members of the gay community. From the priest's point of view, the system seems especially cruel. No wonder that to many of them are more absorbed in their own problems than in the problems of their flocks.

As Lea said, in his three-volume work, *A History of the Inquisition in the Middle Ages*:

> No sooner had the Church . . . succeeded in suppressing the wedlock of its ministers, than we find it everywhere and incessantly busied in the apparently impossible task of compelling their chastity – an effort the futility of which is sufficiently demonstrated by its continuance in modern times.

Priestly Celibacy and Women in the Church

It has often been said that women have a lower place in Catholicism than in any other major institution in the Western world. Even Asian countries, renowned for their neglect of women's rights, have produced prime ministers. In Catholicism, there is no record of any woman directly and of right influencing church policy or any major decision, not even in matters that exclusively affect her sex. Why are women in Catholicism at best patronized and at worst persecuted by male clerics?

The only answer that makes sense is: Celibacy. It is women who have had to bear the brunt over the ages of the painful discipline of priestly celibacy.

In the first place, we noted that priests, especially popes, have developed a cult of the Virgin Mary. For celibates, the ideal woman is an asexual being who gave birth to a child. Mary had a baby without sexual intercourse; this is perfection. In the words of the Catholic liturgy, when becoming a mother 'Mary did not lose the glory of virginity'. She is, unfortunately most often pictured on the model of recent apparitions. A heavenly and hygienic Lady, bustless and dressed in white, she talks sweetly to holy children, has a rosary draped around her unwrinkled hands and wears roses on her feet.

After Mary in importance comes the woman who produces babies without taking pleasure in sex. Owing to the influence of the Fathers and Pope Gregory the Great, this was held throughout church history until modern times as the holiest to which married women could attain. Lower still in the list is the woman who has babies but sins by taking pleasure in the act that brings them into being. Lower still and worthy of all blame are those females who do not have babies but still enjoy or who are paid for the act of sex. In the twentieth century, this position has been modified: women are no longer despised for having pleasurable sex without babies, on one condition: they keep to the clerical method of avoiding conception which, not surprisingly, turns out to be extremely troublesome. More will be said of this later.

We have seen how disgracefully clerical wives were treated over the ages. Early on, popes-elect simply abandoned their wives and children. Especially from the time of Gregory VII, women who had married in good faith were obliged to give up all marital relations with their husbands when they became clerics. Wives' feelings were ignored or trampled on. They were looked on as sinners if they asked for what the New Testament itself made plain was their right before God. But all through history women have been despised for their relationship with priests, while the latter have more or less retained their reputation as 'gentlemen of the cloth'.

The clearest example of the maltreatment of women by a celibate priesthood was in the age of witchcraft. There were appalling pornographic undertones to this persecution. Women were despised by their priestly inquisitors; according to the stereotype, they were tools of Satan, temptresses, sexual traps, especially for men who had chosen to live without female companionship. The persecution of witches shows celibates, with unconscious malevolence, revenging themselves on women for the sacrifice they had made of their own sexuality. They believed Satan was their foe when really it was woman. No other explanation is possible for the ghoulish confessions of witches except that celibates projected their own nightmares on them. Their revulsion made them completely gullible. 'Witches polluted the world' because they themselves had always feared to be polluted by women through the illicit movements of their own flesh. Women, theology assured them, were bent ribs, a sulphurous brood, daughters of Eve. The sheer ugliness and smelliness of those ancient crones must have made the inquisitors detest them that much more. Witches were the worst side of themselves incarnate.

This goes far to explaining why there were so many witches and so few wizards. What convinced priests that witches were more satanic than their male counterparts? Surely it was the Eve complex of the inquisitors to which a man like Sprenger freely admitted. Just as they were brought up to believe the Jews were cursed, so they thought of women as being that much more in league with Satan, so much more likely to be the devil's disciples. Every carnal thought that flitted through the inquisitor's head, every carnal impulse he felt, made him more terrified of witches and more inclined to accept whatever obscenity was said about them during torture. While, therefore, the papacy must take prime responsibility for 'creating' witches through its dogmas, the horrible torments inflicted on them were due to priestly celibacy. 'Good' priests were dedicated to prayer and fasting, to hair-shirts and self-flagellation. What was this for? Why the long vigils, the hard beds, the nights broken up with psalms? Why lower their eyes so that they did not dare even to take in the beauty of the world and the skies? Surely because they had to keep women at bay. Their eyes, the Order's rules said, must not so much as alight on a woman. Their nostrils must not smell their perfume, their hands must not touch their bodies, their imagination must not dwell for an instant on their shape or their feel. One false step and they would be damned. It would reveal that their whole life and all their sacrifices were in vain, that women had conquered them. How wicked must these demons be to do such sacrilegious things.

With hindsight, of course, it is easy to see that 'Satan' was not in the witches but in the flesh of the inquisitors.

If past persecution of women in the church was due, at least substantially, to the repressed sexuality of the celibate, the question arises: In what way are priests continuing this oppression today?

Most priests will find the question itself insulting and preposterous. Priests think of themselves, *rightly*, as, by and large, kind and humane. They fail to see that personal charity is perfectly compatible with institutionalized oppression. Today, the torture-chambers are in the mind. The fires have been internalized. Popes and priests, through their legislation, pitch people into fires that are never quenched.

Priestly antagonism to women today is evidenced in their shunning the idea of women priests. Theologians try to prove from Scripture that women are ineligible. Their arguments are uniformly weak, not to say distasteful. God is masculine, they say. For Jesus was the Icon of God and he was male. The Word incarnate was God's Son not his Daughter. Further, even the Virgin Mary, the holiest of mere mortals, was not admitted to the priesthood. Jesus only chose men as priests. How account for this except that women, however holy, are in God's own design intrinsically unfitted for the ministry?

This male chauvinism, dressed up as theology, finds less and less favour today, even when it comes from bishops and popes. Jesus revealed God not because he was a man but because he was a perfect human being. The notion that God is essentially and eternally Male is a piece of masculine mythology about as acceptable as thinking that the dove is the most sacred animal because the Holy Spirit appeared in the form of a dove. It has caused some women, in despair, to go so far as to suggest that the Bible – and the church's liturgy based on it – has to be scrapped. At the heart of it is a male-superiority syndrome totally alien to the society we live in. Language perpetuates woman's bondage. Christianity, they say, preaches a male chauvinist God and an Incarnation that is not about saving humankind but about preserving the inferiority of women for ever.

Certainly, in a once male-dominated world, men had precedence in everything. It is precisely the realization that we have passed beyond that stage that makes most modern women and many men aware of how relative is the church's insistence that only males can be priests. Further, as has been argued repeatedly, if Jesus' choice of disciples determines all future choices, priests today should all be circumcized Jewish peasants, with a number of married men among them.

It is hard to escape the conclusion that the chief reason the Catholic church, at least in the higher echelons, is opposed to women priests is that it is run exclusively by and for male celibates. From the pope down, with their hearts barbed-wired against women, they are convinced they are superior. Celibacy is a mechanism for proving and maintaining this belief. For women to be granted an equal ministry would destroy this carefully cultivated image of male celibate superiority. The real basis of priests' arguments, in brief, is not theological but sexual. It is not God or Christ but male egotism of a very special sort that makes them oppose the idea of women clergy. Once more, the Catholic church shows itself to be fifty years and more out of date. Today, married men have no objection to their wives being presidents, prime ministers, leading politicians, judges, lawyers, doctors and so on. But celibate priests cannot bear the thought of women, whom they have renounced, being on a par with them. To suggest that, one day, women will be bishops and popes appears to many of them as blasphemy.

The church is the loser because of clerical antagonism to women. The ministry would benefit in every way from womanly wisdom nourishing it. They are, mostly, gentler than men, their detestation of violence is greater, they have profounder insights into young and old people. If these 'virtues' should themselves be considered sexist, women's presence in the ministry would simply be an expression of basic human justice. Apart from anything else, a system that is unjust to women must be bad for the men who devised it and run it.

There is no hope of an immediate change. John Paul II has made it plain that he disapproves from his heart of women priests. In common with many bishops, he seems to think that women can feel perfectly free in the church without any form of representation, without a voice in their own affairs. Men, the pontiff must presume, are best equipped by God to know what is in women's interests.

This helps explain why Catholicism has decimated in recent years the most dedicated body of women in the world. Nuns, the best-educated Catholics, the most apostolic, suffered until they could take no more. They left convents in droves. The figures are startling. In the United States, for example, between 1960 and 1976, there was a drop of 39,500 sisters. They did not mind being servants of the servants of God; they objected to being the lackeys of priests and bishops. Without a single priest among them to minister to their needs, to hear their confession and to say mass for them, nuns were (and are) completely at the mercy of the clergy. They are subject to their every whim not only locally but at the international level, too. They are forbidden to modify their rule and way of life, without getting clearance from the clergy, their 'Cardinal-Protector' and the male-dominated Roman Congregations. Even the length of their skirts is decided by men. This violation of natural justice has led to the massive flight of the church's finest apostles. It is a scandal of which most Catholics are unaware. It must be put down almost entirely to the chauvinism of a male celibate clergy who are so far from accepting women as their equals in the ministry that they even want to dictate to them every detail of their life *as nuns*.

Nuns are not the only female victims; married women suffer equally. Previously, women who had sexual intercourse were obliged to have babies. The logic was that a baby must push out where a man has pushed in. Women must suffer in the place where they have sinned.

The stress on the sinfulness of contraception guaranteed that women would remain socially inferior to men. Repeated pregnancies reduced or eliminated the chances of married women contributing much to society except as wives and mothers. It even led to men assuming that women were genetically inferior to them in intelligence and creativity. Today, oppression of women takes the form of allowing them to use only the clerical method of contraception.

Wives may now have pleasure in sex, even when intending not to procreate. Provided they keep close surveillance of their bodily motions, take their temperature regularly and fill in the calendar, the clergy do not mind. Thus women remain *obedient*. It is the clergy's way – and it is very successful – of keeping sex dangerous and crisis-ridden. Safe sex, they know, risks removing women from ecclesiastical control; it makes them free. It does not seem to worry the higher clergy that many women suffer so much from the safe-period method that they prefer to do without sex altogether, especially when the method does not work for them.

Celibacy Today

For a person to be celibate is a choice of a fine ideal. He may wish to serve Christ and the community with a kind of prophetic witness of poverty and total availability. If he keeps faithful throughout his life, this will prove a blessing to him and perhaps to many others.

The danger only arises when this ideal is institutionalized and, worse, made a condition of receiving orders. Experience over long periods of time shows that only too often this turns out to be a disaster. The individual loses his freedom and often his integrity. He wants desperately to be a priest; part of the package-deal is celibacy, for which he may have little or no inclination. Once ordained, he is a prisoner of the system. It has been remarked that many a priest wishing to defect risks upsetting three very powerful women: Mother Mary, Mother Church and, often, his natural mother who may see her son's vocation as a blessing on her and her whole family. Even if it were no disgrace to leave – and the church does her best to make it so – what will a priest do afterwards? His six- or seven-year training prepared him for a specialized job within the community and he has no taste or expertise for any other. The temptation is to stay in the ministry, even though he cannot fulfil a vital condition: to live chastely. Even the hierarchy tells him that chastity is not so important as celibacy. So he may continue as a celibate while living promiscuously. What is almost as bad is a priest who is so tormented by his own sexual problems that he has little energy left to serve others, which is the whole point of the ministry.

Since a man, *every* man, has a natural right to marry, enforcing celibacy on him against his will is bound to end in tragedy of some sort. Or are all priests so secure as persons that they can dispense with the strength of a woman's love? After all, celibacy is a form of genetic suicide. The celibate spiritually castrates himself and so brings Doomsday to the world in his flesh. Life which has been handed on from generation to generation over millennia enters the cul-de-sac of a celibate's body. He has received the gift of life; he does not hand it on. He blows out the torch. If he is forced to do this against his will, he is likely to be a menace both to himself and to others.

Lea, in his famous study, refrained from commenting in detail on the Catholic clergy of his day. Remarks on such a sensitive subject should be made only in general terms.

Human nature does not change. The Vatican is well aware that there are some dioceses, even some countries, especially in the Third World, where priestly concubinage is practised as widely today as it was in the Middle Ages or the Renaissance. The laity there, no doubt, sympathize with their priest's need for a woman's love. Like lay folk of ages past, they are probably relieved that priests have their own women and so are less likely to poach theirs.

And elsewhere? It would be an injustice to condemn the clergy *en masse*. In fact, many knowledgeable people would say that Catholic priests are one of the finest bodies of men in the world. But it would be naïve to think that today's priests are wholly free from the faults that almost every generation has exhibited since celibacy was made compulsory. Modern priests have far more to contend with than their predecessors. Ours, by common consent, is a permissive age. Logistics alone make unchastity so much easier for everyone, including the clergy. There are reliable, cheap and easy methods of contraception. The telephone makes it simple to fix a meeting and the car to keep it. A priest today can achieve anonymity without difficulty. A half-hour's drive down the motorway and he finds himself in a place where he is unknown. He removes his clerical collar and fuses into the background. It would be surprising if soliciting in the confessional is practised as widely today as it was in nineteenth-century Spain. It is canonically alarming and, unless a priest has a taste for danger, unnecessary.

But the modern priest's chastity is imperilled by something far more devastating than permissiveness; the theological foundations of celibacy have collapsed.

Celibacy sprang from a belief that sex is always and essentially graceless and sordid. This is false.

The church proclaimed that celibacy is essentially higher than marriage, a more perfect state of life, the best way to follow Christ. Few hold this any more.

The church insisted on the conjunction of two totally different vocations: celibacy and ministry. Most people today think this was always highly dangerous, as dangerous as insisting that all doctors or politicians should be celibate.

The church taught that only celibacy is compatible with the ministry. This not only undermined marriage and created an unbridgeable gap between priests and laity; it tempted people to promise celibacy when they could not deliver.

Many men offered themselves for ordination believing the conjunction of celibacy and ministry was biblical, which it isn't, and that celibacy has a long and honourable record of achievement, when it hasn't.

For a long time, priests believed that the church had the warrant to forbid them to marry after ordination. Study of the first millennium shows that the church held then that not even a vow of celibacy invalidates a marriage. A person has the natural right to marry, and not even the church or the pope can take this away from him. John Paul's argument that priests, like married people, must hold equally to their life-long commitment does not hold water. A person who has married has exercised his natural right; one made to remain celibate against his wishes is deprived of his. Apart from this, enforced celibacy is a contradiction in terms. It should be added that celibacy will only be believed in by non-Catholics when it is completely free. John Paul often says that the priest's commitment was made in absolute freedom. If so, why does he not allow priests to leave the ministry? Why compel them to stay on when they themselves can no longer abide the loneliness which God said is not good for man?

Only when the chastity of the clergy is taken as seriously as their celibacy will the Catholic church free itself from peril. By making unchaste priests remain in their posts, the church has undermined respect for celibacy. Instead of forcing priests who are unchaste to stay, the pontiff should insist that *all unchaste priests must leave*.

Enforced celibacy has always led to hypocrisy in the ranks of the clergy. An unchaste priest need never promise a woman that he will marry her. His marriage would not be valid in the eyes of God or the church. A priest can fall a thousand times but he is forbidden by canon law to marry once. It is a sad but notorious fact that any number of women in love with priests are drawn into a web of hypocrisy and suffering because the clergy have to pretend to be other than they really are. These unfortunate women also lead double-lives, often for many years. Their assignations with their priest-lovers are secret. They are unable to explain to their family and friends why they have no boyfriends and no inclination to marry and bring up a family.

There are other disadvantages of celibacy. There are many places where the insistence on ministers being celibate has led to a huge shortfall in the number of priests needed to say mass and administer the sacraments. By not allowing married men to become priests, the papacy continues to assert that this celibate caste, without which the pope would only be the Bishop of Rome, is more important than the most basic needs of the flock. It is better for a church to have no priest than a married priest. This reinforces the impression that celibacy is not primarily about chastity, nor even about benefiting the spiritually poor; it is about control. This is why a relaxation in the law of celibacy would entail a massive change from the idea of a church as power to a church as service.

In this light, the many thousands of priests who asked to be dispensed during Pope Paul's time represented not the destruction but a certain purification of the Roman church. Driving such applicants underground may well have a long-term devastating effect on the morale and the morals of the priesthood.

Finally, not just many lay people but many priests, too, have begun to suspect that a celibate hierarchy is responsible for many phallic fallacies. Catholicism, especially the papacy, seems preoccupied with sex. How could it be otherwise? Lay people are the experts in sexual matters, and their relaxed wisdom has been set aside by a celibate caste. Is it any wonder that papal pronouncements on contraception, divorce, abortion carry no conviction? Can women be expected to obey the official church on matters which intimately concern them when priests continue to tell them to be silent in the church? To ask the laity to give internal assent to priestly pronouncements on sex is rather like asking practitioners to take the word of non-practitioners in, say, medicine or science or mathematics or even a game of football.

Knowledge does not always bring wisdom; ignorance never does.

EPILOGUE

THE WORK OF THE DEVIL'S ADVOCATE IS OVER. He has done his best – or his worst. The Catholic church, with the papacy at its head, has, in the finest Roman tradition, had much dirt thrown at it. It is for the reader to judge how much has stuck and how much fell to the ground. The fact is: the Church of Rome survived as she has survived for nearly two thousand years. She is arguably stronger today than she has ever been, more revered and respected.

The church is made up of millions of devoted men, women and children. In the depths of their being, they need the help and the grace she and she alone can bring. Even the most rigorous of popes touches the hearts of Catholics at a level that no president or member of royalty can begin to reach.

The papacy is a massive rock-like fact of history. Whatever its origins, far more debatable than most Catholics are aware of, it is here to stay. And it has, more than any other religious institution, the capacity to benefit the human race. Whether it will last till the end of time, no one can tell, but one thing is certain: if any of today's institutions is going to survive, the Church of Rome will be it.

Such a conviction should make for peace and generosity towards others. Such virtues have been conspicuously lacking in the past and are not so evident today. But there was that great break in the clouds when John XXIII ascended the papal throne.

John's God was not a tribal deity; He was greater than the church. John's God had a purpose for the whole world, as well as for the church. The Catholic church itself had a vital contribution to make to the world's progress. John's question was always: How can the church help God in His plan that goes beyond the church? Instinctively, he grasped the difference between the church and the Kingdom of God. The church was made up of relatively few; the Kingdom, to which the church is called to contribute, belongs to all people who are meek, and pure, and humble of heart.

This meant that for John the church is never perfect, and is always in need of reformation and updating. But it was still a church. Bishop Creighton would not allow so much. In his *Letters* he said: 'The Roman Church is not a Church at all, but a State, in its organization; and the worst form of State – an autocracy.' Certainly, many popes

435

have given the impression that they were dictators, on the pattern of Gregory VII; and the language used of the hierarchy at Vatican I was all about jurisdiction and dominance, quite out of keeping with the New Testament, which is entirely concerned with lowliness and service.

Pope John's heart was completely in tune with the Gospels. Hence he realized that the papacy is not the only teacher of the world – that would be blasphemy. Since the church does not express God fully in the world, the papacy must be the best of listeners and learners. A pope, he knew, does not have a bagful of truths which he can unload at will whenever the occasion calls for it. He was the first and so far the only pope in modern times who grasped that the world has a message for the church and that the church is also the world's mission-territory. It was because Pope John listened that he was listened to. When he summoned a Council, he begged the bishops to listen to the world in order to grow to their full stature as followers of Christ.

In ancient Israel, the dissenters were never priests but prophets. And, while being an annoying bunch, they were often *right* when the priests were wrong. Jesus was in the line not of priests but of prophets; hence he was looked on as a dissenter. He was crucified for dissent. Pope John recognized that prophets are indispensable to any institution, but especially the church. He did not think the church would be better off without prophets. We, too, need our Micah, our Amos, our Jeremiah, our Jesus. To silence free speech is to silence the voice of prophecy which is the voice of God.

Pope John seemed to take the line that dissent is permissible and fruitful because I am here, and I am your father in God. Other popes have taken the line that dissent is not permissible because I am here as an infallible teacher. But even an infallible teacher cannot say anything of value unless he listens to the word of prophecy. A sixteenth-century Jewish rabbi, Judah Loew, said: 'The elimination of the opinions of those who are opposed to religion undermines religion and weakens it.' But it takes great courage on the part of a pope to listen, to learn, to permit disagreement when he has it within his power to end it with a Bull or an encyclical.

John, in my view, was a man of marvellous detachment. He was Christ's apprentice, full of mercy and love. He died too soon.

Pope Paul VI who succeeded him was a pope in the old style. His first decision was to tell the church and the Council, then in session, to listen to *him*. But because he did not listen to the church, though within his strict 'rights', the church did *not* listen to him, and the world treated his final statement on birth control with a certain derision. *It did not have to be like that.*

Today, Pope John Paul II travels the world and is received with a love and affection that a person would have to be blind to miss. But he is not listened to, because he, too, does not *seem* to be listening. The rapturous masses that turn out to greet him are a sign of what the papacy could be not merely to the church but to everyone. Pope John *was* that to all mankind, even to the communists who met him.

Many Catholics, without any lessening of loyalty, are beginning to feel that an old-style papacy is costing too much. Catholics benefit, or feel they do, from an autocratic office. But it has split Christendom from top to bottom. After Vatican II, can Catholics really go on clinging to the triumphalism of the past, as if the Orthodox and the Protestants have got it all wrong, and there is nothing for them to do except repent and return to the fold of Mother Church? As if they, too, are not the church!

An example of, doubtless, unintended cruelty was Leo XIII's declaration that Anglican orders were null and void. In *Apostolicae Curae* of 1896, he virtually denied that the ancient Church of England existed: it was no Sister Church, nor even a part or branch of the true church. It was at best a well-meaning heretical sect without a share in the true priesthood of Christ. Anglican ministers, on converting to Rome have therefore always been ordained without condition, as if they had never had hands lain on them. In the spirit of Vatican II, Leo XIII's binding decision should be reversed. Rome must admit explicitly at some point that her present stand is mistaken and that she has no wish to convert 'The Church of England' or force submission upon her. Nor must she continue thinking it a good thing when she poaches members from them; this only delays an acceptable solution of an ancient wrong. There must surely come a time, sooner rather than later, when Rome accepts the Church of England as *the* Catholic church in England. It is not Anglicanism that will have to withdraw and stop baptizing new members but what is at present called the Roman Catholic Church.

It is impossible to foresee the details of what will happen, but the principle is clear: the Anglican church, far from withering away, must take her full and rightful place as the Church of Christ in an ancient land in full communion with Rome and all other churches. Just as in her best moments Rome does not think of forcing submission on the Orthodox churches, nor should she think of doing that to the revered and thoroughly evangelical Church of England.

One day, it will be agreed that the validity of orders depends on the validity of the church, and not vice versa. A rigid scholastic view of orders makes specific words and intentions paramount. But this view makes most Catholic orders questionable, too. For who is to know if the priest who baptized Pope John Paul said the right words or had the right intention? Who can be absolutely sure that the bishop who ordained him a priest was not inebriated or out of his mind, unable, therefore, to have any intention? But is one to say that John Paul might not *be* the Bishop of Rome?

What is needed is a Council of the Church. Not a Council of the Roman Catholic Church, even though Vatican II, within limits, achieved marvels. Christians need an Ecumenical Council of all those who profess the name of Jesus and live by his name. Such a Council is already a thousand years and more overdue. In such an assembly, there would be no difficulty agreeing on all vital points of the Gospel message; and what was not agreed would not be of serious importance. The churches are divided by mostly marginal and sectarian issues. In such a Council, there would be such an outpouring of the Spirit that all participants would focus on Jesus Christ. He it is and He alone who can and will make them one.

In such an ecumenical gathering, the pope, bishop of the only remaining apostolic see, would preside, without question. His primacy is not a matter of debate in the great churches. It is his unevangelical supremacy that the Orthodox, the Episcopal and Protestant churches object to. However great the pope's prestige is now, it cannot compare with the prestige and genuine authority he would have if he presided over such a Council with the caring love of Christ, a love that listens and does not want to subjugate. The world would then *see* for the first time in over a millennium that the church is one and that Christians are at least trying to love one another. If the Soviets can talk with the Americans about arms control, cannot Orthodox and Protestants and Romans talk as brothers and sisters about the love and service of Jesus Christ?

The conclusion of this book on the sins of the papacy is the most startling paradox of all. The papacy needs to become greater not less than it is. But the greatness must be on the model of Jesus the Servant of God and men. To extend the paradox: it is not Catholics but other Christians who chiefly can make the papacy what it ought to be – a Peter in the midst of the contemporary church. No one but the pope can represent with love and humility all that the church is struggling to say to itself and the world. Only he can express repentence for the almost inexpressible wrongs that Christians have done throughout the ages and which all human beings continue to do to each other.

Pope John was a rainbow in the night. Perhaps we need an even greater to arise in order to bring his work, God's work, to fulfilment. The task is, humanly speaking, impossible. The greatest crime that Christians can commit is to believe that the Spirit has ceased to blow and their own divisions are everlasting.

Chronology

Dates with asterisks are uncertain

DATE	EVENT	DATE	EVENT
6 BC	Birth of Jesus	161	Persecution by Marcus Aurelius
4 BC	Death of King Herod the Great	189	Election of Victor, first pope to speak Latin
18–37	Caiaphas is Jewish High Priest	248	Rome attacked by Goths
26	Pontius Pilate Prefect in Judaea	250	Christian leaders arrested in Rome Pope Fabian executed 22 January
27–30*	Jesus' ministry		
30*	Jesus is crucified on Golgotha	303	Great Persecution under Diocletian Books surrendered, churches destroyed Clergy are imprisoned
48	Council of Jerusalem Gentiles admitted to the church		
49–58	Paul's missionary journeys		
60–2	Paul in Rome		
63*	Peter in Rome	305–6	Persecution relaxed
64	Great Fire in Rome Nero's persecution of Christians	306–12	Toleration of Christians in Rome and Africa
68	Nero commits suicide	312	Constantine defeats Maxentius Alliance of church and state
70	Jerusalem destroyed by Titus		
74	End of Jewish community at Masada	313	The Edict of Milan Universal toleration
80	Colosseum opens in Rome	314	Council of Arles Council of Ancyra
95	Persecution by Domitian	315	Arch of Constantine in Rome
107	Letters of Ignatius of Antioch	323	Constantine sole emperor

DATE	EVENT	DATE	EVENT
324	Founding of Constantinople (Byzantium)	409–10	Romans leave Britain
		410	Rome sacked by Visigoths
325	Council of Nicaea decides no man may marry after ordination		Alaric takes Rome, 24 August
		430	Death of St Augustine
330	Dedication of Constantinople	431	Hippo falls to Vandals
335	Division of Empire between Constantine's sons and nephews	432	Patrick in Ireland
		440–61	Leo I increases authority of papacy in the West
337	Constantine baptized; dies 22 May	452	Leo meets Attila the Hun, the Scourge of God, and perhaps saves Rome
342	Council of Sardica Augustine of Hippo born at Tagaste		
		476	End of western Empire
361–3	Julian the Apostate grants toleration to all Christian creeds and paganism	480*	Birth of St Benedict
		529	Benedict founds abbey of Monte Cassino
380	Christianity official religion of Roman Empire	547*	Benedict dies
		553	Fifth General Council condemns the Three Chapters
382	Jerome begins to translate the Bible	563	Columba brings Christianity to Scotland
385	Pope Siricius decrees married men, after ordination, must not sleep with their wives	568	Beginning of Lombard invasion of Italy
386	Conversion of Augustine	570–632	Muhammad the Prophet
390–460*	St Patrick		
392	Non-Christian rituals prohibited in Rome	590–604	Pope Gregory the Great decides all sexual desire is sinful in itself – sex is only for the sake of children
392–428	Theodore of Mopsuestia		
395	Augustine consecrated Bishop of Hippo		
		590–615	Mission of Columbanus
401	Augustine writes *On the Good of Marriage*, a Catholic manual of sex	597	Gregory I sends missionaries to Anglo-Saxons

DATE	EVENT	DATE	EVENT
605	Death of Augustine of Canterbury	863–9	Pope deposes and excommunicates Photius, Patriarch of Constantinople, causing a schism
615	Death of Columbanus		
664	Synod of Whitby decides in favour of Roman church over the church of Iona	871–900	Alfred rules Anglo-Saxons
		882	Marinus, first bishop to be elected pope
673–735	Venerable Bede, first English chronicler	892*	Birth of Marozia, whore of Pope Sergius III, mother of Sergius' son, Pope John XI, grandmother of Pope John XII
680	Pope Honorius condemned for heresy by Ecumenical Council		
711	Muslims invade Spain		
732	Victory of Charles Martel over Islam near Tours	910	Foundation of monastery of Cluny
742–814	Charlemagne, Pepin's son	962	Otto I crowned Emperor of West
750*	Forgery of *Donation of Constantine*	1032	Accession of eleven-year-old pope Benedict
754	Pope Stephen III begs Pepin, King of the Franks, for military help	1046	Henry III, King of Germany, Italy and Burgundy, crowned emperor
771	Charlemagne becomes King of the Franks	1047	Henry III deposes Pope Gregory VI
782	Alcuin joins court of Charlemagne	1054	Formal break between East and West Papal legates place pope's excommunication of Michael Cerularius, Patriarch of Constantinople, on altar of St Sophia
787	Second Council of Nicaea, only Council to be called by a woman, Empress Irene		
800	Charlemagne crowned on Christmas Day		
850*	Forgery of *Pseudo-Isidorian Decretals*	1056– 1106	Reign of Emperor Henry IV
855*	Papacy of legendary Pope Joan as Pope John VIII	1070–89	Lanfranc Archbishop of Canterbury

DATE	EVENT	DATE	EVENT
1073	Pope Gregory VII insists word 'pope' is used only of Bishop of Rome	1171	Henry II begins occupation of Ireland
1074	Gregory insists all ordinands pledge themselves to celibacy	1181–1226	St Francis of Assisi
		1182	Crusaders defeated at Horns of Hattin The loss of Jerusalem
1076	Gregory VII excommunicates Henry IV	1189–92	Third Crusade
		1201–4	Fourth Crusade
1077	Henry capitulates at Canossa	1204	Constantinople is sacked by Crusaders
1095–9	Urban II preaches First Crusade	1208	England put under six-year interdict by Innocent III
1099	Crusaders conquer Jerusalem establish Latin Kingdom there	1209	First Albigensian Crusade Massacres at Béziers, Minerve and Lavaur
1100–1200	Foundation of universities	1212	Children's Crusade ends in disaster
1115–53	St Bernard abbot of Clairvaux	1213	King John gives England to Innocent III
1122	Concordat of Worms ends Investiture controversy	1215	Magna Carta signed by King John at Runnymede Fourth Lateran Council decrees laity must confess annually to parish priest
1123	First Lateran Council, first to use Latin as official language For first time, all clerical marriages declared invalid		
1140*	Gratian's *Decretum*	1219	Fifth Crusade
1146–8	Second Crusade	1225–74	Thomas Aquinas
1152–90	Reign of Frederick Barbarossa	1228	Frederick II recovers Jerusalem
1154–89	Reign of Henry II in England	1232	Pope Gregory IX establishes the Inquisition
1154	Adrian IV, English pope, commissions English king to conquer Ireland	1241	First conclave to decide election of pope
1170	Thomas à Becket murdered in Canterbury Cathedral	1244	Final loss of Jerusalem
		1248–51	Fifth Crusade under Saint Louis

DATE	EVENT	DATE	EVENT
1252	Innocent IV allows torture to Inquisition		First pope to grant indulgences to the dead
1265	Birth of Dante		
1300	Boniface VIII declares a Jubilee each century	1474*	Birth of Giulia Farnese, lover of Pope Alexander VI
1302	Bull *Unam Sanctam* Death of Boniface VIII	1474–1504	Isabella, Queen of Castile
1309–78	Papacy in exile in Avignon	1475	Birth of Cesare Borgia, Pope Alexander's most brutal son
1321	Death of Dante		
1331–2	Pope John XXII preaches heresy	1478	Sixtus IV allows Spanish sovereigns to set up Inquisition
1348–9	The Black Death		
1350	Clement VI decrees a Jubilee every fifty years	1480	Birth of Lucrezia Borgia
1374	Death of Petrarch	1483–1546	Martin Luther
1375	Death of Boccaccio	1484	Innocent VIII, first pope to acknowledge his bastards, begins persecution of witches
1378–1417	Great Schism begins with two popes		
1400	Death of Chaucer		
1409	Council of Pisa; three popes	1486	*Witches' Hammer*
1414–18	Council of Constance depose John XXIII	1492	Rodrigo Borgia bribes his way into papacy as Alexander VI Columbus discovers the New World Conquest of Granada by Catholic Kings of Spain
1415	John Huss is burned at Constance		
1420–96	Thomas de Torquemada		
1431	Joan of Arc burned at Rouen as a witch	1493	Alexander VI divides the New World between Spain and Portugal Torquemada appointed General Inquisitor for Spain
1440	Lorenzo Valla proves *Donation of Constantine* is a forgery		
1456	Gutenberg prints the first Bible in Mainz		
1466–1536	Erasmus	1493–5	Pinturicchio decorates the *stanze* of the Vatican Palace
1469–1527	Machiavelli, author of *The Prince*		
1473	Sixtus IV builds Sistine Chapel	1496–1556	Ignatius Loyola

DATE	EVENT	DATE	EVENT
1498	Alexander VI has Savonarola executed	1521	Leo X makes Henry VIII 'Defender of the Faith' for his book on the Seven Sacraments
1503	Julius II bribes his way into the papacy	1527	The sack of Rome
1504	Tetzel begins to sell indulgences	1530	Death of Cardinal Wolsey
1506	Beginning of rebuilding of new St Peter's from sale of indulgences		Henry VIII is Supreme Head of Church of England
1507	Julius II sanctions cult of holy house of Loretto, transported from Holy Land by angels	1533	Henry secretly marries a pregnant Anne Boleyn Birth of their daughter Elizabeth
1508–15	Michelangelo paints ceiling of Sistine Chapel	1534	Ignatius Loyola founds Jesuits Luther's *Bible*
1509–47	John Calvin		Calvin's *Institutes*
1509	Henry VIII married to Catherine of Aragon	1535	More and Fisher executed on Tower Hill
1509–47	Henry VIII King of England	1536	Anne Boleyn executed for adultery
1511	Erasmus' *In Praise of Folly*	1539	Dissolution of English monasteries
1517	Luther's *Ninety-Five Theses against Indulgences* Publication of Lorenzo Valla's book on forgery of *Donation of Constantine*	1542	Paul III establishes first of Roman Congregations, the Inquisition
		1545–63	The Council of Trent Trent finalizes Catholic form of marriage before priest and two witnesses Retains priestly celibacy Declares celibacy and virginity superior to marriage
1519	Charles V elected Holy Roman Emperor		
1520	Leo X excommunicates Luther in Bull *Exsurge Domine* which Luther publicly burns	1555	Paul IV's Bull against the Jews, *Cum nimis absurdum* Ridley and Latimer burned in Oxford

DATE	EVENT	DATE	EVENT
1558	Bloody Mary dies. Elizabeth, aged twenty-five, is Queen of England	1620	*Mayflower* leaves Plymouth for New World
1559	Paul IV introduces Index of Forbidden Books	1621	Paulo Zacchia in Rome is first to suggest soul is infused at conception Rome does not agree
1563	Foxe's *Book of Martyrs*	1632	Galileo's *Dialogue on the Two Chief Systems*
1564	Michelangelo dies. Galileo is born		
1570	Pius V excommunicates Elizabeth in Bull *Regnans in Excelsis*	1633	Inquisition, under Urban VIII, condemns Galileo for saying the sun is centre of universe and the earth moves Urban VIII says Galileo is to be tortured if he does not conform
1577	Massacre of Huguenots in Paris on St Bartholomew's Eve. Pope Gregory XIII decides that to kill embryo of less than forty days is not homicide		
		1641	Blondel, a Calvinist, finally proves Pope Joan did not exist
1582	The Jesuit, Matthew Ricci, enters Imperial Court at Peking	1642	Galileo dies. Newton is born
1587	Execution of Mary Queen of Scots. Edict of Nantes grants religious toleration to all, including Protestants. Clement VIII calls it 'the most cursed edict I could imagine'	1648	Peace of Westphalia grants religious freedom to all citizens. Innocent X condemns its tolerance
		1649	Maryland votes for complete religious freedom for all its citizens. Rome's persecution of witches officially ends
1605	Completion of new St Peter's		
1607	Death of Cardinal Baronius, author of *Ecclesistical Annals*	1685	Revocation of Edict of Nantes
1610	Galileo's *Nuncius Sidereus*	1687	Newton's *Principia*
1614	Roman Ritual imposes box or stall for confession	1691	Penal Code imposed on Catholics in Ireland

DATE	EVENT	DATE	EVENT
1715	Clement XI, by Bull *Ex Illa Die*, puts effective end to Chinese Mission	1845	John Henry Newman joins the Church of Rome
1773	Boston Tea Party Clement XIV suppresses the Jesuit Order numbering 22,589, thus curtailing Catholic missions	1847	Marx's *Communist Manifesto*
		1848	Pius IX exiled in Gaeta
		1850	Pius IX returns to Rome Hierarchy restored in England
1775–81	American War of Independence	1852	Harriet Beecher Stowe's *Uncle Tom's Cabin*
1776	American Declaration of Independence Paine's *Common Sense* Gibbon's *Decline and Fall*	1854	Pius IX is first pope to define on his own a doctrine, Mary's Immaculate Conception
1789	French Revolution	1856–	
1790–2	Llorente, Secretary of Inquisition in Madrid, author of *History of Inquisition*	1939	Sigmund Freud
		1858	Apparitions of Mary at Lourdes
		1859	Darwin's *Origin of Species*
1791–2	Paine's *Rights of Man*	1861	Lincoln President of the United States Cavour occupies most of Papal States
1793	The 'Terror' in France Execution of Louis XVI	1863	Lincoln's Gettysburg address on 19 November
1804	Coronation of Napoleon in Notre-Dame	1864	Pius IX's *Syllabus of Errors* condemns freedom of worship
1805	Battle of Trafalgar	1867	Marx's *Das Kapital*
1809–82	Darwin	1869	First Vatican Council
1814	Congress of Vienna Pius VII restores the Jesuits	1870	Definition of Papal Supremacy and Infallibility Rome falls to New Italy Pope is 'Prisoner of the Vatican'
1815	Battle of Waterloo		
1832	Gregory XVI calls liberty of conscience 'a mad opinion' in *Mirari Vos* Condemnation of de Lamennais		

DATE	EVENT	DATE	EVENT
1878	William Booth founds Salvation Army		Pius XI's *Casti connubii* condemns birth control
1891	Leo XIII's *Rerum Novarum*		Against entire tradition, Pius XI says sex pleasure can be good and holy in itself
1895	Rome decides that to remove a foetus which would otherwise die and kill the mother is immoral	1933	Nazi government in Germany
1896	Leo XIII in *Apostolicae Curae* declares Anglican Orders 'absolutely null and utterly void'	1950	Pius XII defines dogma of Assumption
1903	Franz Josef, last prince to interfere in papal election Abbé Loisy writes *The Gospel and the Church*	1951	In Address to Midwives, Pius XII cautiously sanctions safe-period method of birth control
1905	Mrs Pankhurst starts agitating for Women's Suffrage	1962–5	Second Vatican Council
1907	Pius X publishes *Lamentabili* and *Pascendi* against 'Modernists'	1963	Paul VI withdraws birth control from competence of General Council
1908	Inquisition renamed the Holy Office Pius X excommunicates Loisy Trent's form of marriage is made universal in the church	1964	In Council, several cardinals speak of need to change church's teaching on birth control
1917	New Code of Canon Law	1966	Paul VI discontinues Index of Forbidden Books He allows dispensations from celibacy and there is flood of applicants
1929	Lateran Treaty creates the Vatican State		
1930	Lambeth Conference of Anglican church sanctions birth control	1968	Paul VI's *Humanae Vitae* Complete ban on contraceptives Explosion of disagreement in church

DATE	EVENT	DATE	EVENT
1973	Supreme Court in the United States of America decides human life begins at birth	1986	John Paul removes control of Seattle from Archbishop Hunthausen
1978	John Paul II freezes dispensations from celibacy	1987	Holy Office, with John Paul's approval, condemns test-tube fertilization
1979	John Paul revokes teaching licence of Hans Küng		

The Popes

137	John XIV	983–4
138	John XV	985–96
139	Gregory V	996–9
	John XVI	
	(*antipope*)	997–8
140	Sylvester II	999–1003
141	John XVII	1003
142	John XVIII	1004–9
143	Sergius IV	1009–12
144	Benedict VIII	1012–24
	Gregory	
	(*antipope*)	1012
145	John XIX	1024–32
146	Benedict IX	1032–44;
		1045; 1047–8
147	Sylvester III	1045
148	Gregory VI	1045–6
149	Clement II	1046–7
150	Damasus II	1048
151	Leo IX	1049–54
152	Victor II	1055–7
153	Stephen X	1057–8
	Benedict X	
	(*antipope*)	1058–9
154	Nicholas II	1059–61
155	Alexander II	1061–73
	Honorius II	
	(*antipope*)	1061–72
156	Gregory VII	1073–85
	Clement III	
	(*antipope*)	1080–1100
157	Victor III	1086–7
158	Urban II	1088–99
159	Paschal II	1099–1118
	Theodoric	
	(*antipope*)	1100
	Albert (*antipope*)	1102
	Sylvester IV	
	(*antipope*)	1105–11
160	Gelasius II	1118–19
	Gregory VIII	
	(*antipope*)	1118–21
161	Callistus II	1119–24
162	Honorius II	1124–30
	Celestine II	
	(*antipope*)	1124

163	Innocent II	1130–43
	Anacletus II	
	(*antipope*)	1130–8
	Victor IV	
	(*antipope*)	1138–9
164	Celestine II	1143–4
165	Lucius II	1144–5
166	Eugene III	1145–53
167	Anastasius IV	1153–4
168	Adrian IV	1154–9
169	Alexander III	1159–81
	Victor IV	
	(*antipope*)	1159–64
	Paschal III	
	(*antipope*)	1164–8
	Callistus III	
	(*antipope*)	1168–74
	Innocent IV	
	(*antipope*)	1179–80
170	Lucius III	1181–5
171	Urban III	1185–7
172	Gregory VIII	1187
173	Clement III	1187–91
174	Celestine III	1191–8
175	Innocent III	1198–1216
176	Honorius III	1216–27
177	Gregory IX	1227–41
178	Celestine IV	1241
179	Innocent IV	1243–54
180	Alexander IV	1254–61
181	Urban IV	1261–4
182	Clement IV	1265–8
183	Gregory X	1271–6
184	Innocent V	1276
185	Adrian V	1276
186	John XXI	1276–7
187	Nicholas III	1277–80
188	Martin IV	1281–5
189	Honorius IV	1285–7
190	Nicholas IV	1288–92
191	Celestine V	1294
192	Boniface VIII	1294–1303
193	Benedict XI	1303–4
194	Clement V	1305–14

195	John XXII	1316–34	224	Pius V	1566–72
	Nicholas V		225	Gregory XIII	1572–85
	(*antipope*)	1328–30	226	Sixtus V	1585–90
196	Benedict XII	1334–42	227	Urban VII	1590
197	Clement VI	1342–52	228	Gregory XIV	1590–1
198	Innocent VI	1352–62	229	Innocent IX	1591
199	Urban V	1362–70	230	Clement VIII	1592–1605
200	Gregory XI	1370–8	231	Leo XI	1605
201	Urban VI	1378–89	232	Paul V	1605–21
202	Boniface IX	1389–1404	233	Gregory XV	1621–3
203	Innocent VII	1404–6	234	Urban VIII	1623–44
204	Gregory XII	1406–15	235	Innocent X	1644–55
	Avignon *antipopes*		236	Alexander VII	1655–67
	Clement VII	1378–94	237	Clement IX	1667–9
	Benedict XIII	1394–	238	Clement X	1670–6
		1423	239	Innocent XI	1676–89
	Pisan *antipopes*		240	Alexander VIII	1689–91
	Alexander V	1409–10	241	Innocent XII	1691–1700
	John XXIII	1410–15	242	Clement XI	1700–21
205	Martin V	1417–31	243	Innocent XIII	1721–4
206	Eugene IV	1431–47	244	Benedict XIII	1724–30
	Felix IV (last *antipope*,		245	Clement XII	1730–40
	to date)	1439–49	246	Benedict XIV	1740–58
207	Nicholas V	1447–55	247	Clement XIII	1758–69
208	Callistus III	1455–8	248	Clement XIV	1769–74
209	Pius II	1458–64	249	Pius VI	1775–99
210	Paul II	1464–71	250	Pius VII	1800–23
211	Sixtus IV	1471–84	251	Leo XII	1823–9
212	Innocent VIII	1484–92	252	Pius VIII	1829–30
213	Alexander VI	1492–1503	253	Gregory XVI	1831–46
214	Pius III	1503	254	Pius IX	1846–78
215	Julius II	1503–13	255	Leo XIII	1878–1903
216	Leo X	1513–21	256	Pius X	1903–14
217	Adrian VI	1522–3	257	Benedict XV	1914–22
218	Clement VII	1523–34	258	Pius XI	1922–39
219	Paul III	1534–49	259	Pius XII	1939–58
220	Julius III	1550–5	260	John XXIII	1958–63
221	Marcellus II	1555	261	Paul VI	1963–78
222	Paul IV	1555–9	262	John Paul I	1978
223	Pius IV	1559–65	263	John Paul II	1978–

Ecumenical Councils

(Summoned by civil power. Language: Greek)

1 Nicaea	325	6 Third of Constantinople	680
2 First of Constantinople	381	7 Second of Nicaea	787
3 Ephesus	431	8 Fourth of Constantinople	869
4 Chalcedon	451	(Ecumenicity doubted by East and West)	
5 Second of Constantinople	553		

General Councils of the Roman Church

(Summoned by Popes. Language: Latin)

1	First Lateran	1123
2	Second Lateran	1139
3	Third Lateran	1179
4	Fourth Lateran	1215
5	First of Lyons	1245
6	Second of Lyons	1274
7	Vienne	1311
8	Constance	1414–18

9	Basle (Held ecumenical up to 25th session)	1431
10	Florence (or Ferrara Florence – sometimes held to be continuation of Basle)	1438–42
11	Fifth Lateran	1512–17
12	Trent	1545–63
13	First Vatican	1869–70
14	Second Vatican	1962–5

A Note on Sources

Books on this scale are not of mushroom growth. This one has grown slowly in the mind for over thirty years, nourished by much reading, lectures given by my teachers as well as by discussions with colleagues and my own students over a dozen or more years. My fear is that I do not give credit where it is due. Entire passages may have sprung out of a remark from, say, my tutor in Rome, Frederick Coplestone, SJ, or from an inspired lecture by Bernard Lonergan, SJ, or a student's essay from which I have subconsciously 'borrowed'. If I have overlooked my indebtedness to anyone, I humbly beg his or her pardon.

I remember clearly that *Vicars of Christ* owes its origin to *The Pope and the Council*. This was published in Germany in the year 1869 as *Der Papst und Das Concil* by Janus, the pseudonym of J. H. Ignaz von Döllinger. He was professor of Church History at Munich, the most famous of his day and a fine theologian. For six years, he acted as personal tutor to the future Lord Acton.

Some years ago, I read Döllinger's book three times, finding it at first incredible. I knew that the Vatican, with precision timing, had put it on the Index ten days or so prior to the opening of Vatican I which it was designed to influence. Two years after the Council, Döllinger was excommunicated by his archbishop for not accepting papal infallibility, and a year later he was sacked from his Chair of History. He died aged ninety, still unreconciled. After John Henry Newman was made a cardinal, he made up his mind to visit the ageing Döllinger to tell him that his own moderate views – so close to Döllinger's – were acceptable to the Rome of Leo XIII. Ill-health forced him to cancel the trip. Even after Vatican I, Newman wrote to Mr Daunt on 7 August 1870: 'I do not see why a man who denied it [papal infallibility] might not be as good a Catholic as the man who held it. . . . You put an enormous power into the hands of one man, without check, and at the very time, by your act, you declare that he may use it without special occasion.'

The Pope and the Council contained aspects of papal history completely unknown to me. I had been brought up as a Catholic, had gone through the usual six-year seminary course prior to ordination, had graduated from a Catholic university, the Gregorianum in Rome, and had never come across such ideas. This is partly to be explained by the partisan nature of seminary education and the fact that in such establishments history is a Cinderella subject. The misbehaviour of popes is lightly dwelt on or even excised, rather in the way that Trotsky was cut out of all Soviet history by Stalin. Many young historians in the Soviet Union today have never heard of Trotsky since even his image has been brush-washed out of the 1917 picture in which he stands close to Lenin on the Finland Station in St Petersburg. My ignorance must also be set down to the preference Catholics have for a history of the papacy that can be read with white gloves on. It is not easy to admit that one's leaders were often barbarians, or that the good popes sometimes did far more harm than the bad.

Thus, quite late in my career, I felt obliged to examine the history of Catholic ideas and institutions, the latter of course including the papacy. It was a long and sometimes painful form of self-education. Wartless hagiography can inspire but, as Acton warned, 'History undermines respect'. When he began to edit the *Home and Foreign Review*, he knew he would annoy the hierarchy by his directness. He wrote to Newman, stressing the need for utter honesty in writing about the popes. 'Paul III', he said, 'had a son, not a nephew as he is usually called. I feel very strongly that this ought to be gibbeted, and I cannot avoid pointing out the wilful lie that it involves.' In the end, it was his tutor, Döllinger, who was excommunicated. Acton chose, by a mixture of silence and ambiguity, to avoid the ultimate censure. It is sad to see generations in which more Catholics of greatness were censured or silenced by the church than most other institutions possessed.

In reading Lecky's two-volume classic, *History of European Morals*, I came across a footnote in which he refers to the Philadelphian, Henry Charles Lea. I had never heard of Lea and yet, if Lecky was to be believed, his history of celibacy was the most important work of its kind to come out of the New World. Next, I found that Bishop Mandell Creighton said of him: 'If you don't know Lea's books, read them, for no one knows more about the institutions of the medieval Church.' This praise was reinforced when I came across Acton's review of Lea's magisterial work on the Inquisition. Acton, notoriously backward in commending the works of others, wrote: 'Lea has made the most important contribution of the new world to the religious history of the old. . . . Nothing in European literature can compare with this, the centre and substratum of Mr Lea's great history.'

By common consent, Lea ranks among English-speaking historians with Gibbon and Hallam, Macaulay and Acton. Among Catholics, I dare to say, he is virtually unknown, and heeded still less. This is a pity in that there never was a less propagandist writer than he. It would be hard to find in all his massive works a single sectarian opinion. Unlike

Acton, he felt that the historian's task was to report and not to judge. Judgement belonged to the reader alone.

Lea and his brother Carey were educated at home in Philadelphia by a private tutor. From him, the boys picked up science, mathematics and languages. But Henry, it seemed, was not destined to be a scholar. He was a hard-working publisher; he had a wife and family to support. In his early twenties, he tried combining business and historical research. His health broke down under the strain, and he was always conscious of the possibility that he might crack again if he pushed himself too hard. In view of this, his achievements are astounding.

He interviewed Abraham Lincoln several times for various journals, and was deeply impressed by him as a human being. Only later was Lea able to dedicate more of his time to history. The overriding passion of his life was Justice, hence his interest in the Inquisition which violated every principle he held dear. He did not write his first historical article until he was twenty-four or his first book until he was forty-one. He was self-taught in every way. In the course of his work, he learned a new language as and when it became necessary. He learned German when he was sixty and Dutch when he was eighty.

As a historian, he must be unique. He hardly read the books of others. He always went straight to the original sources in order to make up his own mind. He was also ahead of his time in that he decided from the beginning that the best way to study history is by analysing the institutions, especially the legal institutions in which men and societies express themselves. This may explain the coolness and detachment of his writings which stand out in an age of polemics. Dean Milman confessed that when he started reading Lea he tried to discover on internal evidence whether he was a Catholic or a Protestant, and failed because of Lea's 'fair and candid tone'.

One example of Lea's thoroughness must suffice. According to his biographer, E. C. Bradley, he began his researches into celibacy by reading all 217 volumes of Migne's *Patrologia Latina*. G. P. Gooch, in his monumental survey, *History and Historians in the Nineteenth Century*, says that Lea contributed more to medieval studies than any other writer of his period. His 'works on sacerdotal celibacy, the Spanish Inquisition, Confessions and Indulgences, and the Ordeal repay diligent study. His boundless erudition excites the more astonishment in that it was acquired during the leisure of a publisher's life and his materials for the most part had to be copied and sent across the Atlantic.'

Another American scholar, a contemporary, has also influenced me considerably, though he might say not nearly enough. I suspect that John T. Noonan, Jr, now a federal judge, would say that my conclusions, especially on abortion, differ from his own. Yet with deep gratitude I must pay tribute to the excellence of his researches and measured judgements. His works on contraception, divorce and abortion are models of historical objectivity.

Since *Vicars of Christ* is meant for the general public, references to all sources would have made it unreadable. In particular, an author is indebted to those who have formed the background of his mind. In my case, among the ancients, Plato, Aristotle and Cicero. Among medievals, Thomas Aquinas, whom I used to read for days on end as recreation. In the nineteenth century, Mill's *Essay on Liberty* stands out for me. One sentence of his never ceases to ring in my ears. It provides a kind of touchstone for all that is decent (and indecent) in history, papal or otherwise.

> If all mankind minus one, were of one opinion, and only one person were of the contrary opinion, mankind would be no more justified in silencing that one person, than he, if he had the power, would be justified in silencing mankind.

Among moderns, I owe much to Dietrich Bonhoeffer whose *Letters and Papers from Prison* were anticipated, by two generations and more, by Friedrich Nietzsche. The latter's work was expressed in too polemical a form for Christians to grasp then the immense contribution he was making to purifying the faith of damaging accretions.

One passage in particular inspired the searches that culminated in the writing of this book. It occurs towards the end of *The Pope and the Council*. All my efforts have been directed to discovering whether what Döllinger says in this passage is substantially true or not. It is interesting to note that, while his pupil, Lord Acton, is credited with the statement about absolute power corrupting absolutely, the master said it all nearly twenty years before him.

> All absolute power demoralizes its possessor. To that all history bears witness. And if it be a spiritual power, which rules men's consciences, the danger is only so much greater, for the possession of such a power exercises a specially treacherous fascination, while it is peculiarly conducive to self-deceit, — because the lust of dominion, when it has become a passion, is only too easily in this case excused under the plea of zeal for the salvation of others. And if the man into whose hands this absolute power has fallen cherishes the further opinion that he is infallible, and an organ of the Holy Ghost, — if he knows that a decision of his in moral and religious questions will be received with the general, and what is more, *ex animo* submission of millions, — it seems almost

impossible that his sobriety of mind should always be proof against so intoxicating a sense of power. To this must be added the notion, sedulously fostered by Rome for centuries, that every conclave is the scene of the eventual triumph of the Holy Ghost, who guides the election in spite of the artifices of rival parties, and that the newly elected Pope is the special and chosen instrument of divine grace for carrying out the purposes of God towards the Church and the world. The whole life of such a man, from the moment when he is placed on the altar to receive the first homage by the kissing of his feet, will be an unbroken chain of adulations. Everything is expressly calculated for strengthening him in the belief that between himself and other mortals there is an impassable gulf, and when involved in the cloud and fumes of a perpetual incense, the firmest character must yield at last to a temptation beyond human strength to resist.

Select Bibliography

Only those works easily available are listed

Some Useful Documents

Abbott, W M (ed), *The Documents of Vatican II* (London, 1966).

Baldwin, W M (ed), *Christianity through the Thirteenth Century* (London, 1970).

Baronius, Cardinal Caesar, *Annales Ecclesiasticae,* Vols 1–11 (Paris, 1864–1865).

Bettenson, H, *Documents of the Christian Church* (London, 1947).

Burchard, John, *Diaries, 1483–1492,* trans. A H Matthew (London, 1910).

Butler, C, *The Vatican Council, 1869–1870* (London, 1962).

Davies, J C (ed), *Episcopal Acts Relating to Welsh Dioceses 1066–1272,* 2 vols (1946–8).

Dictionnaire de théologie Catholique (Paris, 1905–60).

Douglas, D C, and Greenaway, G W (eds), *English Historical Documents,* 2 vols (London, 1961).

Ekler, S Z, *Church and State through the Centuries* (London, 1954).

Encyclopaedia Judaica, Vol. 13 'Pope' (Jerusalem, 1971).

Fremantle, Anne, *The Papal Encyclicals in Their Historical Context* (New York, 1956).

Hauben, Paul J. (ed), *The Spanish Inquisition* (Calif., 1969).

Hefele, C J, *A History of the Christian Councils,* 5 vols (Edinburgh, 1950).

Henderson, E F, *Select Historical Documents of the Middle Ages* (London, 1965).

Hillgarth, J N (ed), *The Conversion of Western Europe, 350–750* (New Jersey, 1969).

Jedin, H, *A History of the Council of Trent* (St Louis, Mo, 1957–61).

John, Eric (ed), *The Popes* (London, 1964).

John XXIII, Pope, *The Encyclicals and Other Messages* (Washington, DC, 1964).

Lecky, W E H, *History of European Morals,* 2 vols (London, 1911).

McElrath, Damian, *The Syllabus of Pius IX: Some Reactions in England* (Louvain, 1964).

Manschreck, C L, *A History of Christian Readings in the History of the Church from the Reformation to the Present* (New York, 1964).

Marcus, Jacob R, *The Jew in the Mediaeval World, 315–1791* (Connecticut, 1975).

Mommsen, T E and Morrison, K F, *Imperial Lives and Letters of the Eleventh Century* (New York, 1962).

Olin, John C, *The Catholic Reformation: Savonarola to Ignatius Loyola* (New York, 1969).

Pelikan, J and Lehmann, H, *Luther's Works (The American Edition)* (St Louis, 1955–).

Petry, Ray C (ed), *A History of Christianity: Readings in the History of the Early and Mediaeval Church* (New York, 1962).

Platina, *Lives of the Popes*, 2 vols (London, n.d.).

Pyle, Leo (ed), *Pope and Pill* (London, 1968).

Roncalli, Angelo (John XXIII), *Mission to France*, ed. Don Loris Capovilla (London, 1966).

Rynne, Xavier, *Letters from Vatican City* (London, 1963).

—, *The Second Session* (London, 1964).

—, *The Third Session* (London, 1965).

—, *The Fourth Session* (London, 1966).

Torre, M J de (ed), *The Church Speaks on Marriage and Celibacy* (Philippines, 1976).

Universal Jewish Encyclopaedia, Vol. 8 (New York, 1969), 'Papal Bulls' and 'Popes'.

Vorgrimler, H (ed), *Commentary on the Documents of Vatican II*, 5 Vols (London, 1966–9).

Some Books Consulted

Abel, E, *The Roots of Anti-Semitism* (NJ, 1975).

Ackerman, J S, *The Architecture of Michelangelo* (London, 1970).

Acton, J E (Lord), *Essays in the Liberal Interpretation of History* (Chicago, Ill./London, 1967).

—, *Lectures on Modern History* (London, 1960).

Aquinas, Thomas, *Summa Theologica*, in *Opera Omnia*, ed. Leonina (Rome, 1886–1906).

Atkinson, James, *Martin Luther and the Birth of Protestantism* (London, 1968).

Baker, Leonard, *Days of Sorrow and Pain* (New York, 1978).

Barraclough, G, *The Origins of Modern Germany* (Oxford, 1952).

Bellarmine, Robert, De Controversiis Christianae Fidei, De Romano Pontifice, in *Opera Omnia* (Naples, 1856).

Boase, T S R, *Boniface VIII* (London, 1933).

Boccaccio, Giovanni, *The Decameron*, trans. Mark

Musa and P E Bondanella (New York, 1977).

Bondanella, P E, *Francesco Guicciardini* (Boston, Mass., 1976).

Bradley, E C, *Biography of H C Lea* (Philadelphia, Pa, 1931).

Brent, Peter, *Charles Darwin* (London, 1981).

Brodrick, James, *Robert Bellarmine, 1542–1621*, 2 vols (London, 1950).

—, *Robert Bellarmine, Saint and Scholar* (London, 1961).

Brooke, Z N, *The English Church and the Papacy from the Conquest to the Reign of John* (Cambridge, 1952).

Brown, G K, *Italy and the Reformation to 1550* (Oxford, 1933).

Bultmann, R, *The History of the Synoptic Tradition* (New York, 1968).

Bund, J M W, *The Celtic Church of Wales* (London, 1897).

Burckhardt, Jacob, *The Civilization of the Renaissance in Early Italy* (London, 1878).

—, *The Age of Constantine the Great* (London, 1949).

Callaghan, D, *Abortion: Law, Choice and Morality* (London, 1970).

Carlyle, A J and R W, *A History of Medieval Political Theory in the West*, 6 vols (London, 1903–36).

Chadwick, H, *The Early Christian Church* (London, 1970).

Chadwick, O, *Catholicism and History* (Cambridge, 1978).

—, *The Reformation* (London, 1984).

Chamberlin, E R, *The Bad Popes* (New York, 1969).

Chapman, J, *Studies in the Early Papacy* (London, 1928).

Costello, Con, *In Quest of an Heir* (Cork, 1978).

Coulton, G G, *Inquisition and Liberty* (London, 1959).

—, *The Inquisition* (London, 1974).

Cowan, I B, *The Scottish Reformation* (London, 1982).

Crawford, F M, *Ave Roma Immortalis* (London, 1920).

Creighton, M, *The History of the Papacy during the Reformation* (London, 1882).

—, *A History of the Papacy from the Great Schism to the Sack of Rome* (London, 1899).

Daniel-Rops, H, *The Church in the Dark Ages*, trans. Audrey Butler (London, 1959).

Dante, *Divina Commedia*, various editions.

Davies, J G, *The Early Christian Church* (London, 1965).

Dawson, Christopher, *The Making of Europe* (London, 1944).

—, *The Dividing of Christendom* (New York, 1965).

Deanesly, Margaret, *Sidelights on the Anglo-Saxon Church* (London, 1962).

de Maistre, Joseph, *Letters on the Spanish Inquisition* (1843) (Boston, Mass., 1977).

—, *The Pope* (New York, 1975).

De Rosa, Peter, *Christ and Original Sin* (Milwaukee, Wis., 1967).

—, *Jesus Who Became Christ* (London/New Jersey, 1974).

Döllinger, J H Ignaz von, *The Pope and the Council* (London, 1869).

—, *Fables Respecting the Popes in the Middle Ages* (London, 1871).

Donaldson, Gordon, *The Scottish Reformation* (Cambridge, 1960).

—, *Scotland: Church and Nation through Sixteen Centuries* (London, 1960).

Duchesne, L., *The Beginnings of the Temporal Sovereignty of the Popes, 754–1073* (London, 1908).

—, *The Early History of the Christian Church*, 2 vols (London, 1909).

Dudden, F H, *Gregory the Great*, 2 vols (New York, 1967).

Egner, G, *Birth Regulation and Catholic Belief* (London, 1966).

Einem, Hubert von, *Michelangelo* (London, 1973).

Einstein, Albert, *Essays in Science* (New York, 1962).

Elliot Binns, L, *Innocent III* (London, 1931).

Emerson, E, *The Correspondence of Gregory VII* (New York, 1932).

Falconi, Carlo, *The Popes in the Twentieth Century* (London, 1967).

Ferrara, Orestes, *The Borgia Pope* (London, 1942).

Flannery, E H, *The Anguish of the Jews* (New York, 1963).

Fleming, D H, *The Reformation in Scotland* (London, 1910).

Francome, Colin, *Abortion Freedom: A Worldwide Movement* (London, 1984).

Galileo, *The Sidereal Messenger, with Kepler's Continuation* (Venice, 1610).

—, *Discoveries and Opinions*, trans. Stillman Drake (New York, 1957).

—, *Dialogues Concerning the Two Chief World Systems*, trans. Stillman Drake (Calif., 1962).

Gilbert, Martin, *Auschwitz and the Allies* (London, 1981).

Gill, Joseph, *The Council of Florence* (Cambridge, 1959).

Gooch, G P, *History and Historians in the Nineteenth Century* (London, 1913).

Graetz, H H, *History of the Jews*, 6 vols (Philadelphia, Pa, 1945).

Graham R A, *Vatican Diplomacy* (New Jersey, 1959).

Granfield, David, *The Abortion Decision* (New York, 1969).

Granfield, Patrick, *The Papacy in Transition* (Dublin, 1981).

—, *The Limits of the Papacy* (New York, 1987).

Greeley, A, *The American Catholic* (New York, 1977).

Gregorovius, Ferdinand, *History of the City of Rome in the Middle Ages*, 8 vols (London, 1894–1902).

—, *Lucretia Borgia, According to Original Documents and Correspondence of Her Day* (London, 1903).

Gregory of Tours, *History of the Franks* (Oxford, 1927).

Griesinger, Theodor, *The Mysteries of the Vatican*, 2 vols (London, 1864).

Grünewald, *Complete Edition of the Paintings*, with an introduction by J K Huysmans (London, 1958).

Guicciardini, Francesco, *The History of Italy and the History of Florence* (London, 1986).

Guillemain, B, *La Cour pontificale d'Avignon, 1309–1376* (Paris, 1962).

Gutman, Yisrael, *The Jews of Warsaw, 1939–1943* (Sussex: Harvester Press, 1982).

Hales, E E Y, *The Catholic Church in the Modern World* (London, 1958).

—, *Pope John and His Revolution* (London, 1965).

Hamilton, Bernard, *The Mediaeval Inquisition* (London, 1981).

Hay, M, *Europe and the Jews* (Boston, Mass., 1961).

Hazlitt, William (trans.), *Table Talk of Martin Luther* (London, 1952).

Heath, Peter, *The English Clergy on the Eve of the Reformation* (London, 1969).

Hebblethwaite, P, *The Year of the Three Popes* (London, 1978).

Hebblethwaite, P, and Kaufmann, L, *John Paul II* (New York, 1979).

Hennessy, J, *American Catholics: A History of the Roman Catholic Community in the United States* (New York, 1981).

Herberg, W, *Protestant, Catholic, Jew* (New York, 1955).

Hoess, Rudolf, *Commandant of Auschwitz* (London, 1959).

Hughes, P, *A Short History of the Catholic Church* (London, 1967).

Jalland, T G, *The Church and the Papacy* (London/New York, 1944).

Jedin, H, and Dolan, J, *Handbook of the History of the Church* (London, 1980–1).

Johnson, Paul, *A History of Christianity* (New York, 1977).

—, *Pope John Paul II and the Catholic Restoration* (London, 1982).

Joyce, G H, *Christian Marriage* (London, 1948).

Katz, Robert, *Death in Rome* (London, 1967).

Kitts, Eustace, *In the Days of the Councils* (London, 1908).

—, *Pope John the Twenty-Third* (London, 1910).

Kjeckhefer, R, *European Witch Trials* (London, 1976).

Knowles, David and Obolenski, Dmitri, *The Christian Centuries*, 2 vols (London, 1968–9).

Kobler, Franz, *Napoleon and the Jews* (New York, 1975).

Kristol, Gertrude, *Darwin and the Darwinian Revolution* (London, 1959).

Küng, Hans, *Infallible?* (London, 1971).

Langford, J J, *Galileo, Science and the Church* (New York, 1966).

Lapide, P E, *The Last Three Popes and the Jews* (London, 1967).

Lash, N, *Newman on Development* (London, 1975).

Latourette, K S, *A History of the Expansion of Christianity*, 7 vols (London, 1937–1945).

—, *A History of Christianity* (London, 1950).

—, *Christianity in a Revolutionary Age*, 5 vols (New York, 1957–61).

Lea, H C, *Studies in Church History* (Philadelphia, Pa, 1883).

—, *A History of Auricular Confession and Indulgences in the Latin Church*, 2 vols (Philadelphia, Pa, 1896).

—, *The Eve of the Reformation*, Cambridge Modern History (Cambridge, 1902).

—, *A History of the Inquisition in Spain*, 4 vols (New York, 1906–7).

—, *The Inquisition in the Middle Ages* (New York, 1955).

—, *Materials Towards a History of Witchcraft*, 3 vols (New York, 1957).

Lewy, Guenter, *The Catholic Church and Nazi Germany* (London, 1968).

Liutprand of Cremona, *Works*, trans. T A Wright (London, 1930).

Loisy, Alfred, *The Bible and the Christian Religion* (New York, 1962).

Machiavelli, N, *The Prince*, various editions.

Madden, R M, *Galileo and the Inquisition* (London, 1863).

Malinski, M, *Pope John Paul II* (London, 1979).

Mann, Horace K, *The Lives of the Popes*, 18 vols (London, 1902–32).

Mannix, D, *The History of Torture* (New York, 1964).

Martin, Malachi, *The Decline and Fall of the Roman Church* (London, 1982).

Matthew, A H, *The Life and Times of Rodrigo Borgia* London, n.d.).

Michaelis, Meir, *Mussolini and the Jews, 1922–1945* (Oxford, 1978).

Midelfort, H C E, *Witch Hunting in South-Western Germany, 1562–1684* (Stanford, Calif., 1972).

Milman, H H, *History of the Jews*, Vol 3 (London, 1866).

—, *Savonarola, Erasmus and Essays* (London, 1870).

—, *History of Latin Christianity*, Vols 1–11 (London, 1872).

Milton, John, *English Prose Writings*, ed. H Morley, vol. 5 (London, 1889).

Mitchell, R J, *The Laurels and the Tiara, Pope Pius II, 1458–1464* (London, 1962).

Mollart, G, *Les Papes d'Avignon, 1305–1378* (Paris, 1949).

Morley, J F, *Vatican Diplomacy and the Jews during the Holocaust, 1939–1943* (New York, 1980).

Murphy, Francis X, *The Papacy Today* (London, 1981).

Murray, John C, *We Hold These Truths* (New York, 1960).

Narfon, Julien de, *Pope Leo XIII* (London, 1899).

Newman, John Henry, Cardinal, *An Essay in the Development of Christian Doctrine* (London, 1890).

—, *Letters and Diaries*, ed. C S Dessain, 18 vols (London, 1961–).

Nichols, Peter, *The Politics of the Vatican* (London, 1968).

Nietzsche, Friedrich, *Twilight of the Idols (1889) and The Anti-Christ (1895)* (London, 1968).

Noonan, J T (Jr), *Contraception: A History* (Cambridge, Mass., 1965).

—, *The Morality of Abortion* (Cambridge, Mass., 1970).

—, *Power to Dissolve: Lawyers and Marriages in the Courts of the Roman Curia* (Cambridge, Mass., 1972).

—, *A Private Choice: Abortion in America in the Seventies* (New York, 1979).

Novak, Michael (ed.), *The Experience of Marriage* (New York, 1964).

Nyiszli, Miklos, *Auschwitz: A Doctor's Eye-Witness Account* (New York, 1960).

O'Brien, John A, *Family Planning in an Exploding Population* (New York, 1968).

Oldenberg, Zoe, *Massacre at Monségur*, trans. Peter Green (London, 1961).

Parkes, James, *A History of the Jewish People* (Chicago, Ill., 1962).

Pastor, Ludwig von, *The History of the Popes*, 40 vols (London, 1890–1953).

Pecher, Eric, *John XXIII: A Pictorial Biography* (London, 1959).

Peel, Edgar, and Southern, P, *The Trials of the Lancashire Witches* (Newton Abbot, 1972).

Pieper, Josef, *The Silence of St Thomas* (London, 1957).

Powell, J M (ed.), *Innocent III* (Boston, Mass., 1967).

Powicke, F M, *The Christian Life in the Middle Ages* (Oxford, 1935).

Ranke, Leopold von, *A History of the Popes*, trans. E. Foster, 3 vols (London, 1896).

Richards, Jeffrey, *The Popes and the Papacy in the Early Middle Ages, 476–752* (London, 1979).

Roberts, T D, Archbishop, and others, *Contraception and Holiness* (New York, 1964).

Roo, Peter de, *Pope Alexander VI*, 6 vols (Bruges, 1924).

Roth, Cecil, *A History of the Marranos* (Philadelphia, Pa, 1941).

—, *A History of the Jews in Italy* (Oxford, 1946).

Ruffini, Francesco, *Religious Liberty* (London, 1912).

Runnes, D D, *The Jew and the Cross* (New York, 1966).

Sandmel, Samuel, *We Jews and You Christians* (Philadelphia, Pa/New York, 1967).

Santayana, George, *Interpretation of Poetry and Religion* (New York, 1900).

—, *Little Essays*, ed. L P Smith (London, 1920).

Santillana, G de, *The Crime of Galileo* (Chicago, Ill., 1955).

Shea, William R, *Galileo's Intellectual Revolution* (London, 1972).

Smith, J H, *The Great Schism, 1378* (London, 1970).

Southern, R W, *Western Society and the Church in the Middle Ages* (London, 1970).

Steiner, Jean F, *Treblinka* (London, 1967).

Stokes, A and Pfeffer, L, *Church and State in the United States* (New York, 1964).

Stow, Kenneth R, *Catholic Thought and Papal Jewry Policy, 1555–1593* (New York, 1977).

Strayer, J B, *The Albigensian Crusades* (New York, 1971).

Summers, Montague (trans.), *Malleus Maleficarum of Heinrich Kramer and James Sprenger*, New York, 1971.

Synan, E A, *The Popes and the Jews in the Middle Ages* (New York/London, 1965).

Tatham, E H R, *Francesco Petrarch*, 2 vols (London, 1926).

Thomas, Gordon and Morgan-Witts, Max, *Pontiff* (London, 1983).

—, *The Year of Armageddon: The Pope and the Bomb* (London, 1984).

Tillemann, Helena, *Pope Innocent III* (Amsterdam, 1978).

Tooley, M, *Abortion and Infanticide* (Oxford, 1983).

Trachtenberg, J, *The Devil and the Jews* (New York, 1943).

Trevor, Meriol, *Pope John* (London/New York, 1967).

Ullmann, W, *The Origins of the Great Schism* (London, 1948).

—, *Mediaeval Papalism* (London, 1949).

—, *Growth of Papal Government in the Middle Ages* (London, 1970).

—, *A Short History of the Papacy in the Middle Ages* (London, 1972).

Vaillancourt, Jean-Guy, *Papal Power* (Calif., 1980).

Van de Meer, F, *Augustine the Bishop* (London, 1961).

Vidler, Alec, *A Variety of Catholic Modernists* (Cambridge, 1970).

—, *The Church in an Age of Revolution* (London, 1985).

Voltaire, *Traité sur la tolérance*, various editions.

—, *Selected Works*, trans. J McCabe (London, 1941).

Wakefield, L Walter, *Heresy, Crusade and Inquisition in Southern France, 1100–1250* (Calif., 1974).

Ward, Wilfred, *The Life of John Henry Cardinal Newman*, 2 vols (London, 1912).

Whitehead, A N, *Science and the Modern World* (New York, 1960).

Williams, G H, *The Mind of John Paul II* (New York, 1981).

Wojtyla, Karol, John Paul II, *Segno di Contradizione* (Milan, 1977).

Woodward, G W O, *Dissolution of the Monasteries* (London, 1966).

Zola, Emile, *Rome: A Novel* (London, 1897).

Zweig, Stefan, *Erasmus of Rotterdam* (New York, 1956).

Index

474

477